PONTIAC GTO
RESTORATION
GUIDE—1964-1970

Paul Zazarine & Chuck Roberts

Motorbooks International
Publishers & Wholesalers Inc.
Osceola, Wisconsin 54020, USA ®

First published in 1985 by Motorbooks International Publishers
& Wholesalers Inc, PO Box 2, 729 Prospect Avenue, Osceola, WI
54020 USA

Motorbooks International is a certified trademark, registered
with the United States Patent Office

Printed and bound in the United States of America

The information in this book is true and complete to the best of
our knowledge. All recommendations are made without any
guarantee on the part of the author or publisher, who also dis-
claim any liability incurred in connection with the use of this
data or specific details

Library of Congress Cataloging in Publication Data

Zazarine, Paul
    Pontiac GTO restoration guide, 1964-1970.

    1. Automobiles—Conservation and restoration.
2. GTO automobile.   I. Roberts, Charles
II. Title.
TL152.2.Z39   1985   629.28'722   85-7307
ISBN 0-87938-199-X (pbk.)

Cover photograph by Paul Zazarine

Motorbooks International books are also available at discounts
in bulk quantity for industrial or sales-promotional use. For details write to Special Sales Manager at the Publisher's address

ACKNOWLEDGEMENTS

This book would not have been possible without the help of a number of people. Thanks to Jim Osborne Decals of Georgia for supplying all of the GTO decals illustrated in this book. Thanks to Jerry Drechsler, Brian Tressler, Jeff Lovich, Mark Mento, Wayne Garrison, Perry Roberts and all the other members of the Royal GTO Chapter of the GTO Association of America who let us barge into their homes and photograph their GTO parts. Our heartfelt thanks to Liz Robertson and Dick Thompson at Pontiac Motor Division for supplying us with information whenever possible and for permitting us to use factory text, drawings, bulletins, correspondence and photos.

Finally, a very special thank you to our families. Without their support and encouragement, *Pontiac GTO Restoration Guide* would never have been possible. This book is dedicated to them.

INTRODUCTION

It's hard to imagine that over twenty years have passed since Pontiac introduced the GTO to a performance-hungry America. No one could have predicted the tremendous impact the GTO would have on American automotive philosophy in the sixties. Nearly every automaker rushed to market a GTO-class car to share in the bountiful and profitable youth market. And while the GTO could be beaten in the stoplight drags by 1968, no manufacturer was able to capture the GTO's panache that set it apart from every other Supercar on the market. By the early seventies, the performance market—and the GTO—was virtually legislated into extinction by the overwhelming factions of safety and emission standards, and the astronomical insurance surcharges placed on young drivers of high-performance vehicles.

As the GTO passed into the nether world of used cars, it inevitably ended up in the hands of adolescents whose apparent main mission was to butcher the car in as many ways as possible. Factory Rally wheels, AM/FM radios, Custom Sport steering wheels were all discarded in favor of inferior aftermarket replacements. Desirable engine components (by today's restorers) were tossed for chrome-plated speed shop hardware of usually poor quality, or replaced with Chevrolet engines. Interiors were pillaged with the same ferocity: Camaro highbacks in place of the correct seats and holes cut in door panels for King Kong stereo speakers were some of the first requirements of GTO ownership to the boy racer.

Of the GTOs remaining in the seventies, the number raced, wrapped around poles or hacked and jacked to the junkyard is unfathomable. What was left of the half million GTOs built slowly began falling into the hands of collectors and restorers. These baby boomers, too young to own the GTO of their dreams in high school and college, now could afford to own and restore their favorite GTO. Their work was cut out for them, as few original cars remained.

What compounded the difficulty for these early restorers was the lack of information necessary to correctly restore a GTO to showroom condition. Little or no information was available from Pontiac, and understandably so. When the cars were built, they were simply units to be sold and no one could have possibly foreseen the collectability the GTO would enjoy decades later. Files and records were thrown away, both by Pontiac and its ad agency, depriving today's restorers of invaluable information.

As the ground swell of GTO popularity continued in the early eighties, organizations grew to support the GTO. The largest of these is the GTO Association of America (1634 Briarson Drive, Saginaw, MI 48603). Thanks to clubs like the GTOAA, more collectors, restorers and parts vendors turned to the GTO, reinforcing and accelerating the GTO's popularity. For all the growth in the GTO hobby, however, little research had been done on GTO authenticity. This lack of research and knowledge of authenticity was evident in the GTOs that were winning trophies in show competition. It wasn't unusual for these prize winners to have incorrect master cylinders, carburetors, interior pieces and so on. Components were incorrectly plated or painted, and accessories were incorrectly installed or were installed in models that never offered that particular option or accessory.

As the quality of restoration improved and competition within show classes grew keener, it became abundantly clear that research had to be done on GTO authenticity to provide a reference for the GTO restorer who desired to return his or her car to correct original condition. As we began to gather data, two rules became painfully clear. The first was "never say never," also known as the "'tain't necessarily so" axiom. This theorem states that whenever some assembly, component, color or data should or should not be present, a GTO will surface that was so equipped! This inevitable contradiction is likely because, unlike the Corvette or early Shelby Mustang, the GTO was built at different assembly plants scattered across the United States. These different plants were often supplied by various outside manufacturers, whose product may be similar (meeting GM's requirements) but visually different. Both would be correct.

Build-outs are also a problem in the search for authenticity, and support the Never Say Never axiom. Oftentimes, components still in stock at the end of the model year, instead of going into the parts system, were used on new models until supplies were exhausted. This can explain finding a 1964-design data plate on a 1965 firewall, or C-pillar headliner trim plates on midyear 1966 Fremont-built cars but not on early 1966 Baltimore-built models, or a few early 1970 GTOs with 1969 instruments and so forth.

The second GTO commandment states that no Pontiac part number is guaranteed to remain the same. As the years progressed and supplies dwindled, it wasn't unusual for Pontiac to consolidate parts and reissue older parts with new numbers. Components that fit 1964-66 with one number and 1967-70 with another could, in a few years, be consolidated as servicing 1964-70 with a new part number.

Instead of listing all of the part numbers that could exist for each component, we have listed the original part number whenever possible, for two reasons. First, the number could still be unchanged (if it is still available from GMPD). Second, and most important, we wanted to provide you with original part numbers to prevent the purchase of incorrect parts at a swap meet. Too many times restorers have bought a part that sure looked right, taken it home and discovered it wasn't right, because they didn't know the right part number. Hopefully, this book will save you that hassle. We have made every effort to ensure that all part numbers are correct with no typos, but if some have slipped past, forgive us!

With these two axioms memorized, we set out to write a reference guide that would assist the GTO restorer in making his or her car as authentic as possible. After assembling thousands of part numbers, line drawings and photographs of components; researching thousands of original and magazine photographs; as well as examining original, unrestored GTOs; checking dozens of factory reference manuals; and making every effort to substantiate all data, we believe we have put together a useful and informative tool for the GTO restorer. It is unlikely to be the last book on GTO authenticity, because as the GTO hobby matures and expands, and GTO restoration knowledge becomes more sophisticated, more research and new information will be uncovered.

Paul Zazarine
Chuck Roberts

CONTENTS

Chapter 1
FRAMES AND DATA PLATES

FRAME

1964-65

Both the 1964 and 1965 used a perimeter, swept-hip-design frame. There was one major difference between the frames used for the two years: The 1964 frame used a riveted rear cross-member; the cross-member in 1965 was welded. Convertible frames were boxed, and carried the same part number as the optional 1965 heavy-duty frame (9783404). All frames were painted gloss black.

The serial number was stamped on the left rear rail top. The part number and date of manufacture stamp was located on the side of the left rear rail. According to the factory, "The frame manufacturer's identification will be stamped at the left hand side rail, above the rear bumper bracket attaching slot. Identification information will include the part number, the name of manufacturer: PON-Pontiac; S-A. O. Smith; PPS-Parrish Pressed Steel."

1966-67

The 1966 standard GTO frame (part number 9783502) shared the same design with the 1965 GTO frame. The convertible frame (part number 9783404) was boxed for additional reinforcement.

The standard GTO frame in 1967 was part number 9786302. Two different convertible frames were used, and were boxed like the 1966 GTO. The manual transmission frame (part number 9786304) was different from the automatic transmission frame (part number 9788786); the automatic transmission frame's support cross-member

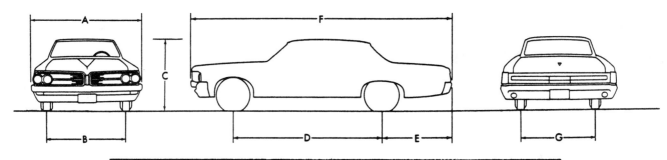

DIMENSION	KEY	Two Door Coupes 2227	Convertibles 2267
Over-All Length	F	203"	203"
Width	A	73.3"	73.3"
Height (Unloaded)	C	53.6"	54.2"
Wheelbase	D	115"	115"
Tread Front	B	58"	58"
Tread Rear	G	58"	58"
Road Clearance	-	6.05"	6.05"
Overhang Front	-	33.2"	33.2"
Overhang Rear	E	54.5"	54.5"
Tire Size	-	7.50 x 14	7.50 x 14

General specifications.

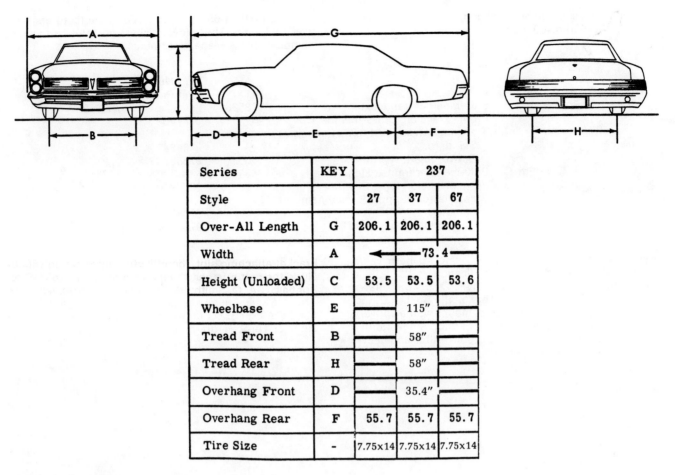

Series	KEY	237		
Style		27	37	67
Over-All Length	G	206.1	206.1	206.1
Width	A	←――73.4――→		
Height (Unloaded)	C	53.5	53.5	53.6
Wheelbase	E	115″		
Tread Front	B	58″		
Tread Rear	H	58″		
Overhang Front	D	35.4″		
Overhang Rear	F	55.7	55.7	55.7
Tire Size	-	7.75x14	7.75x14	7.75x14

1965 basic dimensions.

BASIC DIMENSIONS

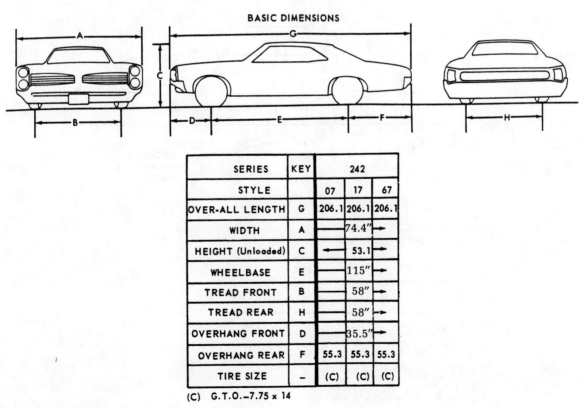

SERIES	KEY	242		
STYLE		07	17	67
OVER-ALL LENGTH	G	206.1	206.1	206.1
WIDTH	A	74.4″		
HEIGHT (Unloaded)	C	←――53.1――→		
WHEELBASE	E	115″		
TREAD FRONT	B	58″		
TREAD REAR	H	58″		
OVERHANG FRONT	D	35.5″		
OVERHANG REAR	F	55.3	55.3	55.3
TIRE SIZE	-	(C)	(C)	(C)

(C) G.T.O.—7.75 x 14

1966-67 basic dimensions (242).

was moved back six inches to accommodate the configuration of the Turbo 400 transmission.

As in 1964-65, three different manufacturers were used for frames. The following chart indicates correct part numbers for the respective frames.

			Part Number	
Manufacturer	Part	RH	One-Piece	LH
Pontiac	Side-member frame extension	9785361		9785362
	Front extension (cross-member)		9787462	
	Transmission support (cross-member)			
	Standard		9788822	
	Convertible/heavy-duty		9788824	
A. O. Smith	Side-member frame extension	3868622		3868661
and Parrish	Front extension (cross-member)		3876916	
	Transmission support (cross-member)			
	Standard		9788822	
	Convertible/heavy-duty		9788824	

The part numbers were the same for both years. Refer to 1964-65 section for identification.

The heavy-duty frame option (RPO 661) was offered for 1966 and 1967. It was available on the Special Equipment order form, and consisted of mounting the convertible frame under a sport coupe or hardtop at the factory. One part number was used for the convertible and heavy-duty frame in 1966: 9783404.

Two heavy-duty frames were used in 1967: 9786304 for manual transmission applications, and 9788786 for Turbo Hydra-matic automatic-transmission applications. These frames were identical to the production frames used for 1967 GTO convertibles with manual transmissions or Turbo Hydra-matics.

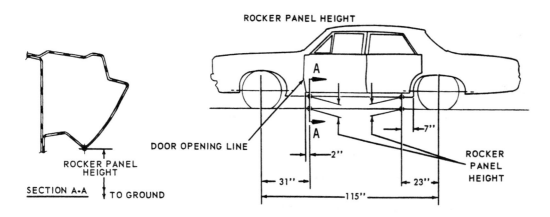

NOTE: DIMENSIONS SHOWN ARE FOR NEW CARS. CARS WITH SERVICE MILES AVERAGE UP TO 1/2" LESS. TOLERANCE OF ± 3/8" ALL DIMENSIONS. MAXIMUM LEFT TO RIGHT VARIATION 3/4".

* CURB LOAD CONDITIONS —
FULL FUEL TANK
SPECIFIED TIRE PRESSURE
STANDARD EQUIP SPRINGS

CURB ROCKER PANEL HEIGHT *(NOMINAL)	
FRONT	REAR
9.50	9.00

1966-67 rocker panel height.

TEMPEST

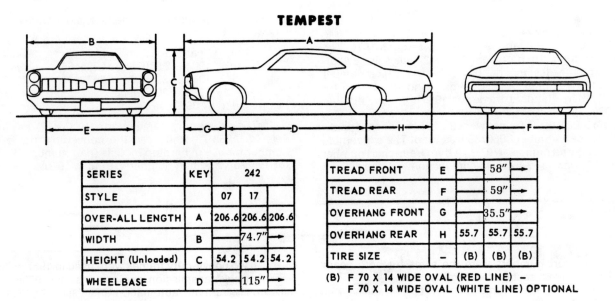

SERIES	KEY	242		
STYLE		07	17	
OVER-ALL LENGTH	A	206.6	206.6	206.6
WIDTH	B	74.7" →		
HEIGHT (Unloaded)	C	54.2	54.2	54.2
WHEELBASE	D	115" →		

TREAD FRONT	E	58" →		
TREAD REAR	F	59" →		
OVERHANG FRONT	G	35.5" →		
OVERHANG REAR	H	55.7	55.7	55.7
TIRE SIZE	–	(B)	(B)	(B)

(B) F 70 X 14 WIDE OVAL (RED LINE) –
F 70 X 14 WIDE OVAL (WHITE LINE) OPTIONAL

1966-67 Tempest basic dimensions.

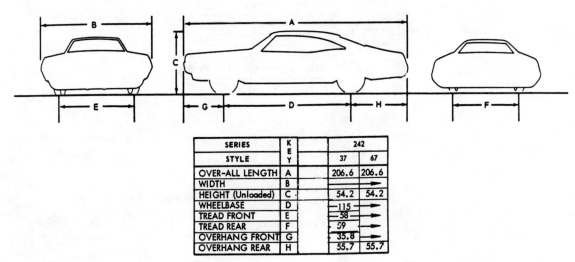

SERIES	KEY	242	
STYLE		37	67
OVER-ALL LENGTH	A	206.6	206.6
WIDTH	B	→	
HEIGHT (Unloaded)	C	54.2	54.2
WHEELBASE	D	115 →	
TREAD FRONT	E	58 →	
TREAD REAR	F	59	
OVERHANG FRONT	G	35.8 →	
OVERHANG REAR	H	55.7	55.7

1968 basic dimensions.

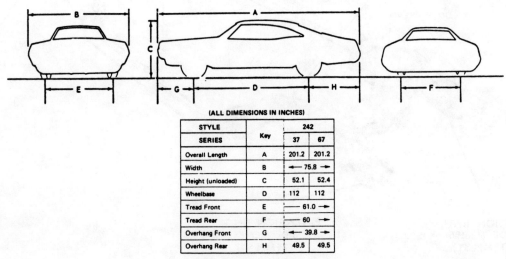

(ALL DIMENSIONS IN INCHES)

STYLE		242	
SERIES	Key	37	67
Overall Length	A	201.2	201.2
Width	B	← 75.8 →	
Height (unloaded)	C	52.1	52.4
Wheelbase	D	112	112
Tread Front	E	← 61.0 →	
Tread Rear	F	← 60	
Overhang Front	G	← 39.8 →	
Overhang Rear	H	49.5	49.5

*2-Door Hardtop 49.6; Convertible 49.5

1969 basic dimensions.

1968-70

The GTO wheelbase was reduced from 115 inches to 112 inches in 1968, and remained so through 1970. The standard frame (part number 3908663) was still a swepthip, perimeter design. The convertible frame (part number 3943347) was built by A. O. Smith, and was boxed for rigidity. The standard frame for 1969 was part number 3943353.

In 1970, three frames were used. For standard applications, part number 3960735 was used. The convertible frame was part number 479715. A third frame, part number 9799986, was used solely in conjunction with the 455 cid engine. The side-member frame extensions were as listed below.

Year	RH	LH
1968	3960284	3925165*
1969	3960284	3960283*
1970	3960284	3977555

*Superseded by 3977555

The heavy-duty frame option (RPO 612) was available for 1968-70, and used the convertible frame part number for use in hardtop models (part number 3943353 for 1968-69, and part number 479715 in 1970).

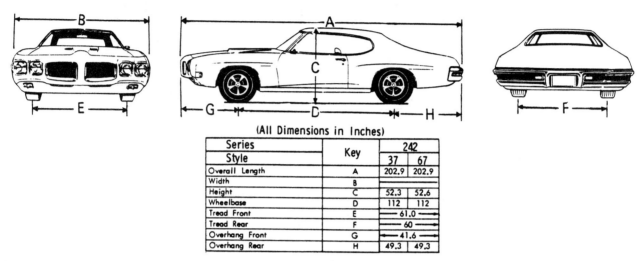

(All Dimensions in Inches)

Series		242	
Style	Key	37	67
Overall Length	A	202.9	202.9
Width	B		
Height	C	52.3	52.6
Wheelbase	D	112	112
Tread Front	E	← 61.0 →	
Tread Rear	F	← 60 →	
Overhang Front	G	← 41.6 →	
Overhang Rear	H	49.3	49.3

1970 basic dimensions.

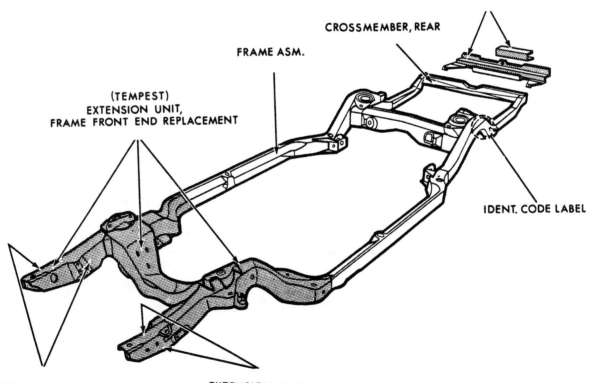

The heavy-duty frame was a Special Equipment option (RPO 661) in 1964. The frame rear cross-member reinforcement was RPO 664. This reinforcement was shipped loose with the car, and was dealer installed.

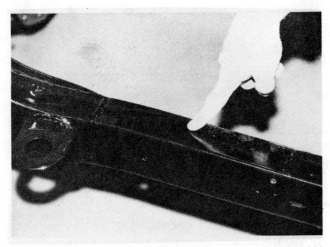

The serial number was stamped on each frame at the top of the LH rear rail, behind body bolt number 6.

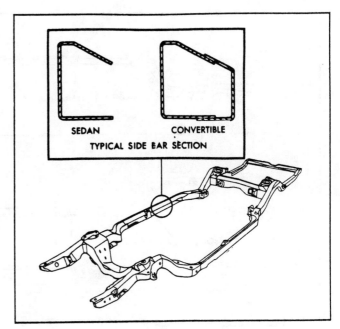

Comparison of side rail design on standard frame and convertible/heavy-duty frame, 1964-67.

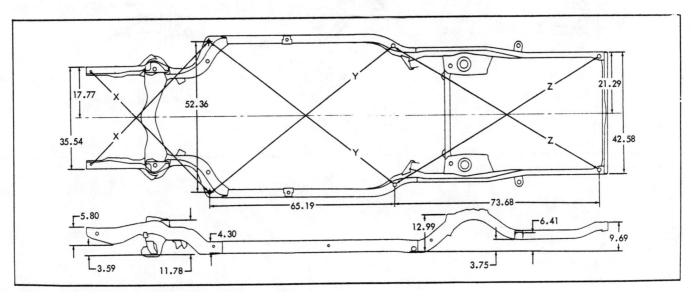

Detail of frame specifications and dimensions of 1964-67 frame.

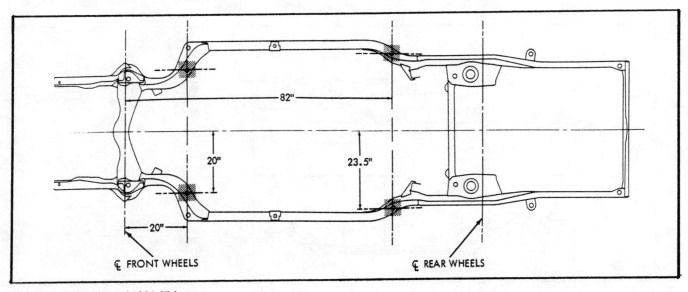

Location of lift points of 1964-67 frame.

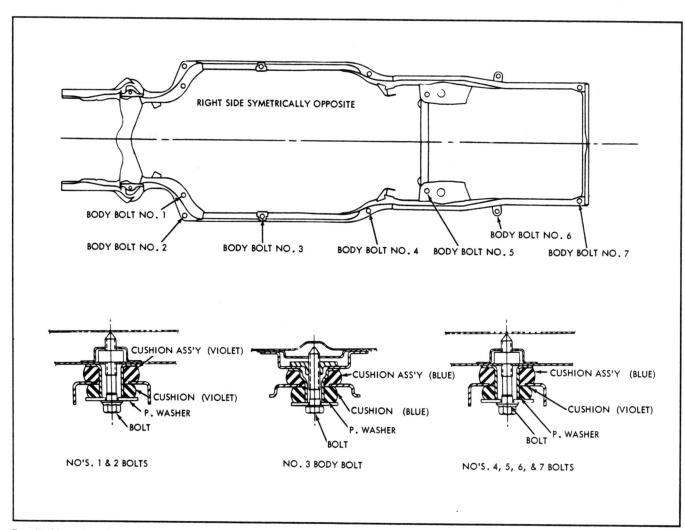

Detail of location of body bolts and their correct installation for
1964-67.

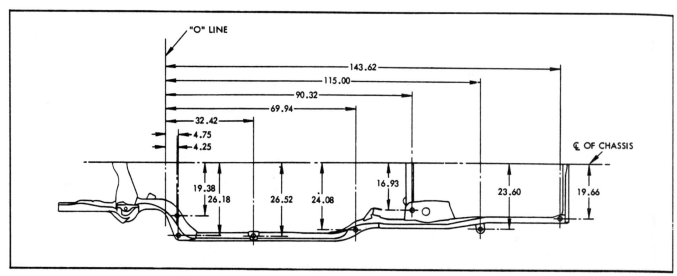

Frame gauge line dimensions for 1964-67 GTO frame.

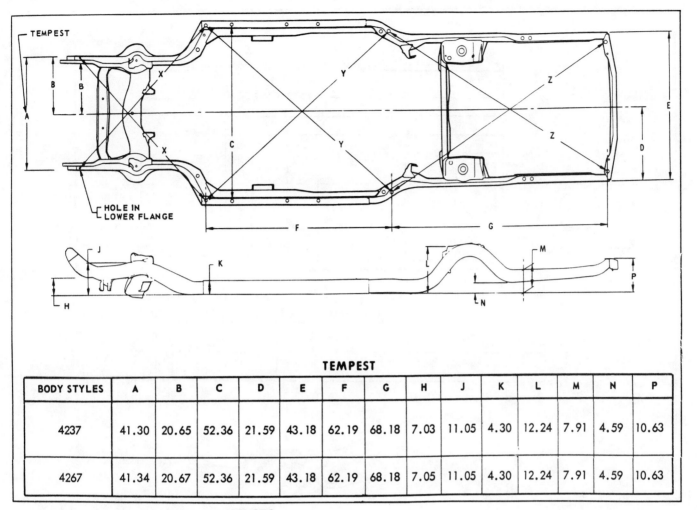

TEMPEST

BODY STYLES	A	B	C	D	E	F	G	H	J	K	L	M	N	P
4237	41.30	20.65	52.36	21.59	43.18	62.19	68.18	7.03	11.05	4.30	12.24	7.91	4.59	10.63
4267	41.34	20.67	52.36	21.59	43.18	62.19	68.18	7.05	11.05	4.30	12.24	7.91	4.59	10.63

Frame alignment chart for 1968 through 1970 GTO.

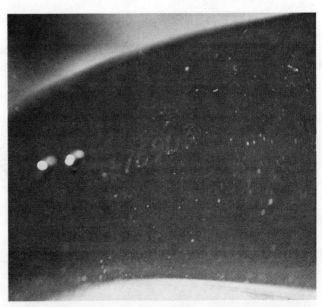

Close-up of frame part number, located on the side of the LH rear frame rail on a 1966.

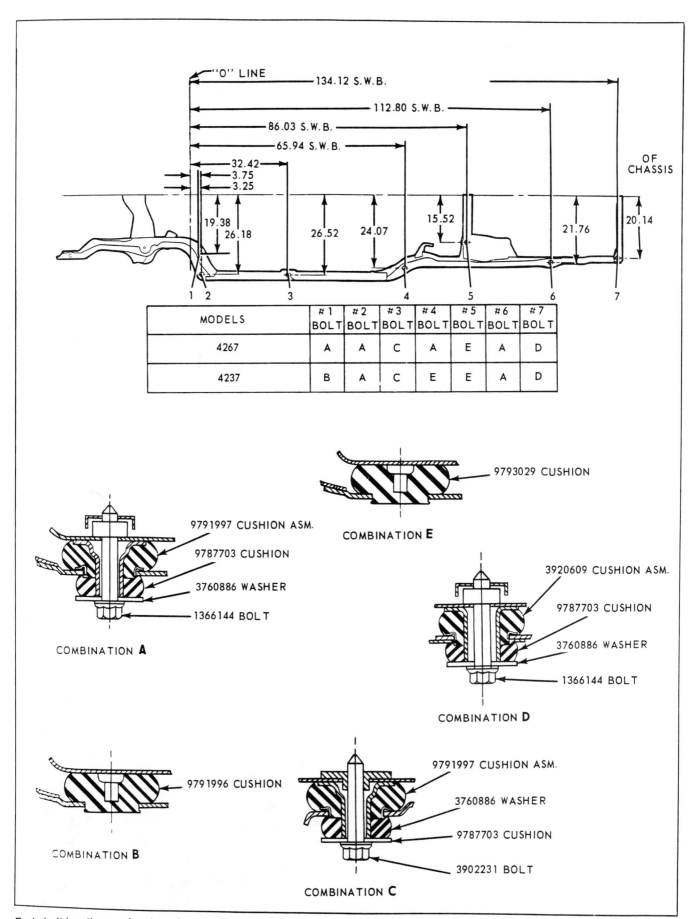

MODELS	#1 BOLT	#2 BOLT	#3 BOLT	#4 BOLT	#5 BOLT	#6 BOLT	#7 BOLT
4267	A	A	C	A	E	A	D
4237	B	A	C	E	E	A	D

COMBINATION A

9791997 CUSHION ASM.
9787703 CUSHION
3760886 WASHER
1366144 BOLT

COMBINATION B

9791996 CUSHION

COMBINATION C

9791997 CUSHION ASM.
3760886 WASHER
9787703 CUSHION
3902231 BOLT

COMBINATION E

9793029 CUSHION

COMBINATION D

3920609 CUSHION ASM.
9787703 CUSHION
3760886 WASHER
1366144 BOLT

Body bolt locations and part numbers for 1968.

20

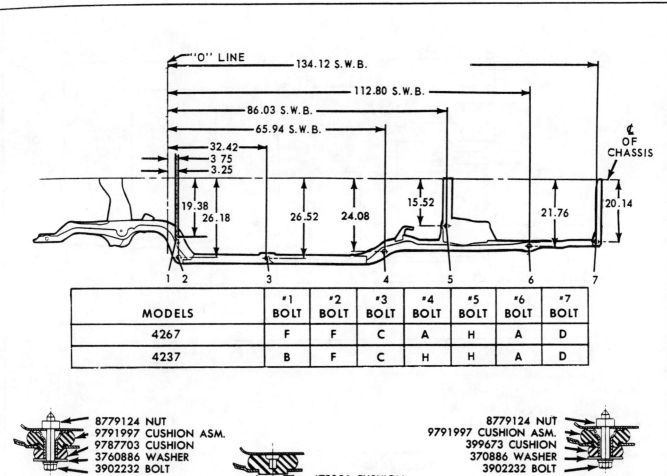

MODELS	#1 BOLT	#2 BOLT	#3 BOLT	#4 BOLT	#5 BOLT	#6 BOLT	#7 BOLT
4267	F	F	C	A	H	A	D
4237	B	F	C	H	H	A	D

8779124 NUT
9791997 CUSHION ASM.
9787703 CUSHION
3760886 WASHER
3902232 BOLT

COMBINATION F

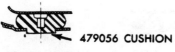

479056 CUSHION

COMBINATION E

8779124 NUT
9791997 CUSHION ASM.
399673 CUSHION
370886 WASHER
3902232 BOLT

COMBINATION J

3920609 CUSHION ASM.
9787703 CUSHION
3760886 WASHER
3902232 BOLT

COMBINATION D

9798420 CUSHION

COMBINATION H

9793708 RESTRICTOR
3920609 CUSHION ASM.
9787703 CUSHION
3760886 WASHER
3902232 BOLT

COMBINATION G

9791997 CUSHION ASM.
9787703 CUSHION
3760886 WASHER
1366144 BOLT

COMBINATION A

479055 CUSHION

COMBINATION B

9791997 CUSHION ASM.
9787703 CUSHION
3760886 WASHER
3902231 BOLT

COMBINATION C

Body bolt locations and part numbers for 1969.

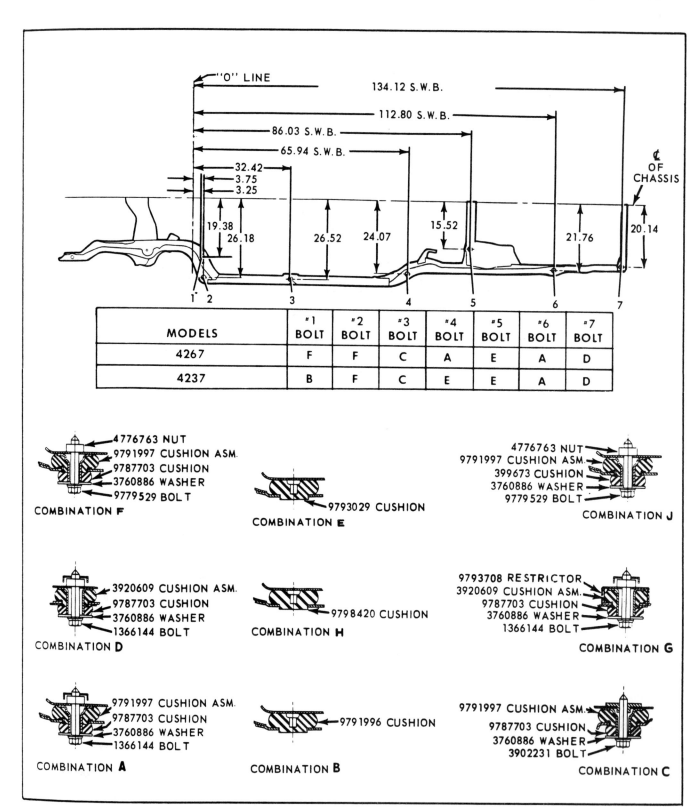

MODELS	#1 BOLT	#2 BOLT	#3 BOLT	#4 BOLT	#5 BOLT	#6 BOLT	#7 BOLT
4267	F	F	C	A	E	A	D
4237	B	F	C	E	E	A	D

COMBINATION F
4776763 NUT
9791997 CUSHION ASM.
9787703 CUSHION
3760886 WASHER
9779529 BOLT

COMBINATION E
9793029 CUSHION

COMBINATION J
4776763 NUT
9791997 CUSHION ASM.
399673 CUSHION
3760886 WASHER
9779529 BOLT

COMBINATION D
3920609 CUSHION ASM.
9787703 CUSHION
3760886 WASHER
1366144 BOLT

COMBINATION H
9798420 CUSHION

COMBINATION G
9793708 RESTRICTOR
3920609 CUSHION ASM.
9787703 CUSHION
3760886 WASHER
1366144 BOLT

COMBINATION A
9791997 CUSHION ASM.
9787703 CUSHION
3760886 WASHER
1366144 BOLT

COMBINATION B
9791996 CUSHION

COMBINATION C
9791997 CUSHION ASM.
9787703 CUSHION
3760886 WASHER
3902231 BOLT

Body bolt locations and part numbers for 1970.

DATA PLATE INFORMATION

1964-65

There is pertinent information contained on the data plate mounted on the LH front of the firewall on all 1964 and 1965 GTOs. Aside from the information listed in the accompanying illustrations, it is also possible to determine when the car was built, the sequence it was in relative to its VIN and the date it was built, and what color the exterior, top and interior should be.

Understanding the time-built code is simple. Assume the date stamped was 10C. The 10 indicated the month of the year (January-December = 1-12), this case being October. The C was the third week of the month (A=1, B=2, C=3, D=4, E=5).

The sequence number was an identification number given to each unit as it was assembled on the line. This, in conjunction with the VIN, allows us to determine what, if any, production changes occurred during the course of the production year.

The VIN identifies the correct engine, the series number, the body style, the model year, the plant in which the car was built and the serial number. All GTOs, since they were equipped with V-8 engines, had VINs that started with the digit 1 (6-cylinder LeMans used the number 6) followed by zeros and the sequential number of V-8s installed by the respective assembly plant during the production year. As an example, we'll analyze the VIN 237375P110034. 23737 indicates a LeMans hardtop coupe (GTO was an option on LeMans in 1964-65); the 5 indicates it was a 1965 model; the P identifies the Pontiac assembly plant; the 1 indicates a V-8 engine was installed, which, when coupled with the rest of the number tells us this was the 10,034th V-8 assembled. The serial numbers for all plants started at 1001 in 1964 and 100001 in 1965. Unfortunately, no breakdown was made as to which sequence V-8s were put in A- or B-bodies. Consequently, they were intermixed within the series. Due to record sales in 1965, V-8 production at the Pontiac, Michigan, plant exceeded 200,000 units on February 8, 1965 (Pontiac Service Management Newsletter number 65-4A dated 2/18/65 advised that cars built after 2/8/65 would start with serial number 200000). By the end of the 1965 production year, V-8 installation exceeded the 300,000 mark.

The engine serial number did not correlate with the VIN in 1964 or 1965. There was no other coding information in the VIN or the engine serial number. Paint and trim codes were stamped on the body identification plate. The paint codes can be deciphered by referring to the section on paint numbers and codes.

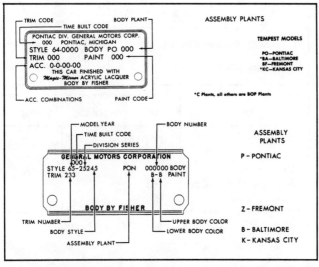

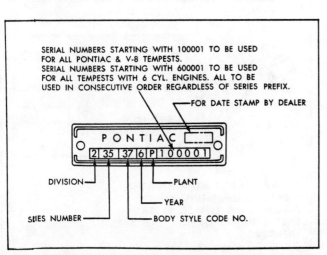

1964 and 1965 body identification plates and assembly plants.

Illustration of 1966 VIN plate located on LH front hinge pillar post. Series number indicates Tempest Custom; GTO would read 42.

Data plate from firewall of 1966 GTO. Date code indicated that this GTO was built the third week of February 1966. It was built at the Baltimore assembly plant, was painted Montero Red with a black top, and had a black interior. Plate was buffed for illustration purposes only; in correct restoration, plate would be painted black as part of firewall. Hole stamped in lower left of plate identified car as having a shoulder harness, a factory-installed provision.

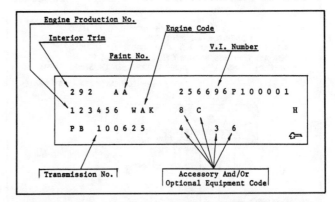

Information shown on the car data plate remained basically the same for 1966, except that the location of the numbers was changed and a new, easier-to-read type was used. Presently, some plates have certain information either omitted or incorrectly positioned. (This information was taken from Pontiac Service Management News Letter number 66-6, dated 10-27-65.)

1966-67

The data plate identification information outlined in the 1964-65 section applied to the 1966 and 1967 models. The only change was the addition of another plant code, G, for the GM Framingham, Massachusetts, A-body assembly plant, which began producing A-body LeMans, Tempest and GTO models at the start of the 1966 production year.

The VIN plate used in the accompanying drawing identifies a B-body Pontiac series. All other VIN information in the drawing is pertinent to the GTO.

The Pontiac, Michigan, home assembly plant exceeded the 200,000 mark for engine sequence serial numbers in 1966.

1968-70

The VIN plate was moved to the LH top of the instrument panel at the windshield in 1968 and remained there through 1970. The data plate was moved from the firewall to the LH top of the cowl near the hood hinge starting in 1968.

Coding information remained the same as in previous years. Beginning with the 1970 models, a label was affixed to the end of the LH door stating that the car complied with all federal government regulations.

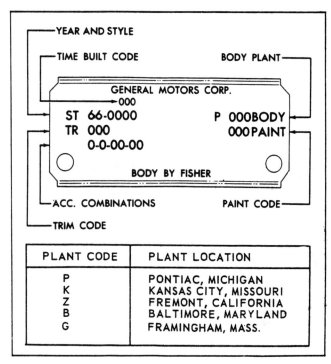

PLANT CODE	PLANT LOCATION
P	PONTIAC, MICHIGAN
K	KANSAS CITY, MISSOURI
Z	FREMONT, CALIFORNIA
B	BALTIMORE, MARYLAND
G	FRAMINGHAM, MASS.

Explanation of 1966 data plate located on LH side of firewall. Note assembly plant codes.

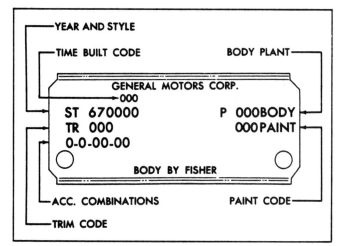

Plant	Code	Pontiac	Tempest
Pontiac	(P)	X	X
Baltimore	(B)		X
Freemont	(Z)		X
Kansas City, Mo.	(K)		X
Framingham	(G)		X

Detail of 1967 data plate and assembly plant codes.

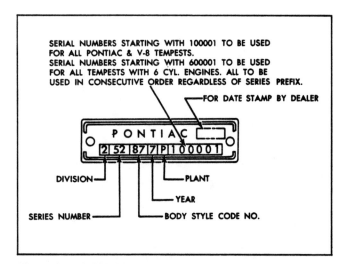

SERIAL NUMBERS STARTING WITH 100001 TO BE USED FOR ALL PONTIAC & V-8 TEMPESTS. SERIAL NUMBERS STARTING WITH 600001 TO BE USED FOR ALL TEMPESTS WITH 6 CYL. ENGINES. ALL TO BE USED IN CONSECUTIVE ORDER REGARDLESS OF SERIES PREFIX.

Illustration of 1967 VIN plate, located in same spot as 1966 plate. Series number is again wrong; should read 42.

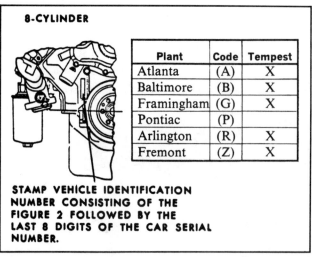

8-CYLINDER

Plant	Code	Tempest
Atlanta	(A)	X
Baltimore	(B)	X
Framingham	(G)	X
Pontiac	(P)	
Arlington	(R)	X
Fremont	(Z)	X

STAMP VEHICLE IDENTIFICATION NUMBER CONSISTING OF THE FIGURE 2 FOLLOWED BY THE LAST 8 DIGITS OF THE CAR SERIAL NUMBER.

Listing of assembly plants and respective codes. Note location of vehicle serial number on engine.

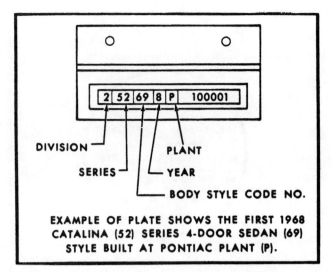

EXAMPLE OF PLATE SHOWS THE FIRST 1968 CATALINA (52) SERIES 4-DOOR SEDAN (69) STYLE BUILT AT PONTIAC PLANT (P).

1968 serial number, assembly plant code and model year identification can be determined from the VIN plate. This plate was fastened to the upper-left instrument panel area, visible through the windshield. The plate had embossed numerals, as shown.

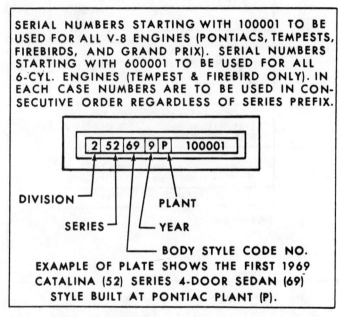

SERIAL NUMBERS STARTING WITH 100001 TO BE USED FOR ALL V-8 ENGINES (PONTIACS, TEMPESTS, FIREBIRDS, AND GRAND PRIX). SERIAL NUMBERS STARTING WITH 600001 TO BE USED FOR ALL 6-CYL. ENGINES (TEMPEST & FIREBIRD ONLY). IN EACH CASE NUMBERS ARE TO BE USED IN CONSECUTIVE ORDER REGARDLESS OF SERIES PREFIX.

EXAMPLE OF PLATE SHOWS THE FIRST 1969 CATALINA (52) SERIES 4-DOOR SEDAN (69) STYLE BUILT AT PONTIAC PLANT (P).

1969 vehicle identification plate.

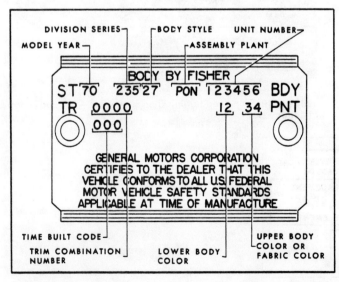

Body data plate was revised in 1970, but still located in same spot as in 1968 and 1969.

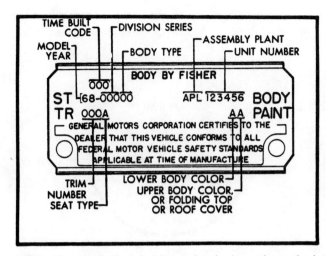

Information as to body style, trim number, body number and paint code may be found stamped on the body identification plate. For 1968, this plate was attached to the left side of the cowl assembly, just below the rear edge of the hood.

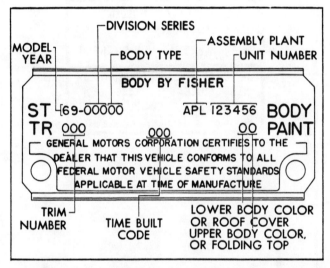

Body data plate for 1969, located on top of cowl near LH hood hinge.

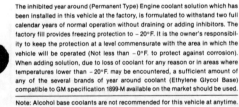

IMPORTANT

The inhibited year around (Permanent Type) Engine coolant solution which has been installed in this vehicle at the factory, is formulated to withstand two full calendar years of normal operation without draining or adding inhibitors. The factory fill provides freezing protection to −20°F. It is the owner's responsibility to keep the protection at a level commensurate with the area in which the vehicle will be operated (Not less than −0°F. to protect against corrosion). When adding solution, due to loss of coolant for any reason or in areas where temperatures lower than −20°F. may be encountered, a sufficient amount of any of the several brands of year around coolant (Ethylene Glycol Base) compatible to GM specification 1899-M available on the market should be used.

Note: Alcohol base coolants are not recommended for this vehicle at anytime.

Checked by Dealer — Date: _____

1964 radiator coolant tag, wired to radiator neck.

USE **CAUTION** ON REMOVING CAP WHEN ENGINE IS **HOT**

If water only is used as coolant GM # 983743 rust inhibitor of equivalent must be used.

1964-66 fan caution decal, located on core support on air-conditioned models. Non-air-conditioned models had the decal affixed to the fan shield, although it has been found on the core support top as well.

All decals were located on the LH inside of the glovebox door.

RECOMMENDED TIRE
PRESSURE (COOL TIRES)
5 PASSENGER LOAD OR LESS

24 P.S.I. - FRONT
22 P.S.I. - REAR

OVER 5 PASSENGER LOAD

26 P.S.I. - FRONT
30 P.S.I. - REAR

1965 tire pressure.

RECOMMENDED TIRE
PRESSURE (COOL TIRES)
5 PASSENGER LOAD OR LESS

24 P.S.I. FRONT — 22 P.S.I. REAR

OVER 5 PASSENGER LOAD

28 P.S.I. FRONT — 32 P.S.I. REAR

VEHICLE LOAD LIMIT: 1100 lbs.

FOR ADDITIONAL DATA
SEE OWNER'S
MANUAL

1966 tire pressure.

VEHICLE LOAD LIMIT 1100 lbs.

STANDARD INFLATION (COLD TIRES)
FULL RATED LOAD (OVER 5 PASSENGERS)

24 P.S.I. FRONT   32 P.S.I. REAR

OPTIONAL INFLATION (COLD TIRES)
REDUCED LOAD (1-5 PASSENGERS)
24 P.S.I. FRONT   24 P.S.I. REAR

See OWNERS MANUAL For Additional Data

1967 tire pressure.

TEMPEST - 6 CYL. with AIR COND. H
& 8 CYL. SEDANS & COUPES   Q

* VEHICLE LOAD LIMIT - 1100 LBS
6 PASS. - (3 Front - 3 Rear & 200 lbs. Luggage)
REDUCED LOAD (1 to 5 Pass. - 750 lbs. MAX.)

RECOMMENDED TIRE PRESSURE
(COLD TIRES)

STANDARD INFLATION		OPTIONAL INFLATION	
(Full Load Limit)		(Reduced Load)	
FRONT	REAR	FRONT	REAR
24 PSI	28 PSI	24 PSI	24 PSI

RECOMMENDED MINIMUM TIRES

| 8.25-14 | 4 PLY RATING | G77-14 | 4 PLY RATING |
| G70-14 | 4 PLY RATING | 205R14 | TYPE "A" |

* If equipped with BUCKET SEATS
VEHICLE LOAD LIMIT - 950 LBS.
5 PASS. - (2 Front - 3 Rear & 200 lbs. Luggage)

See OWNERS MANUAL for Additional Data

1968 tire pressure.

WARNING - ALWAYS CONNECT
POSITIVE TO POSITIVE
NEGATIVE TO NEGATIVE
WHEN USING BATTERY CHARGER OR BOOSTER
TO PREVENT DAMAGE TO ELECTRICAL SYSTEM.

1964-67 battery polarity warning decal, located on core support near battery.

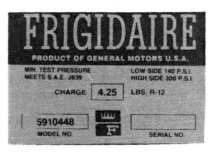

FRIGIDAIRE
PRODUCT OF GENERAL MOTORS U.S.A.

MIN. TEST PRESSURE	LOW SIDE 140 P.S.I.
MEETS S.A.E. J639	HIGH SIDE 300 P.S.I.
CHARGE	4.25	LBS. R-12
5910448		
MODEL NO.		SERIAL NO.

1964 and 1965 air-conditioning charge level decal, located on top of compressor.

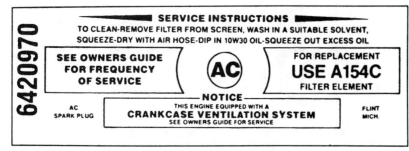

6420970

SERVICE INSTRUCTIONS
TO CLEAN-REMOVE FILTER FROM SCREEN, WASH IN A SUITABLE SOLVENT,
SQUEEZE-DRY WITH AIR HOSE-DIP IN 10W30 OIL-SQUEEZE OUT EXCESS OIL

SEE OWNERS GUIDE
FOR FREQUENCY
OF SERVICE

AC

FOR REPLACEMENT
USE A154C
FILTER ELEMENT

NOTICE

AC
SPARK PLUG

THIS ENGINE EQUIPPED WITH A
CRANKCASE VENTILATION SYSTEM
SEE OWNERS GUIDE FOR SERVICE

FLINT
MICH.

1967 two-barrel foam element service decal, located on outside of air cleaner lid.

WE	WF	WG	WH
YB	YD	YE	YF
YG	YH	XB	XF
XG	HX	ZB	ZF
ZG	ZH	ZK	ZL

WB WD

STANDARD BRAKE LININGS		
Ratio	Std. Axle Code	Saf-T-Track Code
2.56	WB	YB
2.93	WD	YD
3.08	WE	YE
3.23	WF	YF
3.36	WG	YG
3.55	WH	YH

METALLIC BRAKE LININGS		
Ratio	Std. Axle Code	Saf-T-Track Code
3.08	XB	ZB
3.23	XF	ZF
3.36	XG	ZG
3.55	XH	ZH
3.90	(NIA)	ZK
4.33	(NIA)	ZL

Included with the 1965 Tempest GTO axle identification sticker kit were instructions to locate the alphabetical code stamped in the axle housing, just to the right of the carrier case and directly below the brake pipe clip. Then cut out the sticker with the same alphabetical code and apply it to the left rear brake drum facing. The table in the illustration will help identify the codes.

1965-67 transistorized ignition coil decal, located on side of coil.

1965-67 transistorized ignition control amplifier decal, located on amplifier.

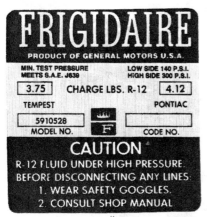

1966 air-conditioning compressor charge and caution decal, located on top of compressor.

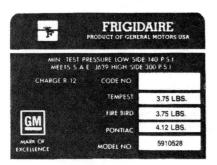

1967 air-conditioning compressor charge and caution decal, located at top of compressor.

1967 fan caution decal, found in the same locations as the 1964-66 decal.

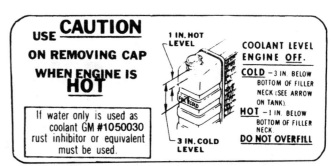

1968 fan caution decal located in core support near the radiator cap.

CAUTION

THIS VEHICLE EQUIPPED WITH LIMITED SLIP DIFFERENTIAL. REAR WHEEL MAY DRIVE IF IN CONTACT WITH GROUND EVEN THOUGH OPPOSITE WHEEL IS RAISED. DO NOT RUN ENGINE WITH VEHICLE ON JACK UNLESS TRANSMISSION IS IN NEUTRAL OR PARK. SEE OWNER'S MANUAL.

PRINTED IN U.S.A.   PART NO. 3745926

1964 positive traction decal, located on underside of deck lid.

AC SPARK PLUG TYPE **A 98 C** **AIR CLEANER**

SERVICE WITH

SERVICE INSTRUCTIONS

INSPECT FILTER ELEMENT EVERY 12,000 MILES MORE OFTEN UNDER SEVERE DUST CONDITIONS TO CLEAN: REMOVE ELEMENT FROM SCREEN, REMOVE OIL AND DIRT BY WASHING ELEMENT IN A SUITABLE SOLVENT SUCH AS KEROSENE — SQUEEZE ELEMENT DRY DIP IN S.A.E. 10 W 30 OIL AND SQUEEZE TO REMOVE EXCESS OIL

FLINT, MICH.   MADE IN U.S.A.

1965-67 standard four-barrel foam element service decal, located at front base of air cleaner.

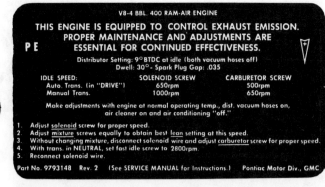

V8-4 BBL. 400 RAM-AIR ENGINE

THIS ENGINE IS EQUIPPED TO CONTROL EXHAUST EMISSION. PROPER MAINTENANCE AND ADJUSTMENTS ARE ESSENTIAL FOR CONTINUED EFFECTIVENESS.

PE

Distributor Setting: 9°BTDC at idle (both vacuum hoses off)
Dwell: 30° - Spark Plug Gap: .035

IDLE SPEED:	SOLENOID SCREW	CARBURETOR SCREW
Auto. Trans. (in "DRIVE")	650rpm	500rpm
Manual Trans.	1000rpm	650rpm

Make adjustments with engine at normal operating temp., dist. vacuum hoses on, air cleaner on and air conditioning "off."

1. Adjust solenoid screw for proper speed.
2. Adjust mixture screws equally to obtain best lean setting at this speed.
3. Without changing mixture, disconnect solenoid wire and adjust carburetor screw for proper speed.
4. With trans. in NEUTRAL, set fast idle screw to 2800rpm.
5. Reconnect solenoid wire.

Part No. 9793148 Rev. 2 (See SERVICE MANUAL for Instructions.) Pontiac Motor Div., GMC

Engine tuning data decal for 1968 Ram Air engine, located on LH top of core support.

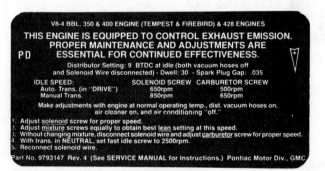

V8-4 BBL. 350 & 400 ENGINE (TEMPEST & FIREBIRD) & 428 ENGINES

THIS ENGINE IS EQUIPPED TO CONTROL EXHAUST EMISSION. PROPER MAINTENANCE AND ADJUSTMENTS ARE ESSENTIAL FOR CONTINUED EFFECTIVENESS.

PD

Distributor Setting: 9 BTDC at idle (both vacuum hoses off and Solenoid Wire disconnected) - Dwell: 30 - Spark Plug Gap: .035

IDLE SPEED:	SOLENOID SCREW	CARBURETOR SCREW
Auto. Trans. (in "DRIVE")	650rpm	500rpm
Manual Trans.	850rpm	650rpm

Make adjustments with engine at normal operating temp., dist. vacuum hoses on, air cleaner on, and air conditioning "off."

1. Adjust solenoid screw for proper speed.
2. Adjust mixture screws equally to obtain best lean setting at this speed.
3. Without changing mixture, disconnect solenoid wire and adjust carburetor screw for proper speed.
4. With trans. in NEUTRAL, set fast idle screw to 2500rpm.
5. Reconnect solenoid wire.

Part No. 9793147 Rev. 4 (See SERVICE MANUAL for Instructions.) Pontiac Motor Div., GMC

Engine tuning decal for 1968 standard four-barrel engine, located on LH top of core support.

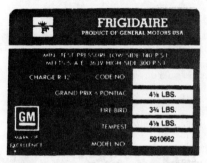

FRIGIDAIRE
PRODUCT OF GENERAL MOTORS USA

MIN. TEST PRESSURE LOW SIDE 140 P.S.I.
MEETS S.A.E. J639 HIGH SIDE 300 P.S.I.

CHARGE R-12	CODE NO.	
GRAND PRIX x PONTIAC		4½ LBS.
FIRE BIRD		3¾ LBS.
TEMPEST		4½ LBS.
MODEL NO.		5910662

GM
MARK OF EXCELLENCE

662

1968-70 air-conditioning compressor charging level and caution decal, located at top of compressor.

PLEASE
DO NOT SPILL GAS
OR DRAG HOSE
ON CAR

1964 gas door decal.

CAUTION

REFRIGERANT FLUID UNDER HIGH PRESSURE
DO NOT DISCONNECT ANY LINES WITHOUT -

1. WEARING PRESCRIBED SAFETY GOGGLES.
2. FOLLOWING PROCEDURE OUTLINED IN THE SHOP MANUAL.

1964-65 charge caution decal, located on top of compressor in front of charge level decal.

THIS ENGINE IS EQUIPPED TO CONTROL **EXHAUST EMISSION** PROPER MAINTENANCE AND ADJUSTMENTS ARE ESSENTIAL FOR CONTINUED EFFECTIVENESS

8 Cyl. Engine
4 Bbl. Carb.
PB

Distributor Setting: 9 BTDC at idle (distributor vacuum hose off)
Dwell: 30 Spark Plug Gap .035

IDLE SETTING	CARB. Setting	MIXTURE Screws
AUTO. TRANS. (In "DRIVE")	675 rpm	650 rpm
MANUAL TRANS.	1050 rpm	950 rpm

Make adjustments with engine at normal operating temperature, distributor vacuum hose off, air cleaner on, and air conditioning off.

1. Disconnect distributor vacuum hose. Plug hose leading to carburetor.
2. Adjust CARBURETOR speed screw for proper speed.
3. Adjust MIXTURE screws to obtain best LEAN setting at this speed.
4. Adjust MIXTURE screws equally (clockwise) to reduce idle rpm to proper speed.
5. With trans in NEUTRAL, set fast idle screw to 2000 rpm on top step of fast idle cam.
6. Reconnect distributor vacuum hose.

Part No. 480918 (See SERVICE MANUAL for instructions) Pontiac Motor Div. G. M. C.

Engine tuning instruction and exhaust emission decal for 1970 standard four-barrel engine, located on LH top of core support.

1967-70 heavy-duty air cleaner element service instructions, located on air cleaner assembly.

1968-70 four-barrel and Ram Air engine air cleaner element service instruction, located on outside of air cleaner body.

1968-69 two-barrel engine air cleaner service instructions, located on air cleaner assembly.

Chapter 2
EXTERIORS

EXTERIOR

1964-65

As part of the LeMans model line-up, the 1964-65 GTO used the same exterior moldings and brightwork not shared with the less expensive Tempest. Wheel opening moldings were polished stainless steel, and shared the same part numbers.

	RH	LH
Front	9774787	9774788
Rear	9775996	9775997

Both years carried the GTO 6.5 liter emblem (part number 9775867) behind the front wheel openings. The 1964 quarter-panel nameplate was mounted in the upper area of the rear quarter panel. In 1965 it was moved down in line with the wraparound taillamp bezel. The nameplate was the same for both years (part number 9775668) and had black letters riding on a chrome bar.

Rocker panel moldings were the same for both years and were made of stainless (part number 9777045 LH and 9777044 RH). The rocker panel moldings were mounted on cadmium-plated clips (package part number 9777046). The front of the molding was mounted by a screw to a nylon insert to a hole in the fender. The rear of the molding was mounted directly to the rocker panel by a chromed Phillips-head screw.

Hoods were different, with the 1964 hood using two simulated scoops made from diecast metal and chromed (part number 9775669 LH and 9775698 RH). The hood emblem (part number 9774297) was also diecast. The 1965 hood used a single ornament in the form of a simulated scoop (part number 9780159) and was painted the exterior color.

Exterior door handles and lock assemblies were identical for both years. The LH handle was part number 5719142, the RH handle was 5719143, and the button shaft assembly used part number 9632427. The lock cylinder cap (part number 230018) used a gasket (part number 4587931). When assembling the lock and handle components, apply strip caulking to the screws. This will seal the handle to the door, making it watertight.

Water leakage into 1965 taillight assemblies was due to a mispositioned gasket, according to Pontiac Service News Flash 65-26, dated 10-13-64. To correct, remove and disassemble the assembly, cement the gasket to the lamp housing in its proper position, and reassemble. Note that it is necessary to lower the rear bumper and remove the rear quarter panel extension.

On September 17, 1964, Pontiac announced to dealers via internal bulletin that the pinstripe on GTOs could be deleted at the buyer's request. Deletion of the pinstripe could be accomplished by writing across the face of the car order, "Do Not Apply Paint Stripe(s)." The deletion of the stripe did not affect the price of the GTO option. Therefore, it technically would not be incorrect for a GTO to be shown without a pinstripe, and points should not be deducted.

The following are the correct code numbers for Cordova top colors:

Code Number	Year	Color
1	1964	Ivory
2	1964	Black
2	1965	Black
6	1965	Beige

1966-67

The GTO graduated from being a LeMans option to a separate series in 1966. While it shared basic trim with the LeMans, it also had some unique trim.

The stainless wheel opening moldings were the same for both 1966 and 1967.

	RH	LH
Front	9785448	9785447
Rear	4227182	4227183

The GTO 6.5 liter emblem (part number 9775867) was located behind the front wheel openings for 1966. The emblem was moved down to the rocker molding behind the front wheel openings in 1967, but used the same part number. The quarter-panel nameplate (part number 9775668) was located in the center rear of the rear quarter panel for both years. The nameplate had black letters on a chrome bar.

Rocker panel moldings were distinctly different for the two years. The rocker molding was retained by cadmium clips and screws in 1966, and only by clips in 1967.

The hood ornament (part number 9780159), was in the form of a simulated hood scoop, and was painted the exterior color. A front hood emblem (part number 9783370), shaped like the Pontiac triangular crest, was brushed diecast metal with a 0° gloss-black painted recess.

Exterior door handles were the same for both years (part number 9706522 RH and 9706523 LH) and were retained by two screws (part number 4430409). All 1967 models had new lock cylinders and keys which would not interchange with earlier years. There was a new keyway design and an increased number of biting depths. This was reported in Dealer Service Information Bulletin number 67-I-5, dated 10-14-66.

	RH	LH
1966	4545370	4545371
1967	7642078	7642079

The push button and shaft assembly was part number 9706042, and was sealed by an O-ring (part number 4156548).

The following are the correct code numbers for Cordova top colors:

Code Number	Year	Color
1	1966	Ivory
2	1966	Black
6	1966	Beige
1	1967	Ivory
2	1967	Black
7	1967	Cream

1968-70

Although the styling of the 1968 and 1969 GTO was quite similar, there were some subtle differences in trim and molding. Dealer Service Information Bulletin number 69-I-66, dated 6-20-69, indicates a production change in front fender moldings. Front fenders (9793405 RH and 9793406 LH) were changed to eliminate the black paint. The unpainted pieces were 478951 RH, and 478952 LH. A car should have the same type of molding on both sides.

Dealer Service Information Bulletin number 69-I-49, dated 2-24-69, reported that the lower rear quarter mold-

COLOR NAME	BODY PLATE PAINT OR TRIM CODE	DU PONT	DITZLER	RINSHED-MASON
EXTERIOR				
Starlight Black	A	88-L	DDL-9300	A-946
Cameo Ivory	C	4024-L	DDL-8259	A-1199
Silvermist Gray	D	4247-L	DDL-32173	A-1477
Yorktown Blue	F	4250-L	DDL-12546	A-1481
Skyline Blue	H	4531-L	DDL-12847	A-1615
Pinehurst Green	J	4532-L	DDL-43264	A-1613
Marimba Red	L	4600-LM (No. 2)	DDL-50684	A-1536 (No. 2)
Sunfire Red	N	4533-LH	DDL-71415	A-1616R
Aquamarine	P	4253-L	DDL-12525	A-1476
Gulfstream Aqua	Q	4529-L	DDL-12848	A-1611
Alamo Beige	R	4526-L	DDL-22391	A-1609
Saddle Bronze	S	4392-L	DDL-22269	A-1537
Singapore Gold	T	4527-L	DDL-22392	A-1610
Grenadier Red	V	4387-LH	DDL-71336	A-1538R
Nocturne Blue	W	4395-L	DDL-12696	A-1539
WHEEL COLORS				
Regent Black	. . . .	93-005	DQE-4000	P-403
Yorktown Blue	. . . .	181-95180	DQE-12546	262V22
Pinehurst Green	. . . .	181-96882	DQE-43264	264V31
Singapore Gold	. . . .	181-96810	DQE-22392	264V82
Gulfstream Aqua	. . . .	181-96812	DQE-12848	264V21
Saddle	. . . .	181-96217	DQE-22269	263V82
INTERIOR (60° GLOSS)				
Parchment	. . . .	900-L	DL-8360	62T82
Starlight Black	214-240-251-253-258-260-268-282-283-285-290-293-299	88-L	DL-9248	400
Yorktown Blue	201-208-221-226-231-236-241-245-249-254-259-261-264-267-278-284-286-289-294	9006-L	DL-12531	62024
Aquamarine	202-209-222-227-232-237-242-246-250-255-262-288	9005-L	DL-12533	62036
Carib Aqua	217-271	9012-LH	DL-12534	62031
Admiral Blue	215-228-269-273-276	96221	DL-12737	63021
Singapore Gold	243-247	4527-L	DL-22454	64082
Saddle (Lt.)	203-206-211-216-224-229-234-238-256-266-270-274-279-295-297	9086-L	DL-22460	64T81
Sunfire Red	205-244-248-281 •	9084-LM	DL-50679	64T61M
Camden Gray	. . . .	9010-L	DL-32186	62012
Oxford Gray	. . . .	9009-L	DL-32194	63T11
Pinehurst Green	223-233-291	4532-L	DL-43294	64031
Belmar Red	204-212-225-230-235-244-248-252-257-263-265-275-281-292-298 •	9090-L	DL-50678	64061M
Burgundy	. . . .	94969-H	DL-50561	62051M
Guard Red	207-218-239-272-277-280-287-296	9016-LH	DL-71276	62T51M
UPPER INSTRUMENT PANEL (0° GLOSS)				
Velvet Black	214-240-258-282-285-299	4428-L	DIA-9317	400
Carib Aqua	202-209-217-222-227-232-237-242-246-288	4429-L	DIA-12753	64T22
Admiral Blue	201-208-215-221-226-228-231-236-241-245-276-286	4430-L	DIA-12754	64T21
Mocha Brown	203-206-211-216-224-229-234-238-243-247-297	4436-L	DIA-22306	64T82
Oxford Gray	205	4433-L	DIA-32319	64T11
Burgundy	204-207-212-218-225-230-235-239-244-248-277-280-298	4431-LH	DIA-50637	64T62M
TRUNK SPATTER FINISH				
Red	. . . .	389-219	DX-1698	833
Blue	. . . .	389-220	DX-1699	834

1964 paint color numbers.

ing was being deleted in production of 1969 models.

The stainless wheel opening moldings were the same for 1968-69, and revised for 1970 to accommodate fender redesign.

Application	Year	RH	LH
Front	1968-69	9793382	9793383
	1970	479176	479177
Rear	1968-69	7795122	7795123
	1970	8702432	8702470

The GTO 6.5 liter emblem (part number 9775867) was located behind the front wheel opening for 1968. This emblem was discontinued in 1969, and replaced by a GTO nameplate in approximately the same location. The letters of the nameplate were white. However, the bar the letters rode on was painted to match the exterior color. There were eighteen part numbers (one for each color nameplate) for 1969.

In 1970, the plate was replaced by a decal, either red (part number 479921), black (part number 479920) or white (part number 479922). If equipped with the optional 455 engine, a GTO 455 decal was used. Three colors were used: red (part number 479918), black (part number 479917) or white (part number 479919).

COLOR NAME	BODY PLATE PAINT OR TRIM CODE	DU PONT	DITZLER	RINSHED-MASON
EXTERIOR				
Starlight Black *	A.	88	DDL-9300	A-946
Blue Charcoal	B.	4622-L	DDL-32448	A-1709
Cameo Ivory *	C.	4024-L	DDL-8259	A-1199
Fontaine Blue	D.	4630-L	DDL-13042	A-1720
Nightwatch Blue	E.	4631-L	DDL-13002	A-1721
Palmetto Green	H.	4633-L	DDL-43391	A-1716
Reef Turquoise	K.	4628-L	DDL-43364	A-1718
Teal Turquoise	L.	4629-L	DDL-13003	A-1719
Burgundy	N.	4624-LH	DDL-50700	A-1711M
Iris Mist	P.	4632-L	DDL-50693	A-1722
Montero Red *	R.	4625-LH	DDL-71472	A-1712M
Capri Gold	T.	4627-L	DDL-22564	A-1714
Mission Beige	V.	4401-L	DDL-22270	A-1530
Bluemist Slate	W.	4623-L	DDL-32461	A-1710
Mayfair Maize	Y.	4620-L	DDL-81500	A-1715
*Pin Stripe Colors				
WHEEL COLORS				
Starlight Black	A.	93-005	DQE-9000	P-403
Fontaine Blue	D.	181-97219	DQE-13042	265B27
Teal Turquoise	L.	181-97218	DQE-13003	265B23
Capri Gold	T.	181-97216	DQE-22564	265B81
Silver Textured (Tempest Rally Wheel)	. . . .	--	--	E28C009
INTERIOR—(60° GLOSS)				
Black	213-218-233-236-241-249-255-256-258-260-261-265-270-274-276-277-281-288-297	88	DL-9248	400-A-946
Blue Charcoal (Gunmetal)	208-235-259-262-279-283-286-290-299	4622-L	DL-32468	65V11
Medium Blue	201-209-219-224-229-237-242-246-251-266-273-292	4630-L	DL-13006	65V22
Medium Green	221-226-294	4633-L	DL-43367	65V32
Medium Turquoise	202-205-210-220-225-230-238-243-247-252-267-278-293. . .	4628-L	DL-43400	65B31
Medium Gold (Fawn)	203-206-211-215-222-227-231-239-244-248-253-263-268-284-291-295	9171-L	DL-22574	65B84
Dark Blue	217.	9172-L	DL-13007	65V23
Dark Turquoise	214-282	9176-L	DL-13008	65B32
Plum	250-264-287	9179-L	DL-50705	65B62M
Red	204-207-212-216-223-228-232-234-240-245-254-257-269-272-275-280-285-289-296-298 . .	9183-LH	DL-71474	65B53R
UPPER INSTRUMENT PANEL (0° GLOSS)				
Blue Charcoal (Gunmetal)	208-235-259-262-279-283-286-290-299	9191-LH	DIA-32466	65V13
Dark Blue	201-209-217-219-224-229-237-242-246-251-266-273-292. . .	9194-LH	DIA-130	65B29
Black	261-265-270-274-276-277-281-288-297	4428-L	DIA-9317	400-A-946
Dark Turquoise	202-205-210-214-220-225-230-238-243-247-252-267-278-282-293.	9197-LH	DIA-43398	65B36
Plum	250-264-287	9200-LM	DIA-50704	65B20
Dark Red	204-207-212-216-223-228-232-234-240-245-254-257-269-272-275-280-285-289-296-298. .	9201-LM	DIA-71486	65B55M
Gold (Dark Fawn)	203-206-211-215-222-227-231-239-244-248-253-263-268-284-291-295	9198-LH	DIA-22533	65B87
Dark Green	221-226-294	9225-LH	DIA-43420	65B35
TRUNK INTERIORS				
Dark Blue, Green Gray	. . . .	389-256	DX-1757	838
ENGINE PAINT				
Blue	. . . .	93-76981	11561	62-015

1965 paint color numbers.

COLOR NAME	BODY PLATE PAINT OR TRIM CODE	DU PONT	DITZLER	RINSHED-MASON
EXTERIOR				
Starlight Black*	A.	88	DDL-9300	A-946
Blue Charcoal	B.	4622-L	DDL-32448	A-1709
Cameo Ivory*	C.	4024-L	DDL-8259	A-1199
Fontaine Blue	D.	4630-L	DDL-13042	A-1720
Nightwatch Blue	E.	4631-L	DDL-13002	A-1721
Palmetto Green	H.	4633-L	DDL-43391	A-1716
Reef Turquoise	K.	4628-L	DDL-43364	A-1718
Marina Turquoise	L.	4703-L	DDL-43496	A-1816
Burgundy	N.	4624-LH	DDL-50700	A-1711M
Barrier Blue	P.	4760-L	DDL-13242	A-1822
Montero Red*	R.	4625-LH	DDL-71472	A-1712M
Martinique Bronze	T.	4706-L	DDL-22660	A-1821
Mission Beige	V.	4401-L	DDL-22270	A-1530
Platinum	W.	4708-L	DDL-32525	A-1819
Candlelite Cream	Y.	4709-L	DDL-81528	A-1824
*Pin Stripe Colors				
WHEEL COLORS				
Starlight Black	A.	93-005	DQE-9300	P-403
Fontaine Blue	D.	181-97219	DQE-13042	E-1720
Marina Turquoise	L.	181-97561-H	DQE-43496	E-1816
Martinique Bronze	T.	181-97591	DQE-22660	E-1821
Silver Textured (Tempest Rally Wheel)	. . . .	--	--	E28C009
INTERIOR—(60° GLOSS)				
Black	223	88	DL-9248	400-A-946
Medium Fawn (Gold)	221			
		9274-LH	DL-22571	66B83
Dark Blue	219	9268-LH	DL-13222	66B21
Dark Turquoise	220	9273-LH	DL-43533	66B31
Red	222			
		9183-LM	DL-71474	65B53R
UPPER INSTRUMENT PANEL (0° GLOSS)				
Blue Charcoal (Gunmetal)		9191-LH	DIA-32466	65V13
Dark Blue				
		9284-LH	DIA-13216	66B27
Black	223			
		4428-L	DIA-9317	400-A-946
Dark Turquoise	220			
		9287-LH	DIA-43532	66B35
		9200-LM	DIA-50704	65B20
Red	222			
		9201-LM	DIA-71486	65B55M
Gold (Dark Fawn)	221			
		9198-LH	DIA-22533	65B87
TRUNK INTERIORS	. . . .			
Dark Blue, Gray Fleck (Tempest)	. . . .	389-259	DX-1758	844
ENGINE PAINT				
Silver Blue	. . . .	181-97219	13255	266T21

1966 paint color numbers.

COLOR NAME	BODY PLATE PAINT OR TRIM CODE	DU PONT	DITZLER	RINSHED-MASON
EXTERIOR				
Starlight Black	A.	88	9300	A-946
Cameo Ivory	C.	4024-L	8259	A-1199
Montreux Blue	D.	4815-L	13349	A-1899
Fathom Blue	E.	4817-L	13346	A-1900
Tyrol Blue	F.	4850-L	13364	A-1920
Signet Gold	G.	4825-L	22818	A-1919
Lindén Green	H.	4816-L	43651	A-1901
Gulf Turquoise	K.	4818-L	43661	A-1903
Mariner Turquoise	L.	4824-L	43659	A-1904G
Plum Mist	M	4832-L	50717	A-1905
Burgundy	N.	4624-L	50700	A-1711M
Silverglaze	P.	4820-L	32603	A-1906
Regimental Red	R.	4822-LH	71583	A-1907R
Champagne	S.	4826-L	22813	A-1908
Montego Cream	T.	4819-L	81578	A-1909
WHEEL COLORS				
Starlight Black	A.	93-005	9300	P-403
Montreux Blue	D.	4815-D	13349	E-1899
Mariner Turquoise	L.	4824-DH	43659	E-1904G
Seneca Bronze	T.	4783-DH	22865	E-1909
INTERIOR—(60° GLOSS)				
Black	235 223			
		88	9248	400-A-946
Signal Blue	219			
Signet Gold	221	9395-LH	13383	67B29
Gulf Turquoise		9390-L	22839	67B78
Mariner Turquoise	202	9399-LH	43680	67B38
		9368-LM	71590	67B56R
Regimental Red	225	9366-LM	71591	67B54R
UPPER INSTRUMENT PANEL (0° GLOSS)				
Black	235 223			
		4428-L	9317	400-A-946
Signal Blue	219			
		9373-LH	13365	67B28
Mariner Turquoise	220	9374-LH	13366	67B31
Champagne	221			
		9376-L	22837	67B72
Burgundy				
		9201-LM	71486	65B55M
TRUNK INTERIORS				
Dark Blue, Gray Fleck	. . . .	389-259	DX-1758	844
ENGINE PAINT				
Silver Blue	. . . .	181-97219	13255	266T21

1967 Pontiac-Tempest paint color numbers.

The same rocker panel molding (part number 9793887 RH and 9793888 LH) was used for 1968 and 1969. This panel was stainless steel. During the 1969 production year, the panel was changed from stainless to aluminum (part number 479366 RH and 479367 LH). The 1970 rocker panel molding (part number 479164 RH and 479165 LH) was revised to accommodate sheet metal changes. The same clip package (part number 8777710) was used from 1967 through 1970.

Dual hood vent ornaments (scoops) were used in 1968-70 (part number 9791143 RH and 9791144 LH). If the optional Ram Air was ordered, the ornaments were opened. The ornaments were painted exterior body color, except on the 1970 Judge option, in which case the ornaments were painted 0° gloss black. When equipped with Ram Air in 1969 or 1970, a decal was affixed to the outboard side of each ornament.

A front bumper emblem (part number 9790459) was used on the Endura bumper in 1968. If the chrome bumper option was ordered, a different emblem (part number 9791833) was installed. The emblem was discontinued after 1968. Both emblems were shaped like the traditional Pontiac crest, and were brushed, diecast metal with the recessed areas of the emblems painted 0° gloss black.

The 1969 urethane bumpers and bumper nose extensions may be subject to yellowing, especially the white ones. To correct, paint the items with three coats of silver urethane paint (part number 1050983), allowing adequate time to dry between coats. Repaint with original exterior color coat, and clear top coat. (This information is from Dealer Technical Bulletin number 69-T-18, dated 1-20-69.)

Exterior door handles were the same for 1968-70 (part number 5719142 RH and 5719143 LH). Care should be taken to inspect these handles if they are ordered

EXTERIOR COLOR (Lower)		STRIPE and/or DECAL COLOR	TRIM COMBINATIONS
A	Starlight Black	Cameo Ivory	219-220-221-223-224-235-236
		Regimental Red	225
C	Cameo Ivory	Regimental Red	225
		Starlight Black	219-220-221-223-224-235-236
D	Alpine Blue	Cameo Ivory	219-224-236
		Starlight Black	223-235
E	Aegena Blue	Cameo Ivory	219-223-224-235-236
F	Nordic Blue	Starlight Black	223-235
		Cameo Ivory	219-224-236
G	April Gold	Starlight Black	223-235
		Cameo Ivory	221-224-236
K	Meridian Turquoise	Starlight Black	223-235
		Cameo Ivory	220-224-236
L	Aleutian Blue	Cameo Ivory	219-223-224-235-236
N	Flambeau Burgundy	Cameo Ivory	223-224-225-235-236
P	Springmist Green	Starlight Black	223-235
		Cameo Ivory	224-236
Q	Verdoro Green	Cameo Ivory	223-224-235-236
R	Solar Red	Starlight Black	223-235
		Cameo Ivory	224-225-236
T	Primavera Beige	Starlight Black	221-223-224-235-236
V	Nightshade Green	Cameo Ivory	223-224-235-236
Y	Mayfair Maize	Starlight Black	223-224-235-236

Paint stripe and decal color usage.

through a dealer today, as the molds are in very poor condition and the quality of the finished product may be low.

The handle was retained to the door skin by two screws (part number 4430409). The button and shaft assembly (part number 9704699) was the same for 1968-69, but was changed to part number 9703519 for 1970. The same sealing ring (part number 4156548) was used for all three years.

COLOR NAME	BODY PLATE PAINT OR TRIM CODE		DU PONT	DITZLER	RINSHED-MASON
	PAINT CODE	MOLDING COLOR			
EXTERIOR					
Starlight Black	A	Black	88-L	9300	A-946
Cameo Ivory	C	Black	4024-L	8259	A-1199
Alpine Blue	D	Teal	4892-L	13512	A-1985
Aegena Blue	E	Black	4899-L	13513	A-1992
Nordic Blue	F	Teal	4901-L	13514	A-1994
April Gold	G	Gold	4896-L	22942	A-1988
Autumn Bronze	I	-	4904-L	60517	A-1996F
Meridian Turquoise	K	Turquoise	4900-L	13517	A-1993
Aleutian Blue	L	Teal	4893-L	13516	A-1986
Flambeau Burgundy	N	Red	4915-LH	50775	A-1999F
Springmist Green	P	Black	4897-L	43774	A-1989
Verdoro Green	Q	Black	4947-LH	43745	A-1936
Solar Red	R	Red	4948-LH	71634	A-1997F
Primavera Beige	T	Gold	4895-L	81617	A-1987
Nightshade Green	V	Black	4898-L	43773	A-1990
Mayfair Maize	Y	Black	4620-L	81500	A-1715
DECK LID OR DOOR CORNER MOLDING					
Dark Teal	. . . .		9571-L - *2 oz.	13628	168V36
Medium Gold	. . . .		9568-L - *1 1/2 oz.	23035	168V74
White	. . . .		9332-L - *1 oz.	8678	168B92
Black	. . . .		9333-L - *2 oz.	9358	168C41
WHEEL COLORS					
Starlight Black	A	. . . .	88-L	9300	P-403
Alpine Blue	D	. . . .	4892-L	13512	E-1985
Nordic Blue	F	. . . .	4901-L	13514	E-1994
April Gold	G	. . . .	4896-L	22942	E-1998
Meridian Turquoise	K	. . . .	4900-L	13517	E-1993
INTERIOR - (30° GLOSS)					
Starlight Black	223	235			
			88-L	9266	A-946
Aleutian Blue	219				
		. . . .	9467-LH	13567	168B29
Laguna Turquoise	220				
			9471-LH	13570	168B35
April Gold	221				
			9478-L	22988	168B74
Regimental Red	225		9366-LH	71591	167B51R
UPPER INSTRUMENT PANEL (0° GLOSS)					
Velvet Black	223				
			4428-L	9317	A-946
Aleutian Blue	219				
			9453-LH	13556	168B22
Laguna Turquoise	220				
			9456-L	43799	168B71
TRUNK INTERIORS					
Dark Blue, Grey Fleck	. . . .		389-259	DX-1758	844
ENGINE PAINT					
Silver Blue	. . . .		181-97219	13255	266T21

* The amount of flattening compound (Dupont #4528) indicated, should be added to one pint of unreduced color to arrive at the correct gloss level.

1968 paint color numbers.

COLOR NAME	BODY PLATE PAINT OR TRIM CODE		DU PONT	DITZLER	RINSHED-MASON
EXTERIOR	PAINT CODE	MOLDING COLOR			
Starlight Black	10 (A)	Black	88-L	9300	A-946
Mayfair Maize	40 (Y)	Black	5036-L	81500	A-1715
Cameo White	50 (C)	Black	5033-L	2058	A-2080
Liberty Blue	51 (E)	Blue	5016-L	2075	A-2098
Matador Red	52 (R)	Red	5009-LH	2076	A-2099R
Warwick Blue	53 (D)	Blue	5015-L	2077	A-2100
Crystal Turquoise	55 (K)	Black	5014-L	2078	A-2101
Midnight Green	57 (M)	Green	5013-L	2079	A-2102
Limelight Green	59 (H)	Green	5012-L	2080	A-2103
Expresso Brown	61 (B)	Brown	5011-L	2081	A-2104
Champagne	63 (S)	Brown	5064-L	22813	A-2105
Antique Gold	65 (G)	Brown	5010-L	2082	A-2106D
Burgundy	67 (N)	Red	5063-LH	50700	A-2107M
Palladium Silver	69 (P)	Black	5032-L	2059	A-2108
Carousel Red	72 (T)	-	5021-LM	2084	A-2111R
Verdoro Green	73 (Q)	Green	5066-LH	2095	A-2110
Goldenrod Yellow	76 (W)	-	5026-LH	2094	A-2119
Claret Red	86 (L)	-	5074-L	71763	169V51R
Windward Blue	87 (F)	-	4962-L	13759	A-2123
Nocturne Blue	88 (V)	-	5075-L	13841	169V29
Castillian Bronze	89 (J)	-	5076-L	23215	169V81
WHEEL COLORS					
Starlight Black	A		93-005	DQE-9300	P-403
Antique Gold	G		5010-D	DQE-2082	E-2106D
Limelight Green	H		5012-D	DQE-2080	E-2103
Crystal Turquoise	K		5014-D	DQE-2078	E-2101
Warwick Blue	D		5009-DM	DQE-2077	E-2100
INTERIOR—(SEMI GLOSS)					
Black		258 268			
Dark Blue		250	88	9266	169C41
			9586LH	13789	169B29
Parchment		257-267			
Medium Gold		252	9401L	22841	167B92
			9594L	23160	169C75
Midnight Green		256			
			9593LH	44010	169V35
Medium Red	254		9528LH	71751	168C51R
INTERIOR—("0" GLOSS)					
Black		258 268			
Dark Blue		250	4428L	9317	168C41
Dark Gold		252	9578LH	13767	169V22
Midnight Green		256	9583L	23143	169C77
Dark Red	254		9582LH	43993	169V36
			9580LM	71643	169B63M
TRUNK INTERIORS Dark Blue & Gray Fleck			389-259	DX-1758	844
ENGINE PAINT Silver Blue			181-97219	13255	266T21

1969 paint color numbers.

The paint colors are identified by letters on Vehicle order form and by numbers on Body Number Plate. Enclosed is a list corresponding one against the other.

Color	Ltr. Code	No. Code	Color	Ltr. Code	No. Code
Starlight Black	A	10	Verdoro Green	Q	73
Expresso Brown	B	61	Matador Red	R	52
Cameo White	C	50	Champagne	S	63
Warwick Blue	D	53	Mayfair Maize	Y	40
Liberty Blue	E	51	Carousel Red	T	72
Antique Gold	G	65	Windward Blue	F	87
Limelight Green	H	59	Goldenrod Yellow	W	76
Crystal Turquoise	K	55	Claret Red	L	86
Midnight Green	M	57	Nocturne Blue	V	88
Burgundy	N	67	Castillian Bronze	J	89
Palladium Silver	P	69			

Dealer Service Information Bulletin number 69-I-16, dated 11-4-68, listed these paint code numbers and corresponding letters for 1969 models.

COLOR NAME	BODY PLATE PAINT OR TRIM CODE		DU PONT	DITZLER	RINSHED-MASON
EXTERIOR	PAINT CODE	MOLDING COLOR			
Polar White	10 (C)	Black	5040-L	8631	A-1802
Palladium Silver	14 (P)	Black	5032-L	2059	A-2108
Starlight Black	19 (A)	Black	99-L	9300	A-946
Bermuda Blue	25 (D)	Dark Blue	5123-L	2165	A-2261
Lucerne Blue	26 (F)	-	5190-L	2213	A-2262
Atoll Blue	28 (E)	Dark Blue	5124-L	2166	A-2264
Mint Turquoise	34 (K)	Black	5119-L	2168	A-2265
Keylime Green	43 (L)	-	5126-L	2170	A-2266
Palisade Green	45 (H)	Dark Green	5122-L	2171	A-2268
Verdoro Green	47 (Q)	Black	5195-LH	2095	A-2110
Pepper Green	48 (M)	Dark Green	5116-L	2173	A-2269
Sierra Yellow	50 (Y)	Dark Gold	5121-L	2175	A-2270D
Goldenrod Yellow	51 (W)	-	5026-LH	2094	A-2119
Coronado Gold	53 (S)	-	5073-L	23211	A-2091F
Baja Gold	55 (G)	Dark Gold	5120-L	2178	A-2271D
Granada Gold	58 (Z)	Dark Gold	5117-L	2179	A-2272
Orbit Orange	60 (T)	-	5210-L	2257	170B770
Palomino Copper	63 (B)	Light Saddle	5125-L	2183	A-2275
Carousel Red	65 (V)	-	5021-LM	2084	A-2111R
Castillian Bronze	67 (J)	-	5076-LH	23215	A-2276G
Cardinal Red	75 (R)	Black	5118-LH	2189	A-2278F
Burgundy	78 (N)	Black	5063-LH	50700	A-2107M
WHEEL COLORS					
Starlight Black	A		99-L	9300	A-946
Atoll Blue	E		5124-L	2166	A-2264
Pepper Green	M		5116-L	2173	A-2269
Granada Gold	Z		5117-L	2179	A-2272
INTERIOR—(SEMI GLOSS)					
Black	268	258	99-L	9266	170B40
Dark Blue		250	9712-LH	13974	170B27
Dark Brown	253		9713-L	23320	170B89
Medium Saddle		255	9714-L	23321	170B800
Dark Sandalwood	257		9727-L	23324	170B78
Dark Green		256	9708-LH	44173	170B300
Medium Red	254		9709-LH	71827	170B51R
INTERIOR—("0" GLOSS)					
Black	268	258	4428-L	9317	168C41
Dark Blue		250	9701-LH	13967	170B24
Dark Brown	253		9702-L	23309	170B87
Dark Saddle		255	9703-L	23310	170B88
Dark Sandalwood		257	9704-L	23311	170B74
Dark Green		256	9697-LH	44169	170B38
Dark Red	254		9699-LH	71826	170B50R
TRUNK INTERIORS					
Black-Gray-Aqua Multiflek	. . . .		389-259	DX-1758	844
ENGINE PAINT					
Silver Blue	. . . .		181-97219	13255	266T21
Orange Red	. . . .		—	60339	—

1970 paint color numbers.

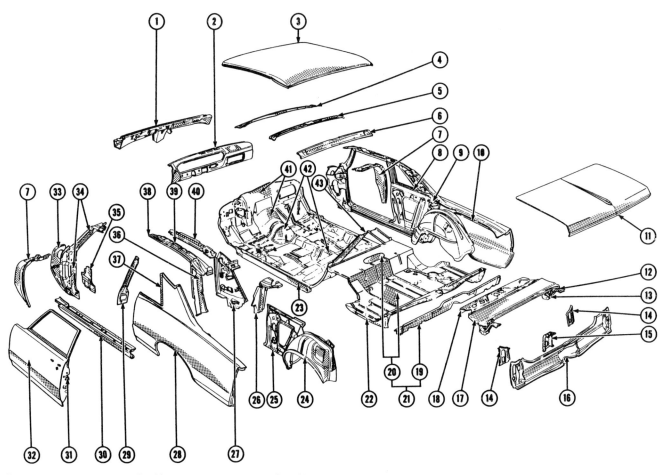

Key	Part Name	Group No.
1 — PANEL ASM., Upper Dash & Duct		12.804
2 — PANEL ASM., Instrument		10.230
3 — PANEL, Roof		12.810
4 — FRAME, Windshield Inner Upper		12.807
5 — BOW, Roof		12.952
6 — PANEL, Back Window Inner		12.964
7 — PANEL, Shroud Side		12.804
8 — FILLER, Quarter Window Lower Rear Corner		12.941
9 — FILLER, Back Window Lower Corner		12.964
10 — GUTTER, Rear Compartment Lid Side		12.996
11 — LID ASM., Rear Compartment		12.181
12 — STRAP, Rear Compartment Lid Hinge		12.187
13 — SUPPORT, Rear Compartment Lid Hinge		12.184
14 — BRACE, Rear Compartment Gutter to Compartment Pan		12.996
15 — PLATE, Rear Compartment Lid Lock Striker Anchor		12.237
16 — PANEL, Rear End		12.966
17 — PANEL, Rear Compartment Front		12.971
18 — PANEL, Rear Seat Back Shelf		12.971
19 — BAR, Rear Cross		12.986
20 — PAN, Rear		12.981
21 — PAN ASM., Rear		12.981
22 — FILLER, Compartment Pan to Quarter Panel		12.981
23 — PANEL, Rocker Inner		12.934
24 — PANEL ASM., Wheelhouse		12.944
25 — PANEL, Rear Quarter Inner		12.941
26 — EXTENSION, Shelf Panel		12.971
27 — RAIL ASM., Side Roof Inner Rear		12.957
28 — PANEL, Quarter Outer		12.940
29 — PANEL ASM., Body Lock Pillar Upper		12.942
30 — PANEL, Door Opening Rocker Outer		12.934
31 — DOOR ASM., Front		10.351
32 — PANEL ASM., Front Door Outer		12.895
33 — PANEL ASM., Shroud Side Duct		12.804
34 — PANEL ASM., Front Body Hinge Pillar		12.840
35 — REINFORCEMENT, Front Body Hinge Pillar to Duct		12.659
36 — RAIL, Side Roof Outer Rear		12.956
37 — MOLDING, Roof Drip Rear		12.075
38 — MOLDING, Roof Drip Front		12.075
39 — RAIL ASM., Side Roof Outer Front		12.956
40 — RAIL, Side Roof Inner Front		12.957
41 — PANEL ASM., Dash Lower		12.804
42 — PAN ASM., Floor		N.S.
43 — BRACE, Rear Seat Back Diagonal		N.S.

Exploded view and parts nomenclature for 1964-65 sheet metal.

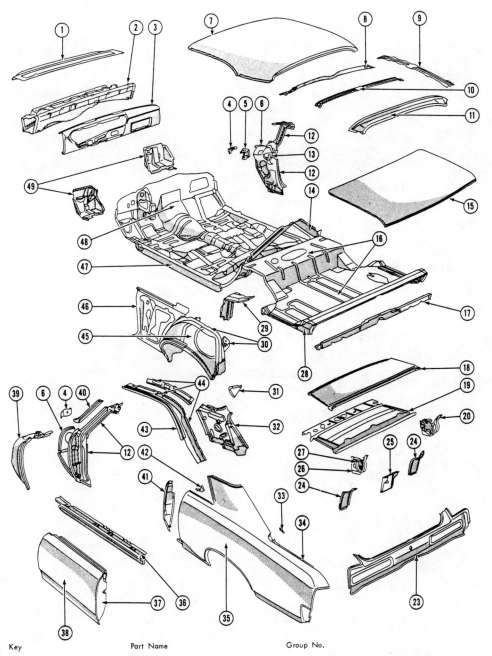

Key	Part Name	Group No.
1 — GRILLE, Shroud Top Vent Louver		12.800
2 — PANEL ASM., Upper Dash and Duct		12.804
3 — PANEL ASM., Instrument		10.230
4 — REINFORCEMENT, Front Body Hinge Pillar to Duct		12.659
5 — REINFORCEMENT, Front Body Hinge Pillar at Upper Hinge		12.659
6 — PANEL ASM., Shroud Vent Duct - Side		12.804
7 — PANEL, Roof		12.810
8 — FRAME, Windshield Inner - Upper		12.807
9 — BOW, Roof Longitudinal		12.952
10 — BOW ASM., Roof		12.952
11 — PANEL, Back Window - Inner		12.964
12 — PANEL ASM., Front Body Hinge Pillar		12.840
13 — SUPPORT ASM., Instrument Panel End		10.230
14 — BRACE, Rear Seat Back - Diagonal		N.S.
15 — LID ASM., Rear Compartment		12.181
16 — PAN ASM., Rear Compartment (Inc. #17)		f2.981
17 — BAR ASM., Rear Cross (Part of #16)		12.986
18 — PANEL, Rear Compartment Front		12.971
19 — PANEL, Rear Seat Back Shelf		12.971
20 — STRAP & LINK, Rear Compartment Lid Hinge		12.187
23 — PANEL ASM., Rear End (4200 Series)		12.966
24 — BRACE, Compartment Gutter to Compartment Pan		12.996
25 — PLATE, Rear Compartment Lid Lock Striker Anchor		12.237
26 — SUPPORT, Rear Compartment Lid Hinge		12.184
27 — PIN, Rear Compartment Lid Hinge		12.186
28 — FILLER, Rear Compartment Pan to Quarter Panel		12.981
29 — EXTENSION, Shelf Panel		12.971
30 — PANEL ASM., Wheelhouse (Inc. #23-45-46)		12.944
31 — FILLER, Rear of Wheelhouse to Quarter Panel		12.940
32 — PANEL, Rear Quarter - Inner Upper		12.941
33 — REINFORCEMENT, Compartment Lid Opening Upper Corner		12.940
34 — GUTTER, Rear Compartment Lid Side		12.996
35 — PANEL, Rear Quarter Side - Outer		12.940
36 — PANEL, Door Opening Rocker Outer		12.934
37 — DOOR ASM., Front (Inc. #38)		10.351
38 — PANEL ASM., Front Door Outer (Part of #37)		12.895
39 — PANEL, Shroud Lower Side		12.804
40 — FRAME, Windshield Outer - Side		12.808
41 — REINFORCEMENT, Body Lock Pillar		12.942
42 — FILLER, Quarter Window Lower Rear Corner		12.941
43 — MOLDING, Roof Drip (Part of #44)		12.075
44 — RAIL ASM., Side Roof (Inc. #43)		12.956
45 — PANEL, Wheelhouse Outer (Part of #30)		12.944
46 — PANEL, Rear Quarter - Inner Lower (Part of #30)		12.941
47 — PANEL, Rocker Inner		12.934
48 — PANEL ASM., Dash - Lower (Inc. #49)		12.804
49 — BRACE ASM., Dash to Chassis (Part of #48)		12.650

Exploded view of 1966-67 sheet metal and correct nomenclature of parts.

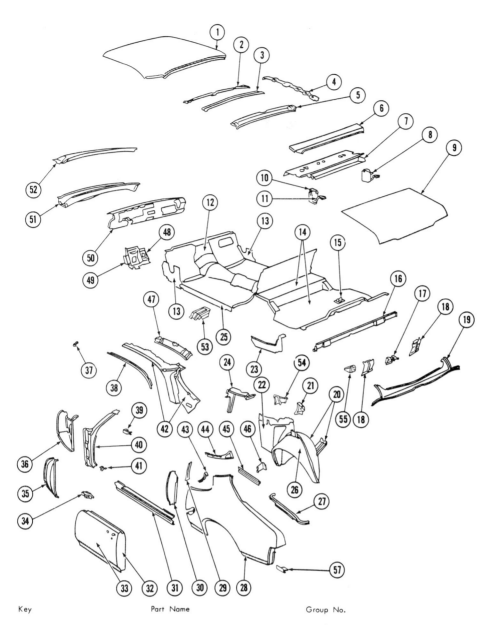

Key	Part Name	Group No.
1 — PANEL, Roof		12.810
2 — FRAME, Windshield Inner Upper		12.807
3 — BOW, Roof		12.952
4 — BOW, Roof Longitudinal		12.952
5 — PANEL, Back Window Inner		12.964
6 — PANEL, Rear Compartment Front		12.971
7 — PANEL, Rear Seat to Back Window		12.971
8 — SUPPORT, Rear Compartment Lid Hinge		12.184
9 — LID ASM., Rear Compartment		12.181
10 — PIN, Rear Compartment Lid Hinge		12.186
11 — STRAP, Rear Compartment Lid Hinge		12.187
12 — PANEL ASM., Dash (Incl. #48)		12.804
13 — REINFORCEMENT, Front Body Hinge Pillar to Rocker		12.659
14 — PAN ASM., Rear Compartment (Incl. #15-16-23)		12.981
15 — SUPPORT, Spare Tire Clamp Anchor Plate (Part of #14)		12.981
16 — BAR ASM., Rear Cross (Part of #14)		12.986
17 — PLATE, Compartment Lid Lock Striker Anchor		12.237
18 — BRACE, Compartment Gutter to Compartment Pan		12.996
19 — PANEL ASM., Rear End		12.966
20 — PANEL ASM., Wheelhouse (Incl. #22-26)		12.944
21 — EXTENSION, Quarter Inner Panel-Rear		12.941
22 — PANEL ASM., Rear Quarter-Inner Lower (Part of #20)		12.941
23 — FILLER, Compartment Pan to Quarter Panel (Part of #14)		12.981
24 — EXTENSION, Rear Seat to Back Window Panel		12.971
25 — PANEL, Rocker-Inner		12.934
26 — PANEL, Wheelhouse-Outer (Part of #20)		12.944
27 — GUTTER, Rear Compartment Lid Side		12.996
28 — PANEL, Rear Quarter Side-Outer		12.940
29 — PANEL ASM., Body Lock Pillar-Upper (27 Styles)		12.942
30 — REINFORCEMENT, Body Lock Pillar		12.942
31 — PANEL, Door Opening Rocker-Outer		12.934
32 — DOOR ASM., Front (Incl. #33)		10.351
33 — PANEL ASM., Front Door-Outer (Part of #32)		12.895
34 — REINFORCEMENT, Front Door Outer Panel-At Vent		10.657
35 — PANEL, Shroud-Lower		12.804
36 — PANEL, Shroud Vent Duct-Side		12.804
37 — SUPPORT, Windshield Glass		10.027
38 — MOLDING, Roof Drip (Part of #42)		12.075
39 — SUPPORT, Instrument Panel End		10.230
40 — PANEL ASM., Front Body Hinge Pillar		12.840
41 — SUPPORT ASM., Front Fender-On Dash		8.141
42 — RAIL ASM., Side Roof (Incl. #38-47)		12.956
43 — FILLER, Quarter Window Lower Rear Corner		12.941
44 — REINFORCEMENT, Rear Quarter Panel-At Belt		12.940
45 — STIFFENER, Quarter Outer Panel		12.940
46 — EXTENSION, Quarter Inner to Outer Stiffener		12.940
47 — RAIL, Side Roof Inner (Part of #42)		N.S.
48 — BRACE ASM., Dash to Chassis Frame (Part of #12-Incl. #49)		12.650
49 — SUPPORT ASM., Front Fender Skirt-On Brace (Part of #48)		8.153
50 — PANEL ASM., Instrument (1968)		10.230
PANEL, Dash – Upper (1969)		12.804
51 — PANEL ASM., Shroud Vent Duct-Center		12.804
52 — PANEL ASM., Shroud-Upper		12.804
53 — REINFORCEMENT, Floor Pan At Lock Pillar (1970)		12.942
54 — BRACE, Body Lock Pillar to Floor Pan (1970)		12.684
55 — REINFORCEMENT ASM., Rear End Panel Outer Corner (1970)		12.966
57 — SUPPORT, Bumper Valance to Quarter Panel Mounting (1970)		12.940

Exploded view of 1968 through 1970 sheet metal, including parts nomenclature.

The following are the correct code numbers for Cordova top colors:

Code Number	Year	Color
1	1968	Ivory-White
2	1968	Black
5	1968	Teal
8	1968	Gold
2	1969	Black
3	1969	Dark Blue
5	1969	Parchment
8	1969	Dark Fawn
9	1969	Dark Green
1	1970	White
2	1970	Black
5	1970	Sandalwood
7	1970	Dark Gold
9	1970	Dark Green

Correct nameplate for rear quarter panel for 1964-67 GTO, with black letters riding on chrome bar.

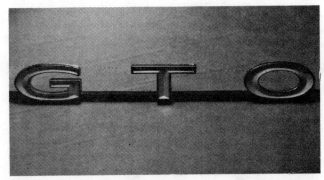

Correct grille nameplate for 1964-66, with white letters riding on black bar.

Close-up detail of rear deck lid nameplate, showing deterioration of factory mold. Nameplate in front is current replacement; nameplate in rear is original replacement. (Note poor quality of mold at top of G.)

Diecast 6.5 liter emblem affixed to front fenders was the same for 1964-68.

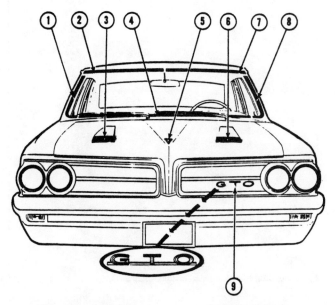

1. 4430500 MOLDING-SIDE
   4-4474354 CLIP
   4-#8-18 x 3/4" SCREW

2. 4430502 MOLDING-UPR.
   4-4474354 CLIP
   4-#8-18 x 3/4" SCREW

3. 9775698 ORNAMENT
   2-446063 NUT
   2-537196 WASHER

4. 4430558 MOLDING-LWR.
   7-4474354 CLIP
   7-#8-18 x 3/4" SCREW

5. 9774297 EMBLEM
   1-3783794 CLIP
   1-274999 NUT

6. 9775699 ORNAMENT
   2-446063 NUT
   2-537196 WASHER

7. 4430503 MOLDING-UPR.
   4-4474354 CLIP
   4-#8-18 x 3/4" SCREW

8. 4430501 MOLDING-SIDE
   4-4474354 CLIP
   4-#8-18 x 3/4" SCREW

9. 9775669 NAME PLATE
   3-9775919 SPACER
   3-9419756 NUT

Identification and parts nomenclature of 1964 GTO exterior trim, front view.

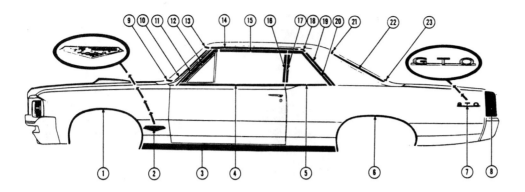

1. 9774787-88 MOLDING 16-588546 SCREW	**7.** 2-9775668 NAME PLATE 3-9419764 NUT	**12.** 4411952-53 MOLDING-FRT.
2. 2-9775867 NAME PLATE 2-3751546 NUT	**8.** 4409934-35 EXTENSION 4426772 GASKET 8-4411489 NUT	**13.** 4430502-03 MOLDING-UPR. 4-4474354 CLIP 4-#8-18 x 3/4" SCREW
3. 9774795-96 MOLDING & CLIP PKG.	**9.** 4430558 MOLDING-LWR. 7-4474354 CLIP 7-#8-18 x 3/4" SCREW	**14.** 4456072-73 MOLDING-FRT.
4. 4410816-17 MOLDING 4-#8-18 x 1/2" SCREW	**10.** 4430500-01 MOLDING-SIDE 4-4474354 CLIP 4-#8-18 x 3/4" SCREW	**15.** 4409816-17 MOLDING-UPR.
5. 4413675-76 MOLDING-LWR. 3-#8-18 x 3/8" SCREW		**16.** 4464153-54 MOLDING-REAR
6. 9775996-97 MOLDING & CLIP PKG.	**11.** 4430532-33 MOLDING	**17.** 4464162-63 MOLDING-FRT. 3-4464403 CLIP
		18. 2-4456067 ESCUTCHEON

19. 4456074-75 MOLDING-REAR	
20. 4411686-87 MOLDING-UPR.	
21. 4430552-53 MOLDING-UPR. 4-4474354 CLIP 4-#8-18 x 3/4" SCREW	
22. 4430544-45 MOLDING-SIDE 3-4474354 CLIP 3-#8-18 x 3/4" SCREW	
23. 4430549 MOLDING-LWR. 4-4474354 CLIP 4-#8-18 x 3/4" SCREW	

Side view of exterior trim and parts nomenclature for 1964 GTO option.

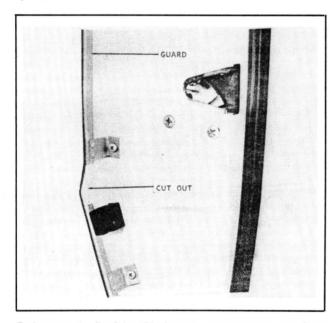

To improve the fit of the 1964 front door-edge guards, a section has been cut out on the interior side at the crease. Start installation at the crease and work up or down from that point to ensure proper fit.

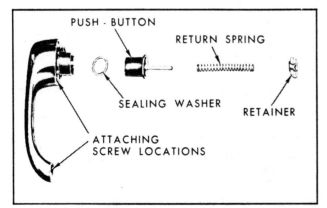

Exploded view of 1964-70 door handle assembly.

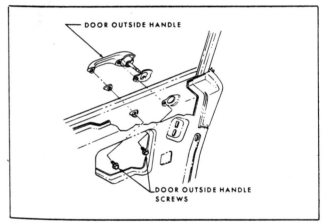

Detail of removal of door handle. Note two attaching screws for door handle and gaskets.

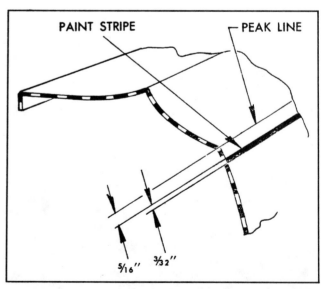

Location and dimensions for 1965 GTO pinstripe. Top of stripe should be 5/16 inch below the accent line on the upper edge of the panel.

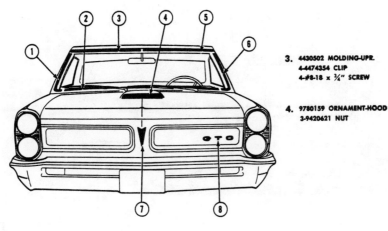

1. 4430500 MOLDING-SIDE
   4-4474354 CLIP
   4-#8-18 x ¾" SCREW
   2-4511999 SPACER

2. 4430558 MOLDING-LWR.
   7-4474354 CLIP
   7-#8-18 x ¾" SCREW
   3-4511999 SPACER

3. 4430502 MOLDING-UPR.
   4-4474354 CLIP
   4-#8-18 x ¾" SCREW

4. 9780159 ORNAMENT-HOOD
   3-9420621 NUT

5. 4430503 MOLDING-UPR.
   4-4474354 CLIP
   4-#8-18 x ¾" SCREW

6. 4430501 MOLDING-SIDE
   4-4474354 CLIP
   4-#8-18 x ¾" SCREW
   2-4511999 SPACER

7. 9780104 EMBLEM
   2-9420621 NUT

8. 9775669 NAME PLATE
   3-9420621 NUT

GTO option for 1965, showing views of exterior trim and parts nomenclature, with second-design painted headlamp bezels.

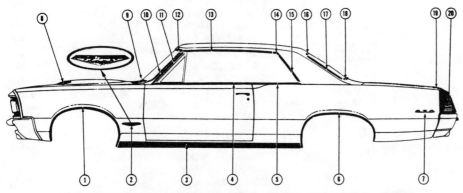

1965 TEMPEST LEMANS 2-DOOR SPORT COUPE - 3737 - G.T.O. OPTION

1. 9774787-88 MOLDING
   16-588546 SCREW

2. 2-9775867 EMBLEM
   4-9420621 NUT

3. 9777044-45 MLDG. & CLIP PKG.
   1-9777046 CLIP PKG.

4. 4453602-03 MOLDING-DOOR
   4-#8-18 x ½" SCREW

5. 4482524-25 MOLDING-QTR.
   6-#8-18 x ¾" SCREW

6. 9775996-97 MLDG. & CLIP PKG.

7. 2-9775668 NAME PLATE
   6-9419764 NUT

8. 9780159 ORNAMENT-HOOD
   3-9420621 NUT

9. 4430558 MOLDING-LWR.
   7-4474354 CLIP
   7-#8-18 x ¾" SCREW
   3-4511999 SPACER

10. 4430500-01 MOLDING-SIDE
    8-4474354 CLIP
    8-#8-18 x ¾" SCREW
    4-4511999 SPACER

11. 4456263-64 MOLDING-FINISH
    6-4825964 SCREW

12. 4430502-03 MOLDING-UPR.
    8-4474354 CLIP
    8-#8-18 x ¾" SCREW

13. 4456072-73 MOLDING-FRT.

14. 2-4456067 ESCUTCHEON

15. 4456074-75 MOLDING-REAR

16. 4430552-53 MOLDING-UPR.
    8-4474354 CLIP
    8-#8-18 x ¾" SCREW
    2-4511999 SPACER

17. 4430544-45 MOLDING-SIDE
    6-4474354 CLIP
    6-#8-18 x ¾" SCREW
    2-4511999 SPACER

18. 4430549 MOLDING-LWR.
    8-4474354 CLIP
    8-#8-18 x ¾" SCREW
    3-4511999 SPACER

19. 4412789 EMBLEM
    2-9419766 NUT
    2-4597477 WASHER

20. 4490940-41 EXTENSION
    2-4490287 GASKET
    1-4506881-82 GASKET
    10-4501682 WASHER
    10-9422265 NUT

Side view and parts nomenclature of exterior trim for 1965 GTO.

1965 license plate mounting brackets (part number 9781771) and accompanying hardware.

Close-up of front hood emblem (part number 9783370) used for 1966 and 1967 GTOs. Emblem was brushed diecast metal, with recessed areas painted 0° gloss black.

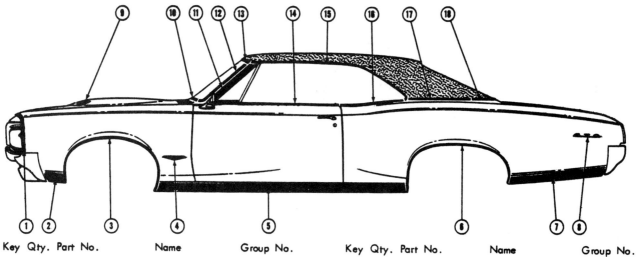

Key	Qty. Part No.	Name	Group No.
1.	9782752-53 BEZEL		2.728
	4—9777486 SCREW		2.729
	4—#8-18 x 2-1/4" SCREW		N.S.
	4—3863669 NUT		2.729
	4—9784299 NUT		2.729
2.	9785123-24 MLDG. & CLIP PKG.		8.147
	4—9420621 NUT		8.148
3.	9785448-49 MLDG. & CLIP PKG.		8.147
	16—588546 SCREW		8.148
4.	2—9775867 EMBLEM		8.147
	4—9420621 NUT		8.148
5.	9785130-31 MLDG. & CLIP PKG.		8.231
	1—9785166 CLIP PKG.		8.231
6.	4227182-83 MLDG. & CLIP PKG.		12.116
	14—588546 SCREW		12.118
7.	4227180-81 MLDG. & CLIP PKG.		12.116
	1—9785178 CLIP PKG.		12.118
8.	2—9775668 NAME PLATE		12.116
	6—9419764 NUT		12.118
9.	9780159 ORNAMENT		8.030
	3—273329 NUT		8.039

Key	Qty. Part No.	Name	Group No.
10.	4430558 MOLDING, Lower		10.093
	7—4474354 CLIP		10.096
	7—#8-18 x 3/4" SCREW		N.S.
	3—4531604 SPACER		10.096
11.	4543088-89 MOLDING, Finish		10.093
12.	4541650-51 MOLDING, Side		10.093
	8—4474354 CLIP		10.096
	8—#8-18 x 3/4" SCREW		N.S.
	4—4531604 SPACER		10.096
13.	4541648-49 MOLDING, Upper		10.093
	8—4474354 CLIP		10.096
	8—#8-18 x 3/4" SCREW		N.S.
14.	7580770-71 MOLDING, Window		10.707
	8—#8-18 x 1/2" SCREW		N.S.
15.	4547733-34 SCALP		12.075
16.	7580593-94 MOLDING, Window		11.031
	6—#8-18 x 1/2" SCREW		N.S.
17.	7589524-25 MOLDING, Belt, Outer		12.116
	8—7594209 CLIP		12.118
18.	7589292-93 MOLDING, Belt, Inner		12.116
	4—7595777 CLIP		12.118
	4—7594209 CLIP		12.118
	4—9419763 NUT		12.118

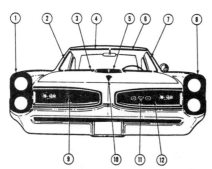

Key	Qty. Part No.	Name	Group No.
1.	9782752 BEZEL		2.728
	2—9777486 SCREW		2.729
	2—#8-18 x 2-1/4" SCREW		N.S.
	2—3863669 NUT		2.729
	2—9784299 NUT		2.729
2.	4541650 MOLDING, Side		10.093
	4—4474354 CLIP		10.096
	4—#8-18 x 3/4" SCREW		N.S.
	2—4531604 SPACER		10.096
3.	4430558 MOLDING, Lower		10.093
	7—4474354 CLIP		10.096
	7—#8-18 x 3/4" SCREW		N.S.
	3—4531604 SPACER		10.096
4.	4541648 MOLDING, Upper		10.093
	4—4474354 CLIP		10.096
	4—#8-18 x 3/4" SCREW		N.S.
5.	9780159 ORNAMENT		8.030
	3—273329 NUT		8.039

Key	Qty. Part No.	Name	Group No.
6.	4541649 MOLDING, Upper		10.093
	4—4474354 CLIP		10.096
	4—#8-18 x 3/4" SCREW		N.S.
7.	4541651 MOLDING, Side		10.093
	4—4474354 CLIP		10.096
	4—#8-18 x 3/4" SCREW		N.S.
	2—4531604 SPACER		10.096
8.	9782753 BEZEL		2.728
	2—9777486 SCREW		2.729
	2—#8-18 x 2-1/4" SCREW		N.S.
	2—3863669 NUT		2.729
	2—9784299 NUT		2.729
9.	9783920 GRILLE (42)		1.266
10.	9783370 EMBLEM		8.030
	2—9420621 NUT		8.039
11.	9775669 NAME PLATE		1.303
	3—9420621 NUT		1.303
12.	9783921 GRILLE (42)		1.266

Views of exteriors and trim with parts nomenclature for 1966 GTO.

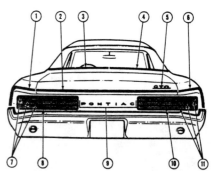

Key	Qty. Part No.	Name	Group No.
1.	4227113 MLDG. & CLIP PKG.		12.116
	1—9785171 CLIP PKG.		12.118
2.	4227150 MLDG. & CLIP PKG.		12.182
	1—9785183 CLIP PKG.		12.183
3.	4541663 MOLDING, Finish (35)		12.116
	4541667 MOLDING, Finish (37 & 42)		12.116
	8—7584999 CLIP		12.118
4.	4541662 MOLDING, Finish (35)		12.116
	4541666 MOLDING, Finish (37 & 42)		12.116
	8—7584999 CLIP		12.118
5.	9775744 NAME PLATE		12.182
	2—9419764 NUT		12.183
6.	4227112 MLDG. & CLIP PKG.		12.116
	1—9785171 CLIP PKG.		12.118

Key	Qty. Part No.	Name	Group No.
7.	3—7620467 MOLDING, Finish		12.182
*8.	4227152 MLDG. & CLIP PKG.		12.182
	1—9785182 CLIP PKG.		12.183
9.	7586857 LETTER "P"		12.182
	7586858 LETTER "O"		12.182
	7586859 LETTER "N"		12.182
	7586860 LETTER "T"		12.182
	7586861 LETTER "I"		12.182
	7586862 LETTER "A"		12.182
	7586863 LETTER "C"		12.182
	7—4528566 NUT		12.183
*10.	4227151 MLDG. & CLIP PKG.		12.182
	1—9785182 CLIP PKG.		12.183
11.	3—7620467 MOLDING, Finish		12.182
	* Less Bright Moldings		

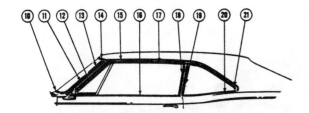

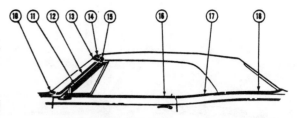

Key	Qty. Part No.	Name	Group No.
10.	4430558	MOLDING, Lower	10.093
	7—4474354	CLIP	10.096
	7—#8-18 x 3/4"	SCREW	N.S.
	3—4531604	SPACER	10.096
11.	4543088-89	MOLDING, Finish	10.093
12.	4547690-91	SCALP, Front	10.707
13.	4541650-51	MOLDING, Side	10.093
	8—4474354	CLIP	10.096
	8—#8-18 x 3/4"	SCREW	N.S.
	4—4531604	SPACER	10.096
14.	4541648-49	MOLDING, Upper	10.093
	8—4474354	CLIP	10.096
	8—#8-18 x 3/4"	SCREW	N.S.
15.	4547733-34	SCALP	12.075
16.	7580768-69	MOLDING, Window	10.707
	8—#8-18 x 1/2"	SCREW	N.S.
17.	4547218-19	SCALP, Upper	10.707
18.	4544920-21	SCALP, Rear	10.707
19.	7581320-21	SCALP, Front	11.031
20.	7580595-96	MOLDING, Window	11.031
	6—#8-18 x 1/2"	SCREW	N.S.
21.	4548436-37	SCALP, Upper	11.031

Key	Qty. Part No.	Name	Group No.
10.	4430558	MOLDING, Lower	10.093
	7—4474354	CLIP	10.096
	7—#8-18 x 3/4"	SCREW	N.S.
	3—4531604	SPACER	10.096
11.	4543092-93	MOLDING, Finish	10.093
12.	4541650-51	MOLDING, Side	10.093
	8—4474354	CLIP	10.096
	8—#8-18 x 3/4"	SCREW	N.S.
	4—4531604	SPACER	10.096
13.	4541648-49	MOLDING, Upper	10.093
	8—4474354	CLIP	10.096
	8—#8-18 x 3/4"	SCREW	10.096
14.	4542518	HEADER, Center	10.093
	4—4409925	SCREW	10.096
15.	4542516-17	HEADER, Side	10.093
	2—4409925	SCREW	10.096
16.	7582451-52	MOLDING, Window	10.707
	8—#8-18 x 1/2"	SCREW	N.S.
17.	4541660-61	MOLDING, Window	11.031
	6—#8-18 x 1/2"	SCREW	N.S.
18.	4541666-67	MOLDING, Finish	12.116
	16—7584999	CLIP	12.118

Comparison of 1966 (left) and 1967 (right) rear of rear wheel-opening molding. Note fluted edge on top of 1966 molding; 1967 molding was rounded with no flute.

Side view of 1968 Endura bumper emblem (part number 9790459). Note thickness of mounting studs.

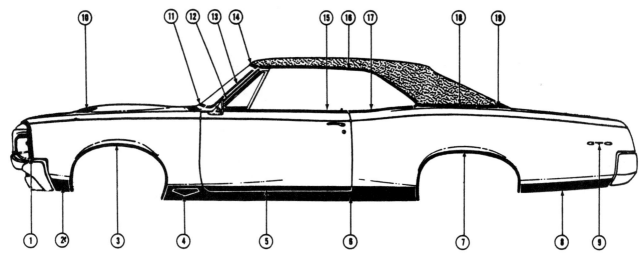

Key	Qty.	Part No.	Name	Group No.
1.		9782752-53	BEZEL	2.728
	4—	9414754	SCREW	8.977
	4—	9423737	SCREW	2.729
	4—	380382	NUT	2.729
	4—	3863669	NUT	2.729
2.		9788957-58	MLDG. PKG., Fender – Lower .	8.147
	4—	9420621	NUT	8.148
3.		9785448-49	MLDG. PKG., W/Opening . . .	8.147
	16—	588546	SCREW	8.148
4.	2—	9775867	EMBLEM, "G.T.O."	8.304
	4—	9420621	NUT	8.148
5.		4229710-11	MLDG. PKG., Door	12.112
	2—	9777696	CLIP PKG.	12.118
6.		9788955-56	MLDG. PKG., Rocker	8.304
	2—	9777712	CLIP PKG.	8.309
7.		4227182-83	MLDG. PKG., W/Opening . . .	12.116
	14—	588546	SCREW	12.118
8.		4229729-30	MLDG. PKG., Rr. of W/Opng..	12.116
	2—	9777698	CLIP PKG.	12.118
9.	2—	9775668	PLATE, "G.T.O."	12.116
	6—	9419764	NUT	12.118
10.		9780159	ORNAMENT, Hood	8.030
	3—	273329	NUT.	8.921

Key	Qty.	Part No.	Name	Group No.
11.		4430558	MOLDING, W/S – Lower	10.093
	7—	4474354	CLIP	10.096
	7—	#8-18 x 3/4"	SCREW	N.S.
	3—	4531604	SPACER	10.096
12.		4543090-91	MOLDING, Pillar – Finish . .'.	10.093
13.		4541650-51	MOLDING, W/S – Side . . .	10.093
	8—	4474354	CLIP	10.096
	8—	#8-18 x 3/4"	SCREW	N.S.
	4—	4531604	SPACER	10.096
14.		4541648-49	MOLDING, W/S – Upper . . .	10.093
	8—	4474354	CLIP	10.096
	8—	#8-18 x 3/4"	SCREW	N.S.
15.		7580770-71	MOLDING, Door – Window. . .	10.707
	8—	#8-18 x 1/2"	SCREW	N.S.
16.		4547733-34	SCALP, Roof	12.075
17.		7580593-94	MOLDING, Qtr. Window	11.031
18.		7589524-25	MOLDING, Belt – Outer . . .	12.116
	8—	7617597	CLIP	12.118
19.		7589292-93	MOLDING, Belt – Inner	12.116
	4—	4817162	CLIP..	12.118
	4—	7617597	CLIP	12.118
	4—	9419763	NUT	12.118

Views of exteriors and trim with parts nomenclature for 1967 GTO.

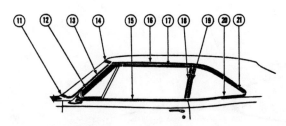

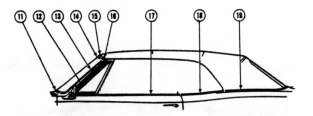

Key	Qty.	Part No.	Name	Group No.
11.		4430558	MOLDING, W/S - Lower	10.093
	7—	4474354	CLIP	10.096
	7—	#8-18 x 3/4"	SCREW	N.S.
	3—	4531604	SPACER	10.096
12.		4547690-91	SCALP, Door - Front	10.707
13.		4541650-51	MOLDING, W/S - Side	10.093
	8—	4474354	CLIP	10.096
	8—	#8-18 x 3/4"	SCREW	N.S.
	4—	4531604	SPACER	10.096
14.		4541648-49	MOLDING, W/S - Upper	10.093
	8—	4474354	CLIP	10.096
	8—	#8-18 x 3/4"	SCREW	N.S.
15.		7580768-69	MOLDING, Door - Window	10.707
	8—	#8-18 x 1/2"	SCREW	N.S.
16.		4547733-34	SCALP, Roof	12.075
17.		4547218-19	SCALP, Door - Upper	10.707
18.		4544920-21	SCALP, Door - Rear	10.707
19.		7581320-21	MOLDING, Qtr. Wind. - Frt.	11.031
20.		7580595-96	MOLDING, Qtr. Window	11.031
	6—	#8-18 x 1/2"	SCREW	N.S.
21.		4548436-37	MOLDING, Qtr. Wind. - Upr.	11.031

Key	Qty.	Part No.	Name	Group No.
11.		4430558	MOLDING, W/S - Lower	10.093
	7—	4474354	CLIP	10.096
	7—	#8-18 x 3/4"	SCREW	N.S.
	3—	4531604	SPACER	10.096
12.		4543092-93	MOLDING, Pillar - Finish	10.093
13.		4541650-51	MOLDING, W/S - Side	10.093
	8—	4474354	CLIP	10.096
	8—	#8-18 x 3/4"	SCREW	N.S.
	4—	4531604	SPACER	10.096
14.		4541648-49	MOLDING, W/S - Upper	10.093
	8—	4474354	CLIP	10.096
	8—	#8-18 x 3/4"	SCREW	N.S.
15.		4542518	HEADER, Center	10.093
	4—	4409925	SCREW	10.096
16.		4542516-17	HEADER, Side	10.093
	2—	4409925	SCREW	10.096
17.		7582451-52	MOLDING, Door - Window	10.707
	8—	#8-18 x 1/2"	SCREW	N.S.
18.		4541660-61	MOLDING, Qtr. Window	11.031
	6—	#8-18 x 1/2"	SCREW	N.S.
19.		4541666-67	MOLDING, Finish	12.116
	16—	7584999	CLIP	12.118

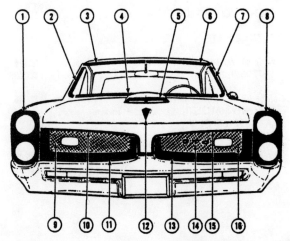

Key	Qty.	Part No.	Name	Group No.
1.		9782752	BEZEL	2.728
	2—	9414754	SCREW	8.977
	2—	9423737	SCREW	2.729
	2—	380382	NUT	2.729
	2—	3863669	NUT	2.729
2.		4541650	MOLDING, W/S - Side	10.093
	4—	4474354	CLIP	10.096
	4—	#8-18 x 3/4"	SCREW	N.S.
	2—	4531604	SPACER	10.096
3.		4541648	MOLDING, W/S - Upper	10.093
	4—	4474354	CLIP	10.096
	4—	#8-18 x 3/4"	SCREW	N.S.
4.		4430558	MOLDING, W/S - Lower	10.093
	7—	4474354	CLIP	10.096
	7—	#8-18 x 3/4"	SCREW	N.S.
	3—	4531604	SPACER	10.096
5.		9780159	ORNAMENT, Hood	8.030
	3—	273329	NUT	8.039
6.		4541649	MOLDING, W/S - Upper	10.093
	4—	4474354	CLIP	10.096
	4—	#8-18 x 3/4"	SCREW	N.S.

Key	Qty.	Part No.	Name	Group No.
7.		4541651	MOLDING, W/S - Side	10.093
	4—	4474354	CLIP	10.096
	4—	#8-18 x 3/4"	SCREW	N.S.
	2—	4531604	SPACER	10.096
8.		9782753	BEZEL	2.728
	2—	9414754	SCREW	8.977
	2—	9423737	SCREW	2.728
	2—	380382	NUT	2.728
	2—	3863669	NUT	2.728
9.		9787759	GRILLE	1.266
10.		9787100	MOLDING, Grille - R.H.	1.268
	5—	9420621	NUT	1.303
11.		9787207	BEZEL, R.H.	1.266
12.		9783370	EMBLEM, Hood	8.055
	2—	9420621		8.039
13.		9787208	BEZEL, L.H.	1.266
14.		9787967	PLATE, "G.T.O."	1.303
	2—	9420621	NUT	1.303
15.		9787101	MOLDING, Grille - L.H.	1.268
	5—	9420621	NUT	1.303
16.		9787759	GRILLE	1.266

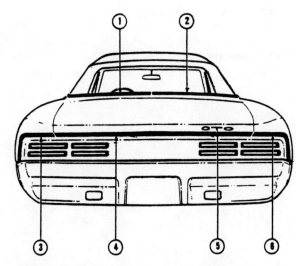

Key	Qty.	Part No.	Name	Group No.
1.		4541663	MOLDING, Finish (35)	12.116
		4541667	MOLDING, Finish (37 & 42)	12.116
	8—	7584999	CLIP	12.118
2.		4541662	MOLDING, Finish (35)	12.116
		4541666	MOLDING, Finish (37 & 42)	12.116
	8—	7584999	CLIP	12.118
3.		4229874	MLDG. PKG., Rear	12.116
	1—	9777700	CLIP PKG.	12.118

Key	Qty.	Part No.	Name	Group No.
4.		4229876	MLDG. PKG., Lid	12.182
	1—	9777701	CLIP PKG.	12.183
5.		7667612	PLATE, "G.T.O."	12.182
	2—	9419763	NUT	8.921
6.		4229873	MLDG. PKG., Rear	12.116
	1—	9777700	CLIP PKG.	12.118

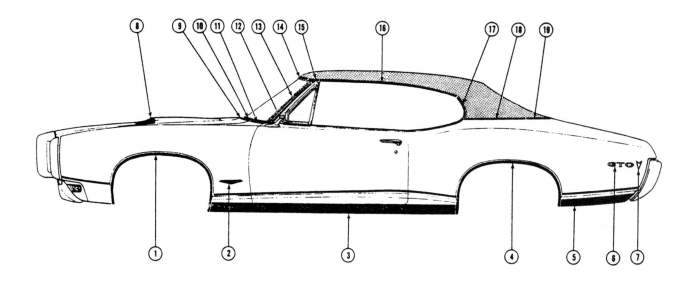

Key	Qty. Part No.	Name	Group No.
1.	9793382-83 MLDG. PKG., W/Opening		8.147
	16—588546 SCREW		8.148
2.	2-97758· ͂MBLEM, "G.T.O."		8.147
	4-9420621 NUT		8.148
3.	9793887-88 MLDG. PKG., Rocker		8.304
	2-9777710 CLIP PKG.		8.309
4.	7795122-23 MLDG. PKG., W/Opening		12.116
	14—588546 SCREW		12.118
5.	7795124-25 MLDG. PKG., Rr. of W/Opng.		12.116
	2-9793351 CLIP PKG.		12.118
6.	2-9788231 LETTERS-"G.T.O.", Black		12.116
	2-9788232 LETTERS-"G.T.O.", Red		12.116
	2-9788233 LETTERS-"G.T.O.", White		12.116
7.	2-5960490 BEZEL, Lamp		2.575
	6-9419764 NUT		8.921
8.	9791143-44 ORNAMENT, Hood		8.030
	6-273329 NUT		8.921
9.	9791870 MOLDING, Hood		8.030

Key	Qty. Part No.	Name	Group No.
10.	7731088 MOLDING, W/S - Lower		10.093
	7—#8-18 x 1/2" SCREW		N.S.
	2-4880689 CLIP		10.096
	2—#8-18 x 3/8" SCREW		N.S.
11.	9793405-06 MLDG. PKG., Fender Rear		8.147
	2-9790369 CLIP PKG.		8.148
12.	7726067-68 SCALP, Pillar - Drip		12.075
13.	7725634-35 MOLDING, W/S - Side		10.093
	8-7730788 CLIP		10.096
	2-7748859 SPACER		10.096
14.	7726034 MOLDING, W/S - Upper		10.093
	7-7730788 CLIP		10.096
	2-7748859 SPACER		10.096
15.	7661072-73 ESCUTCHEON, Roof		12.075
16.	7723586-87 SCALP, Roof		12.075
17.	7741467-68 MOLDING, Qtr. Wind. - Rear		11.031
	2-7747309 CLIP		11.032
	2-7745721 CLIP		11.032
18.	7739442-43 MOLDING, Belt - Front		12.116
	6-7731589 CLIP		12.118
19.	7746858-59 MOLDING, Belt - Rear		12.116
	2-9419764 NUT		12.118

Views of 1968 GTO showing moldings and trim with part numbers.

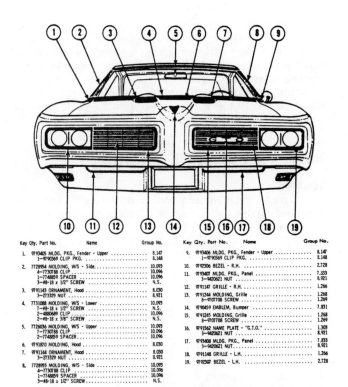

Key	Qty. Part No.	Name	Group No.
1.	9793405	MLDG. PKG., Fender - Upper	8.147
	1—9790369	CLIP PKG.	8.148
2.	7728954	MLDG., W/S - Side	10.093
	4—7730788	CLIP	10.096
	1—7748859	SPACER	10.096
	3—#8-18 x 1/2"	SCREW	N.S.
3.	9791143	ORNAMENT, Hood	8.030
	3—273329	NUT	8.921
4.	7731088	MOLDING, W/S - Lower	10.093
	6—#8-18 x 1/2"	SCREW	N.S.
	2—4880689	CLIP	10.096
	2—#8-18 x 3/8"	SCREW	N.S.
5.	7726036	MOLDING, W/S - Upper	10.093
	7—7730788	CLIP	10.096
	2—7748859	SPACER	10.096
6.	9791870	ORNAMENT, Hood	8.030
7.	9791144	ORNAMENT, Hood	8.030
	3—273329	NUT	8.921
8.	7728955	MOLDING, W/S - Side	10.093
	4—7730788	CLIP	10.096
	1—7748859	SPACER	10.096
	3—#8-18 x 1/2"	SCREW	N.S.
9.	9793406	MLDG. PKG., Fender - Upper	8.147
	1—9790369	CLIP PKG.	8.148
10.	9792306	BEZEL - R.H.	2.728
11.	9793407	MLDG. PKG., Panel	7.333
	3—9420621	NUT	8.921
12.	9791147	GRILLE - R.H.	1.266
13.	9791244	MOLDING, Grille	1.268
	8—9707708	SCREW	1.269
14.	9790459	EMBLEM, Bumper	7.831
15.	9791245	MOLDING, Grille	1.268
	8—9707708	SCREW	1.269
16.	9791562	NAME PLATE - "G.T.O."	1.303
	3—9420621	NUT	8.921
17.	9793408	MLDG. PKG., Panel	7.833
	3—9420621	NUT	8.921
18.	9791148	GRILLE - L.H.	1.266
19.	9792307	BEZEL - L.H.	2.728

Key	Qty. Part No.	Name	Group No.
12.	7728954-55	MLDG., W/S - Side	10.093
	8—7730788	CLIP	10.096
	2—7748859	SPACER	10.096
	6—#8-18 x 1/2"	SCREW	N.S.
13.	7726036	MOLDING, W/S - Upper	10.093
	7—7730788	CLIP	10.096
	2—7748859	SPACER	10.096
14.	7724376-77	MOLDING, Finish	12.116
	8—7742626	CLIP	12.118
	5—#8-18 x 3/8"	SCREW	N.S.

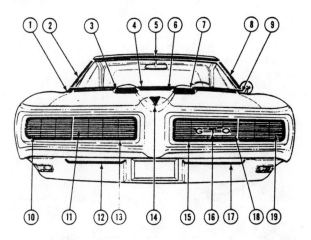

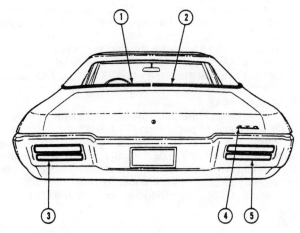

Key	Qty. Part No.	Name	Group No.
2.	7725634	MOLDING, W/S - Side	10.093
5.	7726034	MOLDING, W/S - Upper	10.093
8.	7725635	MOLDING, W/S - Side	10.093
10.	9791178	DOOR ASM., Tilt - R.H.	2.728
11.	9791147	GRILLE - R.H.	1.266
12.	9793407	MLDG. PKG., Panel	7.833
	3—9420621	NUT	8.921
19.	9791179	DOOR ASM., Tilt - L.H.	2.728

Key	Qty. Part No.	Name	Group No.
1.	7724377	MOLDING, Finish	12.116
	4—7742626	CLIP	12.118
	3—#8-18 x 3/8"	SCREW	N.S.
2.	7724376	MOLDING, Finish	12.116
	4—7742626	CLIP	12.118
	3—#8-18 x 3/8"	SCREW	N.S.
3.	5959927	LENS, L.H.	2.682
4.	7758556	NAME PLATE, "G.T.O."	12.182
	2—3/32" I.D. x 13/64" O.D. x 1/16"	WASHER	N.S.
	2—9421827	NUT	8.921
5.	5959928	LENS, R.H.	2.682

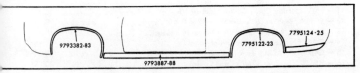

Lower trim molding used on 1969 GTO with part numbers. The rear quarter molding was deleted in mid-1969 production.

Detail of 1969 front fender nameplate. The crossbar was painted to match the exterior color.

OUTSIDE MIRROR

1964-65

The standard outside mirror (RPO 602) was mounted in the same location for 1964 and 1965. It was a dealer-installed option (accessory part number 984087 or part number 9770283 in 1964). This mirror could be mounted on either side. If a remote-control mirror was ordered, a RH door-mounted mirror that matched the remote style was available (part number 9775629 or accessory package part number 984089). This mirror was not, however, a remote-control mirror. It only matched the style of the LH remote mirror.

The 1965 mirror used the same part number, 9770283, and the accessory part number was 984369 or 984612. It was used for both sides, and was door mounted.

1966-67

The LH outside rearview mirror was standard equipment for the GTO. The original replacement part number for the 1966 coupe and hardtop was 4440430; the convertible used part number 4548218. These part numbers were superseded by 9770283. A matching-style RH mirror was available as a dealer-installed option (accessory package part number 984612). The mirror assembly was mounted on a black plastic pad, and was retained by a number 8 32x¾ inch chrome Phillips-head screw to a mounting bracket (part number 9774116). The bracket was mounted to the door by two number 10 16x⅝ inch Phillips screws.

The 1967 LH standard mirror used a slightly different style and design; part number 7729443 for coupes and hardtops and 7729448 for convertibles. These numbers were superseded by 9787901 for all applications. A matching RH mirror was available as a dealer-installed option (accessory package part number 984758). The 1967 mirror used the same mounting hardware as the 1966.

1968-70

A LH outside rearview mirror was standard equipment for all three years. The 1968 mirror was identical to the 1967 mirror (part number 9787901). A matching RH mirror was available as a dealer-installed option. For 1969-70, a rectangular, chromed LH mirror assembly (part number 9782390) was standard. A matching RH mirror was available as a dealer-installed option (accessory package number 988596).

Detail of 1964-66 outside LH mirror (part number 9770283). Mirror was optional for 1964-65, standard in 1966. It was available as a dealer accessory package in 1964 (part number 984087) and 1965 (984369 or 984612).

The 1968 mirror was mounted exactly like the 1966-67 mirror. A pad (part number 9782534) was used in 1969-70. The pad went between the mirror and the outer door panel. A number 8 32x¾ inch chrome Phillips-head screw (part number 9785422) was used to retain the mirror to the mounting bracket (part number 9794690). The bracket was retained to the door by two number 10 16x⅝ inch cadmium screws (part number 162906).

REMOTE-CONTROL MIRROR

1964-65

The 1964 LH remote-control mirror (RPO 444) was mounted on the front fender. The control was routed under the dash. Three different control styles were used, although the head design remained the same. Three different part numbers were used for replacement head and control.

	1st Design	2nd Design	3rd Design
Mirror	9775009	9777367	9780431
Control	9773476	9775541	9780430

The mounting bracket (part number 9775134) and mounting pad (part number 9775131) were used regardless of design.

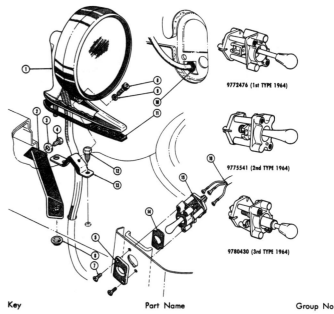

9772476 (1st TYPE 1964)

9775541 (2nd TYPE 1964)

9780430 (3rd TYPE 1964)

Key	Part Name	Group No.
1 — MIRROR & CABLE ASM., Outside Rear View		10.186
2 — BRACE, Cable Controlled Mirror to Fender		10.186
3 — WASHER, Brace to Fender (1/4")		8.929
4 — SCREW, Brace to Fender (#14-10 x 3/4")		8.977
5 — ESCUTCHEON ASM., Rear View Mirror Control		10.186
6 — NUT, Mirror to Fender (1/4"-20 stamped)		8.921
7 — SCREW, Control to Instrument Panel (#10-24 x 3/8")		N.S.
8 — SCREW, Mirror to Bracket (#10-32 x 5/8")		10.186
9 — LOCKWASHER, Mirror to Bracket (#10)		8.931
10 — GROMMET, Mirror Cable to Hinge Pillar		10.186
11 — PAD, Outside Cable Controlled Rear View Mirror Mtg.		10.186
12 — SCREW, Bracket to Fender (#10-12 x 1/2")		8.977
13 — BRACKET, Remote Controlled Mirror to Fender		10.186
14 — GASKET, Control to Instrument Panel		10.186
15 — CONTROL ASM., Remote Control Mirror Cable		10.186
16 — HOUSING, Rear View Mirror Cable		10.186

1964 fender-mount remote-control mirror, showing the three designs used in 1964 for the control assembly.

The 1965 LH remote mirror had a first and second design also, but these differed only in the manner in which the mirror was mounted to the door.

	1st Design	2nd Design
Mirror	9780185	9792562
Bracket	9780131	9784859
Pad	9787795	9787795
Screw	9781380	9784907

The control cables were routed through the door. The control was mounted in the door panel through a metal retainer (part number 4526624), and held in place by the chromed escutcheon (part number 9780181).

1966-67

The optional remote-control mirror (RPO 394) was mounted on the LH door panel, next to the leading edge of the vent window. The 1966 unit was identical in all respects to the 1965 second-design remote mirror.

The 1967 mirror (part number 9787846) was mounted in the same location as the 1966. The pad, mounting bracket and interior door panel escutcheon were the same as the 1965. The retainer (part number 4526624) was the same for 1965-68.

The control cables for 1966 and 1967 were routed through the door. The remote-control mirror could be either factory or dealer installed. The 1966 accessory package part number was 984455; for 1967, 984752. Remote-control mirrors installed by a dealer were not necessarily mounted in exactly the same location as a factory-installed mirror.

1968-70

Remote-Control Mirror
RPO 424   1968-69
RPO 444   1970
UPC D33   1969-70

The remote-control mirror was available for all three years. The 1968 mirror (part number 9792564) was factory

Detail of 1965-68 remote-control mirror. Small hole in mirror body allowed water to drain.

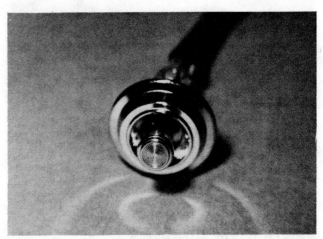

Close-up of 1965-68 remote-control mirror cable control with escutcheon.

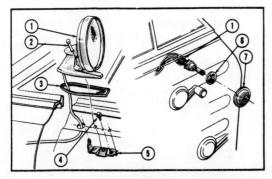

Key	Part Name	Group No.
1 — MIRROR ASM., Rear View (Includes Control)		10.186
2 — SCREW, Cable Control Mirror Bracket		10.186
3 — PAD, Outside Mirror Mounting		10.186
4 — SCREW, Bracket to Door (#10 – 24 x 1/2") .		8.977
5 — BRACKET, Mirror to Door		10.186
6 — RETAINER, Front Door Mirror – Inner		10.186
7 — ESCUTCHEON, Control to Door Trim Pad. .		10.186

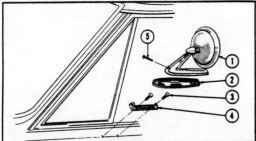

Key	Part Name	Group No.
1 — MIRROR ASM., Outside Rear View		10.185
2 — PAD, Outside Rear View Mirror Mounting (5 1/4" long).		10.186
3 — SCREW, Bracket to Door (#10 – 16 x 5/8") .		8.977
4 — BRACKET, Outside Rear View Mirror Mounting		10.186
5 — SCREW, Outside Rear View Mirror (#8 – 32 x 3/4")		10.186

Exploded view and parts nomenclature for 1965 second-design remote-control mirror used through 1968, and 1964-67 standard mirror.

or dealer installed (accessory part number 984974). It used the same mounting hardware as the 1967 mirror.

The 1969-70 remote mirror (part number 9796802) was available either as a factory- or dealer-installed option (accessory package 988563). The mounting pad (part number 9782534) was the same for both years. The mirror was attached to a bracket (part number 9794690) by means of a screw. The bracket mirror assembly was retained to the door by two Phillips-head cadmium screws.

The control cables were routed through the door, and a prestamped hole was knocked out of the inside of the door panel. The 1968 escutcheon and retainer were identical to the 1967 units. The escutcheon was redesigned in 1969 and carried over to 1970. The cable was held to the interior door panel by a retainer (part number 9784178). The cable control fit through the escutcheon (part number 9784388) and was retained by a nut (part number 9787449).

Detail of 1967 outside rearview mirror.

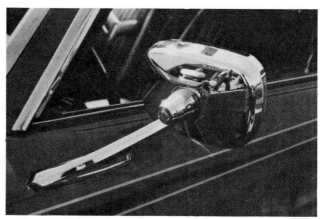

Detail of 1969-70 remote outside rearview mirror (part number 9796802).

VENTILATOR WINDOWS

1964-68

The vent window was used from 1964 through 1968. The 1964-65 models used a different vent window assembly for hardtops and convertibles (part number 4411072 RH and 4411073 LH) and sedans (part number 4493026 RH and 4493027 LH). The vent window assemblies were serviced without glass.

The 1966-67 sedan assembly was part number 9705684 (RH) and 9705685 (LH). The hardtop and convertible assembly was part number 9706198 (RH) and 9706199 (LH). The 1968 assembly was part number 9712502 (RH) and 9712503 (LH) for hardtops. The convertible assembly

was part number 9712544 (RH) and 9712545 (LH). These were also serviced without glass.

The vent frame and channel assemblies were chromed. The channel and scalp assembly was a multi-piece unit capped with stainless molding. A vent window handle was chromed and used from 1964 through 1967. A window crank was used in 1968 with color-keyed knobs to match interior trim.

The 1964-65 vent handle mounting stud was serviced with the vent frame assembly. The stud and cap assembly was part number 9707826 for 1966-67. The 1968 ventilator regulator was part number 7719731 (RH) and 7719732 (LH).

Year	Part	RH	One-Piece	LH
1964-65	handle	4305052		4305053
1966-67	handle	9706878		9706879
1968	crank, black		7752486	
	red		7765716	
	turquoise		7765717	
	blue		7765719	
	teal		7765726	
	gold		7765728	
	parchment		7765729	
Front Door Ventilator Glass Channel				
1964-65	sedan	5718112		5718113
	hardtop/convertible	5717994		5717995
1966-67	sedan	9705714		9705715
	hardtop/convertible	9706224		9706225
1968	all	9712532		9712533

Vent Window Weatherstrip

1964-65	sedan	5717252		5717253
	hardtop/convertible	5717170		5717171
1966-67	sedan	9706494		9706495
	hardtop/convertible	9706596		9706597
1968	all	9712506		9712507

Division Channel Weatherstrip

1964-65	all	5717194		5717195
1966-67	sedan	9706496		9706497
	hardtop/convertible	9706502		9706503
1968	all	9712524		9712525

Front Glass Run Channel

1964-65	sedan		5717239	
	hardtop/convertible		5717179	
1966-67	sedan		9705708	
	hardtop/convertible		9711387	
1968	all (upper)	9712986		9712987
	(lower)		9713647	

Roof Rail Weatherstrip

1964-65		4409034		4409035
1966-67		7725458		7725459
1968		7717780		7717781
1969-70		8723732		8723733

Door Hinge Assembly

1964-65	upper		4409743	
	lower	4506971		4506972
1966-67	upper		7642529	
	lower	7663424		7663425
1968-70	upper		7722170	
	lower	7722087		7722088

For owners of 1964-66 models who may want to update their cars, the 1967 safety door-lock feature can easily be installed. With this feature, the door can't be opened from inside when the door is locked. To install, use the 1967 lock assembly (part number 7642078) and lock rod (part number 7656078). This will hook right up to the lock control.

Inner Door-lock Handle

1964	4760518	
1965-67	4468414	
1968-70	RH-7743520	LH-7743521

Door Weatherstrip
Front Door Glass Outer Weatherstrip

1964-65	sedan (rubber)	5717616		5717617
1964-65	hardtop (rubber) and convertible	5718952		5718953
1966-67	sedan	9706668		9706669
	hardtop/convertible	9706672		9706673
1968	all (rubber)	7726810		7726811
1969	all (rubber)	8723391		8723392
1970	all (rubber)	8807626		8807627

Front Door Glass Inner Weatherstrip

1964	sedan (rubber)	4456247		4456248
	hardtop/convertible	4456250		4456251
1965	sedan		4405917	
	hardtop/convertible	4407833		4407834
1966	all	7617628		7617629
1967	all	7672606		7672607
1968	all (rubber)	7759720		7759721
1969-70	all (rubber)		8765653	

Door Window Glass Run Channel Assembly

1964-67	sedan		4439775	

Door Weatherstrip

1964-65	sedan	4892622		4892623
	hardtop/convertible	4894905		4894906
1966-67	sedan	4550804		4540805
	hardtop/convertible	4540544		4540545
1968	all	7717756		7717757
1969-70	all	8781168		8781169

QUARTER WINDOWS

1964-70

Front Vertical Weatherstrip

1964-65	hardtop	4407840	4407841
	convertible	4407842	4407843
1966-67	hardtop/convertible	4542975	4542976
1968	all	7763303	7763304
1969-70	all	8734084	8734085

Front Sash Channel (Chrome)

1964-65	convertible	4496436		4496437
	hardtop	4496438		4496439
	sedan		4543162	
1966-67	hardtop/convertible	7632212		7632213
	sedan	7582170		7582171
1968	all	7763301		7763302
1969-70	all	8734082		8734083

Rear Upper Weatherstrip

1964	sedan	4528438	4528439
1965	sedan	4505822	4505823
1966-67	sedan	7583542	7583543

Outer Belt Weatherstrip
(note: also serviced with moldings listed in 1964-67 Exterior section)

1964-67	sedan	5718032	5718033
	convertible	5718078	5718079
	hardtop	5718050	5718051
1966-67	sedan	9706616	9706617
	hardtop	9706618	9706619
	convertible	9706528	9706529
1968	hardtop	7726042	7726043
1968-69	convertible	7725568	7725569
1969	hardtop	8730934	8730935
1970	hardtop	8807650	8807651
	convertible	8807640	8807641

Inner Weatherstrip

1964	sedan (rubber)		4460788	
	convertible (rubber)	4465756		4461679
	hardtop (rubber)	4465756		4465757
1965	sedan	4415853		4415854
	convertible		4412568	
	hardtop	4508687		4508688
1966-67	sedan	7592442		7592443
	convertible	7591082		7591083
	hardtop	7592444		7592445
1968-70	hardtop (rubber, inner rear vertical)	7730295		7730296
	hardtop (rubber, inner)	7726038		7726039
	convertible	7726205		7726206

WINDOW TRIM

1964-65

The front windshield stainless trim was the same for 1964 and 1965.

	RH	One-Piece	LH
Upper	4430502		4430503
Side	4430500		4430501
Lower		4430558	

A-Pillar Drip Molding

	RH	LH
Convertible	4456265	4456266
Hardtop	4456263	4456264
Sedan	7626294	7626295

Drip Rail Moldings, front

	RH	LH
Hardtop	4456072	4456073
Sedan	4456072	4456073

Drip Rail Moldings, rear

	RH	LH
All except 1967	4456074	4456075

The escutcheon was the same for both sides and top (part number 4456067).

Upper Door and Quarter Trim—Hardtop

	Door	Quarter
LH	4453603	4482525
RH	4453602	4482524

Upper Door and Quarter Trim—Convertible

	Door	Quarter	Pinchweld Finish Molding
LH	4453605	4483675	4407519
RH	4453604	4483674	4407518

The pinchweld finish molding package carried part number 3853121. All moldings came on cars in stainless steel. Replacement moldings were made from aluminum.

Upper Door and Quarter Trim—Sedan

	Door	Quarter
LH	4410817	4413676
RH	4410816	4413675

Front Door Vertical Scalp Molding—Sedan
4411952   4411953

Front Door Upper Scalp Molding—Sedan
4409816   4409817

Front Vertical Quarter Reveal Molding
4464162   4464163

Upper Quarter Reveal Molding

	LH	RH
1964	4496256	4411688
1965	4496257	4496258

Back Window Reveal Moldings

	Upper	Side	Lower
LH	4430553	4430545	4430549 one piece
RH	4430552	4430544	

Rear Quarter Belt Reveal Molding
(used with Cordova top or two-tone paint)

LH	RH
4437501	4437502

Center molding (part number 4440332) was one piece.

1966-67

All exterior window brightwork was the same for 1966 and 1967.

Windshield Molding

	RH	One-Piece	LH
Upper	4541648		4541649
Side	4541650		4541651
Lower, one piece		4430558	

Windshield Pillar Finish Molding

Sedan	4543088	4543089
Hardtop	4543090	4543091
Convertible	4543092	4543093

Roof Drip Scalp Molding—Sedan/Hardtop
LH   4547734
RH   4547733

Upper Door and Quarter Trim—Hardtop

Door	7580770	7580771
Quarter	7580593	7580594

Upper Door and Quarter Trim—Convertible

Door	7582451	7582452
Quarter	4541660	4541661

Upper Door and Quarter Trim—Sedan

Door	7580768	7580769
Quarter	7580595	7580596

Pinchweld Finish Molding—Convertible
LH   4541667
RH   4541666

Front Door Front Vertical Scalp Molding—Sedan
LH   4547691
RH   4547690

Front Door Upper Scalp Molding—Sedan
LH   4547219
RH   4547218

Front Door Rear Vertical Scalp Reveal Molding—Sedan
LH   4544921
RH   4544920

Upper Rear Quarter Reveal Molding—Sedan
LH   4548437
RH   4548436

Rear Quarter Window Reveal
Front Vertical Molding—Sedan
LH   7581321
RH   7581320

Back Window Reveal Molding

Upper	7580180	7580181
Lower	7581670	7581670

Rear Quarter Belt Reveal Molding
(Used with Cordova top or two-tone paint)

Inner	7589292	7589293
Outer	7589524	7589525

1968-70

The numbers below are for the 1968-70 GTO. A number of trim pieces were used for all three years.

Windshield Molding

All upper, side and lower moldings were the same for 1968-70. A 1969 windshield garnish molding production change was indicated by Dealer Service Information Bulletin number 69-I-74, dated 5-14-69. The vinyl-coated windshield side garnish moldings were changed to painted steel units.

Roof Drip Scalp Molding

All years the same.

Convertible Pinchweld Molding

Year	RH	LH
1968	3940526	3940525
1969-70	3962892	3962893

Rear Window Reveal Molding

All years the same.

Rear Quarter Belt Reveal Molding
(Used with two-tone paint or Cordova top)

Front	1968-69	7739442	7739443
Rear	1968-69	7746858	7746859
	1970	8789242*	8789243*

*Includes rear section wraparound to rear end belt.

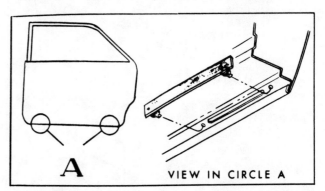

Door drain holes sealing strip; part number 4489247 was used for all GTOs.

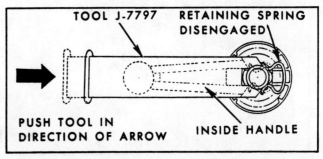

Use of special tool to remove inside door handles and window cranks. Tool can be purchased in most auto parts stores.

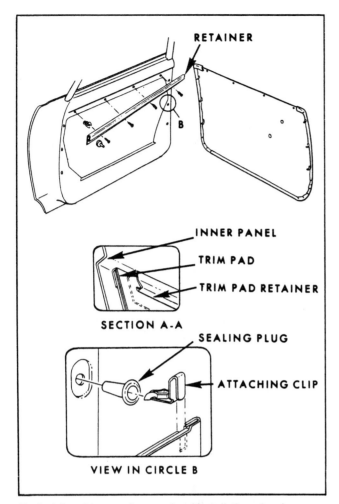

Typical door trim panel removal and installation, showing upper stainless retainer molding, sealing plugs (part number 4853962) and attaching clips (part number 4840575).

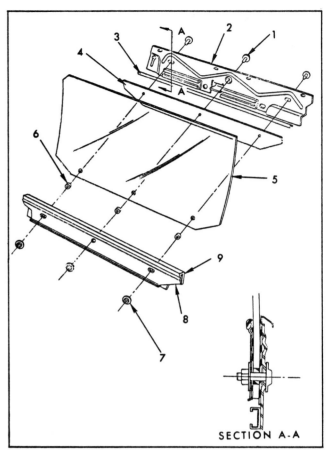

1. Lower Sash Channel to Glass Attaching Bolt
2. Lower Sash Channel Assembly
3. Lower Sash Channel Finishing Molding
4. Lower Sash Channel Outer Filler
5. Door Window Glass
6. Glass to Sash Channel Spacers (3)
7. Lower Sash Channel to Glass Attaching Bolt Nut
8. Lower Sash Channel Inner Filler Support
9. Lower Sash Channel Inner Filler

Exploded view of 1964-65 hardtop and convertible door glass, attaching parts and lower sash assembly.

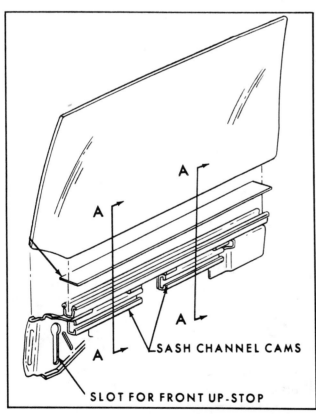

Exploded view of 1966-67 hardtop and convertible door glass and their attachment to sash channel.

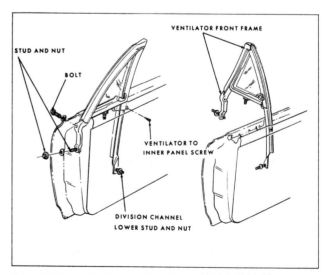

Removal of typical vent window assembly for 1964-68.

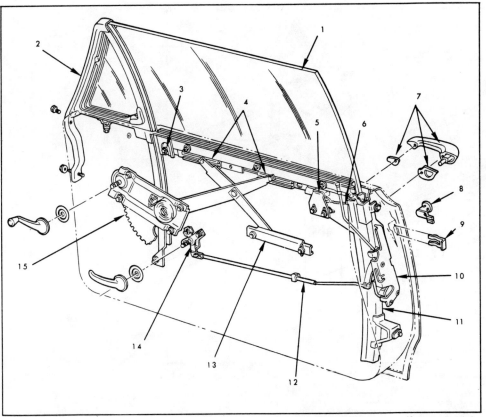

1. Window Assembly	6. Window Guide Plate	9. Lock Cylinder Retainer	13. Inner Panel Cam
2. Ventilator Assembly	7. Outside Handle and	10. Door Lock	14. Remote Control
3. Front Up-Travel Stop	Sealing Gaskets	11. Glass Run Channel	15. Door Window
4. Lower Sash Channel Cams	8. Lock Cylinder	12. Remote Control	Regulator
5. Rear Up-Travel Stop	Assembly	Connecting Rod	

1964-65 hardtop and convertible internal window and door lock
hardware. Design of lock cylinder retainer (number 9) was used
only on 1964 models.

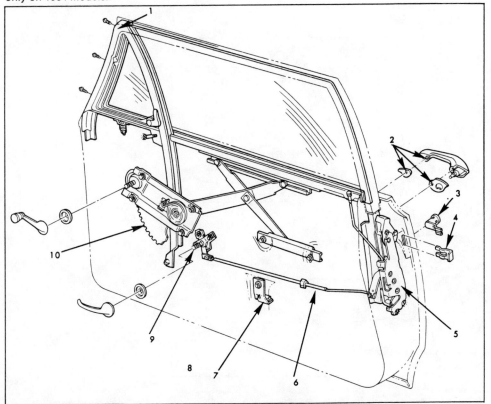

1. Front Door Ventilator Assembly	4. Front Door Lock Cylinder Retainer	7. Front Door Window Lower Stop
2. Front Door Outside Handle and	5. Front Door Lock Assembly	8. Front Door Inner Panel Cam
Sealing Gaskets	6. Front Door Remote Control	9. Front Door Remote Control Assembly
3. Front Door Lock Cylinder Assembly	Connecting Rod	10. Front Door Window Regulator Assembly

1964-65 closed-style (sedan) window and door lock hardware.
Note that illustration depicts 1964 door with a lock cylinder
retainer (number 4) and a 1964-style door handle and window
crank.

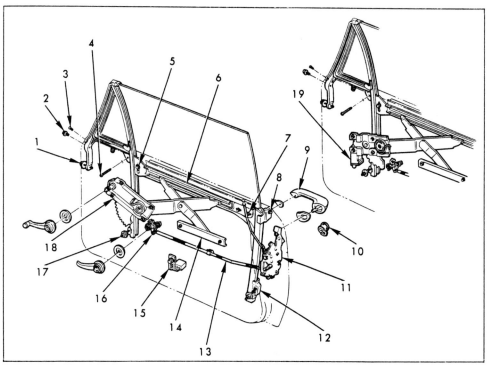

1. Ventilator Frame Lower Adjusting Stud and Nut	5. Window Front Up-Stop	11. Lock
2. Ventilator Frame Upper Attaching Bolt	6. Window Sash Channel Cam	12. Glass Rear Run Channel Lower Adjusting Stud and Nut
3. Ventilator Frame to Inner Panel Screw	7. Window Rear Guide	13. Lock to Remote Control Connecting Rod
4. Ventilator to Door Inner Panel Attaching Screw	8. Glass Rear Run Channel Upper Bolt	14. Inner Panel Cam
	9. Outside Handle Assembly	
	10. Lock Cylinder	

15. Window Lower Stop	
16. Remote Control	
17. Ventilator Division Channel Lower Adjusting Stud and Nut	
18. Window Regulator (Manual)	
19. Window Regulator (Electric)	

View of 1966-67 hardtop and convertible window and lock hardware, with parts nomenclature.

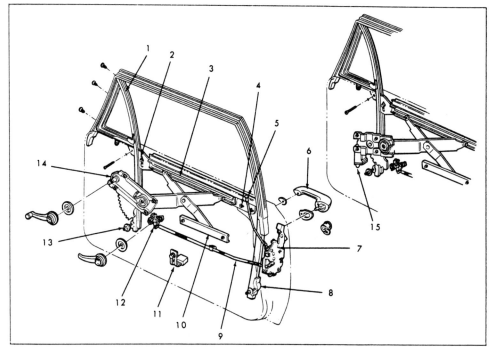

1. Ventilator Assembly	6. Outside Handle and Sealing Gaskets	10. Inner Panel Cam
2. Window Front Up-Stop	7. Lock	11. Window Lower Stop
3. Sash Channel Cam	8. Rear Glass Run Channel	12. Remote Control
4. Rear Guide	9. Remote Control Connecting Rod	13. Ventilator Division Channel
5. Lock to Locking Lever Rod		

14. Window Regulator (Manual)
15. Window Regulator (Electric)

Sedan models in 1966-67 used this hardware for window and door assemblies. Note difference between this front door vent frame and that of hardtop or convertible.

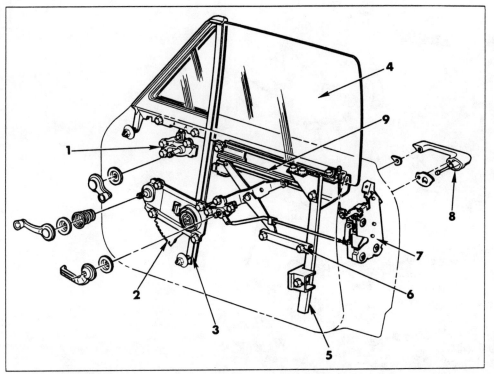

1. Ventilator Regulator
2. Window Regulator
3. Ventilator Division Channel
4. Front Door Window Assembly
5. Rear Guide
6. Inner Panel Cam
7. Door Lock
8. Door Outside Handle
9. Lower Sash Channel Cam

1968 window and door lock hardware with parts nomenclature.
1968 was last year for vent window.

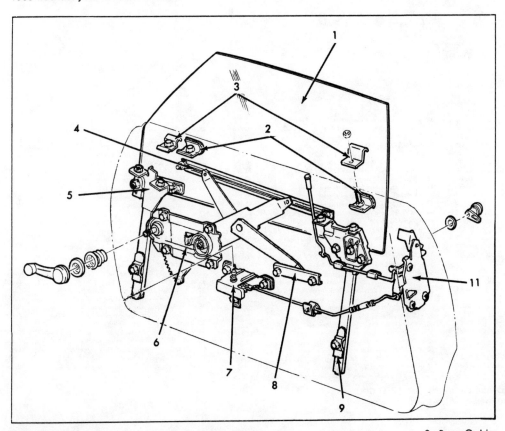

1. Window Assembly
2. Stabilizer Strips
3. Trim Pad Adjusting Plates
4. Lower Sash Channel Cam
5. Front Guide
6. Window Regulator
7. Door Lock Remote Control (Squeeze Type)
8. Inner Panel Cam
9. Rear Guide
11. Door Lock

Typical 1969 hardtop and convertible window and door lock
mechanisms.

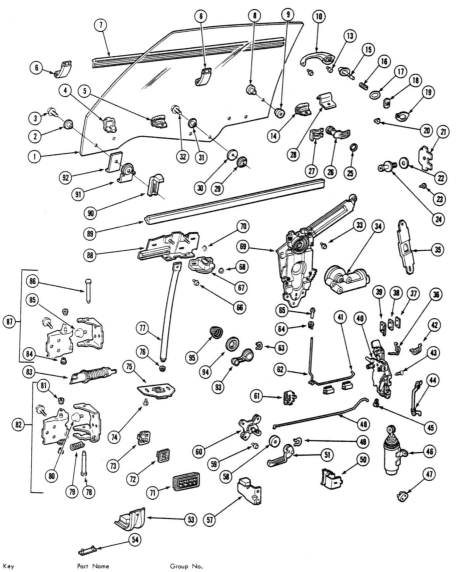

Key	Part Name	Group No.
1 — GLASS, Front Door Window	10.681
2 — SPACER, Window Up Stop to Glass	10.685
3 — BOLT, Window Up Stop to Glass	10.685
4 — RETAINER, Belt Trim Support – Front	14.683
5 — STRIP ASM., Window Anti-Rattle – Front	10.710
6 — PLATE ASM., Window Guide Front and Rear	10.728
7 — SEALING STRIP ASM., Window Outer – At Belt	10.710
8 — FASTENER, Window Glass Bearing	10.685
9 — CAP, Window Glass Bearing Fastener	10.685
10 — HANDLE, Door Outside – Less Push Button	10.527
13 — SCREW, Outside Handle to Panel	10.527
14 — STRIP ASM., Window Anti-Rattle – Rear	10.710
15 — BUTTON & SHAFT ASM., Door Handle Push	10.529
16 — SPRING, Door Handle Push Button	10.529
17 — RING, Door Handle Push Button Sealing	10.529
18 — WASHER, Door Handle Push Button Stop	10.529
19 — GASKET, Outside Handle to Panel – Rear	10.537
20 — GASKET, Outside Handle to Panel – Front	10.537
21 — PLATE, Door Lock Striker Anchor	10.571
22 — WASHER, Door Lock Striker	10.571
23 — FASTENER, Weatherstrip to Lock Pillar	10.695
24 — STRIKER ASM., Door Lock	10.569
25 — GASKET, Lock Cylinder to Door	10.529
26 — KIT, Door Lock Cylinder	10.550
27 — RETAINER, Lock Cylinder	10.551
28 — RETAINER, Belt Trim Support – Rear	14.683
29 — NUT, Window Plate Assembly to Glass	10.685
30 — WASHER, Window Plate Assembly to Glass	10.685
31 — SPACER, Window Plate Assembly to Glass	10.685
32 — BOLT, Window Plate Assembly to Glass	10.685
33 — SCREW, Regulator to Inner Panel	10.783
34 — MOTOR ASM., Window Regulator – Electric	10.783
35 — RETAINER, Remote Control Rod	10.565
36 — SPRING, Lock Push Button Return	10.474
37 — SPACER, Door Wedge Plate Door Side (67 Style)	10.584
38 — PLATE, Door Wedge Body Side (67 Style)	10.584
39 — PLATE, Door Wedge Door Side (67 Style)	10.584
40 — LOCK ASM., Front Door	10.470
41 — CLIP, Inside Locking Rod to Inner Panel	10.565
42 — SPRING, Door Lock Over Center	10.474
43 — SCREW, Door Lock to Inner Panel	10.474
44 — ROD, Electric Actuator to Lock	10.485
45 — CLIP, Door Lock Spring	10.474
46 — ACTUATOR ASM., Door Electric Lock	10.485
47 — BUMPER, Door Lock Pillar Door Side	10.587
48 — ROD, Lock Remote Control to Lock	10.506
49 — SPRING, Remote Control Handle Retaining	10.513
50 — CHANNEL ASM., Door Window Anti-Rattle	10.701
51 — HANDLE ASM., Door Lock Remote Control	10.512
53 — SUPPORT ASM., Door Window Bumper – Front	10.716
54 — SEALING STRIP, Door Bottom Drain Hole	10.694
57 — SUPPORT ASM., Door Window Bumper – Rear	10.716
58 — WASHER, Remote Control Hole Sealing	10.517
59 — SCREW, Remote Control to Inner Panel	10.506
60 — CONTROL ASM., Door Lock Remote	10.500
61 — CLIP, Remote Control Rod to Panel	10.565
62 — ROD ASM., Inside Locking to Lock	10.563
63 — SPRING, Regulator Handle Retaining	10.513
64 — FERRULE ASM., Inside Locking Rod Knob	10.560
65 — KNOB, Door Inside Locking Rod	10.559
66 — SCREW, Window Guide Tube Upper to Panel	10.728
67 — GUIDE ASM., Window Lower Sash – Upper	10.685
68 — NUT, Window Lower Sash Upper Guide	10.685
69 — REGULATOR ASM., Door Window	10.783
70 — NUT, Lower Sash Guide Plate	10.685
71 — SWITCH & ESCUTCHEON ASM., Door Window	10.777
72 — REINFORCEMENT, Door Trim at Window Switch	10.777
73 — RETAINER, Window Switch Escutcheon	10.777
74 — SCREW, Lower Sash Guide to Plate	10.685
75 — GUIDE ASM., Window Lower Sash Lower	10.685
76 — NUT, Window Guide Tube Lower to Panel	10.728
77 — TUBE ASM., Door Window Guide	10.728
78 — PIN, Door Lower Hinge (Part of #82)	N.S.
79 — SPRING, Door Lower Hinge	10.460
80 — SCREW, Lower Sash Guide Plate	10.463
81 — BUSHING, Door Lower Hinge (Part of #82)	N.S.
82 — HINGE ASM., Door – Lower	10.454
83 — CONDUIT, Door Electric Wiring	10.778
84 — BUSHING, Door Upper Hinge	10.464
85 — SCREW, Upper Hinge to Body & Door	10.463
86 — PIN, Door Upper Hinge	10.466
87 — HINGE ASM., Door – Upper	10.450
88 — PLATE ASM., Window Lower Sash Guide	10.728
89 — SEALING STRIP ASM., Window Inner – At Belt	10.710
90 — STOP, Door Window Up – On Glass	10.716
91 — PLATE, Door Window Up Stop Retainer	10.685
92 — FILLER, Door Up Stop Retaining Plate	10.685
93 — HANDLE ASM., Door Window Regulator	10.797
94 — PLATE, Regulator Handle Bearing	10.515
95 — SPRING, Window Regulator Handle	10.806

Complete parts breakdown and nomenclature for 1970 door, including window regulation and lock hardware. Power window controls and motor are shown.

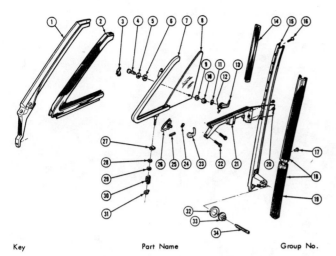

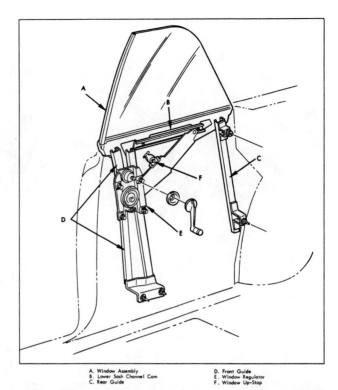

Key	Part Name	Group No.
1 — FRAME, Door Vent		10.656
2 — WEATHERSTRIP ASM., Door Vent (Incl. #14 on 07-17-37-39-67 Styles)		10.652
3 — SUPPORT, Door Vent Upper Pivot (35 & 69 Styles)		10.669
4 — STUD & CAP, Vent Glass Channel Handle (07-17-37-39-67 Styles)		10.664
5 — GASKET, Glass Channel Handle (07-17-37-39-67 Styles)		10.664
6 — INSERT, Glass Channel Handle (07-17-37-39-67 Styles)		10.664
7 — CHANNEL ASM., Door Vent Glass (Incl. #23-24-25-26 on 35 & 69 Styles)		10.655
8 — GLASS, Door Vent		10.658
9 — WASHER, Glass Channel Handle (07-17-37-39-67 Styles)		10.664
10 — SPACER, Glass Channel Handle (07-17-37-39-67 Styles)		10.664
11 — WASHER, Glass Channel Handle (07-17-37-39-67 Styles)		10.664
12 — PIN, Glass Channel Handle (07-17-37-39-67 Styles)		10.664
13 — HANDLE, Glass Channel (07-17-37-39-67 Styles)		10.664
14 — WEATHERSTRIP, Division Channel (35 & 69 Styles)		10.652
15 — CHANNEL & SCALP ASM., Vent Division		10.688
16 — SCREW, Division Channel to Frame		10.688
17 — RIVET, Division to Glass Run Channel		10.688
18 — CHANNEL ASM., Door Window Glass Run Front (07-17-37-39-67 Styles)		10.688
19 — CHANNEL, Glass Run Front Lower (35 & 69 Styles)		10.688
20 — RIVET, Division Channel to Support		10.688
21 — SUPPORT, Division Channel		N.S.
22 — SCREW, Support to Frame		N.S.
23 — HANDLE, Glass Channel (35 & 69 Styles)		10.664
24 — WASHER, Glass Channel Handle (35 & 69 Styles)		10.364
25 — PIN, Glass Channel Handle (35 & 69 Styles)		10.664
26 — SUPPORT, Vent Locking Handle (35 & 69 Styles)		10.664
27 — WASHER, Vent Spring Retainer		10.660
28 — WASHER, Vent Friction Unit		10.660
29 — STOP, Vent Friction Unit		10.660
30 — SPRING, Vent Friction Unit		10.660
31 — WASHER, Vent Friction Unit Tab		10.660
32 — WASHER, Stud Nut to Door Inner Panel		N.S.
33 — NUT, Stud to Door Inner Panel		N.S.
34 — STUD, Door Vent to Inner Panel - Front Lower		10.670

A. Window Assembly
B. Lower Sash Channel Cam
C. Rear Guide
D. Front Guide
E. Window Regulator
F. Window Up-Stop

Rear quarter window glass and hardware for 1964-65 convertible.

Exploded view and parts nomenclature of 1964-67 vent window assembly.

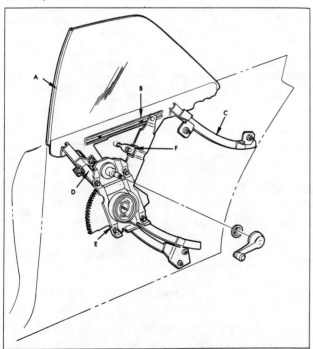

Detail of 1964-65 quarter window glass and hardware for hardtop models.

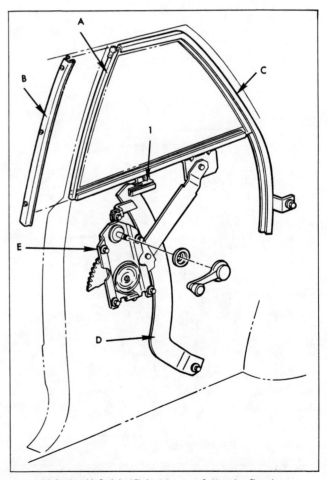

A. Window Assembly (Includes "Clothespin" Nylon Guide at "1")
B. Front Run Channel
C. Upper Run Channel
D. Window Guide Assembly
E. Window Regulator Assembly

Rear quarter glass and hardware for 1964-65 sedan.

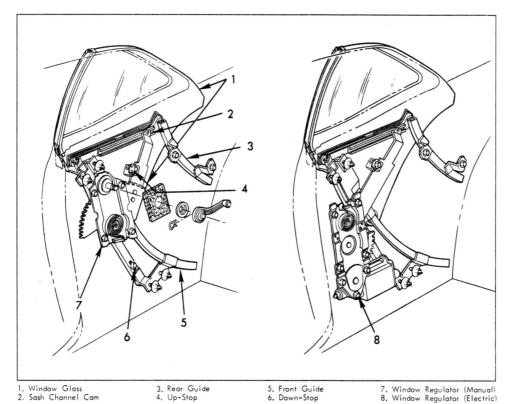

1. Window Glass	3. Rear Guide	5. Front Guide
2. Sash Channel Cam	4. Up-Stop	6. Down-Stop

7. Window Regulator (Manual)
8. Window Regulator (Electric)

1966-67 hardtop quarter-window regulation hardware for both manual and power-operated types.

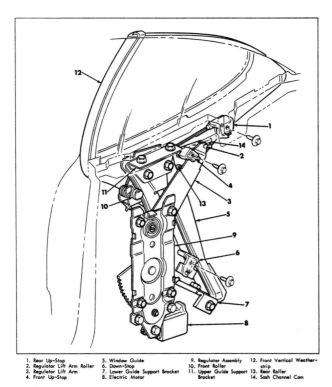

1. Rear Up-Stop	5. Window Guide	9. Regulator Assembly	12. Front Vertical Weather-strip
2. Regulator Lift Arm Roller	6. Down-Stop	10. Front Roller	13. Rear Roller
3. Regulator Lift Arm	7. Lower Guide Support Bracket	11. Upper Guide Support Bracket	14. Sash Channel Cam
4. Front Up-Stop	8. Electric Motor		

The quarter-window regulation assemblies were the same from 1968 through 1970, for both hardtop and convertible applications.

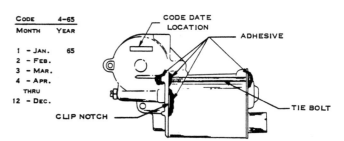

CODE	4-65
MONTH	YEAR
1 – JAN.	65
2 – FEB.	
3 – MAR.	
4 – APR.	
THRU	
12 – DEC.	

If the power window motor must be replaced because of water entry, apply black weatherstrip adhesive to both ends of the "tie bolts" and at the brush holder clip on *all* service replacement motors with two "tie bolts." The improved replacement motors with three "tie bolts," built prior to April 1965, will also require additional sealing. (These replacement motors manufactured prior to April 1965, can easily be identified by the code date stamped in the diecast gear housing; for example, 4-65). Note: Power window motors should be replaced as an assembly, not repaired. (Service News Flash 65-132 dated 12-15-65.)

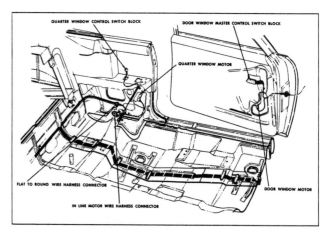

Detail of power window wiring harness for 1966-67 GTO convertibles.

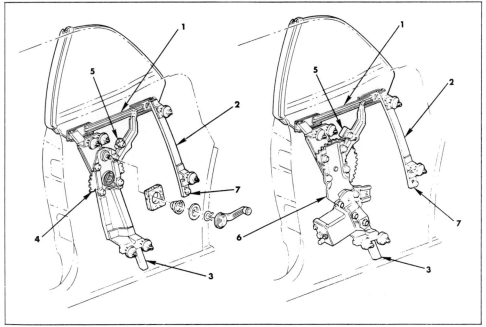

1. Sash Channel Cam
2. Rear Guide
3. Front Guide
4. Window Regulator (Manual)
5. Up-Stop
6. Window Regulator (Electric)
7. Rear Guide Lower Stop

Detail of 1967 manual and power quarter-window hardware used for convertible models.

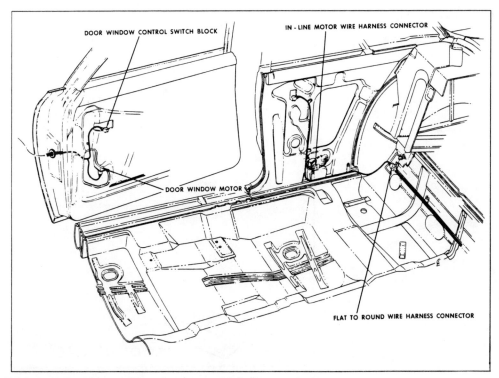

DOOR WINDOW CONTROL SWITCH BLOCK

IN - LINE MOTOR WIRE HARNESS CONNECTOR

DOOR WINDOW MOTOR

FLAT TO ROUND WIRE HARNESS CONNECTOR

RH side view of typical 1964-67 power window harness for both door and quarter window.

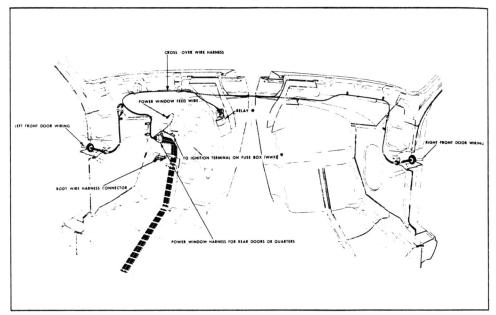

Front view of typical 1964-67 power window harness. Note routing of harness along with main body harness.

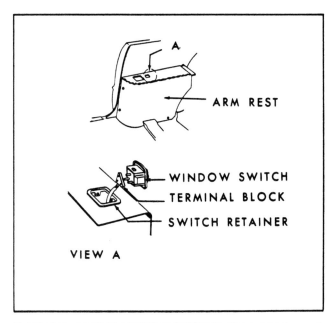

Detail of power window switch and wiring on rear-quarter armrest to rear of ashtray for 1964-70.

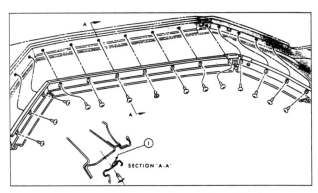

View of 1964-65 roof rail retainer for weatherstrip, with screws.

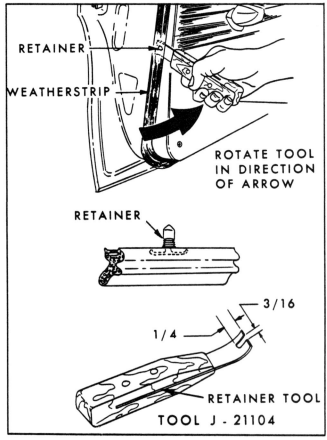

Removal of door weatherstrip was facilitated by use of a special tool. Illustration demonstrates removal of weatherstrip and construction of a facsimile of the factory tool.

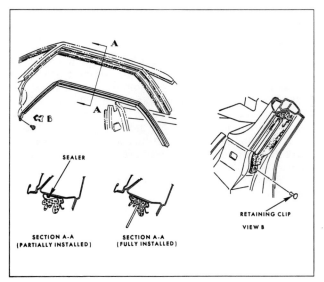

Installation of 1964-65 (typical 1966-70) roof rail weatherstrip into weatherstrip retainer, and glass positioning.

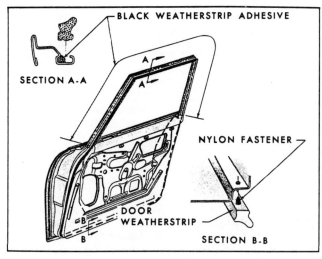

Installation and alignment of 1964-67 sedan door weatherstrip.

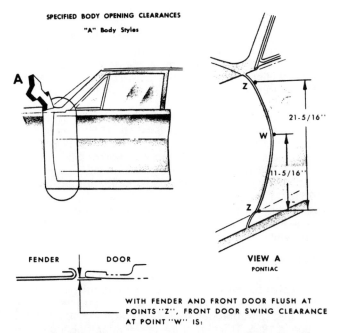

Alignment of door to fender with clearance specified by factory for 1969 GTO.

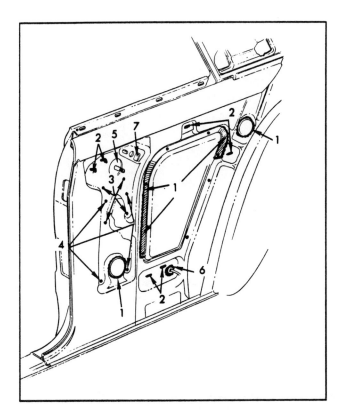

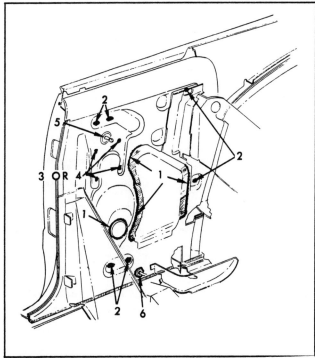

1. Access Hole Cover and Sealing Plugs
2. Window Guide and Glass Run Channel Attaching Screws
3. Window Regulator Attaching Screws (Manual)
4. Window Regulator Attaching Screws (Electric)
5. Window Regulator Spindle Hole Sealing Washer
6. Wire Harness and Grommet Hole (Power Operated Windows Only)
7. Regulator Lift Arm Up-Travel Stop

Hardtop and convertible rear-quarter inner sealing panel and plugs for 1964.

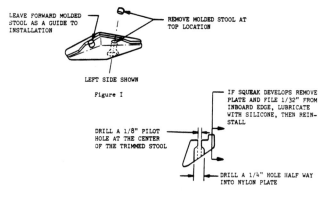

LEAVE FORWARD MOLDED STOOL AS A GUIDE TO INSTALLATION

REMOVE MOLDED STOOL AT TOP LOCATION

LEFT SIDE SHOWN

Figure I

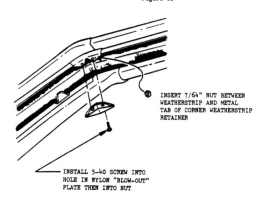

IF SQUEAK DEVELOPS REMOVE PLATE AND FILE 1/32" FROM INBOARD EDGE, LUBRICATE WITH SILICONE, THEN REINSTALL

DRILL A 1/8" PILOT HOLE AT THE CENTER OF THE TRIMMED STOOL

DRILL A 1/4" HOLE HALF WAY INTO NYLON PLATE

Figure II

INSERT 7/64" NUT BETWEEN WEATHERSTRIP AND METAL TAB OF CORNER WEATHERSTRIP RETAINER

INSTALL 5-40 SCREW INTO HOLE IN NYLON "BLOW-OUT" PLATE THEN INTO NUT

Figure III

Service Kit #8704194 (F) consists of:

One replacement black nylon upper corner "blow-out" guide plate.

One slotted head counter-recessed 5-40 x 1/4" screw.

One 7/64" nut with 5-40 thread.

To replace a broken "blow-out" plate, utilizing Service Kit #8704194, proceed as follows:

1. Depending on which side the "blow-out" plate is being replaced, determine which molded stool is at the top and chisel it off flush to the nylon surface. The other stool at the forward side of the plate will remain as a guide and support (Fig. 1).

2. Using a 1/8" drill bit, drill through the plate at the center of the trimmed stool location.

3. Using the 1/8" hole as a guide, from the opposite side (lower surface or plate) drill halfway into the plate with a 1/4" bit. (Fig. 2).

4. Insert the 7/64" nut between the side roof rail weatherstrip and the metal tab of the "blow-out" plate retainer (Fig. 3).

5. Insert the screw into the nylon plate, then into the nut, and tighten.

NOTE: After installation, if there is a squeak between the nylon plate and glass, remove the plate and file approximately 1/32" from the inboard surface of the "blow-out" plate; liberally lubricate with spray or tube type silicone; and reinstall into the upper corner retainer (see Fig. 2).

Dealer Technical Bulletin number 70-T-10, dated 5-27-70, reported this procedure for replacing broken blow-out plates on 1969 and 1970 hardtop models.

REAR DECK LID

1964-67

The GTO nameplate was mounted on the right rear of the deck lid. Three different part numbers existed for the same nameplate. The original part number was 9775744. This number was replaced in 1967 by 7667612. The final and current number is 8701433. The first and second part numbers are more desirable than the third, as the mold for this nameplate has deteriorated over the years, to the point where there are "pits" on the leading edges of the nameplate.

Both 1964 and 1965 used the same emblem (part number 4412789) on the center rear of the deck lid.

The GTO deck lid nameplate for 1966-67 was the same as for 1964-65. The deck lid molding was stainless steel (part number 4227150 for 1966 and 4229876 for 1967).

1968-70

A rear deck lid molding (part number 8701363) was used on some—but not all—1969 GTOs. The molding ran across the rear center lip of the deck lid. An extension ran across the tops of the taillamps on the deck lid (part number 8701361 RH and 8701362 LH). The entire deck lid molding was joined at the rear of each rear quarter by a molding (part number 8701012 RH and 8701013 LH).

The traditional GTO nameplate (part number 8701433) was attached to the right rear of the deck lid. This plate was used in 1968 and 1969.

In 1970, a decal took the place of the nameplate on the deck lid. One of three colors was used, depending on exterior color: red (479921), black (479920), white (479922).

REAR END

1964-65

The rear end design was the same for the GTO and the LeMans for 1964 and 1965. The 1964 taillamp saw a production change relative to design. The reflector on the first type was in the side of the taillamp lens. The second type had the reflector in the center of the lens. Only the second-design lamp assembly was serviced by part number 9710761 LH and 9710762 RH.

It was possible to replace the first type of lens with part number 5955622 RH and 5955621 LH. The second-type taillamp lens used part number 5955650 for both sides since the reflector was in the center of the lens.

The RH and LH taillamp housings were separated by the fuel filler door which came in two pieces: the fuel filler door (part number 4417537) and the fuel filler door nameplate (part number 4453753).

The 1965 rear end used quarter-panel extensions (part number 4490941 LH and 4490940 RH). The taillamp bezels (part number 5956831 LH and 5956832 RH were chromed, and held the taillamp lens (part number 5956829 LH and 5956830 RH).

The center rear body panel molding (part number 9781577) separated the taillamp bezels. The panel was painted black between the chrome ribs, and carried the name Pontiac in white letters. The GTO rear panel has six ribs, while the Tempest has ten.

1966-67

The GTO in 1966 and 1967 used a rear end design exclusive to the 242 GTO series to identify it from the Tempest and LeMans series. A diecast chrome "dogleg" molding (part number 4227112 RH and 4227113 LH) was used in 1966. The rear of the rear fender molding in 1967 was part number 4229873 (RH) and 4229874 (LH).

The rear end design of the 1966 GTO consisted of a rear panel (part number 7584633) which was painted the exterior color. The taillamp molding package (part number 4227151 RH and 4227152 LH) mounted to the rear panel with a gasket (part number 5957994 RH and 5957993 LH). It fit over the taillamp lens (part number 5957992 RH and 5957991 LH) and was retained by eight ⅞ inch speed nuts (part number 7616775). The taillamp molding package was painted the exterior color, and had three finishing moldings (part number 7620467) that snapped on each side over the taillamp lens openings.

Individual chrome letters spelling out the name Pontiac were mounted on the rear panel with the letter T directly under the trunk lock. The letters were retained by a ⅜ inch speed nut (part number 4528566). The part numbers and corresponding letters are listed below.

P	7586857
O	7586858
N	7586859
T	7586860
I	7586861
A	7586862
C	7586863

The 1967 GTO rear end was redesigned and had a cleaner appearance. The rear panel (part number 7551686) was painted to match the exterior color. The taillamp assembly consisted of a lamp lens (part number 5958606 RH and 5958605 LH) and a gasket (part number 5958610 RH and 5958609 LH). These were encased in a housing assembly (part number 5958448 RH and 5958447 LH), which was mounted to the inside of the rear panel by means of twelve clips (part number 7616775) and twelve nuts (part number 7731439). Eight screws (part number 5942132) retained the taillamp lens to the housing.

1968-70

Unlike earlier models, the 1968-70 GTO did not incorporate a rear end panel design. The rear taillamps were integrated into the bumper in 1968. They were redesigned to "float" between the rear bumper and the trailing edge of the deck lid in 1969, but returned to the confines of the bumper in 1970.

The 1968 taillamp housing (part number 5959922 RH and 5959921 LH) encased the taillamp lens (part number 5959928 RH and 5959927 LH), which was sandwiched by a lens gasket (part number 5959926). The assembly went toward the housing, and a lamp mounting gasket (part number 5959771) sealed against the inside of the rear bumper. The entire assembly was held to the bumper by a ¼ inch 20x⅞ inch screw and a 9/32 inch inside-diameter and ¾ inch outside-diameter washer.

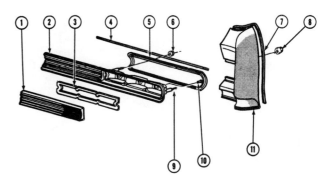

BACK-UP LAMP

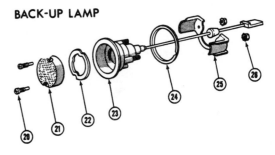

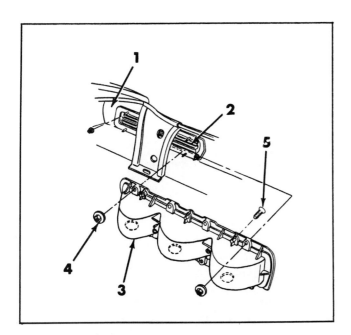

1. Rear End Inner Panel
2. Rear End Outer Panel Finishing Molding
3. Rear Lamp Housing
4. Housing Nut
5. Lens Screw

Detail of taillamp housing mounting. Taillamp housing was installed after the trunk compartment was painted on the assembly line; housing appearance should be white metal, with no trunk paint on housing.

Key	Part Name	Group No.
1 — LENS ASM., Tail Lamp		2.682
2 — HOUSING ASM., Tail Lamp		N.S.
3 — GASKET, Tail Lamp Lens		2.684
4 — GASKET, Tail Lamp Mounting — Inner		2.660
5 — GASKET, Tail Lamp Mounting		2.660
6 — NUT, Lamp Asm. to Body		N.S.
7 — GASKET, Rear Quarter Extension at Tail Lamp		2.697
8 — NUT, Quarter Outer Panel Extension at Tail Lamp		2.688
9 — STUD, Lamp Housing to Rear End Panel		N.S.
10 — SCREW, Tail Lamp Lens (#8-18 x 3/4" W/Sealer)		2.688
11 — EXTENSION, Rear Quarter Outer Panel		2.681
20 — SCREW, Back-Up Lamp Lens		2.697
21 — LENS, Back-Up Lamp		2.697
22 — GASKET, Back-Up Lamp Lens		2.697
23 — HOUSING ASM., Back-Up Lamp		N.S.
24 — SEAL, Back-Up Lamp to Bumper		2.697
25 — BRACKET, Back-Up Lamp Mounting		2.697
26 — NUTS & LOCK WASHER, Housing to Bracket (#10-24)		8.915

1964 taillamp assembly and optional backup lamp assembly with parts nomenclature.

The 1969 assembly was similar in structure, but mounted differently. The taillamp lens (part number 5961048) was retained to the housing assembly (part number 5960986) by screws. The taillamp bezel (part number 5961091 RH and 5961092 LH) used a gasket (part number 5960991) for sealing against the rear pan. Studs from the bezel extruded through the pan. The housing assembly mounted on these studs and was retained by nuts.

The 1970 taillamp package (part number 911330 RH and 911329 LH) was serviced as an assembly. Individual components could be serviced separately, with the exception of the housing assembly.

The lamp lens (part number 5962274 RH and 5962273 LH) mounted to the housing with a gasket (part number 5962271). A bracket (part number 9799076 RH and 9799077 LH) was used to retain the lamp assembly to the rear bumper.

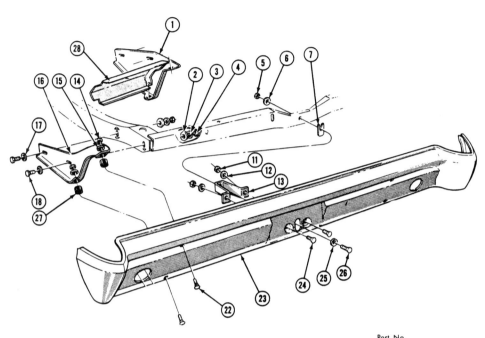

Key	Part Name	Part No. 1964	Part No. 1965	Group No.
1 — BAR, Rear Bumper Impact Bar to Frame - Outer (w/Station Wagon)		9773904 R.H.	9773904 R.H.	7.836
		9773905 L.H.	9773905 L.H.	7.836
2 — WASHER, Bumper Adjusting		3838450	3838450	7.836
3 — WASHER, Frame Bar to Frame (17/32" I.D. x 1-1/4" O.D.)		1362249	1362249	7.831
4 — NUT, Frame Bar to Frame (1/2"-13)		9414511	9414511	8.916
5 — NUT, Center Bracket to Frame (7/16"-14)		9424985	9424985	8.915
6 — WASHER, Lower Impact Bar to Frame Bar		531315	531315	7.831
7 — SHIM, Center Bracket to Frame (.060)		540803	540803	8.143
11 — NUT, Lower Impact Bar to Frame Bar (7/16"-14)		9424985	9424985	8.915
12 — WASHER, Lower Impact Bar to Frame Bar		531315	531315	7.831
13 — BRACKET, Impact Bar to Frame Center		9773976	9773976	7.836
14 — NUT, Lower Impact Bar to Frame Bar (7/16"-14)		9424985	9424985	8.915
15 — WASHER, Lower Impact Bar to Frame Bar		531315	531315	7.831
16 — BAR, Rear Bumper Impact Bar to Frame - Outer		9773978 R.H.	9773978 R.H.	7.836
		9773979 L.H.	9773979 L.H.	
17 — WASHER, Frame Bar to Frame		—	—	N.S.
18 — BOLT, Frame Bar to Frame (1/2"-13 x 1-1/4")		455000	455000	8.900
22 — BOLT, Impact Bar to Frame Bar - Outer		9775533	9775533	7.852
23 — BAR, Rear Bumper Impact - Exc. Back-up Lamps		9773217	—	7.831
BAR, Rear Bumper Impact - With Back-up Lamps		9773428	—	7.831
BAR, Rear Bumper Impact - 2035, 2135, 3335, 3535		9774004	9774004	7.831
24 — BOLT, Impact Bar to Center Bracket (7/16"-14 x 1")		126433	126433	8.902
25 — WASHER, Center Bracket to Frame		—	—	N.S.
26 — BOLT, Center Bracket to Frame		—	—	N.S.
27 — SPACER, Bumper Bar-Cut to 5/32" Thickness		540114	540114	7.831
28 — SHIELD, Rear Frame Bar Rear Qtr. Panel Splash (w/Station Wagon)		—	9781356	12.944
SHIELD, Rear Frame Bar Rear Qtr. Panel Splash (All exc. Station Wagon)		—	—	N.S.

Exploded view and parts nomenclature of 1964 rear bumper. Brackets were painted gloss black.

1) R & R tail light assembly.

2) Disassemble tail light assembly, removing lens and weatherstripping.

3) Clean panels and mask black painted areas.

4) Remove red paint with a commercial stripping agent, such as DUPONT 999 PAINT & VARNISH REMOVER, using No. 1 steel wool.

5) Rinse with water and dry thoroughly.

6) Condition the metal with DUPONT VM 5717 METAL CONDITIONER or a similar product. Dry thoroughly.

   CAUTION: This metal conditioner is an acidic concentrate and care must be exercised to avoid skin contact.

Here is a method for refinishing the 1964 taillight bezel assembly. It is taken from Pontiac Service News Flash number 64-106, dated 9-15-64.

7) Mask panel area not to be painted.

8) Spray with DUPONT 577 WASH PRIMER (818-012). This primer must be mixed in a 5:1 ratio (5 parts thinner to 1 part primer) and should be used or thrown away within six hours after mixing to avoid spray equipment contamination.

9) Wipe chrome ribs clean with rag dampened with thinner using care to avoid contacting the recessed area.

10) Spray with standard primer and wipe off chrome ribs

11) Paint panel with Marimba Red (Code L) and wipe off chrome ribs.

    CAUTION: Avoid any paint contact with black area.

12) Force dry at 180°F for 15 minutes.

13) Reassemble tail light assembly installing lens and weatherstripping

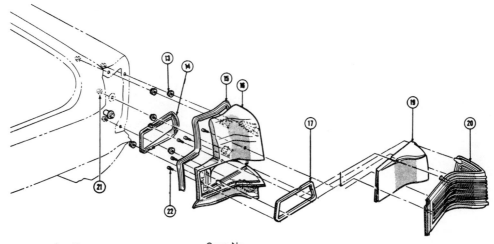

Key	Part Name	Group No.
10 — GASKET, Rear Quarter Extension at Tail Lamp		2.660
11 — NUT, Quarter Outer Panel Extension at Tail Lamp		2.688
12 — SCREW, Quarter Panel Extension at Tail Lamp		2.688
13 — WASHER, Quarter Outer Panel Extension at Tail Lamp		2.688
14 — GASKET, Rear Quarter Extension at Rear End - R.H.		2.660
15 — GASKET, Rear Quarter Extension at Tail Lamp		2.660
16 — EXTENSION, Rear Quarter Outer at Tail Lamp		2.681
17 — GASKET, Tail Lamp Lens		2.684
19 — LENS, Tail Lamp (3700 Series)		2.682
20 — BEZEL, Tail Lamp (3700 Series)		2.681
21 — NUT, Quarter Outer Panel Extension at Tail Lamp		2.688
22 — SCREW, Tail Lamp Bezel (#8-32 x 5/8")		2.688

1965 rear lamp assembly and installation with parts nomenclature.

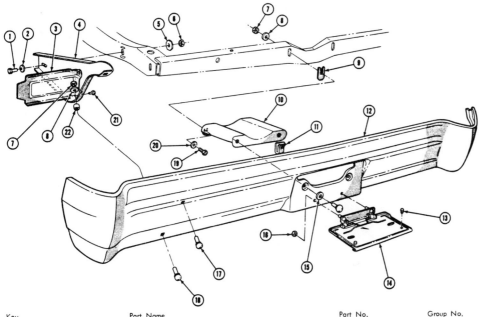

Key	Part Name	Part No.	Group No.
1—BOLT, Outer Bar to Frame (1/2"-13 x 1 3/8")		427566	8.900
2—WASHER, Rear Frame Bar to Frame (17/32" I.D. x 1 1/4" O.D.)		1362249	7.831
3—SHIELD, Rear Frame Bar to Rear Qtr. Panel Splash		9778877	12.944
4—BAR, Rear Bumper to Frame - Outer		9778828 RH	7.836
		9778829 LH	7.836
5—WASHER, Rear Bumper Adjusting		3838450	7.836
6—NUT, Outer Bar to Frame Bolt (1/2"-13)		9422301	8.917
7—NUT, Center Bracket to Frame Bolt (7/16"-14)		9424985	8.915
8—WASHER, Rear Bumper Bar to Frame		531315	7.831
9—SHIM, Rear Bumper Bar Center Bracket to Frame (1/16")		540803	7.831
10—BRACKET, Rear Bumper to Frame - Center		9778391	7.836
11—NUT, Rear Bumper to Center Bracket		9794251	7.852
12—BAR, Rear Bumper Impact - Exc. Back-Up Lamps		9778096	7.831
BAR, Rear Bumper Impact - With Back-Up Lamps		9778491	7.831
13—BUMPER, Fuel Tank Filler Door		9777365	12.945
14—DOOR ASM., Fuel Tank Filler		9797235	12.945
15—WASHER, (Flat 7/16")		120388	8.929
16—NUT, (1/4"-20 Spec. Lock)		-	N.S.
17—BOLT, Rear Bumper to Frame Outer Bar (7/16"-14 x 1 1/4")		9775533	7.852
18—BOLT, Rear Bumper to Frame Outer Bar (7/16"-14 x 1")		9425343	7.852
19—BOLT, Center Bracket to Frame Bar (7/16"-14 x 1 1/2")		427555	8.900
20—WASHER, Rear Frame Bar to Frame (17/32" I.D. x 1 1/4" O.D.)		1362249	7.831
21—SCREW, (1/4"-14 x 5/8" Hex. Washer Hd. Tapping)		-	N.S.
22—SPACER, Rear Bumper to Frame Outer Bar - Cut to 5/32" Thickness		540114	7.831

Exploded view and part numbers for 1965 rear bumper. Bumper is shown without optional backup lamps.

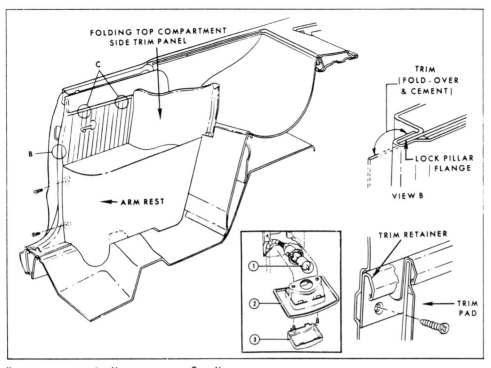

Key	Part Name	Group No.
1 — BULB, Quarter Arm Rest Lamp (No. 68)		8.991
2 — REFLECTOR, Quarter Arm Rest Lamp		11.927
3 — LENS, Quarter Arm Rest Lamp		11.928

Detail of 1964-70 rear-quarter panel and trim.

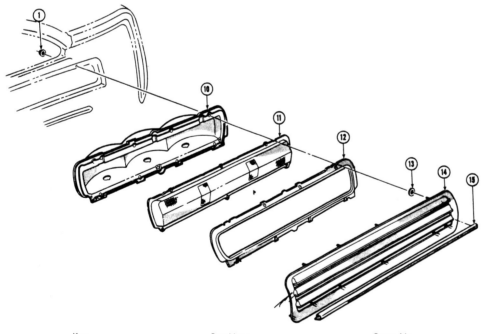

Key	Part Name	Group No.
1 — NUT, Rear Qtr. Outer Ext. to Panel	12.118
10 — HOUSING, Tail Lamp	2.681
11 — LENS, Tail Lamp	2.682
12 — GASKET, Tail Lamp Lens and Mtg.	2.684
13 — WASHER, Tail Lamp Mtg.	12.183
14 — MOLDING & CLIP PKG., Tail Lamp	12.182
15 — MOLDING, Tail Lamp Finishing	12.182

Exploded view of 1966 taillamp assembly. Note snap-on molding (number 15) that is used on molding package.

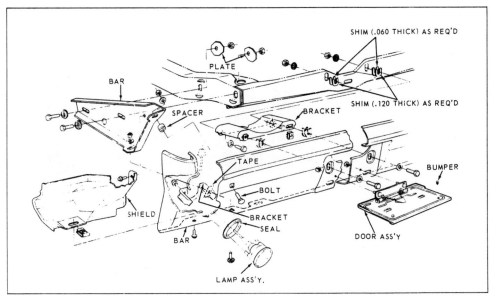

Exploded view of 1966 rear bumper installation. Plates were mounted on inside of frame rail. Shield was black; fuel filler door assembly was 60° gloss black. All mounting brackets and bars were painted 60° gloss black. (Also typical of 1967.)

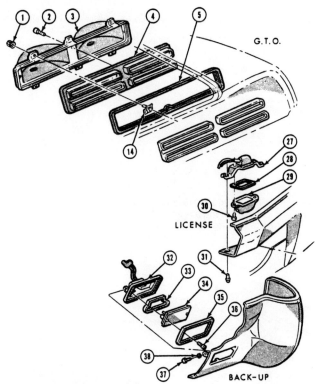

Key	Part Name	Group No.
1 — NUT, Tail Lamp Clip to Pocket		12.118
2 — SCREW, Tail Lamp Lens		2.688
3 — HOUSING, Tail Lamp		2.681
4 — LENS, Tail Lamp		2.682
5 — GASKET, Tail Lamp Lens		2.684
14 — CLIP ASM., Tail Lamp		12.118
27 — HOUSING ASM., License Lamp		N.S.
28 — GASKET, License Lamp Lens		2.707
29 — LENS, License Lamp		2.709
30 — SCREW, License Lamp Lens to Housing (#8-15 x 5/8" Rd. Hd.)		8.977
31 — SCREW, License Lamp to Bumper (#8-18 x 1/2")		8.977
32 — HOUSING ASM., Back-Up Lamp		2.697
33 — GASKET, Back-Up Lamp Lens		2.697
34 — LENS, Back-Up Lamp		2.697
35 — GASKET, Back-Up Lamp Mounting		2.697
36 — SCREW, Back-Up Lamp Lens		2.585
37 — SCREW, Back-Up Lamp Housing to Bumper (1/4"-14 x 5/8")		8.977
38 — WASHER, Back-Up Lamp Housing to Bumper (1/4" Ext. Tooth)		8.932

Exploded view of 1967 GTO taillamp assembly. Note detail of backup lamp, tag bracket and lamp assembly.

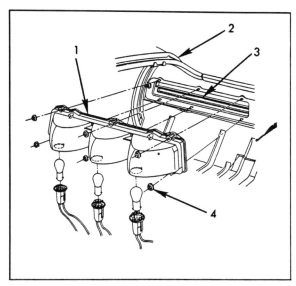

1. Lamp Housing
2. Quarter Panel
3. Rear End Panel
   Molding
4. Lamp Housing Nut

Installation of 1967 taillamp housing to rear end panel. Correct bulb for taillamp was 1157.

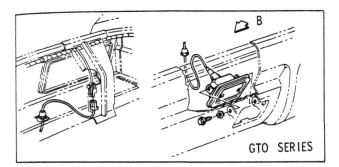

GTO SERIES

Detail of 1967 GTO backup lamp assembly. All GTOs in 1966 and 1967 came standard with backup lamps. When purchasing a rear 1967 bumper, make sure it has provision for mounting backup lamp, as Tempest rear bumper had none.

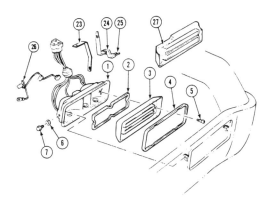

Key	Part Name	Group No.
1	HOUSING, Tail Lamp	2.681
2	GASKET, Tail Lamp Lens	2.684
3	LENS, Tail Lamp	2.682
4	GASKET, Tail Lamp Mounting	2.660
5	SCREW, Tail Lamp Lens	2.688
6	WASHER, Housing to Bumper (9/32" I.D. x 3/4" O.D.)	8.929
7	SCREW, Housing to Bumper (1/4"-20 x 7/8")	N.S.
23	STRAP, Tail Lamp Ground - Inboard (G.T.O.)	2.664
24	TUBE, Outboard Ground Strap Insulator	N.S.
25	STRAP, Tail Lamp Ground - Outboard (G.T.O.)	2.664
26	WIRE ASM., Lamp Ground (1969)	2.694
27	BEZEL, Tail Lamp (1969)	2.681

Exploded view of 1968 taillamp components and parts nomenclature.

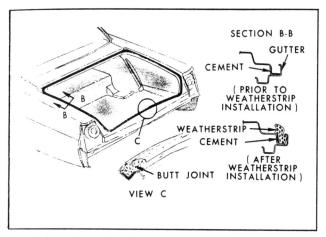

Installation of weatherstrip (part number 7726266 in 1968 and 8723802 in 1969-70) for rear compartment lid. All weatherstrip part numbers were superseded by part number 9825829, which was used in 1964-70 and was installed similarly.

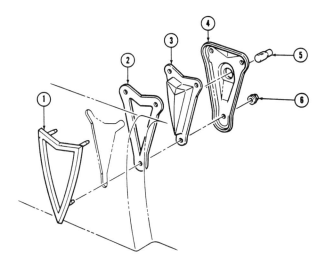

Key	Part Name	Group No.
1	BEZEL, Rear Side Marker Lamp	2.575
2	GASKET, Side Marker Lamp Mounting	2.575
3	LENS, Rear Side Marker Lamp	2.575
4	HOUSING, Rear Side Marker Lamp	2.575
5	BULB, Rear Side Marker Lamp (#194)	8.991
6	NUT, Lamp to Quarter Panel (#10)	8.921

Exploded view of 1968 rear quarter marker lamps.

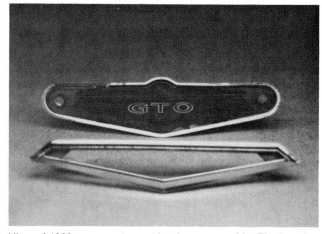

View of 1969 rear quarter marker lamp assembly. The housing was part number 5961778, and the lens was part number 5961779.

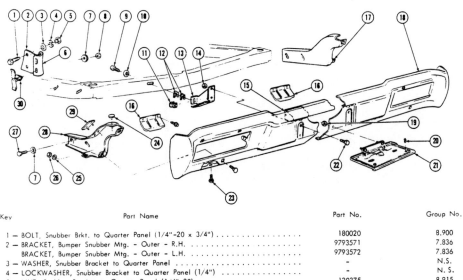

Key	Part Name	Part No.	Group No.
1 — BOLT, Snubber Brkt. to Quarter Panel (1/4"-20 x 3/4")		180020	8.900
2 — BRACKET, Bumper Snubber Mtg. - Outer - R.H.		9793571	7.836
BRACKET, Bumper Snubber Mtg. - Outer - L.H.		9793572	7.836
3 — WASHER, Snubber Bracket to Quarter Panel		-	N.S.
4 — LOCKWASHER, Snubber Bracket to Quarter Panel (1/4")		-	N.S.
5 — NUT, Snubber Bracket to Quarter Panel (1/4"-20)		120375	8.915
6 — SNUBBER, Impact Bar to Body - Outer		9793538	7.836
7 — WASHER, Frame Bar to Frame		1362249	7.831
8 — NUT, Frame Bar to Frame (1/2"-13)		9414511	8.916
9 — BOLT, Center Bracket to Frame (7/16"-14 x 1 3/8")		-	N.S.
10 — WASHER, Center Bracket to Frame (7/16" I.D. x 1" O.D.)		120388	8.929
11 — NUT ASM., Impact Bar to Center Bracket (7/16"-14 "U")		9794251	7.852
12 — SHIM, Center Bracket to Frame - .060		540803	8.143
13 — BRACKET, Bumper Bar to Frame - Center		9790225	7.836
14 — NUT, Impact Bar to Bracket (7/16"-14)		9422299	8.917
15 — SNUBBER, Impact Bar to Body - Center		9793483	7.836
16 — SHIELD, Tail Lamp Splash		9792633	2.664
17 — BAR, Bumper to Frame - Outer - R.H.		9797165	7.836
18 — BAR, Rear Bumper Impact		9790051	7.831
19 — NUT, Door to Impact Bar (1/4"-20)		120375	8.915
20 — BUMPER, Fuel Filler Door		9777945	12.945
21 — DOOR ASM., Fuel Tank Filler		9797235	12.945
22 — BOLT, Impact Bar to Bracket (7/16"-14 x 7/8")		180144	8.900
23 — BOLT, Impact Bar to Frame Bar (7/16"-14 x 1")		9425343	8.902
24 — INSULATOR, Bumper to Frame Bar - Upper (Round)		9790141	7.865
25 — WASHER, Impact Bar to Frame Bar		531315	7.831
26 — NUT, Impact Bar to Frame Bar (7/16"-14)		9422299	8.917
27 — BOLT, Frame Bar to Frame (1/2"-13 x 1 3/8")		427566	8.900
28 — BAR, Bumper to Frame - Outer - L.H.		9790121	7.836
29 — INSULATOR, Bumper to Frame Bar - Lower (Oblong)		9794220	7.865
30 — CLIP, Snubber to Bracket		480534	12.801

Exploded view of 1968 GTO rear bumper with part numbers.

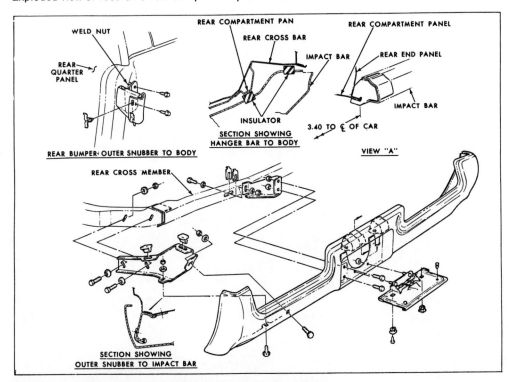

Installation instructions for the 1969 GTO rear bumper. Note location of insulators and shims used with center mounting bracket. License plate door and bumper brackets were painted 60° gloss black.

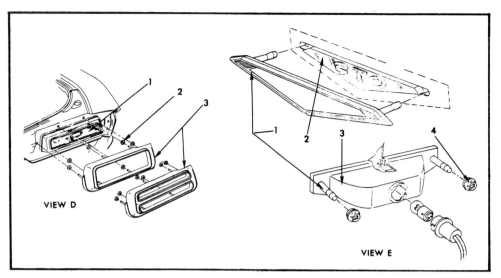

Exploded view of rear taillamp installation and rear quarter marker lamps for 1969 GTO.

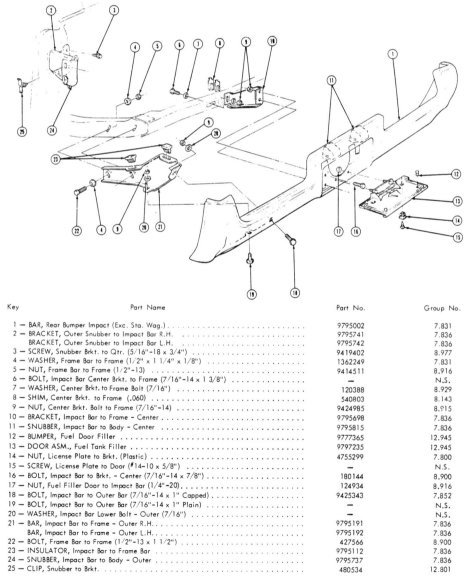

Key	Part Name	Part No.	Group No.
1 — BAR, Rear Bumper Impact (Exc. Sta. Wag.)		9795002	7.831
2 — BRACKET, Outer Snubber to Impact Bar R.H.		9795741	7.836
BRACKET, Outer Snubber to Impact Bar L.H.		9795742	7.836
3 — SCREW, Snubber Brkt. to Qtr. (5/16"-18 x 3/4")		9419402	8.977
4 — WASHER, Frame Bar to Frame (1/2" x 1 1/4" x 1/8")		1362249	7.831
5 — NUT, Frame Bar to Frame (1/2"-13)		9414511	8.916
6 — BOLT, Impact Bar Center Brkt. to Frame (7/16"-14 x 1 3/8")		—	N.S.
7 — WASHER, Center Brkt. to Frame Bolt (7/16")		120388	8.929
8 — SHIM, Center Brkt. to Frame (.060)		540803	8.143
9 — NUT, Center Brkt. Bolt to Frame (7/16"-14)		9424985	8.915
10 — BRACKET, Impact Bar to Frame - Center		9795698	7.836
11 — SNUBBER, Impact Bar to Body - Center		9795815	7.836
12 — BUMPER, Fuel Door Filler		9777365	12.945
13 — DOOR ASM., Fuel Tank Filler		9797235	12.945
14 — NUT, License Plate to Brkt. (Plastic)		4755299	7.800
15 — SCREW, License Plate to Door (#14-10 x 5/8")		—	N.S.
16 — BOLT, Impact Bar to Brkt. - Center (7/16"-14 x 7/8")		180144	8.900
17 — NUT, Fuel Filler Door to Impact Bar (1/4"-20)		124934	8.916
18 — BOLT, Impact Bar to Outer Bar (7/16"-14 x 1" Capped)		9425343	7.852
19 — BOLT, Impact Bar to Outer Bar (7/16"-14 x 1" Plain)		—	N.S.
20 — WASHER, Impact Bar Lower Bolt - Outer (7/16")		—	N.S.
21 — BAR, Impact Bar to Frame - Outer R.H.		9795191	7.836
BAR, Impact Bar to Frame - Outer L.H.		9795192	7.836
22 — BOLT, Frame Bar to Frame (1/2"-13 x 1 1/2")		427566	8.900
23 — INSULATOR, Impact Bar to Frame Bar		9795112	7.836
24 — SNUBBER, Impact Bar to Body - Outer		9795737	7.836
25 — CLIP, Snubber to Brkt.		480534	12.801

View of 1969 rear bumper with associated part numbers.

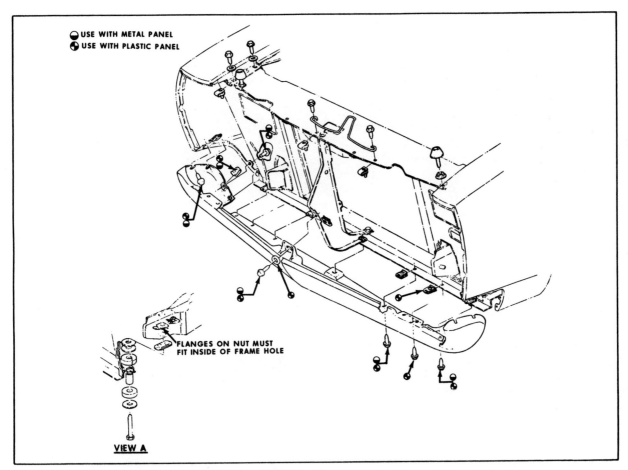

○ USE WITH METAL PANEL
◑ USE WITH PLASTIC PANEL

FLANGES ON NUT MUST
FIT INSIDE OF FRAME HOLE

VIEW A

Installation of 1969 valance panel (part number 9795655). All
GTO valance panels were steel.

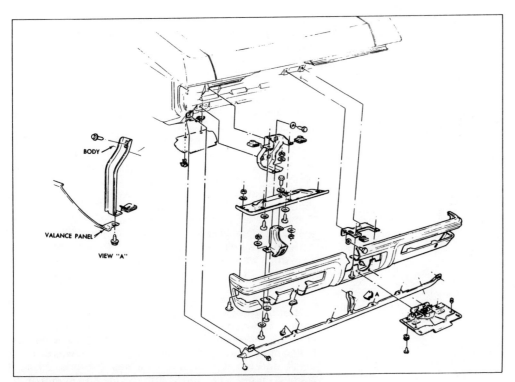

BODY

VALANCE PANEL

VIEW "A"

Installation of 1970 GTO rear bumper. GTO rear valance (part
number 478953) was different than that of the standard LeMans;
rear exhaust splitters extruded past the GTO valance.

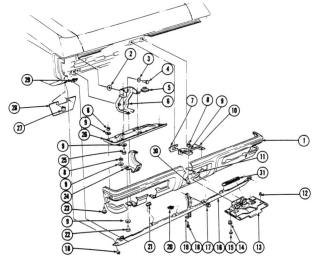

Key	Part Name	Part No.	Group No.
1 — BAR, Rear Bumper		484946	7.831
2 — WASHER, (1/2" I.D. x 1-7/8" O.D. x 1/8")		—	N.S.
3 — WASHER, (1/2" I.D. x 1-1/4" O.D. x 3/16")		120389	8.929
4 — BOLT, (7/16" — 14 x 1-1/2")		3955019	7.874
5 — NUT, (7/16" — 14 — "U")		480567	7.852
6 — BRACKET, Impact Bar - Outer		481177	7.836
7 — SHIM, Center Brkt. to Frame (.060)		540803	8.143
8 — NUT, (7/16" — 14)		124834	8.916
9 — WASHER, (7/16" I.D. x 1" O.D. x 1/8")		531315	7.831
10 — BRACKET, Impact Bar Mtg. - Center		9799071	7.836
11 — SCREW, (1/4" — 14 x 1/2")		—	N.S.
12 — BUMPER, Filler Door to Impact Bar		9777365	12.945
13 — DOOR ASM., Fuel Tank Filler		9797235	12.945
15 — SCREW, (#14-10 x 5/8")		—	N.S.
16 — PANEL, Rear Valance (G.T.O.)		478953	7.833
17 — SCREW, (#10-16 x 1/2")		9419303	8.977
18 — SCREW ASM., (#10-16 x 3/4")		—	N.S.
19 — STRAP, Panel to Body		477668	7.833
20 — NUT, (#10-16 — "U")		9422836	8.921
21 — NUT, Panel to Bumper (Plastic)		1377030	7.833
22 — BOLT, (7/16" — 14 x 7/8" Hex)		—	N.S.
23 — BOLT, (7/16" — 14 x 7/8" Rd.)		—	N.S.
24 — REINFORCEMENT, Rear Impact Bar		9799088R.H. - 9799089L.H.	7.836
25 — BOLT, (7/16" — 14 x 1")		454944	8.900
26 — BRACKET, Tail Lamp to Bumper		9799076R.H. - 9799077L.H.	2.664
27 — CLIP, Lamp Splash Shield		480534	12.801
28 — SHIELD, Lamp Splash (G.T.O.)		479302	2.664
29 — NUT, (#10-16 — "U")		546156	7.833
30 — BOLT, (7/16" — 14 x 1")		9425343	8.902
31 — GUARD, Valance		480590	7.833

Exploded view of 1970 GTO rear bumper with associated part nomenclature and numbers.

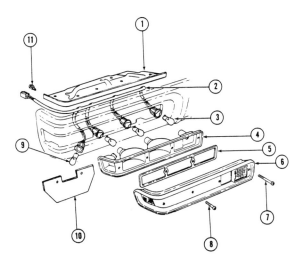

Key	Part Name	Group No.
1 — BRACKET, Lamp to Rr. Bumper Mounting		2.664
2 — WIRE ASM., Tail Lamp		2.480
3 — BULB, Tail Stop or Back Up Lamp (#1157)		8.991
4 — HOUSING, Tail Lamp (Part of Lamp Asm. - 2.679)		N.S.
5 — GASKET, Tail Lamp Lens		2.684
6 — LENS, Tail Lamp		2.682
7 — SCREW, Tail Lamp Lens Mounting (Inboard)		2.688
8 — SCREW, Tail Lamp Lens		2.688
9 — BULB, Side Marker Lamp (#194)		8.991
10 — SHIELD, Tail Lamp Splash		2.664
11 — SCREW, Lamp Housing to Bumper (5/16"-12 x 1 1/8")		N.S.

Exploded view of 1970 taillamp components and part nomenclature. Splash shield was painted 60° gloss black.

GRILLE

1964-65

To differentiate the GTO from the rest of the LeMans model line-up, Pontiac painted the grille's center bars matte black except for the thick center horizontal bar and the headlamp-surround openings. The LH grille carried the white-lettered GTO emblem on a black connecting bar (part number 9775669).

The 1965 GTO used the LeMans grilles with no change except the inclusion of the same white-lettered GTO nameplate. The Tempest grilles were not used on the GTO.

There were two styles of headlamp doors in 1965. The differences were in paint trim. One, used on the GTO, was blacked-out in the ribbed area between the headlamp openings (part number 5957313). The other, standard on the Tempest, was blacked-out between the ribs only. The replacement door (service number 5956794) matched the Tempest door, painted to match the correct trim style for the GTO. The gasket (part number 5958116) mounted between the headlamp door and the front fender. Guide T-3 lamps were used for both years.

1966-67

The GTO became a separate series in 1966, and as a part of the model identification, a new, distinctive grille design was used. The GTO grille was all plastic, and used an egg-crate design, with the housing for the parking lamps molded into the grille. The grille itself was 0° gloss black, and the surrounding area was low-gloss silver. A stainless molding snapped into the leading edges of the grille assembly on three sides.

The 1967 used a completely different grille assembly. The bezel was cast in gloss-black plastic. The wire mesh assembly bolted directly to the bezel. The parking lamp housing and related components were mounted on the mesh grille. Chrome Phillips-head screws were used to retain the bezel to the housing. The parking lamp assembly was serviced by five components, and used a 1157A bulb.

	RH	LH
Housing	5959494	5959493
Reflector	5958195	
Gasket	5956522	
Lens and shield assembly	5956205	
Bezel	5956521	

Headlamp bezels were interchangeable between 1966 and 1967. Guide T-3 headlamps were used for both years.

1968-70

As part of the new styling for 1968, the GTO grilles were entirely redesigned. Standard grilles had fixed headlamps using Guide T-3 lamps. Optional was the disappearing headlamp package (RPO 414). The same grille assembly was used for both applications.

The Endura bumper could be deleted in 1968, in which case a different grille assembly was used. (Refer to illustration of 1968 GTO grille with chrome bumper option.)

For 1969, the grille design was retained. However, a thin horizontal bar was highlighted in the center of the grilles. The chrome bumper option was discontinued. The same grilles were used for the standard headlamps or the hideaway option (RPO 414). Guide T-3 lamps were used.

The 1970 GTO grilles were redesigned, using an egg-crate design. The grilles were mounted by means of two brackets at the top of the grille to the front bumper reinforcement. Two U-type nuts were attached to the bottom of the grilles, and were retained by bolts through the lower brackets.

FRONT SHEET METAL AND ENGINE COMPARTMENT

1964-67

The inner fender skirt for 1964-67 carried part number 9781456 (RH) and 9781457 (LH). The 1967 LH fender skirt was redesigned, with a dimple in the rear of the skirt to accommodate the larger power brake booster used in 1967, and was part number 9785739. This part number superseded the 9781457 number for replacement purposes.

	RH	LH
1964	9774178	9774179
1965	9779332	9779333
1966	9782603	9782604
1967	9786937	9786938

The cowl hood ledge seal was the same for 1964-67 (part number 3819258). Although unpopular with restorers, an underhood insulator pad was used on the GTO. The 1964 pad was part number 9775371; the 1965-67 pad was part number 9780586. Ten pad retaining clips (part number 9784547) were used for all four years.

The 1964 hood stood alone in its application (part number 9775716), but there was a multitude of part numbers for 1965-67 hoods. The 1965 hood (original part number 9779558) had no holes in the front, since no emblem was used. The 1966 hood (original part number 9783744) had predrilled holes for mounting the hood emblem. An original part number also exists for the 1967 hood (9787268), although there are no known differences between it and the 1966 hood.

Sometime during 1969, a consolidated part number was assigned to a hood for use on all 1965-67 GTOs. This

hood (part number 9789954) had no holes in the outer skin, but had provisions for the 1966-67 hood emblem studs in the inner frame structure; thus, it was a correct replacement for all three years.

The hood hinge and spring were the same for 1964-67. The hinge was part number 391107 (LH) and 391106 (RH). The spring was the same for both sides (part number 3848272). Replacement hinges and springs were plated in black cadmium, while original springs and hinges were natural metal in appearance.

The black-rubber front fender upper control arm opening cover, or filler (replacement part number 9785863), was the same for 1964-67. It did, however, differ from the original style used in production, as it was rectangular in shape and didn't fold down over the control arm. Four rubber bumpers, two per side, were used on the fenders to cushion the hood-to-fender contact. For 1964, 1965 and 1967, part number 9773912 was used. The 1966 application was part number 9785480.

According to the Pontiac News Flash number 64-21, dated 10-25-63, the routing of the 1964 front wire harness behind the fender cross-brace (in front of the radiator top tank) could result in the wires being pinched between the radiator and the fender cross-brace. These wires should be routed on the underside of the cross-brace. To do this, remove the radiator top bracket, then remove the center wire clip from the back of the cross-brace and reinstall it in the same hole from the opposite side.

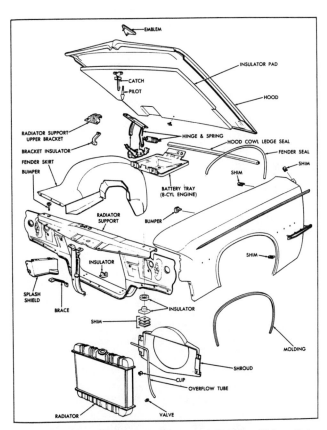

Exploded view of 1964 front sheet metal. Fender skirt, radiator support, metal fan shroud and splash shields were all painted 60° gloss black. The underside of the hood was not painted, but left in factory-black primer. Overspray at front of underhood was correct. Shims were plated in silver cadmium, and radiator was painted 60° gloss black. A coolant tag was affixed to the radiator neck in 1964.

Sheet Metal

1964 body styles	2227 Sports Coupe
	2237 Hardtop Sports Coupe
	2267 Convertible
1965 body styles	23727 Sports Coupe
	23737 Hardtop Coupe
	23767 Convertible

Roof Panel
All 27 and 37   4333802

Rear Compartment Lid Assembly

1964	1965
4892674	4468421

Rear End Panel

1964	1965
4477611	4487775

Rear Pan Assembly

1964	1965
4407330	7624713

Front Door Outer Panel Assembly

27 styles	RH	LH
Both years	4461228	4461229

37 & 67 styles	RH	LH
Both years	4461232	4461233

Outer Quarter Panels

Year	Style	RH	LH
1964	27	4511961	4511962
		4452569	4452568
	37	4489368	4489369
	67	4452570	4452571
1965	27	4511961	4511962
	37	4489368	4489369
	67	4489370	4489371

Sheet Metal
1966 and 1967 body style numbers

24207	Sport Coupe
24217	Hardtop Coupe
24267	Convertible

Roof Panel

1966-67	07	4534268
	17	4534268

Rear Compartment Lid Assembly

1966	4523788
1967	7699422

Rear End Panel

1966	7584633
1967	7651686

Rear Pan Assembly

1966	4545408
1967	7651684

Front Door Outer Panel Assembly

Year	Style	RH	LH
1966-67	24207	7580480	7682142
	24217	7580482	7682143
	24267	7580482	7682143

Outer Quarter Panels

Year	Style	RH	LH
1966	24207	4543266	4543267
	24217	4543268	4543269
	24267	4543272	4543273
1967	24207	7598574	7598575
	24217	7598580	7598581
	24267	7598586	7598587

1968-70

The 1968, 1969 and 1970 body style numbers were 24237 (hardtop coupe) and 24267 (convertible).

Roof Panel   7790418

Rear Compartment Lid Assembly

1968	7775812
1969	7774807
1970	8761217 (superseded by 9613616)

Rear Pan Assembly

1968	7762545
1969	8789245
1970	9814135

Front Door Outer Panel Assembly

	RH	LH
1968	7742326	7742327
1969	8716932	8716933
1970	8809740	8809741

Outer Quarter Panels

Year	Style	RH	LH
1968	24237	8745796	8745797
	24267	7721648	7721649

During the 1969 production year, the rear of the rear wheel opening quarter-panel moldings were discontinued. Consequently, quarter panels were offered with or without piercing for trim attachment.

1969	24237	8769022*	8784755*
	24237	9813864	9813865
	24267	8769024*	8769025*
	24267	9813866	9813867
1970	24237	9817322	9817323
	24267	9817374	9817375

*With piercings

Front Sheet Metal and Engine Compartment Fenders

1968-69	9794027	9794028
1970	9799852	9799853

Inner Fender Skirts

1968-69	9794119	9794120
1970	9799055	9799056

Detail of T-3 sealed beam unit (part number 5956001). High-beam unit was part number 5956002. T-3 sealed beam shown was first design without ribs in triangle.

A body-to-hood seal (part number 9791342) was used for 1968-70. An underhood pad (part number 9791485) was used, and was retained by eight black plastic clips (part number 9784547). On 1969 and 1970 GTOs with hood-mounted tachometer, a pad-to-tach retainer (part number 546499) was used.

The standard GTO hood (part number 9790349) was used for 1968-70. The 1969 and 1970 Ram Air hood used part number 9797791, which was modified underneath for the baffle assembly and the inlet door assembly.

The hood hinges (part number 9794024 RH and 9794025 LH) were black cadmium. Hinge springs (part number 3926800) were either silver cadmium or natural metal in appearance.

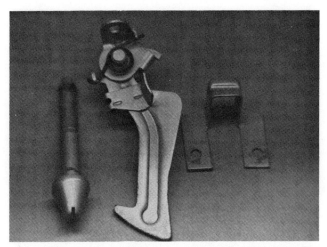

Detail of front hood latch assembly: pilot (part number 536129), left; safety catch assembly (part number 9776327) center; hood safety catch stop, used in 1965 only (part number 9777358), right.

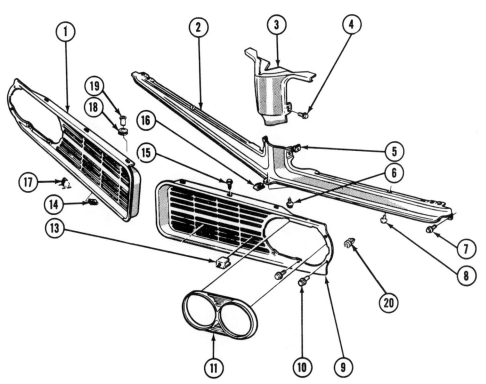

Key	Part Name	Part No.	Group No.
1 — GRILLE, Radiator - R.H.		9774149 (20-21 Series)	1.266
		9775271 (22 Series)	
2 — PANEL, Radiator Grille - Lower		9773980	1.266
3 — PANEL ASM., Radiator Grille - Center		9773947	1.266
4 — BOLT, Center Panel to Lower Panel (1/4"-20 x 1/2")		180016	8.900
5 — NUT ASM., Center Panel to Lower Panel (1/4"-20)		—	N.S.
6 — SCREW, Lower Panel to Support (5/16"-18 x 5/8")		—	N.S.
7 — SCREW, Lower Panel to Fender (5/16"-18 x 5/8")		—	N.S.
8 — SCREW, Grille to Lower Panel (#14-10 x 1/2")		—	N.S.
9 — GRILLE, Radiator - L.H.		9774150 (20-21 Series)	1.266
		9775272 (22 Series)	
10 — SCREW, Grille to Fender (#8-15 x 3/4")		—	N.S.
11 — BEZEL, Headlamp Door		9773990	2.728
13 — SPACER, Grille Name Plate		—	N.S.
14 — NUT, Grille to Lower Panel (#14-10 "J" Shape)		454421	8.921
15 — SCREW, Cross Brace to Grille (#14-10 x 1/2")		9416677	8.977
16 — NUT ASM., Lower Panel to Support		—	N.S.
17 — CUSHION, Rad. Grille to Lower Panel-Rubber		—	N.S.
18 — GROMMET, Rad. Grille to Front Fender Cross Brace		9776267	9.775
19 — SLEEVE, Rad. Grille Front Fender Cross Brace		9776268	1.268
20 — NUT, Grille to Fender Headlamp Opening Reinforcement		9774436	1.269

Exploded view of 1964 grille and front panel. GTO nameplate was placed in LH grille.

1964-67 hood hinge assembly. Hinge was natural metal in appearance. Note underhood pad and black retaining clip.

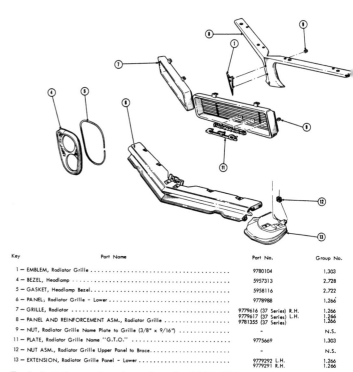

Key	Part Name	Part No.	Group No.
1 — EMBLEM, Radiator Grille		9780104	1.303
4 — BEZEL, Headlamp		5957313	2.728
5 — GASKET, Headlamp Bezel		5958116	2.722
6 — PANEL, Radiator Grille - Lower		9778988	1.266
7 — GRILLE, Radiator		9779616 (37 Series) R.H.	1.266
		9779617 (37 Series) L.H.	1.266
8 — PANEL AND REINFORCEMENT ASM., Radiator Grille		9781355 (37 Series)	1.266
9 — NUT, Radiator Grille Name Plate to Grille (3/8" x 9/16")		-	N.S.
11 — PLATE, Radiator Grille Name "G.T.O."		9775669	1.303
12 — NUT ASM., Radiator Grille Upper Panel to Brace		-	N.S.
13 — EXTENSION, Radiator Grille Panel - Lower		9779292 L.H.	1.266
		9779291 R.H.	1.266

Exploded view and part numbers for 1965 GTO grilles and front panel assembly.

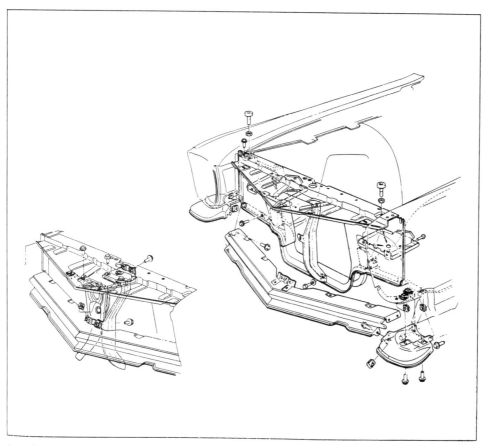

Installation of cross-brace and baffle assembly. Lower grille panel and fender extensions were painted to match the exterior trim. Hood bumpers were the same for 1964-65 (part number 533596); bumpers were changed for 1966 (part number 9785479).

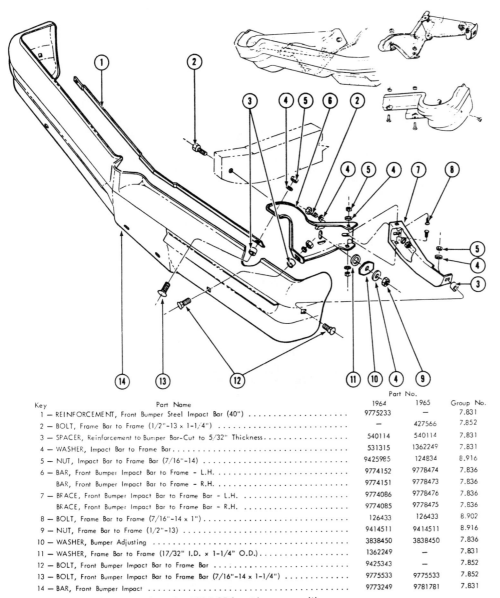

Key	Part Name	Part No.		Group No.
		1964	1965	
1 — REINFORCEMENT, Front Bumper Steel Impact Bar (40")		9775233	—	7.831
2 — BOLT, Frame Bar to Frame (1/2"-13 x 1-1/4")		—	427566	7.852
3 — SPACER, Reinforcement to Bumper Bar-Cut to 5/32" Thickness		540114	540114	7.831
4 — WASHER, Impact Bar to Frame Bar		531315	1362249	7.831
5 — NUT, Impact Bar to Frame Bar (7/16"-14)		9425985	124834	8.916
6 — BAR, Front Bumper Impact Bar to Frame - L.H.		9774152	9778474	7.836
BAR, Front Bumper Impact Bar to Frame - R.H.		9774151	9778473	7.836
7 — BRACE, Front Bumper Impact Bar to Frame Bar - L.H.		9774086	9778476	7.836
BRACE, Front Bumper Impact Bar to Frame Bar - R.H.		9774085	9778475	7.836
8 — BOLT, Frame Bar to Frame (7/16"-14 x 1")		126433	126433	8.902
9 — NUT, Frame Bar to Frame (1/2"-13)		9414511	9414511	8.916
10 — WASHER, Bumper Adjusting		3838450	3838450	7.836
11 — WASHER, Frame Bar to Frame (17/32" I.D. x 1-1/4" O.D.)		1362249	—	7.831
12 — BOLT, Front Bumper Impact Bar to Frame Bar		9425343	—	7.852
13 — BOLT, Front Bumper Impact Bar to Frame Bar (7/16"-14 x 1-1/4")		9775533	9775533	7.852
14 — BAR, Front Bumper Impact		9773249	9781781	7.831

Exploded view and part numbers for 1964-65 front bumper, with 1965-design brackets shown in upper RH corner.

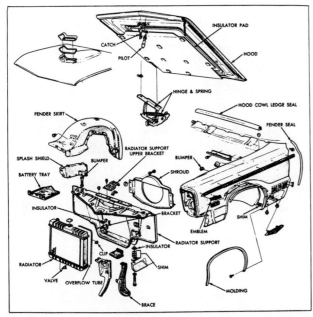

Exploded view of 1965 front sheet metal. Detailing of compartment was the same as 1964. Emblem on front of fender was not used on GTO, nor were molding and louvers on side of fender.

Close-up of parking lamp bezel and lamp lens for 1966 and 1967 GTOs. Bezel was made of diecast metal and was chrome (part number 5956521). The lens (part number 5956205) had a built-in shield. The correct bulb was amber, 1157A.

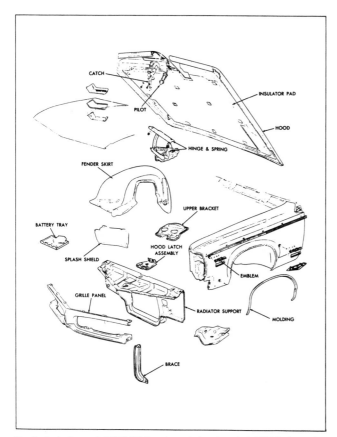

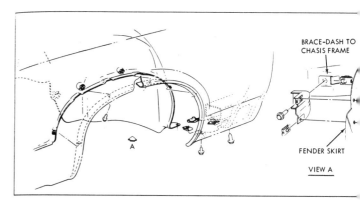

Detail of front fender inner skirt retention, 1966-67. Note use of dash-to-chassis-frame brace.

Exploded view of 1966-67 front end sheet metal (1966 shown). Fender molding and engine emblems were used on Tempest and LeMans only. GTO used 6.5 liter emblem behind front wheel opening.

Detail of 1966 242176B105833 engine compartment. Note positioning of upper control arm opening cover on LH fender skirt and routing of brake lines from master cylinder to the block and across front frame cross-member.

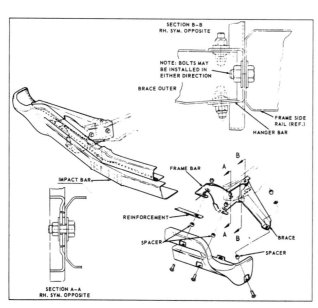

Detail of 1966-67 front bumper mounting components. Note instructions for mounting brackets to the frame rail; bolts could have been installed in either direction. This mounting procedure was used from 1964 to 1967.

Another view of 242176B105833. Notice location of horns (part number 9000500 LH low-note, and 9000513 RH high-note). The horns and bracket were painted 60° gloss black. Note heavy-duty radiator lower brackets and insulators.

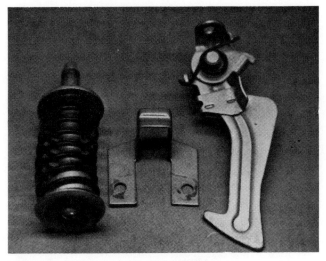

Hood latch components for 1966 and 1967.

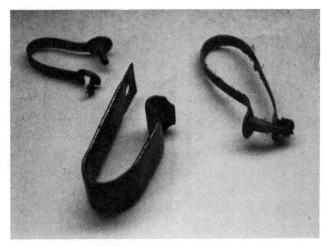

Clips used for harness retention in engine compartment. Firewall harness clip (center) was either rubber coated or plain metal; all original clips were black.

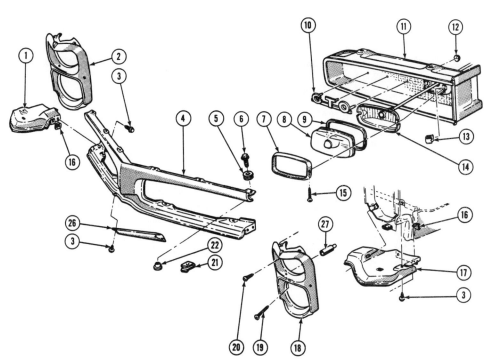

Key	Part Name	Part No.	Group No.
1 — PANEL, Rad. Grille Lower Extension – R.H.		9782624	1.266
2 — BEZEL, Head Lamp – R.H.		9782752	2.728
3 — SCREW, Panel to Extension (5/16"-12 x 5/8")		9422232	8.977
4 — PANEL, Radiator Grille		9782741	1.266
5 — GROMMET, Grille to Lower Panel.		9776267	9.775
6 — SCREW, Grille to Grille Panel (5/16"-18 x 7/8")		9411835	8.977
7 — BEZEL, Parking Lamp (42 Series)		5956521	2.593
8 — LENS & SHIELD, Parking Lamp (42 Series)		5956205	2.589
9 — GASKET, Parking Lamp Lens (42 Series)		5956522	2.590
10 — NAMEPLATE, Rad. Grille – "G.T.O."		9775669	1.303
11 — GRILLF ASM., Radiator – L.H. (42 Series)		9783921	1.266
GRILLE ASM., Radiator – R.H. (42 Series)		9783920	1.266
13 — NUT, Lamp Bezel to Rad. Grille (#8-18-J)		9784284	2.587
14 — REFLECTOR & WIRE, Parking Lamp (42 Series)		5958195	2.596
15 — SCREW, Bezel to Rad. Grille (#8-18 x 1/2")		9414752	8.977
16 — NUT, Extension to Fender (5/16"-12-"U")		9424314	8.921
17 — PANEL, Rad. Grille Lower Extension – L.H.		9782625	1.266
18 — BEZEL, Headlamp – L.H.		9782753	2.728
19 — SCREW, Bezel to Fender (#8-18 x 2-1/8")		9415475	8.977
20 — SCREW, Bezel to Reinforcement (#8-15 x 3/4")		9414754	8.977
21 — NUT, Grille to Brace or Panel (5/16"-18)		9782648	1.269
22 — SLEEVE, Rad. Grille to Lower Panel		9776268	1.268
26 — BRACE, Rad. Grille Panel		9784627	1.268
27 — NUT, Bezel to Fender Opening Reinforcement—Lower		3863669	2.729

Exploded view and part number breakdown for the 1966 GTO front end grille assembly.

Close-up of 1967 washer jar. Jar was mounted on LH fender skirt in 1967, except with AIR California GTOs, which mounted the jar on the RH side of the core support.

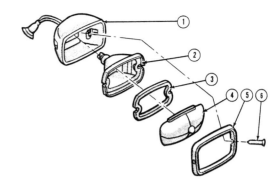

Key	Part Name	Group No.
1 — HOUSING, Parking & Signal Lamp		2.586
2 — REFLECTOR & WIRING ASM., Parking & Signal Lamp		2.596
3 — GASKET, Parking Lamp Lens		2.590
4 — LENS & SHIELD ASM., Parking & Signal Lamp		2.589
5 — BEZEL, Parking & Signal Lamp		2.593
6 — SCREW, Bezel to Housing		8.977

Exploded view of 1967 parking lamp assembly.

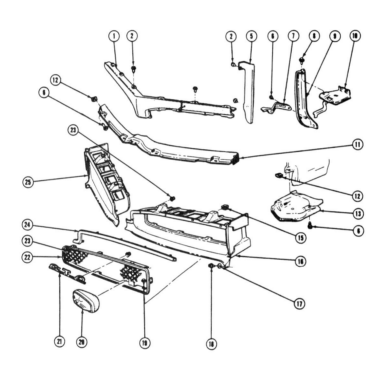

Key	Part Name	Part No	Group No.
1 — PANEL, Radiator Grille - 42		9787040	1.266
2 — SCREW, Panel to Baffle (1/4"-14 x 5/8")		—	N.S.
5 — FILLER, Radiator to R.H. Baffle		9780505	1.274
6 — SCREW, Brace to Support (1/4"-14 x 5/8")		—	N.S.
7 — BRACE, Sheet Metal Lower Reinforcement		9786986	1.268
8 — SCREW, Sheet Metal to Support (5/16"-18 x 3/4")		3960314	1.276
9 — SUPPORT, Sheet Metal Brace		9782327	8.155
10 — LATCH ASM., Hood		9786964	8.083
11 — REINFORCEMENT, Sheet Metal - Lower		9787077	1.266
12 — NUT, Extension to Fender (5/16"-12 "U")		9424314	8.921
13 — EXTENSION, Sheet Metal Lower Reinforcement - R.H.		9786931	1.266
EXTENSION, Sheet Metal Lower Reinforcement - L.H.		9786932	1.266
15 — NUT, Grille to Brace or Panel (5/16"-18)		9782648	1.269
16 — BEZEL, Radiator Grille - 42 - L.H.		9787208	1.266
17 — WASHER, Bezel to Extension (.339 x 1-1/8" x 1/16")		—	N.S.
18 — SCREW, Bezel to Extension (5/16"-12 x 7/8")		—	N.S.
19 — SCREW, Grille to Bezel (#8-18 x 9/16")		—	N.S.
20 — LAMP ASM., Parking-42 (Serviced in Components)		—	2.585
21 — PLATE, Radiator Grille Name - "G.T.O."		9787967	1.303
22 — GRILLE ASM., Radiator - 42		9787759	1.266
23 — NUT, Plate & Molding to Grille (3/16")		9420621	8.921
24 — MOLDING, Radiator Grille Panel - L.H.		9787101	1.268
MOLDING, Radiator Grille Panel - R.H.		9787100	1.268
25 — BEZEL, Radiator Grille - 42 - R.H.		9787207	1.266

1967 GTO grille assembly and related components, with part numbers.

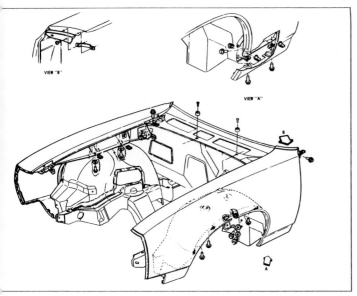

Installation of 1968 GTO front end sheet metal (typical of 1969 also).

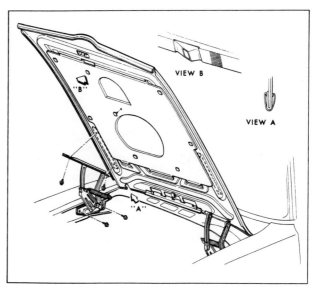

Installation of 1968-70 GTO hood, with alignment instructions for underhood insulator pad. Underside of hood to be painted 30° gloss black.

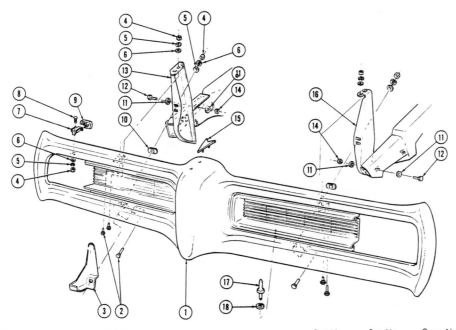

Key	Part Name	Part No. 1968	Part No. 1969	Group No.
1 —	BAR ASM., Front Bumper Impact (Unpainted)*	9794971	9794971	7.831
2 —	BOLT, Impact Bar to Frame Bar (7/16"-14 x 1 1/4")	9427908	9427908	8.902
3 —	BRACKET, Frt. Bumper Support	9793307R.H.	9793307R.H.	7.831
	BRACKET, Frt. Bumper Support	9793308L.H.	9793308L.H.	7.831
4 —	NUT, Reinforcement to Frame Bar (7/16"-14)	9422299	9422299	8.917
5 —	LOCKWASHER, Reinforcement to Frame Bar (7/16")	120383	120383	8.931
6 —	WASHER, Impact Bar to Frame Bar (7/16")	531315	531315	7.831
7 —	BRACKET, Front Bumper Stabilizer	9791658	9791658	7.831
8 —	BOLT, Bracket to Reinforcement (7/16"-14 x 1")	9425343	9425343	8.902
9 —	STABILIZER, Front Bumper	9791639	9791639	7.831
10 —	NUT, Reinforcement to Frame Bar (7/16")	—	528579	N.S.
11 —	WASHER, Frame Bar to Frame	1362249	1362249	7.831
12 —	BOLT, Frame Bar to Frame (1/2"-13 x 1-3/8")	427566	427566	8.900
13 —	BAR, Bumper Bar to Frame – exc. Tilt Door	9790316R.H.	9790316R.H.	7.836
	BAR, Bumper Bar to Frame – with Tilt Door	9794209R.H.	9794209R.H.	7.836
14 —	NUT, Frame Bar to Frame (1/2"-13)	9422301	9422301	8.917
15 —	EMBLEM, Front Bumper	9790459		7.831
16 —	BAR, Bumper to Frame – exc. Tilt Door	9790317L.H.	9790317L.H.	7.836
	BAR, Bumper Bar to Frame – with Tilt Door	9794210L.H.	9794210L.H.	7.836
17 —	STABILIZER, Frt. Valance Panel		9798082	7.833
18 —	NUT, Valance Panel Stabilizer (1/4")		9428794	7.833

*PAINT TO MATCH

Exploded view of 1968-69 GTO Endura front bumper with parts nomenclature.

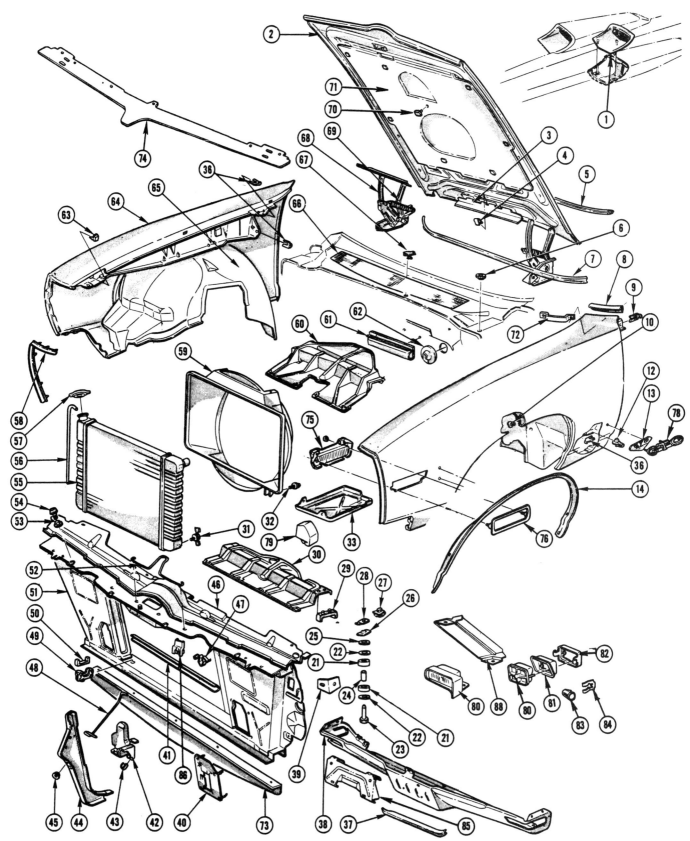

Exploded view of 1968 and 1969 front end sheet metal and parts nomenclature. Note engine wire harness retainer (number 61), part number 9791666, used in 1968.

Key	Part Name	Group No.
1 — ORNAMENT, Hood Top Vent – L.H.	8.030
2 — PANEL ASM., Hood	8.000
3 — FILLER, Hood to Shroud (27 5/8" Long)	8.021
4 — CLIP, Hood Shroud Filler to Hood	8.021
5 — MOLDING, Hood Panel – Rear	8.054
6 — PLUG, Front Fender Skirt & Cowl	8.153
7 — SEAL, Body to Hood	12.801
8 — MOLDING PKG., Front Fender – Upper Rear	8.147
9 — SHIM, Front Fender	8.143
10 — NUT, Skirt to Fender	N.S.
12 — NUT ASM., Fender to Lower Shroud (3/8"-16 "U")	8.143
13 — EMBLEM, Front Fender – "G.T.O."	8.147
14 — MOLDING PKG., Front Fender Wheel Opening	8.147
21 — INSULATOR, Rad. Support to Frame (2 7/32" O.D. x 9/16" Thick)	1.270
22 — SHIM, Radiator Support Bracket to Frame (.120 Thick)	.270
23 — BOLT, Radiator Support to Frame (7/16"-14 x 3 1/2")	8.900
24 — SLEEVE, Radiator Support to Frame	1.270
25 — SHIM, Radiator Support Bracket to Frame – (.120 Thick)	1.270
26 — NUT, Radiator Support Insulator	N.S.
27 — NUT, Radiator Support to Frame Insulator (7/16"-14 "U")	1.270
28 — PLATE, Radiator Support Insert	1.270
29 — INSULATOR, Radiator Mounting Upper	1.270
30 — PANEL, Radiator Upper Mounting & Fan Guard	1.277
31 — DRAIN COCK, Radiator	1.229
32 — CLIP, Shroud to Baffle	N.S.
33 — TRAY, Battery	2.333
36 — SHIM, Front Fender	8.143
37 — MOLDING PKG., Front Bumper Valance Panel – L.H. (42)	7.833
38 — PANEL, Front Bumper Valance	7.833
39 — BRACKET, Radiator Support to Fender	1.274
40 — SEAL & CLIP ASM., Radiator Baffle to Frame Bar	1.274
41 — SEAL, Radiator Support to Radiator	1.274
42 — LATCH ASM., Hood	8.083
43 — CLIP, Hood Latch Release Lever	8.083
44 — SUPPORT, Front End Sheet Metal Vertical	8.155
45 — GROMMET, Hood Latch Release Lever	8.083
46 — FILLER, Front End Sheet Metal Brace to Bumper	8.155

Key	Part Name	Group No.
47 — CLIP, Seal to Baffle	N.S.
48 — LEVER, Hood Latch Release	8.083
49 — BRACKET, Radiator Support – Lower	1.274
50 — INSULATOR, Radiator Support Bracket – Lower	1.270
51 — SUPPORT ASM., Radiator – w/Baffle & Seals	1.270
52 — SPRING, Hood Pop-Up	8.083
53 — NUT, Bumper & Bolt to Baffle (5/16"-18)	8.916
54 — BUMPER & BOLT, Hood Adjustable	8.024
55 — RADIATOR ASSEMBLY	1.219
56 — TUBE, Radiator Overflow	1.240
57 — CAP ASM., Radiator	1.203
58 — FILLER, Front Fender to Bumper	8.153
59 — SHROUD, Radiator Fan	1.277
60 — PANEL, Radiator Upper Mounting & Fc Guard	1.277
61 — RETAINER, Engine Wire Harness	2.482
62 — GROMMET, Accessory Wire Thru Dash	9.775
63 — BUMPER, Hood to Fender Side	8.024
64 — FENDER ASM., Front	8.130
65 — SKIRT, Front Fender	8.153
66 — SCREEN, Shroud Vent	12.800
67 — CLIP, Screen to Shroud Panel	N.S.
68 — HINGE ASM., Hood	8.015
69 — SPRING, Hood Hinge	8.013
70 — CLIP, Hood Insulator Pad Retainer	8.021
71 — PAD, Hood Insulator	8.021
72 — NUT, Speed – Frt. Fender Upper Rear Mldg.	8.148
73 — BAFFLE, Valance Panel to Front End Sheet Metal (42)	7.833
74 — FILLER, Front End Sheet Metal Brace to Bumper	8.155
75 — HOUSING, Cornering	2.586
76 — BEZEL, Corner Lamp	2.593
78 — NAME PLATE, Front Fender (G.T.O.)	8.147
79 — SPACER, Front Fender to Radiator Support	8.155
80 — LAMP, Parking	2.585
81 — FILLER, Parking Lamp	2.587
82 — BRACKET, Lamp Mounting	2.587
83 — LAMP ASM., Side Marker – Front	2.575
84 — RETAINER, Side Marker Lamp	2.575
85 — BRACKET, License Plate Mounting	7.800
86 — RETAINER, Radiator Insulator Mounting	1.270
88 — SUPPORT, Valance Panel to Bumper Bar – L.H.	7.833

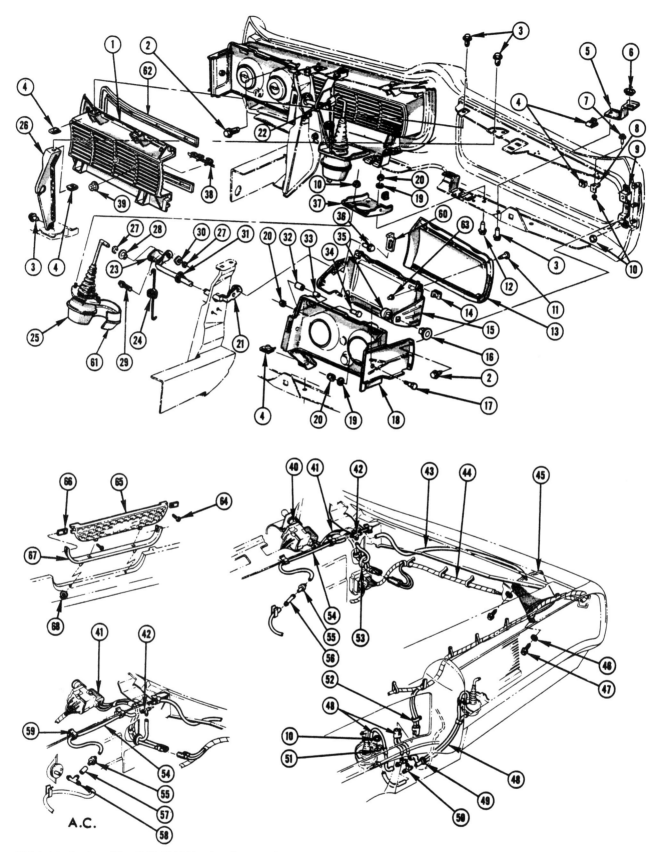

This intricate view of the 1968-69 hidden headlamp option details
the hardware used and parts nomenclature.

A.C.

Key	Part Name	Part No. 1968	Part No. 1969	Group No.
1	GRILLE ASM., Radiator (w/Silver Bars)	9791147R.H. - 9791148L.H.	9795733R.H. - 9795734L.H.	1.266
	GRILLE ASM., Radiator (w/Black Bars)	-	9794650R.H. - 9794651L.H.	1.266
2	SCREW, Headlamp Body to Bracket (1/4"-14 x 5/8")	-	-	N.S.
3	SCREW, Grille to Reinforcement (1/4"-14 x 3/4")	-	-	N.S.
4	NUT, Grille to Reinforcement (1/4"-14 "U")	9422619	9422619	8.921
5	BRACKET, Radiator Grille Mounting	9791777R.H. - 9791778L.H.	9791777R.H. - 9791778L.H.	1.266
6	GROMMET, Grille Mounting Bracket	9791341	9791341	1.268
7	SCREW, Lamp Mounting Bracket to Reinforcement (1/4"-20 x 5/8")			N.S.
8	BRACKET, Headlamp Mounting	9792249R.H. - 9792250L.H.	9792249R.H. - 9792250L.H.	2.726
9	STOOL, Tilt Drive Torsion Rod	9791691	9791691	2.765
10	NUT, Bracket to Reinforcement (1/4"-20")	120375	120375	8.915
11	SCREW, Door to Reinforcement (#8-18 x 5/8")	9428582	9428582	8.977
12	BOLT, Bracket to Reinforcement (1/4"-20 x 5/8")	180018	180018	8.900
13	DOOR ASM., Headlamp Tilt (w/Silver Bars)	9791178R.H. - 9791179L.H.	9795835R.H. - 9795836L.H.	2.728
	DOOR ASM., Headlamp Tilt (w/Black Bars)	-	9794644R.H. - 9794645L.H.	2.728
14	NUT, Door to Reinforcement (#8-18 "U")	9417488	9417488	8.921
15	REINFORCEMENT, Headlamp Tilt Door...........	9791704R.H. - 9791705L.H.	9791704R.H. - 9791705L.H.	2.726
16	BUSHING, Tilt Door Pivot	9791496	9791496	2.765
17	BOLT, Headlamp Door Pivot (1/4"-20 x 1 1/8")	9791498	9791498	2.765
18	BODY ASM., Headlamp	9797258R.H. - 9797259L.H.	9797258R.H. - 9797259L.H.	2.726
19	WASHER, Door to Rein. (9/32" I.D. x 1/2" O.D.)	-	-	N.S.
20	NUT, Door to Reinforcement (1/4"-20)	120375	120375	8.915
21	ROD ASM., Tilt Drive Torsion.	9791700R.H. - 9791701L.H.	9791700R.H. - 9791701L.H.	2.765
22	BRACKET, Torsion Rod Over - Center Spring - L.H.	9791739	9791739	2.765
23	BRACKET, Torsion Rod Over - Center Spring - R.H.	9791738	9791738	2.765
24	SPRING, Tilt Door Over - Center	9791946	9791946	2.765
25	ACTUATOR ASM., Tilt Door	5638258	5638258	2.760
26	SUPPORT, Tilt Drive Torsion Rod	9791696R.H. - 9791697L.H.	9791696R.H. - 9791697L.H.	2.765
27	RETAINER, Actuator to Torsion Rod (5/16" Ring)	274560	274560	8.934
28	BUSHING, Adjusting Bracket to Actuator	9791494	9791494	2.765
29	SCREW, Over-Center Spring Brkt. to Rod (1/4"-20 x 5/8") ..	-	-	N.S.
30	WASHER, Tilt Door Actuator.	9791169	9791169	2.765
31	BUSHING, Torsion Rod to Bracket	9787022	9787022	2.765
32	STOP, Tilt Door.	9791495	9791495	2.775
33	SPACER, Tilt Door	9791499	9791499	2.765
34	SCREW, Door to Bracket (1/4"-20 x 1 1/8").	-	-	N.S.
35	WASHER, Tilt Door Pivot	9791497	9791497	2.765
36	SCREW, Torsion Rod to Reinforcement (1/4"-20 x 5/8")	-	-	N.S.
37	BRACKET, T.H. Door Actuator Mounting	9791698R.H. - 9791699L.H.	9791698R.H. - 9791699L.H.	2.760
38	PLATE, Radiator Grille Name "GTO"	9791562	9791562	1.303
39	NUT, Name Plate to Grille (3/16").	9420621	9420621	8.921
40	SWITCH ASM., Headlamp	1995169	1995156	2.485
41	HOSE ASM., Switch to Front End Harness	6290614	6290614	2.765
42	TEE, Headlamp Vacuum Feed	391779	391779	12.243
43	HOSE, Switch Feed Line to Reserve Tank (5/32" x 36")	3987363	3987363	8.962
44	HARNESS, Front End	6295402	6297478	2.480
45	TANK & BRACKET ASM., Headlamp Vacuum Reserve	9785022	9785022	9.281
46	WASHER, Reserve Tank to Skirt (9/32" I.D. x 1" O.D.).	-	-	N.S.
47	SCREW, Reserve Tank to Skirt (1/4"-14 x 3/4")	-	-	N.S.
48	HOSE ASM., Actuator to Frt. End Harness	6295551	6295551	2.765
49	GROMMET, Actuator to Frt. End Harness Hose	9789775	9789775	9.775
50	TEE, L.H. Hose to R.H. Hose (3/16" x 3/16" x 3/16").	540581	540581	3.440
51	RETAINER, Actuator to Frt. End Vacuum Hose	9792143R.H. - 9792144L.H.	9792143R.H. - 9792144L.H.	2.765
52	CLIP, Harness to Cross Brace	3816659	3816659	2.559
53	GROMMET, Headlamp Vacuum Line (On Fire Wall).	9788842	9788842	2.765
54	HOSE, Vacuum Source to Feed Line (5/32" x 36").	3987363	3987363	8.962
55	VALVE ASM., Tilt Door Vacuum Check	9782793	9782793	9.281
56	REDUCER, Vacuum Feed to Check Valve Hose	9783465	9783465	3.765
57	HOSE, Feed Line to Check Valve (7/32" x 3 1/2")	3987364	3987364	8.962
58	TEE, Vacuum Hose to Vacuum Valve	534145	534145	10.155
59	CLIP, Vacuum Hose to Dash	9793032	9793032	2.765
60	STOP, Headlamp Tilting Door.	9793735	9793735	2.775
61	COVER, Headlamp Door Actuator	9793558	9793558	2.760
62	MOLDING, Radiator Grille.	9791244R.H. - 9791245L.H.	9791244R.H. - 9791245L.H.	1.268
63	COVER, Headlamp Door to Door Reinf. Screw.	9798964	9798964	2.729
64	SCREW, Grille to Valance Panel Molding	-	9417479	8.977
65	GRILLE, Front Bumper Valance Panel	-	9798092R.H. - 9798093L.H.	7.833
66	CLIP, Grille to Valance Panel Molding	-	9798064	7.833
67	MOLDING PKG., Front Bumper Valance Panel	-	9794804R.H. - 9794805L.H.	7.833
68	NUT, Grille to Valance Panel.	-	9420621	8.921

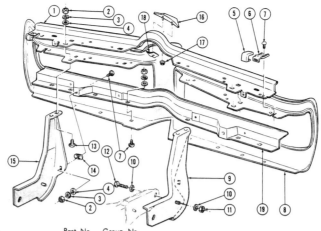

Key	Part Name	Part No. 1968	Group No.
1 — REINFORCEMENT, Front Bumper Bar - Upper		9790872	7.831
2 — NUT, Reinforcement to Frame Bar (7/16"-14)		9422299	8.917
3 — LOCKWASHER, Reinforcement to Frame Bar (7/16")		120383	8.931
4 — WASHER, Impact Bar to Frame Bar		531315	7.831
5 — STABILIZER, Front Bumper		9791639	7.831
6 — BRACKET, Front Bumper Stabilizer		9791658	7.831
7 — BOLT, Bracket to Reinforcement (7/16"-14 x 1")		9425343	8.902
8 — BAR, Front Bumper Impact		9790045	7.831
9 — BAR, Front Bumper to Frame - R.H.		9790316	7.836

Key	Part Name	Part No.	Group No.
10 — WASHER, Frame Bar to Frame		1362249	7.831
11 — NUT, Frame Bar to Frame (1/2"-13)		9422301	8.917
12 — BOLT, Frame Bar to Frame (1/2"-13 x 1-3/8")		427566	8.900
13 — BOLT, Impact Bar to Frame Bar (7/16"-14 x 1-1/4")		9427908	8.902
15 — BAR, Front Bumper to Frame - L.H.		9790317	7.836
16 — EMBLEM, Front Bumper		9791833	7.831
17 — NUT, Emblem to Bumper (3/16")		9420621	8.921
18 — RETAINER, Emblem to Bumper		9785896	7.831
19 — REINFORCEMENT, Front Bumper Bar - Lower		9790873	7.831

In 1968, the Endura bumper could be replaced with a chrome bumper, as shown.

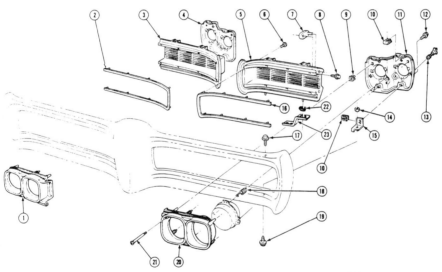

Key	Part Name	1968 Part No.	1969 Part No.	Group No.
1 — BEZEL, Headlamp - R.H.		9792306	9796397	2.728
2 — MOLDING, Radiator Grille - R.H.		9791244	9791244	1.268
3 — GRILLE ASM., Radiator - R.H. (w/Silver Bars)		9791147	9795733	1.266
GRILLE ASM., Radiator - L.H. (w/Black Bars)		-	9794651	1.266
4 — BODY ASM., Headlamp - R.H.		9792480	9796615	2.726
5 — GRILLE ASM., Radiator - L.H. (w/Silver Bars)		9791148	9795734	1.266
GRILLE ASM., Radiator - R.H. (w/Black Bars)		-	9794650	1.266
6 — SCREW, Molding to Grille		9707708	9707708	1.269
7 — PIN, Rad. Grille Locator		9792519	9792519	1.269
8 — SCREW, Locator Pin to Grille (#10-24 x 1/2")		455380	455380	8.977
9 — NUT, Bezel to Body - Nylon		380382	380382	10.275
10 — NUT, Body to Reinforcement (1/4"-14-"U")		9422619	9422619	8.921
11 — BODY ASM., Headlamp - L.H.		9792481	9796616	2.726
12 — SCREW, Body to Bracket (1/4"-14 x 5/8")				N.S.
13 — NUT & SCREW ASM., Mounting Ring to Housing		5953005	1235816	2.737
14 — NUT, Bracket to Bumper (1/4"-20)		193232	193232	8.916
15 — BRACKET, Headlamp Mounting		9792249RH - 9792250LH	9792249RH - 9792250LH	2.726
16 — MOLDING, Radiator Grille - L.H.		9791245	9791245	1.268
17 — SCREW, Reinforcement to Body (1/4"-14 x 3/4")		9425451	9425451	8.977
18 — SPRING, Headlamp Adjuster		9790354	9790354	2.737
19 — SCREW, Bracket to Reinforcement (1/4"-20 x 5/8")		-	-	N.S.
20 — BEZEL, Headlamp - L.H.		9792307	9796398	2.728
21 — SCREW, Bezel to Body (#8-18 x 2 1/4")		9792502	9792502	2.729
22 — GROMMET, Grille Mounting Bracket		9791341	9791341	1.268
23 — BRACKET, Radiator Grille Mounting		9791777RH - 9791778LH	9791777RH - 9791778LH	1.266

Exploded diagram and part numbers for the 1968-69 GTO standard front grilles.

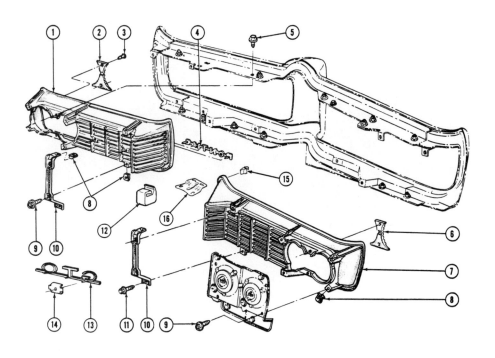

Key	Part Name	Part No. 1968	Part No. 1969	Group No.
1 — GRILLE, Radiator - L.H. (Shadow Silver - 1969)		9790382	546146*	1.266
2 — ESCUTCHEON, Radiator Grille		9790379	-	1.268
3 — SCREW, Escutcheon to Grille (#8-18 x 5/8")		9790767	-	1.269
4 — PLATE, Radiator Grille Name - "Pontiac"		9791371	9796046	1.303
5 — SCREW, Reinforcement to Bracket (1/4"-14 x 3/4")		9425451	9425451	8.977
6 — ESCUTCHEON, Radiator Grille		9790379	-	1.268
7 — GRILLE, Radiator - R.H. (Shadow Silver - 1969)		9790381	9795678	1.266
GRILLE, Radiator - R.H. (Oxford Gray)		-	546145	1.266
8 — NUT, Grille Mounting Bracket (1/4"-14 "U")		9422619	9422619	8.921
9 — SCREW, Mounting Bracket to Grille (1/4"-14 x 3/4")		9425451	9425451	8.977
10 — BRACKET, Radiator Grille Mounting		9791335	9795664	1.266
11 — SCREW, Grille to Reinforcement (1/4"-14 x 3/4")		9425451	9425451	8.977
12 — SPACER, Grille to Bumper Reinforcement		9793806	-	1.268
13 — PLATE, Radiator Grille Name - "G.T.O." (w/Chrome Bumper)		9791562	9791562	1.303
14 — BRACKET, Grille Name Plate Mounting (w/Chrome Bumper)		9791875	-	1.303
15 — BUMPER, Radiator Grille to Impact Bar			9797086	1.269
16 — BRACKET, Radiator Grille Mounting - Lower		-	9786392	1.266

*Paint to match - Oxford Gray for 1969

Exploded diagram of 1968 GTO grilles with chrome bumper option. Chrome bumper was only offered in 1968.

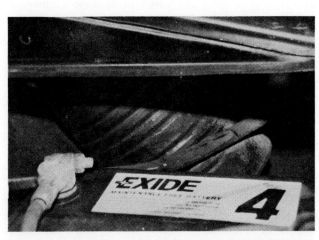

Location of vacuum canister used for 1968-69 hidden headlamp option.

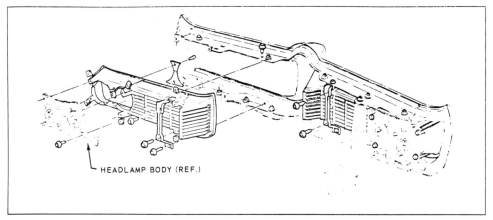

HEADLAMP BODY (REF.)

Installation guide for 1968 GTO with chrome bumper option.

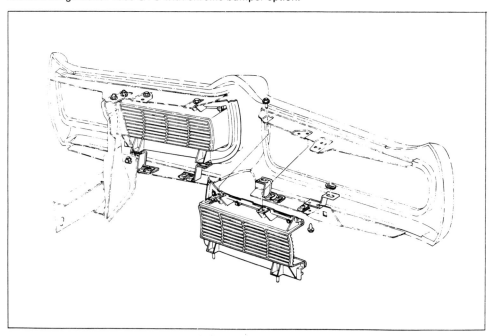

Installation instructions for alignment of 1968 grilles with Endura bumper.

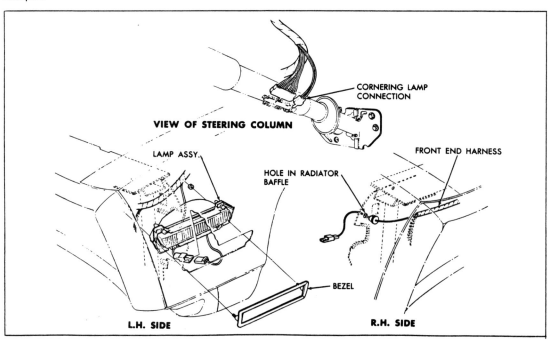

CORNERING LAMP CONNECTION

VIEW OF STEERING COLUMN

LAMP ASSY.

HOLE IN RADIATOR BAFFLE

FRONT END HARNESS

BEZEL

L.H. SIDE

R.H. SIDE

Installation instructions for 1968 cornering lamp option (RPO 651). Lamp option was also available in 1969 (RPO 651, UPC T-87). Components were interchangeable between the two years.

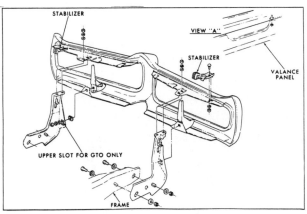

Installation instructions for the 1968-69 GTO front bumper. Note indexing of bracket to frame bolts and nuts.

Here is a list of Endura bumper materials descriptions and their part numbers.

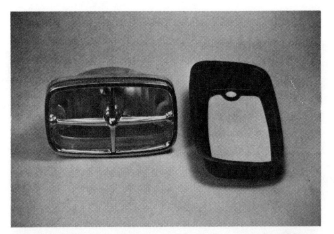

Detail of 1969 parking lamp assembly (part number 916735) and filler (part number 9796262 RH and 9796263 LH). The bezel (part number 5961607) and lens (part number 5961605) were interchangeable between 1969-70. However, the housing assemblies were not. The 1970 assembly part number was 917247.

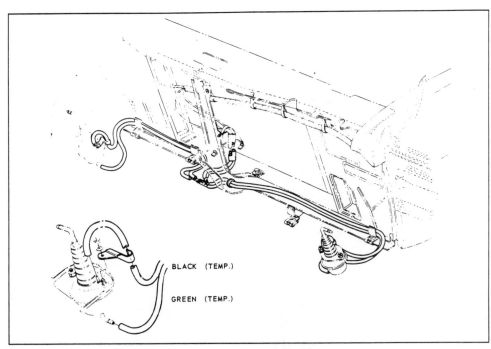

Routing directions for hideaway headlamp option for 1969 GTO.

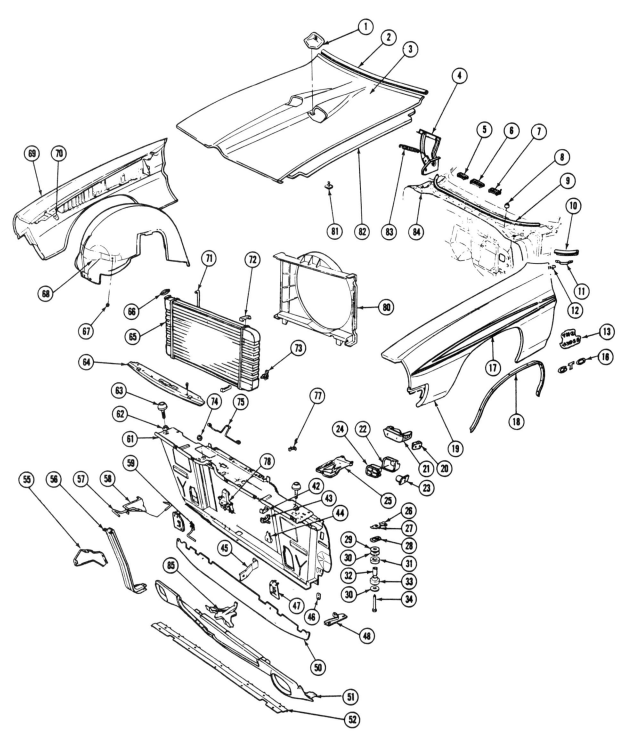

Exploded view of 1970 GTO front sheet metal and parts
nomenclature.

Key	Part Name	Group No.
1 — ORNAMENT, Hood Top Vent – L.H.		8.030
2 — MOLDING, Hood Panel – Rear		8.054
3 — PANEL, Hood		8.000
4 — HINGE ASM., Hood		8.015
5 — SCREEN, Shroud Top Vent – R.H.		12.800
6 — SCREEN, Shroud Top Vent – Center		12.800
7 — SCREEN, Shroud Top Vent – L.H.		12.800
8 — BUMPER, Hood Rear		8.024
9 — SEAL, Body to Hood		12.801
10 — MOLDING PKG., Front Fender – Upper Rear		8.147
11 — NUT, Front Fender Upper Rear Molding		8.148
12 — SHIM, Front Fender Alignment		8.143
13 — DECAL, Front Fender Name "The Judge"		8.147
16 — DECAL, Front Fender "G.T.O."		8.147
17 — MOLDING PKG., Front Fender Side		8.147
18 — MOLDING PKG., Front Fender Wheel Opening		8.147
19 — FENDER ASM., Front		8.130
20 — LAMP ASM., Side Marker		2.575
21 — LAMP ASM., Parking & Direction Signal		2.585
22 — FILLER, Parking Lamp		2.587
23 — LAMP ASM., Side Marker		2.575
24 — LAMP ASM., Parking & Direction Signal		2.585
25 — TRAY ASM., Battery		2.333
26 — NUT, Rad. Supt. to Frame Insul. (7/16"-14-"U")		1.270
27 — CLIP & NUT ASM., Radiator Supt. to Frame		1.274
28 — NUT, Radiator Supt. to Frame (7/16"-14)		N.S.
29 — SHIM, Radiator Supt. Brkt. to Frame - .060		1.270
30 — WASHER, Radiator Supt. Brkt. to Frame - .120		1.270
31 — INSULATOR, Radiator Supt. to Frame - Upper		1.270
32 — SLEEVE, Radiator Supt. to Frame		1.270
33 — INSULATOR, Radiator Supt. to Frame - Lower		1.270
34 — BOLT, Radiator Supt. to Frame (7/16"-14 x 3 1/2")		8.900
42 — INSULATOR, Radiator Mtg.		1.270
43 — BRACKET, Radiator Mtg. Lower		1.274
44 — RETAINER, Radiator Insulator Mtg.		1.270

Key	Part Name	Group No.
45 — SUPPORT, Upper Grille Panel – Outer		1.266
46 — BRACKET, Radiator Supt. Air Baffle		1.272
47 — SEAL & CLIP ASM., Radiator Baffle to Frame		1.270
48 — BRACKET, Radiator Supt. to Front Fender – R.H. (G.T.O.)		1.274
50 — BAFFLE, Radiator Supt. Air		1.272
51 — PANEL ASM., Front Bumper Valance (G.T.O.)		7.833
52 — BAFFLE, Radiator Supt. Air		1.272
55 — SUPPORT, Upper Grille Panel – Center		1.266
56 — SUPPORT, Front End Sheet Metal – Vertical		8.155
57 — LEVER, Hood Latch Release (G.T.O.)		8.083
58 — BRACKET ASM., Hood Release (G.T.O.)		8.083
59 — GROMMET, Hood Release Bracket		8.083
61 — SUPPORT ASM., Radiator – W/Baffle		1.270
62 — NUT, Bumper & Bolt to Baffle		8.916
63 — BUMPER & BOLT, Hood Adjustable		8.024
64 — FILLER, Front End Sheet Metal Brace to Bumper		8.155
65 — RADIATOR ASM.		1.219
66 — CAP ASM., Radiator		1.203
67 — PLUG, Front Fender Skirt		8.153
68 — SKIRT, Front Fender		8.153
69 — FENDER ASM., Front		8.130
70 — BUMPER, Hood to Fender Side		8.024
71 — TUBE, Radiator Overflow		1.240
72 — INSULATOR, Radiator Mounting Upper		1.270
73 — DRAIN COCK, Radiator		1.229
74 — PLUG, Front End Sheet Metal Cross Brace		N.S.
75 — SPRING, Hood Pop – Up		8.083
77 — INSULATOR, Radiator Mounting Upper		1.270
78 — LATCH ASM., Hood		8.083
80 — SHROUD, Radiator Fan		1.277
81 — CLIP, Hood Insulator Pad Retainer		8.021
82 — PAD, Hood Insulator		8.021
83 — SPRING, Hood Hinge		8.013
84 — PLUG, Front Fender Skirt & Cowl		8.153
85 — BRACKET, Valance Panel Center Mounting		7.833

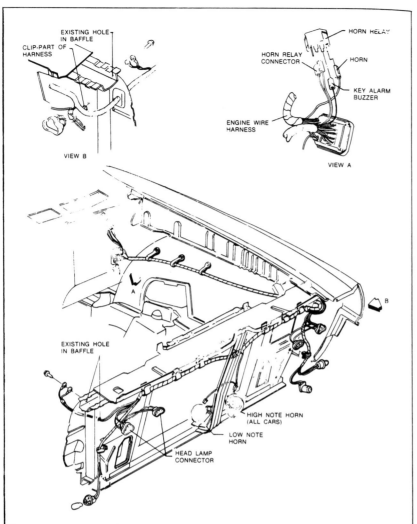

Installation and routing of 1970 front end harness. Note use of clips on fender skirt.

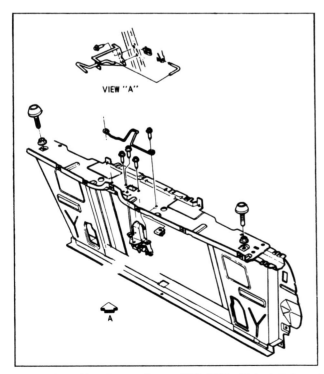

Installation of hood extension on 1970 GTO with installation of hood adjustment bumper (part number 9785479) used on all 1968-70 models. Extension was painted 60° gloss black.

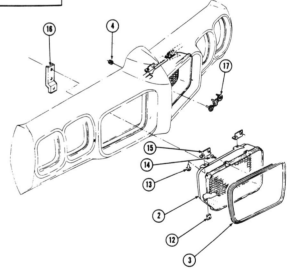

Key	Part Name	Part No. 1970	Group No.
2 —	GRILLE, Radiator (G.T.O.) R.H. (Silver)	9799789	1.266
	GRILLE, Radiator (G.T.O.) L.H. (Silver)	9799790	1.266
	GRILLE, Radiator (G.T.O.) R.H. (Black)	480680	1.266
	GRILLE, Radiator (G.T.O.) L.H. (Black)	480681	1.266
3 —	MOLDING PKG., Grille R.H.	479178	1.268
	MOLDING PKG., Grille L.H.	479179	1.268
4 —	NUT (3/16")	9420621	8.921
12 —	NUT (1/4"-14-"U")	9422619	8.921
13 —	SCREW (1/4"-14 x 3/4")	9783400	1.269
14 —	SCREW (#8-32 x 1/2")	9707708	1.269
15 —	BRACKET, Grille, Mtg. Upper - R.H.-(G.T.O.)	477712	1.266
	BRACKET, Grille Mtg. - Upper - L.H.-(G.T.O.)	477713	1.266
16 —	BRACKET, Grille Mtg. - Lower - (G.T.O.)	477689	1.266
17 —	PLATE PKG., Grille Name "GTO"	479184	1.303

Exploded drawing of 1970 grille with part numbers.

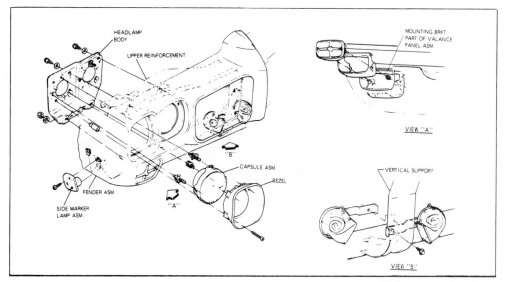

Installation of 1970 front lamps and horns. Horns and brackets were painted 60° gloss black. High-note horn was part number 9000011; low-note horn carried part number 9000239. The parking lamp assembly was part number 917247; replacement lens was available as part number 5961605, also used in 1969.

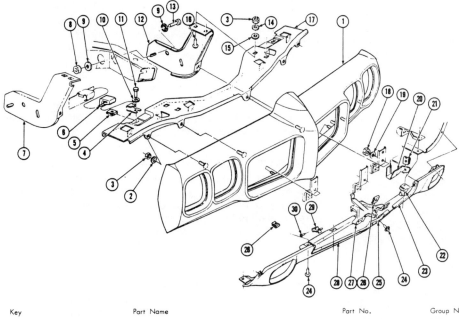

Key	Part Name	Part No.	Group No.
1 — BAR, Front Bumper Impact	....	9799427	7.831
2 — WASHER, (7/16" I.D. x 1" O.D. x 1/8")	....	531315	7.831
3 — NUT, (7/16" – 14)	....	124834	8.916
4 — BRACKET, Stabilizer to Bumper	....	477620	7.831
5 — NUT, (7/16" – 14 "U")	....	—	N.S.
6 — STABILIZER, Bumper	....	9799960	7.831
7 — BAR, Impact Bar to Frame	....	9799767R.H.	7.836
8 — NUT, (1/2" – 13)	....	9414511	8.916
9 — WASHER, Bumper Adj.	....	1362249	7.831
10 — WASHER, Bumper Adj.	....	1362249	7.831
11 — BOLT, (7/16" – 14 x 1")	....	454944	8.900
12 — BAR, Impact Bar to Frame	....	9799768L.H.	7.836
13 — BOLT, (1/2" – 13 x 1-1/2")	....	427566	8.900
14 — LOCKWASHER, (7/16")	....	120383	8.931
15 — WASHER, Bumper Adj.	....	1362249	7.831
16 — BOLT, (7/16" – 14 x 1")	....	9425343	8.900
17 — REINFORCEMENT, Impact Bar (Upper)	....	9799703	7.831
18 — NUT, (5/16" – 18)	....	124824	8.916
19 — WASHER, (5/16" I.D. x 5/8" O.D.)	....	—	N.S.
20 — STABILIZER, Valance Panel	....	480791R.H. – 480792L.H.	7.833
21 — NUT, (1/4" – 14 – "U")	....	9422619	8.921
22 — SCREW, (1/4" – 14 x 3/4")	....	9425451	8.977
23 — MOLDING PKG., Valance Panel	....	479794L.H.	7.833
24 — SCREW, (5/16"– 12 x 1")	....	9796223	1.269
25 — PANEL ASM., Bumper Valance	....	478435	7.833
26 — NUT, (5/16" – 12 "U")	....	9424314	8.921
27 — BRACKET, Valance Panel Center Mtg.	....	478498	7.833
28 — MOLDING PKG., Valance Panel	....	479793R.H.	7.833
29 — RETAINER, (Incl. in #23 & 28 Mldg. Pkgs.)	....	—	N.S.
30 — SCREW, (#10 – 16 x 1/2")	....	9419303	8.977

Detailed view of 1970 front bumper with impact bar reinforcement and valance panel with part numbers.

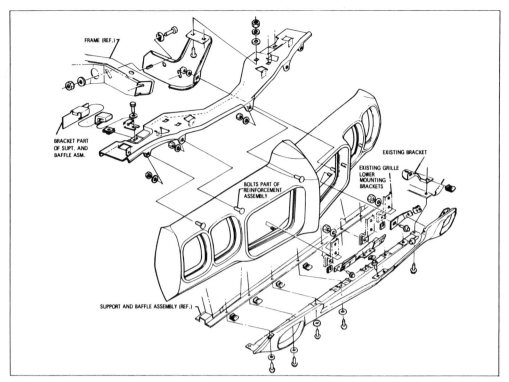

Installation and alignment instructions for the 1970 front bumper and valance panel.

FOLDING TOP

1964-65

All GTOs used a power top; no manually operated tops were ever used on the GTO. The frame assemblies were all painted gloss black. The sunshade support assembly with striker was the same for 1964 and 1965 (part number 4523878 LH and 4523877 RH). The header center molding part number was 4407522, and the corner moldings carried part number 4407349 LH and 4407348 RH.

The front roof rail lock was painted gloss black, and carried part number 4484804 LH and 4484803 RH. The hook was chrome part number 5716613.

The hydraulic pump and motor assembly (part number 7595117) was mounted on rubber grommets to the pan (mounting package part number 3698109). Two different motor shields were used in 1964: steel and cardboard. There were no replacement part numbers. The cardboard shield was used on all 1965 models. The lift assemblies (part number 4407818) were interchangeable.

The power top switch (part number 9774483 in 1964 and 9781368 in 1965) was mounted on the underside of the instrument panel, to the left of the steering column opening.

The rear quarter armrest lamp reflector (part number 4636293) and the lens (part number 4482877) were mounted in the upper front of the panel. The ashtray (part number 4725854) was mounted in a chrome escutcheon (part number 4146967). The lamp was activated by either the instrument panel headlamp knob or by opening either door.

The folding top boot bag (part number 4485356) was the same for 1964 and 1965.

Folding Top Weatherstrip

	RH	One-Piece	LH
Pillar Post	4409036		4409037
Side Roof Rail, front	4407736		4407737
Side Roof Rail, center	4477662		4477663
Side Roof Rail, rear	4477664		4477665
Center Header		4406207	

Convertible sun visors were not as long as those found in hardtops or coupes. They were shorter to clear the top lock mechanisms.

1966-67

The sunshade support with striker was chrome, and carried part number 4548356 (RH) and 4548357 (LH) for 1966 and 1967. The windshield header center moldings were 4542357 (RH) and 4542517 (LH).

The front roof rail lock was painted (part number 7590745 RH and 7590746 LH). The hook (part number 5716613) could be serviced separately if necessary.

The hydraulic pump and motor assembly with shield was identical to the 1965 GTO, as were the lift assemblies.

The power top wire and switch assembly (part number 9782978) was mounted in a chrome bezel (part number 9784641). The chrome knob was part number 9784535. The bezel was mounted on the underside of the dash pad.

The quarter armrest lamp assembly, ashtray and escutcheon, and top boot bag were identical to 1965.

Folding Top Weatherstrip

	RH	One-Piece	LH
Pillar Post	7615143		7615144
Side Roof Rail, front	4548205		4548206
Side Roof Rail, center	4548205		4548206
Side Roof Rail, rear	4548207		4548208
Center Header		7615002	

1968-70

The 1968-70 sunshade support was part number 7735476 (RH) and 7735477 (LH). The striker was serviced separately and carried part number 7740912 (RH) and 7740913 (LH).

The upper windshield garnish moldings were painted gloss black (part number 7742776 RH and 7742777 LH), as were the roof rail locks (part number 7762242 RH and 7762243 LH). The hook (part number 5716613) was chrome.

The hydraulic pump and motor assembly (part number 7710923) mounted to the pan on four rubber grommets (part number 3698109).

The 1968 power top wire and switch assembly (part number 9790871) came with an integral chrome bezel and mounted under the dash pad ledge between the center and RH instrument pods.

The 1969-70 switch and wire assembly (part number 9797081) mounted in the instrument panel to the right of the steering column.

The quarter armrest courtesy lamp for 1968-70 was the same as for 1964 models. The chromed ashtray used in the rear-quarter armrest was part number 8761458 (1968) and 8801663 (1969-70). No escutcheon was used. The convertible top boot bag was the same as 1964-67.

Lift cylinders were interchangeable and were the same (part number 9812594) for 1968-70.

Folding Top Weatherstrip

	RH	One-Piece	LH
Pillar Post			
1968*	7726960		7726961
1969-70	9823138		9823139
Side Roof Rail, front			
1968*	7783476		7783477
1969-70	8715372		8715373
Side Roof Rail, center			
1968-70	7783478		7783479
Side Roof Rail, rear			
1968-70	8796920		8796921
Center Header		7726803	

*Vent window discontinued after 1968 model year.

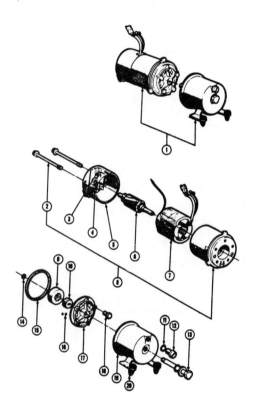

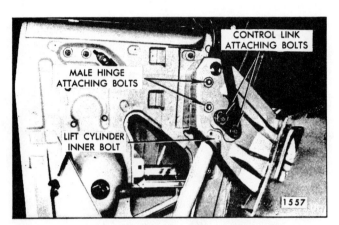

Note control link attaching bolts and inner bolt of lift cylinder. Cylinder was interchangeable between all GM A-bodies.

Key	Part Name	Group No.
1 — MOTOR & PUMP ASM., Hydraulic		14.481
2 — BOLT ASM., Motor Case		N.S.
3 — SPRING, Pump Motor Brush		14.482
4 — BRUSH, Pump Motor		14.482
5 — CASE ASM., Brush Holder		14.482
6 — ARMATURE, Pump Motor		14.482
7 — FIELD, Pump Motor		14.482
8 — MOTOR ASM., Hydraulic Pump		14.481
9 — ROTOR, Pump Motor - Outer		14.482
10 — ROTOR, Pump Motor - Inner		14.482
11 — SEAL, Pump Reservoir		14.486
12 — FILLER PLUG, Pump Reservoir		14.486
13 — BOLT, Pump Reservoir		14.486
14 — SEAL, Pump Motor Shaft		14.482
15 — SEAL, Pump Reservoir		14.486
16 — BALL, Hydraulic Pump		14.482
17 — COVER PLATE ASM., Pump		14.482
18 — BOLT, Pump Cover Attaching		N.S.
19 — RESERVOIR ASM., Hydraulic Pump		14.486
20 — GROMMET, Pump Mounting Rubber		14.482

Exploded view of 1964-70 folding-top hydraulic pump and motor assembly.

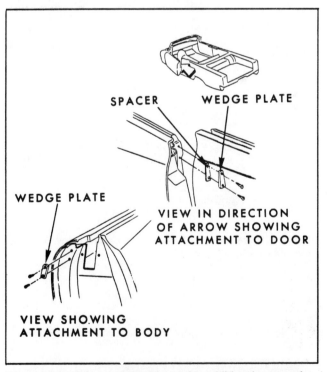

Door wedge plates were used to provide additional support for convertible-style doors when they were closed. The plates were installed with screws to the door and body lock pillars just below the beltline. The body wedge plate was metal; the door wedge plate was nylon. If necessary, shims could be installed 1/32 inch interference. These shims are available today as a service part. To remove either wedge plate, simply remove the exposed screws.

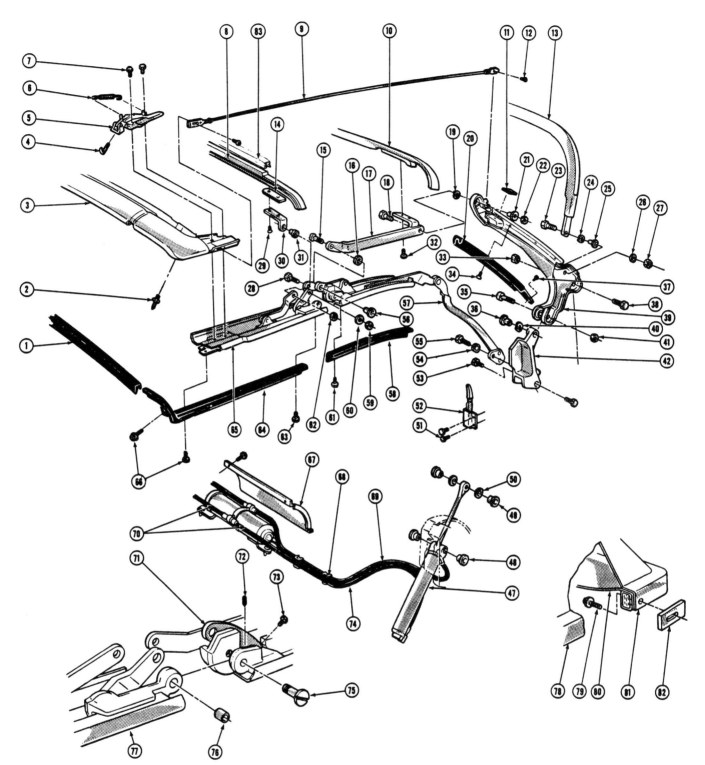

Frame rail assemblies for 1964-65 were painted black. Back window was plastic for both years.

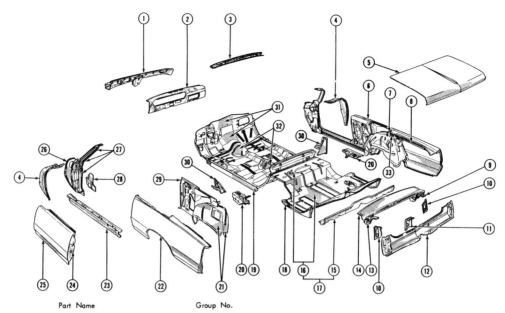

Key	Part Name	Group No.
1 — PANEL, Dash & Duct - Upper		12.804
2 — PANEL ASM., Instrument		10.230
3 — FRAME, Windshield Inner Upper		12.807
4 — PANEL, Shroud Vent Duct - Side		12.804
5 — LID ASM., Rear Compartment		12.181
6 — REINFORCEMENT, Quarter Outer Panel at Belt		N.S.
7 — PANEL, Folding Top Compartment Rear		12.989
8 — GUTTER, Rear Compartment Lid Side		12.996
9 — STRAP, Rear Compartment Lid Hinge		12.187
10 — BRACE, Rear Compartment Gutter to Compartment Pan		12.996
11 — PLATE, Rear Compartment Lid Lock Striker Anchor		12.237
12 — PANEL, Rear End		12.966
13 — SUPPORT, Rear Compartment Lid Hinge		12.184
14 — PANEL, Rear Compartment Front		12.971
15 — BAR, Rear Cross		12.986
16 — PAN, Rear Compartment		12.981

Key	Part Name	Group No.
17 — PAN ASM., Rear Compartment		12.981
18 — FILLER, Compartment Pan to Quarter Panel		12.981
19 — PANEL, Rocker Inner		12.934
20 — BRACE, Folding Top Compartment to Wheelhouse Outer		12.768
21 — PANEL ASM., Wheelhouse		12.944
22 — PANEL, Rear Quarter Outer		12.940
23 — PANEL, Door Opening Rocker Outer		12.934
24 — DOOR ASM., Front		10.351
25 — PANEL ASM., Front Door Outer		12.895
26 — PANEL ASM., Shroud Side Duct		12.804
27 — PANEL ASM., Front Body Hinge Pillar		12.840
28 — REINFORCEMENT, Front Body Hinge Pillar to Duct		12.659
29 — PANEL ASM., Rear Quarter Inner Front		12.941
30 — BRACE, Body Lock Pillar to Floor Pan		12.684
31 — PANEL ASM., Dash Lower		12.804
32 — PAN ASM., Floor		N.S.
33 — FILLER, Folding Top Compartment Side to Rear Panel		12.768

Exploded view of 1964-65 convertible sheet metal and parts nomenclature.

A little-known and extremely rare option was the tonneau cover offered for GTO convertibles. It was dealer installed only and offered from 1964 through 1967.

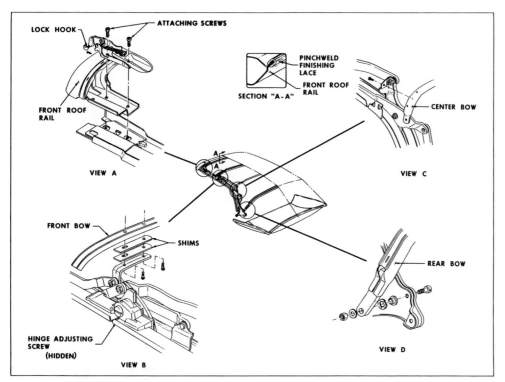

Detail of 1966-67 folding top assembly. Lock hook could be serviced separately, if necessary. Attaching screws were chromed.

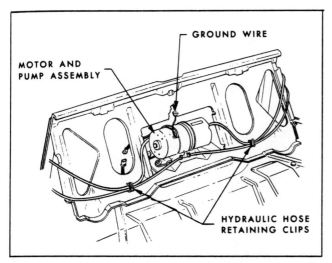

Drawing of 1968-70 hydraulic pump and motor assembly, with hose routing.

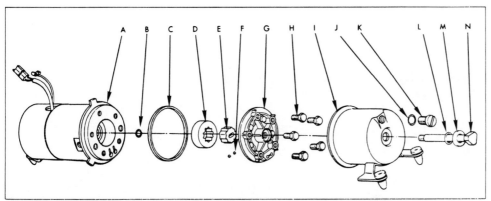

A. Motor Assembly
B. Motor Shaft "O" Ring Seal
C. Reservoir Seal
D. Outer Pump Rotor
E. Inner Pump Rotor
F. Fluid Control Valve Balls
G. Pump Cover Plate Assembly
H. Pump Cover Attaching Screws
I. Reservoir Tube and Bracket Assembly
J. Reservoir Filler Plug
K. Reservoir End Plate Attaching Bolt "O" Ring Seal
L. Reservoir End Plate Attaching Bolt Washer
M. Reservoir End Plate Attaching Bolt

Exploded view of pump assembly for convertible top.

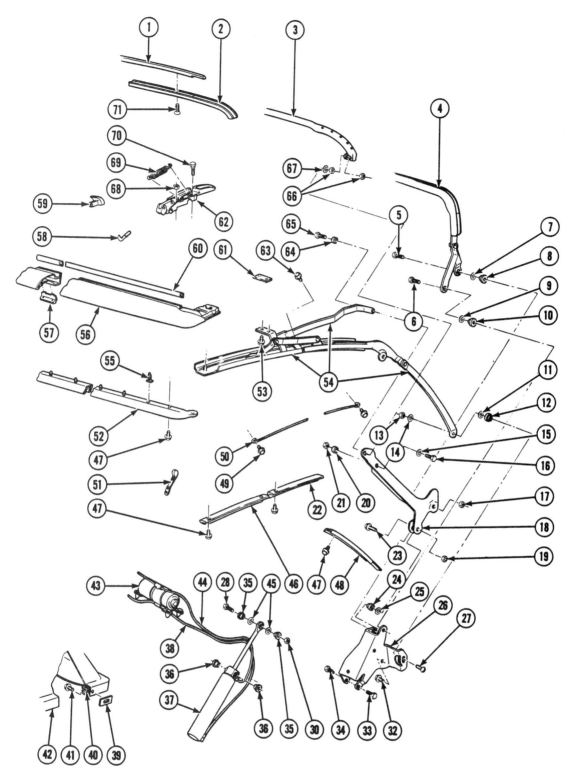

Exploded view and nomenclature of folding top frame and associated hardware for 1968-70.

Key	Part Name	Group No.
1 — RETAINER, Front Bow Material		14.130
2 — BOW ASM., Front		14.130
3 — BOW ASM., Center		14.215
4 — BOW ASM., Rear		14.340
5 — BOLT, Rear Bow to Rear Rail		14.155
6 — BOLT, Rear Bow Control Link to Male Hinge		14.155
7 — WASHER, Rear Bow to Rear Rail		14.155
8 — BUSHING, Rear Bow to Rear Rail		N.S.
9 — WASHER, Rear Bow Control Link to Male Hinge		N.S.
10 — BUSHING, Rear Bow Control Link to Male Hinge		14.160
11 — WASHER, Center Rail to Male Hinge-Spring		14.162
12 — BUSHING, Center Rail to Male Hinge		14.160
13 — NUT, Center Rail to Male Hinge		14.157
14 — WASHER, Center Rail to Male Hinge-Flat		N.S.
15 — WASHER, Center Rail to Rear Rail		14.162
16 — BOLT, Center Rail to Rear Rail		14.155
17 — NUT, Rear Bow to Rear Rail		14.157
18 — RAIL ASM., Side Roof Rear		14.170
19 — NUT, Rear Rail to Male Hinge		14.157
20 — BUSHING, Center Rail to Rear Rail		14.160
21 — NUT, Center Rail to Rear Rail		N.S.
22 — WEATHERSTRIP ASM., Side Roof Rail-Center		14.190
23 — BOLT, Rear Rail to Male Hinge		14.155
24 — BUSHING, Rear Rail to Male Hinge		14.160
25 — WASHER, Rear Rail to Male Hinge		14.162
26 — HINGE ASM., Male		14.310
27 — BOLT, Center Rail to Male Hinge		14.155
28 — BOLT, Lift to Rear Rail		14.155
32 — BOLT, Male Hinge to Mounting Support		14.155
33 — BOLT, Lift to Male Hinge		14.155
34 — BOLT, Lift to Male Hinge-Shoulder		14.155
35 — BUSHING, Lift to Rear Rail		14.160
36 — BUSHING, Lift to Male Hinge		14.160
37 — LIFT ASM., Folding Top-Hydraulic		14.475
38 — HOSE ASM., Pump to Bottom of Lift		14.472
39 — FILLER, Trimstick to Quarter Panel		N.S.
40 — TRIMSTICK, Quarter Belt Rail-Rear		12.946
41 — SCREW, Trimstick to Quarter Panel		N.S.
42 — TRIMSTICK, Quarter Belt Rail-Front		12.946
43 — MOTOR & PUMP ASM., Folding Top Lift		14.481
44 — HOSE ASM., Pump to Top of Lift		14.472
45 — WASHER, Hydraulic Lift to Rear Rail		14.162
46 — WEATHERSTRIP ASM., Side Roof Rail-Front		14.120
47 — SCREW, Roof Rail Weatherstrip to Rail		N.S.
48 — WEATHERSTRIP ASM., Side Roof Rail-Rear		14.260
49 — SCREW, Hold Down Cable to Rail		N.S.
50 — CABLE, Top Trim Hold Down		14.102
51 — CATCH ASM., Center Rail		14.310
52 — WEATHERSTRIP ASM., Front Roof Rail		14.060
53 — SCREW, Front Bow to Rail		14.155
54 — RAIL ASM., Side Roof Front & Center		14.100
55 — FASTENER, Front Roof Rail Weatherstrip		14.060
56 — RAIL ASM., Front Roof		14.050
57 — SPACER, Front Roof Rail-Center		14.090
58 — HOOK, Lock Handle (Also Part of #62)		14.080
59 — STRIKER, Lock		14.080
60 — LACE, Front Roof Rail-Rear		14.650B
61 — SPACER, Front Bow		14.130
62 — LOCK & HANDLE ASM., Front Roof Rail (Incl. #58 & 62)		14.080
63 — SCREW, Side Roof Front Rail Hinge Set		14.155
64 — BUSHING, Control Link to Rear Rail		14.160
65 — BOLT, Control Link to Rear Rail		14.155
66 — NUT, Control Link to Rear Rail		N.S.
67 — WASHER, Control Link to Rear Rail		14.162
68 — NUT, Front Rail Lock Handle		N.S.
69 — SPRING, Lock Handle Return (Also Part of #62)		14.080
70 — BOLT, Front Roof Rail Handle & Lock		14.080
71 — SCREW, Front Bow Material Retainer		N.S.

1964 Folding Tops came in six colors and codes:

CODE	COLOR
1	Ivory
2	Black
4	Blue
5	Aqua
6	Beige
7	Saddle

1965 Folding Tops came in five colors and codes:

CODE	COLOR
1	White
2	Black
4	Blue
5	Turquoise
6	Beige

The boots matched the interior trim color.

1966 Folding Tops came in five colors and codes:

CODE	COLOR
1	White
2	Black
4	Blue
5	Turquoise
6	Beige

1967 Folding Top colors and codes:

CODE	COLOR
1	Ivory White
2	Black
4	Blue
5	Turquoise
7	Cream

1968 Folding Top colors and codes:

CODE	COLOR
1	Ivory White
2	Black
5	Teal
8	Gold

1969 Folding Top colors and codes:

CODE	COLOR
1	Ivory White
2	Black
3	Dark Blue
9	Dark Green

1970 Folding Top Colors and codes:

CODE	COLOR
1	White
2	Black
5	Sandalwood
7	Dark Gold

Colors and color codes for GTO folding tops for 1964 through 1970 models.

WHEELS

1964-65

A stamped steel wheel measuring 14x6 inches (part number 3871919) was standard equipment for all 1964 and 1965 GTOs. The wheel was painted 60° gloss black. Five lug nuts (part number 358501) were used per wheel.

1966-67

The standard stamped steel wheel (part number 3871919) measured 14x16 inches. When equipped with front disc brakes, stamped steel wheel part number 9773690 was used in 1967. This wheel also measured 14x6 inches, and was stamped DB. Lug nuts for standard wheels used part number 358501.

1968-70

The standard stamped steel wheel for 1968 and 1969 (part number 9791450) measured 14x6 inches, and was stamped HF. The stamp was located near the valve stem hole. The 1970 stamped wheel also measured 14x6 inches, but used a Chevrolet part number (3928297). The same lug nut was used 1968-70 (part number 358501). The Space Saver wheel (part number 9793592) was the same for all three years, and was stamped KC.

WHEEL DISCS

1964-65

A simulated wire wheel disc option was offered in 1964 (RPO 411). This wheel disc had a separate two-ear spinner with a Mylar decal in the center of the spinner. The decal was composed of the word Pontiac above a silver-and-red-checkered field.

A change was made in the wire wheel disc in 1965 with the addition of cooling slots, and the checkered field in the spinner insert was now black and red. The RPO number remained the same for 1965. The wire wheel disc part number was 9771087, which also served as the 1964 replacement. This part number was also used for the 1966 disc. A repair package (part number 9776024) was available for the spinner. The accessory package part number for 1964 and 1965 was 983938.

Two other wheel disc options were offered in 1964, a Deluxe Wheel disc (RPO 462, accessory package part number 984128) and the more expensive Custom Wheel disc (RPO 521, accessory package part number 984129). The Deluxe disc carried part number 9774074. The Custom disc was identified as part number 9774611. The center ornament was a spinner design and was serviced by replacement part number 9774614.

In 1965, the Deluxe and Custom wheel disc options were again available. While the RPO numbers remained the same, the design and the part numbers were changed.

The Deluxe disc (part number 9780913, accessory package part number 984490) had the words Pontiac Motor Division stamped into the center ornament. The Custom Wheel disc (part number 9780724) also had the words Pontiac Motor Division stamped into a three-ear spinner which could be serviced by part number 9780818.

1966-67

The 1966 wire wheel disc was identical in all respects to the 1965 disc. The only difference was the RPO number in 1966 (452).

The wire wheel disc offered on the Senior Pontiacs was introduced into the A-body line-up in 1967. This disc had no spinner and was serviced by part number 9781478. The RPO number was 452 and the accessory package part number 984528.

The Deluxe Wheel disc (RPO 461) and the Custom Wheel disc (RPO 458) were revised for 1966 and were assigned new accessory package part numbers. The Deluxe disc (part number 9783391, accessory package part number 984609) was similar in design to the 1985 disc but the center ornament was blank. The Custom Wheel disc was totally redesigned (part number 9783624, accessory package part number 985610).

The RPO numbers remained the same for 1967. However, the disc designs were again changed. The Deluxe disc (part number 9786453, accessory package part number 984775) had a six-slot design. The redesigned Custom Wheel disc (part number 9787697) had a three-eared spinner which could be serviced by replacement part number 9778677. The disc could be ordered as a dealer-installed accessory (package part number 984773).

1968-70

The Wire Wheel disc option for 1968-70 was unchanged in design and was serviced by the same part number (9781478) and carried the same accessory package part number (984528). The RPO numbers were 452 in 1968; RPO 453 UPC N95 in 1969; RPO 473 UPC N95 in 1970.

The Deluxe Wheel disc (RPO 461) and the Custom Wheel disc (RPO 458) were restyled for 1968. The Deluxe disc could be ordered as a dealer-installed accessory package (984913) and carried part number 9714122.

The Custom Wheel disc was a step-up option and used part number 9791006. It could be ordered from the dealer as accessory package part number 984912.

The Deluxe Wheel and Custom Wheel disc options were restyled in 1969 and were continued unchanged in 1970. The Deluxe disc had an RPO of 451 in 1969 and 471 in 1970. The UPC code was P01 for both years. Both years shared the same accessory package part number (988609). The Custom Wheel disc was identified as RPO 452 in 1969 and RPO 472 in 1970. The UPC code was P02. The replacement part number for this disc was 9795997 and the accessory package part number was 988607.

RALLY WHEEL

1965

A new road wheel option (RPO 691) was introduced with the 1965 model year. Dubbed the Rally wheel, this stamped steel wheel was painted Silver Textured (Rinshed-Mason E28C009) and measured 14x6 inches. The Rally wheel was composed of three components: a rim (part number 9781246), a trim ring (part number 9781480) and a center cap (part number 9781249). The special lug nuts were part number 9780732.

1966-67

The optional Rally wheel was again offered in 1966. The wheel, trim ring and lug nuts were unchanged. However, the center cap was now blacked-out and carried a new part number (9785501). In 1966, brake drums were painted red when Rally wheels were mounted. The Rally wheel was unchanged for 1967. However, it was now designated Rally I to differentiate it from the newly introduced Rally II mag-style wheel. The Rally I was available on models equipped with or without disc brakes.

The Rally II wheel was introduced in 1967. The wheel (part number 9787279) was stamped JA and measured 14x6 inches. It could be ordered on models equipped with or without disc brakes. The tops of the lug nuts (part number 9789086) were filled with red paint. The 1967 Rally II center cap could be serviced as an assembly (part number 9787940), or just the PMD medallion could be replaced (using part number 9787941).

1968-70

The optional Rally I wheel continued to be offered in 1968. The wheel (part number 9781246) measured 14x6 inches, and was stamped KB. The center cap (part number 9785501) was identical to the 1966-67 cap. The trim ring (part number 9781480) was interchangeable with the 1967-69 Rally II trim ring. Five 20x7/16 inch hex-crown lug nuts were used (part number 9780732).

The Rally II wheel was optional for 1968-70. Two Rally II wheels were used in 1968. Wheel part number 9787279 was used when the disc brake option was ordered. This wheel was identified by a two-letter code, JA, stamped on the rim. When front drum brakes were used, Rally II wheel part number 9789329 was installed. This wheel carried stamp code JC on the rim, and was carried over for 1969 for all applications. For 1970, Rally II wheel part number 546494 was used, and it measured 14x6 inches. No 14x7 inch Rally II wheels were used on the GTO. The lug nut (part number 9789086) was the same for all three years, 20x7/16 inch with a hex crown. This nut

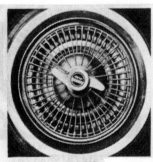

9774074
(984128)

9774611
(984129)

9771087
(983938)

Here are the wheel covers, and RPO numbers, for 1964. Left to right: Deluxe (462), Custom (521) and wire (411).

TEMPEST DELUXE
9780913 (984490)

TEMPEST CUSTOM
9780724 (984491)

CAP 9781249
TRIM RING 9781480

Carried over from 1964 was the wire wheel disc; new for 1965 were, left to right: Deluxe (462), Custom (521) and Rally (691).

should not be confused with the Rally I nut, as it had a much higher profile and an insert.

CAPS, ORNAMENTS AND TRIM RINGS

The standard wheel cover offered from 1964 to 1970 was the "poverty cap" design, which covered the wheel hub and lug nuts only. Part number 9774609 was used for all 1964-70 GTO applications.

The 1968 Deluxe wheel disc medallion was serviced by replacement part number 9714056. The 1968-70 wire wheel disc ornament (part number 9777270) had a red background with black PMD letters. The Rally II ornament (part number 9787941) was black with red PMD letters from 1968 through mid-1970, when it was changed to a red background with black letters. The black ornament could be serviced with the bezel as an assembly, part number 9792996, and part number 480301 serviced the red-background ornament and bezel. The bezel could also be replaced separately (part number 9787942).

The 1968-69 Rally II trim ring (part number 9781480) was brushed stainless. The 1970 Rally II trim ring (part number 545910) was rounded at the outside edge and was polished stainless.

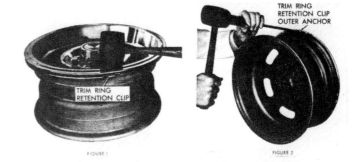

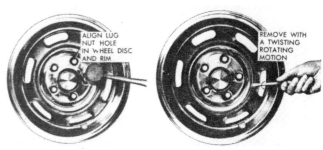

Pontiac Service News Flash number 65-43, dated 11-24-64, warned that the Custom wheel discs were designed to leave ⅛ to ¼ inch clearance between the disc and the wheel rim. Attempts to eliminate this gap will result in a damaged wheel disc.

Close-up detail of 1967 Rally II lug nuts. Top of nut was painted red.

When installing the trim ring assembly (5 per car) or the wheel disc (4 per car) on a Tempest Rally Wheel, the following recommended procedure should be followed in order to avoid any unnecessary damage:

TRIM RING INSTALLATION -

1. Place the trim ring on the rim properly aligning the valve stem holes.

2. Attach the retention clips located on the back of the trim ring to the rim (Figure 1)) making sure that the two outer retaining anchors are located on the outer portion of the rim, while the center curled section is positioned beneath.

3. Using a rubber mallet, tap the trim ring lightly only in the retainer area until the clip is properly seated on the rim.

   NOTE: Excessive hammering or striking in any other area could cause unnecessary distortion.

4. Use the same procedure on the remaining attachment clips again exercising care to avoid any possible trim ring damage.

TRIM RING REMOVAL -

The use of a screwdriver and rubber mallet will facilitate easy removal of the trim ring. Simply position the screwdriver along side the retention clip and tap lightly (Figure 2).

NOTE: Do NOT pry or use excessive force as this may cause unnecessary damage.

WHEEL DISC INSTALLATION -

1. Place the wheel disc on the rim in the proper position, making sure that the disc indentations and lug nut holes are properly aligned.

2. Using a rubber mallet, tap the wheel disc lightly in a rotating motion until properly seated on the rim (Figure 3).

WHEEL DISC REMOVAL -

The wheel disc may be removed from the rim assembly by placing a screwdriver under the lip of the disc and applying a twisting motion while rotating around the disc (Figure 4).

NOTE: Care should be exercised so as not to damage the wheel disc or any other decorative components of the Rally Wheel.

Whenever it is necessary to remove a tire from the rim, all decorative chrome components <u>must</u> be removed from the Rally Wheel assembly.

Pontiac Service News Flash number 65-91, dated 4-8-65, reported these procedures for installing the trim ring assemblies or wheel discs on the Rally wheels. This advice should be followed in order to avoid unnecessary damage.

  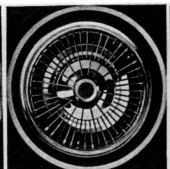 

TEMPEST DELUXE	TEMPEST CUSTOM	TEMPEST WIRE	RALLY I
9783391 (984609)	9783624 (984610)	9771087 (983938)	9785501 CAP 9781480 T/RING

For 1966 the following were designated for GTOs, left to right: Deluxe (461), Custom (458), wire (452) and Rally (454).

  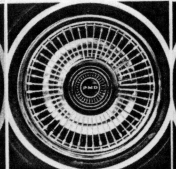 

TEMPEST DELUXE	TEMPEST & FIREBIRD CUSTOM	PONTIAC, TEMPEST & FIREBIRD WIRE	RALLY II
9786453 (984775)	9787697 (984773)	9781478 (984528)	9787941 MED. 9781480 T/RING

The Rally I wheel (454) was carried over into 1967; new were, left to right: Deluxe (461), Custom (458), wire (452) and Rally II (453).

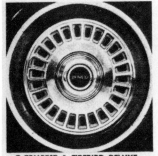  

● TEMPEST & FIREBIRD DELUXE	TEMPEST & FIREBIRD CUSTOM	ALL RALLY 11
9714122	9791006	9792996 ORN. 9781480 T/RING

Newly restyled for 1968 were, left to right: Deluxe (461), Custom (458), and Rally II (453). Carried over were the wire disc and Rally I wheel.

TEMPEST & FIREBIRD DELUXE	TEMPEST & FIREBIRD CUSTOM
9718045	9795997

1969 and 1970 had the same wheel covers and the Rally II wheel (RPO 454 in 1969, and 474 in 1970; UPC N98 both years). Carried over from 1968, besides the Rally II, was the wire wheel cover (RPO 453 in 1969, and 473 in 1970; UPC N95 both years). New were Deluxe (RPO 451 in 1969, and 471 in 1970; UPC P02 both years) and Custom (RPO 452 in 1969, and 472 in 1970; UPC P01 both years).

THE JUDGE

The Judge (RPO 554, UPC WT1 in 1969 and RPO 332, UPC WT1 in 1970) was released in the middle of the 1969 production year. Although originally intended as a low-priced, junior Supercar to compete against the Plymouth Road Runner, by the fall of 1968 it was decided to incorporate the package that eventually would be named The Judge into the GTO option list.

The initial 2,000 units were "planned" models, and were all painted Carousel Red, a Firebird color. Early production Judges not equipped with air conditioning had the GTO nameplate (part number 9798895) above the heater controls on the instrument panel. This nameplate was deleted from production in mid-February 1969.

Because of supplier difficulties, the The Judge glovebox emblem (part number 479376) wasn't installed on production-line Judges until early February; therefore, it was possible to have both the nameplate and the emblem installed on some Judges built before mid-February of 1969. No very early production Judge had the glovebox emblem installed. Along the same lines, there were no production-line Judges sequenced before January of 1969. This is the easiest method for spotting a bogus Judge.

After initial sales, the Judge was offered to buyers in any GTO exterior color. This policy was carried through to the 1970 model year; however, Carousel Red was not offered in 1970. Because of buyer demand, a new color, Orbit Orange, was offered. Pontiac Sales Promotion Blueprint number 70-20, dated 10-24-69, reported the availability of Orbit Orange as a special color for RPO 332, UPC WT1. Paint code T was given to Orbit Orange. Recommended interior trims were: Sandalwood with bucket seats (257) or bench seat (267); and Black with bucket seats (258) or bench seat (268). Recommended Cordova or Convertible top colors were White (1), Black (2) or Sandalwood (5). There were no two-tone combinations available.

The Judge package was comprised of a rear deck airfoil, distinctive stripes and decals, and other minor trim items. The airfoil was mounted on the rear deck. A pad (part number 545739) was used on each leg of the airfoil, and each leg was retained to the deck lid by a nut and sealer (part number 4801719).

Because of design differences between hardtop and convertible quarter panels, two different airfoils were used in 1969. These could also be ordered as accessory packages. The hardtop used part number 545647 (accessory package 988719) and the convertible airfoil was part number 545032 (accessory package 988718).

The airfoil was redesigned for 1970. One part number was used for both body styles (part number 480473). The accessory package was 988806. An accessory package number (988833) was released for the 1970 convertible, but no package is known to exist. On white 1970 Judges, some airfoils were painted matte black and some were painted white.

Because of the additional weight of the airfoil, the Judge deck lid used heavier torque rods for both years. The 1970 Judge required the heavy-duty rod on the LH side only.

Year	Style	RH	LH
1969	Hardtop	8790659	8790660
	Convertible	8790132	8790133
1970	Hardtop		8733945
	Convertible		7765576

A Judge decal was applied to the top RH side of the airfoil, and used the same part numbers as the front fender decal in 1969 (545898 blue and 545899 black). The decal was moved from the airfoil to the deck lid in 1970 and replaced the GTO nameplate decal (part number 480290

orange, 480291 blue, 480292 black and 480293 yellow).

The front fender decal in 1969 was mounted in front of the wheel opening (part number 545897 olive, 545898 blue and 545899 black). The decal was moved in 1970 to the rear of the front wheel opening and took the place of the GTO nameplate decal. The decal came in four colors (part number 479950 orange, 479951 blue, 479952 black and 479953 yellow).

In the mid-seventies, the individual stripe component part numbers were discontinued in favor of stripe package part numbers.

Year	Color	RH	LH
1969	White/Yellow/Green	490869	490870
	Yellow/Red/Blue	490871	490872
	White/Red/Black*	490873	490874
1970	Blue/Orange/Pink	490855	490856
	Yellow/Blue/Red	490857	490858
	Yellow/Black/Red	490859	490860
	Green/Yellow/White	490861	490862

*Also available as optional stripe package for early production 1970 GTO.

The Ram Air III engine was standard, as were Rally II wheels without trim rings, G70x14 blackwall fiberglass belted tires, Hurst T-handle shift lever (either with the standard three-speed gearbox or the optional 4-speed) and blacked-out grilles. The hideaway headlamp option was also available for the Judge in 1969, and used blacked-out headlamp doors to match the grilles. The 1970 Judge grilles differed from the standard GTO grilles, as the Argent Silver grille surrounds were blacked out.

Year	Description	LH	RH
1969	Grille	9794650	9794651
	Headlamp Door	9794644	9794645
1970	Grille	480680	480681

The hood scoop ornaments were painted exterior color in 1969 and 0° gloss black in 1970. Ram Air and Ram Air IV decals were applied to the outboard sides of the hood scoops on all Judges, depending on which engine was installed. A front spoiler (part number 480463) was installed on some—but not all—1970 GTO Judges. This spoiler was either painted matte black or to match the exterior color.

It was possible to order the body stripe option (RPO 422, UPC D98) in 1970 for standard GTO models. During the first half of the production year, the upper beltline slash stripe as used on the 1969 Judge was applied. However, in the second half of the year, this was discontinued in favor of the "eyebrow" stripes over the wheel openings as used on the 1970 Judge.

Close-up detail of 1969 front fender Judge decal.

1969 rear deck airfoil. Note absence of downward curl on sides of foil; preproduction design was pronounced.

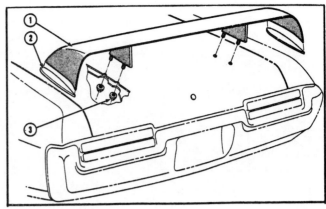

Key	Part Name	Group No.
1 — SPOILER ASM., Compartment Lid	. . . .	12.180
2 — PAD, Spoiler to Rear Qtr. Panel	. . . .	12.181
3 — NUT, Spoiler to Lid	. . . .	12.181

View of the 1969 airfoil, pad, and nut and sealer components. Preliminary drawing shows prototype airfoil design; downward curve on rear of foil on each side didn't see production.

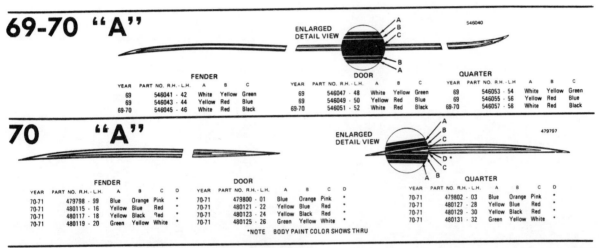

69-70 "A"

ENLARGED DETAIL VIEW

546040

	FENDER					DOOR					QUARTER			
YEAR	PART NO. R.H. - L.H.	A	B	C	YEAR	PART NO. R.H. - L.H.	A	B	C	YEAR	PART NO. R.H. - L.H.	A	B	C
69	546041 - 42	White	Yellow	Green	69	546047 - 48	White	Yellow	Green	69	546053 - 54	White	Yellow	Green
69	546043 - 44	Yellow	Red	Blue	69	546049 - 50	Yellow	Red	Blue	69	546055 - 56	Yellow	Red	Blue
69-70	546045 - 46	White	Red	Black	69-70	546051 - 52	White	Red	Black	69-70	546057 - 58	White	Red	Black

70 "A"

ENLARGED DETAIL VIEW

479797

	FENDER						DOOR						QUARTER				
YEAR	PART NO. R.H. - L.H.	A	B	C	D	YEAR	PART NO. R.H. - L.H.	A	B	C	D	YEAR	PART NO. R.H. - L.H.	A	B	C	D
70-71	479798 - 99	Blue	Orange	Pink	*	70-71	479800 - 01	Blue	Orange	Pink	*	70-71	479802 - 03	Blue	Orange	Pink	*
70-71	480115 - 16	Yellow	Blue	Red	*	70-71	480121 - 22	Yellow	Blue	Red	*	70-71	480127 - 28	Yellow	Blue	Red	*
70-71	480117 - 18	Yellow	Black	Red	*	70-71	480123 - 24	Yellow	Black	Red	*	70-71	480129 - 30	Yellow	Black	Red	*
70-71	480119 - 20	Green	Yellow	White	*	70-71	480125 - 26	Green	Yellow	White	*	70-71	480131 - 32	Green	Yellow	White	*

*NOTE BODY PAINT COLOR SHOWS THRU

In 1969 and 1970, as well as into the mid-seventies, individual stripe components could be ordered separately. After that, the stripes were serviced as packages. This illustration shows the original part numbers for the stripes and a detailed enlargement of a stripe.

Front three-quarter view of 1969 Judge shows location of front fender decal and stripe package. A total of 6,725 hardtop Judges was produced in 1969, along with 108 convertibles.

Rear three-quarter view of 1969 Judge showing "dechromed" Rally II wheels and rear deck lid airfoil. Diecast deck lid nameplate was used in 1969.

Close-up of the Judge glovebox emblem (part number 479376) used in both 1969 and 1970.

View of 1970 airfoil with Judge decal on deck lid.

Factory photograph of 1970 Judge. Hood scoop ornaments were painted black, as was the rear deck airfoil. There were 3,629 hardtops and 168 convertibles built in 1970 with the Judge option. Note the absence of a front spoiler.

114

EXTERIOR COLOR	COLOR CODE	DECAL & STRIPE COLOR
PALOMINO COPPER	B	
BAJA GOLD	G	
PALISADE GREEN	H	
PEPPER GREEN	M	YELLOW
VERDORO GREEN	Q	
SIERRA YELLOW	Y	
GRANADA GOLD	Z	
BURGUNDY	N	
CARDINAL RED	R	BLACK
BERMUDA BLUE	D	
ATOLL BLUE	E	
MINT TURQUOISE	K	ORANGE
ORBIT ORANGE	T	
STARLIGHT BLACK	A	
POLAR WHITE	C	BLUE
PALLADIUM SILVER	P	

Bulletin number 70-49 dated 10-27-69 listed these decal and stripe usage combinations for Judge models.

BODY COLOR	STRIPE/DECAL COLOR
1969	
LIMELIGHT GREEN	
MIDNIGHT GREEN	
VERDORO GREEN	OLIVE
MAYFAIR MAIZE	
STARLIGHT BLACK	
CAMEO WHITE	
WARWICK BLUE	
LIBERTY BLUE	BLUE
CRYSTAL TURQUOISE	
PALLADIUM SILVER	
CAROUSEL RED	
EXPRESSO BROWN	
ANTIQUE GOLD	
BURGUNDY	BLACK
MATADOR RED	
CHAMPAGNE	
1970	
PALAMINO COPPER	
BAJA GOLD	
PALISIDE GREEN	
PEPPER GREEN	YELLOW
VERDORO GREEN	
SIERRA YELLOW	
GRANADA GOLD	
STARLIGHT BLACK	
POLAR WHITE	BLUE
PALLADIUM SILVER	
BURGUNDY	
CARDINAL RED	BLACK
BERMUDA BLUE	
ATOLL BLUE	
MINT TURQUOISE	ORANGE
ORBIT ORANGE	

    Stripes and decals were multicolored and are identified by the prominent color:

                                   1969

            White/Yellow/OLIVE*
            Yellow/Red/BLUE
            White/Red/BLACK

                    1970-'71

            Blue/ORANGE/Pink
            Yellow/BLUE/Red
            Yellow/BLACK/Red
            Green/YELLOW/White

    *Sometimes referred to in factory literature as Green.

These are the factory recommended Judge stripe/decal and body color combinations for 1969-70.

Chapter 3

INTERIORS

CONSOLE, AUTOMATIC TRANSMISSION

1964-65

The automatic console (RPO 601) was identical for 1964 and 1965, except for paint trim. The 1964 console top (part number 9774249) was painted bluish gray with chrome trim. The 1965 top (part number 9781523) was 60° gloss black with chrome trim.

The shift-indicator assembly used a clear plastic lens (part number 9774971) with white letters on a light blue background. The gear shift opening escutcheons were physically the same, but again were painted the correct color for their respective years. The 1964 escutcheon carried part number 9776298; the 1965 was 9781520. The plastic console base (part number 9774128) was the same for both years. It was painted to match the interior trim, and was mounted into the mounting brackets and floor pan by chrome-plated Phillips-head screws.

Finally, all consoles used a courtesy lamp at the rear of the console, activated by either the lamp switch at the instrument panel or the opening of a door. Some courtesy lamps had a switch at the lamp itself, but not all GTOs came with this switch. The lamp assembly was part number 543336 in 1964. The 1965 lamp was serviced in parts: The lens was part number 543243 and the housing was part number 9776397.

1966-67

The 1966 GTO used the same automatic console assembly as the 1965, except that the console top carried a different part number (9781523). The gear shift escutcheon was the same, but the shift knob (part number 9779345) and the button (part number 9777515) were unique to the 1966.

With the introduction of the three-speed Turbo Hydra-matic in 1967, the entire console assembly was redesigned. The console (part number 9789202) had an imitation-wood veneer along the entire top. The gearshift opening escutcheon (part number 9790373) also had an imitation-wood insert, and used four Phillips-head chrome screws to attach the escutcheon to the shifter assembly.

The console tops were the same for the LeMans two-speed automatic console and the GTO Turbo Hydra-matic, but modifications must be made to the LeMans console top. The shifter opening has to be enlarged, and the divider bar must be removed to accommodate the Hurst Dual Gate shifter.

The shift indicator, which was part of the shift lever indicator housing (part number 9777906), had a gray-blue background with white letters. The shift lever (part number 9777924) was chrome and had the Hurst name stamped on it. A black lever knob (part number 9777921) was used. The console base (part number 9789201) was painted to

match the interior trim, except for RPO 224 parchment, in which case the base was painted black.

The console was mounted to the floor by a bracket (part number 9774564) and was used for 1966 and 1967. The consoles also used four number 10 16x½ inch chrome-plated Phillips-head screws (part number 9414768), two per side.

The console compartment door was black with chrome ribs in 1966 to match the console top (part number 9781521). To match the wood trim in 1967, the door also had an imitation-wood insert (part number 9788023). Both years used the same opening spring assembly (part number 9775946).

A courtesy lamp was used at the rear of the console for both years, and was activated by either the headlamp rheostat or by the opening of a door. The housing assembly (part number 9776397) was the same for both years, as was the lamp lens (part number 543243). There was no switch used on the lamp assembly itself.

Difficulty in obtaining an adequate ground circuit on the 1967 courtesy lamp resulted in Dealer Service Information Bulletin number 67-I-49, dated 3-27-67. On some occasions the plastic lens was eliminated on the courtesy lamp brackets. On others an O-ring was inserted to avoid interference between bulb and lens. Brackets should not be replaced as defective parts. The socket was later changed to adequately clear the bulb.

1968-70

The components that made up the automatic transmission console used from 1968 through 1970 varied little in design.

The console body itself was identical for all three years, and was color keyed to match the interior trim (except that parchment interiors used black).

The console compartment door was padded and matched the console color. A compartment box (part number 9790838) was used for all three years.

Three fixes for the problem with the 1968 console door not closing completely were reported in Dealer Technical Bulletin number 68-T-1, dated 10-11-67. (1) Replace console light switch with part number 9791219 (F3) which has a gray plastic base. (2) Crimp the door hinge spring location to increase spring tension. (3) Provide more clearance by cutting material away from the notch in the compartment box to prevent interference of box to spring. Dealer Service Information Bulletin 68-I-52, dated 3-22-68, reported that the console compartment lamp had been canceled and the lamp lead cut off the production wiring harness.

The 1968 console used the Hurst Dual Gate shifter (part number 9791438). The indicator housing was identical to and interchangeable with the 1967 unit. The gearshift opening escutcheon (part number 9791636) was not interchangeable with the 1967 unit, as the 1968 was bolted from underneath. A black shift knob (part number 9793565) was used on the Dual Gate.

The Dual Gate was dropped in 1969 for the factory Rally Sport shifter, which was also used in 1970. The shifter assembly (part number 9782398 in 1969 and 481176 in 1970) used the same gearshift opening escutcheon (part number 9797272) for both years. The lever was chrome, and used a wood knob (part number 9796831). A black button (part number 9797194) on the top of the knob was depressed to engage the shifter out of park or into reverse. A PMD emblem was laminated onto the button.

The console was mounted to the floor by a support bracket (part number 7768476) and two number 10 16x⅝ inch hex-head screws in 1968. A front bracket (part number 9791364) was used for 1968-70, with a number 10 16x¾ inch hex-head screw retaining the console to the bracket.

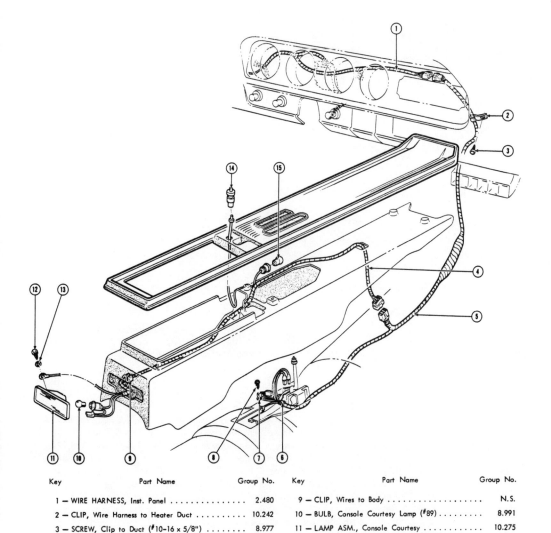

Key	Part Name	Group No.
1 — WIRE HARNESS, Inst. Panel		2.480
2 — CLIP, Wire Harness to Heater Duct		10.242
3 — SCREW, Clip to Duct (#10-16 x 5/8")		8.977
4 — WIRE HARNESS, Console		13.090
5 — WIRE HARNESS, Console Jumper		13.090
6 — CLIP, Wires to Floor Pan		N.S.
7 — LOCKWASHER, Shift Lever Bracket to Body (1/4")		8.932
8 — SCREW, Shift Lever Bracket to Body (1/4"-14 x 29/32")		N.S.

Key	Part Name	Group No.
9 — CLIP, Wires to Body		N.S.
10 — BULB, Console Courtesy Lamp (#89)		8.991
11 — LAMP ASM., Console Courtesy		10.275
12 — SCREW, Ground Wire to Lamp (#10-12 x 1/2")		8.977
13 — LOCKWASHER, Ground Wire to Lamp (#10)		8.932
14 — SWITCH & LAMP ASM., Console Compt.		10.275
15 — BULB, Shift Indicator Lamp (#1895)		8.991

Exploded view and parts nomenclature for 1964-66 automatic transmission console electrical components. This glovebox switch and lamp assembly (part number 3870209) was used for 1964-66.

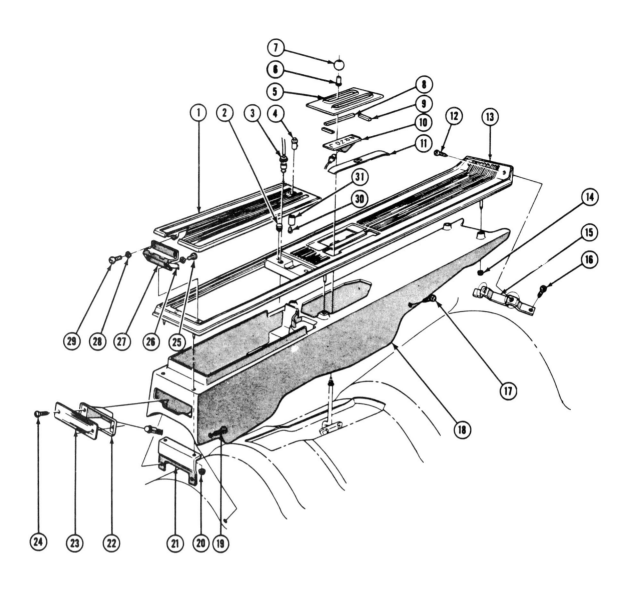

Key	Part Name	Group No.
1 – DOOR, Trans. Console Compartment		10.242
2 – BUMPER, Compartment Door to Top Molding		10.263
3 – SWITCH & LAMP ASM., Console Compartment		10.275
4 – CYLINDER, Compartment Lock		10.266
5 – ESCUTCHEON, Console Gearshift Opening		10.240
6 – BUTTON, Shift Lever Knob		4.006
7 – KNOB, Trans. Shift Lever		4.006
8 – SEAL, Gearshift Opening Escutcheon to Lens-Side		10.240
9 – SEAL, Gearshift Opening Escutcheon to Lens-Front & Rear		10.240
10 – HOUSING ASM., Console Shift Lever Indicator		4.020
11 – SEAL, Trans. Shift Lever		4.015
12 – SCREW, Top Molding to Bracket		N.S.
13 – Molding, Console Top		10.240
14 – NUT, Console Molding		10.240
15 – BRACKET, Console Top Molding		10.240
16 – SCREW & SEALER ASM., Bracket to Floor Pan		N.S.

Key	Part Name	Group No.
17 – SCREW & SEALER ASM., Console to Floor (#10-12 x 1-1/2)		8.977
18 – CONSOLE, Transmission Floor		10.240
19 – SCREW & SEALER ASM., Console to Floor (#10-12 x 1")		8.977
20 – NUT, Console Molding		10.240
21 – RETAINER, Console Courtesy Lamp		10.275
22 – LAMP ASM., Console Courtesy		10.275
23 – LENS, Console Courtesy Lamp		10.275
24 – SCREW, Lamp Asm. to Lamp Retainer (#8-15 x 5/8")		8.977
25 – SCREW, Hinge to Top Molding (#10-24 x 1/4")		8.977
26 – SPRING, Compt. Door Hold-Open		10.242
27 – HINGE ASM., Console Compartment Door		10.242
28 – WASHER, Hinge to Top Molding (#10)		8.929
29 – SCREW, Hinge to Top Molding (#10-24 x 3/8")		8.977
30 – SCREW, Compartment Door Lock to Lock Retainer		10.267
31 – RETAINER, Compartment Door Lock		10.267

Exploded view and parts nomenclature for 1964-66 automatic transmission console.

1964-66 GTO automatic shift indicator assembly, broken down to show housing and indicator plate.

Detail of courtesy lamp housing with switch used in some 1964-65 automatic transmission consoles.

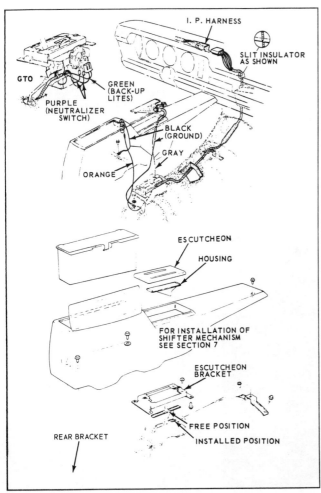

Installation and wire routing instructions for 1968 GTO automatic transmission console. Rear bracket was welded to floor pan.

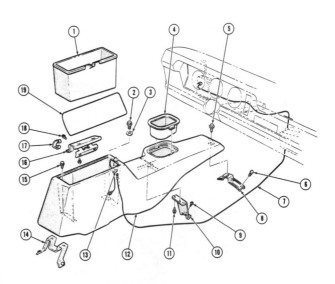

Key	Part Name	Group No.
1 — BOX, Console Compartment		10.240
2 — SCREW, Console to Floor (#10-16 x 5/8" Hex. Hd.)		8.977
3 — WASHER, Console to Floor (7/32" I.D. x 9/16" O.D. x 13/32")		N.S.
4 — ESCUTCHEON, Trans. Floor Console		10.240
5 — SCREW, Console to Mounting Brkt. Front (#10-16 x 3/4" Hex. Hd.)		N.S.
6 — SCREW & SEALER ASM., Console Front Mounting Bracket to Floor		14.630
7 — WIRE HARNESS, Console Jumper		13.090
8 — BRACKET, Console to Floor Mounting - Front		10.240
9 — SCREW, Console Support Brkt. to Floor (#10-16 x 5/8" Hex. Hd.)		8.977
10 — BRACKET, Console Support		10.240
11 — SCREW, Console Support Brkt. to Console (#10-16 x 1/2" Hex. Hd.)		N.S.
12 — CONSOLE, Transmission Floor		10.240
13 — SWITCH ASM., Console Compt. Lamp		10.275
14 — SUPPORT, Console to Floor Mounting - Rear (Welded to Floor Pan)		10.240
15 — SCREW, Console to Mounting Brkt. - Rear (#10-16 x 5/8" Hex. Hd.)		8.977
16 — HINGE ASM., Console Compt. Door		10.242
17 — SPRING, Console Compt. Door		10.242
18 — SCREW, Console Door Hinge to Door (#8-18 x 1/2" Rd. Hd.)		8.977
19 — DOOR, Console Compartment Box		10.242

Compartment box and console door were interchangeable with automatic console parts for 1968-70.

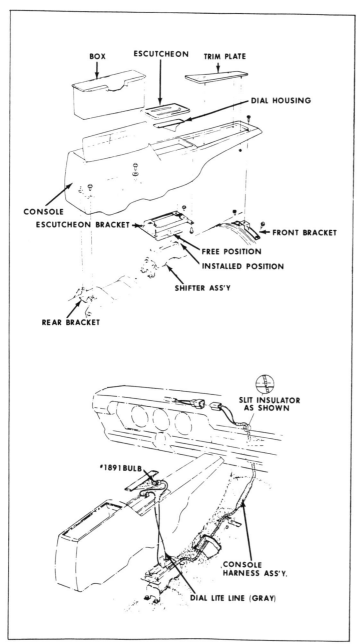

Installation of 1969 automatic console.

View of 1969-70 Rally Sport shifter used for all GTO automatic transmission applications.

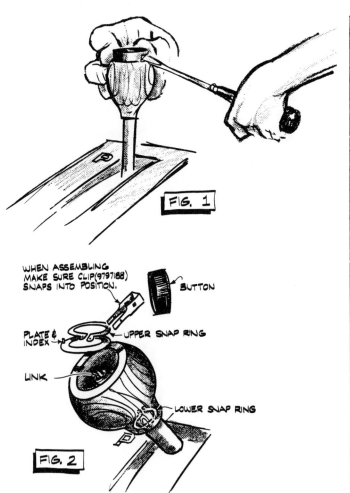

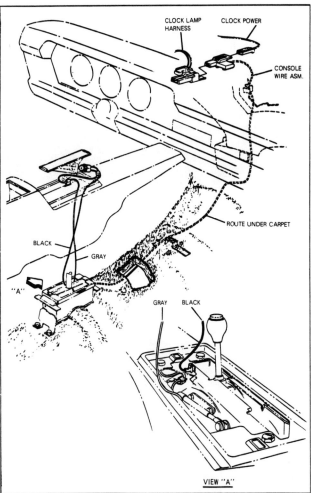

Dealer Service Information Bulletin number 69-I-18, dated 11-10-68, reported this procedure for removing the 1969 floor shift knob on models with the console and Turbo Hydra-matic transmission. First, place the selector in Park position and insert a screw driver into each notch located on each side of the center button and pry button off. Remove retaining clip (9797188) from center actuator link; in some cases the clip will come off when center button is removed. Then remove upper snap ring located inside the shift knob and lift special plate and knob off shift lever. If console is to be removed also remove the lower snap ring from the shift lever. When reassembling do not attach clip to knob and try to install as a sub-assembly to link, as this will cause the clip to bend or break.

While this installation for 1970 was almost identical to the 1969, it did not interconnect to the instrument panel harness.

CONSOLE, MANUAL TRANSMISSION

1964-65

As was the case with the automatics, manual transmission consoles shared many similarities. The 1964 console top had a bluish-gray tint; the 1965 console had a black and chrome motif.

The 1964 two-piece console top (part number 9774725 front and 9774793 rear) used a gray shift lever opening cover (part number 9776823) that slid under the console opening with the movement of the shift lever. The console door (part number 9774188) was also chrome ribbed, with gray trim.

The 1965 console top (part number 9780589 front and 9781522 rear) used a removable escutcheon (part number 9780577) painted 60° gloss black. No shift lever opening cover was used, as had been in 1964.

The plastic console base (part number 9774995) was shared by both years, and was painted to match the interior color. Parchment interiors had black console bases.

The courtesy lamp at the rear of the console was serviced with the same part numbers as the automatic console courtesy lamp.

1966-67

The 1966 manual transmission console was identical in all respects to the 1965. The 1967 console used the same base (part number 9774995), but had a wood insert on the console top (part number 9788092), and was serviced as one assembly. The console compartment door was identical to the one used on automatic consoles.

The gearshift opening escutcheon (part number 9788042) was redesigned in 1967 to accommodate the flat console top. It also had different mounting stud placement, and the bottom of the escutcheon had a wider opening. The escutcheon was painted 0° gloss black for both years.

The courtesy lamp at the rear of the console was serviced by the same part numbers as the automatic console.

1968-70

The console design was the same for 1968-70, and was color keyed to match the interior trim (except with parchment interiors, which used a black console). The console compartment box and lid were the same as for the 1968-70 automatic console, and used the same part numbers. The shifter opening escutcheon (part number 9791125) was the same for all three years, and was painted black with chrome trim around the inside lip.

The console was mounted to the floor by a center support bracket (part number 9791203) using a number 10 16x½ inch hex-screw, and by a front floor-to-console bracket (part number 9791364), using a number 10 16x¾ inch hex-head screw.

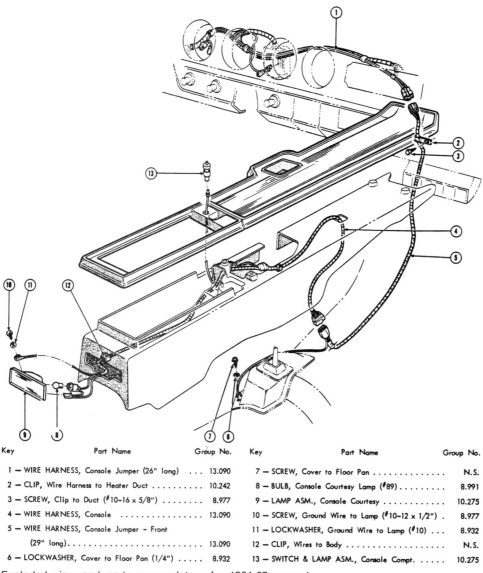

Key	Part Name	Group No.	Key	Part Name	Group No.
1 — WIRE HARNESS, Console Jumper (26" long)		13.090	7 — SCREW, Cover to Floor Pan		N.S.
2 — CLIP, Wire Harness to Heater Duct		10.242	8 — BULB, Console Courtesy Lamp (#89)		8.991
3 — SCREW, Clip to Duct (#10-16 x 5/8")		8.977	9 — LAMP ASM., Console Courtesy		10.275
4 — WIRE HARNESS, Console		13.090	10 — SCREW, Ground Wire to Lamp (#10-12 x 1/2")		8.977
5 — WIRE HARNESS, Console Jumper - Front			11 — LOCKWASHER, Ground Wire to Lamp (#10)		8.932
(29" long)		13.090	12 — CLIP, Wires to Body		N.S.
6 — LOCKWASHER, Cover to Floor Pan (1/4")		8.932	13 — SWITCH & LAMP ASM., Console Compt.		10.275

Exploded view and parts nomenclature for 1964-67 manual transmission console (1964 shown). Note routing of harness for glovebox and courtesy lamps.

Shift lever knobs used in 1964-66. Three-speed knob on left (part number 9781840) was used in 1966 only. White four-speed knob (part number 9776121) was used 1964-66.

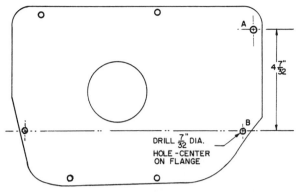

1964 Tempests built before October 7, 1963, with a three- or four-speed synchromesh transmission and console, or a four-speed floor shift, used a screw at (A) to attach the transmission shift control cover to the floor pan. (See Figure 7-11, 1964 Tempest Chassis Shop Manual.) However, this rearmost screw was located directly over the propeller shaft and, under certain conditions, the shaft could hit the screw resulting in a damaged propeller shaft. All cars should be inspected for this condition and reworked as follows: Remove those parts necessary to perform the following steps. Remove screw at (A) and fill hole with body sealer. Drill a 7/32-inch-diameter hole on the center of the flange at (B). Install screw and sealer at (B). (This information and illustration taken from Pontiac Service News Flash number 64-20 dated 10-23-63.)

Manual transmission shifter seal used in 1964-65 (part number 9771974). Seal was used in 1964 with or without optional console; in 1965, without console only. Pictured chrome retainer plate (part number 535910) was used in 1964-65 nonconsole applications. A black retainer plate (part number 9775002), identical in shape, was used in 1964 console applications.

Detail of face of console-mounted optional vacuum gauge. Gauge was located on console top ahead of shifter opening, and was available 1964-67 as accessory package number 984326 (1964), 984547 (1965), 984699 (1966) and 984814 (1967).

Close-up of 1965-66 shifter seal (part number 9780575) used with console. Black retainer plate (part number 9780576) was used for console applications for 1965-66.

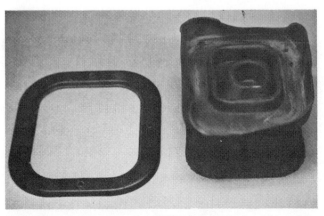

1967 shifter seal (part number 9788235) and black retainer plate (part number 9787707), used with console.

1967 nonconsole seal and retainer plate. The 1967 seal (original part number 9788170, replacement part number 9795407) could be used in place of the 1966 seal (part number 9784914). The retainer plate was chrome (part number 9780055) and was used for 1966 and 1967.

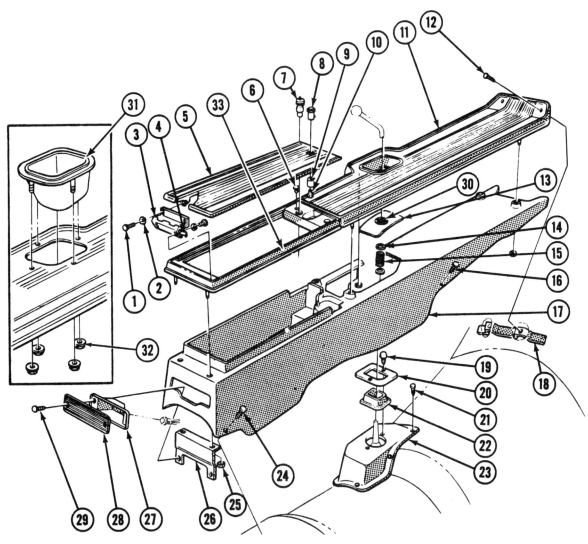

Key	Part Name	Group No.
1 — SCREW, Door to Hinge (#10-24 x 3/8")		8.977
2 — LOCKWASHER, Door to Hinge (#10)		8.932
3 — HINGE ASM., Console Compartment Door		10.242
4 — SPRING, Compt. Door Hold Open		10.242
5 — DOOR, Trans. Console Compt.		10.242
6 — BUMPER, Compt. Door to Top Molding		10.263
7 — SWITCH & LAMP ASM., Console Compartment		10.275
8 — CYLINDER, Console Lock		10.266
9 — RETAINER, Door Lock Retainer		10.267
10 — SCREW, Compt. Lock Retainer		10.267
11 — MOLDING, Console Top – Front		10.240
12 — SCREW, Molding to Floor Bracket (#10-12 x 3/4")		8.977
13 — COVER, Shift Lever Opening		10.240
14 — WASHER, Gearshift Opening Cover Spring (1-1/8" I.D. x 21/32" O.D.)(Early Production)		4.046
15 — SPRING, Gearshift Opening Cover		4.027
16 — SCREW & SEALER ASM., Console to Floor (#10-12 x 1 1/2")		8.977

Key	Part Name	Group No.
17 — CONSOLE, Transmission Floor		10.240
18 — BRACKET, Console Top Molding		10.240
19 — SCREW, Trim Plate to Cover (#8-15 x 5/8")		8.977
20 — PLATE, Control Lever Trim		4.017
21 — SCREW, Cover to Floor Pan		N.S.
22 — SEAL, Trans. Control Lever to Floor		4.015
23 — COVER, Trans. Shift Control		4.010
24 — SCREW & SEALER ASM., Console to Floor (#10-12 x 1")		8.977
25 — NUT, Console Molding		10.240
26 — RETAINER, Console Courtesy Lamp		10.275
27 — LAMP ASM., Console Courtesy		10.275
28 — LENS, Console Courtesy Lamp		10.275
29 — SCREW, Lamp Asm. to Lamp Retainer (#8-15 x 5/8")		8.977
30 — GROMMET, Shift Lever Opening Cover		4.010
31 — ESCUTCHEON, Trans. Floor Console		10.240
32 — NUT, Escutcheon to Console (3/16")		8.921
33 — MOLDING, Console Rear		10.240

Hardware and parts nomenclature for 1964-67 manual transmission console. Note that shift lever opening cover grommet (number 30) was used in 1964 only.

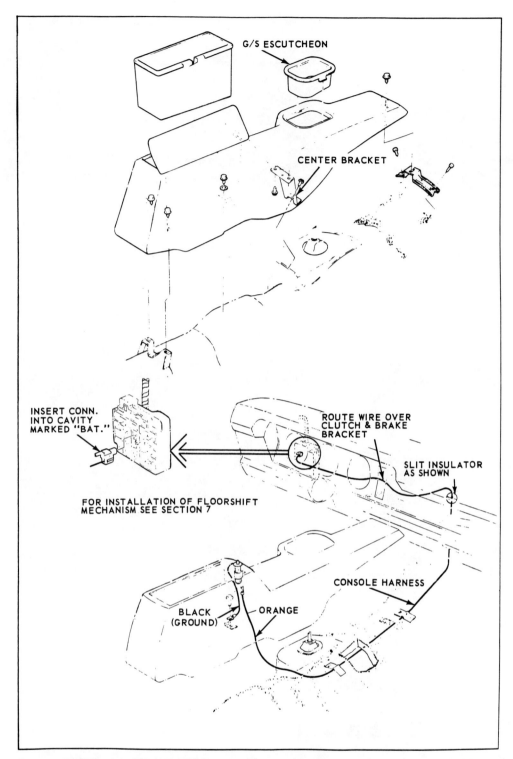

G/S ESCUTCHEON

CENTER BRACKET

INSERT CONN.
INTO CAVITY
MARKED "BAT."

ROUTE WIRE OVER
CLUTCH & BRAKE
BRACKET

SLIT INSULATOR
AS SHOWN

FOR INSTALLATION OF FLOORSHIFT
MECHANISM SEE SECTION 7

CONSOLE HARNESS

BLACK
(GROUND)   ORANGE

Console used for the 1968 and 1970 four-speeds was virtually
identical. Gearshift opening escutcheon was 0° gloss black, with
the inside lip chromed.

Close-up of 1966-68 walnut wood shift knob (accessory part number 984700).

Hurst Dual Gate shifter and opening escutcheon used in 1968 GTO. Compare opening cover to 1967 design.

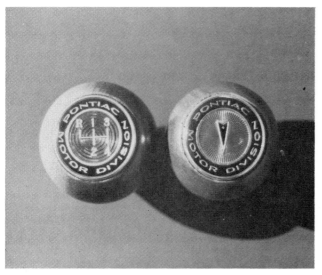

Knob on left is 1969 and 1970 four-speed wood; knob on right is 1969 and 1970 three-speed wood. Note absence of shift pattern on three-speed knob.

Close-up of wood shift knob (part number 9794301) used in 1969-70.

1969 manual transmission and console in the Judge. Note correct deletion of parking brake pedal trim plate, and incorrect after-market radio.

INSTRUMENT PANEL

1964-65

Dash and instrument panel designs were somewhat similar in the 1964 and 1965 GTO. The upper instrument panel assembly was painted 0° gloss. The remainder was done in 60° gloss. The instrument cluster housing assembly was painted 0° gloss. In 1964, an aluminum-turned instrument panel insert was used exclusively on the GTO. The insert was not available under a separate part number, but could be ordered as part of the instrument cluster housing assembly (part number 6408519). A GTO equipped with air conditioning used a different housing assembly (part number 6408520). Replacement housing assemblies were chromed, then painted to match instrument panel trim. Raised areas were left chrome, and then the insert was installed.

Instead of aluminum, the 1965 insert came in one of two versions. The first was a real-wood veneer with open grain on an aluminum backing. The second version was a smooth, paper-backed imitation-wood grain. Both were used in production, and either one came as a replacement. Part number 9781823 was used for cars without air conditioning. Two numbers were used for air-condition-equipped cars: 9781824 LH and 9781825 RH. The housing assembly was again available chrome plated, paint to match (part number 6457246 and 6457247 for air-condition-equipped cars).

Instrument panel molding was of the same design for both years, but the 1964 models had a gray-blue tint between the panel ribs, and 1965 models had black between the chrome ribs.

The 1964 had a wedge-shaped GTO emblem (part number 9775808) mounted flush on the panel above the glovebox. This was not the same as the GTO 6.5 liter emblem on the front fenders.

The 1965 dash panel did not use the emblem. Instead, a nameplate (part number 9783028) was mounted with a grab bar that matched the interior trim. Dash pads were optional and matched the interior trim color. There was a variance in the texture of the Morrokide grain between the 1964 and 1965 pads, but they were interchangeable. There were no parchment (white) dash pads in production models.

1966-67

Dash and instrument panel designs were very similar for 1966 and 1967. The upper instrument panel was painted 0° gloss. The remainder of the panel was 60° gloss. The components of the instrument panel were painted to match interior trim, except when the interior was RPO 224 parchment, in which case all instrument components were black. In 1966, an instrument cluster insert of real-wood veneer on an aluminum backing was used (part number 6457392) and the instrument cluster housing assembly was part number 6457394. If equipped with air conditioning, a larger heater and air conditioning control assembly was used (part number 6457393 for the insert and 6457395 for the instrument cluster housing). Replacement cluster housing assemblies were chromed, then painted to match the interior trim color after which the insert was installed.

Although fundamentally the same in physical appearance and dimensions, the 1967 cluster housing assembly was different. The upper overhang was eliminated, the directional signal indicator was enlarged and split by a thin, chromed bar, and the assembly was covered by an imitation-wood veneer.

As in the case of the 1966 model, there were two different housings, heater controls and inserts used with or without air conditioning.

	With	Without
Instrument cluster housing	6458942	6458941
Heater control assembly insert	6458962	6458961

The instrument panel and housing assembly were painted according to 1966 instructions.

Both years used a GTO nameplate (part number 9783028 in 1966 and 9787400 in 1967) with a grab bar color keyed to match the instrument panel trim color. This assembly was mounted directly above the instrument panel compartment door (part number 4410954).

Instrument panel pads were standard equipment in both 1966 and 1967, and were not interchangeable. Pads matched the instrument panel trim color.

1968-70

The instrument panel was redesigned in 1968. The top of the panel was painted 0° gloss. All other surfaces were painted 60° gloss to match the interior trim color—except when the interior was parchment, in which case all instrument panel components were painted 60° gloss black.

A wood veneer (part number 6481428) was used on the instrument panel. It extended across the glovebox door insert (part number 6481429) and ended in a RH extension insert (part number 6481431). If no radio was ordered, a woodgrain cover plate (part number 9792116) was used. The instrument panel insert was applied to a plate (part number 9790405), which was mounted on the instrument panel. A replacement plate was available (part number 9790319), which came complete with wood insert.

There were two designs in the instrument panel pad for 1968, with or without air conditioning. Due in part to poor air distribution, the inner outlet duct length was changed from 10⅞ inches to 13⅞ inches. This change correlated with the pad change, although research does not show why the change was made to the pad design, as all other parts remained the same. It is not known at this time when the change was made during the production year. However, the vehicle identification numbers are known.

Models built before VIN B (Baltimore) 109291, K (Kansas City) 112258, Z (Fremont) 114472, G (Framingham) 118664 and P (Pontiac) 194379 used the first-design pad. Units built after these VINs used the second-design pad. The two series of pad numbers are listed below.

Color	1st Design	2nd Design
black	9790741	9794179 (AC)
red	9791439	9794154
blue	9791440 (AC)	9794181 (AC)
	9791445	9794155
teal	9794182 (AC)	9794182 (AC)
turquoise	9791442	9794157
	9791447 (AC)	9794183 (AC)

There were some pads that remained unaffected by the change. Their part numbers were as follows.

Color	Air Conditioning	No Air Conditioning
black		9794153
red	9794180	
teal		9794156
gold	9794184	9794158

Early-production GTOs had a few pads that were similar in texture and grain to the Cordova top. Later pads, such as the second-design, had a "pinpoint" grain, similar to the grain used on the 1966-67 pads.

The 1968 pad for cars not equipped with air conditioning used a courtesy lamp assembly in the center of the pad. Pads with air-conditioned models used a center outlet nozzle in the same location.

The 1969 instrument panel was redesigned, and used no insert or plate around the instrumentation. A wood insert molding was used on the lower section of the

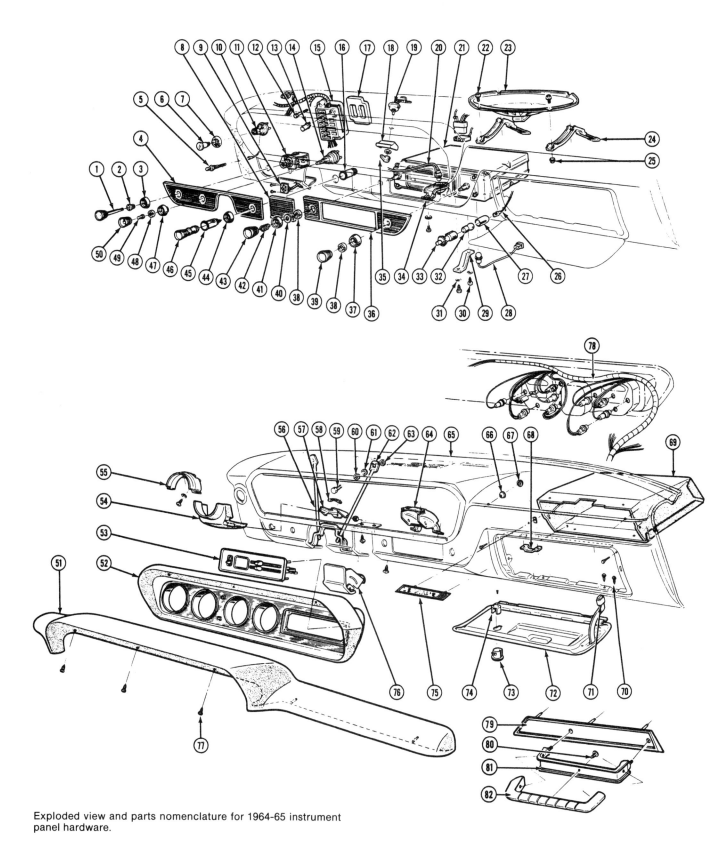

Exploded view and parts nomenclature for 1964-65 instrument panel hardware.

Key	Part Name	Group No.
1 — KNOB, Headlamp Switch Control	2.486
2 — BUSHING, Switch Mounting Nut	2.487
3 — BEZEL, Headlamp Switch	2.487
4 — MOLDING, Inst. Panel-L.H.	10.252
5 — SWITCH ASM., Door Jamb-Front (Single Contact).	11.950
6 — CYLINDER, Ignition Lock	2.188
7 — FERRULE, Ignition Switch	2.192
8 — MOLDING, Ash Tray	10.252
9 — SWITCH ASM., Window-W/Wire	12.195
10 — SWITCH, Starter and Ignition	2.188
11 — SWITCH, Headlamp	2.485
12 — SCREW, Fuse Block to Dash (#10-16 x 1-3/4")	N.S.
13 — FLASHER, Directional Signal	2.892
14 — SWITCH ASM., Windshield Wiper	10.163
15 — BLOCK, Fuse (Part of Inst. Panel Wire Harness)	2.480
16 — RETAINER, Lighter Clamping	9.709
17 — GASKET, Inst. Panel Main Wire Asm. Fuse Panel	2.483
18 — BEZEL, Antenna Switch	9.647
19 — SWITCH AND WIRE ASM., Antenna	9.647
20 — SOCKET AND WIRE ASM., Courtesy Lamp	10.275
21 — RECEIVER, Radio...(Serviced in Accessory Package Only)	
22 — SCREW, Bracket to Inst. Panel (#10-24 x 7/8")	8.977
23 — SPEAKER ASM., Radio-Front	9.650
24 — BRACKET, Radio Speaker Mounting	9.655
25 — NUT, Speaker to Bracket (#10-24)	8.921
26 — WIRE ASM., Inst. Panel Compartment (45" long)	10.275
27 — HOOD, Inst. Panel Compartment Lamp	10.275
28 — WIRE ASM., Radio Lamp (15-1/2" long)	9.650
29 — SUPPORT, Radio Receiver	9.667
30 — SCREW, Support to Radio (#10-12 x 5/8")	8.977
31 — WASHER, Support to Radio (13/64 I.D. x 15/32"O.D.)	N.S.
32 — BULB, Inst. Panel Compt. Light (#1895)	8.991
33 — SWITCH AND LAMP ASM., Inst. Panel Compt.	10.275
34 — LENS AND RETAINER ASM., Inst. Panel Courtesy	10.275
35 — KNOB, Antenna Control	9.647
36 — MOLDING, Inst. Panel-w/Radio-R.H.	10.252
37 — KNOB, Radio Dummy	9.649
38 — NUT, Radio Dummy Knob	9.649
39 — KNOB, Tuning and Volume Control	9.649
40 — SPACER, Radio Tone Control	9.649
41 — KNOB, Radio Tone Control	9.649

Key	Part Name	Group No.
42 — SPRING, Control Knob	9.649
43 — KNOB, Tuning and Volume Control	9.649
44 — BEZEL, Lighter to Inst. Panel	9.709
45 — HOUSING ASM., Cigar Lighter	9.709
46 — KNOB, PLUG AND ELEMENT, Cigar Lighter	9.709
47 — BEZEL, Windshield Wiper Switch	10.166
48 — NUT, Windsheild Wiper Control (1/2"-28 x 5/8")	10.151
49 — BUTTON, Wiper Control Knob	10.164
50 — KNOB, Windshield Wiper and Washer	10.164
51 — PAD PKG., Inst. Panel (Incl. #66-67)	14.655
52 — *HOUSING ASM., Inst. Cluster	9.743
53 — CONTROL ASM., Heater	8.849
54 — COVER, Inst. Panel Strg. Col. Opening-Lower	6.758
55 — COVER, Inst. Panel Strg. Col. Opening-Upper	6.758
56 — SUPPORT, Steering Column - L.H.	6.750
57 — RETAINER, Inst. Panel Strg. Col. Opening Cover	6.758
58 — RETAINER, Strg. Col. Cover to Inst. Panel-Upper	6.750
59 — BOLT, Support to Dash (5/16"-18 x 3/4")	8.900
60 — LOCKWASHER, Support to Dash (5/16")	8.931
61 — WASHER, Support to Dash (5/16")	8.929
62 — SUPPORT, Steering Column - R.H.	6.750
63 — GASKET, Support to Plenum	6.761
64 — RETAINER ASM., Ash Tray	12.009
65 — PANEL, Instrument	10.230
66 — WASHER, Bezel to Inst. Panel	10.252
67 — NUT, Bezel to Inst. Panel (#10-24)	8.921
68 — STRIKER, Inst. Panel Compt. Door Lock	10.268
69 — COMPARTMENT, Instrument Panel	10.260
70 — SCREW, Compt. Door to Panel (#8-15 x 7/16")	10.260
71 — BUMPER, Compt. Door Stop	10.268
72 — DOOR ASM., Inst. Panel Compartment	10.261
73 — CASE, Inst. Panel Compt. Door	10.266
74 — RETAINER, Inst. Panel Compt. Door Lock	10.267
75 — PLATE, Inst. Panel Name	10.254
76 — ASH TRAY ASM., Inst. Panel (Incl. Ash Box)	12.009
77 — SCREW, Cushion to Housing (#10-12 x 7/8")	8.977
78 — WIRE HARNESS, Inst. Panel	2.480
79 — PLATE ASM., Inst. Panel Name	10.252
80 — SCREW, Assist Grip Pad to Handle (#8-18 x 1/2")	8.977
81 — HANDLE, Assist Grip	14.660
82 — PAD ASM., Assist Grip	14.655

panel (part number 9796906 RH and 9796907 LH). If the GTO was not equipped with a radio, RH molding part number 9797794 was used. No cover plate was necessary with this molding. Early-production GTOs had a nameplate (part number 9798895) located above the heater control assembly on non-air-conditioned models only. This nameplate was discontinued in mid-February 1969 (as reported in Dealer Service Information Bulletin number 69-I-49, dated 2-24-69).

In 1970, the panel was again redesigned. The instrument panel plate (part number 480298 with air conditioning and 480295 without air conditioning) was covered with a woodgrain insert. Non-air-conditioned models had a black Pontiac nameplate to cover the center air-conditioning duct opening. The instrument panel molding was engine-turned-aluminum appliqué.

The heater control assemblies were different for each year, with and without air conditioning.

Year	With	Without
1968	7306722	7306002
1969	7307822	7307802
1970	7311882	7311872

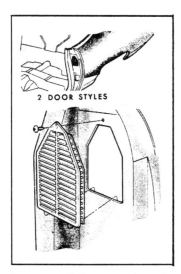

Pressure relief system aided flow-through ventilation. Grilles were cast in black plastic, but for restoration they can be painted 60° gloss black.

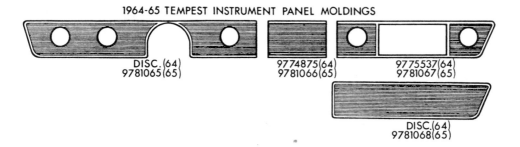

1964-65 TEMPEST INSTRUMENT PANEL MOLDINGS

DISC. (64) 9781065(65)

9774875(64) 9781066(65)

9775537(64) 9781067(65)

DISC.(64) 9781068(65)

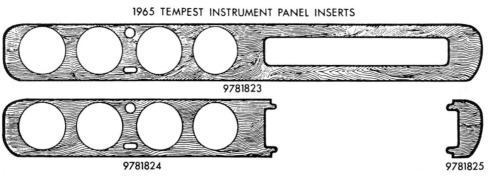

1965 TEMPEST INSTRUMENT PANEL INSERTS

9781823

9781824

9781825

1964-65 instrument panel moldings and part numbers. Some 1964 parts were discontinued.

Optional 1964-67 courtesy lamp (RPO 491), mounted on bottom of instrument panel, was activated by headlamp switch or open door. It was standard on convertibles.

Detail of 1964 GTO. Note incorrect pedal pads and that air conditioning nozzles are painted, rather than chromed.

Interior of 1964 GTO. Note correct GTO emblem above glovebox door, and location of vacuum gauge.

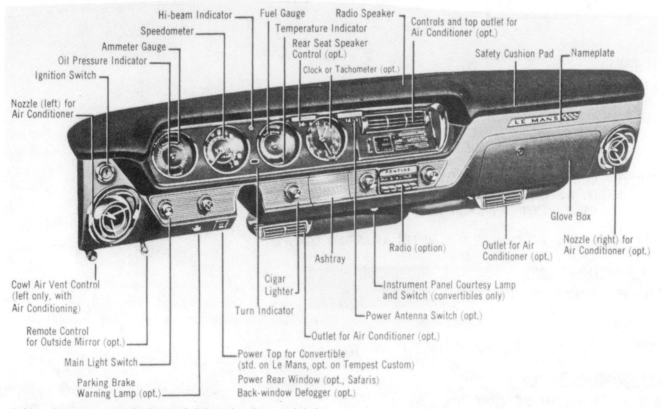

LeMans instrument panel with the full line of options and their correct locations. LeMans nameplate would be replaced by GTO plate in same location.

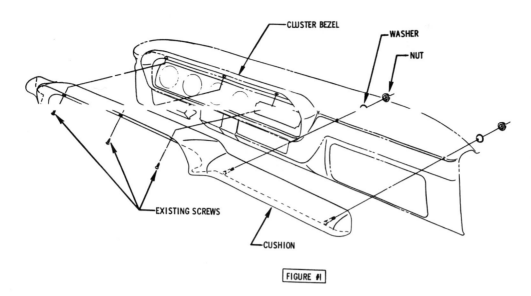

FIGURE #1

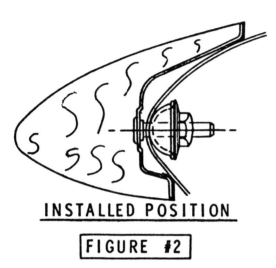

INSTALLED POSITION

FIGURE #2

ALL CARS

STEP #1 - CHALK THE ENDS OF THE TWO STUDS ON THE CUSHION.

STEP #2 - ALIGN THE THREE HOLES IN THE CUSHION WITH THE CORRESPONDING THREE SCREWS IN THE CLUSTER BEZEL AND TRANSFER THE CHALK ON THE STUD ENDS TO THE INSTRUMENT PANEL.

STEP #3 - CENTERPUNCH THESE LOCATIONS AT THE CENTER OF THE ROUND EDGE ON THE INSTRUMENT PANEL (FIGURE #2) AND DRILL 1/4 DIAMETER HOLES USE CAUTION TO PREVENT DAMAGE TO OBJECTS BEHIND THE PANEL.

STEP #4 - REMOVE THE CLUSTER BEZEL UPPER ATTACHING SCREWS.

AIR CONDITIONED CARS

STEP #5 - REMOVE THE GLOVE BOX.

ALL CARS

STEP #6 - INSTALL THE CUSHION (FIGURES #1 AND #2).

AIR CONDITIONED CARS

STEP #7 - REINSTALL THE GLOVE BOX.

Field installation instructions. (This information and these illustrations were taken from GMC Instruction Sheet number 9775098, revision number 1, dated 6-18-63.)

Components of 1965 instrument panel. Headlamp switch knob (part number 9773884) was interchangeable with 1964. LH molding (part number 9781065) was unique to 1965.

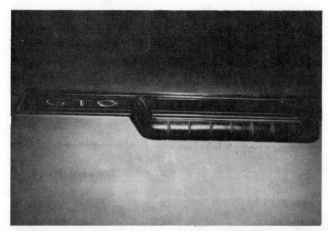

1965 grab bar was made up of three components: a nameplate (part number 9777154), an assist grip handle (part number 9777164) and an assist grip pad, which was color keyed to match the instrument panel trim.

A. LOOSENESS -

1. Carefully lift the insert away from the instrument panel.

2. Apply a thin layer of trim cement (3M VINYL TRIM ADHESIVE, 3M SUPER WEATHERSTRIP ADHESIVE, or equivalent) to the instrument panel and also to the wood insert.

3. Let stand a few moments until cement becomes tacky.

4. Carefully press the insert into place.

B. REPLACEMENT - NEW INSERT -

1. Remove original wood grain insert from the instrument panel.

2. Remove the paper from the new aluminum-backed wood grain insert and apply a thin layer of trim cement.

3. Also apply a thin layer of trim cement to the instrument panel.

4. Let stand for a few moments until cement becomes tacky.

5. Align the wood grain insert with the instrument panel and carefully press into place.

This is the procedure for reapplying or replacing the wood-grain instrument panel insert, as reported in Pontiac Service News Flash number 65-107, dated 6-9-65.

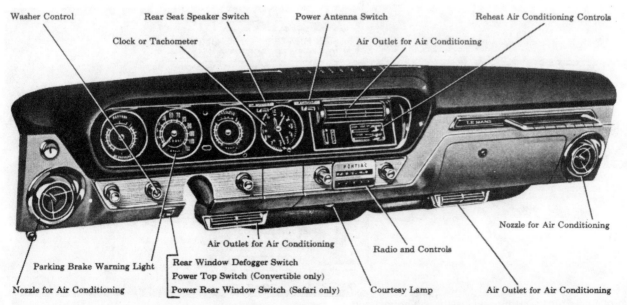

Washer Control
Rear Seat Speaker Switch
Power Antenna Switch
Reheat Air Conditioning Controls
Clock or Tachometer
Air Outlet for Air Conditioning
Nozzle for Air Conditioning
Air Outlet for Air Conditioning
Parking Brake Warning Light
Rear Window Defogger Switch
Power Top Switch (Convertible only)
Power Rear Window Switch (Safari only)
Radio and Controls
Nozzle for Air Conditioning
Courtesy Lamp
Air Outlet for Air Conditioning

1965 instrument panel showing most available options and their correct location on panel. LeMans nameplate next to assist han- dle was later replaced by GTO plate, and wood-grain insert was later used around instrument pods.

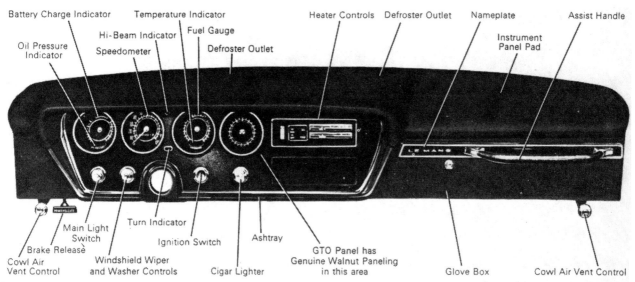

Battery Charge Indicator
Temperature Indicator
Heater Controls
Defroster Outlet
Nameplate
Assist Handle
Oil Pressure Indicator
Hi-Beam Indicator
Fuel Gauge
Instrument Panel Pad
Speedometer
Defroster Outlet

Main Light Switch
Turn Indicator
Brake Release
Ignition Switch
Ashtray
Cowl Air Vent Control
Windshield Wiper and Washer Controls
Cigar Lighter
GTO Panel has Genuine Walnut Paneling in this area
Glove Box
Cowl Air Vent Control

Illustration of typical 1966-67 LeMans/GTO standard instrument panel and related components. Note radio opening cover plate. Cowl vent control handles were not located under instrument panel in 1967. Nameplate above glovebox read GTO on 242 models.

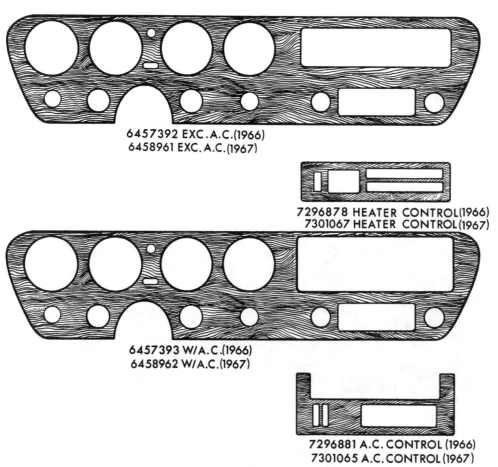

6457392 EXC. A.C. (1966)
6458961 EXC. A.C. (1967)

7296878 HEATER CONTROL (1966)
7301067 HEATER CONTROL (1967)

6457393 W/A.C. (1966)
6458962 W/A.C. (1967)

7296881 A.C. CONTROL (1966)
7301065 A.C. CONTROL (1967)

Drawing of 1966-67 instrument panel inserts with correct part numbers. Note difference in design of heater control and air-conditioning control inserts.

Close-up of 1966 cowl vent knob and bracket. Knob was identical to instrument panel knob design.

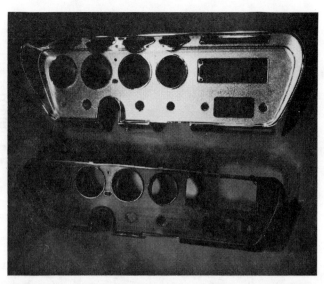

Comparison of 1966 (upper) and 1967 (lower) instrument cluster housing assemblies. Note that 1967 housing did not overhang above instrument pod openings as did 1966. Also, directional signal indicator was enlarged and split by chrome bar. 1966 housing was chromed in preparation for painting. 1967 housing had an enlarged opening for heater and air conditioning control assembly.

Grouping of 1966 instrument panel knobs. Headlamp switch and shaft are on left, with windshield washer button in front of wiper control knob. Rear RH knob and front bezels were for radio.

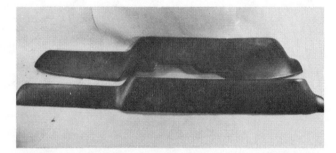

Comparison of 1966 (top) and 1967 dash pads. Photo angle makes 1966 pad appear shorter but both were same length.

Standard instrumentation bale used in right-center pod of instrument panel for 1966-67.

Close-up of standard instrumentation bale used in far LH pod of 1966-67 instrument panel.

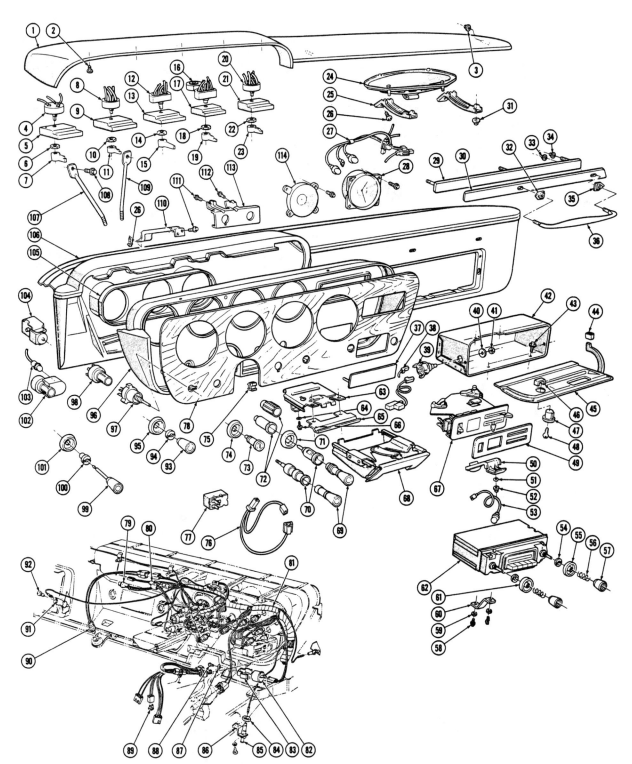

Exploded view of 1967 GTO instrument panel. (Typical for 1966 also, with the exception of instrument panel pad and instrument cluster housing.)

Key	Part Name	Group No.
1	PAD, Instrument Panel Trim	14.655
2	SCREW, Bezel to Cluster Asm. (#10-16 x 7/8")	N.S.
3	NUT, Bezel to Inst. Panel (#10-24)	8.921
4	SWITCH ASM., End Gate Window – w/Wire	12.195
5	BEZEL, Rear Window Switch	12.195
6	NUT, Window Switch to Inst. Panel (3/8"÷32)	12.195
7	KNOB, Rear Window Switch	12.195
8	SWITCH & WIRE ASM., Rear Window Defogger Blower	9.778
9	BEZEL, Rear Window Defogger	9.778
10	NUT, Defogger Switch to Inst. Panel (3/8"÷32)	9.778
11	KNOB, Rear Window Defogger Switch	9.778
12	SWITCH & WIRE, Rear Seat Reverberator	9.665
13	BEZEL, Radio Reverberation Switch	9.649
14	NUT, Rear Seat Speaker Switch to Panel	9.665
15	KNOB, Rear Seat Speaker Switch	9.649
16	SWITCH & WIRE, Rear Seat Speaker	9.665
17	BEZEL, Rear Seat Speaker Switch	9.649
18	NUT, Rear Seat Speaker Switch to Panel	9.665
19	KNOB, Rear Seat Speaker Switch	9.649
20	SWITCH & WIRE ASM., Antenna	9.647
21	BEZEL, Antenna Switch	9.647
22	NUT, Antenna Switch to Inst. Panel	9.647
23	KNOB ASM., Antenna Switch	9.647
24	SPEAKER ASM., Radio – Front	9.650
25	BRACKET, Radio Speaker Mounting	9.655
26	SCREW, Bracket to Inst. Panel (#14-10 x 5/8")	8.977
27	WIRE ASM., Clock	9.772
28	CLOCK ASM., Instrument Panel	9.772
29	PLATE, Inst. Panel Name – "Tempest or Custom"	10.254
30	PLATE, Inst. Panel Name – "Le Mans-Safari or G.T.O."	10.254
31	NUT, Speaker to Bracket (#10-24)	8.921
32	BEZEL, Inst. Panel Assist Grip Mounting – L.H.	14.660
33	NUT, Assist Grip to Inst. Panel (#10-24)	8.921
34	NUT, Name Plate to Inst. Panel (3/16")	8.921
35	BEZEL, Inst. Panel Assist Grip Mounting – R.H.	14.660
36	HANDLE & PAD ASM., Assist Grip	14.660
37	PLATE, Radio Opening Cover	10.256
38	WIRE ASM., Deck Lid Release	12.243
39	SWITCH, Deck Lid Release	12.243
40	WASHER, Lid Switch to Inst. Panel Compt.	12.243
41	NUT, Lid Switch to Inst. Panel Compt. (1/2" x 28)	12.243
42	COMPARTMENT, Inst. Panel	10.260
43	SCREW, Compartment to Inst. Panel	10.260
44	BUMPER, Compartment Door Stop	10.268
45	DOOR ASM., Inst. Panel Compartment	10.261
46	RETAINER, Inst. Panel Compt. Door Lock	10.267
47	CASE, Inst. Panel Compt. Door Lock	10.266
48	KEY, Inst. Panel Compt. (Round)	10.266
49	INSERT, Heater Control Panel	10.252
50	LENS & RETAINER ASM., Inst. Panel Courtesy	10.275
51	WASHER, Lamp to Inst. Panel (13/64" I.D. x 9/16" O.D.)	N.S.
52	SCREW, Lamp to Inst. Panel (#10-16 x 1/2")	8.977
53	WIRE ASM., Radio Lamp Jumper	9.650
54	NUT, Receiver to Inst. Panel	9.667
55	KNOB, Radio Dummy	9.649
56	SPRING, Radio Control Knob	9.649
57	KNOB, Radio Tuning Control	9.649
58	SCREW, Support to Radio Receiver (#10-16 x 5/8")	8.977
59	WASHER, Support to Radio Receiver (13/64" I.D. x 9/16" O.D.)	N.S.
60	SUPPORT, Radio Receiver	9.667
61	KNOB, Radio Tone Control	9.649
62	RECEIVER, Radio (Serviced in Accessory Pkg. Only.)	
63	RETAINER & BRACKET ASM., Inst. Panel Ash Tray	12.009
64	WASHER, Bracket to Inst. Panel (13/64" I.D. x 9/16" O.D.)	N.S.
65	SHIELD, Ash Tray to Inst. Panel	12.009
66	SCREEN, Bracket to Inst. Panel (#8-18 x 1/2")	8.977
67	CONTROL ASM., Heater	8.849
68	TRAY ASM., Inst. Panel Ash	12.009
69	KNOB & ELEMENT, Cigar Lighter	9.709
70	BASE ASM., Cigar Lighter	9.709
71	BEZEL ASM., Cigar Lighter	9.709
72	RETAINER, Cigar Lighter	9.709
73	CYLINDER, Ignition Lock	2.188
74	FERRULE, Ignition & Starter Switch	2.192
75	NUT, Cluster & Housing to Inst. Panel	9.743
76	WIRE ASM., Safeguard Speedometer	2.480
77	BUZZER ASM., Safeguard Speedometer	9.762
78	INSERT, Inst. Panel Cluster	10.252
79	BULB, Inst. Panel Lamp (#1895)	8.991
80	LAMP & WIRE ASM., Ash Tray & Cigar Lighter	12.009
81	HARNESS ASM., Inst. Panel Wire	2.480
82	FLASHER, Direction Signal	2.892
83	CLIP, Direction Signal Flasher Mounting	2.892
84	NUT, Switch to Mounting Brkt. (5/16"-18)	8.915
85	SWITCH ASM., Parking Brake Warning Lamp	4.589
86	BRACKET, Brake Warning Switch Mounting	4.589
87	WASHER, Flasher Clip to Inst. Panel (13/64" I.D. x 9/16" O.D.)	N.S.
88	SCREW, Flasher Clip to Inst. Panel (#10-16 x 1/2")	8.977
89	TERMINAL, Neutral Safety Switch Jumper	2.530
90	SOCKET & WIRE ASM., Courtesy Lamp	10.275
91	SWITCH & LAMP ASM., Inst. Panel Compartment	10.275
92	BULB, Inst. Panel Compt. Lamp (#1895)	8.991
93	KNOB ASM., Windshield Wiper & Washer	10.164
94	NUT, Wiper Control Switch to Panel	10.166
95	BEZEL, Windshield Wiper Switch	10.166
96	HOUSING, Instrument Cluster	9.743
97	SWITCH ASM., Windshield Wiper & Washer	10.163
98	SWITCH, Starter & Ignition (Less Light)	2.188
99	KNOB, Headlamp Switch Control	2.486
100	NUT & BUSHING ASM., Light Switch Mtg.	2.487
101	BEZEL, Light Switch	2.487
102	SWITCH, Starter & Ignition (With Light)	2.188
103	WIRE ASM., Ignition Switch Lamp	2.189
104	SWITCH, Headlamp	2.485
105	CLUSTER ASM., Instrument (Serviced by Components)	
106	PANEL, Instrument	10.230
107	SUPPORT, Steering Column – L.H.	6.760
108	SCREW, Support to Dash (5/16"-18 x 3/4")	8.977
109	SUPPORT, Steering Column – R.H.	6.760
110	BRACE, Speedometer Case	9.743
111	SCREW, Brace to Inst. Panel (#8-18 x 1/2")	8.977
112	SCREW, Support to Cluster Hsg. (#6-32 x 1/2")	N.S.
113	SUPPORT, Inst. Panel Cluster Housing	9.743
114	PLATE, Tachometer or Clock Opening Cover	10.256

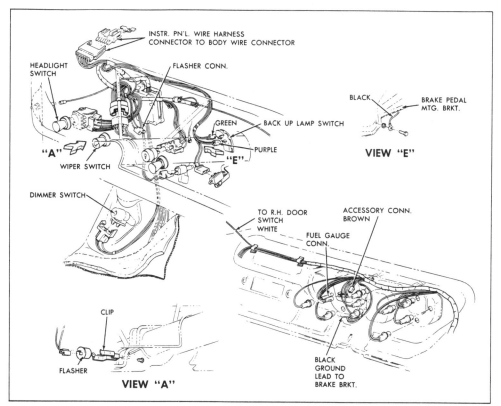

INSTR. PN'L. WIRE HARNESS
CONNECTOR TO BODY WIRE CONNECTOR

HEADLIGHT
SWITCH

FLASHER CONN.

BLACK

BRAKE PEDAL
MTG. BRKT.

BACK UP LAMP SWITCH

GREEN

PURPLE

VIEW "E"

"A"

WIPER SWITCH

"E"

DIMMER SWITCH

TO R.H. DOOR
SWITCH
WHITE

ACCESSORY CONN.
BROWN

FUEL GAUGE
CONN.

CLIP

FLASHER

VIEW "A"

BLACK
GROUND
LEAD TO
BRAKE BRKT.

Drawing of rear of instrument panel, showing wiring harness and
routing for 1966.

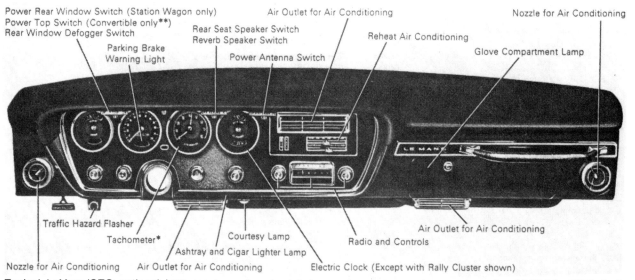

Power Rear Window Switch (Station Wagon only)
Power Top Switch (Convertible only**)
Rear Window Defogger Switch

Parking Brake
Warning Light

Rear Seat Speaker Switch
Reverb Speaker Switch

Power Antenna Switch

Air Outlet for Air Conditioning

Reheat Air Conditioning

Nozzle for Air Conditioning

Glove Compartment Lamp

Traffic Hazard Flasher

Tachometer*

Ashtray and Cigar Lighter Lamp

Courtesy Lamp

Radio and Controls

Air Outlet for Air Conditioning

Nozzle for Air Conditioning

Air Outlet for Air Conditioning

Electric Clock (Except with Rally Cluster shown)

Typical LeMans/GTO optional instrument panel and related
components. Note location of traffic-hazard warning flasher
(accessory package part number 984598 in 1966); flasher was
built into steering column in 1967 and was standard equipment.

1967 interior view showing air conditioning, Custom Sport wheel,
Rally gauges and Hurst Dual Gate shifter.

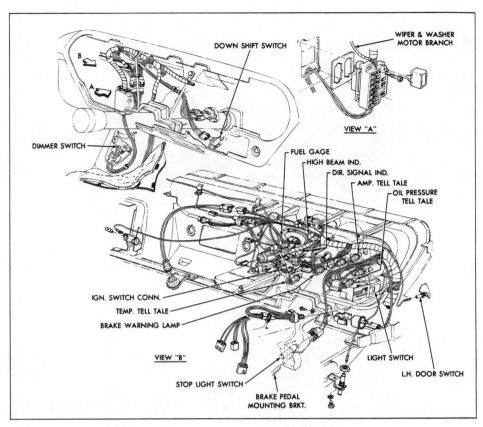

Drawing of 1967 harness. Note location of courtesy lamp option and hazard flasher to fuse block.

Detail of instrument panel cluster housing sticker for 1968; letters were orange. Standard instrumentation is shown.

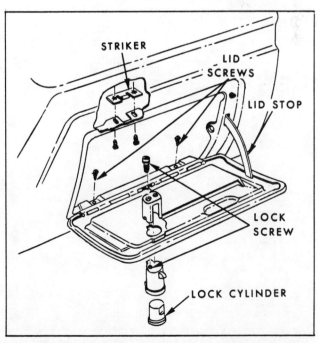

Glovebox door and lock assembly. The case and bolt assembly was the same for 1964-66, part number 4099315. The 1967 part number was 7652251.

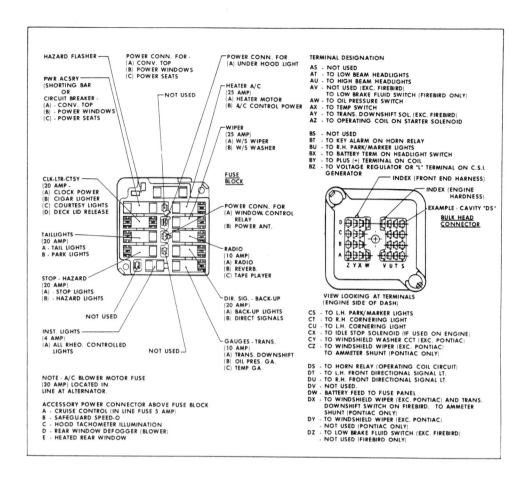

HAZARD FLASHER

PWR ACSRY
(SHORTING BAR
OR
CIRCUIT BREAKER -
(A) - CONV. TOP
(B) - POWER WINDOWS
(C) - POWER SEATS

POWER CONN. FOR -
(A) CONV. TOP
(B) POWER WINDOWS
(C) POWER SEATS

NOT USED

POWER CONN. FOR
(A) UNDER HOOD LIGHT

HEATER A/C
(25 AMP)
(A) HEATER MOTOR
(B) A/C CONTROL POWER

WIPER
(25 AMP)
(A) W/S WIPER
(B) W/S WASHER

CLK-LTR-CTSY
(20 AMP) -
(A) CLOCK POWER
(B) CIGAR LIGHTER
(C) COURTESY LIGHTS
(D) DECK LID RELEASE

FUSE
BLOCK

POWER CONN. FOR
(A) WINDOW CONTROL RELAY
(B) POWER ANT.

RADIO
(10 AMP)
(A) RADIO
(B) REVERB.
(C) TAPE PLAYER

TAILLIGHTS
(20 AMP)
A - TAIL LIGHTS
B - PARK LIGHTS

STOP - HAZARD
(20 AMP)
(A) - STOP LIGHTS
(B) - HAZARD LIGHTS

NOT USED

DIR. SIG. - BACK-UP
(20 AMP)
(A) BACK-UP LIGHTS
(B) DIRECT SIGNALS

INST. LIGHTS
(4 AMP)
(A) ALL RHEO. CONTROLLED
LIGHTS

NOT USED

GAUGES - TRANS.
(10 AMP)
(A) TRANS. DOWNSHIFT
(B) OIL PRES. GA.
(C) TEMP GA.

NOTE - A/C BLOWER MOTOR FUSE
(30 AMP) LOCATED IN
LINE AT ALTERNATOR.

ACCESSORY POWER CONNECTOR ABOVE FUSE BLOCK
A - CRUISE CONTROL (IN LINE FUSE 5 AMP)
B - SAFEGUARD SPEED-O
C - HOOD TACHOMETER ILLUMINATION
D - REAR WINDOW DEFOGGER (BLOWER)
E - HEATED REAR WINDOW

TERMINAL DESIGNATION
AS - NOT USED
AT - TO LOW BEAM HEADLIGHTS
AU - TO HIGH BEAM HEADLIGHTS
AV - NOT USED (EXC. FIREBIRD)
TO LOW BRAKE FLUID SWITCH (FIREBIRD ONLY)
AW - TO OIL PRESSURE SWITCH
AX - TO TEMP SWITCH
AY - TO TRANS. DOWNSHIFT SOL. (EXC. FIREBIRD)
AZ - TO OPERATING COIL ON STARTER SOLENOID

BS - NOT USED
BT - TO KEY ALARM ON HORN RELAY
BU - TO R.H. PARK/MARKER LIGHTS
BX - TO BATTERY TERM ON HEADLIGHT SWITCH
BY - TO PLUS (+) TERMINAL ON COIL
BZ - TO VOLTAGE REGULATOR OR "L" TERMINAL ON C.S.I.
GENERATOR

INDEX (FRONT END HARNESS)
INDEX (ENGINE HARDNESS)
EXAMPLE - CAVITY "DS"
BULK HEAD CONNECTOR

Z Y X W   V U T S

VIEW LOOKING AT TERMINALS
(ENGINE SIDE OF DASH)

CS - TO L.H. PARK/MARKER LIGHTS
CT - TO R.H CORNERING LIGHT
CU - TO L.H. CORNERING LIGHT
CX - TO IDLE STOP SOLENOID (IF USED ON ENGINE)
CY - TO WINDSHIELD WASHER CCT (EXC. PONTIAC)
CZ - TO WINDSHIELD WIPER (EXC. PONTIAC)
TO AMMETER SHUNT (PONTIAC ONLY)

DS - TO HORN RELAY (OPERATING COIL CIRCUIT)
DT - TO L.H. FRONT DIRECTIONAL SIGNAL LT.
DU - TO R.H. FRONT DIRECTIONAL SIGNAL LT.
DV - NOT USED.
DW - BATTERY FEED TO FUSE PANEL
DX - TO WINDSHIELD WIPER (EXC. PONTIAC) AND TRANS.
DOWNSHIFT SWITCH ON FIREBIRD. TO AMMETER
SHUNT (PONTIAC ONLY)
DY - TO WINDSHIELD WIPER (EXC. PONTIAC)
- NOT USED (PONTIAC ONLY)
DZ - TO LOW BRAKE FLUID SWITCH (EXC. FIREBIRD)
- NOT USED (FIREBIRD ONLY)

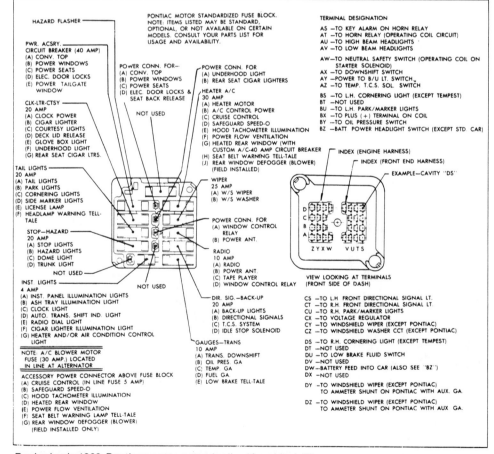

HAZARD FLASHER

PONTIAC MOTOR STANDARDIZED FUSE BLOCK.
NOTE: ITEMS LISTED MAY BE STANDARD,
OPTIONAL, OR NOT AVAILABLE ON CERTAIN
MODELS. CONSULT YOUR PARTS LIST FOR
USAGE AND AVAILABILITY.

PWR. ACSRY
CIRCUIT BREAKER (40 AMP)
(A) CONV. TOP
(B) POWER WINDOWS
(C) POWER SEATS
(D) ELEC. DOOR LOCKS
(E) POWER TAILGATE
WINDOW

POWER CONN. FOR-
(A) CONV. TOP
(B) POWER WINDOWS
(C) POWER SEATS
(D) ELEC. DOOR LOCKS &
SEAT BACK RELEASE

NOT USED

POWER CONN. FOR
(A) UNDERHOOD LIGHT
(B) REAR SEAT CIGAR LIGHTERS

HEATER A/C
30 AMP
(A) HEATER MOTOR
(B) A/C CONTROL POWER
(C) CRUISE CONTROL
(D) SAFEGUARD SPEED-O
(E) HOOD TACHOMETER ILLUMINATION
(F) POWER FLOW VENTILATION
(G) HEATED REAR WINDOW (WITH
CUSTOM A/C-40 AMP CIRCUIT BREAKER
(H) SEAT BELT WARNING TELL-TALE
(J) REAR WINDOW DEFOGGER (BLOWER)
(FIELD INSTALLED)

CLK-LTR-CTSY
20 AMP
(A) CLOCK POWER
(B) CIGAR LIGHTER
(C) COURTESY LIGHTS
(D) DECK LID RELEASE
(E) GLOVE BOX LIGHT
(F) UNDERHOOD LIGHT
(G) REAR SEAT CIGAR LTRS.

TAIL LIGHTS
20 AMP
(A) TAIL LIGHTS
(B) PARK LIGHTS
(C) CORNERING LIGHTS
(D) SIDE MARKER LIGHTS
(E) LICENSE LAMP
(F) HEADLAMP WARNING TELL-
TALE

WIPER
25 AMP
(A) W/S WIPER
(B) W/S WASHER

POWER CONN. FOR
(A) WINDOW CONTROL
RELAY
(B) POWER ANT.

RADIO
10 AMP
(A) RADIO
(B) POWER ANT.
(C) TAPE PLAYER
(D) WINDOW CONTROL RELAY

STOP—HAZARD
20 AMP
(A) STOP LIGHTS
(B) HAZARD LIGHTS
(C) DOME LIGHT
(D) TRUNK LIGHT

NOT USED

INST LIGHTS
4 AMP
(A) INST. PANEL ILLUMINATION LIGHTS
(B) ASH TRAY ILLUMINATION LIGHT
(C) CLOCK LIGHT
(D) AUTO. TRANS. SHIFT IND. LIGHT
(E) RADIO DIAL LIGHT
(F) CIGAR LIGHTER ILLUMINATION LIGHT
(G) HEATER AND/OR AIR CONDITION CONTROL
LIGHT

NOT USED

DIR. SIG. —BACK-UP
20 AMP
(A) BACK-UP LIGHTS
(B) DIRECTIONAL SIGNALS
(C) T.C.S. SYSTEM
(D) IDLE STOP SOLENOID

GAUGES—TRANS
10 AMP
(A) TRANS. DOWNSHIFT
(B) OIL PRES. GA
(C) TEMP. GA
(D) FUEL GA.
(E) LOW BRAKE TELL-TALE

NOTE: A/C BLOWER MOTOR
FUSE (30 AMP.) LOCATED
IN LINE AT ALTERNATOR

ACCESSORY POWER CONNECTOR ABOVE FUSE BLOCK
(A) CRUISE CONTROL (IN LINE FUSE 5 AMP)
(B) SAFEGUARD SPEED-O
(C) HOOD TACHOMETER ILLUMINATION
(D) HEATED REAR WINDOW
(E) POWER FLOW VENTILATION
(F) SEAT BELT WARNING LAMP TELL-TALE
(G) REAR WINDOW DEFOGGER (BLOWER)
(FIELD INSTALLED ONLY)

TERMINAL DESIGNATION
AS —TO KEY ALARM ON HORN RELAY
AT —TO HORN RELAY (OPERATING COIL CIRCUIT)
AU —TO HIGH BEAM HEADLIGHTS
AV —TO LOW BEAM HEADLIGHTS

AW —TO NEUTRAL SAFETY SWITCH (OPERATING COIL ON
STARTER SOLENOID)
AX —TO DOWNSHIFT SWITCH
AY —POWER TO B/U LT. SWITCH
AZ —TO TEMP. T.C.S. SOL. SWITCH

BS —TO L.H. CORNERING LIGHT (EXCEPT TEMPEST)
BT —NOT USED
BU —TO L.H. PARK/MARKER LIGHTS
BX —TO PLUS (+) TERMINAL ON COIL
BY —TO OIL PRESSURE SWITCH
BZ —BATT POWER HEADLIGHT SWITCH (EXCEPT STD. CAR)

INDEX (ENGINE HARNESS)
INDEX (FRONT END HARNESS)
EXAMPLE—CAVITY "DS"

Z Y X W   V U T S

VIEW LOOKING AT TERMINALS
(FRONT SIDE OF DASH)

CS —TO L.H. FRONT DIRECTIONAL SIGNAL LT.
CT —TO R.H. FRONT DIRECTIONAL SIGNAL LT.
CU —TO R.H. PARK/MARKER LIGHTS
CX —TO VOLTAGE REGULATOR
CY —TO WINDSHIELD WIPER (EXCEPT PONTIAC)
CZ —TO WINDSHIELD WASHER CCT (EXCEPT PONTIAC)

DS —TO R.H. CORNERING LIGHT (EXCEPT TEMPEST)
DT —NOT USED
DU —TO LOW BRAKE FLUID SWITCH
DV —NOT USED
DW—BATTERY FEED INTO CAR (ALSO SEE "BZ")
DX —NOT USED

DY —TO WINDSHIELD WIPER (EXCEPT PONTIAC)
TO AMMETER SHUNT ON PONTIAC WITH AUX. GA.
DZ —TO WINDSHIELD WIPER (EXCEPT PONTIAC)
TO AMMETER SHUNT ON PONTIAC WITH AUX. GA.

Beginning in 1968, Pontiac went to a standardized fuse block. The
1968 block (part number 6294006) stood alone. The 1969 (top)
and 1970 (bottom) blocks (part number 8905772) were interchangeable.

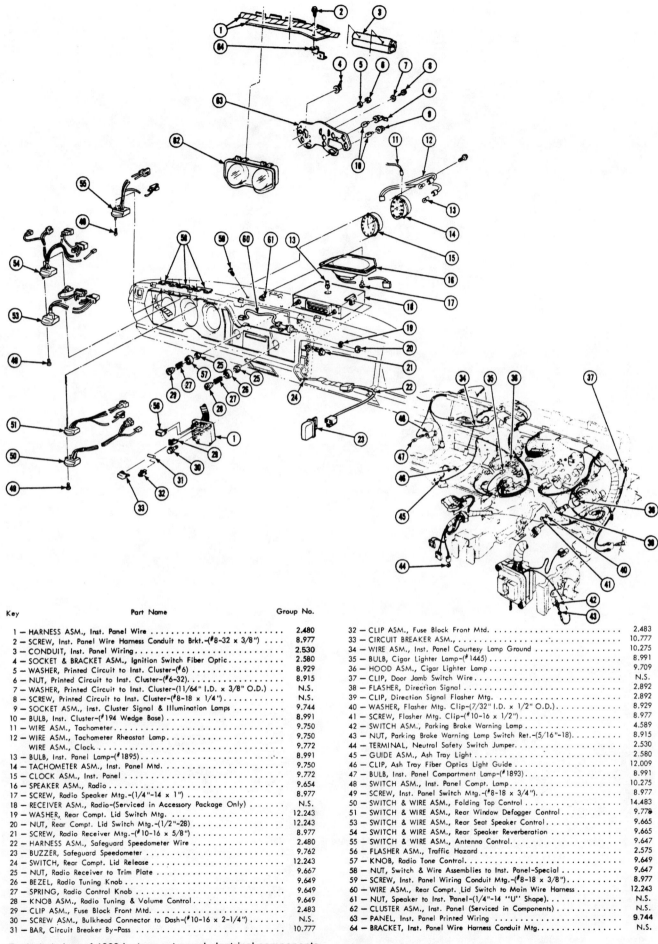

Key	Part Name	Group No.
1 — HARNESS ASM., Inst. Panel Wire		2.480
2 — SCREW, Inst. Panel Wire Harness Conduit to Brkt.-(#8-32 x 3/8")		8.977
3 — CONDUIT, Inst. Panel Wiring		2.530
4 — SOCKET & BRACKET ASM., Ignition Switch Fiber Optic		2.580
5 — WASHER, Printed Circuit to Inst. Cluster-(#6)		8.929
6 — NUT, Printed Circuit to Inst. Cluster-(#6-32)		8.915
7 — WASHER, Printed Circuit to Inst. Cluster-(11/64" I.D. x 3/8" O.D.)		N.S.
8 — SCREW, Printed Circuit to Inst. Cluster-(#8-18 x 1/4")		N.S.
9 — SOCKET ASM., Inst. Cluster Signal & Illumination Lamps		9.744
10 — BULB, Inst. Cluster-(#194 Wedge Base)		8.991
11 — WIRE ASM., Tachometer		9.750
12 — WIRE ASM., Tachometer Rheostat Lamp		9.750
WIRE ASM., Clock		9.772
13 — BULB, Inst. Panel Lamp-(#1895)		8.991
14 — TACHOMETER ASM., Inst. Panel Mtd.		9.750
15 — CLOCK ASM., Inst. Panel		9.772
16 — SPEAKER ASM., Radio		9.654
17 — SCREW, Radio Speaker Mtg.-(1/4"-14 x 1")		8.977
18 — RECEIVER ASM., Radio-(Serviced in Accessory Package Only)		N.S.
19 — WASHER, Rear Compt. Lid Switch Mtg.		12.243
20 — NUT, Rear Compt. Lid Switch Mtg.-(1/2"-28)		12.243
21 — SCREW, Radio Receiver Mtg.-(#10-16 x 5/8")		8.977
22 — HARNESS ASM., Safeguard Speedometer Wire		2.480
23 — BUZZER, Safeguard Speedometer		9.762
24 — SWITCH, Rear Compt. Lid Release		12.243
25 — NUT, Radio Receiver to Trim Plate		9.667
26 — BEZEL, Radio Tuning Knob		9.649
27 — SPRING, Radio Control Knob		9.649
28 — KNOB, Radio Tuning & Volume Control		9.649
29 — CLIP ASM., Fuse Block Front Mtd.		2.483
30 — SCREW ASM., Bulkhead Connector to Dash-(#10-16 x 2-1/4")		N.S.
31 — BAR, Circuit Breaker By-Pass		10.777
32 — CLIP ASM., Fuse Block Front Mtd.		2.483
33 — CIRCUIT BREAKER ASM.,		10.777
34 — WIRE ASM., Inst. Panel Courtesy Lamp Ground		10.275
35 — BULB, Cigar Lighter Lamp-(#1445)		8.991
36 — HOOD ASM., Cigar Lighter Lamp		9.709
37 — CLIP, Door Jamb Switch Wire		N.S.
38 — FLASHER, Direction Signal		2.892
39 — CLIP, Direction Signal Flasher Mtg.		2.892
40 — WASHER, Flasher Mtg. Clip-(7/32" I.D. x 1/2" O.D.)		8.929
41 — SCREW, Flasher Mtg. Clip-(#10-16 x 1/2")		8.977
42 — SWITCH ASM., Parking Brake Warning Lamp		4.589
43 — NUT, Parking Brake Warning Lamp Switch Ret.-(5/16"-18)		8.915
44 — TERMINAL, Neutral Safety Switch Jumper.		2.530
45 — GUIDE ASM., Ash Tray Light		2.580
46 — CLIP, Ash Tray Fiber Optics Light Guide		12.009
47 — BULB, Inst. Compartment Lamp-(#1893)		8.991
48 — SWITCH ASM., Inst. Panel Compt. Lamp.		10.275
49 — SCREW, Inst. Panel Switch Mtg.-(#8-18 x 3/4")		8.977
50 — SWITCH & WIRE ASM., Folding Top Control		14.483
51 — SWITCH & WIRE ASM., Rear Window Defogger Control		9.779
53 — SWITCH & WIRE ASM., Rear Seat Speaker Control		9.665
54 — SWITCH & WIRE ASM., Rear Speaker Reverberation		9.665
55 — SWITCH & WIRE ASM., Antenna Control		9.647
56 — FLASHER ASM., Traffic Hazard		2.575
57 — KNOB, Radio Tone Control		9.649
58 — NUT, Switch & Wire Assemblies to Inst. Panel-Special		9.647
59 — SCREW, Inst. Panel Wiring Conduit Mtg.-(#8-18 x 3/8")		8.977
60 — WIRE ASM., Rear Compt. Lid Switch to Main Wire Harness		12.243
61 — NUT, Speaker to Inst. Panel-(1/4"-14 "U" Shape)		N.S.
62 — CLUSTER ASM., Inst. Panel (Serviced in Components)		N.S.
63 — PANEL, Inst. Panel Printed Wiring		9.744
64 — BRACKET, Inst. Panel Wire Harness Conduit Mtg.		N.S.

Exploded view of 1968 instrument panel electrical components
and parts nomenclature.

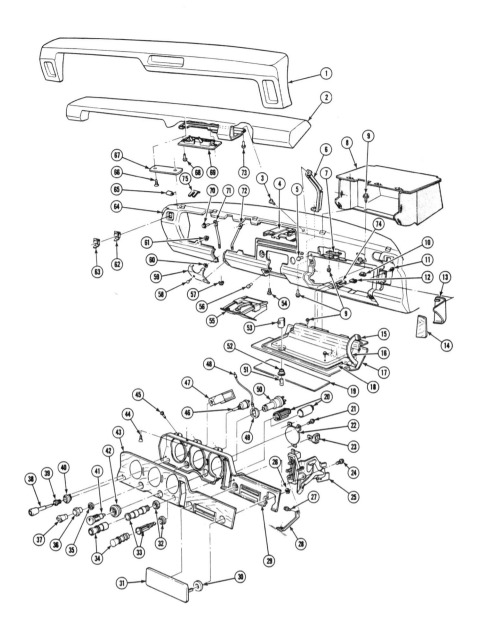

Key	Part Name	Group No.
1 — PAD, Inst. Panel – Upper (w/A.C.)		14.655
2 — PAD, Inst. Panel – Upper (exc. A.C.)		14.655
3 — SCREW, Radio Receiver Brace Mtg. (1/4"–14 x 5/8")		N.S.
4 — RETAINER & BRACKET ASM., Inst. Panel Ash Tray		12.009
5 — BUMPER, Inst. Panel Compartment Door		10.263
6 — BRACE, Radio Receiver		9.667
7 — STRIKER, Inst. Panel Compartment Door Lock		10.268
8 — BOX ASM., Inst. Panel Compartment		10.260
9 — SCREW, Inst. Panel Compt. Door Lock Striker or Inner Panel (#8-18 x 1/2")		N.S.
10 — NUT, Trim Pad to Inst. Panel – Plastic		10.252
11 — SCREW, Inst. Panel Trim Plate Extension Mtg. – (#8-32 x 3/8")		8.977
12 — NUT, Inst. Panel Compt. Door Hinge – (#8-18 "U" Shape)		N.S.
13 — EXTENSION, Inst. Panel Trim Plate		10.252
14 — INSERT, Inst. Panel Trim Plate Extension		10.252
15 — GROMMET, Inst. Panel Compartment Door Stop		10.268
16 — STOP, Inst. Panel Compartment Door		10.268
17 — PANEL, Inst. Panel Compartment Door – Outer		10.261
18 — PANEL ASM., Inst. Panel Compartment Door – Inner		10.261
19 — INSERT, Inst. Panel Compartment Door		10.261
20 — RETAINER, Cigar Lighter to Inst. Panel		9.709
21 — SCREW, Clock Opening Cover Plate Mtg. (#8-18 x 5/8")		N.S.
22 — PLATE, Clock Opening Cover		10.256
23 — CLIP, Inst. Panel Wire Retainer		2.482
24 — SCREW, Heater Control Mtg. (#8-32 x 1/2")		8.977
25 — CONTROL ASM., Heater		8.849
26 — NUT, Radio Opening Cover Plate Mtg. – (#10-24 Stamped)		8.921
27 — SCREW, Control Stabilizer Bracket – (#10-16 x 5/8")		8.977
28 — BRACKET, Heater and Air Conditioner Control Stabilizer		8.852
29 — PLATE, Inst. Panel		10.252
30 — WASHER, Radio Opening Cover Plate Spacer – (7/32" I.D. x 1-1/4" O.D.)		N.S.
31 — PLATE, Radio Opening Cover		10.256
32 — BEZEL, Cigar Lighter to Inst. Panel		9.709
33 — CASE, Cigar Lighter – (Rochester)		9.709
HOUSING, Cigar Lighter – (Casco)		9.709
34 — KNOB, PLUG & ELEMENT ASM., Cigar Lighter		9.709
35 — NUT, Windshield Wiper Control Switch to Inst. Panel		10.166
36 — BEZEL, Windshield Wiper Switch		10.166
37 — KNOB, Windshield Wiper & Washer		10.164
38 — KNOB ASM., Headlamp Switch		2.486
39 — NUT & BUSHING ASM., Headlamp Switch Mtg.		2.487
40 — BEZEL, Headlamp Switch		2.487
41 — CYLINDER, Ignition Lock – Uncoded		2.188
42 — FERRULE, Ignition and Starter Switch		2.192
43 — INSERT, Inst. Panel Trim Plate		10.252
44 — SCREW, Inst. Panel Trim Plate Mtg. – (#8-18 x 1/2")		8.977
45 — SCREW, Inst. Panel Trim Plate Mtg. – (#10-16 x 5/8")		8.977
46 — SWITCH ASM., Windshield Wiper & Washer		10.163
47 — SWITCH ASM., Headlamp		2.485
48 — GUIDE, Ignition Switch Light		2.580
49 — BRACKET, Ignition Switch Light Guide		2.188
50 — SWITCH ASM., Ignition & Starter		2.188
51 — CYLINDER, Compartment Door Lock – Uncoded		10.266
52 — ESCUTCHEON, Inst. Panel Compt. Door Knob		10.267
53 — CASE & BOLT ASM., Inst. Panel Compartment Door		10.26/
54 — SCREW, Ash Tray Retainer & Bracket Mtg. – (#8-18 x 1/2")		N.S.
55 — ASH TRAY ASM., Inst. Panel		12.009
56 — BUMPER, Inst. Panel Ash Tray		12.009
57 — NUT, Strg. Column Support to Support Bracket		6.760
58 — SCREW, Strg. Column Opening Cover Mtg. – (#8-18 x 5/8")		8.977
59 — COVER, Strg. Column Opening		6.760
60 — NUT, Strg. Column Opening Cover to Inst. Panel		6.760
61 — NUT, Inst. Panel Trim Plate to Inst. Panel – (#10-24 Stamped)		8.921
62 — CLIP, Upper Pad to Inst. Panel		14.655
63 — CLIP, Upper Pad to Inst. Panel		14.655
64 — PANEL, Instrument		10.230
65 — PAD, Inst. Panel to Pad – Anti-Squeak		10.252
66 — SCREW, Courtesy Lamp Opening Cover Plate Mtg. – (#8-18 x 5/8")		8.977
67 — PLATE, Inst. Panel Courtesy Lamp Opening Cover		10.256
68 — SCREW, Inst. Panel Courtesy Lamp Mtg. – (#8-18 x 5/8")		8.977
69 — LAMP ASM., Inst. Panel Courtesy		10.275
70 — SCREW, Steering Column Support Mounting (5/16"-18 x 3/4")		8.977
71 — SUPPORT, Steering Column – L.H.		6.760
72 — SUPPORT, Steering Column – R.H.		6.760
73 — SCREW, Inst. Panel Pad to Panel – (#8-18 x 1/2")		N.S.
74 — SHIM, Compartment Door Hinge		10.262
75 — SHIM, Inst. Panel Trim Plate to Panel		10.252

Exploded view of 1968 instrument panel hardware and parts nomenclature. Note difference between air-conditioned and non-air-conditioned instrument panel pads.

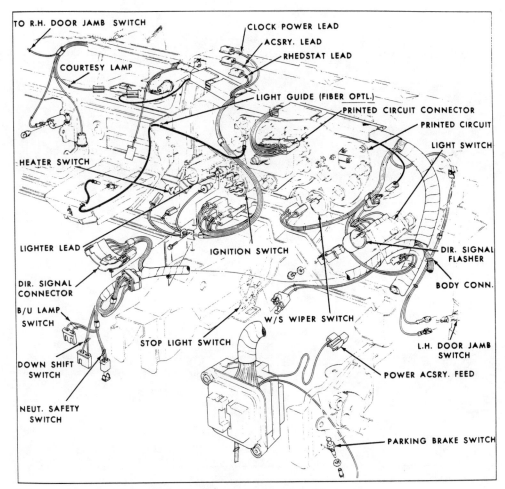

Instrument panel wiring harness for 1968. Note fiber optic guide for ashtray (part number 6293310).

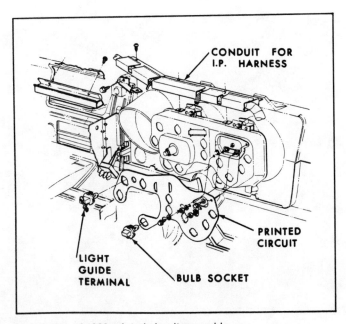

Installation of 1968 printed circuit assembly.

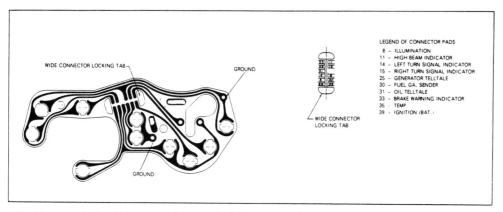

LEGEND OF CONNECTOR PADS

8 – ILLUMINATION
11 – HIGH BEAM INDICATOR
14 – LEFT TURN SIGNAL INDICATOR
15 – RIGHT TURN SIGNAL INDICATOR
25 – GENERATOR TELLTALE
30 – FUEL GA. SENDER
31 – OIL TELLTALE
33 – BRAKE WARNING INDICATOR
35 – TEMP.
39 – IGNITION (BAT.)

1968-70 printed circuit for use with standard instrumentation
(part number 6295409).

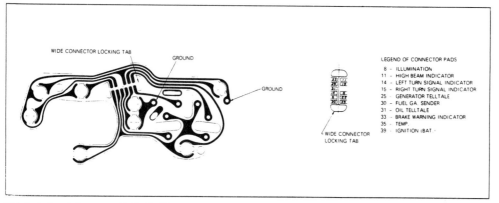

LEGEND OF CONNECTOR PADS

8 – ILLUMINATION
11 – HIGH BEAM INDICATOR
14 – LEFT TURN SIGNAL INDICATOR
15 – RIGHT TURN SIGNAL INDICATOR
25 – GENERATOR TELLTALE
30 – FUEL GA. SENDER
31 – OIL TELLTALE
33 – BRAKE WARNING INDICATOR
35 – TEMP.
39 – IGNITION (BAT.)

Printed circuit for use with Rally Cluster was the same for 1968-70
(part number 6295410).

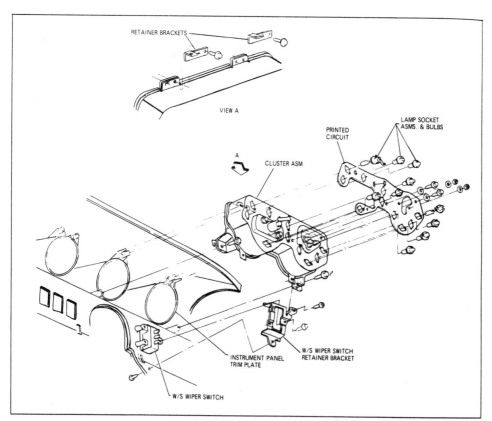

Installation of printed-circuit-to-cluster assembly. Shown is 1970;
1968 and 1969 installations were identical.

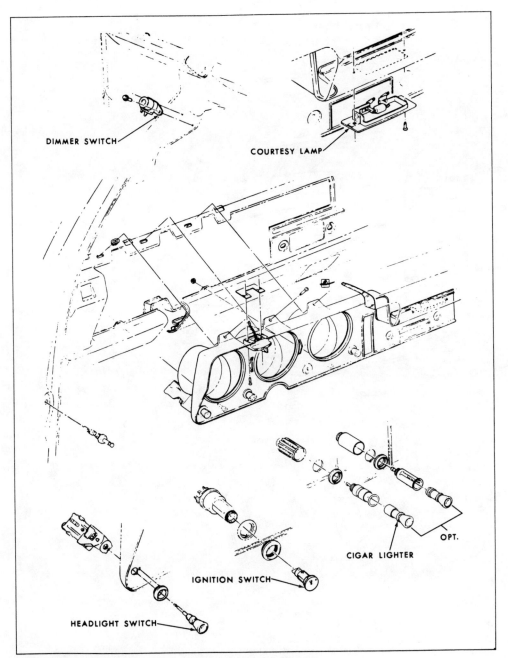

DIMMER SWITCH

COURTESY LAMP

CIGAR LIGHTER

OPT.

IGNITION SWITCH

HEADLIGHT SWITCH

Exploded drawing detailing installation of 1968 instrument panel plate to panel. There were two designs used for the headlamp bezel: The first was the same as that used in 1967, with black letters (part number 9786945). The second design used white letters (part number 9791107).

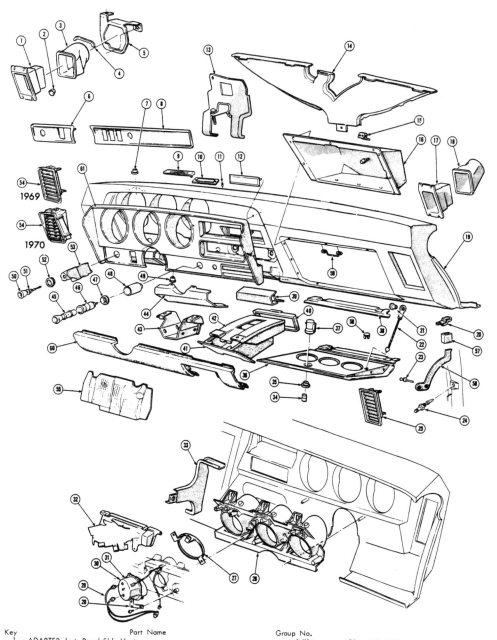

Key	Part Name	Group No.
1 — ADAPTER, Inst. Panel Side Vent		9.786
2 — NUT, Outer Side Adapter to Inst. Panel (# 10-24)		8.921
3 — DUCT, Inst. Panel Side Vent - L.H.		9.786
4 — INSULATOR, Inst. Panel Side Vent Duct to Brkt. - L.H.		9.786
5 — BRACKET, Inst. Panel Side Vent Duct - L.H.		9.786
6 — MOLDING, Inst. Panel - Lower - L.H.		10.252
7 — NUT, Upper Inst. Panel to Dash Attaching		10.252
8 — MOLDING, Inst. Panel - Lower - R.H.		10.252
9 — BEZEL, Vehicle Identification Number		10.252
10 — PLATE, Vehicle Identification Number		N.S.
11 — RIVET, Vehicle Identification Plate to Dash		N.S.
12 — PLATE ASM., Inst. Panel Name		10.254
13 — SUPPORT ASM., Steering Column Upper		6.760
14 — NOZZLE ASM., Defroster Air		9.779
15 — STRIKER, Inst. Panel Comp. Door Lock		10.268
16 — COMPARTMENT ASM., Inst. Panel		10.260
17 — ADAPTER, Inst. Panel Side Vent		9.786
18 — DUCT, Inst. Panel Side Vent - R.H.		9.786
19 — PAD, Instrument Panel		14.655
20 — SUPPORT, Inst. Panel Courtesy Lamp		10.275
21 — RIVET, Inst. Panel Comp. Door Check to Panel		N.S.
22 — STOP ASM., Inst. Panel Compt. Door Cable		10.268
23 — RIVET, Stop Cable End at Door		N.S.
24 — SWITCH ASM., Courtesy Light Door Jamb		10.275
25 — DEFLECTOR, Inst. Panel Side Outer Air		9.264-9.786
26 — ADAPTER, Inst. Cluster		9.743
27 — PLATE, Clock Opng. Cover		10.252
28 — STRAP, Clock to Inst. Panel Bezel - Ground		9.743
29 — WIRE ASM., Clock Lighting		9.772
30 — CLOCK ASM., Inst. Panel		9.772
31 — TACHOMETER ASM.,		9.750
32 — CONTROL ASM., Heater		8.849
33 — SUPPORT, Heater Control		8.852
34 — CYLINDER, Compt. Door Lock (Uncoded)		10.266
35 — ESCUTCHEON, Inst. Panel Compt. Door Knob		10.267
36 — PANEL ASM., Inst. Panel Compt. Door - Outer		10.261
37 — CASE & BOLT ASM., Inst. Panel Compt. Door		10.266
38 — REINFORCEMENT, Inst. Panel Compt. Hinge		10.262
39 — GUARD, Inst. Panel Ash Tray Opng.		12.009
40 — BEZEL, Heater Control Opng.		8.852
41 — ASH TRAY ASM., Instrument Panel		12.009
42 — RETAINER, Instrument Panel Ash Tray		12.016
43 — BRACKET ASM., Steering Column Support - Lower		6.760
44 — COVER, Steering Column Lower Finish		6.760
45 — KNOB, PLUG & ELEMENT ASM., Cigar Lighter		9.709
46 — CASE, Cigar Lighter		9.709
47 — BEZEL, Cigar Lighter to Inst. Panel		9.709
48 — RETAINER, Cigar Lighter Case to Inst. Panel		9.709
49 — NUT, Strg. Col. Cover to Inst. Panel Attach.		10.252
50 — KNOB ASM., Headlamp Switch		2.486
51 — NUT & BUSHING ASM., Headlamp Switch Mtg.		2.487
52 — BEZEL, Headlamp Switch		2.487
53 — SWITCH ASM., Headlamp		2.485
54 — DEFLECTOR, Inst. Panel Side Outer Air		9.264-9.786
55 — COVER, Dash Insulator at Strg. Col. (Plastic)		6.758
56 — PLUG, Compartment Door Stop Hole		10.268
57 — SLEEVE, Compartment Door Stop (1970-72)		10.268
58 — STOP, Compartment Door (1970-72)		10.268
59 — STRIKER, Compartment Door Lock (1970-72)		10.268
60 — COVER, Instrument Panel - Lower (Black) (1970-72)		6.760
61 — PLATE, Instrument Panel Trim (1970-72)		10.252

Exploded view and parts nomenclature for 1969-70 instrument panel components. A number of components were interchangeable from 1970 to 1972.

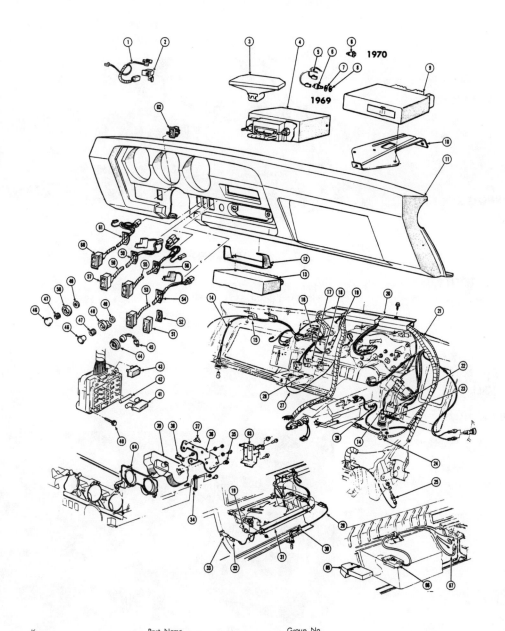

Key	Part Name	Group No.
1 — WIRE HARNESS ASM., Safeguard Speedometer		2.480
2 — BUZZER ASM., Safeguard Speedometer		9.762
3 — SPEAKER, Radio Front		9.654
4 — RECEIVER ASM., Radio	(Serviced in Accessory Pkg. Only)	
5 — WIRE ASM., Rear Compt. Lid Switch to Main Wire Harness		12.243
6 — SWITCH, Rear Compt. Lid Switch		12.243
7 — WASHER, Rear Compt. Lid Switch		12.243
8 — NUT, Rear Compt. Lid Switch		12.243
9 — AMPLIFIER, Reverberation Unit	(Serviced in Accessory Pkg. Only)	
10 — BRACKET, Reverb. Amplifier Mtg.		9.667
11 — PANEL, Instrument		10.230
12 — BRACKET, Stereo Multiplex Adapter		9.667
13 — ADAPTER, Stereo Multiplex	(Serviced w/Radio in Accessory Pkg. Only)	
14 — SOCKET & WIRE ASM., Courtesy Lamp		10.275
15 — CLIP, Engine Wire Harness		2.482
16 — WIRE ASM., Clock		9.772
17 — BULB, Cigar Lighter Asm. (#1445)		8.991
18 — HOOD ASM., Cigar Lighter Lamp		9.709
19 — BULB, Clock Asm.(#1895)		8.991
20 — HARNESS ASM., Inst. Panel Wire		2.480
21 — WIRE ASM., Trans. Neutral Switch (M.T.)		4.054
22 — CLIP, Dir. Signal Flasher Mounting		2.892
23 — FLASHER, Direction Signal		2.892
24 — BULB, Courtesy Lamp (#89)		8.991
25 — SWITCH ASM., Emer. Brake Warning Lamp		4.589
26 — CLIP, Stop Light Wire Harness Lead to Pedal Mtg. Brkt.		2.559
27 — GUIDE ASM., Ash Tray Light		2.580
28 — CLIP, Ash Tray Fiber Optics Light Guide		12.009
29 — SOCKET & WIRE ASM., Courtesy Lamp		10.275
30 — CLIP, Courtesy Light Harness to Inst. Panel		N.S.
31 — CONDUIT, Instrument Panel Wiring		2.482
32 — BULB, Glove Box Lamp (#1891)		8.991
33 — SWITCH ASM., Glove Box Lamp		10.275
34 — STRAP, Wiper Switch to Inst. Cluster		9.735
35 — SOCKET ASM., Inst. Cluster Signal & Illumination Lamps		9.744
36 — PANEL, Inst. Panel Printed Wiring		2.480
37 — SOCKET & BRACKET ASM., Fiber Optic Light Guide		2.480
38 — BRACKET, Inst. Panel Wire Harness		2.482
39 — CLUSTER ASM., Inst. Panel (Serviced in Components)		N.S.
40 — SCREW, Fuse Block to Dash Panel Attaching(#10-16 x 2 1/4" Hex.)		N.S.
41 — CIRCUIT BREAKER, Main Wire Harness - Use w/Power Seat, Windows & End Gate Wind.		10.777
42 — BAR, Circuit Breaker By-Pass - w/Conv. Folding Top		14.483
43 — FLASHER, Direction Signal		2.892
44 — BEZEL, Rear Speaker Fader Control		9.649
45 — CONTROL ASM., Rear Speaker Fader		9.665
46 — KNOB ASM., Radio Tuning & Volume Control		9.649
47 — SPRING, Radio Control Knob		9.649
48 — BEZEL, Radio Tuning Knob		9.649
49 — NUT, Radio Receiver to Trim Plate		9.667
50 — KNOB, Radio Tone Control		9.649
51 — SWITCH ASM., Rear Speaker Reverb. Control		9.665
52 — CLIP, Switch to Inst. Panel Ret.		9.665
53 — SWITCH & WIRE ASM., Power-Flow Vent Control		9.790
54 — CLIP, Switch to Inst. Panel Ret.		9.790
55 — SWITCH & WIRE ASM., Rear Window Defogger		9.778
56 — CLIP, Switch to Inst. Panel Ret.		9.778
57 — SWITCH & WIRE ASM., Power End Gate Window Control		12.195
58 — SWITCH & WIRE ASM., Convertible Top Motor Control		14.483
59 — CLIP, Switch to Inst. Panel Ret.		12.195-14.483
60 — SWITCH & WIRE ASM., Power Antenna Control		9.647
61 — CLIP, Switch to Inst. Panel Ret.		9.647
62 — SWITCH ASM., Windshield Wiper & Washer		10.163
63 — BRACKET, Trim Plate to Pad (1970-71)		10.252
64 — RETAINER, Cluster Face Lens		9.747
65 — LAMP ASM., Utility - Rechargeable Travelite		N.S.
66 — RECEPTACLE ASM., Travelite		8.890
67 — WIRE ASM., Travelite		8.890

Components used in electrical applications for 1969 and 1970, along with parts nomenclature. This instrument panel is correct for 1969.

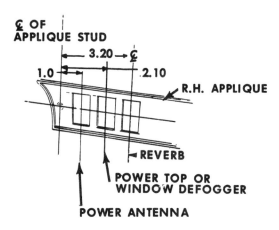

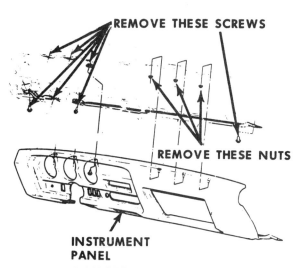

Installation of 1969 GTO instrument panel. Panel was one-piece design; it did not use panel plate, as in 1968 and 1970.

PROCEDURE FOR PIERCING CUTOUTS.

1. LOCATE & PUNCH CENTER OF CUTOUT

2. DRILL 9/16" HOLE THRU DASH & APPLIQUE

3. ASSEMBLE SQUARE STUD OF TOOL J 23118 THRU FEMALE PORTION OF TOOL & INSTALL STUD THRU DRILLED HOLE FROM BEHIND DASH.

4. INSTALL MALE CUTTER & NUT ON STUD.

5. CAREFULLY ALIGN PUNCH WITH OTHER CUTOUTS IN DASH.

6. WHILE HOLDING TOOL FROM ROTATING, TIGHTEN NUT TO PIERCE CUTOUT.

Accessory switch cutout templates for 1969 instrument panel.

LH instrument panel molding on 1969 GTO, showing correct wiper/washer switch and headlamp switch. Hole between controls is incorrect.

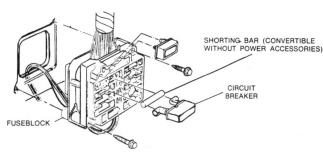

A zinc-coated shorting bar approximately ¼ inch in diameter by 1¼ inches long was used in the circuit breaker fuse block cavity on 1969 convertibles that did not have other power accessories on the same circuit. The power top motor had a self-contained circuit breaker. Convertibles equipped with other accessories (power seats, windows, and so on) used a circuit breaker (part number 1476675) in place of the shorting bar. If accessories were added in the shorting bar circuit, a circuit breaker was substituted for the shorting bar. (This information and illustration taken from Dealer Service Information Bulletin number 69-I-87 dated 8-4-69.)

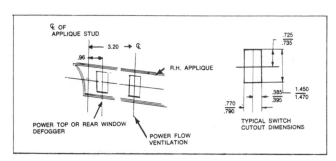

Dimensions for 1970 accessory cutout templates were slightly different from 1969. This 1970 shows only two cutouts. Procedures were the same as 1969.

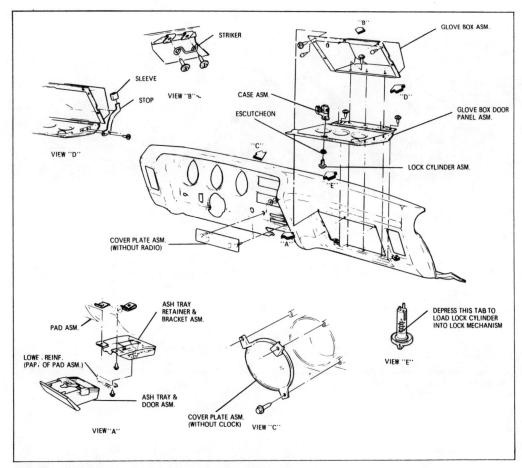

STRIKER

SLEEVE

STOP

VIEW "B"

VIEW "D"

"C"

"B"

GLOVE BOX ASM.

CASE ASM.

ESCUTCHEON

"D"

GLOVE BOX DOOR
PANEL ASM.

LOCK CYLINDER ASM.

"E"

"A"

COVER PLATE ASM.
(WITHOUT RADIO)

PAD ASM.

ASH TRAY
RETAINER &
BRACKET ASM.

LOWER REINF.
(PART OF PAD ASM.)

ASH TRAY &
DOOR ASM.

COVER PLATE ASM.
(WITHOUT CLOCK)

VIEW "A"

VIEW "C"

DEPRESS THIS TAB TO
LOAD LOCK CYLINDER
INTO LOCK MECHANISM

VIEW "E"

Related hardware of 1970 instrument panel. A clock cover was installed when Rally Clock was not ordered on standard instrumentation.

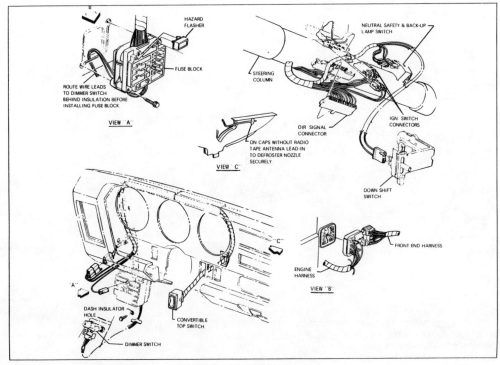

HAZARD
FLASHER

NEUTRAL SAFETY & BACK-UP
LAMP SWITCH

FUSE BLOCK

STEERING
COLUMN

ROUTE WIRE LEADS
TO DIMMER SWITCH
BEHIND INSULATION BEFORE
INSTALLING FUSE BLOCK.

VIEW "A"

DIR SIGNAL
CONNECTOR

IGN SWITCH
CONNECTORS

ON CARS WITHOUT RADIO
TAPE ANTENNA LEAD-IN
TO DEFROSTER NOZZLE
SECURELY

VIEW "C"

DOWN SHIFT
SWITCH

"C"

FRONT END HARNESS

ENGINE
HARNESS

VIEW "B"

DASH INSULATOR
HOLE

CONVERTIBLE
TOP SWITCH

DIMMER SWITCH

Installation of 1970 instrument panel wire harness connections.

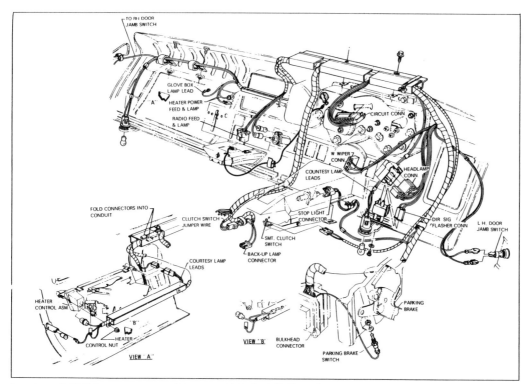

Routing of 1970 instrument panel harness. Note installation of instrument panel courtesy lamp behind glovebox at bottom of panel.

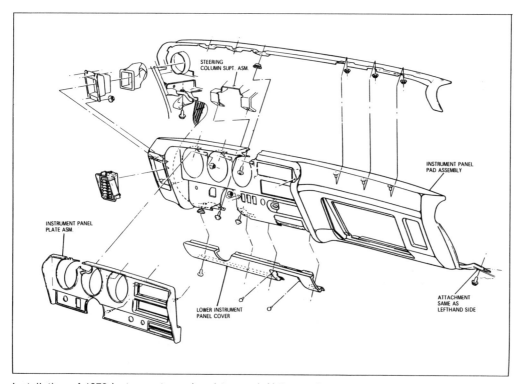

Installation of 1970 instrument panel pad to panel. Note panel plate assembly; air-conditioned plate is shown. Non-air-conditioned models used black Pontiac nameplate in place of outlet duct.

INSTRUMENTATION

1964-65

For 1964-65 the instruments were housed in four round pods recessed in the instrument panel. In the far left pod were the ammeter lamp (upper) and the oil pressure lamp (lower). The left-center pod contained the speedometer. Between the left-center and right-center pods were the Hi-Beam indicator (upper) and the turn indicator (lower). The right-center pod contained the fuel gauge (upper) and the temperature lamp (lower). The far RH pod was either blank or contained the optional clock (RPO 604) or optional tachometer (RPO 452).

In the center of the housing assembly was the heater or heater and air conditioning controls, depending on how the car was equipped. Air-conditioned cars had an outlet vent positioned directly above the control assembly.

The standard dash layout was carried over to 1965. However, with the introduction of the Rally Cluster (RPO 504) the location of the instruments was changed. The background was black—as opposed to the gray-blue background of the standard instrumentation—and the characters were white. The Rally Cluster layout had the fuel gauge (upper) and the battery lamp (lower) in the far LH pod. The speedometer, with one unfurled checkered flag, was above the center of the dial, with provision for the optional brake warning lamp at the bottom of the gauge. The right-center pod held the 8000 rpm tachometer, and the RH pod contained the temperature gauge (upper) and the oil pressure gauge (lower).

Pontiac Service News Flash number 65-27, dated 10-13-64, reported that some early 1965 models had the wrong oil-pressure sending unit installed. The correct one for the GTO was the 93 ohm unit. The correct unit can best be identified by its copper dust cap. Having the incorrect one installed will result in an oil pressure reading about one-third of normal.

There were two different faces used for the tachometer in 1965 Rally Clusters. The first version had a green band around the numbers with no redline shift point on the gauge face. In mid-1965 this face was discontinued in favor of a green band around the numbers that changed to red at 5200 rpm and ended at 8000 rpm. The tachometer part numbers for the 1964 were 6411951 with standard ignition and 6411950 with transistorized ignition. The 1965 tachometers can be identified by the checkered flag and the part number (6412412 with standard ignition and 6412413 with transistorized ignition).

Dash Pad Colors And Part Numbers

1964	Black	9775215
	Aqua	9775350
	Blue	9775351
	Brown	9775352
	Burgundy	9775353
	Gray	9775354
1965	Hampton Blue	9780534
	Teal Turquoise	9780535
	Burgundy	9780536
	Blue Charcoal	9780537
	Bronze	9780538
	Velvet Black	9781469

1966-67

The four-pod design from previous years was carried over into 1966-67. The far LH pod contained the battery charge lamp (upper) and the oil-pressure lamp (lower). The left-center pod housed the speedometer and the optional parking brake warning lamp. Between the center pods were the Hi-Beam indicator (upper) and the directional signal indicator (lower). The right-center pod held the fuel gauge (upper) and the temperature indicator lamp (lower). The far RH pod was either blank (using a cover, part number 9770401) or housed the optional Rally clock (RPO 444).

To the right of the far RH instrument pod was the heater or heater and air conditioning control assembly. Any GTO equipped with air conditioning had an outlet vent directly above the control assembly.

Available for both years was the optional Rally Cluster (RPO 448 in 1966 and RPO 444 in 1967). The background was gray-blue with white letters for both years. The Rally Cluster layout used the fuel gauge (upper) and battery warning lamp (lower) in the far LH pod, a redesigned speedometer face with brake warning lamp in the left-center pod, and the Hi-Beam indicator (upper) and directional signal indicator (lower) between the left-center and right-center pod. The right-center pod contained the 8000 rpm tachometer with a redline band beginning at 5200 rpm and sweeping to the 8000 mark. The far RH pod held the water temperature gauge (upper) and the oil pressure gauge (lower). The oil pressure gauge read from zero to sixty pounds of pressure in 1966 and zero to eighty pounds of pressure in 1967. However, a few 1967 original Rally Clusters have turned up with the sixty-pound gauge.

There were some subtle differences between the two years for the Rally Cluster, such as the oil pressure gauge variations noted earlier. The other difference was in the Rally Cluster cases. Because of the repositioning of the 1967 directional signal indicator, the cardboard tube for for the directional lamp was changed, as was the cluster case.

Year	Case Part Number	Lens Assembly with Set Pointer
1966	6455807	6456167
1967	6458930	6458933
1967	6481312*	—

*This cluster case was for the hood-mounted tachometer only Pontiac had planned to release a Rally Cluster with factory-installed hood tachometer and a Rally Clock in the instrument cluster, as was done in 1968. However, for reasons unknown, the hood-mounted tachometer was offered only as a dealer-installed option until April of 1967, when it became a Regular Production Option (RPO 704; list price $63.19), and could be installed on the assembly line. At least one example of this second-design Rally Cluster is known to exist, although no RPO code has yet been discovered for this option.

The oil and temperature gauge cluster case lens assembly was the same for both years (part number 6456176).

The dealer-installed hood tachometer (accessory package part number 984829) was introduced in the beginning of the 1967 model year. The replacement lens assembly was part number 6468453. The face of the tachometer was gray-blue with white numbers. The name Pontiac was at the bottom of the face and the redline started at 5200 rpm and swept to 8000 rpm. The 1967 tachometer was pop riveted to the hood, and stood approximately three inches high.

The following chart indicates tachometer part numbers and their respective years.

Year	Mounting	With Transistorized Ignition	Without
1966	Cluster	6412944	6412943
1967	Cluster	6468597	6468597
1967	Hood	6468410	6468410

When the standard instrumentation was utilized the Safeguard Speedometer (RPO 441 in 1966 and RPO 442 in

1967) was available. The Safeguard was a preset speed-warning device that would buzz if the preset speed was exceeded. A low-fuel warning lamp was available as part of this option in 1966 only. It could not be ordered with the Rally Cluster.

Instrument Panel Pads

	Color	Part Number
1966	Velvet Black	9782641
	Commodore Blue	9783018
	Marina Turquoise	9783019
	Burgundy	9783020
	Sierra Bronze	9783022
1967	Signal Blue	9788079
	Mariner Turquoise	9788080
	Midnight Champagne	9788081
	Burgundy	9788082
	Black	9788458

1968-70

Beginning in 1968, a three-pod design was used to house instrumentation. In 1968, the standard instrumentation was laid out as described below.

The LH pod held the fuel gauge (upper), the oil telltale lamp (right), the generator lamp (lower) and the temperature telltale lamp (left). The left turn indicator lamp separated the LH and center pods. The center pod contained the 120 mph speedometer and the emergency brake warning lamp. The right turn signal indicator separated the center and RH pods. The RH pod used an opening cover plate (part number 9790952) if the optional Rally Clock (RPO 474) was not ordered.

Two different Rally Clusters were available in 1968. Both were factory installed. A Rally Gauge Cluster with the Rally Clock (RPO 484) placed the fuel gauge (upper), eighty-pound oil pressure gauge (right), generator telltale lamp (lower) and temperature gauge (left) in the LH pod. The speedometer design was unchanged in the Rally Cluster. The RH pod contained the clock.

The other available Rally Cluster (RPO 444) used an 8000 rpm tachometer in the RH pod in place of the clock. The redline band on the inside of the division marks began at 5100 rpm and swept to 8000 rpm.

The instrumentation layouts, both standard and Rally, were similar in 1969. In standard form, the fuel gauge and telltale lamps were located in the same order. However, the divisions in the dial face were increased in number and were all of uniform length. The speedometer remained in the center pod, and contained the directional signal indicators. If the optional Rally Clock was not ordered, a clock cover plate (part number 9784399, also used in 1970) was installed.

The background color of the instruments changed from the steel-blue of 1968 to black for 1969 and 1970. The characters remained white.

If the Rally Cluster was ordered with instrument panel tachometer (RPO 444, UPC U30), the layout was the same as 1968—as was the case with the Rally Cluster with Rally Clock (RPO 484, UPC W63). The temperature gauge used two markings, 100 degrees and 250 degrees. The tachometer used a red-and-white-band redline, beginning at 5100 rpm and sweeping to 8000 rpm.

The 1970 instrument layout was again similar to 1969. The standard instrumentation used the same format in the LH pod, although face design was slightly changed. The speedometer read to an optimistic 140 mph, as opposed to the 120 mph speedo used in previous years. A cover plate (part number 9784399) was used in 1969 if the Rally Clock (RPO 492, UPC U35) was not ordered.

When the Rally Gauge Cluster with tachometer was ordered (RPO 484, UPC U30), the gauge package was in the LH pod, and was almost identical to the 1969 cluster. The speedometer was unchanged in the center pod, and the tachometer was in the RH pod. The numbers on the face of the tach were slightly fatter than in previous years, as was the redline band, which again began at 5100 rpm and ended at 8000 rpm.

The hood-mounted tachometer (RPO 434 in 1968; RPO 471, UPC UB5 in 1969; RPO 491, UPC UB5 in 1970) was available as either a factory- or dealer-installed option. Research done by Padgett Peterson indicates the use of three types of hood tachs in 1968. Early-production (until approximately mid-December 1967) hood tachs used a case size of about two inches. The part number on the rear of the tach face (6469012-H) identified it as an early-production hood tach. The characters were circular in shape and the sweep needle was approximately ¼ inch shorter than other 1968 needles. Redline began at 5100 rpm.

In mid-December 1967, a second-design tach was released, identifiable by oval-shaped characters, a slightly longer sweep needle and its part number on the rear of the tach face (6469012-L). This tach was used on all GTO standard, HO and Ram Air I engines until the end of the production year.

The third tachometer used in 1968 hood applications was released in mid-March 1968 with the Ram Air II engine. This tach also stood two inches high, but used a redline of 5500 rpm. The tach face was a six-cylinder design with the redline recalibrated for use with the Ram Air II. It was identifiable by its part number on the rear of the tach face (6469025-K). It was used for Ram Air II production (when ordered) until the end of the production year.

The 1968 unit used a steel-blue face with white characters and the name Pontiac in white above the white rpm letters. The 1969 and 1970 units were similar, except they had black faces with white characters. The hood-mounted tachometer was pop riveted to the hood. The following chart indicates part numbers and accessory package part numbers for the respective years.

Year	Part Number	Accessory Part No.	Mounting
1968	6469694*	988559	Hood
	6468834		Cluster
1969	6469694	988662	Hood
	6469500		Cluster
1970	5657097	988748	Hood
	5657064		Cluster

*Research did not turn up any other replacement part numbers for the other two 1968 tachs. This replacement number carried a 5100 rpm redline.

Dashpad Colors And Part Numbers

Year	Color	All	With A/C	Without A/C
1969	black		9797683	9797673
1969	blue		9797684	9797674
1969	gold		9797685	9797676
1969	red		9797686	9797677
1969	green		9797687	9797675
1970	saddle	477871		
1970	sandalwood	477873		
1970	dk. blue	477867		
1970	dk. green	477863		
1970	black	9799462		
1970	dk. brown	477869		
1970	dk. red	477865		

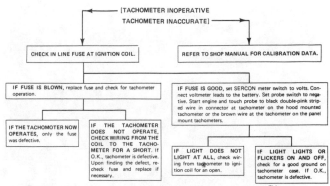

Hood and instrument panel tachometer troubleshooting guide.

Detail of 1964-67 clock opening cover plate (part number 9770401).

Close-up of Rally Clock (RPO 444 in 1966 and RPO 474 in 1967). Clock was not available with Rally Cluster.

1966 Rally Cluster speedometer. Examination of instrument code stickers XL and XN indicates speedometers were the same (part number 6457730-W). These were production part numbers, and were not used for replacement parts.

Close-up of identification sticker for XN, used for transistorized tachometer Rally Cluster in 1966.

Close-up of sticker XL, used for standard ignition Rally Clusters in 1966. Not shown is sticker XE, affixed to standard instrumentation cluster.

Standard instrumentation speedometer for 1966. XE sticker on cluster case indicates that the production part number for this speedometer was 6408209-W. Designs of numbers and sweep band were completely different from Rally Cluster speedometer.

1966 transistorized ignition tachometer (part number 6412944). Tachometer was easily identifiable from standard ignition tachometer which had a longer needle.

Close-up of rear of 1966 tachometer (6412944). Two terminals were used for this tachometer; a single terminal was used on standard ignition tachometer.

Close-up of 1966 standard ignition Rally Cluster tachometer. Compare needle length with that of transistorized ignition tachometer.

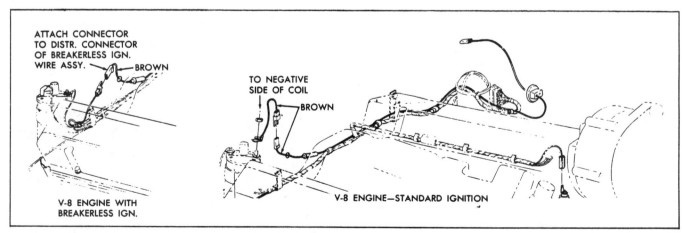

Diagram of 1966 tachometer installation. Jumper lead from coil to tachometer wire assembly.

Detail of rear of 1966-67 standard ignition tachometer with one terminal design.

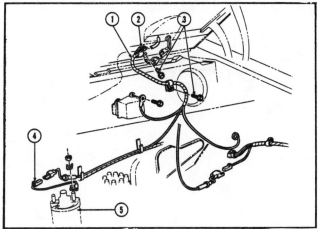

Key	Part Name	Group No.
1 — WIRE ASM., Tachometer	. . . .	9.750
2 — CLIP, Wire to Hood & Dash (1/4").	. . . . . .	N.S.
3 — Screw, Clip to Hood & Dash (#10-16 x 1/2")		8.977
4 — WIRE ASM., Tachometer Coil Jumper	. . . . .	9.750
5 — COIL ASM., Ignition	. . . .	2.170

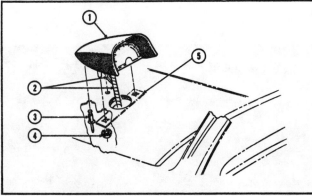

1 — HEAD ASM., Tachometer (Paint to Match)		9.750
2 — WIRE ASM., Tach. to Engine Harness . . .		9.750
3 — RIVET, Tach. to Hood		N.S.
4 — NUT & LOCKWASHER ASM., Tach. to Hood (#10-24)		8.915
5 — RETAINER, Hood Pad to Tachometer		8.021

Detail drawings of 1967 hood-mounted tachometer installation. Note attachment of tachometer to hood.

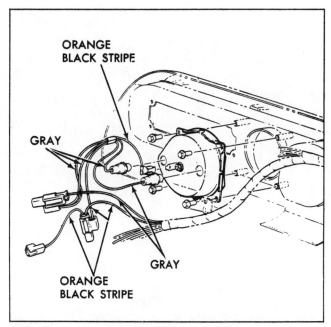

Installation instructions for 1966-67 Rally Clock.

Assembly for 1967 Rally Cluster. Label was white with green letters. Speedometer part number was for assembly plant identification only.

1967 Rally Cluster water temperature and oil pressure gauge assembly. Temperature divisions were different from 1966, and oil pressure went to 80 pounds. Not all 1967 Rally Clusters used these gauges; some used the 1966 markings.

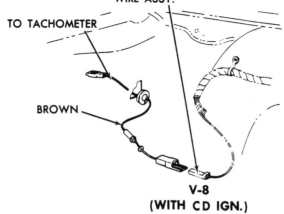

PART OF BREAKERLESS IGN.
WIRE ASSY. REMOVE TAPE
HOLDING THIS LEAD TO
WIRE ASSY.

TO TACHOMETER

BROWN

V-8
(WITH CD IGN.)

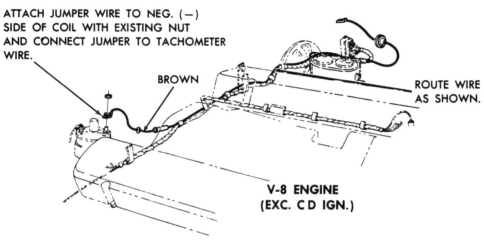

ATTACH JUMPER WIRE TO NEG. (—)
SIDE OF COIL WITH EXISTING NUT
AND CONNECT JUMPER TO TACHOMETER
WIRE.

BROWN

ROUTE WIRE
AS SHOWN.

V-8 ENGINE
(EXC. CD IGN.)

Tachometer installation in 1967 GTO. Tachometer lead ran directly to coil; jumper not used in 1967.

1968 speedometer (part number 6480585) used for all applications except Safeguard option.

Close-up of 1968 Rally Clock (part number 9790760).

Detail of gauge cluster used for 1968 standard instrumentation.

1968 tachometer. Face was steel-blue with white characters.

Detail of 1968 Rally Gauge Cluster. Cluster was serviced by individual components.

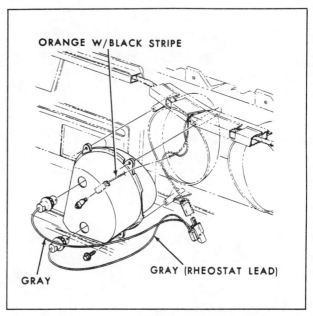

Rally Clock installation for 1968. Clock replacement part number was 9790760.

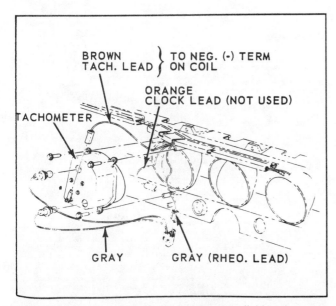

Instrument-panel-mounted tachometer was available only as part of the Rally Cluster. Shown is a 1968 installation.

Close-up of 1969 optional hood-mounted tachometer.

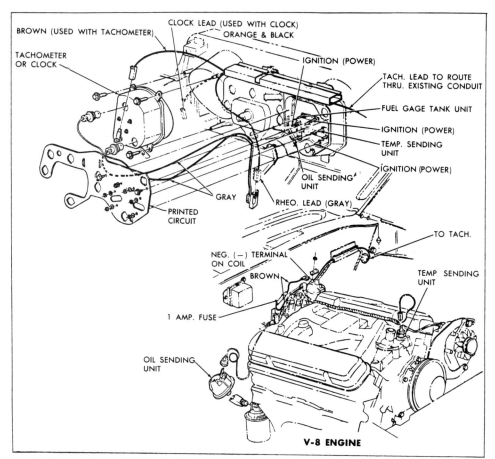

Detail of installation of 1969 Rally Cluster.

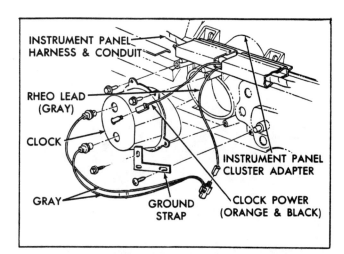

Installation of 1969 Rally Clock (part number 9796785). Note design of ground strap.

1. Diagnosis

Inoperative

Check for power at tach connector (pink wire at hood tach or brown at I. P. tach) with engine running. I. P. tach brown lead should not have a red connector. Red connectors are for accessory power leads only. If no power at tach, trace wire back to distributor side (neg. terminal) of coil - including: check in-line fuse. Be sure tach is connected to distributor side of coil. Check tach for proper ground. If tach has power, good ground, is connected properly, and is still inoperative, remove it and send to a UMS Service Station for repair.

Fogged Lens on Hood Tach

Slight fogging is normal under some conditions such as high humidity and/or rapid changes in temperature (car wash on hot hood). If fogging is excessive, remove hood tachometer (pop rivet must be drilled out) and dry out. Do not use heat lamp as this will damage unit. Seal edges of base plate to housing with windshield sealer, and reinstall tach to hood. Be sure to use a new pop rivet to preserve the anti-theft feature of this tach.

2. Calibration

Without removing tach, hook up an accurate shop tach to the engine, in addition to the vehicle's tachometer. Note reading on vehicle's tachometer at 3500 r.p.m., as indicated on shop tach. If difference is not more than 200 r.p.m., calibration is o.k. Neither the hood nor the I. P. tach used in 1968 and 1969 can be field calibrated. If calibration is more than 200 r.p.m. off, it will be necessary to remove the tach and send it to a UMS Service Station.

CAUTION: Do not exceed 3500 r.p.m. without load on engine, and operation at this speed should be as short as possible, or serious damage to the engine may result.

Dealer Technical Bulletin number 69-T-9, dated 11-15-68, outlined these procedures for servicing the 1969 GTO tachometer.

Close-up of 1970 tachometer. Face was black with white characters.

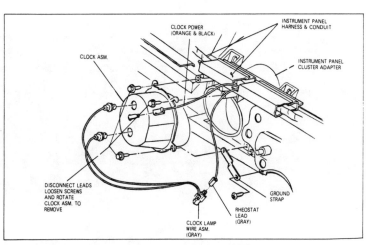

Installation of 1970 Rally Clock (part number 9799921). Compare the design of ground strap to that used for 1969.

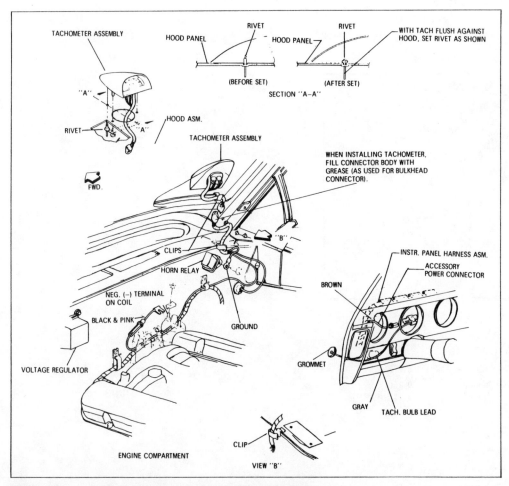

GTO hood-mounted tach installation instructions for 1970. Installation was almost the same for 1968 and 1969. However, the 1968 used the voltage regulator bracket screw for a ground; horn relay mounting screw was used for 1969 and 1970.

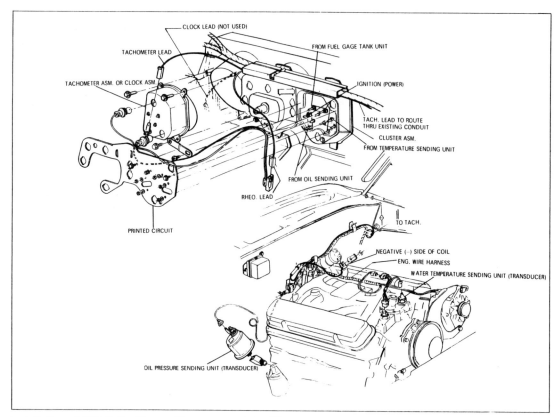

Installation of 1970 Rally Cluster. There were subtle differences between the installation of the 1970 option and the 1969 unit. Compare routings of engine harness and the ground strap used for each tachometer.

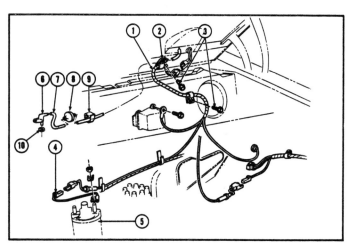

Key	Part Name	Group No.
1 — WIRE ASM., Tachometer	. . . .	9.750
2 — CLIP, Wire to Hood & Dash (1/4").	. . . . . .	N.S.
3 — Screw, Clip to Hood & Dash (#10–16 x 1/2")		8.977
4 — WIRE ASM., Tachometer Coil Jumper.	. . . .	9.750
5 — COIL ASM., Ignition	. . . .	2.170
6 — CONNECTOR, Hose to Inlet.	. . . .	9.750
7 — HOSE, Tach to Connector (7/32" I.D.)	. . . .	9.750
8 — FILTER, Hood Tachometer Air Hose	. . . . .	9.750
9 — CLIP, Vacuum Hose to Dash	. . . .	2.765
10 — WASHER, Air Hose Connector	. . . .	9.750

Installation drawing for hood-mounted tachometer. Note use of hose and filter arrangement (numbers 6–10) used in 1970 to eliminate condensation build-up on the tach glass.

SAFEGUARD SPEEDOMETER

The Safeguard Speedometer option was available only when the Rally Cluster option was not ordered. It was operated by setting a predetermined speed, using a pointer. When the speed was exceeded, a warning buzzer would sound.

The Safeguard Speedometer was easily recognized by the odometer placement (above the center of the speedometer) and by its unique pointer and knob assembly.

For 1968 the Safeguard Speedometer carried RPO 442; 1969, RPO 442 UPC U15; 1970, RPO 482 UPC U15.

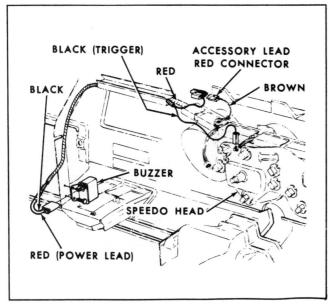

Installation of Safeguard Speedometer in 1968 GTO. This option was not available with Rally Cluster.

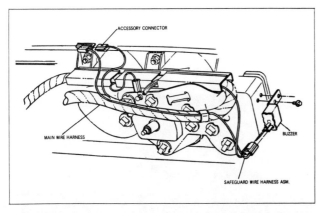

1970 Safeguard Speedometer was installed differently than in previous models. Buzzer assembly was mounted to side of speedometer cluster.

UNDERSTANDING INTERIOR TRIM CODES

Interior trim combinations were relatively uniform in the sense that, with the exception of parchment, all interior combinations were one color. Dash pads, instrument panels, seats, door panels, kick panels, package shelves and carpets were all color keyed.

With parchment (white) interiors, this color-key rule changed. When the parchment interior was ordered, the following components were black: carpets, console base, instrument panel, steering column and Deluxe steering wheel. Windlace, headliner and finishing moldings were white.

Since only bucket seat interiors were offered in 1964 and 1965 GTOs, there were no exceptions to the interior codes. Although a Strato Bench seat (RPO 568) was available in 1966, no changes were made in interior trim coding to identify bench seat from bucket seat interiors. This changed beginning in 1967, with the use of the notchback bench seat (RPO 568). Two special interior codes were assigned to differentiate bench seat interiors from the standard bucket seat format. Two colors were offered, RPO 235 for black bench seat interior and RPO 236 for white bench seat interior.

This practice was continued through the 1970 model, allowing the GTO restorer today the opportunity to identify the correct interior format for any 1967-70 GTO.

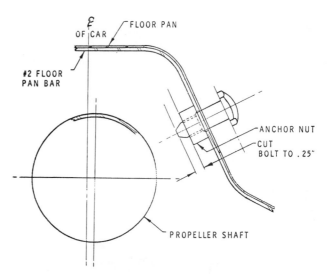

Under certain conditions, the propeller shaft on a 1964 may contact the bolt that attaches the inner front seat belt at the tunnel. If interference is found, proper clearance should be provided by cutting the bolt so that it protrudes no more than ¼ inch beyond the bottom of the nut. Caution: Do not back bolt off to obtain this dimension. (This information and illustration taken from Dealer Service Information Bulletin number 64-37 dated 12-4-63.)

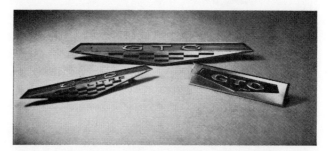

Emblems used for interior trim, 1964-70. LH emblem used for door trim, 1965-68. Center emblem used above glovebox door, 1964. RH emblem used as door panel trim, 1969-70.

INTERIOR COMB. NO.	SEAT TRIM	DOOR TRIM		HEADLINING	FLOOR COVERING
	Expanded Morrokide	Lower Carpet	Center Vinyl Coated Fabric	"Astral" Pattern Vinyl Coated Fabric (2227 Sports Coupe)	Tacoma Weave Nylon Blend Loop Pile Carpet
14	Black	Black	Black	Silver	Black
15	Dark Blue	Blue	Dark Blue	Medium Blue	Blue
16	Saddle	Saddle	Saddle	Parchment	Saddle
17	Dark Aqua	Aqua	Dark Aqua	Light Aqua	Aqua
18	Red	Red	Red	Ivory	Red
19	Parchment	Black	Parchment	Parchment	Black

1964 interiors.

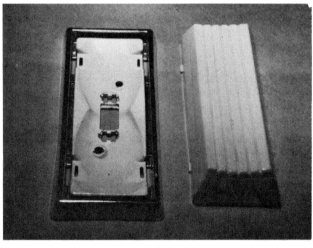

1964-67 dome lamp reflector (part number 4409950) and dome lamp lens (part number 4817415) used in hardtop and sedan models.

Detail of 1964 dome and reading lamp (RPO 484).

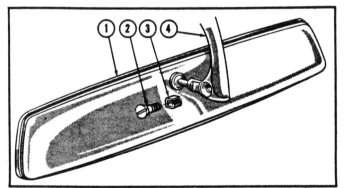

Key	Part Name	Group No.
1 —	MIRROR ASM., Inside Rear View	10.185
2 —	SCREW, Inside Mirror to Bracket (#10 - 32 x 9/16")	10.186
3 —	BUSHING, Inside Rear View Mounting . . .	10.186
4 —	SUPPORT, Inside Rear View Mirror	10.187

Mounting detail of 1964-70 inside rearview mirror.

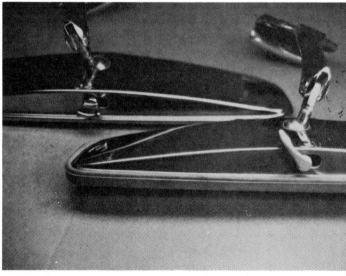

Comparison of day/night lever on 1964-66 (left) and 1967. Lever was rubber coated in 1967.

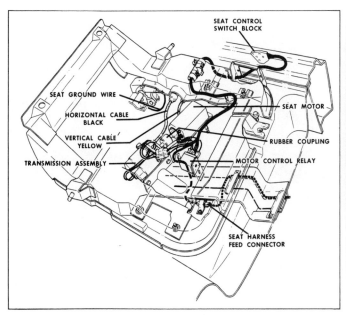

Electrical wiring routing for 1964-65 power bucket seat option.

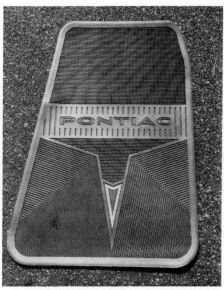

Typical passenger floor mat used in all Pontiac models. Floor mat shape differed from year to year, but rib and emblem design remained the same.

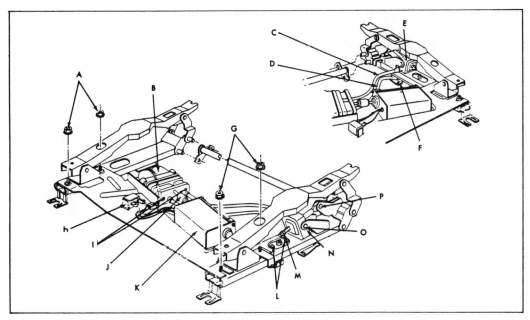

A. Motor and Transmission Support Inboard Attaching Nuts
B. Transmission Assembly
C. Vertical Drive Cable
D. Horizontal Drive Cable
E. Vertical Gearnut
F. Horizontal Actuator
G. Motor and Transmission Support Outboard Attaching Nuts

H. Motor Relay
I. Transmission End Plate Screws
J. Rubber Coupling
K. Motor
L. Horizontal Actuator Attaching Screws
M. Jackscrew Down Stop
N. Vertical Gearnut
O. Shoulder Screw
P. Jackscrew-To-Adjuster Rivet

Components and parts nomenclature for 1964-65 power bucket seat assembly.

INTERIOR COMBINA-TION NO.	SEAT TRIM	DOOR TRIM		HEADLINING	FLOOR COVERING
			Center Vinyl-coated Fabric	*Whipcord Perforated Vinyl-coated Fabric*	*Tacoma Weave Nylon Blend Loop Pile Carpet*
	Expanded Morrokide	*Lower Carpet*			
30	Black	Black	Black	Medium Slate	Black
36	Dark Turquoise	Turquoise	Dark Turquoise	Medium Turquoise	Turquoise
34	Gold	Bronze	Gold	Gold	Bronze
35	Red	Red	Red	Parchment	Red
33	Dark Blue	Dark Blue	Dark Blue	Medium Blue	Dark Blue
3E	Parchment	Parchment	Parchment	Parchment	Black

1965 interiors.

1965 Visor Vanity mirror was available as RPO 441 or as a dealer-installed option (accessory package part number 984338). The word Pontiac graced the top of some of the mirror frames.

Detail of 1965 Deluxe seat belt buckle, with Fisher body logo in insert.

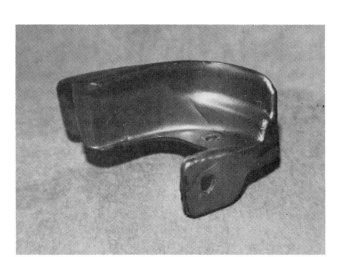

1965 body lock pillar trim cap was cast in a color to match the interior trim.

Detail of 1966 Deluxe seat belt with retractor and boot. Note year on label located on belt; all years carried the identifying label.

Detail of original headliner for 1965 GTO coupe. Chrome coat hook (part number 4840719) was used for 1964-66, with number 8 18x¾ inch chrome screw (part number 9414754).

INTERIOR COMB. NO.	SEAT TRIM	DOOR TRIM		HEADLINING	FLOOR COVERING
	Expanded Morrokide	*Lower: Carpet*	*Center: Vinyl Coated Fabric*	*Taffeta Perforated Vinyl Coated Fabric**	*Tacoma Weave Nylon Blend Loop Pile Carpet*
219	Dark Blue	Dark Blue	Dark Blue	Dark Blue	Dark Blue
220	Dark Turquoise	Dark Turquoise	Dark Turquoise	Dark Turquoise	Dark Turquoise
221	Bronze	Bronze	Bronze	Bronze	Bronze
222	Medium Red	Red	Medium Red	Medium Red	Medium Red
223	Black	Black	Black	Black	Black
224	Parchment	Black	Parchment	Parchment	Black

*Sports Coupe (24207) and Hardtop Coupe (24217) only

1966 interiors.

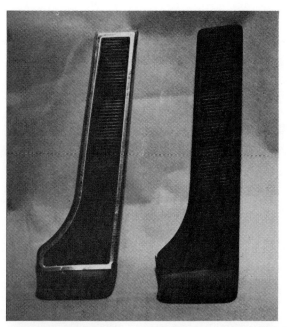

Comparison of 1964-65 accelerator pedals. When power brakes were ordered, pedal with trim plate (part number 9775550) was used. When not equipped with power brakes, pedal part number 9774234 was used.

Comparison of 1966 custom seat belt (left) and two designs used for 1967. Center buckle has GM logo; RH buckle has GM logo and words Mark of Excellence. Both are correct for 1967.

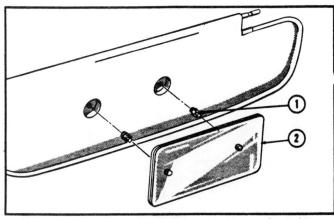

Key	Part Name	Group No.
1	NUT, Vanity Mirror to Visor	10.195
2	MIRROR, Visor Vanity	10.195

Diagram of 1966-67 Visor Vanity mirror (accessory package part number 984571 in 1966 and 984873 in 1967).

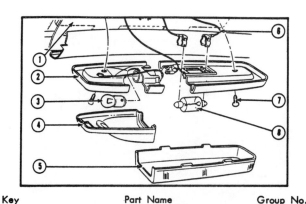

Key	Part Name	Group No.
1	SUPPORT, Side Roof Rail Lamp	12.953
2	REFLECTOR, Side Roof Rail & Reading Lamp-w/Switch	11.927
3	BULB, Side Roof Rail Lamp (No. 1004)	8.991
4	HOUSING ASM., Side Roof Rail & Reading Lamp	11.927
5	LENS, Side Roof Rail & Reading Lamp	11.928
6	WIRE HARNESS, Roof Rail & Reading Lamp	13.090
7	SCREW, Reflector to Support	N.S.
8	BULB, Side Roof Rail Lamp (No. 212)	8.991

Exploded drawing of 1966-67 roof rail and map reading lamp.

As of February 1, 1966, all bodies have been built incorporating anchorage provisions (anchor nuts) for the installation of front seat shoulder straps, on both the driver and passenger sides of the vehicle. As of March 1, 1966, front seat shoulder straps have become available as factory or dealer installed options.

Units which incorporate the shoulder strap provisions in the body structure can be identified by a 3/16 inch diameter hole stamped in the body number plate (Figure I).

NOTE: SHOULDER STRAPS ARE NOT TO BE INSTALLED ON ANY VEHICLE NOT EQUIPPED WITH THE ANCHORAGE PROVISION.

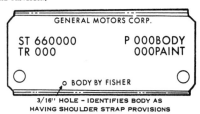

GENERAL MOTORS CORP.

ST 660000   P 000BODY
TR 000   000PAINT

o BODY BY FISHER

3/16" HOLE – IDENTIFIES BODY AS HAVING SHOULDER STRAP PROVISIONS

Information regarding introduction of front seat shoulder belts effective February 1, 1966. (This information and illustration taken from Dealer Service Information Bulletin number 66-55 dated 4-5-66.)

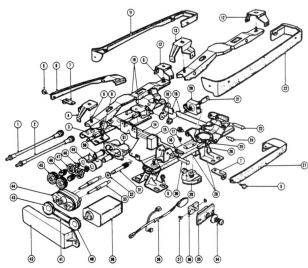

Comparison of 1966-70 accelerator pedals. Stainless trim plate was used only when model was equipped with power brakes.

Key	Part Name	Group No.
1	CABLE ASM., Seat Adj. Trans. to Left Adj. - Vertical	11.561
2	CABLE ASM., Seat Adj. Trans. to Left Adj. - Horizontal	11.561
3	SHOE, Driver Seat Inner Adj. Lower Channel	11.561
4	SUPPORT, Driver's Seat Adj. Track - Upper Inner Cover - Front	11.573
5	FASTENER, Seat Adjuster Track Cover	11.573
6	COVER, Driver's Seat Adj. Track - Inner Lower	11.573
7	SUPPORT, Driver's Seat Adj. Track - Lower Cover - Front	11.573
8	BOLT, Adjuster to Side Bar	11.561
9	BOLT, Adjuster to Floor Pan Bar	11.561
10	ADJUSTER ASM., Driver Seat - Inner (Inc. #3)	11.561
11	COVER, Driver's Seat Adj. Track - Inner Upper	11.573
12	SUPPORT, Driver's Seat Adj. Track - Upper Cover - Rear	11.573
13	SUPPORT, Driver's Seat Adj. Track - Upper Outer Cover - Front	11.573
14	SUPPORT, Seat Adjuster Transmission	11.556
15	RELAY ASM., Driver's Seat Adjuster Motor	13.095
16	SCREW, Seat Adjuster Trans. Support	11.556
17	SCREW, Driver's Outer Seat Adj. Actuator	11.561
18	STOP, Driver Outer Seat Adj. Jackscrew - Front	11.561
19	TUBE ASM., Driver's Seat Adjuster Torque	11.561
20	GEARNUT ASM., Driver's Outer Seat Adj. Jackscrew	11.561
21	JACKSCREW, Driver's Outer Seat Adjuster	11.561
22	COVER, Driver's Seat Adj. Track Outer Upper	11.573
23	PIN, Driver's Outer Adj. Top Plate - Rear	11.561
24	RIVET, Driver's Outer Adjuster Jackscrew	11.561
25	SCREW, Driver's Outer Adjuster Gearnut	11.561
26	SHOE, Driver's Seat Outer Adj. Lwr. Channel	11.561
27	COVER, Driver's Seat Adj. Track - Outer Lower	11.573
28	ADJUSTER ASM., Driver Seat Outer (Inc. #17-18-20-21-23-24-25-26-29-30)	11.561
29	ACTUATOR ASM., Driver's Outer Seat Adjuster	11.561
30	PIN, Driver's Outer Seat Adj. Top Plate - Front	11.561
31	GEAR, Seat Adj. Transmission Driving	11.556
32	WASHER, Seat Adj. Trans. Drive Gear Thrust	11.556
33	SHAFT, Seal Adjuster Transmission Clutch	11.556
34	BUTTON ASM., Driver's Outer Seat Switch	11.558
35	ESCUTCHEON, Driver's Outer Seat Switch	11.558
36	BASE ASM., Driver's Outer Seat Switch	11.558
37	CLIP, Driver Outer Seat Switch to Escutcheon	11.558
38	HARNESS ASM., Four Way Seat Adj. Wiring	13.090
39	MOTOR ASM., Driver's Seat Adj. Horizontal and Vertical	11.556
40	PULLEY, Seat Adj. Trans. at Motor	11.556
41	RING, Seat Adj. Trans. Pulley Rubber	11.556
42	COVER, Seat Adj. Trans. Pulley	11.556
43	PULLEY, Seat Adj. Trans. at Trans.	11.556
44	TRANS. ASM., Driver's Seat Adj. (Inc. #31-32-33-45-46-47-48-49-50)	11.556
45	GEAR, Seat Adj. Trans. - Horizontal & Vertical	11.556
46	SPRING, Seat Adj. Trans. Clutch Shaft	11.556
47	DOG, Seat Adj. Trans. Shaft	11.556
48	WASHER, Seat Adj. Trans. Clutch Shaft	11.556
49	SOLENOID ASM., Seat Adj. Transmission	11.556
50	PLUNGER ASM., Seat Adj. Trans. Clutch Shaft	11.536
51	HOUSING, Seat Adj. Transmission	N.S.

Exploded view and parts nomenclature for 1966-70 Strato-Bucket power seat. Note use of adjustment track cover, which was painted to match seat color.

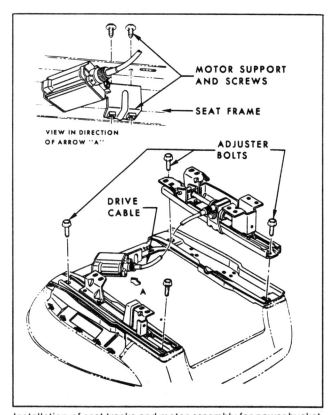

MOTOR SUPPORT AND SCREWS

SEAT FRAME

VIEW IN DIRECTION OF ARROW "A"

ADJUSTER BOLTS

DRIVE CABLE

Installation of seat tracks and motor assembly for power bucket seat used from 1966 to 1970.

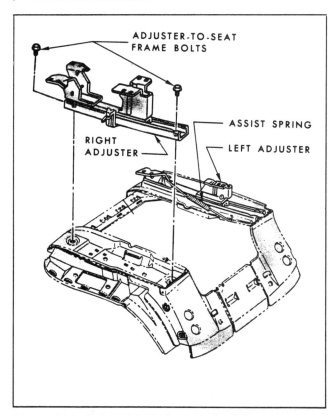

ADJUSTER-TO-SEAT FRAME BOLTS

RIGHT ADJUSTER

ASSIST SPRING

LEFT ADJUSTER

Seat track installation of 1966-70 manual bucket seat.

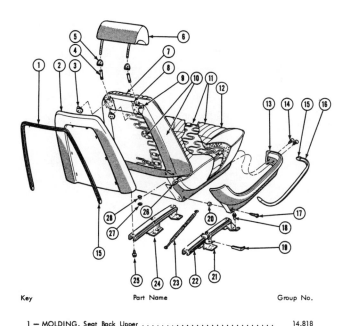

Key	Part Name	Group No.
1 — MOLDING, Seat Back Upper		14.818
2 — PANEL, Seat Back		11.358
3 — SUPPORT, Seat Back Panel - Upper		11.368
4 — TUBE, Seat Back Headrest Support Guide		11.376
5 — ESCUTCHEON, Seat Back Headrest Panel Support		11.376
6 — HEADREST ASM., Seat Back		14.924
7 — COVER, Seat Back		14.800
8 — SPRING, Seat Back Headrest Stop		11.376
9 — GUIDE ASM., Seat Back Headrest Support		11.376
10 — SPRING & FRAME, Seat Back		N.S.
11 — SPRING & FRAME, Seat Cushion		N.S.
12 — COVER, Seat Cushion		14.880
13 — PANEL, Seat Side		11.362
14 — SCREW, Seat Side Panel		N.S.
15 — CAP, Seat Back & Back Panel End		14.818
16 — MOLDING, Seat Side Panel Finishing		14.818
17 — SCREW, Seat Side Panel		N.S.
18 — BOLT, Seat Adjuster to Floor Pan		11.561
19 — KNOB, Seat Adjuster Panel		11.588
20 — SPACER, Seat Side Panel		11.362
21 — ADJUSTER ASM., Seat Outer - Manual		11.561
22 — SPRING, Seat Outer Adjuster Lock Bar		11.581
23 — SPRING, Seat Adjuster Assist		11.581
24 — ADJUSTER ASM., Seat Inner - Manual		11.561
25 — BOLT, Seat Adjuster to Side Bar		11.561
26 — SUPPORT, Seat Side Panel - Rear Outer		11.368
27 — WASHER, Seat Reclining Back Control Cable Trim Grommet		11.377
28 — GROMMET, Seat Reclining Back Control Cable Trim		11.377
29 — HINGE ASM., Seat Reclining Back Outer		11.377
30 — CLIP, Passenger Seat Back Retaining		11.375
31 — PIN, Seat Back Position Unit to Seat		11.377
32 — BUMPER, Seat Reclining Back Frame Outer		11.381
33 — POSITION UNIT ASM., Seat Reclining Back (Inc. #34)		11.377
34 — CABLE, Seat Reclining Back Control (Part of #33)		11.377
35 — STRAP, Seat Reclining Back Cable to Position Unit		11.377
36 — SCREW, Seat Reclining Back Control Handle		11.377
37 — HANDLE, Seat Reclining Back Control		11.377
38 — GUIDE, Seat Reclining Back Control Cable		11.377
39 — WASHER, Seat Reclining Back Control		11.377
40 — RING, Seat Reclining Back Control		11.377
41 — SUPPORT ASM., Seat Reclining Back Control		11.377
42 — CONTROL ASM., Seat Reclining Back		11.377
43 — HINGE ASM., Seat Reclining Back Inner		11.377
44 — BUMPER, Seat Reclining Back Frame Inner		11.381

Exploded view of 1966-68 Strato Bucket seat and related hardware, including reclining LH bucket seat option.

Interior of 242176B105833. Note headrests, floor mats and Custom Sport steering wheel. Carpeting was aftermarket installation; location of front and rear carpet joint is incorrect.

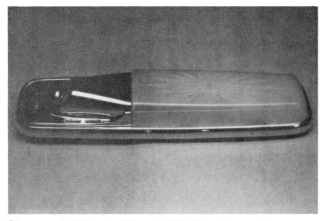

Close-up of 1966 roof rail lamp (RPO 404) with map light in front of assembly. Lens was serviced separately. Dome lamp was not used when roof rail lamp option was ordered. Option was not dealer installed.

Detail of 1966-68 LH seat recliner assembly.

INTERIOR COMB. NO.	SEAT TRIM	DOOR TRIM		HEADLINING	FLOOR COVERING

GTO Sports Coupe (24207), Hardtop Coupe (24217) and Convertible (24267)—Strato-bucket Seats—Expanded Morrokide

	Expanded Morrokide	Lower: Carpet	Center: Vinyl Coated Fabric	Taffeta Perforated Vinyl Coated Fabric*	Tacoma Weave Nylon Blend Loop Pile Carpet
219	Dark Blue	Dark Blue	Dark Blue	Dark Blue	Dark Blue
220	Dark Turquoise	Dark Turquoise	Dark Turquoise	Dark Turquoise	Dark Turquoise
221	Medium Gold	Medium Dark Gold	Medium Gold	Medium Gold	Medium Dark Gold
223	Black	Black	Black	Black	Black
224	Parchment	Black	Parchment	Parchment	Black
225	Medium Red	Medium Red	Medium Red	Medium Red	Medium Red

*Not applicable to convertible model.

GTO Sports Coupe (24207), Hardtop Coupe (24217) and Convertible (24267)—Notch-back Front Seat with Center Armrest—Expanded Morrokide

	Expanded Morrokide	Lower: Carpet	Center: Vinyl Coated Fabric	Taffeta Perforated Vinyl Coated Fabric*	Tacoma Weave Nylon Blend Loop Pile Carpet
235	Black	Black	Black	Black	Black
236	Parchment	Black	Parchment	Parchment	Black

*Not applicable to convertible model.

1967 interiors.

Optional 1967 seat belt retractor.

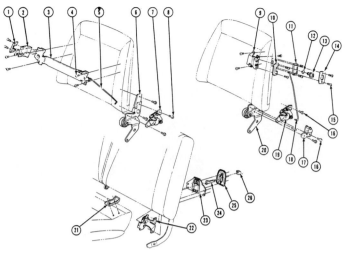

Key	Part Name	Group No.
1 — TRIMSTICK, Seat Reclining Back Lock Control Support		N.S.
2 — SUPPORT, Seat Reclining Back Lock Control		11.390
3 — CONTROL ASM., Seat Reclining Back Lock		11.390
4 — SCREW, Seat Reclining Back Lock Control Support		N.S.
5 — ROD, Seat Reclining Back Locking		11.390
6 — HINGE ASM., Seat Reclining Back - Inner		11.377
7 — LOCK ASM., Seat Reclining Back		11.390
8 — SCREW, Seat Back Lock to Hinge		11.390
9 — CONTROL ASM., Seat Back Lock		11.390
10 — SUPPORT, Seat Back Lock Control		11.390
11 — RETAINER, Seat Back Trim at Lock Knob		11.390
12 — FERRULE, Seat Back Lock Knob		11.390
13 — KNOB ASM., Seat Back Lock Rod Push Button		11.390
14 — ESCUTCHEON, Seat Back Lock Knob		11.390
15 — SCREW, Lock Knob Escutcheon		N.S.
16 — SCREW, Lock Striker to Hinge		N.S.
17 — STRIKER ASM., Seat Back Lock		11.390
18 — ROD, Seat Back Locking		11.390
19 — LOCK ASM., Seat Back		11.390
20 — HINGE ASM., Seat Back		N.S.
21 — STRIKER, Seat Back Lock		11.390
22 — LOCK ASM., Seat Back		11.390
23 — SUPPORT, Seat Back Lock Handle & Escutcheon		11.390
24 — HANDLE, Seat Back Lock		11.390
25 — ESCUTCHEON, Seat Back Lock Handle		11.390
26 — KNOB, Seat Back Lock Handle		11.390

Exploded views of 1967 seatback locks for standard bucket seat, reclining bucket seat and bench seat.

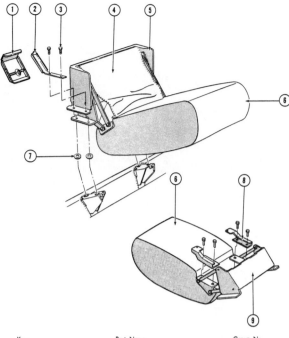

Key	Part Name	Group No
1 — COVER, Arm Rest Trim Finish (Pontiac)		14.900
2 — COVER, Arm Rest Trim Finish (Tempest)		14.900
3 — SCREW, Finish Cover to Seat Brace (1/4" - 20 x 3/4")		N.S.
4 — CURTAIN, Arm Rest		14.900
5 — COVER & TRIM ASM., Arm Rest Back		14.900
6 — TRIM ASM., Center Seat Arm Rest		14.900
7 — WASHER, Arm Rest to Seat Brace (5/16" I.D. x 3/4" O.D.)		8.929
8 — PLATE, Arm Rest Side Finish		14.900
9 — SPRING & PANEL, Center Seat Arm Rest		11.422

Detail of front seat armrest used in 1967 front bench seat option.

YEAR	COLOR	TRIM CODE
1968	TEAL	219
1968	TURQUOISE	220
1968	GOLD	221
1968	BLACK	223
1968	PARCHMENT	224
1968	RED	225
1968	BLACK	235*
1968	PARCHMENT	236*
1969	BLUE	250
1969	GOLD	252
1969	RED	254
1969	GREEN	256
1969	PARCHMENT	257
1969	BLACK	258
1969	PARCHMENT	267*
1969	BLACK	268*
1970	BLUE	250
1970	SADDLE	255
1970	GREEN	256+
1970	SANDALWOOD	257
1970	BLACK	258
1970	BROWN	253+
1970	RED	254
1970	SANDALWOOD	267*
1970	BLACK	268*

* DENOTES BENCH SEAT INTERIOR
+ DENOTES NOT AVAILABLE IN 1970 CONVERTIBLE MODELS

These codes correspond with the 1968-70 interior trim code information found on the firewall data plate to determine correct interior trim color.

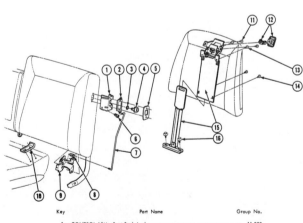

Key	Part Name	Group No.
1 — CONTROL ASM., Seat Back Lock		11.390
2 — RETAINER, Seat Back Panel Trim at Lock Knob		11.390
3 — FERRULE, Seat Back Lock Knob		11.390
4 — KNOB ASM., Seat Back Lock Rod Button		11.390
5 — ESCUTCHEON, Seat Back Lock Knob		11.390
6 — CLIP, Seat Back Lock Spring		11.390
7 — ROD, Seat Back Locking (Incl. clip for 1971-72)		11.390
8 — CLIP, Seat Back Lock Spring		11.390
9 — LOCK ASM., Seat Back		11.390
10 — STRIKER, Seat Back Lock		11.390
11 — SCREW, Seat Back Center Lock to Upper Bar		N.S.
12 — BUTTON ASM., Seat Back Lock Push		11.390
13 — SCREW, Seat Back Center Lock to Upper Bar Reinf.		N.S.
14 — SCREW, Seat Back Center Lock to Lower Bar		N.S.
15 — LOCK ASM., Seat Back Center		11.390
16 — SCREW, Seat Back Center Lock to Bottom Frame		N.S.

Exploded view of 1968-70 notch-back front seatback lock and 1969-70 Strato Bucket seatback lock. The 1968 seatback lock was similar to the 1967 Strato Bucket seat lock.

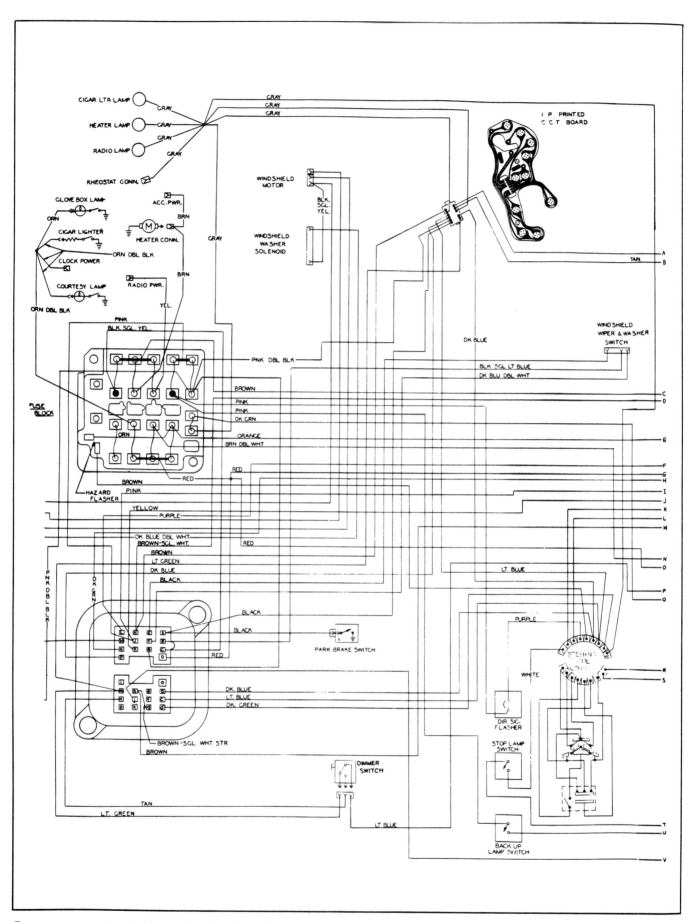

Passenger compartment wiring diagram for 1968 GTO.

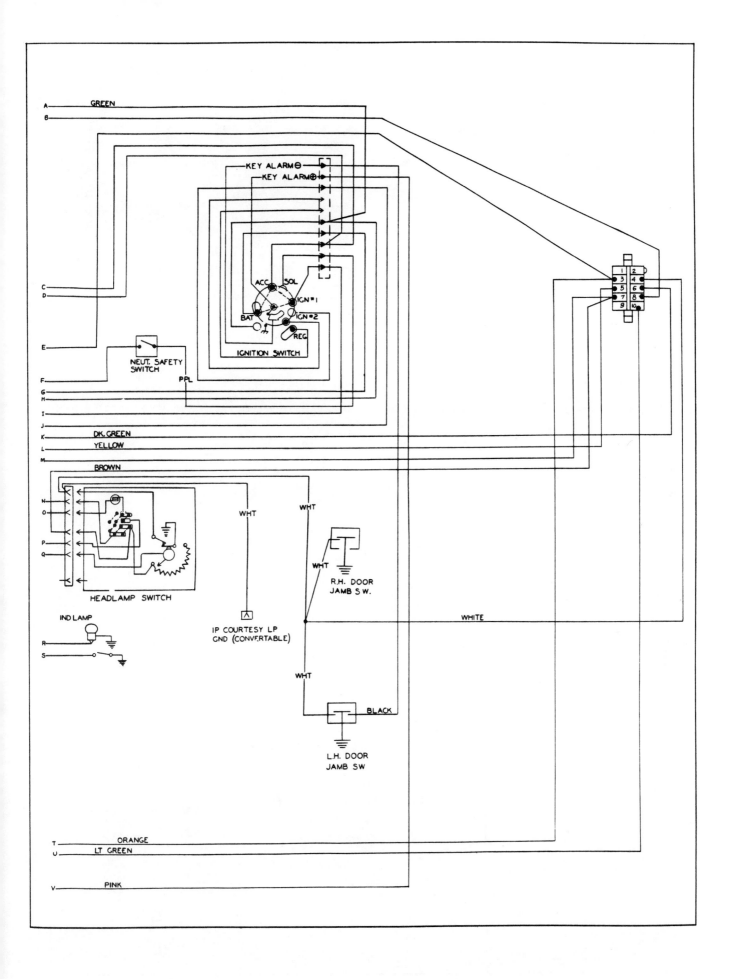

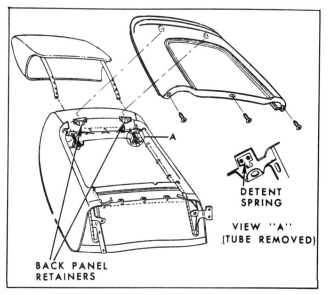

Head restraint installation for 1968 Strato Bucket seat.

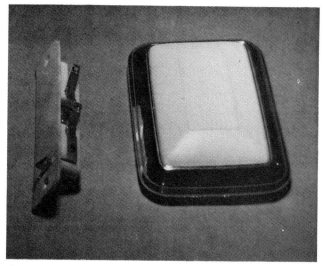

Close-up of 1968 courtesy lamp at instrument panel (left) and dome lamp assembly. Courtesy lamp assembly (part number 9790368) was used for 1968 only.

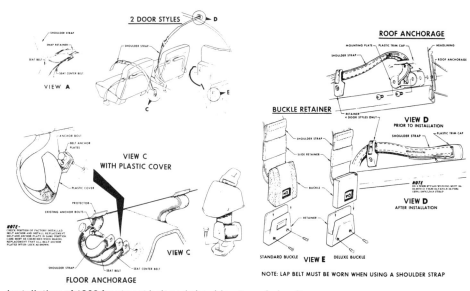

Installation of 1968 front seat belt and shoulder straps in hardtop models.

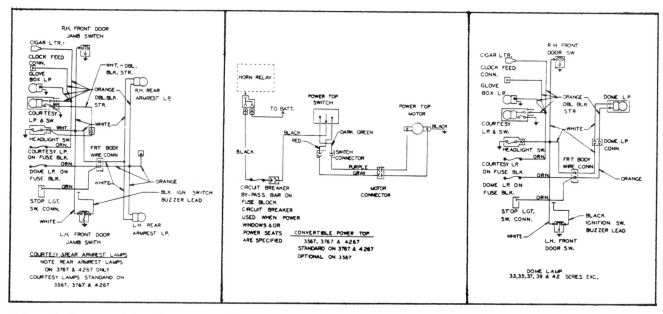

Schematic diagrams of dome lamp, convertible power top and courtesy lamps used in 1968 GTO.

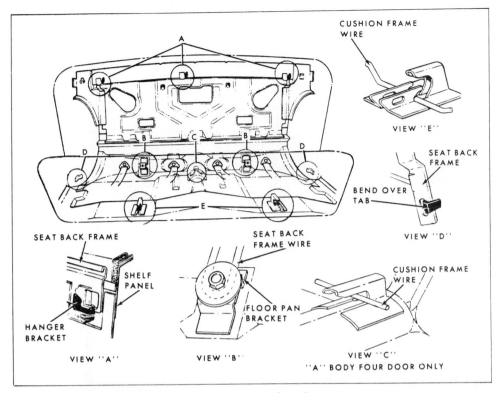

CUSHION FRAME WIRE

VIEW "E"

SEAT BACK FRAME

BEND OVER TAB

VIEW "D"

SEAT BACK FRAME

SHELF PANEL

HANGER BRACKET

VIEW "A"

SEAT BACK FRAME WIRE

FLOOR PAN BRACKET

VIEW "B"

CUSHION FRAME WIRE

VIEW "C"
"A" BODY FOUR DOOR ONLY

Installation of rear seat and seatback. View C applies to four-door
models of LeMans and Tempest only.

View of 1969 interior. Note correct floor mats, and stereo tape
player mounted on console.

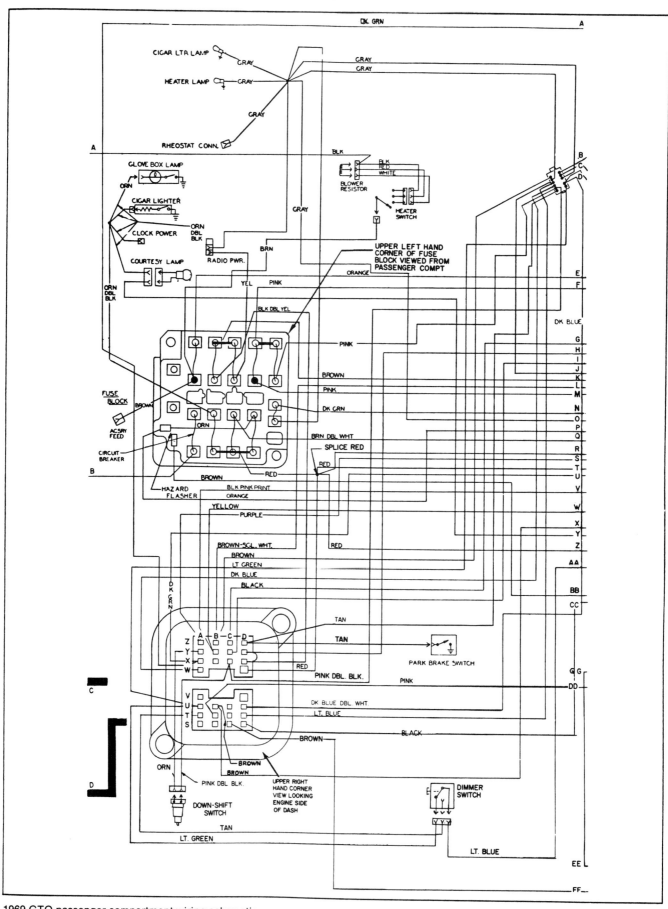

1969 GTO passenger compartment wiring schematic.

174

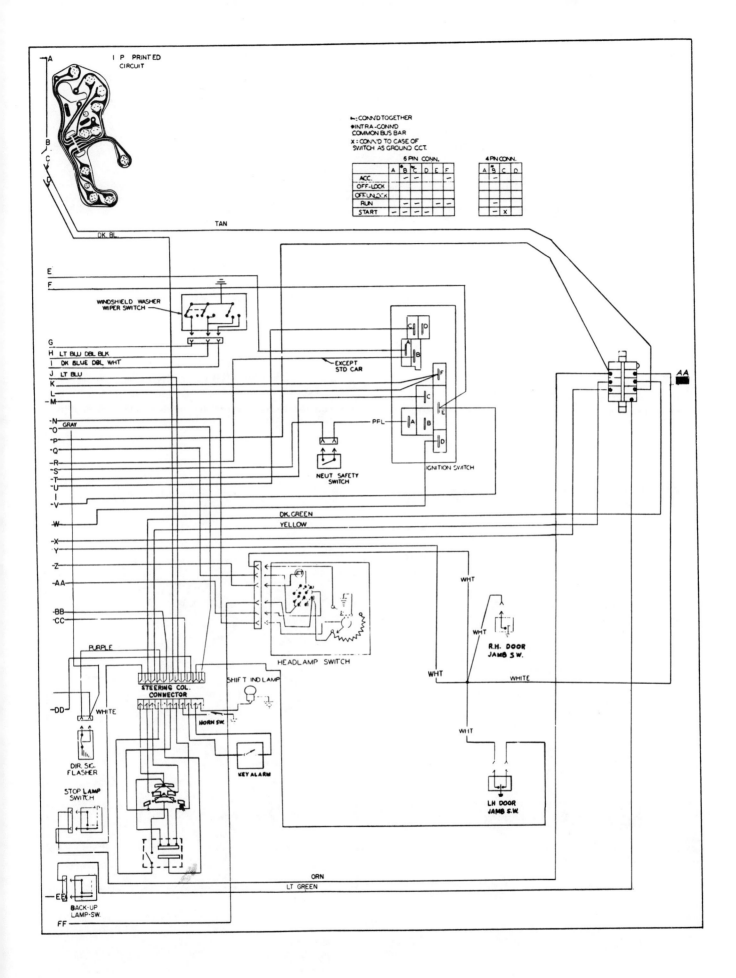

QUARTER ANCHORAGE

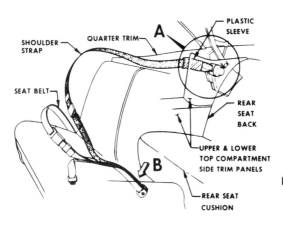

SHOULDER STRAP
QUARTER TRIM — **A**
PLASTIC SLEEVE
SEAT BELT
REAR SEAT BACK
UPPER & LOWER TOP COMPARTMENT SIDE TRIM PANELS
B
REAR SEAT CUSHION

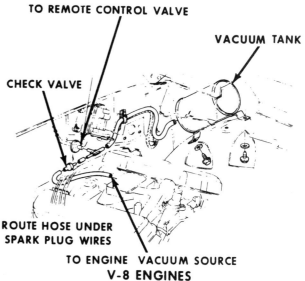

TO REMOTE CONTROL VALVE
VACUUM TANK
CHECK VALVE
ROUTE HOSE UNDER SPARK PLUG WIRES
TO ENGINE VACUUM SOURCE
V-8 ENGINES

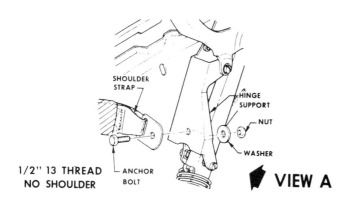

SHOULDER STRAP
HINGE SUPPORT
NUT
WASHER
ANCHOR BOLT

1/2" 13 THREAD NO SHOULDER

▶ **VIEW A**

SYSTEM TEST
SYSTEM SHOULD LOCK AND UNLOCK
DOORS TWICE AFTER ENGINE IS TURNED OFF.

Vacuum door locks were optional equipment in 1969 only (RPO 541, UPC A93).

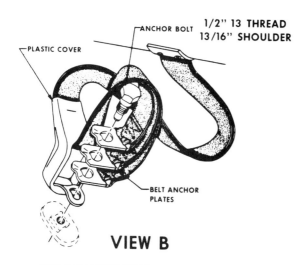

PLASTIC COVER
ANCHOR BOLT
1/2" 13 THREAD 13/16" SHOULDER
BELT ANCHOR PLATES

VIEW B

FLOOR ANCHORAGE

Installation and anchorage of 1968-69 front seat shoulder straps used in convertibles.

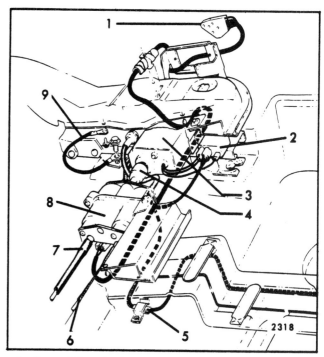

2318

1. Control Switch Block
2. Motor Control Relay
3. Motor
4. Rubber Coupler
5. Harness Feed Connector
6. Vertical Drive Cable (Yellow)
7. Horizontal Drive Cable (Black)
8. Transmission Assembly
9. Seat Ground Wire

Wiring routing and parts breakdown for 1968-70 four-way power bench seat.

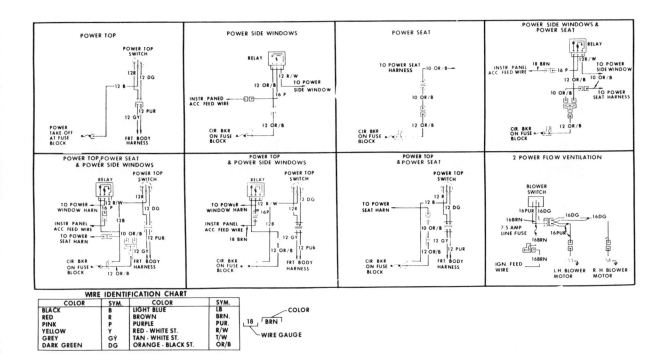

Schematic diagram for wiring 1969 options.

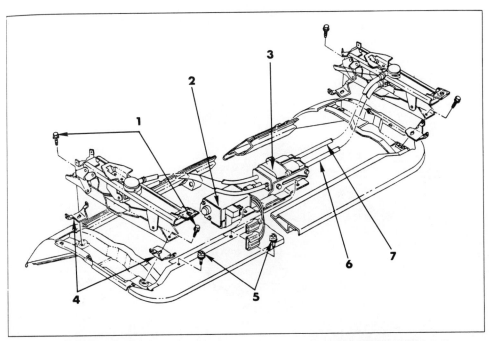

1. Adjuster to Seat Frame Attaching Bolts
2. Motor Assembly
3. Transmission Assembly
4. Track Cover Supports
5. Motor and Transmission Support Attaching Screws
6. Vertical Cable (Yellow)
7. Horizontal Cable (Black)

Power bench seat components and parts nomenclature for 1969-70.

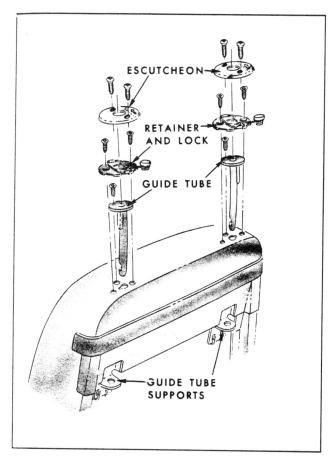

Typical 1969-70 head restraint installation. Escutcheon was chromed.

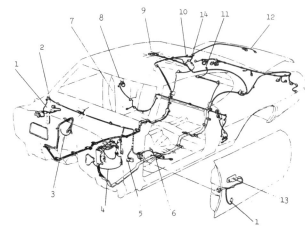

1. Door Window Motor Connector
2. Door Window Control
3. Antenna & Speaker Connectors
4. Main Body & Feed Wire Connectors
5. Ignition Relay
6. Power Seat Feed
7. Quarter Window Motor Connector
8. Quarter Window Control
9. Dome Lamp Connectors
10. Antenna Connectors
11. Rear Defogger Connector
12. Electric Deck Lid Release
13. Master Window Control
14. Rear Speaker Connector

Overall wiring harness layout and routing for 1970 GTO hardtop. Note power window and rear defogger connections.

Comparison of 1964-66 (right) and 1967 lock knobs.

1970 GTO convertible interior. Note optional Formula wheel and clock cover in RH instrument pod. Radio is incorrect.

Condition: Battery discharging while vehicle is parked because lamp remains on with glovebox door closed.

Cause: Switch plunger is not sufficiently long enough to be activated by glovebox door.

Corrective Procedure: Using small flat bladed screwdriver, pry under chrome outer disc of switch assembly. This will release the spring retaining clips and allow the entire assembly to be disengaged from retaining hole. Install "O" ring, part number 3140748, as a spacer for the switch assembly. This can be worked over the disc from the plunger side of the switch and seated against the back of the disc (as shown). Push entire assembly back into the retainer hole.

Parts Required: A/C expansion valve "O" ring, part number 3140748 (available through your Zone warehouse). It is also a component of "O" ring package 540999. (5/8" O.D.)

Dealer Technical Bulletin 70-T-1, dated 9-15-69 reported this problem and cure for the 1970 glovebox lamp.

KICK PANEL

1964-65

The interior kick panels for 1964 and 1965 were not interchangeable because of the windlace. Ventilator control knobs were black plastic in 1964 and chrome-plated plastic to match the design of the instrument panel knobs in 1965.

1966-67

The interior kick panels were not interchangeable between 1966 and 1967. In 1966, a separate vent knob and cable assembly mounted to the underside of the instrument panel and ran to the vent assembly behind the kick panel. In 1967, the knob and cable assembly was mounted in the kick panel itself. The kick panel vent grille was removable in 1967 only, and the vent assembly was part of the kick panel.

On air-conditioned models for both years, there was no provision for a vent, and the panel was molded to cover part of the heater core and case assembly for the RH side. On 1967 air-condition-equipped models, the LH kick panel was a 1965-66 design, eliminating the built-in ventilator and knob assembly. A block-off plate on the cowl was used, and no vent control was offered on these models.

The vent control knobs were chromed and matched the instrument panel knob design. The panels were color-cast plastic, and matched the instrument panel trim color.

Close-up of power window control assembly (part number 4432791). This switch assembly was used from 1964 to 1967.

1968-70

The 1968 kick panel was similar in design to the 1967 panels, with the single vent control knob integrated into the panel design. With air conditioning, the vent was eliminated.

With the deletion of vent windows in 1969, the kick panel was redesigned to contain two vent control knobs integrated into the panel design. The upper knob controlled the flow of air in the instrument panel vents, while the lower one controlled airflow through the kick panel. This design was carried through into 1970. The kick panels on all 1968-70 models was keyed to match instrument panel trim color.

Individual power window switch (part number 4432790). Switch was interchangeable for 1964-67.

1964 interior door panel. GTO 6.5 liter emblem was not used in 1964.

Comparison of 1964 (top) and 1965-66 window cranks.

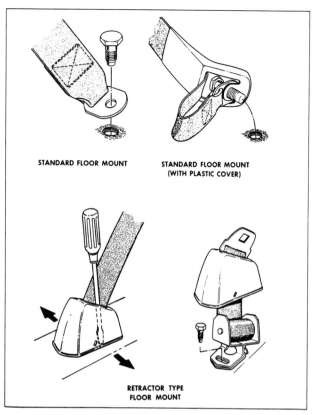

STANDARD FLOOR MOUNT

STANDARD FLOOR MOUNT
(WITH PLASTIC COVER)

RETRACTOR TYPE
FLOOR MOUNT

Installation instructions for outboard seat belt floor mounting.

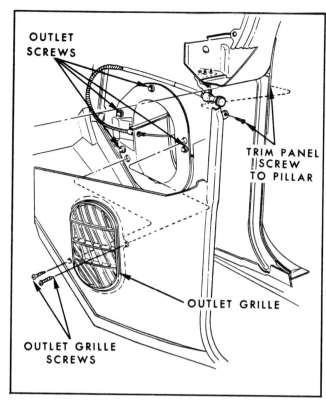

OUTLET
SCREWS

TRIM PANEL
SCREW
TO PILLAR

OUTLET GRILLE

OUTLET GRILLE
SCREWS

Installation of kick panel in non-air-conditioned 1964-66 GTO.
Note location of control cable and routing to outlet door.

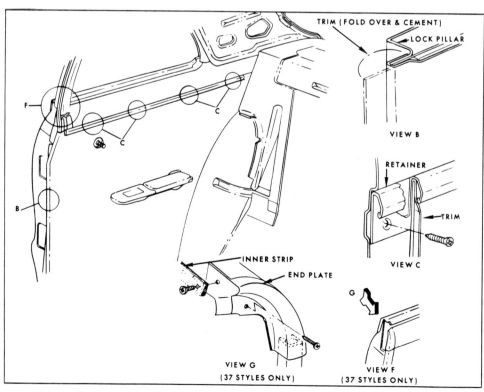

TRIM (FOLD OVER & CEMENT)

LOCK PILLAR

VIEW B

RETAINER

TRIM

VIEW C

INNER STRIP

END PLATE

VIEW G
(37 STYLES ONLY)

VIEW F
(37 STYLES ONLY)

Installation of 1965 quarter trim assemblies.

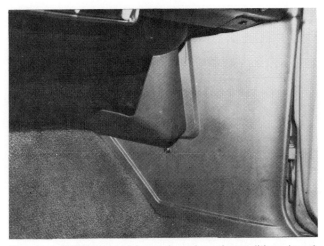

Close-up of 1965 right kick panel used on air-conditioned models. Non-air-conditioned models had a vent and grille in the panel. 1965 and 1966 black panels were interchangeable.

1967 interior door panel. Armrest base was chrome-plated plastic. 6.5 liter emblem (original part number 4485306) was used for 1965-66. Part number 7656954 was used in 1967 and 1968 and replaced original number.

View of 1968 rear quarter armrest assembly and ashtray.

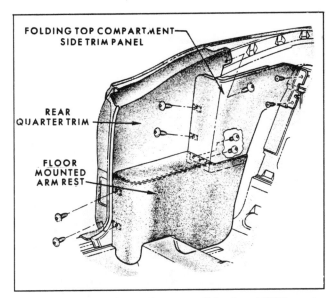

Typical rear quarter trim used on convertibles from 1968 through 1970. Trim lacks courtesy lamp and ashtray.

Detail of 1968 door panel design. 6.5 liter emblem replacement part number was the same for 1965-68. Remote mirror escutcheon (part number 9780181) was the same as for 1965-68.

1968 convertible rear quarter trim, armrest, courtesy lamp and ashtray.

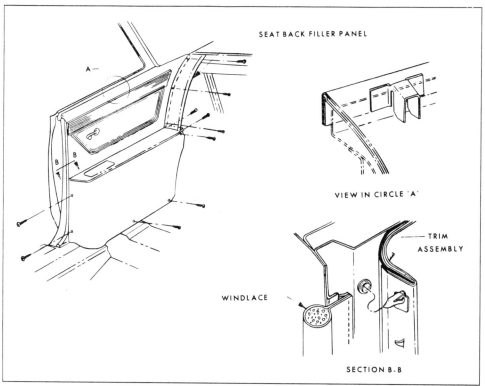

Typical rear quarter trim installation for 1968-70. Note windlace alignment.

Close-up of 1969-70 remote-control mirror escutcheon (part number 9784388). This escutcheon was used only on hardtop and convertible models. 1969-70 LeMans and Tempest sedans, station wagons and four-door hardtops all used the 1965-68 design escutcheon, and did not interchange with the GTO.

Detail of 1969 door panel. Note redesign of GTO nameplate emblem on door panel (part number 7790996), also used in 1970.

Detail of 1970 door panel. Note placement of remote-control mirror escutcheon.

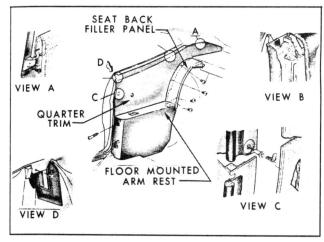

Rear quarter trim used in 1970 GTO hardtop; unit was one piece.

PACKAGE SHELF

1964-67

Package shelves for 1964-67 came in two forms. Cars equipped from the factory with no rear seat speaker received a plain cardboard package shelf painted 0° gloss to match the interior trim. This held true with or without installation of the rear window defogger option. Dealer-installed rear speakers used a grille painted to match the interior trim.

A GTO equipped from the factory with a rear seat speaker used a package shelf with a weave design, painted to match the interior trim.

1968-70

As in previous years, package shelves came in two forms for 1968-70. When ordered with no rear seat speaker, a plain cardboard shelf was installed, painted 0° gloss to match the interior trim, unless the interior was parchment.

When any type of factory-installed radio, tape player or reverb option using a rear seat speaker was ordered, a package shelf with a mesh design was used. Holes were punched through the cardboard for the speaker, but were screened from view by the mesh. The shelf was painted 0° gloss to match the interior trim.

SEATS

1964-65

All Morrokide vinyl bucket seats were standard on 1964 and 1965 GTOs. A chrome trim plate ran up the side of the seat backs. Seat upholstery patterns were restyled for 1965.

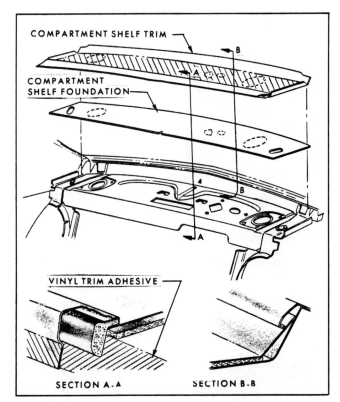

Typical 1968-70 package shelf installation. In GTOs, the foundation and the mesh trim were one piece.

1966-67

Seat design was changed in 1966. The new design was carried over into 1967, with minor changes in upholstery pattern, and the addition of locking seatbacks.

1968-70

The Strato Bucket seat was primarily unchanged for 1968-70, except for yearly variations in seat-covering patterns. A notchback bench seat was available for all three years. Headrests were standard equipment beginning in 1969.

TRUNK COMPARTMENT

1964-67

A two-piece floor mat (part number 4412119 rear and 4412108 front) was used in all 1964 and 1965 GTOs. It was made of rubber, and had a hound's-tooth-check pattern in black and gray. The trunk in the 1964 GTO was painted the exterior color; the 1965 was finished in gray and green spatter.

For 1966, a two-piece floor mat (part number 4412108 front and 4545492 rear) was used. It was made of rubber and had a turquoise and black hound's-tooth-check pattern. The 1967 used the same pattern. However, the front mat was no longer used, and the rear mat was part number 7696447. Trunk compartments for 1966 and 1967 were painted dark-blue-and-gray-fleck spatter.

The spare tire was mounted on the RH side of the trunk floor as described on the jacking and tire stowage decal affixed to the underside of the deck lid. All bumper jack bases were painted blue and measured 6x6 inches. However, three different racks were used: a T-shape rack (base part number 9774441) used in 1964 only; a rounded keystone-shape rack (base part number 9783363) used with some 1965-67 GTOs; and a square rack (base part number 9781295) used in other 1965-67 GTOs.

The jack handle (part number 9775167) was the same for 1964-67. It was painted blue and had a socket on one end that doubled as a lug nut wrench. It was encased in a black rubber sleeve (part number 9785869) in 1966 and 1967 only. The anchor bolt secured the spare to the trunk floor (part number 535782) and was natural metal in appearance. It measured 5½ inches long and was used for 1964 through 1966 applications. In 1967, the bolt was six inches long, was natural metal in appearance and used part number 9789921. The hold-down wing nut was natural metal in appearance (part number 9785616) and was used 1964-67.

A spare tire lock was available beginning in 1965 (accessory package part number 984538 for 1965-66 and 984701 for 1967) as a dealer-installed option. A spare tire cover was offered (RPO 572 for 1964-65 and RPO 372 in 1966) as a factory-installed option in 1964-66 and matched the color and pattern of the trunk mat. The cover could also be installed by the dealer as accessory package part number 983587 in 1964 and 984321 in 1965-67. It was offered only as a dealer-installed option in 1967. New for 1967 was an optional factory-installed (RPO 362) or dealer-installed (accessory package part number 984826) auxiliary trunk floor mat. This mat was black-ribbed rubber, with the Pontiac emblem in white on the left and right halves of the mat.

1968-70

A hound's-tooth-check, one-piece floor mat (part number 7731767) was used in 1968. If the optional Space Saver spare was ordered, a different mat (part number 7790900) was installed, as the spare was moved from the usual RH flat mounting to the Space Saver LH vertical mount.

The standard mat used in 1969 was part number 8769527; in 1970, part number 8801975. If the Space Saver was ordered in 1970, mat part number 8801977 was installed. The mat was dark gray in appearance.

The standard spare tire was mounted on the RH trunk floor. The jack assemblies were different for all three years.

Year	Part Number	Manufacturer
1968	9793539	Ryerson and Haynes
1969	9798342	Universal Tool and Stamping
1970	9798138	Auto Specialties

The bumper jack bases were painted blue. However, each year used a slightly different design. The 1968 base (part number 9793349) used a keystone-shape rack. Two different bases were used in 1969-70: A T-design rack used base part number 9794472; the more common keystone-shape rack used base part number 9794471. The same jack handle (part number 9775167) was used as in previous years.

The hold-down bolt varied in length and application. The 1968-70 bolt (part number 9792305) was eight inches long. For the Rally II spare wheel in 1970, a 9½ inch bolt (part number 9797612) was used. All bolts used the same wing nut (part number 9785616). The wing nut was natural metal in appearance, as was the hold-down bolt.

The Space Saver spare tire option (RPO 702 in 1968; RPO 704, UPC N65 in 1969-70) was available from 1968-70. A collapsible tire was mounted vertically in the LH side of the rear compartment. A support bracket (part number 9793622 in 1968-69, and 478715 in 1970) mounted on the metal bracing and trunk pan lip. A variety of clamp bolts was used throughout the three years for hardtop and convertible applications.

Year	Body Style	Length (inches)	Part Number
1968	All	10¾	9793621
1969	24237	9¼	9797771
1970	24237	6½	480865
	24267	10⅛	480138

The jack was mounted next to the LH lid opening, and was retained by two brackets, one at the front and one at the rear. In convertibles, center and rear brackets were employed. The tire inflater (accessory package 984922) was the same for all three years.

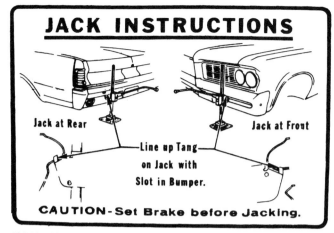

1964 jacking instructions, located on RH underside of deck lid.

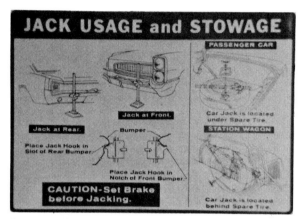

Detail of 1966 jack usage and stowing decal located on underside of deck lid. Research indicates at least two different decals were used for 1966. Currently only one design is being reproduced; either one is correct.

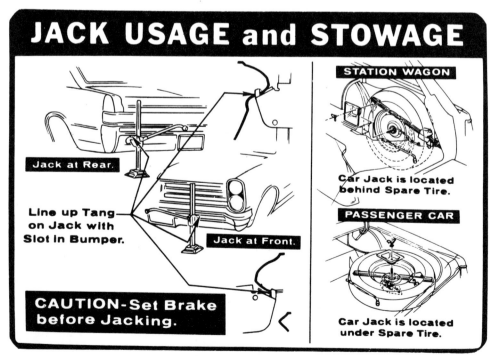

1965 jacking instructions and spare tire storage, located on RH underside of deck lid.

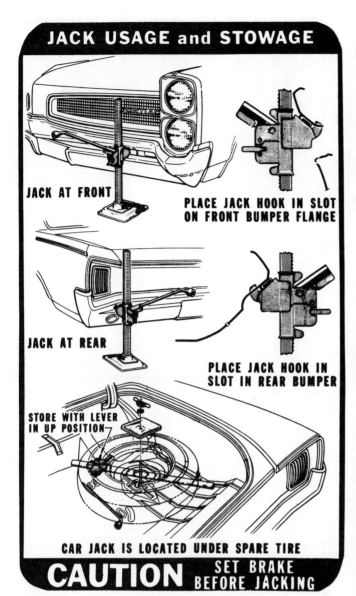

JACK USAGE and STOWAGE

JACK AT FRONT

PLACE JACK HOOK IN SLOT ON FRONT BUMPER FLANGE

JACK AT REAR

PLACE JACK HOOK IN SLOT IN REAR BUMPER

STORE WITH LEVER IN UP POSITION

CAR JACK IS LOCATED UNDER SPARE TIRE

CAUTION SET BRAKE BEFORE JACKING

1966 jacking and spare tire storage, located in center underside of deck lid.

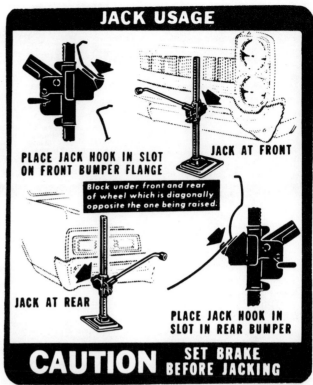

JACK USAGE

PLACE JACK HOOK IN SLOT ON FRONT BUMPER FLANGE

JACK AT FRONT

Block under front and rear of wheel which is diagonally opposite the one being raised.

JACK AT REAR

PLACE JACK HOOK IN SLOT IN REAR BUMPER

CAUTION SET BRAKE BEFORE JACKING

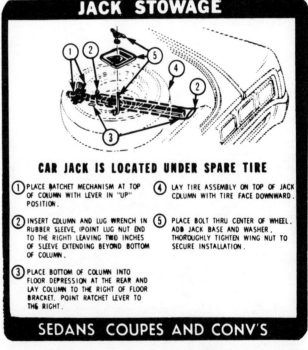

JACK STOWAGE

CAR JACK IS LOCATED UNDER SPARE TIRE

1. PLACE RATCHET MECHANISM AT TOP OF COLUMN WITH LEVER IN "UP" POSITION.

2. INSERT COLUMN AND LUG WRENCH IN RUBBER SLEEVE, (POINT LUG NUT END TO THE RIGHT) LEAVING TWO INCHES OF SLEEVE EXTENDING BEYOND BOTTOM OF COLUMN.

3. PLACE BOTTOM OF COLUMN INTO FLOOR DEPRESSION AT THE REAR AND LAY COLUMN TO THE RIGHT OF FLOOR BRACKET. POINT RATCHET LEVER TO THE RIGHT.

4. LAY TIRE ASSEMBLY ON TOP OF JACK COLUMN WITH TIRE FACE DOWNWARD.

5. PLACE BOLT THRU CENTER OF WHEEL. ADD JACK BASE AND WASHER. THOROUGHLY TIGHTEN WING NUT TO SECURE INSTALLATION.

SEDANS COUPES AND CONV'S

Two-piece 1967 jacking and spare tire storage instructions, located on the center underside of the deck lid.

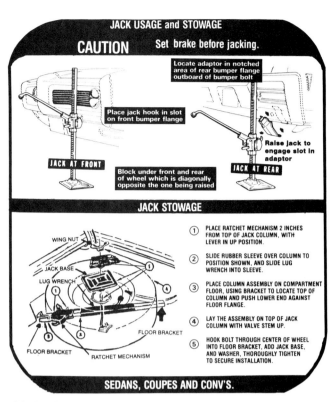

JACK USAGE and STOWAGE

CAUTION — Set brake before jacking.

Locate adaptor in notched area of rear bumper flange outboard of bumper bolt

Place jack hook in slot on front bumper flange

JACK AT FRONT

Raise jack to engage slot in adaptor

JACK AT REAR

Block under front and rear of wheel which is diagonally opposite the one being raised

JACK STOWAGE

WING NUT
JACK BASE
LUG WRENCH
FLOOR BRACKET
FLOOR BRACKET
RATCHET MECHANISM

① PLACE RATCHET MECHANISM 2 INCHES FROM TOP OF JACK COLUMN, WITH LEVER IN UP POSITION.

② SLIDE RUBBER SLEEVE OVER COLUMN TO POSITION SHOWN, AND SLIDE LUG WRENCH INTO SLEEVE.

③ PLACE COLUMN ASSEMBLY ON COMPARTMENT FLOOR, USING BRACKET TO LOCATE TOP OF COLUMN AND PUSH LOWER END AGAINST FLOOR FLANGE.

④ LAY THE ASSEMBLY ON TOP OF JACK COLUMN WITH VALVE STEM UP.

⑤ HOOK BOLT THROUGH CENTER OF WHEEL INTO FLOOR BRACKET, ADD JACK BASE, AND WASHER, THOROUGHLY TIGHTEN TO SECURE INSTALLATION.

SEDANS, COUPES AND CONV'S.

1968 jacking and spare tire storage instructions, located on the center underside of deck lid.

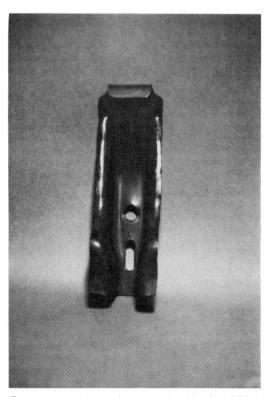

Bumper jack adapter for use only with 1968 GTO (part number 9790394).

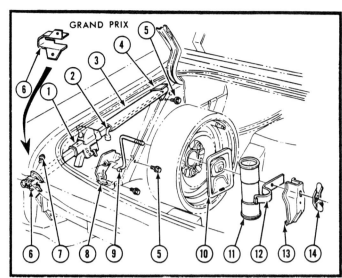

GRAND PRIX

Key	Part Name	Group No.
1 — JACK ASM., Bumper		8.820
2 — HANDLE, Jack		8.820
3 — SLEEVE, Jack Post & Handle		8.820
4 — BRACKET, Jack Retaining - Front		8.820
5 — SCREW, Bracket to Body (1/4"-14 x 5/8")		N.S.
6 — BRACKET, Jack Retaining - Rear		8.820
7 — SCREW & SEALER ASM., Bracket to Body		N.S.
8 — SUPPORT ASM., Spare Wheel Hold Down		7.629
9 — BOLT, Spare Wheel Clamp (10 3/4")		7.632
10 — BASE ASM., Bumper Jack		8.820
11 — TIRE INFLATOR, Space Saver	See Accessory Section	
12 — RETAINER, Tire Inflator		5.880
13 — ADAPTER, Jack to Rear Bumper		8.820
14 — NUT, Spare Wheel Clamp Bolt		7.633

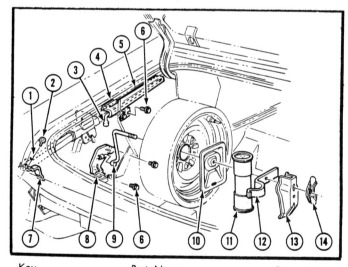

Key	Part Name	Group No.
1 — JACK ASM., Bumper		8.820
2 — SCREW & SEALER ASM., Bracket to Body		N.S.
3 — HANDLE, Jack		8.820
4 — BRACKET, Jack Retaining - Front		8.820
5 — SLEEVE, Jack Post & Handle		8.820
6 — SCREW, Bracket to Body (1/4" - 14 x 5/8")		N.S.
7 — BRACKET, Jack Retaining - Rear		8.821
8 — SUPPORT ASM., Spare Wheel Hold Down		7.629
9 — BOLT, Spare Wheel Clamp (10 3/4")		7.632
10 — BASE ASM., Bumper Jack		8.820
11 — TIRE INFLATOR, Space Saver	See Accessory Section	
12 — RETAINER, Tire Inflator		5.880
13 — ADAPTER, Jack to Rear Bumper		8.820
14 — NUT, Spare Wheel Clamp Bolt		7.633

Exploded views of 1968-70 hardtop and convertible Space Saver spare tire components and parts nomenclature. Adapter was used in 1968 only for jack to bumper.

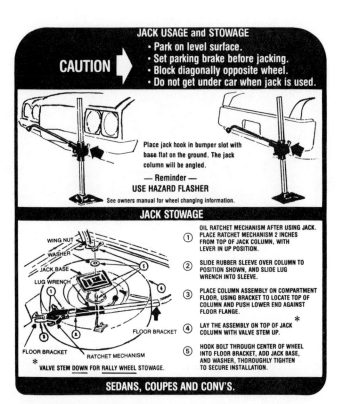

1969 jacking and spare tire storage instructions, located in center underside of deck lid.

1970 jacking and spare tire storage instructions, located in center underside of deck lid.

LUGGAGE LAMP

1964-65

A luggage lamp (RPO 481) was available for 1964 and 1965. It was also part of the 084 Lamp Group. It was mounted in a recess on the inside of the LH rear deck lid, with the wire running down the inside of the deck lid, emerging at the LH strap, and into the trunk.

1966-67

The optional luggage lamp (RPO 401) was available for both years as a factory-installed option, as part of the 074 Lamp Group or as a dealer-installed option (accessory package 984709 for both years). It was mounted the same as the 1964-65 unit.

1968-70

The 1968 luggage compartment lamp was identical in all respects to the 1966-67 assembly. The lamp assembly for 1969-70 was redesigned, and mounted on the LH deck lid hinge bracket. When the lid was raised, an arm riding on the hinge would activate the luggage lamp. The accessory part number for the luggage lamp was 988678 in 1969, and 988730 in 1970. It was also a factory-installed option, coded as RPO 652 for 1968 through 1970.

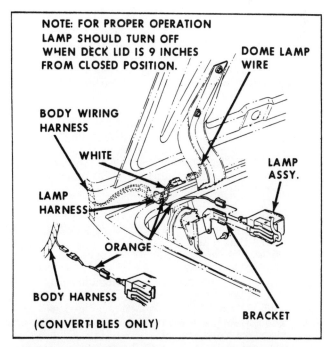

Installation of accessory package part number 988678 luggage lamp for 1969. Note difference from 1970 installation.

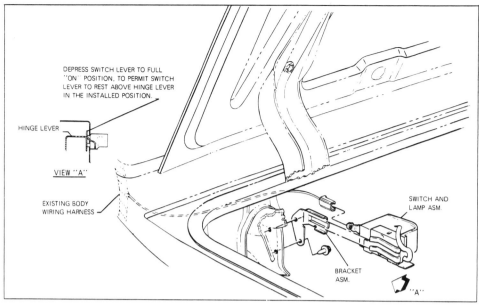

Installation of 1970 luggage compartment lamp (accessory package part number 988730).

REAR DECK LID RELEASE

1964-65

The optional rear deck lid release (RPO 451) was cable operated and was available from the dealer (1964 accessory package number 984268 and 1965, 984446). The cable and handle assembly (part number 9775285 in 1964 and 4506983 in 1965) was mounted through a bracket (part number 9775284) that was attached to the instrument panel. The cable was routed down the cowl and under the RH sill plate to the rear trunk panel. The rear compartment lid lock was activated by pulling the handle and turning the lid release lever and coupling (part number 9776228 in 1964 and 4506985 in 1965). A release-cable return spring (part number 4472714) then returned the assembly to the closed position.

1966-67

Two different types of rear deck releases were used in 1966 (RPO 422): a cable release, identical in design to the 1965 system, and a vacuum-operated unit.

The cable release differed from the 1965 unit only in the cable and handle assembly (part number 7584076) and the lever and coupling assembly (part number 9584504). The 1965 system ran to the underside of the deck lid, and the 1966 system ran to the rear end panel where the lock assembly was situated.

The second type of rear deck lid release was vacuum operated. A chromed lid-release control assembly (part number 9785611) was mounted in the glovebox and connected to a 3/32 inch inside-diameter hose, which went to a reducer (part number 9781073). A 3/16 inch inside-diameter hose (part number 534679) ran to the rear compartment to a vacuum-release power unit (part number 4482923), mounted on the anchor plate.

The 1967 GTO used an electric lid release (RPO 492). The switch (original part number 9787827, replacement part number 478282) mounted in the glovebox. A wire assembly (part number 9788061) ran to the main wire harness from the switch. A second wire lead (part number 9774600) went from the switch, along the RH passenger compartment floor, into the trunk along the LH gutter, and through a plastic connector to the electric rear compartment lid lock (part number 7660686), which was mounted to the lid lock anchor plate.

1968-70

For 1968-70, the deck lid release option was similar to the 1967 unit (RPO 492 in 1968; RPO 492, UPC A90 in 1969; and RPO 554, UPC A90 in 1970). The switch and the wire assembly were the same until 1970. The wire from the lid lock to the switch (part number 9792899) was different for 1970. The thirty-one-inch wire from the harness to the switch (part number 9788060) was also unique for 1970.

The 1968-70 lock lid release was the same as the 1967 unit. However, it was located in the deck lid in place of the standard lock lid assembly.

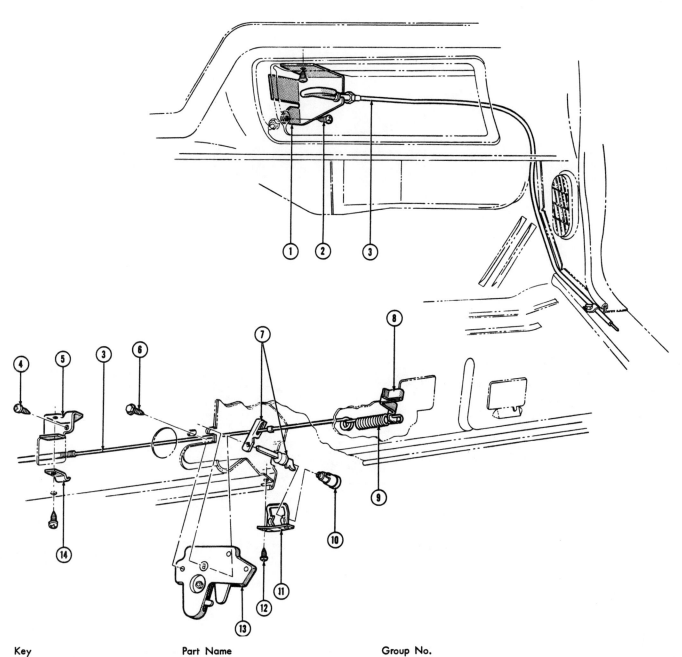

Key	Part Name	Group No.
1 — BRACKET, Release Control		12.243
2 — SCREW, Bracket ot Inst. Panel (#8-18 x 1/2")		8.977
3 — CABLE & HANDLE ASM., Release		12.243
4 — SCREW, Support to Compt. Lid (#8-18 x 1/2")		8.977
5 — SUPPORT, Lid Release Cable		12.243
6 — SCREW, Lid Lock to Reinforcement		12.237
7 — LEVER & COUPLING, Lid Release		12.243
8 — CLIP, Cable to Lid		N.S.
9 — SPRING, Release Cable Return		12.243
10 — CYLINDER, Rear Compt. Lock		12.248
11 — RETAINER, Lid Lock Cylinder		12.249
12 — SCREW, Retainer to Compt. Lid (#8-18 x 1/2")		8.977
13 — LOCK, Rear Compt. Lid		12.242
14 — CLIP, Release Cable		12.243

Installation and routing of cable-controlled rear deck lid release
used in 1964-65.

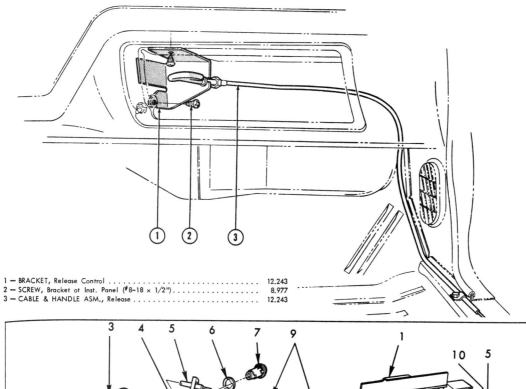

1 — BRACKET, Release Control 12.243
2 — SCREW, Bracket ot Inst. Panel (#8-18 x 1/2") 8.977
3 — CABLE & HANDLE ASM., Release 12.243

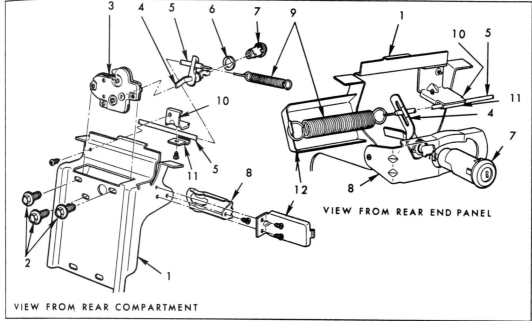

VIEW FROM REAR END PANEL

VIEW FROM REAR COMPARTMENT

1. Compartment Lid Anchor Plate - Body Side
2. Rear Compartment Lock Attaching Screws
3. Rear Compartment Lock
4. Release Coupling and Lever Assembly
5. Release Cable
6. Sealing Gasket
7. Lock Cylinder
8. Lock Cylinder Retainer
9. Return Spring
10. Release Cable Support
11. Release Cable Support Clip
12. Return Spring Retainer

Installation of 1966 cable rear deck lid release, showing installation of release unit on anchor plate in rear compartment.

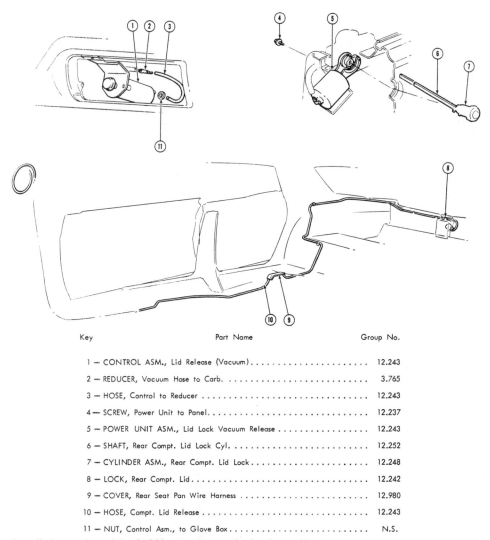

Key	Part Name	Group No.
1 — CONTROL ASM., Lid Release (Vacuum)		12.243
2 — REDUCER, Vacuum Hose to Carb.		3.765
3 — HOSE, Control to Reducer		12.243
4 — SCREW, Power Unit to Panel		12.237
5 — POWER UNIT ASM., Lid Lock Vacuum Release		12.243
6 — SHAFT, Rear Compt. Lid Lock Cyl.		12.252
7 — CYLINDER ASM., Rear Compt. Lid Lock		12.248
8 — LOCK, Rear Compt. Lid		12.242
9 — COVER, Rear Seat Pan Wire Harness		12.980
10 — HOSE, Compt. Lid Release		12.243
11 — NUT, Control Asm., to Glove Box		N.S.

Installation and routing of 1966 vacuum rear deck release. Note difference in glovebox control assembly mounting to cable unit.

Detail of 1967-70 electric rear deck release lid lock and glovebox-mounted release switch.

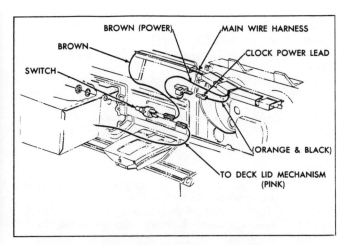

Installation of 1969 deck lid release. Compare to installation of 1970 unit. Switch design was changed for 1970.

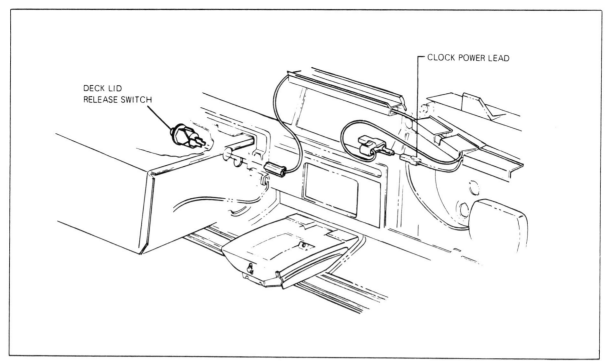

DECK LID RELEASE SWITCH

CLOCK POWER LEAD

Installation of 1970 remote-control deck lid release switch and wire assembly. Note routing of wire through conduit.

STEERING WHEEL

1964-65

All 1964 GTOs came standard with the LeMans Deluxe steering wheel. Optional was the Custom Sport wheel, made of a woodlike plastic with four brushed metal spokes. The wheel carried the 9741648 part number, the center horn button was 9774390, and the insert (emblem) was 9774073.

The Deluxe wheel was again standard in 1965, and the Custom Sport wheel was redesigned. The new wood-like wheel was much deeper, with three spokes of diecast metal and a redesigned center horn cap. The wheel carried part number 9780784, the horn button bezel assembly was 9779777, and the horn switch housing was 9780556.

Pontiac Service News Flash number 65-31, dated 10-19-64, reported that some early-production 1965 models had the wrong horn switch installed. The correct switch for the 235 and 237 Series was part number 9781837(Z-3), which was either black oxide or copper color. For the Custom Sport wheel the correct switch was number 9780171(Z-3), which was colored olive dichromate.

A production change occurred in mid-1964, and a new cancel cam was used in production. The standard column cam (part number 382931) was of a different design than the tilt cam (part number 9774458); the tilt cam was the same for 1964 and 1965. A standard column cam could not be used in tilt column applications.

1966-67

The 1966 GTO came standard with the LeMans Deluxe steering wheel. Available as an extra-cost option was the Custom Sport steering wheel (RPO 471). This "wood" wheel was identical in all respects to the 1965 wheel.

The 1967 GTO followed the same pattern as the 1966, using the LeMans Deluxe wheel as standard equip-

ment. A redesigned Custom Sport steering wheel (RPO 471) was available. The spoke and horn button and bezel were completely different in 1967.

Canceling cams for the directional signal assembly were carried over from 1965 for use in the 1966 GTO. The 1967 used different designs, as the column was also redesigned for 1967.

Year	Application	Part Number
1966	With tilt column	9774458
	Without tilt column	382931
1967	With tilt column	9788414
	Without tilt column	9787615

1968-70

All GTOs came standard with the Deluxe steering wheel in 1968-70. The 1968 wheel was identical in style to the 1967 wheel—with the exception of the horn buttons, which were color keyed to match the interior trim.

The 1969 and 1970 Deluxe wheels were identical in design, however, since the wheels and horn covers were color keyed to match the trim colors of the interior (except parchment). The only wheels interchangeable between the two years were black.

The Custom Sport steering wheel option was available for all three years. The 1968 wheel (part number 5464470, RPO 471) was much shallower than earlier wheels. (Dealer Product Campaign Bulletin number 68-C-4, dated 4-3-69, reported on problems with the 1968 Custom Sport steering wheel—one or all of the spokes could break adjacent to the hub. This wheel was replaced with an improved version, part number 546470). The horn button bezel (part number 9792775) was different than the 1967 bezel in surface texture.

The 1969 and 1970 Custom Sport steering wheels (part number 9795885; RPO 462 UPC N34) were identical in all respects. The horn button bezel was color keyed to match the interior trim (with the exception of parchment).

The insert for the bezel was black, with the letters PMD in red.

A second steering wheel option was available in 1970, the Formula wheel (RPO 464, UPC NK3). This wheel was identical in all respects to the wheel used on the 1969 Firebird Trans Am. The padded rim (part number 546296) used a horn button cover (part number 480479) with the Pontiac crest in the center of the insert. This wheel was only available in black and only with power steering.

Directional signal canceling cams were different and not interchangeable between the 1968 and the 1969-70 columns.

Year	Application	Part Number
1968	With tilt column	399294
	Without tilt column	399292
1969-70	With tilt column	7805224
	Without tilt column	7804768

Detail of 1964 Custom Sport wood wheel (RPO 524). Spokes were made of stainless steel. Available in 1964 only.

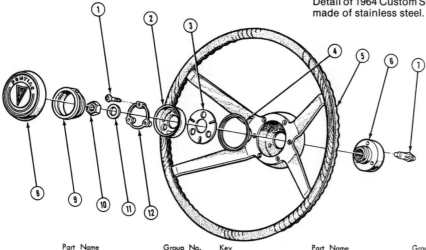

Key	Part Name	Group No.
1 — SCREW, Horn Ring Spacer Bushing (#10-32 x 3/4")		2.821
2 — CUP, Horn Button Contact		2.821
3 — SPRING, Horn Button		2.819
4 — INSULATOR, Horn Contact Spring		2.819
5 — WHEEL, Steering (Wood)		6.513
6 — HUB, Steering Wheel		N.S.

Key	Part Name	Group No.
7 — CONTACT & SPRING ASM., Horn Button		2.819
8 — CAP, Steering Wheel-Includes Ornament		2.817
9 — RETAINER, Horn Button Cap		2.821
10 — NUT, Wheel Asm. to Steering Shaft (1/2"-20)		6.515
11 — WASHER, Wheel Asm. to Steering Shaft (17/32" I.D. x 15/16" O.D.)		6.515
12 — BUSHING, Horn Button Cup Spacer		2.821

Exploded view of 1964 Custom Sport steering wheel and parts nomenclature.

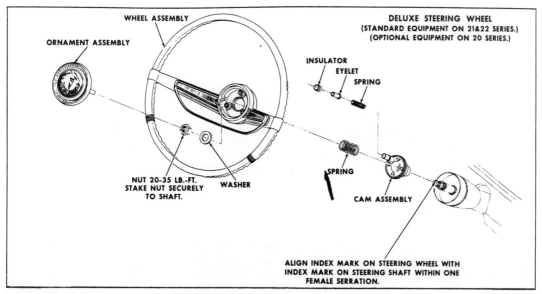

Installation of 1964 GTO Deluxe steering wheel. The horn ring used part number 9740478, and the ornament was serviced by part number 9774189.

For 1965, the Custom Sport wheel was redesigned to be bigger in diameter and deeper. RPO was 524, available 1965 and 1966.

Close-up of 1967 GTO standard wheel ornament bezel (part number 9787953). Bezel was metal, with the Pontiac emblem against a green background and the words energy absorbing beneath the emblem.

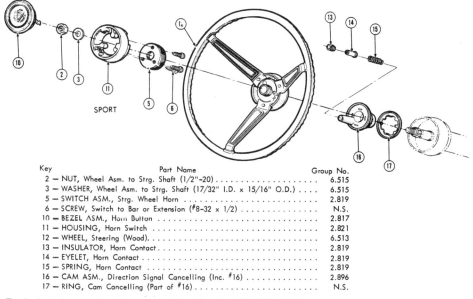

Key	Part Name	Group No.
2 — NUT, Wheel Asm. to Strg. Shaft (1/2"-20)		6.515
3 — WASHER, Wheel Asm. to Strg. Shaft (17/32" I.D. x 15/16" O.D.)		6.515
5 — SWITCH ASM., Strg. Wheel Horn		2.819
6 — SCREW, Switch to Bar or Extension (#8-32 x 1/2)		N.S.
10 — BEZEL ASM., Horn Button		2.817
11 — HOUSING, Horn Switch		2.821
12 — WHEEL, Steering (Wood)		6.513
13 — INSULATOR, Horn Contact		2.819
14 — EYELET, Horn Contact		2.819
15 — SPRING, Horn Contact		2.819
16 — CAM ASM., Direction Signal Cancelling (Inc. #16)		2.896
17 — RING, Cam Cancelling (Part of #16)		N.S.

Exploded view and parts nomenclature for the 1965-66 Custom Sport steering wheel.

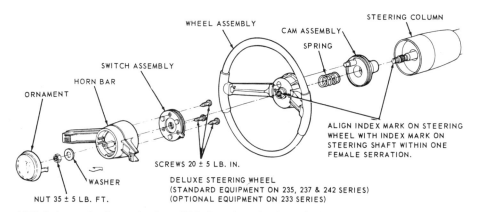

1966 Deluxe wheel, standard on GTO. Steering wheel matched the instrument panel trim color. The horn bar (part number 9783137) was chrome with the pebble-grain insert painted black. Wood inserts had been planned for the horn bar to match the GTO instrument panel veneer—as was done in the Grand Prix and Bonneville—but were scrapped before production began. The ornament carried part number 9783134.

194

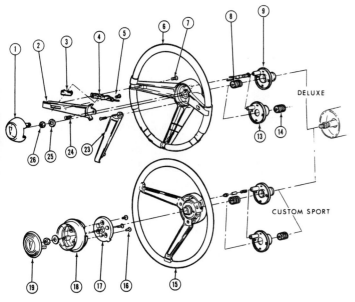

Comparison of 1967 (right) and 1968 Custom Sport horn button bezels. The 1968 was easily identifiable by the brushed-metal appearance around the bezel; 1967 bezels were chromed and polished.

Key	Part Name	Group No.
1 —	BEZEL ASM., Steering Wheel Ornament	2.817
2 —	COVER, Steering Wheel Spoke Trim & Horn Switch	2.830
3 —	BUTTON ASM., Horn	2.819
4 —	SWITCH ASM., Steering Wheel Horn	2.819
5 —	SCREW, Switch to Hub (#8-32 x 7/16")	N.S.
6 —	WHEEL ASM., Steering - Deluxe	6.513
7 —	SCREW, Cover to Spoke (#8-32 x 11/16")	N.S.
8 —	SPRING, Steering Shaft Upper Bearing (Exc. Tilt Wheel) - 7/8" Long	6.526
9 —	CAM ASM., Direction Signal Cancelling (Exc. Tilt Wheel)	2.896
13 —	CAM ASM., Direction Signal Cancelling (With Tilt Wheel)	2.896
14 —	SPRING, Direction Signal Cancelling Cam Retainer (With Tilt Wheel)	2.896
15 —	WHEEL ASM., Steering - Custom Sport (Wood)	6.513
18 —	HOUSING, Horn Switch	2.821
19 —	BEZEL ASM., Horn Button	2.817
23 —	COVER, Steering Wheel Spoke Trim	2.830
24 —	SCREW, Cover to Hub (#8-32 x 7/16")	N.S.
25 —	WASHER, Steering Wheel to Shaft	6.515
26 —	NUT, Steering Wheel to Shaft (1/2"-20)	8.916

Deluxe wheel (top) was standard on all 1967 GTOs. The horn buttons (part number 9787958) mounted in the brushed-metal spoke covers (part number 9787961). A lower spoke cover (part number 9787962) completed the spoke trim. The Custom Sport wood wheel (bottom) was redesigned for 1967. Spoke design was different. The wheel part number was 9787429, the horn switch housing was 9787428, and the bezel was 9787425.

Custom Sport steering wheel for 1968 was shallower than 1965-67 wheels.

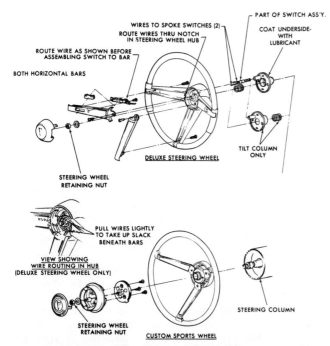

Detail of 1969-70 Custom Sport steering wheel horn button bezel. Bezels were color keyed to match the interior trim—except for parchment interiors, which used black bezels.

Exploded views of 1968 Deluxe and Custom Sport steering wheels. The spoke covers for the Deluxe wheel were part number 9793040 for the horizontal bars, and 9793041 for the lower spoke cover. The ornament bezel was part number 9793036. The spoke covers and the bezel were brushed metal.

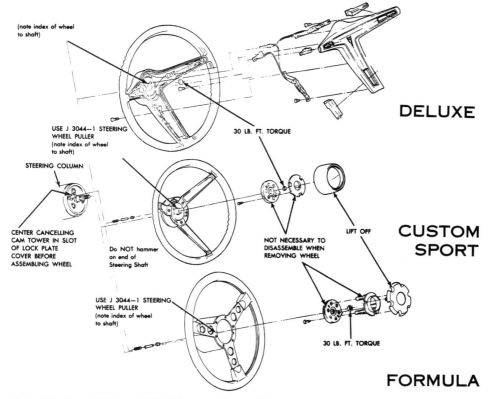

(note index of wheel to shaft)

USE J 3044—1 STEERING WHEEL PULLER (note index of wheel to shaft)

30 LB. FT. TORQUE

DELUXE

STEERING COLUMN

CENTER CANCELLING CAM TOWER IN SLOT OF LOCK PLATE COVER BEFORE ASSEMBLING WHEEL

Do NOT hammer on end of Steering Shaft

NOT NECESSARY TO DISASSEMBLE WHEN REMOVING WHEEL

LIFT OFF

CUSTOM SPORT

USE J 3044—1 STEERING WHEEL PULLER (note index of wheel to shaft)

30 LB. FT. TORQUE

FORMULA

Exploded view of 1969 and 1970 Deluxe and Custom Sport steering wheels. Formula wheel at bottom was used on 1970 only.

Detail of 1970 Formula wheel. Wheel was only available in black.

STEERING COLUMN

1964-65

The steering columns used in 1964 and 1965 had the same physical appearance from the outside, and they shared the same dimensions. However, there was one major internal difference, and that was in the directional signal switch assembly. The 1964 switch was serviced as a complete assembly. The 1965 directional switch assembly was diecast, with the upper bearing mounted on the turn signal switch, and was serviced without the upper collar.

The column jackets were painted the interior trim color, and the shaft and flange assembly was natural metal in appearance.

The steering column opening covers were different for the two years. The 1964 cover was a two-piece design (part number 9775063 and 9775064) made of diecast metal, and was painted to match the interior trim. The 1965 unit was serviced with the two-piece cover. Some 1965 GTOs were equipped with a one-piece plastic cover, with a standard column.

Tilt steering columns were identical for both years externally, with one internal difference in the horn button contact assembly (part number 5679863 in 1964 and 5694239 in 1965). Both years used the same two-piece steering column opening cover (part number 9775063 and 9775064).

The same release lever (part number 9776105) was used both years. It was possible for a GTO to come equipped with the automatic column shift with a tilt option. The tilt column jacket, cover and bowl assembly was painted to match the interior trim color. The shaft and flange were natural metal.

1966-67

The 1966 standard and tilt columns were almost identical to the 1965 columns. The only exception was the tilt column release lever (part number 9785257), which was slightly longer in length in 1966.

The 1967 columns were redesigned to meet federal safety standards relative to the column's ability to absorb energy and collapse in the event of a frontal impact. The length of the column was the same for 1966. However, the jacket and bowl were wider, and a traffic hazard warning flasher switch was incorporated into the jacket.

Two different types of flasher switches were used, one chrome (part number 398165), the other black plastic. The chrome switch was the most prevalent, although either was correct for 1967. No steering column opening cover was used in 1967, and two different steering-column mounting brackets were used, with or without air conditioning.

The 1966 used an all-chrome directional signal control lever; the 1967 lever was chrome with a black plastic knob:

Year	Application	Part Number
1966	With tilt column	9780280
	Without tilt column	9784709
1967	With cruise control	6465256
	Without cruise control	9786981

Steering column jackets were painted to match the interior trim at 60° gloss—except the RPO 224 parchment interior, in which case the column was painted 60° gloss black. The shaft and flange were natural metal in appearance.

1968-70

As federal safety standards began to come more into play in the late sixties, steering columns were subject to change almost at an annual rate. An exception was the energy-absorbing column introduced in 1967; the 1968 column was almost a carbon copy of it.

In 1969 the ignition lock was moved from the instrument panel to the steering column. The column and column cover diameters were increased to accommodate the directional signal assembly and the steering column lock mechanism.

One peculiarity of the 1968 column was in conjunction with the optional cornering lamp option. Because of different directional switch and harness assemblies, columns without the cornering lamps were not interchangeable with models using cornering lamps. This lack of interchangeability went as far as entire column assemblies, not only individual components.

The directional signal lever was chrome with a dull-black plastic knob (part number 9786981 for 1968-70 GTOs without cruise control). Lever part number 6465256 was used with cruise control. This lever had a button at the end of the stalk, which was depressed to activate the cruise control.

The steering column jackets were painted 60° gloss to match the upper instrument panel trim color. The shaft and flange were natural metal in appearance.

Detail of directional signal switch used for tilt column applications, 1964-66 (part number 1993624).

Canceling cam used for 1964-66 tilt column applications only.

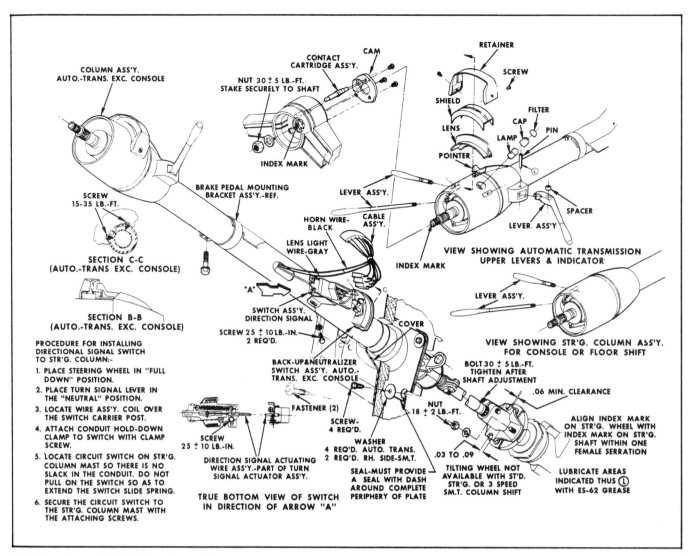

COLUMN ASS'Y. AUTO.-TRANS. EXC. CONSOLE

NUT 30 ± 5 LB.-FT. STAKE SECURELY TO SHAFT

CONTACT CARTRIDGE ASS'Y.

CAM

INDEX MARK

RETAINER

SCREW

SHIELD

LENS

POINTER

FILTER

CAP

LAMP

PIN

SPACER

LEVER ASS'Y

VIEW SHOWING AUTOMATIC TRANSMISSION UPPER LEVERS & INDICATOR

SCREW 15-35 LB.-FT.

SECTION C-C (AUTO.-TRANS EXC. CONSOLE)

SECTION B-B (AUTO.-TRANS. EXC. CONSOLE)

BRAKE PEDAL MOUNTING BRACKET ASS'Y.-REF.

HORN WIRE-BLACK

LENS LIGHT WIRE-GRAY

LEVER ASS'Y.

CABLE ASS'Y.

INDEX MARK

LEVER ASS'Y.

VIEW SHOWING STR'G. COLUMN ASS'Y. FOR CONSOLE OR FLOOR SHIFT

"A"

SWITCH ASS'Y. DIRECTION SIGNAL

SCREW 25 ± 10 LB.-IN. 2 REQ'D.

BACK-UP&NEUTRALIZER SWITCH ASS'Y. AUTO.-TRANS. EXC. CONSOLE

COVER

BOLT 30 ± 5 LB.-FT. TIGHTEN AFTER SHAFT ADJUSTMENT

.06 MIN. CLEARANCE

ALIGN INDEX MARK ON STR'G. WHEEL WITH INDEX MARK ON STR'G. SHAFT WITHIN ONE FEMALE SERRATION

PROCEDURE FOR INSTALLING DIRECTIONAL SIGNAL SWITCH TO STR'G. COLUMN:-

1. PLACE STEERING WHEEL IN "FULL DOWN" POSITION.
2. PLACE TURN SIGNAL LEVER IN THE "NEUTRAL" POSITION.
3. LOCATE WIRE ASS'Y. COIL OVER THE SWITCH CARRIER POST.
4. ATTACH CONDUIT HOLD-DOWN CLAMP TO SWITCH WITH CLAMP SCREW.
5. LOCATE CIRCUIT SWITCH ON STR'G. COLUMN MAST SO THERE IS NO SLACK IN THE CONDUIT. DO NOT PULL ON THE SWITCH SO AS TO EXTEND THE SWITCH SLIDE SPRING.
6. SECURE THE CIRCUIT SWITCH TO THE STR'G. COLUMN MAST WITH THE ATTACHING SCREWS.

FASTENER (2)

SCREW-4 REQ'D.

SCREW 25 ± 10 LB.-IN.

DIRECTION SIGNAL ACTUATING WIRE ASS'Y.-PART OF TURN SIGNAL ACTUATOR ASS'Y.

TRUE BOTTOM VIEW OF SWITCH IN DIRECTION OF ARROW "A"

NUT 18 ± 2 LB.-FT.

WASHER 4 REQ'D. AUTO. TRANS. 2 REQ'D. RH. SIDE-SM.T.

.03 TO .09

SEAL-MUST PROVIDE A SEAL WITH DASH AROUND COMPLETE PERIPHERY OF PLATE

TILTING WHEEL NOT AVAILABLE WITH ST'D. STR'G. OR 3 SPEED SM.T. COLUMN SHIFT

LUBRICATE AREAS INDICATED THUS Ⓛ WITH ES-62 GREASE

Details of typical 1964-66 tilt column. Note release lever (part number 9785257) and design of canceling cam.

Detail of two-piece diecast steering column opening cover used on all 1964 and 1965 tilt column applications. Cover was painted to match the interior trim. Note pads on upper assembly per Dealer Service Information Bulletin 64-96.

Compare steering column insulator cover (part number 3850999), noting different designs. Application was 1964 through 1966; a third style, unribbed, was also known to exist. Letters MMP were stamped on rear of ribbed cover. The 1967 cover was part number 3897543, and was a similar design.

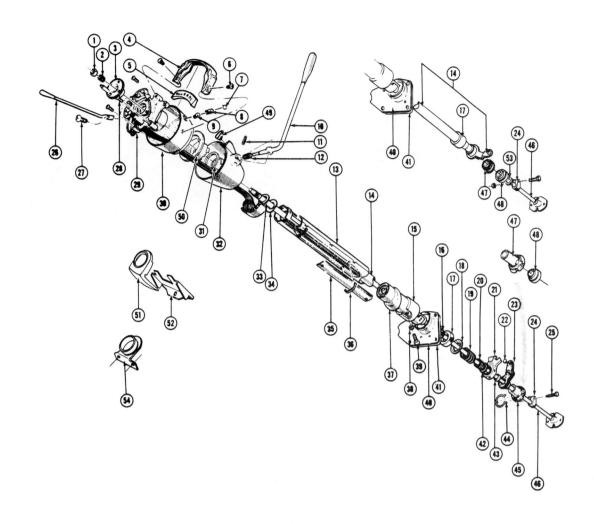

Key	Part Name	Group No.
1 — NUT, Steering Wheel to Steering Shaft (1/2" x 20) .		6.515
2 — SPRING, Steering Shaft Upper Bearing		6.526
3 — CAM ASM., Direction Signal Cancelling		2.896
4 — RETAINER, Gearshift Indicator Dial		4.020
5 — DIAL, Gearshift Indicator		4.020
6 — SCREW, Retainer to Housing (#8-32 x 1/4")		8.977
7 — FILTER, Indicator Dial Lamp		N.S.
8 — CAP, Indicator Dial Lamp		4.020
9 — BULB, Indicator Lamp (#53)		8.991
10 — LEVER ASM., Gearshift Control Upper		4.006
11 — PIN, Gearshift Lever Pivot		4.008
12 — SPRING, Gearshift Lever Anti-Rattle		4.008
13 — JACKET ASM., Steering Column		6.518
14 — TUBE ASM., Gearshift		4.025
15 — SLEEVE, Steering Column Jacket		
(2-1/4" O.D. x 1-1/2 Long)		6.760
16 — SEAL, Steering Shaft		6.758
17 — SEAL, Steering Column Gearshift Tube		4.027
18 — SEAT, Gearshift Tube Return Sprg-Upr.(Part of #14) .		N.S.
19 — SPRING, Gearshift Tube Return-Outer (Part of #14) .		N.S.
20 — SPRING, Gearshift Tube Return (Part of #14)		N.S.
21 — PLATE, Control Selector (Part of #14)		N.S.
22 — BUSHING, Gearshift Lever to Rod		
(5/16" I.D. x 13/16" O.D.)		4.037
23 — LEVER, Gearshift Tube (Part of #14)		N.S.
24 — CLAMP, Steering Shaft Lower Bearing		6.526
25 — SCREW, Clamp to Shaft (#14-10 x 1")		8.977
26 — LEVER, Direction Signal Control		2.897
27 — SCREW, Signal Lever to Switch Asm. (#8-32 x 1/2")		8.977
28 — SCREW, Switch to Housing		N.S.
29 — CONTROL ASM., Direction Signal (Inc. #30)		2.895
30 — HOUSING, Direction Signal Control (Part of #29) . .		N.S.
31 — WASHER, Gearshift Control Thrust		2.895
32 — BOWL, Gearshift Lever		4.010
33 — WASHER, Gearshift Control Spring		4.012
34 — WASHER, Gearshift Control Retainer		4.012
35 — COVER, Steering Column Wiring		2.906
36 — RETAINER, Steering Column Wiring Cover		2.901
37 — GROMMET, Steering Column		6.758
38 — LOCKWASHER, Jacket to Tube (1/4")		8.931
39 — SCREW, Jacket to Tube (1/4"-28 x 3/8")		8.977
40 — COVER, Steering Column to Toe Pan		6.758
41 — SEAL, Cover to Floor		6.758
42 — SEAT, Gearshift Tube Return Spring - Lower		
(Part of #14)		N.S.
43 — SLEEVE, Gearshift Tube Return Spring (Part of #14) .		N.S.
44 — RETAINER, Steering Column Lower Bearing		4.027
45 — ADAPTER ASM., Steering Column Lower		
Bearing (Inc. #47 - 48)		6.521
46 — SHAFT AND FLANGE ASM., Steering		6.524
47 — ADAPTER, Strg. Column Lower Bearing		6.525
48 — BEARING ASM., Strg. Shaft Lower Adapter		6.525
49 — POINTER, Indicator		4.020
50 — PLATE, Shift Lever Stop		4.027
51 — COVER, Steering Column Opening-Upper (1964-65) .		6.758
52 — COVER, Steering Column Opening-Lower (1964-65) .		6.758
53 — WASHER, Steering Column Lower Bearing Ret.		6.525
54 — COVER, Steering Column Opening (1966)		6.758

Exploded view of 1964-66 standard steering column, with parts
nomenclature for automatic transmission application with column
shift.

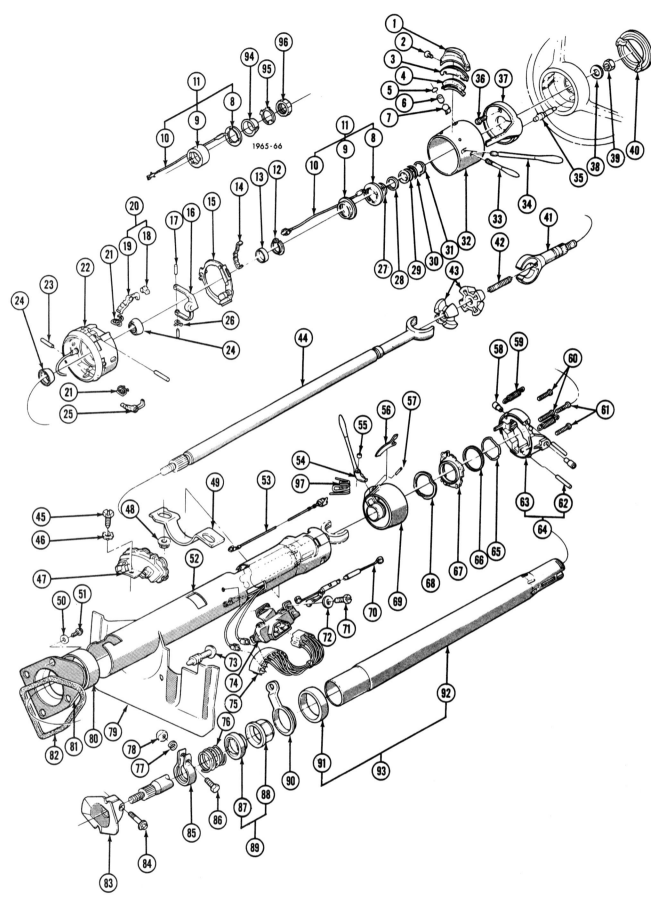

Exploded view of 1964-66 tilt steering column. Note difference in 1965-66 horn contact assembly from that used in 1964. When purchasing a used tilt column, make sure that item numbers 37 and 75 are included with column.

1965-66

Key	Part Name	Group No.
1 — RETAINER, Gearshift Indicator Lens	4.020
2 — SCREW, Retainer to Cover (#6-32 x 1/4")	8.977
3 — SHIELD, Gearshift Indicator Lens Light	4.020
4 — LENS, Gearshift Indicator	4.020
5 — FILTER, Gearshift Indicator Lens Lamp	4.020
6 — CAP, Gearshift Indicator Lens Lamp	4.020
7 — BULB, Gearshift Indicator Lamp (#53)	8.991
8 — PLATE, Horn Button Upper Bearing Contact	N.S.
9 — INSULATOR, Horn Button Contact	N.S.
10 — CABLE ASM., Horn Button Contact	N.S.
11 — CONTACT ASM., Horn Button	2.819
12 — SEAT, Steering Column Upper Bearing Spring	6.526
13 — RACE, Steering Shaft Upper Bearing Inner	6.521
14 — SPRING, Direction Signal Detent	2.910
15 — YOKE ASM., Direction Signal Actuator	2.910
16 — ACTUATOR, Shoe Release (Part of #22)	N.S.
17 — PIN, Actuator (3/16" x 7/8") (Part of #22)	8.939
18 — STOP, Wheel Tilt	N.S.
19 — SHOE, Steering Wheel Lock - Upper	N.S.
20 — SHOE ASM., Steering Wheel Lock	6.514
21 — SPRING, Steering Wheel Lock Shoe	6.514
22 — HOUSING ASM., Direction Signal Actuator	2.895
23 — PIN, Steering Wheel Shoe Dowel	6.514
24 — BEARING ASM., Steering Shaft - Upper	6.521
25 — SHOE, Steering Wheel Lock - Lower	6.514
26 — SPRING, Actuator (Part of #22)	N.S.
27 — RETAINER, Bearing Preload Capsule Washer..(▲)	6.526
28 — WASHER, Bearing Preload Capsule - Rubber...(▲)	6.526
29 — CAPSULE, Steering Column Preload (▲)	N.S.
30 — WASHER, Bearing Preload Capsule Retainer...(▲)	6.526
31 — RING, Preload Capsule Retaining (▲)	N.S.
32 — COVER, Direction Signal Control	2.906
33 — LEVER ASM., Steering Wheel Release	6.514
34 — LEVER ASM., Direction Signal Control	2.897
35 — CARTRIDGE ASM., Horn Contact	2.819
36 — SCREW, Cam to Steering Wheel (#6 - 32 x 3/8")	N.S.
37 — CAM, Direction Signal Cancelling	2.896
38 — WASHER, Steering Shaft to Wheel (17/32" I.D. x 15/16" O.D.)	6.515
39 — NUT, Steering Shaft to Wheel (1/2" - 20)	6.515
40 — ORNAMENT ASM., Strg. Wheel Horn Ring	2.817
41 — SHAFT, Steering Column Upper	6.524
42 — SPRING, Steering Shaft Joint Preload	6.524
43 — SPHERE, Steering Shaft Centering (▲)	N.S.
44 — SHAFT & YOKE ASM., Steering Column	6.524
45 — SCREW, Switch to Jacket (#10-24 x 3/8")	8.977
46 — LOCKWASHER, Switch to Jacket (#10 Ext.)	N.S.
47 — SWITCH ASM., Trans. Neutralizer and Back-up Lamp	2.695
48 — NUT, Steering Column Upper Clamp to Support	6.761
49 — CLAMP, Steering Column	6.761
50 — WASHER, Cover to Toe Pan	N.S.
51 — SCREW, Cover to Toe Pan (#10-16 x 1/2")	8.977
52 — JACKET, Steering Column	6.518
53 — SOCKET & WIRE ASM., Gearshift Indicator	4.020
54 — LEVER ASM., Gearshift Control Upper	4.006
55 — SPACER, Gearshift Lever Anti-Rattle	4.008
56 — POINTER, Gearshift Indicator	4.020
57 — PIN, Gearshift Lever Fulcrum (3/16" x 15/16")	8.939
58 — PIN, Steering Column Pivot	6.514
59 — SPRING, Steering Column Wheel Tilt	6.514
60 — SCREW, Steering Column Support (#8-32 x 7/8")	6.521
61 — SCREW, Steering Column Support (#10-32 x 1-1/4")	6.521
62 — PIN, Steering Column Support Asm.	N.S.
63 — SUPPORT, Steering Column Bearing Housing	N.S.
64 — SUPPORT ASM., Steering Column	6.521
65 — RING, Gearshift Tube Retaining	4.027
66 — WASHER, Steering Column Bowl Thrust	4.012
67 — PLATE, Steering Column Lock	6.521
68 — WASHER, Steering Column Wave	4.012
69 — BOWL ASM., Gearshift Lever	4.010
70 — WIRE ASM., Direction Signal Switch Actuating	2.895
71 — SCREW, Switch to Jacket (#10-16 x 3/8")	8.977
72 — LOCKWASHER, Switch to Jacket (#10 Ext.)	N.S.
73 — FASTENER, Dash Insulator Cover	6.758
74 — SWITCH ASM., Direction Signal	2.895
75 — WIRE ASM., Signal Switch Jumper	2.895
76 — SPRING, Steering Column Bearing	6.526
77 — LOCKWASHER, Clamp to Steering Shaft (1/4" Int.)	8.932
78 — NUT, Clamp to Steering Shaft (1/4"-20)	8.915
79 — COVER, Dash Ins. at Strg. Col.	6.758
80 — SLEEVE, Steering Column Jacket	6.750
81 — COVER, Steering Column to Toe Pan	6.758
82 — SEAL, Cover to Floor	6.758
83 — FLANGE, Steering Shaft Upper	6.525
84 — BOLT, Flange to Shaft Clamping	6.525
85 — CLAMP, Steering Column Lower Bearing	6.525
86 — BOLT, Clamp to Steering Shaft (1/4"-20 x 11/16")	8.900
87 — BEARING ASM., Steering Shaft	6.525
88 — ADAPTER, Steering Column Shift Tube	6.525
89 — ADAPTER ASM., Steering Column Lower Shift Tube	6.525
90 — LEVER, Gearshift Lower Shift (Part of #93)	N.S.
91 — SEAL, Steering Column Lever (Part of #93)	4.017
92 — TUBE, Gearshift (Part of #93)	N.S.
93 — TUBE ASM., Gearshift (Inc. #83-84-85)	4.025
94 — SEAT, Steering Shaft Upper Bearing Race - Inner	6.521
95 — WASHER, Steering Column Bearing Lock Tab	6.521
96 — NUT, Steering Shaft Upper Bearing	6.521
97 — SPRING, Gearshift Lever Bowl (5-coils)	4.010

(▲) STEERING COLUMN CENTERING SPHERE SHIM KIT-6.525

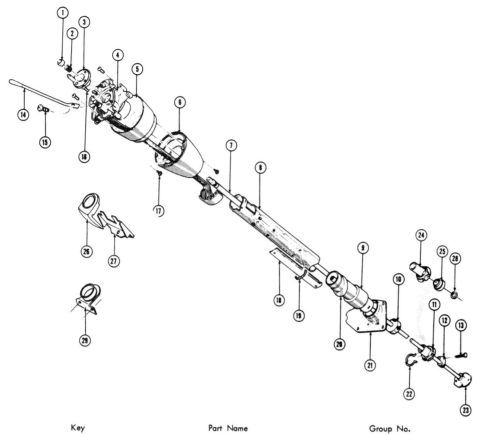

Key	Part Name	Group No.
1 — NUT, Steering Wheel to Steering Shaft (1/2" - 20)		6.515
2 — SPRING, Steering Shaft Upper Bearing		6.526
3 — CAM ASM., Direction Signal Cancelling		2.896
4 — CONTROL ASM., Direction Signal (Inc. #5)		2.895
5 — HOUSING, Direction Signal Control		N.S.
6 — EXTENSION ASM., Steering Column Jacket		6.518
7 — SHAFT & FLANGE ASM., Steering		6.524
8 — JACKET, Steering Column		6.518
9 — SLEEVE, Steering Column Jacket (2-1/4" O.D. x 1-1/2" Long)		6.760
10 — SEAL, Steering Shaft		6.519
11 — ADAPTER ASM., Steering Column Lower Bearing (Inc. #24 - 25)		6.521
12 — CLAMP, Steering Shaft Lower Bearing		6.526
13 — SCREW, Clamp to Shaft (#14 - 10 x 1")		8.977
14 — LEVER, Direction Signal Control		2.897
15 — SCREW, Signal Lever to Switch Asm. (#8 - 32 x 1/2")		8.977
16 — SCREW, Switch Asm. to Extension		N.S.
17 — SCREW, Extension to Control Asm. (#10 - 16 x 3/8")		8.977
18 — COVER, Steering Column Wiring		2.906
19 — RETAINER, Steering Column Wiring Cover		2.901
20 — GROMMET, Steering Column		6.758
21 — COVER, Steering Column to Toe Pan - w/A.T.		6.758
22 — RETAINER, Steering Column Lower Bearing		6.525
23 — FLANGE, Steering Shaft (Part of #7)		N.S.
24 — ADAPTER, Steering Column Lower Bearing		6.525
25 — BEARING ASM., Steering Shaft Lower Adapter		6.525
26 — COVER, Steering Column Opening-Upper (1964-65)		6.758
27 — COVER, Steering Column Opening-Lower (1965-66)		6.758
28 — WASHER, Steering Column Lower Bearing Retaining		6.525
29 — COVER, Steering Column Opening (1966)		6.758

Exploded view of standard steering column with floor shift, with
parts nomenclature used from 1964-66.

LOOSE TEMPEST STEERING COLUMN OPENING COVERS

Reports are being received that the Tempest steering column opening cover 9775064-F is rattling requiring the installation of screws.

Screws should not be necessary as the cover is held in place by the lower bezel 9775063-F. Adhesive backed foam pads installed under the tabs of the upper cover by the assembly plants provide the anti-rattle requirement. In cases where the foam pads have not been installed and a rattle is found, make and install foam rubber pads from existing stock.

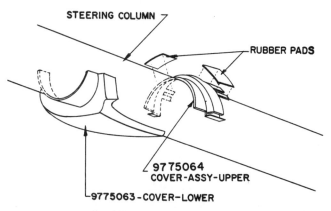

Installation of these foam-rubber pads may be necessary to stop rattling of the 1964 steering column. (This information taken from Dealer Service Information Bulletin number 64-96, dated 4-30-64.)

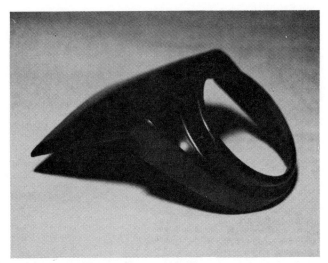

1965 second-design plastic steering column opening cover, painted to match the instrument panel trim.

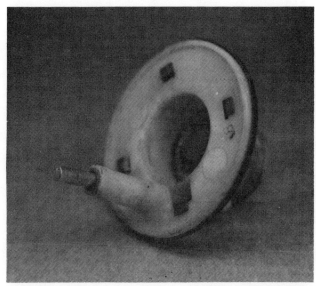

Close-up of 1966 standard steering column directional signal canceling cam.

Close-up of 1966 standard steering column directional signal assembly in column. While this column was removed from 242176B105833 equipped with console shift, the provision for column shift indicator bulb was still installed by the factory, as the bulb socket (one o'clock position) and wire assembly are clearly visible.

1966 steering column at instrument panel opening cover for 1966 (part number 9785452). Cover was used for all column applications, and was painted to match the instrument panel trim color. Cover was made of plastic. No opening cover was used on the 1967 GTO.

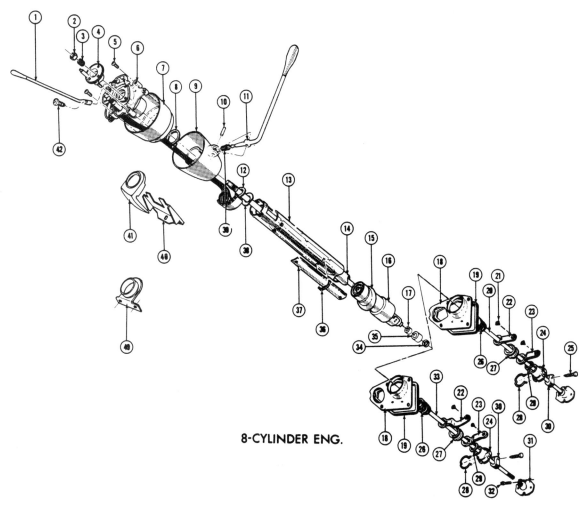

8-CYLINDER ENG.

Key	Part Name	Group No.
1 — LEVER, Direction Signal Control		2.897
2 — NUT, Steering Wheel to Steering Shaft (1/2"-20)		6.515
3 — SPRING, Steering Shaft Upper Bearing		6.526
4 — CAM ASM., Direction Signal Cancelling		2.896
5 — SCREW, Switch to Housing		N.S.
6 — CONTROL ASM., Directional Signal (Incl. #7) . .		2.895
7 — HOUSING, Direction Signal Control		2.906
8 — WASHER, Gearshift Control Thrust		4.012
9 — BOWL, Steering Column Gearshift Lever		4.010
10 — PIN, Gearshift Lever Pivot		4.008
11 — LEVER, Gearshift Control - Upper		4.006
12 — WASHER, Control Lever Housing Ret. – Wave . . .		4.012
13 — JACKET, Steering Column		6.518
14 — TUBE ASM., Gearshift		4.025
15 — GROMMET, Steering Column		N.S.
16 — SLEEVE, Steering Column Jacket (2 1/4 O.D. x 1 1/2" long)		6.760
17 — SEAL, Steering Shaft		6.519
18 — PLATE, Steering Col. to Toe Pan Cover		6.758
19 — SEAL, Steering Col. Cover to Floor		6.758
20 — SHAFT & FLANGE, Steering Gear Upper		6.524
21 — BUSHING, Gearshift Lever to Rod (1 7/16" I.D. x 13/16" O.D.)		4.037
22 — LEVER, Gearshift - 2nd and 3rd		4.030
23 — LEVER, Gearshift - 1st and Reverse		4.030
24 — ADAPTER ASM., Steering Col. Lower Bearing		6.525
25 — SCREW, Clamp to Shaft (#14 - 10 x 1").		8.977
26 — SPRING, Gearshift Tube Return		N.S.
27 — SPACER, Gearshift Tube Lever (1964)		4.027
28 — RETAINER, Steering Column Lower Bearing		6.525
29 — WASHER, Strg. Col. Shift Cont. Spring Lower. . .		4.032
30 — CLAMP, Steering Shaft Lower Bearing.		6.526
31 — FLANGE, Steering Shaft.		6.524
32 — BOLT, Lower Flange to Shaft Clamping		6.525
33 — SHAFT, Steering		6.524
34 — SEAT, Gearshift Tube Return Spring		N.S.
35 — SEAL, Gearshift Tube.		4.027
36 — RETAINER, Steering Col. Wiring Cover		2.906
37 — COVER, Steering Column Wiring		2.906
38 — WASHER, Control Lever Housing - Retainer. . . .		4.012
39 — SPRING, Gearshift Lever Anti-Rattle		4.008
40 — COVER, Steering Column Opening - Lower (1964–65)		6.758
41 — COVER, Steering Column Opening - Upper (1964–65)		6.758
42 — SCREW, Signal Lever to Switch (#8 - 32 x 1/2") .		8.977
43 — ADAPTER, Steering Column Lower Bearing		6.525
44 — BEARING, Steering Shaft Adapter - Lower		6.525
45 — WASHER, Gearshift Lever Housing & Steering Column Wave		4.012
46 — SPACER, Gearshift Tube Levers		4.032
47 — RING, Shifter Tube Adjusting		4.027
48 — WASHER, Steering Column Lower Bearing Retaining		6.525
49 — COVER, Steering Column Opening (1966)		6.758

Exploded view of standard steering column with parts nomenclature used for 1966 GTO with standard three-speed shifter on column.

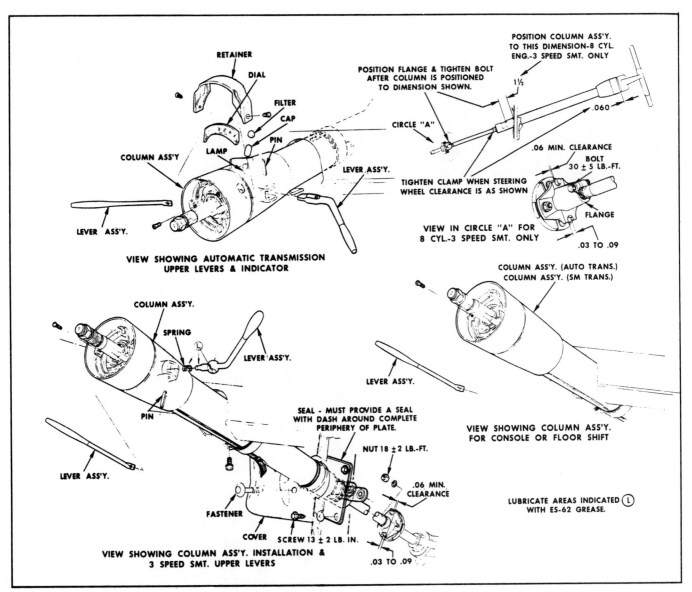

RETAINER

DIAL

FILTER

CAP

COLUMN ASS'Y

PIN

LAMP

LEVER ASS'Y.

LEVER ASS'Y.

VIEW SHOWING AUTOMATIC TRANSMISSION
UPPER LEVERS & INDICATOR

POSITION COLUMN ASS'Y.
TO THIS DIMENSION-8 CYL.
ENG.-3 SPEED SMT. ONLY

POSITION FLANGE & TIGHTEN BOLT
AFTER COLUMN IS POSITIONED
TO DIMENSION SHOWN.

CIRCLE "A"

1½

.060

.06 MIN. CLEARANCE

BOLT
30 ± 5 LB.-FT.

TIGHTEN CLAMP WHEN STEERING
WHEEL CLEARANCE IS AS SHOWN

FLANGE

VIEW IN CIRCLE "A" FOR
8 CYL.-3 SPEED SMT. ONLY

.03 TO .09

COLUMN ASS'Y.

SPRING

LEVER ASS'Y.

PIN

LEVER ASS'Y.

FASTENER

COVER   SCREW 13 ± 2 LB. IN.

SEAL - MUST PROVIDE A SEAL
WITH DASH AROUND COMPLETE
PERIPHERY OF PLATE.

NUT 18 ± 2 LB.-FT.

.06 MIN.
CLEARANCE

.03 TO .09

VIEW SHOWING COLUMN ASS'Y. INSTALLATION &
3 SPEED SMT. UPPER LEVERS

COLUMN ASS'Y. (AUTO TRANS.)
COLUMN ASS'Y. (SM TRANS.)

LEVER ASS'Y.

VIEW SHOWING COLUMN ASS'Y.
FOR CONSOLE OR FLOOR SHIFT

LUBRICATE AREAS INDICATED ⓁWITH ES-62 GREASE.

Details of 1966 standard steering column. Note details of automatic column shift.

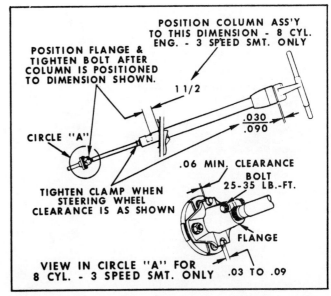

POSITION COLUMN ASS'Y
TO THIS DIMENSION - 8 CYL.
ENG. - 3 SPEED SMT. ONLY

POSITION FLANGE &
TIGHTEN BOLT AFTER
COLUMN IS POSITIONED
TO DIMENSION SHOWN.

1 1/2

.030
.090

CIRCLE "A"

.06 MIN. CLEARANCE
BOLT
25-35 LB.-FT.

TIGHTEN CLAMP WHEN
STEERING WHEEL
CLEARANCE IS AS SHOWN

FLANGE

VIEW IN CIRCLE "A" FOR
8 CYL. - 3 SPEED SMT. ONLY   .03 TO .09

Installation of 1967 column. Compare measurements to 1966 column.

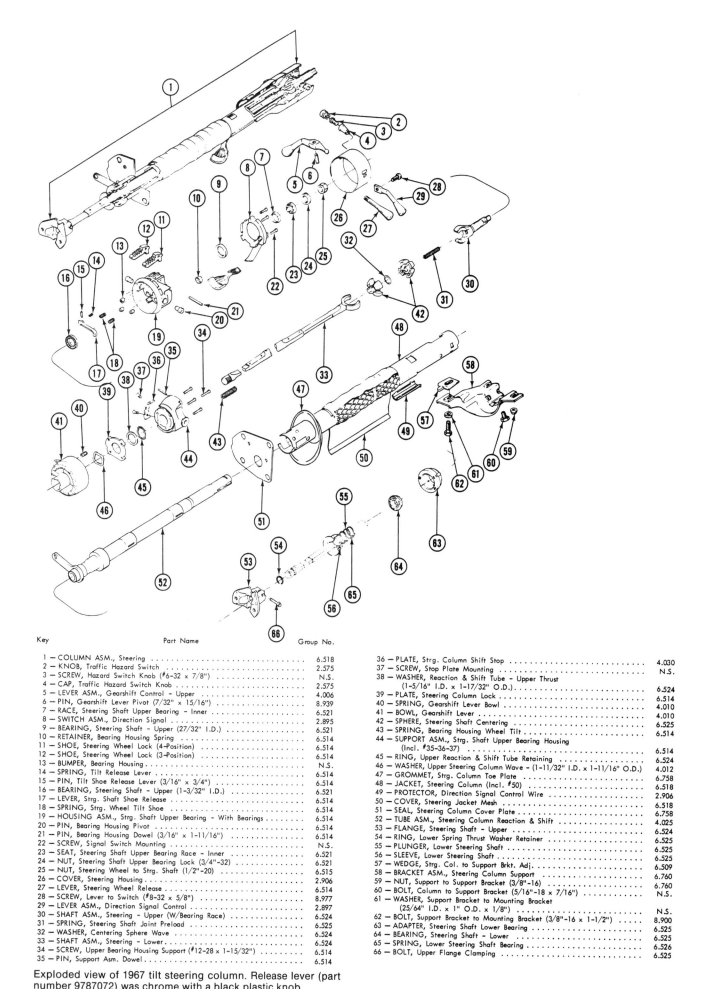

Key	Part Name	Group No.
1 — COLUMN ASM., Steering		6.518
2 — KNOB, Traffic Hazard Switch		2.575
3 — SCREW, Hazard Switch Knob (#6-32 x 7/8")		N.S.
4 — CAP, Traffic Hazard Switch Knob		2.575
5 — LEVER ASM., Gearshift Control - Upper		4.006
6 — PIN, Gearshift Lever Pivot (7/32" x 15/16")		8.939
7 — RACE, Steering Shaft Upper Bearing - Inner		6.521
8 — SWITCH ASM., Direction Signal		2.895
9 — BEARING, Steering Shaft - Upper (27/32" I.D.)		6.521
10 — RETAINER, Bearing Housing Spring		6.514
11 — SHOE, Steering Wheel Lock (4-Position)		6.514
12 — SHOE, Steering Wheel Lock (3-Position)		6.514
13 — BUMPER, Bearing Housing		N.S.
14 — SPRING, Tilt Release Lever		6.514
15 — PIN, Tilt Shoe Release Lever (3/16" x 3/4")		6.514
16 — BEARING, Steering Shaft - Upper (1-3/32" I.D.)		6.521
17 — LEVER, Strg. Shaft Shoe Release		6.514
18 — SPRING, Strg. Wheel Tilt Shoe		6.514
19 — HOUSING ASM., Strg. Shaft Upper Bearing - With Bearings		6.514
20 — PIN, Bearing Housing Pivot		6.514
21 — PIN, Bearing Housing Dowel (3/16" x 1-11/16")		6.514
22 — SCREW, Signal Switch Mounting		N.S.
23 — SEAT, Steering Shaft Upper Bearing Race - Inner		6.521
24 — NUT, Steering Shaft Upper Bearing Lock (3/4"-32)		6.521
25 — NUT, Steering Wheel to Strg. Shaft (1/2"-20)		6.515
26 — COVER, Steering Housing		2.906
27 — LEVER, Steering Wheel Release		6.514
28 — SCREW, Lever to Switch (#8-32 x 5/8")		8.977
29 — LEVER ASM., Direction Signal Control		2.897
30 — SHAFT ASM., Steering - Upper (W/Bearing Race)		6.524
31 — SPRING, Steering Shaft Joint Preload		6.525
32 — WASHER, Centering Sphere Wave		6.524
33 — SHAFT ASM., Steering - Lower		6.524
34 — SCREW, Upper Bearing Housing Support (#12-28 x 1-15/32")		6.514
35 — PIN, Support Asm. Dowel		6.514

Key	Part Name	Group No.
36 — PLATE, Strg. Column Shift Stop		4.030
37 — SCREW, Stop Plate Mounting		N.S.
38 — WASHER, Reaction & Shift Tube - Upper Thrust (1-5/16" I.D. x 1-17/32" O.D.)		6.524
39 — PLATE, Steering Column Lock		6.514
40 — SPRING, Gearshift Lever Bowl		4.010
41 — BOWL, Gearshift Lever		4.010
42 — SPHERE, Steering Shaft Centering		6.525
43 — SPRING, Bearing Housing Wheel Tilt		6.514
44 — SUPPORT ASM., Strg. Shaft Upper Bearing Housing (Incl. #35-36-37)		6.514
45 — RING, Upper Reaction & Shift Tube Retaining		6.514
46 — WASHER, Upper Steering Column Wave - (1-11/32" I.D. x 1-11/16" O.D.)		4.012
47 — GROMMET, Strg. Column Toe Plate		6.758
48 — JACKET, Steering Column (Incl. #50)		6.518
49 — PROTECTOR, Direction Signal Control Wire		2.906
50 — COVER, Steering Jacket Mesh		6.518
51 — SEAL, Steering Column Cover Plate		6.758
52 — TUBE ASM., Steering Column Reaction & Shift		4.025
53 — FLANGE, Steering Shaft - Upper		6.524
54 — RING, Lower Spring Thrust Washer Retainer		6.525
55 — PLUNGER, Lower Steering Shaft		6.525
56 — SLEEVE, Lower Steering Shaft		6.525
57 — WEDGE, Strg. Col. to Support Brkt. Adj.		6.509
58 — BRACKET ASM., Steering Column Support		6.760
59 — NUT, Support to Support Bracket (3/8"-16)		6.760
60 — BOLT, Column to Support Bracket (5/16"-18 x 7/16")		N.S.
61 — WASHER, Support Bracket to Mounting Bracket (25/64" I.D. x 1" O.D. x 1/8")		N.S.
62 — BOLT, Support Bracket to Mounting Bracket (3/8"-16 x 1-1/2")		8.900
63 — ADAPTER, Steering Shaft Lower Bearing		6.525
64 — BEARING, Steering Shaft - Lower		6.525
65 — SPRING, Lower Steering Shaft Bearing		6.526
66 — BOLT, Upper Flange Clamping		6.525

Exploded view of 1967 tilt steering column. Release lever (part number 9787072) was chrome with a black plastic knob.

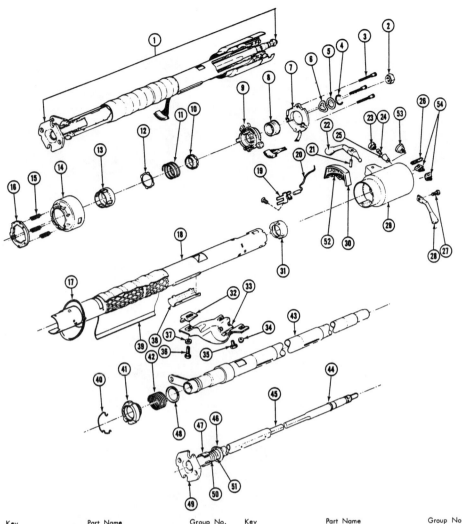

Key	Part Name	Group No.	Key	Part Name	Group No.
1 — COLUMN ASM., Steering.		6.518	28 — LEVER ASM, Dir. Signal Control		2.897
2 — NUT, Steering Wheel to Strg. Shaft (1/2"-20). .		6.515	29 — BOWL, Gearshift Lever		4.010
3 — SCREW, Direction Signal Switch Mounting.		N.S.	30 — RETAINER, Gearshift Indicator Lens (Tempest) . .		4.020
4 — RING, Upper Bearing Retaining		6.521	31 — BEARING, Shift Bowl - Lower		6.518
5 — WASHER, Strg. Shaft Upper Thrust		6.521	32 — WEDGE, Strg. Col. to Support Brkt. Adj.		6.509
6 — WASHER, Strg. Shaft Upper - Wave		6.521	33— BRACKET ASM., Strg. Column Support		6.760
7 — SWITCH ASM., Direction Signal		2.895	34 — NUT, Supt. to Supt. Bracket (3/8"-16)		6.760
8 — BEARING, Strg. Shaft - Upper		N.S.	35 — BOLT, Column to Supt. Brkt. (5/16"-18 x 7/16")		N.S.
9 — HOUSING, Direction Signal Control (Incl.			36 — BOLT, Supt. Brkt. to Mtg. Brkt. (3/8"-16 x 1-1/2")		8.900
#8-10-11-12-13)			37 — WASHER, Supt. Brkt. to Mtg. Brkt.		
. . . .		2.906	(25/64" I.D. x 1" O.D. x 1/8")		N.S.
10 — BEARING, Shift Bowl - Upper		N.S.	38 — PROTECTOR, Dir. Signal Control Wire.		2.906
11 — SPRING, Shift Bowl Centering		6.521	39 — COVER, Jacket Mesh		6.518
12 — RING, Spring Thrust		6.521	40 — CLIP, Lower Bearing Adapter		6.525
13 — SHELL, Spring Retainer		6.521	41 — ADAPTER, Strg. Shaft Lower Bearing		6.525
14 — COVER, SWITCH & HOUSING ASM., Direction			42 — SPRING, Reaction & Shift Tube Return		6.518
Signal.		2.895	43 — TUBE ASM., Strg. Col. Reaction & Shift		4.025
15 — SPRING, Switch Cover Retaining		6.526	44 — RING, Upper Strg. Shaft Retaining		6.521
16 — PLATE, Lock		6.514	45 — SHAFT ASM., Steering - w/Flange (Incl. #49).		6.524
17 — GROMMET, Strg. Col. Toe Plate		6.758	46 — BEARING, Strg. Shaft - Lower		6.525
18 — JACKET, Steering Column (Incl. #31-39).		6.518	47 — SLEEVE, Steering Shaft Lower		6.525
19 — CLAMP, Indicator to Shift Tube		4.020	48 — WASHER, Reaction & Shift Tube Thrust		6.518
20 — POINTER, Gearshift Indicator		4.020	49 — FLANGE, Lower Steering Shaft		N.S.
21 — PIN, Gearshift Lever Pivot (7/32" x 15/16"). . .		8.939	50 — PLUNGER, Lower Steering Shaft		6.525
22 — LEVER ASM., Gearshift Control Upper		4.006	51 — SPRING, Lower Strg. Shaft Bearing		6.526
23 — KNOB, Traffic Hazard Switch (Flat Black)		2.575	52 — LENS, Gearshift Indicator (Tempest).		4.020
24 — SCREW, Hazard Switch Knob (#6-32 x 7/8"). . .		N.S.	53 — KNOB, Traffic Hazard Switch (Chrome)		2.575
25 — CAP, Traffic Hazard Switch Knob (Flat Black) . .		2.575	54 — SPRING, Shift Indicator to Signal Switch Hsg.		
26 — SPRING, Gearshift Lever Bowl		4.010	(Tempest)		4.020
27 — SCREW, Lever to Switch (#8-32 x 5/8")		8.977			

Exploded view of 1967-68 GTO standard column.

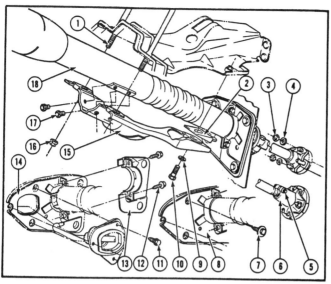

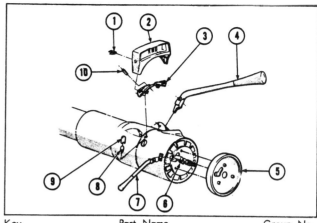

Key	Part Name	Group No.
1 — SPRING, Gearshift Indicator Lens Retainer		4.022
2 — INDICATOR ASM., Gearshift		4.020
3 — BRACKET, Gearshift Indicator Lens Retainer . .		4.022
4 — LEVER ASM., Gearshift Control - Upper		4.006
5 — COVER & SCREW ASM., Strg. Column Lock Plate .		6.500
6 — SCREW, Direction Signal Control Lever to Switch (8-32 x 5/8)		N.S.
7 — LEVER ASM., Direction Signal Control		2.897
8 — BULB, Gearshift Indicator Lamp (#1893)		8.991
9 — CAP, Gearshift Indicator Lens Lamp		4.022
10 — PIN, Gearshift Upper Lever Pivot (7/32" x 15/16)		4.008

Key	Part Name	Group No.
1 — SUPPORT, Steering Col.-Upr.-L.H.		6.760
2 — WEDGE, Strg. Col. to Supt. Brkt. Adj. . .		6.760
3 — NUT, Flange to Strg. Gear (3/8"-24)		8.916
4 — LOCKWASHER, Flange to Strg. Gear (3/8")		8.931
5 — BOLT, Flange to Shaft Clamping		6.525
6 — FLANGE, Strg. Shaft - Lower		6.525
7 — SCREW ASM., Cover to Dash (1/4"-14 x 3/4")		8.977
8 — PLATE & CLAMP ASM., Strg. Col.-Outboard (A.T.)		6.758
9 — WASHER, Supt. Brkt. to Pedal Brkt.		6.760
10 — BOLT, Supt. Brkt. to Pedal Brkt. (3/8"-16 x 1 1/2")		8.900
11 — SCREW, Cover to Dash (1/4"-14 x 3/4") . .		N.S.
12 — SCREW, Cover to Inner Clamp (1/4"-14 x 1")		8.977
13 — PLATE & CLAMP ASM., Strg. Col.-Inboard .		6.758
14 — PLATE & CLAMP ASM., Strg. Col.-Outboard (S.T.)		6.758
15 — BRACKET ASM., Strg. Col. Supt.		6.760
16 — NUT, Strg. Col. Supt. to Supt. Brkt.		6.760
17 — BOLT, Supt. Brkt. to Col. (5/16"-18 x 7/16")		N.S.
18 — COLUMN ASM., Steering		6.518

Drawings of steering column and cover plates for 1967 GTO.

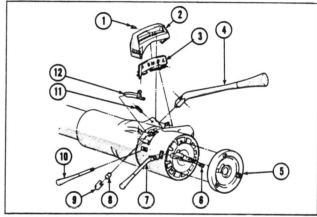

Key	Part Name	Group No.
1 — CLIP, Gearshift Indicator Lens to Retainer		4.022
2 — RETAINER, Gearshift Indicator Lens		4.022
3 — LENS, Gearshift Indicator		4.020
4 — LEVER ASM., Gearshift Control - Upper		4.006
5 — COVER & SCREW ASM., Strg. Column Lock Plate .		6.500
6 — SCREW, Direction Signal Control Lever to Switch (#8-32 x 5/8")		N.S.
7 — LEVER ASM., Direction Signal Control		2.897
8 — BULB, Gearshift Indicator		8.991
9 — CAP, Gearshift Indicator Lens Lamp		4.022
10 — LEVER ASM., Tilt Wheel Release		6.514
11 — PIN, Gearshift Upper Lever Pivot (7/32" x 15/16")		4.008
12 — POINTER, Gearshift Indicator		4.020

Exploded views of automatic upper gearshift controls for 1969 and 1970 GTOs with or without tilt column.

Close-up of 1968 steering column opening cover (part number 9791435).

1969-70 dash insulator at steering column cover. Cover was black plastic.

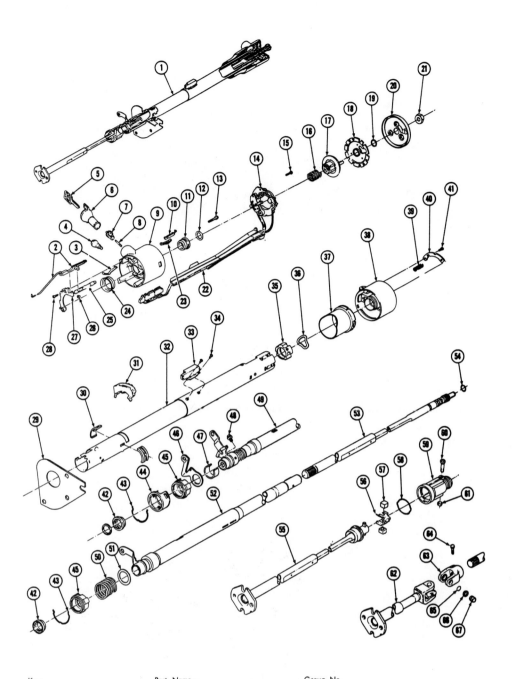

Key	Part Name	Group No.
1 — COLUMN ASM., Steering		6.518
2 — RACK ASM., Shaft Lock		2.195
3 — SPRING, Housing Rack Preload		2.195
4 — KNOB, Hazard Flasher		2.575
5 — KEY, Ignition		2.187
6 — CYLINDER ASM., Ignition		2.188
7 — SECTOR, Ignition Switch Actuator		2.195
8 — SHAFT, Ignition Switch Actuator Sector		2.195
9 — HOUSING, Steering Column		2.906
10 — SWITCH ASM., Ignition Buzzer		2.195
11 — BEARING ASM., Steering Shaft Upper		6.521
12 — WASHER, Steering Shaft Upper Thrust		6.521
13 — SCREW, Upper Brg. Housing Support		N.S.
14 — SWITCH ASM., Directional Signal		2.895
15 — SCREW, Turn Signal Switch		2.895
16 — SPRING, Steering Shaft Upper Bearing		6.521
17 — CAM ASM., Turn Signal Cancelling		2.896
18 — LOCK, Steering Shaft		6.500
19 — RING, Upper Steering Shaft Retaining		6.521
20 — COVER ASM., Steering Column Lock Plate (W/Screw)		6.500
21 — NUT, Steering Shaft to Wheel		6.515
22 — PROTECTOR, Turn Signal Control Wire		2.195
23 — CLIP, Ignition Buzzer Switch Retainer		2.906
24 — CUP, Turn Signal Housing Thrust		2.906
25 — SPRING & BOLT ASM., Steering Column Housing		6.500
26 — WASHER, Housing Rack Spring Thrust		6.500
27 — GATE, Turn Signal Housing Shift Lever		4.027
28 — SCREW, Turn Signal Housing Shift Lever Gate		2.195
29 — SEAL, Steering Column to Dash		6.758
30 — GROMMET, Neutral & Back-Up Lamp Retainer		2.698
31 — SWITCH ASM., Trans. Neutralizer & Back-Up Lamp		2.698
32 — JACKET ASM., Steering Column		6.518
33 — SWITCH ASM., Ignition		2.188
34 — SCREW, Ignition Switch to Steering Column		N.S.
35 — BEARING, Steering Column Bowl Lower		6.521
36 — WASHER, Steering Column Bowl (Wave)		4.012
37 — SHROUD, Steering Column Bowl		4.010
38 — BOWL, Gear Shift Lever		4.010
39 — SPRING, Upper Gearshift Lever		4.008
40 — PLATE, Gearshift Lever Bowl		4.010
41 — SCREW, Gearshift Lever Bowl Plate		4.012
42 — BEARING, Steering Shaft Adapter - Lower		6.521
43 — CLIP, Steering Column Lower Brg. Adapter		6.521
44 — RETAINER, Steering Column Lower Brg. Adapter		6.521
45 — ADAPTER, Steering Column Lower Brg.		6.521
46 — LEVER, Steering Column Lower Shift		4.030
47 — SPACER, Steering Column Shift Lever		4.032
48 — SCREW & WASHER, to Shift Tube (1/4"-20 x 1/2")		8.977
49 — TUBE ASM., Gearshift		4.025
50 — SPRING, Steering Column Shift Tube Return		4.027
51 — WASHER, Steering Column Shift Tube Return Spring Thrust		4.027
52 — TUBE ASM., Gearshift - Upper		4.025
53 — SHAFT ASM., Steering - Upper		6.524
54 — RING, Upper Steering Shaft Retaining		6.521
55 — SHAFT ASM., Steering - Intermediate		6.524
56 — SPRING, Intermediate Steering Shaft Coupling		6.525
57 — BEARING, Intermediate Steering Shaft Coupling		6.525
58 — RING, Intermediate Shaft Seal Retainer		6.525
59 — CLAMP, PLUG & COUPLING, Intermediate Shaft		6.525
60 — BOLT, Coupling to Upper Shaft		N.S.
61 — NUT, Coupling to Upper Shaft		N.S.
62 — SHAFT ASM., Steering - Intermediate		6.524
63 — YOKE, Intermediate Shaft - Upper		6.525
64 — BOLT, Intermediate Shaft		N.S.
65 — SEAL, Intermediate Steering Shaft "U/J" Oil		6.525
66 — RING, Intermediate Steering Shaft "U/J" Retaining		6.525
67 — BEARING, Intermediate Steering Shaft "U/J"		6.525

Exploded view and parts nomenclature for 1969-70 standard
column.

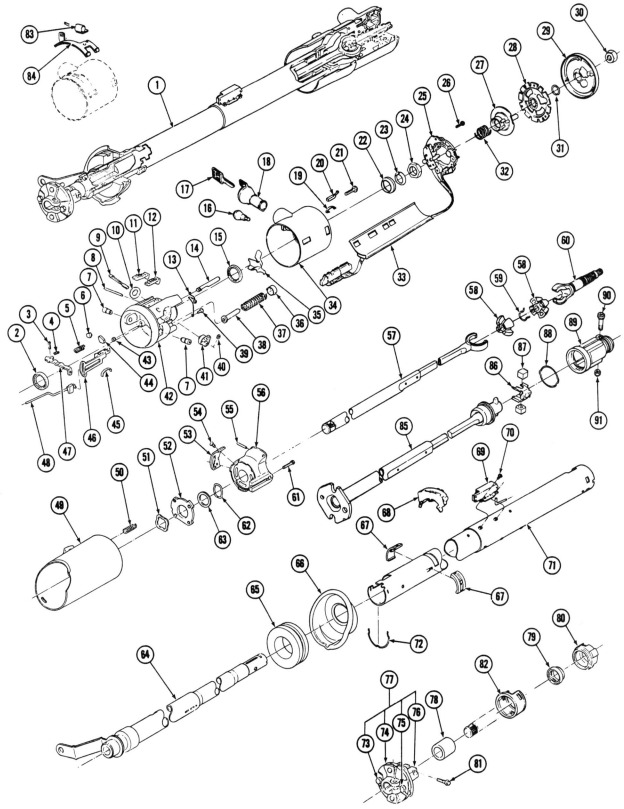

Exploded view of typical 1969-70 tilt steering column, with parts nomenclature.

Chapter 4

EXTERIOR MECHANICAL AND STEERING

1964-65

STANDARD BRAKE

All GTO brakes were manufactured by Delco Morraine. The standard brakes were the same for 1964 and 1965. The master cylinder assembly (part number 5465180) was painted black. The reservoir cap (5462994) was gold cadmium, the cap retainer (5462996) was natural metal. The brake pipe was natural metal and ran to the brass junction block (1366288).

POWER BRAKE

Both 1964 and 1965 models used Delco Morraine master cylinders (5465085) with gold cadmium vacuum booster (5465080), gold cadmium reservoir cap (5462994), natural-metal retainer (5462996) and white plastic check valve. The brake line pipe was natural metal and ended in the brass junction block (1366288). The vacuum fitting for the four-barrel carburetor (535247) was brass, as was the Tri-Power fitting (538958).

Brake drums were the same diameter (9.5 inches) and carried the same part number (9776701 front and 9776704 rear). Metallic linings were available both years, and used identical assemblies, except for the return spring. Metallic brakes were not available on cars equipped with 3.08:1 rear end ratios. The factory suggested the use of power brakes when metallic linings were ordered, due to high pedal pressure. The 1965 GTOs offered an aluminum front drum option; the replacement part number for the drum was 9781513.

A few 1964 models built at the Kansas City plant were assembled with Buick and Oldsmobile power brake units. They were the same as GTO units except for the location where the pipe from the connector attached to the master cylinder—the GTO pipe being on the outboard side. If a new pipe needs to be formed because of a kink or inadequate clearance from the steering shaft, it should be ¼-inch-diameter steel tubing, about twenty inches long. The minimum bend radius should be ⅞ inch. (This information is from Pontiac file reference 5A, number 64-25.)

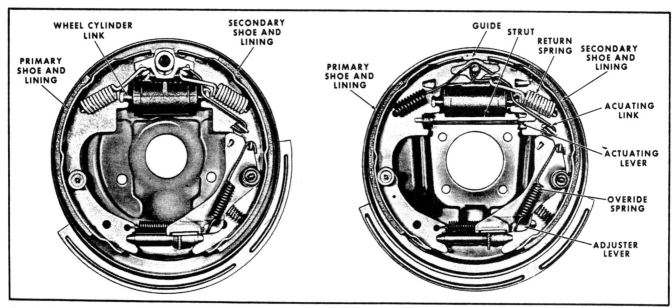

Detail of 1964-70 drum brakes, front (left) and rear (right).

PARKING BRAKE

Parking brake pedals were different both years. In 1964, a square pedal was used, with a wide-rib top and bottom, and narrow ribs in between. No trim plate was offered. In 1965, the parking brake pedal emulated the clutch and brake pedals in shape; it used the same rib design and had a trim plate like the two other pedals when so equipped.

The ratchet and pedal assembly was not interchangeable between 1964 and 1965. The 1964 version used an assembly similar to that used on early Tempests, and was designated by part number 9776459. The pad number was 9770817. The parking brake pedal assembly was redesigned for 1965, and used part number 9781452. The pad number was 9781282, and the trim plate was 9781281. Parking brake handles were different, and no replacement was offered by Pontiac. When necessary, a Chevrolet replacement was used, which had a different configuration.

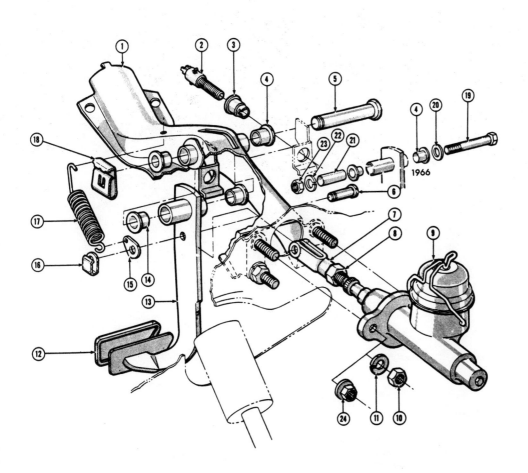

Key	Part Name	Group No.
1 — BRACKET ASM., Brake Pedal Mounting		4.634
2 — SWITCH ASM., Stop Light		2.447
3 — CLIP, Switch to Bracket		2.447
4 — BUSHING, Brake Pedal Shaft		4.626
5 — SHAFT, Brake Pedal Pivot		4.634
6 — PIN, Brake Master Cylinder Clevis to Pedal		4.662
7 — CLEVIS, Pedal to Push Rod		4.662
8 — NUT, Clevis Adjusting (3/8"-24)		8.915
9 — CYLINDER ASM., Brake Master		4.650
10 — NUT, Mounting Bracket Asm. to Dash (3/8"-16)		8.915
11 — LOCKWASHER, Mounting Bracket Asm. to Dash (3/8")		8.931
12 — PAD, Brake & Clutch Pedal		4.630
13 — ARM ASM., Brake Pedal		4.625
14 — BUSHING, Brake Pedal Shaft		4.626
15 — EXTENSION, Brake Pedal Return Spring		4.639
16 — RETAINER, Clevis to Pedal		4.662
17 — SPRING, Brake Pedal Return		4.639
18 — RETAINER, Pedal Shaft to Mounting Bracket		4.634
19 — BOLT, Arm to Bracket (7/16"-14 x 4 1/4")		0.833
20 — WASHER, Arm to Bracket (7/16" I.D. x 1" O.D.)		N.S.
21 — SPACER, Brake Pedal		4.625
22 — LOCKWASHER, Arm to Bracket (7/16")		8.931
23 — NUT, Arm to Bracket (7/16"-14)		8.915
24 — NUT, Cylinder to Bracket (3/8"-16)		N.S.

Exploded view of 1964-66 standard brake master cylinder and pedal assembly.

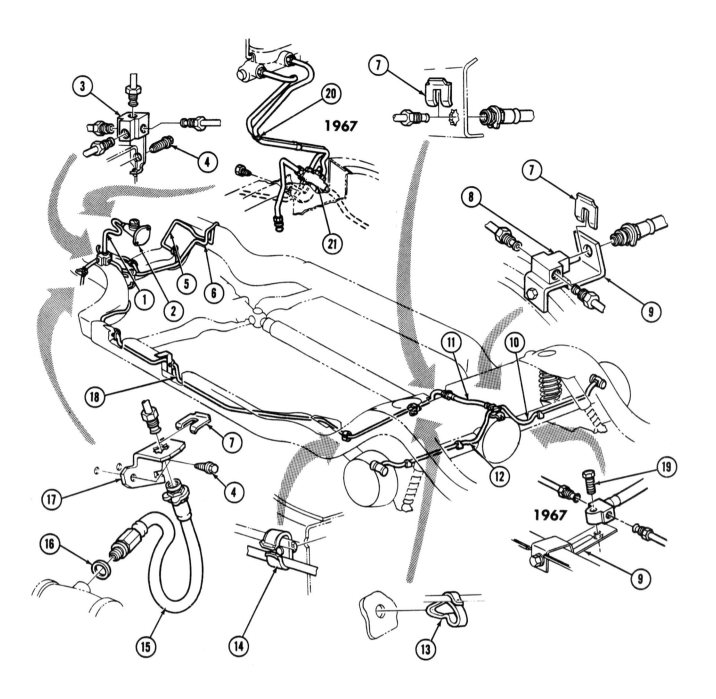

Diagram of 1964-67 brake pipe routing. Note differences in brake pipe distribution and in rear brake hose fitting at rear axle.

Key	Part Name	Group No.
1 — PIPE, Master Cyl. to Distributor		4.685
2 — CYLINDER ASM., Brake Master		4.650
3 — FITTING ASM., Brake Pipe Dist.-- Front		4.686
4 — SCREW, Fitting to Frame (5/16"-18 x 9/16")		8.977
5 — PIPE, Front Brake (8-Cyl. Engine)		4.685
6 — PIPE, Dist. to Right Front Wheel (6-Cyl. Engine)		4.685
7 — SPRING, Hose to Bracket		N.S.
8 — TEE, Rear Brake Hose to Rear Pipes		4.686
9 — BRACKET, Rear Brake Hose		4.681
10 — PIPE, Rear Brake - R.H.		4.685
11 — HOSE, Brake Rear		4.680

Key	Part Name	Group No.
12 — PIPE, Rear Brake - L.H.		4.685
13 — CLIP, Pipe to Frame		N.S.
14 — CLIP, Brake Pipe to Frame		4.686
15 — HOSE, Brake Front		4.680
16 — WASHER, Pipe Conn. & Front Hose (29/64" I.D. x 45/64" O.D. x 21/64")		4.671
17 — BRACKET, Front Brake Hose Support		4.681
18 — PIPE, Rear Brake - Center		4.685
19 — BOLT, Rear Brake Hose to Axle Housing (5/16"-18 x 1")		8.900
20 — CLIP, Master Cyl. Frt. to Rear Pipes ("S" type).		3.162
21 — DISTRIBUTOR & SWITCH, Brake Pipe		4.874

1964 brake warning lamp (RPO 494) mounted at bottom of instrument panel, to left of steering column opening.

Correct pads and trim plates for 1964-70 applications: parking brake pad for 1965-67; automatic pad for 1964-70 at top; clutch and brake pads and trim plates for 1964-70 at bottom.

Detail of brake pipe routing and attachment at rear cross-member.

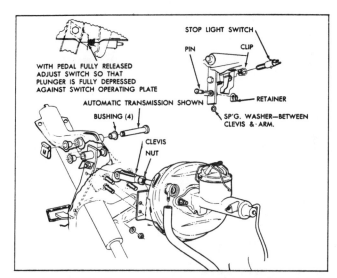

Drawing of 1964-66 power brake system. Note use of pivot shaft and retaining clip for brake pedal in 1964-65 as opposed to 1966-67 use of a bolt and nut assembly.

1964 parking brake release handle. Note cowl vent handle to left.

1964 parking brake pedal and pad. Note difference from 1965 pad; no trim plate used for 1964 pad.

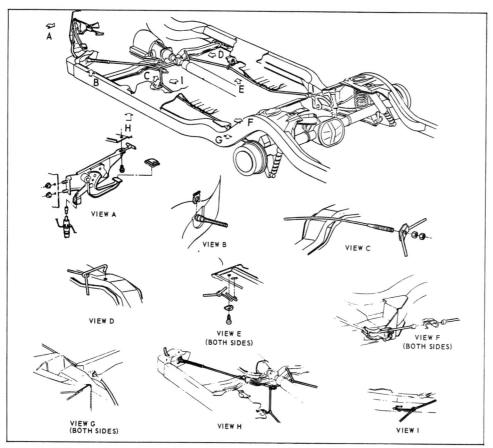

VIEW A

VIEW B

VIEW C

VIEW D

VIEW E
(BOTH SIDES)

VIEW F
(BOTH SIDES)

VIEW G
(BOTH SIDES)

VIEW H

VIEW I

1964-68 parking brake system. Cable clips were cadmium plated.
View I was for use with 1967-68 Turbo Hydra-matic applications.

1966-1967

STANDARD BRAKE

The standard Delco Morraine brakes for 1966-67 were identical in all respects to the brakes used on the 1965 GTO, with the exceptions of the distribution block and the rear hose, which was enlarged to 3/16 inch. (Refer to the 1964-65 section for detail.)

A dual-cylinder master cylinder was introduced for 1967 as one of seventeen new safety features mandated by the federal government, and was used for both standard and power brake applications. The master cylinder (part number 5458522) was painted black. The master cylinder cover (part number 5452320) was plated gold cadmium. The cover retainer (part number 5468053) was natural metal in appearance. The brake pipes (part number 1382515 front and 1382516 rear) were natural metal, and ran to the distributor and switch assembly on the front LH frame rail.

POWER BRAKE

The 1966 power brake system was the same as that used on the 1965 GTO, except for the revision to the rear brake line and block as specified earlier. Also, the master cylinder carried a different part number (5467918), as did the brake cylinder vacuum diaphragm housing shell (part number 5464349 front and 5467997 rear). Refer to the 1965 section for appearance details.

The 1967 power brake system was completely different. The master cylinder was the same as the standard unit, unless the front disc brake option (RPO 521) was ordered. In that case, master cylinder part number 5445784 was used, along with the gold cadmium cover (part number 5455517) and the natural-metal retainer (part number 5455518). The vacuum diaphragm housing shell (part number 5467850 front and 5453683 rear) was again gold cadmium. This master cylinder was immediately identifiable from the standard or power brake master cylinder, as it was somewhat larger.

Two designs were used in 1967 GTO disc brake front hoses. (Refer to Service Bulletin 67-I-61.) This production change occurred approximately the second week of April 1967. GTOs built in 1967 with the disc brake options and data plate built code O4B or later should have the second-design hoses.

The disc brake option used a pressure-metering valve to the distributor and switch (part number 1381584). The pipe from the master cylinder to the valve was part number 1381585. Two front RH brake hoses to the distributor and switch assembly were used: Standard 335 hp models used part number 9778575, Ram Air or HO models used a heavier-duty hose (part number 9778815 RH and 1380567 LH).

The brake pedal assembly for 1966 GTOs equipped with standard transmissions was part number 9775901. For automatic-transmission-equipped versions using standard brakes, the pedal assembly was part number 9776112. Those with power brakes used a slightly different design, part number 9775902. The 1967 manual-transmission brake pedal assembly was part number 1381464. One pedal assembly was used for automatics, part number 1381466. The assemblies for both years were painted 60°

216

gloss black. Pedal pads were the same for both years. Manual transmissions used part number 9776819, and automatics used part number 9774235.

Pedal pad trim plates were again used for GTOs equipped with power brakes. The trim plates used for the manual transmission pedals carried part number 9775737 (1966) or 9778267 (1967). There was no appreciable difference in the trim plates, and they could be interchanged. The automatic brake pedal pad trim plate (part number 977556) was the same for both years.

Brake drums were 9.5 inches in diameter. Radial fins were introduced in 1966 and carried over into 1967 (part number 9785109). The 1967 front disc brake and hub assembly measured 11¼ inches (part number 1381730) and came with power assist. The aluminum front brake drum (RPO 651) was again offered in 1966 (see 1965 section for detail). All brake drums were painted red on 1966 GTOs when equipped with RPO 454 Rally I wheels.

METALLIC BRAKE LINING

Metallic brake linings (RPO 484) were available in 1966, but only in conjunction with RPO 731 Safe-T-Track limited slip differential. The brake drum for the metallic lining option (part number 9785375) was identified by a white dab of paint on the fins. Brake springs were of a heavier-duty design to accommodate the higher temperatures encountered with the metallic linings. This option was discontinued at the end of 1966 production.

PARKING BRAKE

The parking brake lever assembly (part number 9781452) was carried over from 1965, and remained unchanged through 1967. The lever assembly was painted 60° gloss black. The switch for the parking brake warning lamp (part number 9781678) was the same for 1966 and 1967. The pedal pad (part number 9781282) and the trim plate (part number 9781281) were the same for both years. The parking brake handle release was black with the words brake release inlaid in white. The handle and cable assembly were not serviced by Pontiac; instead, a Chevrolet replacement was used, which was designed differently from the Pontiac version.

With the introduction of the Turbo Hydra-matic transmission in 1967, the transmission support crossmember was moved six inches toward the rear of the car. Consequently, the parking brake center cable was shorter than that used in 1966 (or 1967 manual transmissions), and the front cable was longer.

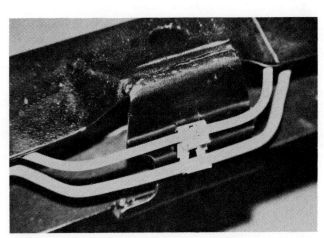

Detail of 1966 brake line routing, using clip (part number 537296) to retain pipes to frame.

An aluminum front drum was available for 1965-66, and was natural aluminum in appearance for both years—except in 1966 when ordered in conjunction with Rally I wheels, in which case it was painted red.

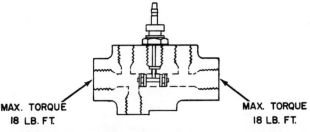

MAX. TORQUE 18 LB. FT.　　MAX. TORQUE 18 LB. FT.

To avoid damage to the internal parts of the 1967 brake line distributor and switch assembly, use the correct torque specifications on the fittings. Should a torque greater than 18 lb. ft. be required to stop leaks on these fittings, the brake line distributor and switch assembly must be replaced. (This information and illustration taken from Dealer Service Information Bulletin number 67-I-40, dated 2-17-67.)

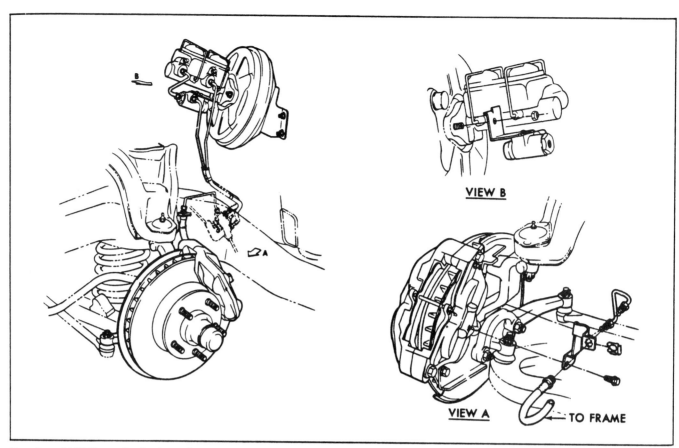

VIEW B

VIEW A ← TO FRAME

Drawing of 1967 front disc brake option.

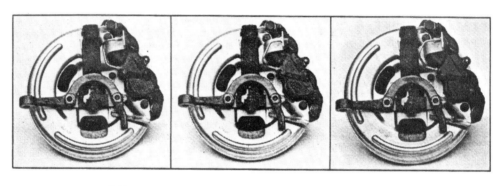

CORRECT INST.   WRONG END OF   OPPOSITE SIDE
                       PIPE IN CALIPER   PIPE INST.

TEMPEST RH ASSEMBLY SHOWN

	1ST. TYPE	2ND. TYPE
Inboard Caliper Housing	5462043 RH	5468364 RH
	5462042 LH	5468363 LH
Pipe	1381726 RH	1382794 RH
	1381727 LH	1382795 LH

Two disc brake caliper housings and pipes (hose to caliper) were produced in 1967. Original pipe nuts and caliper housings had ⅜-inch-diameter threads. The new *right side* pipe nut and caliper housings had 7/16-inch-diameter threads and new *left side* pipe nut and caliper housings had ½-inch-diameter threads. These new caliper housings and pipes eliminated the possibility of installing the pipe upside down or on the wrong side. When replacing inboard caliper housing or pipe, be sure proper mating part is also used. When installing the first-type pipe (⅜-inch-diameter tube nuts), some difficulty may arise as to identification of left and right pipe and/or which end is the *caliper* end of the pipe. To install correctly, make sure the contour of the pipe follows the contour of the caliper housing. The pipe should be installed without any bending. If bending appears necessary, either the pipe is being installed upside down or the opposite-side pipe is being used. (This information and illustration taken from Dealer Service Information Bulletin number 67-I-61, dated 4-21-67.)

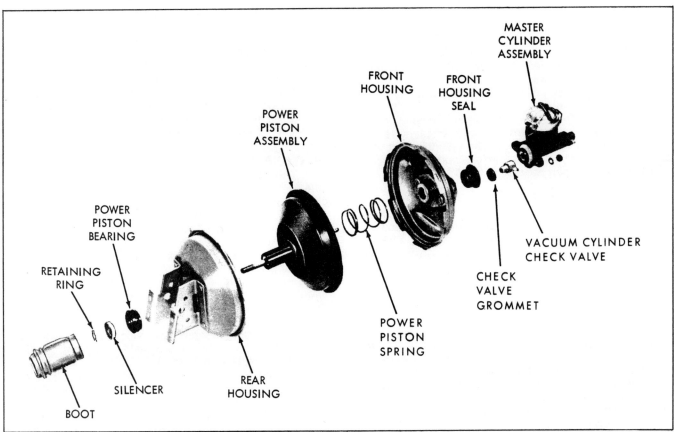

MASTER
CYLINDER
ASSEMBLY

FRONT
HOUSING

FRONT
HOUSING
SEAL

POWER
PISTON
ASSEMBLY

POWER
PISTON
BEARING

RETAINING
RING

VACUUM CYLINDER
CHECK VALVE

CHECK
VALVE
GROMMET

POWER
PISTON
SPRING

SILENCER

REAR
HOUSING

BOOT

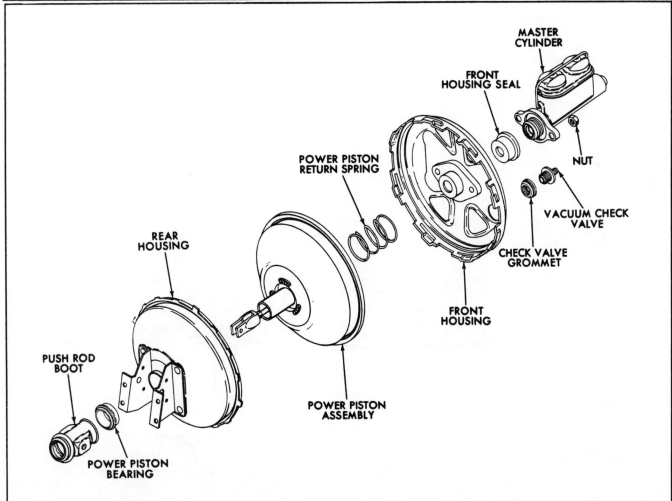

MASTER
CYLINDER

FRONT
HOUSING SEAL

POWER PISTON
RETURN SPRING

NUT

VACUUM CHECK
VALVE

CHECK VALVE
GROMMET

REAR
HOUSING

FRONT
HOUSING

POWER PISTON
ASSEMBLY

PUSH ROD
BOOT

POWER PISTON
BEARING

Comparison of 1964-66 and 1967 power brake assemblies. Note
difference of front vacuum diaphragm housing design.

1968-70

STANDARD BRAKE

All GTOs built from 1968 through 1970 used Delco Morraine master cylinders. The 1968-70 GTO standard brake master cylinder was identical to the 1967 unit, and carried the same part number, as did the master cylinder cover and cover retainer.

The distributor and switch assembly, located on the LH frame rail behind the front cross-member, was the same regardless of brake system. The 1968-69 distributor and switch assembly was the same (part number 3934089). The 1970 unit was part number 1234388.

POWER DRUM BRAKE

The master cylinder used for 1968 power drum brake applications was the same as that used for standard brakes, as were the cover and cover retainer. (See 1968-70 standard brakes.) The vacuum diaphragm, or booster (part number 5468816), was gold cadmium plated and stood alone in its application.

A different type of hub and drum assembly was installed on 1968 models in a *limited* quantity beginning with V.I. number P268122. The major difference between these assemblies and those normally installed was that the drum could be serviced separately from the hub (similar to rear brake drums). Since the new drum could be removed separately, it is important that the alignment index on the drum web lines up with the hole in the hub upon reassembly. The part numbers were:
Drum—3853799 [M-CX] (Gp. No. 5.809)
Hub Assembly—3887867 [Z-CX] (Gp. No. 6.307)
Front Hub Bolt—3851677 [Z-CX] (Gp. No. 5.812)
If it became necessary to turn or replace a brake drum of this type, the hub and drum had to be properly indexed and turned as an assembly. Install all wheel nuts and torque to 35 lb. ft. before machining is performed. In case a hub bolt became damaged or broken, service the hub by

removing the hub bolt(s) with a press or hammer. These bolts were not peened into the hub. Use care not to damage wheel mounting surface on hub flange. Install new serrated bolt into hole in hub. Tap lightly with a hammer to start bolt serrations into hole, making sure that bolt is square with hub flange. Press bolt into flange until head is fully seated against hub flange. The procedure for replacing and part numbers for front bearings and races did not change. (This information taken from Dealer Service Information Bulletin number 68-I-69 dated 5-13-68.)

DISC BRAKE

The disc brake option for 1968 (RPO 521) was available with or without power assist. (Refer to master cylinder usage chart.) When power brakes were ordered, master cylinder part number 5468774 was used, which was painted 60° gloss black. The master cylinder cover (part number 5455517) was gold cadmium. The cover retainer (part number 5455518) was natural metal. An acceptable alternative to natural metal is silver cadmium plate. A metering valve (part number 3905525) was located directly beneath the master cylinder. The vacuum diaphragm housing assembly (part number 5468817) was plated with gold cadmium.

This housing assembly was also used for 1969 and 1970. Power brakes were only available with front discs in 1969 (RPO 511, UPC JL2) and 1970 (RPO 502, UPC JL2).

The master cylinder for 1969 (part number 5469344) had a two-letter code, EA, stamped on the end of the cylinder. The master cylinder cover was identical to the 1968 unit, but used a different retainer (part number 5468305). The metering valve was the same as that used in 1968.

The 1970 vacuum housing assembly was the same as used in 1968-69. The black master cylinder (part number 5470664) used a gold cadmium cover (part number 5470405). This cover was easily distinguishable from earlier covers because it was slightly larger and more squared-

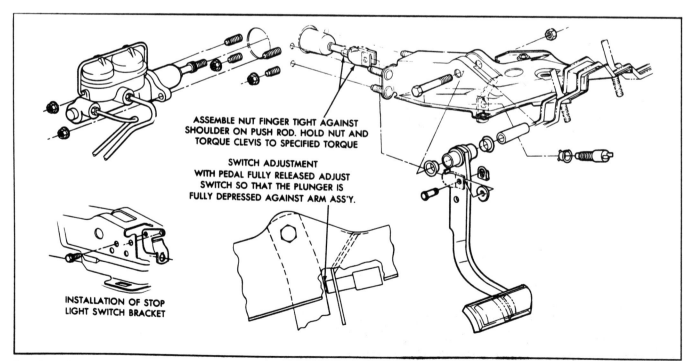

ASSEMBLE NUT FINGER TIGHT AGAINST
SHOULDER ON PUSH ROD. HOLD NUT AND
TORQUE CLEVIS TO SPECIFIED TORQUE

SWITCH ADJUSTMENT
WITH PEDAL FULLY RELEASED ADJUST
SWITCH SO THAT THE PLUNGER IS
FULLY DEPRESSED AGAINST ARM ASS'Y.

INSTALLATION OF STOP
LIGHT SWITCH BRACKET

Drawing of 1968 standard brake master cylinder and pedal assembly.

off in appearance. The retainer was natural metal in appearance (part number 5470407). While specifications for the brake system remained constant, a different metering valve (part number 1233464) was used in 1970.

Service Bulletin number 70-I-14 dated 9-23-69 pointed out that the 1970 disc brakes were produced with either two- or one-piece hub and rotor assemblies installed in like pairs. The one- and two-piece rotors were not interchangeable, because of differences in the splash shield design.

The brake pedal assembly for 1968 through 1970 was identical: part number 1381466 for automatic transmissions, 1386088 for manual transmissions. The brake pedal assemblies were painted 60° gloss black. Pedal pads were the same for all years; part number 9774235 for automatic transmission pedals and 9776819 for manual transmission pedals.

Pedal pad trim plates were the same from 1968 to 1970. The automatic transmission pedal pad trim plate was part number 9788316; manual transmission pedal pad plate, 9778267.

Front brake drums measured 9.5 inches in diameter for all three years. During the later part of 1968 model production, a limited run of front drums was used at the Pontiac assembly plant on A-bodies with vehicle identification number (VIN) P268122 and on. These units were unique to Pontiac design, as the drum could be serviced separately from the hub.

The regular-production front drums were part number 9790983 (1968) and 9798690 (1969-70). The 9798690 part number was superseded by 481832. The 9790983 part number is currently being used for all 1966-68 replacements.

Rear brake drums also measured 9.5 inches in diameter, and were the same for all three years (part number 9788681). Early-production 1968 GTOs may have been affected by a coding error on the rear brake drum. Certain early-production Tempests were built using Kelsey-Hayes rear brake drums coded with the identification letter F, rather than the specified identification KH. Later rear drums manufactured by Kelsey-Hayes incorporated the code letters KH-F as an optional identification.

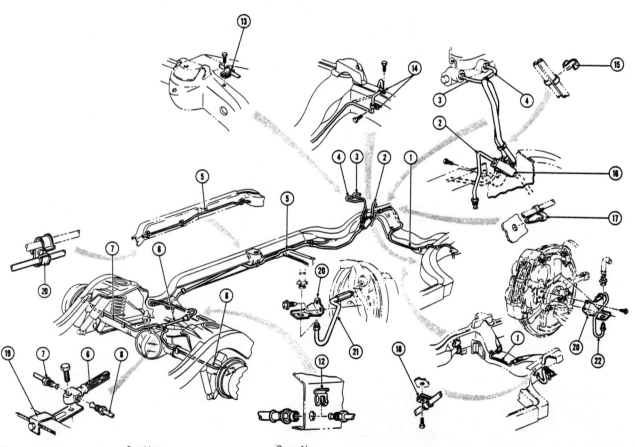

Key	Part Name	Group No.
1	PIPE, Distributor & Switch to Front Brake - R.H.	4.685
2	PIPE, Distributor & Switch to Front Brake - L.H.	4.685
3	PIPE, Master Cyl. to Distributor & Switch - Front	4.685
4	PIPE, Master Cyl. to Distributor & Switch - Rear	4.685
5	PIPE, Rear Brake Center	4.685
6	HOSE, Brake - Rear	4.680
7	PIPE, Rear Brake - L.H.	4.685
8	PIPE, Rear Brake - R.H.	4.685
12	YOKE, Front Brake Hose to Support Bracket	4.681
13	CLIP, Brake Pipe to Frame (3/16" Closed)	N.S.
14	CLIP, Brake Pipe to Frame (13/64" Open)	N.S.
15	CLIP, Front & Rear Brake Pipe (1/4" x 3/8" - "S")	N.S.
16	DISTRIBUTOR & SWITCH ASM., Brake Pipe	4.874
17	CLIP, Brake Pipe to Frame (3/16" - "E")	N.S.
18	CLIP, Brake Pipe to Frame (1/4" - Closed)	N.S.
19	BRACKET, Rear Brake Hose	4.681
20	BRACKET, Front Brake Hose to Backing Plate	4.681
21	PIPE, Front Brake Hose to Backing Plate Bracket	4.685
22	PIPE, Caliper to Front Brake Hose Bracket	4.685

Installation and nomenclature for 1968 GTO brake pipes and attaching parts.

Kelsey-Hayes drums with any one of these three codes should not cause concern regarding the variation of code between right and left rear drums.

Front hub and disc assemblies were different for all three years. The 1968 hub and disc assembly (part number 1381730) measured 11.12 inches in diameter. This unit used the two-piece four-piston caliper design carried over from 1967.

A floating, single caliper disc brake was introduced in 1969. A one-piece hub and disc assembly (part number 405824) was used. This assembly measured 10.94 inches in diameter.

In 1970, according to Service Bulletin 70-I-14, both one- and two-piece hub and disc assemblies were used in production. The one- and two-piece rotors were not interchangeable due to differences in the splash shield design. The 1970 replacement part number was 9794943. By 1972, this number was superseded by a one-piece design (part number 405824), which necessitated the installation of splash shields (part number 5463565 LH and 5463566 RH) on GTOs originally equipped with two-piece hub and disc assemblies.

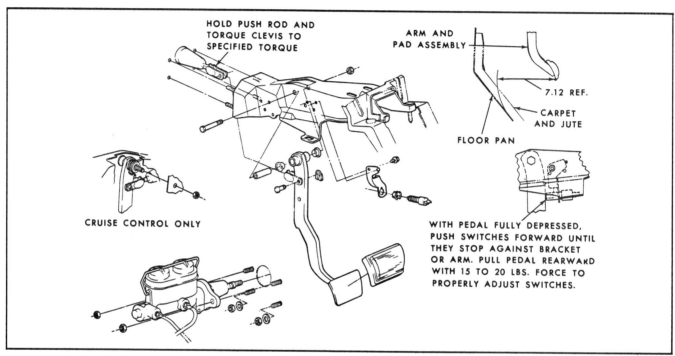

1969 and 1970 manual brake system.

1967 (left) and 1968-69 (right) disc brake master cylinder and power booster assemblies. 1967 unit had valve mounted on LH side, 1968-70 on RH side. External appearance was the same.

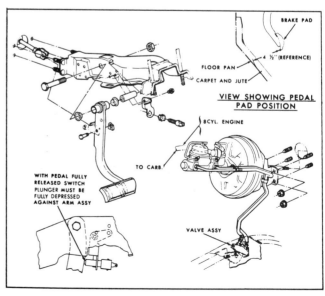

View of 1968 power booster and brake components. Note pedal height adjustment and routing of steel lines to valve assembly.

PARKING BRAKE

The parking brake lever assembly (part number 1383868) was the same for all three years, and was painted 60° gloss black. The switch for the parking brake warning lamp was part number 9781678 for 1968. The switch was modified for 1969-70, and used part number 9795358.

The parking brake release handle was black with the words BRAKE RELEASE inlaid in white. The parking brake pedal pad was the same for 1968 and 1969 (part number 9791740). The 1970 pad had the word PARK embossed on it and used part number 1378903. The pedal pad trim plate (part number 9781281) was used in all 1968 GTOs equipped with power brakes. A running change was made in 1969: Early-production cars equipped with power brakes used the same trim plate as in 1968, but sometime in late January or early February of 1969 (as reported in the Dealer Service Information Bulletin number 69-I-49, dated 2-24-69), the trim plate was deleted from production and was not used at all in 1970 models.

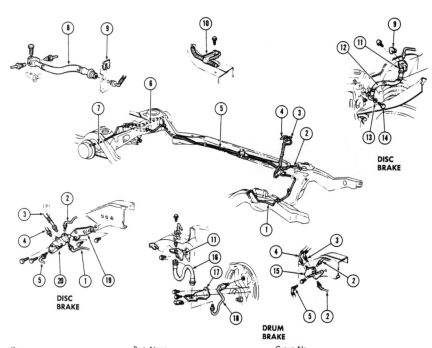

Key	Part Name	Group No.
1 — PIPE ASM., Valve to Front Brake - R.H.		4.685
2 — PIPE ASM., Valve to Front Brake - L.H.		4.685
3 — PIPE ASM., Hyd. Cyl. to Distributor - Front		4.685
4 — PIPE ASM., Hyd. Cyl. to Distributor - Rear		4.685
5 — PIPE ASM., Distributor to Rear Brake Hose		4.685
6 — PIPE ASM., Rear Brake - L.H.		4.685
7 — PIPE ASM., Rear Brake - R.H.		4.685
8 — HOSE, Brake - Rear		4.680
9 — YOKE, Hose Retainer (Spring Type)		4.681
10 — CLIPS, Brake & Fuel Pipes to Frame		4.686
11 — BRACKET, Front Hose		4.681
12 — HOSE, Front Brake (Disc Brakes)		4.680
13 — WASHER, Pipe Conn. Front Hose (Small) (Copper)		4.671
14 — BOLT, Front Hose		4.681
15 — DISTRIBUTOR & SWITCH ASM., Brake Pipe (Drum Brakes)		4.874
16 — HOSE, Front Brake (Drum Brakes)		4.680
17 — BRACKET, Front Hose to Backing Plate		4.681
18 — PIPE ASM., Front Brake Hose to Backing Plate Bracket		4.685
19 — BRACKET, Valve to Frame		4.690
20 — VALVE, Brake Pressure Metering & Combination (Disc Brakes)		4.690

Drawing of 1969-70 brake pipes. Note difference between disc and drum setups.

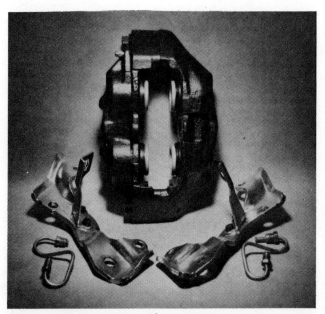

View of 1968 disc brake caliper with RH and LH mounting brackets, and tubes from caliper to hose.

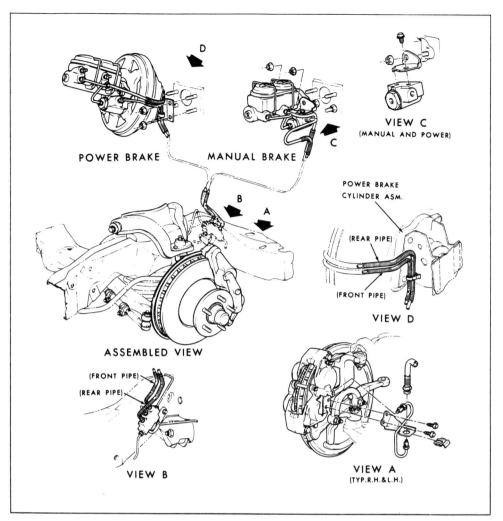

VIEW C
(MANUAL AND POWER)

POWER BRAKE   MANUAL BRAKE

POWER BRAKE
CYLINDER ASM.

(REAR PIPE)

(FRONT PIPE)

VIEW D

ASSEMBLED VIEW

(FRONT PIPE)
(REAR PIPE)

VIEW B

VIEW A
(TYP. R.H. & L.H.)

1968 power and manual front disc brake line routing.

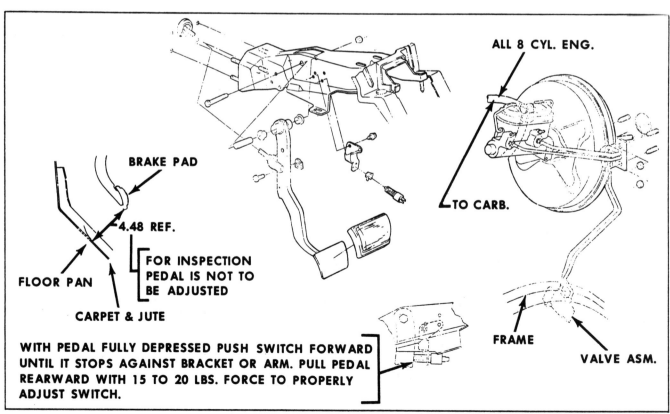

ALL 8 CYL. ENG.

BRAKE PAD

4.48 REF.

FOR INSPECTION
PEDAL IS NOT TO
BE ADJUSTED

FLOOR PAN

CARPET & JUTE

TO CARB.

FRAME

VALVE ASM.

WITH PEDAL FULLY DEPRESSED PUSH SWITCH FORWARD
UNTIL IT STOPS AGAINST BRACKET OR ARM. PULL PEDAL
REARWARD WITH 15 TO 20 LBS. FORCE TO PROPERLY
ADJUST SWITCH.

Components and adjustments for 1969 power brake system.

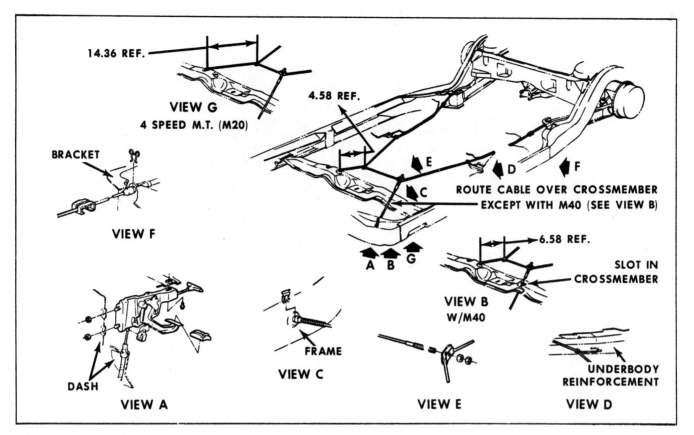

Diagram of 1969 parking brake cables and related components. 1970 used same arrangement. Note routing of front cable for automatic transmission applications.

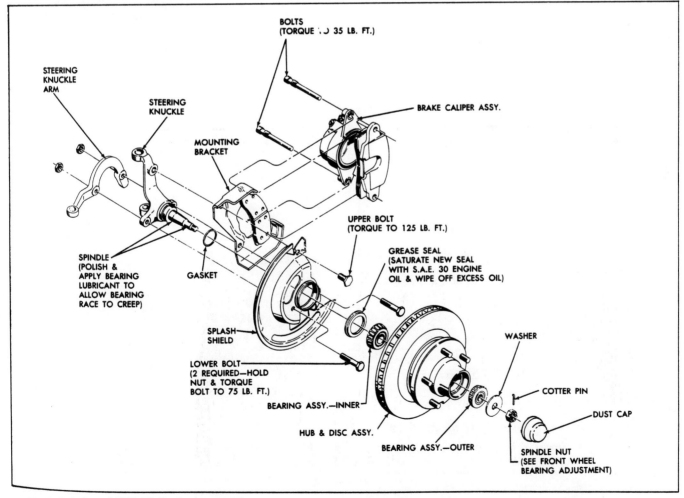

Exploded view of 1969-70 disc brake mounting.

REAR SUSPENSION

1964-65

The rear suspension used the standard Pontiac-designed four-link system. The entire assembly was painted black—with the exception of the shocks, which were gray. Original lower control arms were unboxed (not reinforced) and carried part number 9781339 for 1964 and 1965. The upper arm in 1964 was part number 9773166, and the unchanged 1965 arm was issued part number 9780959.

In midyear, the 1965 GTO had a production change, with the introduction of a reinforcement bracket (LH 3909669, RH 3909670, complete package 9777613) for all manual transmission models. The field part number was LH 3869875 and RH 3869876. These reinforcement brackets were designed to provide extra rigidity and improved load distribution in the frame rear cross-member and lower control arm area. The brackets attached between the frame rear cross-member and the lower control arm bracket on each side, utilizing the forward upper and lower control arm attachments. Be sure to check for proper brake line clearance before installation.

1966-67

The 1966-67 rear suspension was nearly identical to the 1965 in all respects. The 1966-67 lower control arms switched part number to 9777905. One change was in the 1967 upper control arm: When the 3.36:1, 3.55:1, 3.90:1 or 4.33:1 heavy-duty rear axle was used, a different-sized upper arm (part number 9788993) was installed.

The Delco gray spiral-design rear shock absorbers were original equipment. Both years used part number 3192445 for standard suspension and 3192458 for heavy-duty suspension.

The reinforcement package was again applied to all 1966 and 1967 GTOs with standard transmission. The 1967 package was part number 3909670 (RH) and 3909669 (LH).

1969	Firm Ride	9793101

1968-70

There were no major changes to the basic design of the 1968-70 rear suspension. The 1968 and 1969 lower control arm was the same (part number 9790375), while the 1970 arm was changed to part number 9791773. The 1970 arm was boxed and had holes to accommodate the rear stabilizer bar (part number 394926), which measured 0.875 inch in diameter.

The same upper control arm (part number 9790152) was used 1968-70. When the C-type twelve-bolt rear was used, upper control arm part number 478276 was employed. As in earlier years, the rear suspension was painted 60° gloss black.

Rear Coil Spring Usage

Year	Model	Part Number
1968	all	9788447
1969	all	9788447
1969	Ram Air	9793101
1969	Firm Ride	9793101

Delco shocks were used for all three years, and were the familiar gray color with a spiral design.

Year	Standard	Ram Air	Firm Ride
1968	3192840		3192842
1969-70	3192921		3192917
1969 only		3292917	

The rear cross-member reinforcement bracket used for the manual-transmission-equipped GTO was the same for all three years (part number 3918062 RH and 3918061 LH).

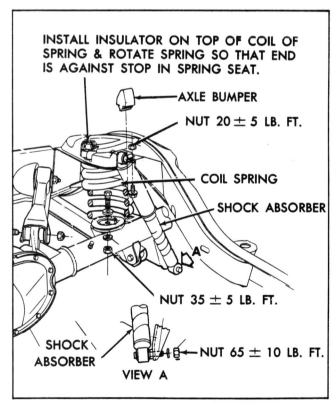

INSTALL INSULATOR ON TOP OF COIL OF SPRING & ROTATE SPRING SO THAT END IS AGAINST STOP IN SPRING SEAT.

AXLE BUMPER
NUT 20 ± 5 LB. FT.
COIL SPRING
SHOCK ABSORBER
A
NUT 35 ± 5 LB. FT.
SHOCK ABSORBER
NUT 65 ± 10 LB. FT.
VIEW A

Detail of rear suspension, illustrating shock absorber installation and torque specifications. Spiral design of shock, and lower coil spring perch installation are incorrect.

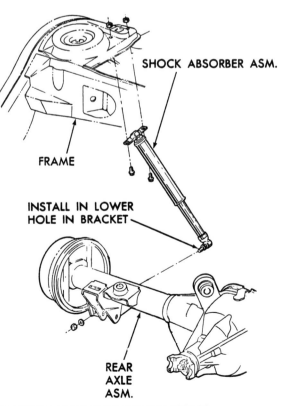

SHOCK ABSORBER ASM.
FRAME
INSTALL IN LOWER HOLE IN BRACKET
REAR AXLE ASM.

Installation of rear shock absorber, 1967-70.

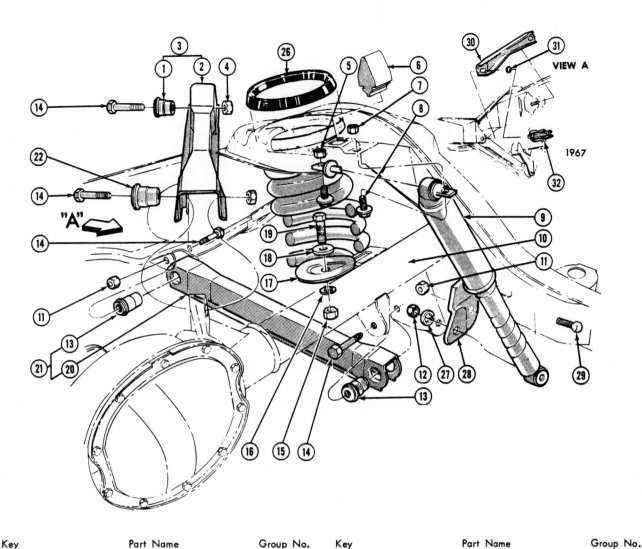

Key	Part Name	Group No.	Key	Part Name	Group No.
1 — BUSHING ASM., Rear Axle Control Arm-Upper . .		5.381	17 — CLAMP, Rear Spring Lower (1964-66)		7.518
2 — ARM, Rear Axle Upper Control		N.S.	18 — WASHER, Rear Spring Lower Clamp (33/64" I.D. x 1-1/2" O.D. x 3/16")		7.518
3 — ARM ASM., Rear Axle Upper Control (Inc #1) . .		5.382	19 — BOLT, Clamp to Lower Control Arm (1/2" x 13 x 1-3/4")		8.900
4 — NUT, Control Arm to Frame & Brackets (1/2"-13)		8.916	20 — ARM, Rear Axle Lower Control		N.S.
5 — NUT, Shock Absorber to Frame (5/16"-18)		8.915	21 — ARM ASM., Rear Axle Lower Control (Inc #13) . . .		5.382
6 — BUMPER, Rear Axle		5.395	22 — BUSHING, Rear Axle Control Arm-On Housing .		5.381
7 — SCREW & WASHER ASM., Shock Absorber to Frame		N.S.	26 — INSULATOR, Rear Spring (1964-66)		7.545
8 — SPRING, Rear Coil		7.503	27 — LOCKWASHER, Extension to Axle Housing (9/32" I.D. x 3/8" O.D.)		N.S.
9 — SHOCK ABSORBER, Pkg.		7.345	28 — EXTENSION, Superlift Shock to Axle Housing . .		7.346
10 — CARRIER, CAPS & TUBES ASM., Differential (Reference)		5.387	29 — BOLT, Extension to Axle Housing(1/2"-20 x 1-5/8")		8.900
11 — NUT, Control Arm to Frame & Brackets (1/2"-13) .		8.916	30 — REINFORCEMENT, Rear Suspension Frame		7.039
12 — NUT, Shock Absorber to Axle Housing (1/2"-20). .		8.915	31 — WASHER, Reinf. to Lwr. Arm Frame Brkt.		7.039
13 — BUSHING, Rear Axle Control Arm - Lower		5.381	32 — GUIDE, Parking Brake Cable-Rear		4.785
14 — BOLT, Control Arm to Frame & Brackets (1/2"-13 x 3-3/4")		8.900			
15 — NUT, Clamp to Lower Control Arm (1/2"-13) . . .		8.916			
16 — LOCKWASHER, Clamp to Lower Control Arm (1/2")		8.931			

Exploded view of 1964-67 rear suspension with parts nomenclature. Rear-axle-to-frame reinforcement (number 30) was used on manual-transmission-equipped GTOs.

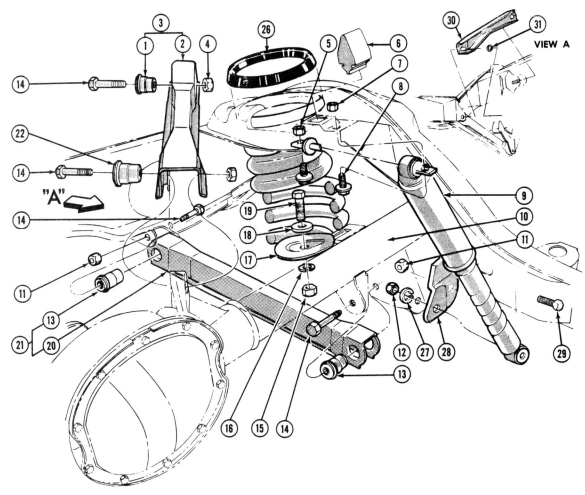

VIEW A

"A"

Key	Part Name	Group No.
1 — BUSHING ASM., Rear Axle Control Arm–Upper		5.381
2 — ARM, Rear Axle Upper Control		N.S.
3 — ARM ASM., Rear Axle Upper Control (Inc #1)		5.382
4 — NUT, Control Arm to Frame & Brackets (1/2"-13)		8.916
5 — NUT, Shock Absorber to Frame (5/16"-18)		8.915
6 — BUMPER, Rear Axle		5.395
7 — SCREW & WASHER ASM., Shock Absorber to Frame		N.S.
8 — SPRING, Rear Coil		7.503
9 — SHOCK ABSORBER, Pkg.		7.345
10 — CARRIER, CAPS & TUBES ASM., Differential (Reference)		5.387
11 — NUT, Control Arm to Frame & Brackets (1/2"-13)		8.916
12 — NUT, Shock Absorber to Axle Housing (1/2"-20)		8.915
13 — BUSHING, Rear Axle Control Arm – Lower		5.381
14 — BOLT, Control Arm to Frame & Brackets (1/2"-13 x 3-3/4")		8.900
15 — NUT, Clamp to Lower Control Arm (1/2"-13)		8.916
16 — LOCKWASHER, Clamp to Lower Control Arm (1/2")		8.931

Key	Part Name	Group No.
17 — CLAMP, Rear Spring Lower (1964-66)		7.518
18 — WASHER, Rear Spring Lower Clamp (33/64" I.D. x 1-1/2" O.D. x 3/16")		7.518
19 — BOLT, Clamp to Lower Control Arm (1/2" x 13 x 1-3/4")		8.900
20 — ARM, Rear Axle Lower Control		N.S.
21 — ARM ASM., Rear Axle Lower Control (Inc #13)		5.382
22 — BUSHING, Rear Axle Control Arm–On Housing		5.381
26 — INSULATOR, Rear Spring (1964-66)		7.545
27 — LOCKWASHER, Extension to Axle Housing (9/32" I.D. x 3/8" O.D.)		N.S.
28 — EXTENSION, Superlift Shock to Axle Housing		7.346
29 — BOLT, Extension to Axle Housing(1/2"-20 x 1-5/8")		8.900
30 — REINFORCEMENT, Rear Suspension Frame		7.039
31 — WASHER, Reinf. to Lwr. Arm Frame Brkt.		7.039

Typical 1964-67 GTO four-link rear suspension. The Superlift extension (number 28) was not used on 1967 Superlift installations.

MODEL SERIES	STANDARD	AIR COND.	RIDE & HANDLING PACKAGE
4207	9776201	(All Applications)	
4217	9776201	(All Applications)	
4267	9776201	(All Applications)	

1964 rear coil spring usage chart.

MODEL SERIES	STANDARD	AIR COND.	RIDE & HANDLING PACKAGE
3727	9776201	9776201	9781727
3737	9776201	9776201	9781727
3767	9776201	9776201	9781728

1965 rear coil spring usage chart.

MODEL SERIES	STANDARD	AIR COND.	RIDE & HANDLING PACKAGE
4207	9785487	9785487	9781727
4217	9785487	9785487	9781727
4267	9785487	9785488	9773998

1966 rear coil spring usage chart.

MODEL SERIES	STANDARD	AIR COND.	RIDE & HANDLING PACKAGE
4207	9788589	(All Applications)	
4217	9788589	(All Applications)	
4267	9788590	(All Applications)	

1967 rear coil spring usage chart.

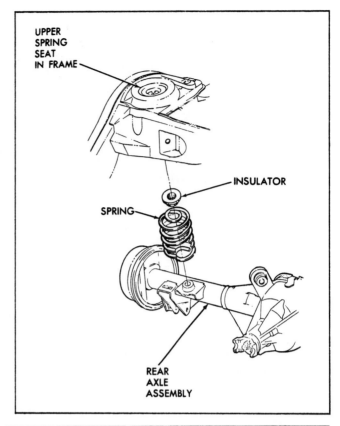

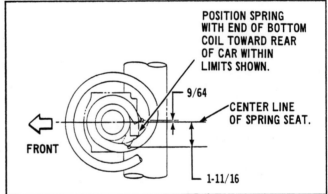

Installation and positioning of rear coil springs, 1967-70.

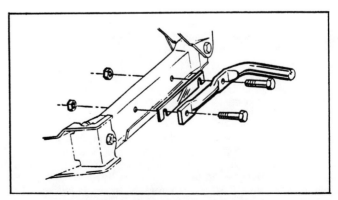

Installation of 1970 rear stabilizer bar to lower control arm using shims (part number 385967).

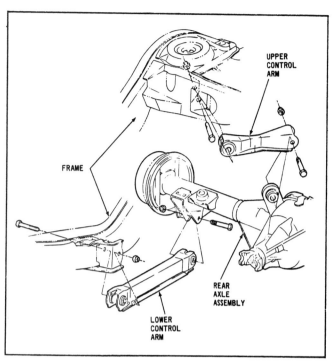

Installation of upper and lower control arms for 1968-70 GTO.

```
-----------------------------------------------------------------------------
MODEL     STANDARD  R    455 H.P.   RIDE AND HANDLING     HEAVY LOAD
SERIES    4  4      A      E  W     4   4                 400 ENG.
          0  5      M      X         0   5
          0  5      A      C  J     0   5
                    I      J  U
                    R      U  D
                           D  G
                           G  E
                           E
-----------------------------------------------------------------------------
4237  R    NN#    NZ   NN*  P8        P8#               NR#
      L    NN#    NZ   PC#  P8        NZ#               NR#
-----------------------------------------------------------------------------
4267  R    NN#    NZ   NN*  P8        P8#               NR#
      L    NN#    NZ   PC#  P8        NZ#               NR#
-----------------------------------------------------------------------------
4237  R    NN*    NZ   NN#  P8        P8                NX*
      L    NN*    NZ   PC*  P8        P8                NX*
-----------------------------------------------------------------------------
4267  R    NN*    NZ   NN*  P8        P8                NX*
      L    NN*    NZ   PC*  P8        P8                NX*
-----------------------------------------------------------------------------
# EXCEPT 455 HP 4 SPEED AND SPECIAL AXLE
* WITH 455 HP 4 SPEED AND SPECIAL AXLE

        SPRING CODES
NN - 9777794    NR - 9792491    NX - 9792855
NZ - 9789814    PC - 9777794    P8 - 9793101
```

1970 rear coil spring usage chart.

SUPERLIFT

The Superlift option was offered from 1964 through 1969. However, it was only a dealer-installed option in 1970.

1964-65   RPO 622
1966-68   RPO 634
1969   RPO 634 UPC G66

An extension bracket (part number LH 9776475 and RH 9776474) was used on the lower shock mount as an adapter for 1964-66. The package part number for 1964-66 was 3186486. The 1967 package part number was 3186525.

The replacement part numbers for the Superlift shocks were RH 3178552 and LH 3178551 in 1964; and RH 3186599 and LH 3186598 in 1965-66.

The 1967 shocks were issued new part numbers, as they were longer in length and didn't require the extension package to fit the rear suspension. The 1967 part numbers were 3186523 (RH) and 3186522 (LH).

The Superlift option for 1968-70 used the same accessory package part number, 3197570. The replacement Superlift shocks were RH 3186581 and LH 3186580 for 1968; and RH 3197570 and LH 3197569 for 1969-70.

These accessory package numbers were Delco part numbers. There were no Pontiac accessory part numbers for the Superlift package.

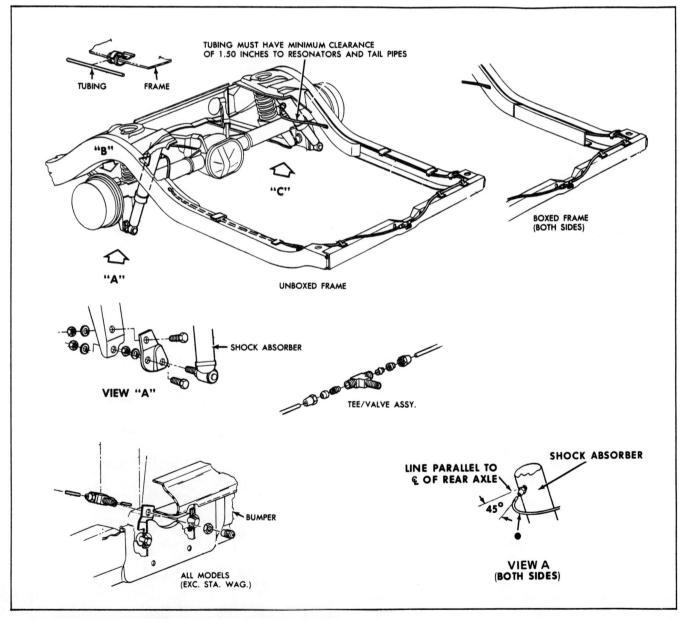

Superlift package used from 1964 to 1970. The 1967-70 GTO did not use the extension package (view A), because its shocks were longer than those used in 1964-66.

Detail of Superlift extension brackets.

FRONT SUSPENSION

1964-70

All GTOs used the General Motors Corporation front suspension—a ball-joint, independent type, with upper control arms pivoted on rubber bushings. While there was no apparent difference, the spindle carried a different part number in 1964 (385091) than in 1965-66 (9780078). In 1967, the spindle was redesigned. With drum brakes, part number 9778569 was used, and with disc brakes, part number 396887 was installed. They were not interchangeable.

In the mid-seventies, Pontiac changed spindle part number designations several times. Instead of listing the many diverse part numbers, the following breakdown should suffice for most replacement applications: 1967-70 drum brake spindles used part number 9799305; 1967-70 disc brake spindles used part number 478171.

The upper control arms were the same for 1964-66 (original part number RH 384444 and LH 384445). For the sake of originality and correctness, the original-design ⅜ inch bolt and washer for upper control arm bushing retention should be retained.

The GTO restorer has three choices when it comes to replacing the 1964-66 upper control arms. The best is to use the replacement upper control arms with a riveted ball joint from Chevrolet (part number 3974217 LH and RH 3877062), which comes with no upper shaft or bushings; then purchase the upper shaft package (part number 3849412). Another alternative is to rebuild the existing original control arms and lose the correctness of a riveted ball joint. The third possibility is to use the 1967-70 upper control arm assembly (RH 404124 and LH 404125) to replace 1964-66 applications. However, this unit utilizes the 1967-and-later-design control arm shaft, consisting of a large studded shaft with a nut and washer arrangement.

Another important area of front suspension restoration is the lower control arm. The 1964-67 GTO had a small-diameter hole for shock absorber installation. Current replacement lower arms use a later-model, large-hole design. For originality and correctness, the small shock hole should be used. However, utilization of the replacement later-model design with the larger shock hole will allow use of bigger shocks, which can improve handling.

The lower control arms were the same for 1964-67, part number RH 9784869 and LH 9784870. These numbers were replaced by RH 402038 and LH 402039, and were used for 1968-70 replacement as well. The original 1968-70 part numbers were RH 402964 and LH 402965.

The front stabilizer bar for 1964-67 was the same (part number 397705), with an outside diameter of 15/16 inch. In 1968, the bar diameter increased to 1.0 inch (part number 401194), and was carried over to 1969. In 1970, the bar diameter was increased again to 1⅛ inch (part number 402544). The replacement stabilizer link package part number was 487128 for 1964-70.

The 1968 GTO used spring part number 400880 for all hardtop applications without air conditioning, and 400881 for convertibles. When air conditioning was ordered, part number 400980 was used for hardtops and convertibles.

Beginning in 1969, Pontiac began fine tuning front suspension components by computer. Before that, front coil springs had come in matched pairs. With the advent of new sophistication in springing, the factory designed special spring rates for the LH and RH sides for different applications.

For detailing, all front suspension components were painted 60° gloss black.

Delco shocks with a one-inch piston diameter were used in all GTOs, and were painted gray. The chart below gives the correct part numbers for GTO front shock applications.

Year	Standard	Heavy-Duty	Ram Air
1964-67	3186721	3166593	—
1968	3192974	3182027	—
1969	—	—	3182027
1969-70	3182145	3182027	—

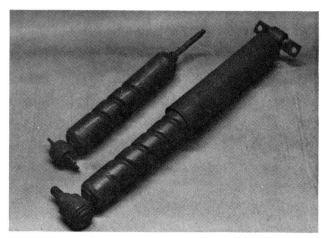
Correct AC Delco front (left) and rear shocks for all GTOs, 1964-65. Front shock for standard suspension was 3186721. Firm ride was part number 3166593. Rear shock was part number 3192445 with the standard package, and part number 3192458 with the optional handling package for 1964-67.

Detail of steering linkage shock absorber package with components. Option was available only on standard steering GTOs. It was dealer installed 1964-65; factory installed in 1964 only.

STANDARD	AIR COND. WITH M.T.	AIR COND WITH A.T.
384543	384544	384752

M.T. = MANUAL TRANSMISSION
A.T. = AUTOMATIC TRANSMISSION

1964 front coil spring usage chart.

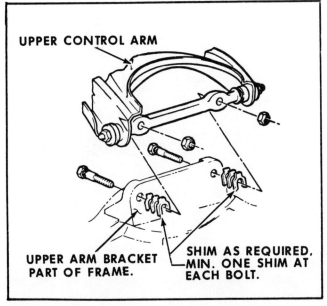

UPPER CONTROL ARM

UPPER ARM BRACKET PART OF FRAME.

SHIM AS REQUIRED, MIN. ONE SHIM AT EACH BOLT.

Installation and positioning of shims for upper control arm, 1964-70.

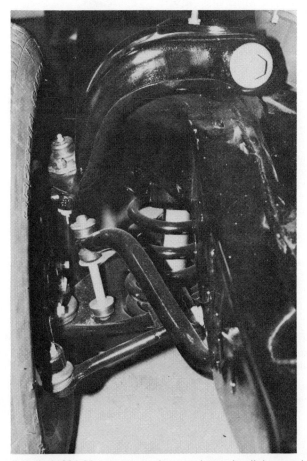

Detail of 1964-65 upper control arm and sway bar link assembly. Note larger diameter of sway bar; application 1970, but will bolt up to earlier suspensions, as shown here. Control arm position is incorrect as illustrated; this photo was taken of a bare frame, without body.

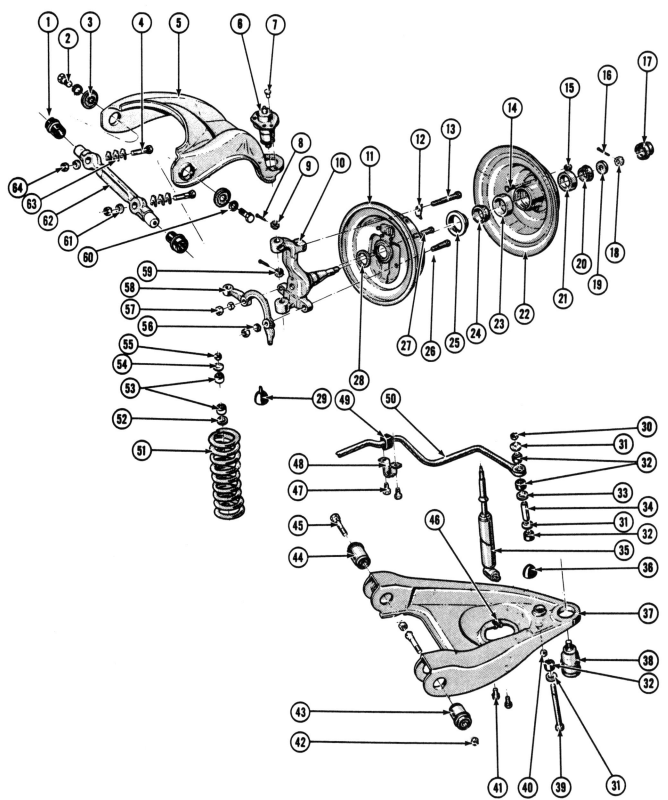

Exploded view and parts nomenclature for 1964-67 front suspension. All components except the shocks were painted 60° gloss black. 1967-70 upper control arm used a different shaft mounting package. Shock absorbers were the gray spiral design manufactured by AC Delco.

Key	Part Name	Group No.
1 — BUSHING ASM., Upper Control Arm Shaft (Part of #5) (B)		6.164
2 — BOLT, Bushing Asm. to Control Arm Shaft (3/8"-24 x 7/8") (B)		8.900
3 — RETAINER, Steering Knuckle Upper Control (Part of #5) (B)		6.163
4 — BOLT, Control Arm Shaft to Frame (7/16"-14 x 2-1/4")		6.178
5 — ARM ASM., Front Susp. Upper Control (Inc. #1-2-3-6-7-60-62)		6.178
6 — BALL JOINT PKG., Upper Control Arm (Part of #5)		6.178
7 — RIVET, Ball Joint to Control Arm (Part of #5)		N.S.
8 — COTTER PIN, Control Arm to Steering Knuckle (1/8" x 1")		8.938
9 — NUT, Control Arm to Steering Knuckle - Upper (1/2"-20)		8.917
10 — KNUCKLE, Steering		6.020
11 — BRAKE ASM., Front		N.S.
12 — PLATE, Front Brake to Strg. Knuckle Anchor Bolt Lock		5.002
13 — BOLT, Front Brake to Steering Knuckle Anchor		5.002
14 — BOLT, Front Wheel Hub		6.335
15 — NUT, Wheel Hub		5.813
16 — COTTER PIN, Hub & Drum Asm., to Steering Knuckle (1/8" x 1-1/8")		N.S.
17 — CAP, Front Wheel Hub Grease		6.330
18 — NUT, Steering Knuckle Spindle		6.022
19 — WASHER, Steering Knuckle Spindle		6.321
20 — BEARING & RACE ASM., Front Wheel Outer Bearing - Inner		6.319
21 — RACE, Front Wheel Outer Bearing - Outer		6.317
22 — HUB & DRUM ASM., Front Brake		6.306
23 — RACE, Front Wheel Inner Bearing - Outer		6.316
24 — BEARING & RACE ASM., Front Wheel Inner Bearing - Inner		6.318
25 — SEAL ASM., Front Wheel Inner Bearing		6.326
26 — BOLT, Brake Asm. to Steering Knuckle & Arm (7/16"-14 x 2-1/4")		8.900
27 — BOLT, Brake Asm. to Steering Knuckle & Arm (7/16"-14 x 2-1/2")		8.900
28 — GASKET, Front Brake Support to Knuckle		5.002
29 — BUMPER, Front Suspension Upper Arm.		6.176
30 — NUT, Front Stabilizer Link (5/16"-18) (A)		7.238
31 — RETAINER, Front Stabilizer Link Grommet (A)		7.245
32 — GROMMET, Front Stabilizer Link (A)		7.244
33 — RETAINER, Front Stabilizer Link Grommet (A)		7.245
34 — SPACER, Front Stabilizer Link (A)		7.240
35 — SHOCK ABSORBER ASM., Front		7.345
36 — BUMPER, Lower Control Arm.		6.176
37 — ARM ASM., Front Suspension Lower Control (Inc. #38-43-44-46)		6.168
38 — BALL JOINT ASM., Lower Control Arm (Part of #37)		6.174
39 — LINK, Stabilizer to Control Arm (A).		7.240
40 — NUT, Bumper to Lower Arm (3/8"-16)		8.916
41 — BOLT, Shock to Control Arm (5/16"-18 x 7/8")		N.S.
42 — NUT, Arm Asm. to Frame (1/2"-13)		8.916
43 — BUSHING, Front Suspension Lower Control Arm - Rear (Part of #37)		6.169
44 — BUSHING, Front Suspension Lower Control Arm - Front (Part of #37)		6.169
45 — BOLT, Arm Asm. to Frame (1/2"-13 x 3-3/4")		6.172
46 — NUT, Front Shock Absorber to Lower Arm (Part of #37)		7.395
47 — SCREW, Front Stabilizer Shaft Bracket (5/16"-18 x 1-1/8")		8.977
48 — BRACKET, Front Stabilizer Shaft		7.242
49 — BUSHING, Front Stabilizer Shaft		7.243
50 — SHAFT, Front Stabilizer (7/8" Dia.)		7.241
51 — SPRING, Front Coil		7.412
52 — RETAINER, Shock Absorber Grommet		7.377
53 — GROMMET, Front Shock Upper Mounting to Bracket		7.377
54 — RETAINER, Shock Absorber Grommet		7.377
55 — NUT, Shock Absorber to Frame (3/8"-24)		7.395
56 — LOCKWASHER, Brake Asm. to Strg. Knuckle & Arm (7/16")		8.931
57 — NUT, Brake Asm. to Steering Knuckle & Arm (7/16"-14)		8.917
58 — ARM, Steering		6.103
59 — NUT, Control Arm to Steering Knuckle - Lower (9/16"-18)		8.917
60 — LOCKWASHER, Bushing Asm. to Control Arm Shaft (3/8") (B)		8.931
61 — LOCKWASHER, Control Arm Shaft to Frame (7/16")		8.931
62 — SHAFT, Front Suspension Upper Arm (B)		6.178
63 — SHIMS, Front Suspension Upper Arm Shaft		6.178
64 — NUT, Control Arm Shaft to Frame (7/16"-14)		8.915
(A) LINK PKG., Front Stabilizer		7.240
(B) SHAFT PKG., Steering Knuckle Upper Control Arm		6.178

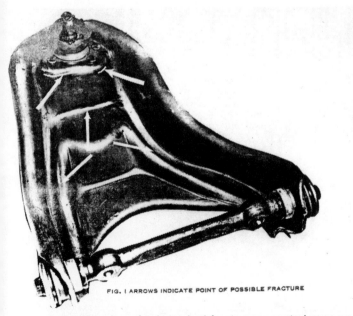

FIG. I ARROWS INDICATE POINT OF POSSIBLE FRACTURE

A small number of substandard front upper control arms was produced in the early 1964 production. Units built after the following were satisfactory: Pontiac (P) 12160, Fremont (F) 1582, Kansas City (M) 1475 and Baltimore (B) 2338. Units built prior to these numbers should be checked by raising the car and looking for metal tear or fracture in the areas indicated. It may be necessary to clean the affected areas of grit and black paint. (Information taken from letter to dealers from J. C. Bates, General Service Manager, dated 10-1-63.)

MODEL	STANDARD	AIR COND.
3727	384543	388283
3737	384543	388283
3767	384543	388283

AUTOMATIC TRANSMISSIONS		
3727	384543	384752
3737	384543	384752
3767	384543	384752

1965 front coil spring usage chart.

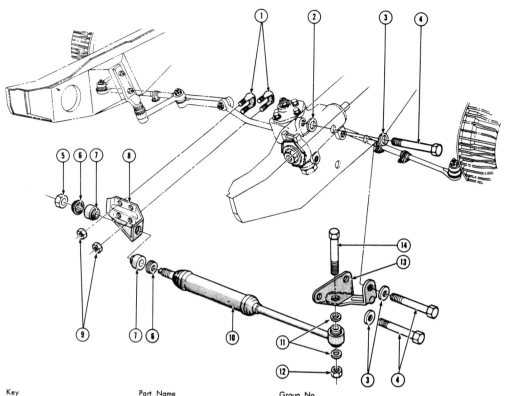

Key	Part Name	Group No.
1 — "U" BOLT, Bracket to Steering Connecting Rod		6.865
2 — WASHER, Bolt to Steering Gear (31/32"O.D. x 15/32"I.D. x 1/8"thick)		N.S.
3 — WASHER, Steering Gear to Frame		6.509
4 — BOLT, Steering Gear to Frame (7/16"-14 x 4 1/2")		N.S.
5 — NUT, Absorber to Stabilizer Brkt. & Conn. Rod Brkt. (3/8"-24)		6.865
6 — RETAINER, Absorber grommet to Stabilizer Brkt. & Conn. Rod Brkt.		6.865
7 — GROMMET, Absorber to Stabilizer Brkt. & Conn. Rod Brkt.		N.S.
8 — BRACKET, Absorber to Connecting Rod		6.865
9 — NUT, "U" Bolt to Bracket & Connecting Rod (5/16"-18)		8.915
10 — SHOCK ABSORBER PKG., Steering Linkage		6.865
11 — WASHER, Bracket to Absorber (17/32"I.D. x 1 1/8"O.D. x 9/64" thick)		6.178
12 — NUT, Frame Bracket Bolt to Absorber (1/2"-13)		8.915
13 — BRACKET, Shock Absorber to Frame		6.865
14 — BOLT, Absorber to Frame Bracket (1/2"-13 x 2 3/4")		N.S.

Standard steering linkage shock absorber used in 1964 and 1965.

```
MANUAL TRANSMISSIONS
```

MODEL	STANDARD	AIR COND.	SOFT RIDE WITH A/C	SOFT RIDE NO A/C
4207	384543	388283		
4217	384543	388283		
4267	388281	388283		

```
AUTOMATIC TRANSMISSIONS
```

MODEL	STANDARD	AIR COND.	SOFT RIDE WITH A/C	SOFT RIDE NO A/C
4207	388281	388283	381940	381946
4217	388281	384752	381946	381946
4267	388281	384752	381946	381946

1966 front coil spring usage chart.

1967 GTO front suspension. Note upper control arms and shaft packages.

MANUAL TRANSMISSIONS - NO A.I.R.

MODEL	STANDARD	AIR COND.	
4207	388283	386288	
4217	388283	386288	
4267	384752	388284	

MANUAL TRANSMISSION - WITH A.I.R.

4207	388283	386288	
4217	388283	386288	
4267	384752	388284	

1967 front coil spring usage chart.

AUTOMATIC TRANSMISSIONS - NO A.I.R.

MODEL	STANDARD	AIR COND.	
4207	384752	388284	
4217	384752	388284	
4267	386288	388284	

AUTOMATIC TRANSMISSION - WITH A.I.R.

4207	384752	388284	
4217	384752	388284	
4267	386288	388284	

1967 front coil spring usage chart.

AUTOMATIC TRANSMISSIONS

MODEL	STANDARD 400	R A M A I R	HEAVY LOAD NO A/C	HEAVY LOAD WITH A/C	FIRM RIDE WITH A/C	FIRM RIDE NO A/C	AIR COND. 400	R A M A I R
4237 R	LY	SC			SF	SC	SB	SF
L	SB	SF			SF	SF	SF	SF
4267 R	LY	SC			SF	SC	SB	SF
L	SB	SF			SN	SF	SF	SN

LY 400881   SB 400882   SC 400975
SF 400980   SN 401174

1969 front coil spring usage chart.

MODEL	STANDARD 400 / RAM AIR		HEAVY LOAD NO A/C	HEAVY LOAD WITH A/C	FIRM RIDE WITH A/C	FIRM RIDE NO A/C	AIR COND. 400 / RAM AIR	
4237								
R	LY	SC			SF	SC	SB	SF
L	SB	SF			SF	SF	SF	SF
4267								
R	LY	SC			SF	SC	SB	SF
L	SB	SF			SN	SF	SF	SN

LY 400881   SB 400882   SC 400975
SF 400980   SN 401174

1969 front coil spring usage chart.

MODEL	STANDARD 400 / RAM AIR		455	HEAVY LOAD NO A/C	HEAVY LOAD WITH A/C	FIRM RIDE WITH A/C	FIRM RIDE NO A/C	AIR COND. 400 / RAM AIR		455
4237										
R	LT*	SC	SC*	SF	SK	SF	SC	LX*	SF	SF#
L	LT*	SF	SF*	SN	SK	SN	SF	LA*	SN	SN#
4267										
R	LT*	SC	SC*	SF	SK	SF	SC	LX*	SF	SF#
L	LT*	SF	SF*	SN	SK	SN	SF	LA*	SN	SN#

LA 400876   LT 400872   SC 400975
SF 400980   SK 401174   SN 401174
* EXCEPT JUDGE OPTION
# WITH JUDGE OPTION

1970 front coil spring usage chart.

MODEL	STANDARD 400 / RAM AIR		455	HEAVY LOAD NO A/C	HEAVY LOAD WITH A/C	FIRM RIDE WITH A/C	FIRM RIDE NO A/C	AIR COND. 400 / RAM AIR		455
4237										
R	LT	SC	*	SF	SN	SF	SC	LT	SF	*
L	LT	SC	*	SN	SK	SN	SC	LA	SN	*
4267										
R	LT	SC	*	SF	SN	SF	SC	LT	SF	*
L	LT	SC	*	SN	SK	SN	SC	LA	SN	*

LA 400876   LT 400872   SC 400975
SF 400980   SK 401174   SN 401174

* WITH 455 ENGINE
STANDARD - WITH JUDGE - R SC
                        L SC

         EXCEPT JUDGE - R LT
                        L LT

AIR CONDITIONED - WITH JUDGE - R SF
                               L SN

              EXCEPT JUDGE - R LT
                             L LA

1970 front coil spring usage chart.

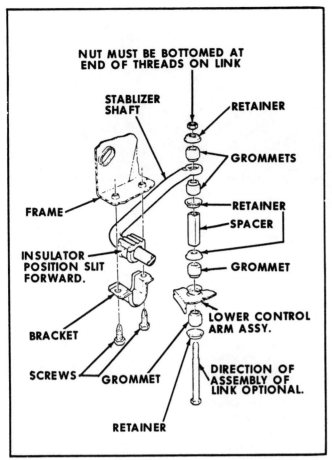

NUT MUST BE BOTTOMED AT
END OF THREADS ON LINK

STABLIZER
SHAFT

RETAINER

GROMMETS

FRAME

RETAINER

SPACER

INSULATOR
POSITION SLIT
FORWARD.

GROMMET

LOWER CONTROL
ARM ASSY.

BRACKET

SCREWS

GROMMET

DIRECTION OF
ASSEMBLY OF
LINK OPTIONAL.

RETAINER

Exploded view of front stabilizer link package. Rubber bushings were used for the stabilizer bracket; nylon bushings were used in 1970 for the link grommets.

STEERING BOX

1964-67

There were no external differences in the 1964 and 1965 steering boxes. Three versions were used: a standard box with 24:1 ratio, a standard quick box of 20:1 ratio and a 17.5:1 box available with power steering only. The steering box was painted gloss black, with the lower end plug and side cover in natural aluminum.

The steering linkages were the same for both years. The entire assembly was painted gloss black. An interesting and rare option was the standard steering, steering linkage shock absorber. Its purpose was to dampen road shock transmitted to the steering wheel. In 1964, the absorber was available either factory installed or dealer installed (package number 3857174, replacement number 3186732). In 1965 it was a dealer-installed option only, and the package part number was 9777411.

Steering box design for 1966-67 was identical to the 1964-65 GTO.

The steering linkage shock absorber was again offered as a dealer-installed option in 1966 only. The part numbers were the same as for the 1965 unit.

1968-70

Manual steering boxes were serviced by individual components. Power steering gearboxes were different for 1968-70. The 1968 box had a 17.5:1 ratio (part number 5696003). The 1969 box (part number 7807029) was unique to the GTO alone; it used a ratio of 15:1, while all other Tempests and LeMans used a 17.5:1 box. The 1970 steering box (part number 7807439) was a variable-ratio box, using ratios of 16:1 to 12.4:1, providing faster response without a change in effort.

While it is next to impossible to identify a steering box by sight alone, there is one foolproof way of determining the model year of a box: On the top inboard side of the box is a machined pad. On the pad is the date code of the box. A code may read 1578, indicating it was built the 157th day of 1968—obviously a 1968 box. A code reading 2978 would indicate the box was built the 297th day of 1968, identifying it as a 1969 box.

The steering box was painted 60° gloss black—with the exception of the top and end plugs, which were natural aluminum in appearance.

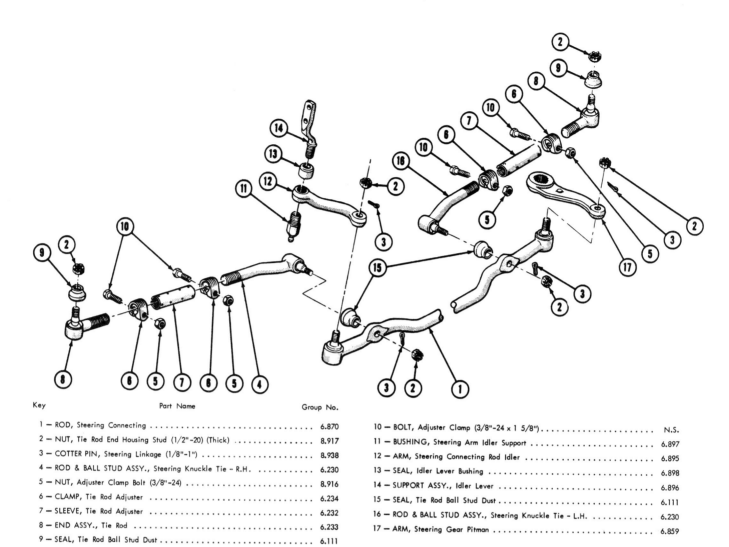

Key	Part Name	Group No.
1 — ROD, Steering Connecting		6.870
2 — NUT, Tie Rod End Housing Stud (1/2"-20) (Thick)		8.917
3 — COTTER PIN, Steering Linkage (1/8"-1")		8.938
4 — ROD & BALL STUD ASSY., Steering Knuckle Tie - R.H.		6.230
5 — NUT, Adjuster Clamp Bolt (3/8"-24)		8.916
6 — CLAMP, Tie Rod Adjuster		6.234
7 — SLEEVE, Tie Rod Adjuster		6.232
8 — END ASSY., Tie Rod		6.233
9 — SEAL, Tie Rod Ball Stud Dust		6.111

10 — BOLT, Adjuster Clamp (3/8"-24 x 1 5/8")		N.S.
11 — BUSHING, Steering Arm Idler Support		6.897
12 — ARM, Steering Connecting Rod Idler		6.895
13 — SEAL, Idler Lever Bushing		6.898
14 — SUPPORT ASSY., Idler Lever		6.896
15 — SEAL, Tie Rod Ball Stud Dust		6.111
16 — ROD & BALL STUD ASSY., Steering Knuckle Tie - L.H.		6.230
17 — ARM, Steering Gear Pitman		6.859

Exploded view and parts nomenclature for 1964-67 steering linkage. Assembly was painted 60° gloss black.

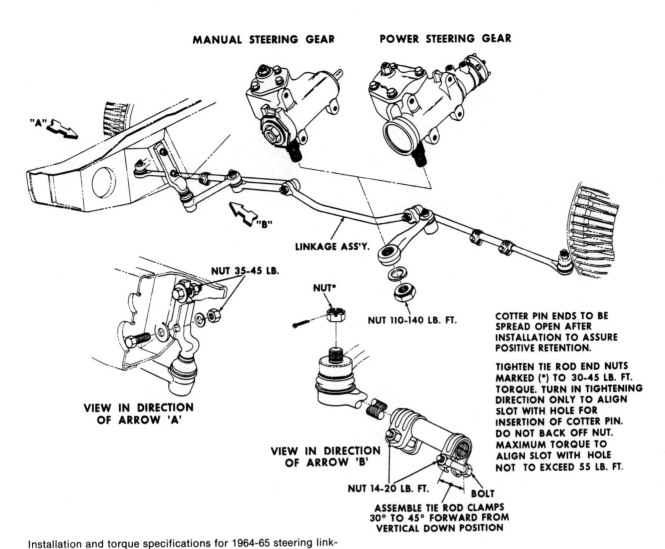

MANUAL STEERING GEAR

POWER STEERING GEAR

"A"

"B"

LINKAGE ASS'Y.

NUT 35-45 LB.

NUT*

NUT 110-140 LB. FT.

VIEW IN DIRECTION OF ARROW 'A'

VIEW IN DIRECTION OF ARROW 'B'

NUT 14-20 LB. FT.

BOLT

ASSEMBLE TIE ROD CLAMPS 30° TO 45° FORWARD FROM VERTICAL DOWN POSITION

COTTER PIN ENDS TO BE SPREAD OPEN AFTER INSTALLATION TO ASSURE POSITIVE RETENTION.

TIGHTEN TIE ROD END NUTS MARKED (*) TO 30-45 LB. FT. TORQUE. TURN IN TIGHTENING DIRECTION ONLY TO ALIGN SLOT WITH HOLE FOR INSERTION OF COTTER PIN. DO NOT BACK OFF NUT. MAXIMUM TORQUE TO ALIGN SLOT WITH HOLE NOT TO EXCEED 55 LB. FT.

Installation and torque specifications for 1964-65 steering linkage. Note alignment of tie rod clamps.

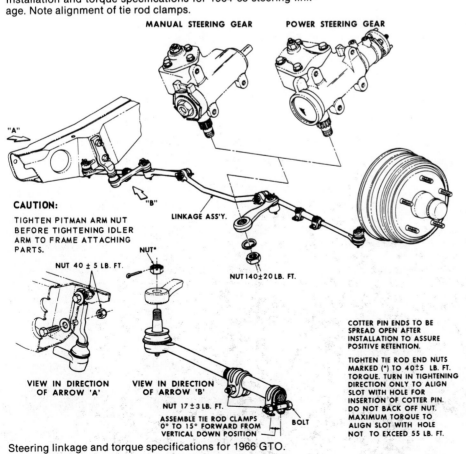

MANUAL STEERING GEAR

POWER STEERING GEAR

"A"

"B"

LINKAGE ASS'Y.

CAUTION:

TIGHTEN PITMAN ARM NUT BEFORE TIGHTENING IDLER ARM TO FRAME ATTACHING PARTS.

NUT 40 ± 5 LB. FT.

NUT*

NUT 140±20 LB. FT.

VIEW IN DIRECTION OF ARROW 'A'

VIEW IN DIRECTION OF ARROW 'B'

NUT 17 ± 3 LB. FT.

BOLT

ASSEMBLE TIE ROD CLAMPS 0° TO 15° FORWARD FROM VERTICAL DOWN POSITION

COTTER PIN ENDS TO BE SPREAD OPEN AFTER INSTALLATION TO ASSURE POSITIVE RETENTION.

TIGHTEN TIE ROD END NUTS MARKED (*) TO 40±5 LB. FT. TORQUE. TURN IN TIGHTENING DIRECTION ONLY TO ALIGN SLOT WITH HOLE FOR INSERTION OF COTTER PIN. DO NOT BACK OFF NUT. MAXIMUM TORQUE TO ALIGN SLOT WITH HOLE NOT TO EXCEED 55 LB. FT.

Steering linkage and torque specifications for 1966 GTO.

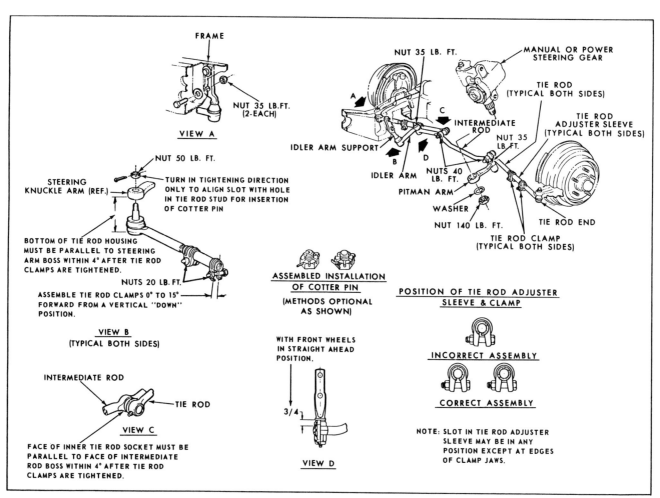

Typical 1968-70 steering linkage components and assembly instructions, including torque requirements. All linkage pieces were painted 60° gloss black.

POWER STEERING BELT AND PULLEY

1964-70

The 1964 GTO used two different belt and pulley configurations. Those built before February 1, 1964, without air conditioning, used a double-groove dual-belt-drive assembly. A double-groove pulley, 5⅞ inches in diameter (part number 9774775), drove the power steering pump. A double-groove pulley (1962998) was also used for the alternator. Air-conditioned cars used a single, ½ inch groove pulley (part number 54840) measuring 6 21/32 inches in diameter.

A GTO built after February 1, 1964, used a single-groove pulley (9778378) for the power steering pump and a single-groove pulley (1949357) for the alternator. A separate belt was run to each pulley. The water pump and balancer pulleys remained the same. This second type of design was carried over into the 1965 model run. The water pump pulley was painted gloss black; the balancer pulley, engine-blue; the alternator pulley, natural; and the power steering pump pulley, gloss black.

The 1965 single-groove pulley without air conditioning was 9777401, measured 5⅞ inches in diameter and had a ⅜ inch groove. The air conditioning pulley measured 7⅜ inches in diameter, used a ½ inch single groove, and was identified by part number 9779020. The pump, bracket and pulley were gloss black, the reservoir cap was natural metal.

Pontiac Service News Flash number 65-99, dated 5-17-65, reported on the best way to deal with a flipped or rolled-over drive belt on 1965 models. All the spacers between the power steering pump bracket and the cylinder head should be removed. Then inspect for bent pulleys (generator, power steering pump, air conditioner compressor). With a straightedge, check for pulley misalignment. And replace the belt using only a wrapped-type (Gates).

For 1966-67 the water pump pulley was gloss black; the balancer pulley, engine-blue; and the power steering pulley, gloss black.

For 1968-70, power steering belts and pulleys were identical in appearance to those used in 1966-67.

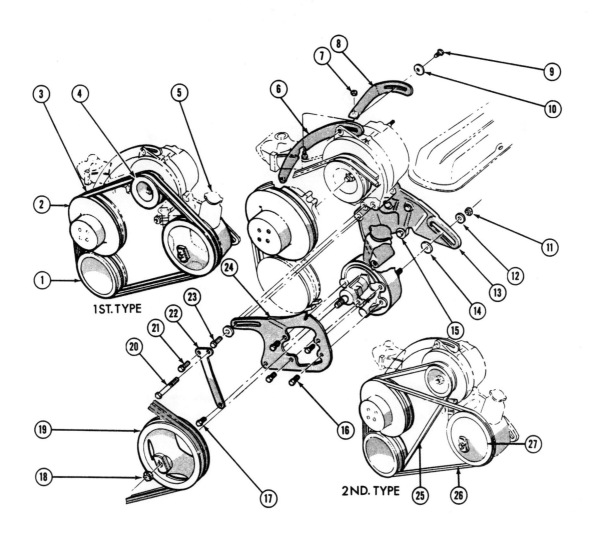

Key	Part Name	Group No.
1 — BALANCER ASM., Harmonic		0.659
2 — PULLEY, Water Pump and Fan		1.062
3 — BELTS, Water Pump, Alt. & Strg. Pump Drive (57-1/2") (1st Type)		1.066
4 — PULLEY, Alternator		2.274
5 — PUMP ASM., Steering Gear Oil		6.605
6 — STRAP, Alternator Belt Adjusting-Front		2.317
7 — NUT, Strap to Water Outlet Stud (3/8"-16)		8.915
8 — STRAP, Alternator Belt Adjusting-Rear		2.317
9 — WASHER, Alternator to Adjusting Straps (11/32" I.D. x 3/4" O.D.)		2.277
10 — BOLT, Alternator to Adjusting Straps (5/16"-18 x 1-1/8")		8.900
11 — NUT, Steering Pump to Bracket (3/8"-16)		8.915
12 — WASHER, Steering Pump to Mounting Bracket (1" O.D. x 13/32" I.D.)		6.606
13 — BRACKET, Steering Pump Mounting		6.606
14 — WASHER, Steering Pump to Bracket (3/8" I.D. x1-3/16" O.D. x 3/16" cup)		6.606

Key	Part Name	Group No.
15 — BOLT, Steering Pump Bracket to Cylinder Head (3/8"-16 x 1-1/8")		8.900
16 — BOLT, Strg. Pump to Support (3/8"-16 x 3/4")		8.900
17 — BOLT, Brace to Support and Steering Pump (3/8"-16 x 7/8")		8.900
18 — NUT, Pump Pulley to Pump (9/16"-18)		8.917
19 — PULLEY, Power Steering Pump (1st Type)		6.655
20 — BOLT, Alternator to Bracket and Brace (3/8"-16 x 3-1/4")		8.900
21 — BOLT, Alternator Support Brace (3/8"-16 x 7/8")		8.900
22 — BRACE, Alternator Support		2.277
23 — WASHER, Support to Bracket (13/32" I.D. x 3/4" O.D.)		2.277
24 — SUPPORT, Power Steering Pump		6.606
25 — BELT, Water Pump, Fan & Alt. (50-13/16") (2nd Type)		1.066
26 — BELT, Water Pump, Fan & Strg. Pump (55-1/2") (2nd Type)		1.066
27 — PULLEY, Power Steering Pump (2nd Type)		6.655

Power steering pump and drive assemblies for 1964, showing first- and second-design. The pump mounting bracket (part number 545313) was natural aluminum in appearance, and the front alternator mounting strap (part number 9774972) and the rear strap (part number 9775526 for four-barrel engines, part number 9775611 for Tri-Power) were painted 60° gloss black.

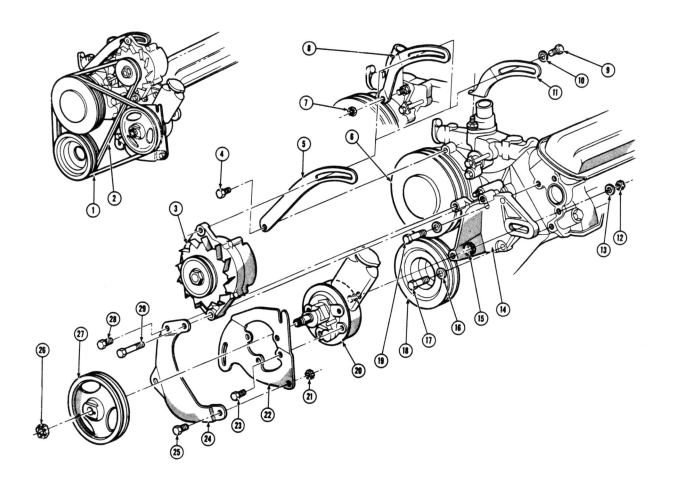

Key	Part Name	Group No.
1 — BELT, Waterpump, Fan & Power Steering Pump		1.066
2 — BELT, Waterpump, Fan & Delcotron Drive		1.066
3 — DELCOTRON ASSEMBLY		2.275
4 — BOLT, Delcotron Belt Adj. Strap - (3/8" - 16 x 1 1/8")		8.900
5 — STRAP, Delcotron Belt Adj. - Front		2.317
6 — PULLEY, Waterpump and Fan		1.062
7 — NUT, Delcotron Belt Adj. Strap - w/3/2 B.C. - (3/8" - 16)		8.917
8 — STRAP, Delcotron Belt Adj. - Rear		2.317
9 — BOLT, Delcotron Belt Adj. Strap - (5/16" - 18 x 1 1/8")		8.900
10 — WASHER, Delcotron Adj. Strap to Delcotron		2.317
11 — STRAP, Delcotron Belt Adj. - Rear - w/2 and 4 B.C.		2.317
12 — NUT, Power Steering Pump to Bracket - (3/8" - 16)		8.917
13 — WASHER, Power Steering Pump to Bracket		6.606
14 — BRACKET, Power Steering Pump Mounting		6.606

Key	Part Name	Group No.
15 — WASHER, Power Steering Pump to Bracket		6.606
16 — WASHER, Pump Mounting Bracket		6.606
17 — BOLT, Pump Mounting Bracket-(3/8"-16 x 1 1/2")		8.900
18 — BALANCER ASM., Harmonic		0.659
19 — BOLT, Pump Mtg. Bracket - (3/8" - 16 x 1 7/8")		8.900
20 — PUMP ASM., Power Steering		6.605
21 — NUT, Pump Mtg. Plate to Pump Support - (3/8"-16)		8.917
22 — SUPPORT, Power Steering Pump - Front		6.606
23 — BOLT, Pump Support to Pump Asm. (3/8"-16 x 3/4")		8.900
24 — PLATE, Power Steering Pump Mounting		6.606
25 — BOLT, Pump Mtg. Plate to Pump Support - (3/8" - 16 x 7/8")		8.900
26 — NUT, Power Steering Pump Pulley - (9/16" - 18)		8.917
27 — PULLEY, Power Steering Pump		6.655
28 — BOLT, Pump Mounting Plate to Pump Mounting Bracket - (3/8" - 16 x 1 3/8")		8.900
29 — BOLT, Pump Mounting Plate to Delcotron - (3/8" - 16 x 3 1/4")		8.900

1965 and 1966 power steering pump and drive assemblies were detailed similarly to the 1964 unit. However, the pump mounting bracket was part number 9778848 (9782660 with AIR) in 1966. The alternator mounting straps (part number 9778851 front, 9778852 for four-barrel and 9778853 for Tri-Power) were painted 60° gloss black. Power steering pulley in this illustration is incorrect.

PRESSURE & RETURN HOSES
SHOULD BE POSITIONED SO
THEY DO NOT CONTACT.

DO NOT REMOVE CAPS &
PLUGS UNTIL IMMEDIATELY
BEFORE ASSEMBLING HOSES.

AFTER INSTALLATION IS
COMPLETE, & WITH FRONT
WHEELS IN STRAIGHT AHEAD
POSITION, FILL PUMP
RESERVOIR TO FULL MARK.

BLEED SYSTEM WITH ENGINE
OPERATING BY TURNING
FRONT WHEELS FULL LEFT
AND HOLDING AGAINST
STOP FOR 10 SECONDS.
REFILL PUMP TO INDICATED LEVEL.

INSPECT SYSTEM FOR LEAKS,
ESPECIALLY AT HOSE
CONNECTIONS & FITTINGS.

GEAR ASSY.

VIEW "A"
(8 CYL. ENG.)

€ OF PUMP

PARALLEL

VIEW "C"
(ALL ENGINES)

FRAME

"A"

Detail of 1967 power steering pump and related assemblies. Alignment of pressure hose (part number 7800108) was parallel to center line of pump. The return hose (part number 9788836) clamped onto the fitting running underneath the reservoir and out to the LH side of the pump.

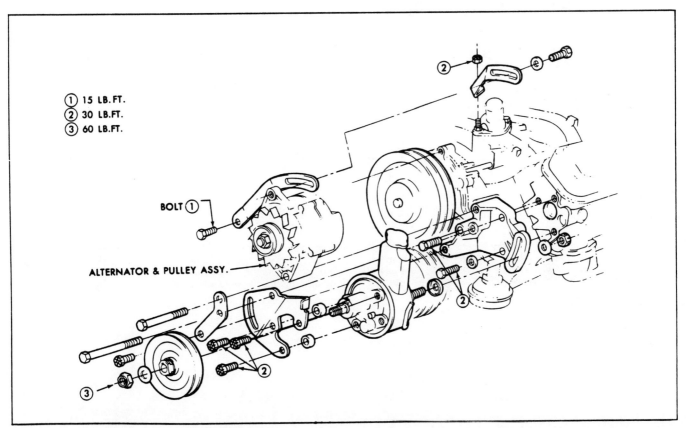

① 15 LB.FT.
② 30 LB.FT.
③ 60 LB.FT.

BOLT ①

ALTERNATOR & PULLEY ASSY.

Installation of 1968-69 power steering pump and alternator. All pulleys, bolts and brackets were painted 60° gloss black—with the exception of the pump-mounting bracket to the cylinder head, which was aluminum. Alternator bracket was 60° gloss black as well. Alternator was natural metal, with no gloss.

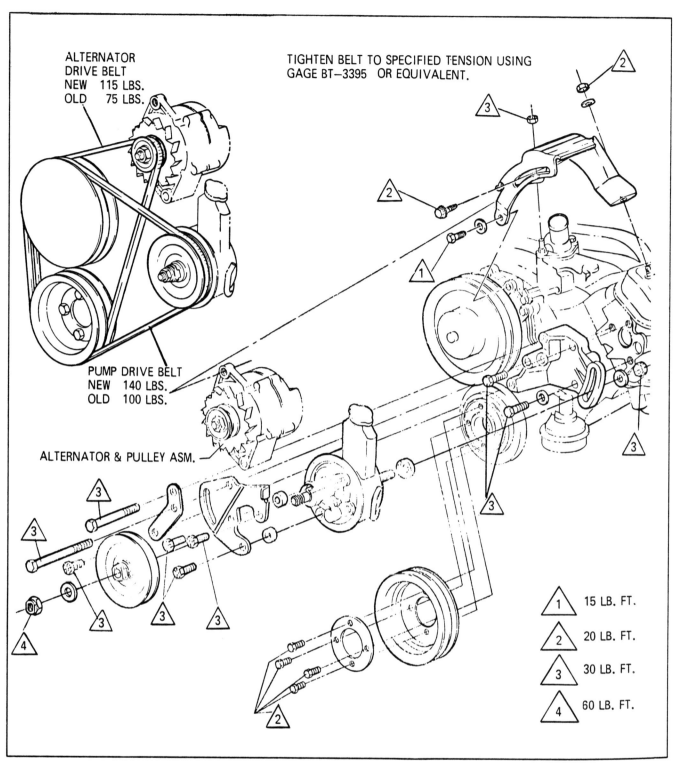

ALTERNATOR
DRIVE BELT
NEW   115 LBS.
OLD   75 LBS.

TIGHTEN BELT TO SPECIFIED TENSION USING
GAGE BT—3395 OR EQUIVALENT.

PUMP DRIVE BELT
NEW   140 LBS.
OLD   100 LBS.

ALTERNATOR & PULLEY ASM.

1 15 LB. FT.

2 20 LB. FT.

3 30 LB. FT.

4 60 LB. FT.

Installation of 1970 power steering and alternator assemblies. While basic installation was the same as 1968-69, note use of alternator mounting and adjustment bracket (part number 546479); bracket was painted 60° gloss black. Note balancer pulley and weight. Pulley was 60° gloss black, retainer plate was engine-blue, bolts were silver cadmium.

POWER STEERING PUMP

1964-70

A different power steering pump was used in 1964 and 1965. The 1964 version used part number 5692883, and the pressure hose was 5692716. The pump and its mounting brackets were gloss black; the cap, natural.

In 1965, the pump used different mounting brackets, and the reservoir design was changed. Two power steering pumps were used in 1965; each had different rotator, vane and pressure plate assemblies. The two correct pump numbers were 5693871 and 5696861. The complete pumps were interchangeable on the 1965 GTO.

The 1966 pump (part number 5696861) was identical to the 1965 pump. It could be identified by grooves on the head of the orifice fitting. The 1967 pump (part number 5698070) was not interchangeable with the 1966 unit, as the housing and reservoir were completely redesigned, with a fitting running underneath the bottom of the reservoir for the return hose.

Mounting brackets and plates were not interchangeable, as the 1966 pump adjusted horizontally in the bracket and the 1967 adjusted vertically.

The power steering pump pulley varied in size, depending on the use of air conditioning or AIR (air induction reactance).

The 1968 and 1969 pumps were identical, using part number 5698070, which was also used in 1967.

Because the control valve was changed in the 1970 pump, it was assigned a new number (7808043). It was externally identical to earlier pumps.

The pump, pulley and assorted bolts and brackets were painted 60° gloss black—with the exception of the pump mounting bracket (part number 9786903), which was natural aluminum in appearance.

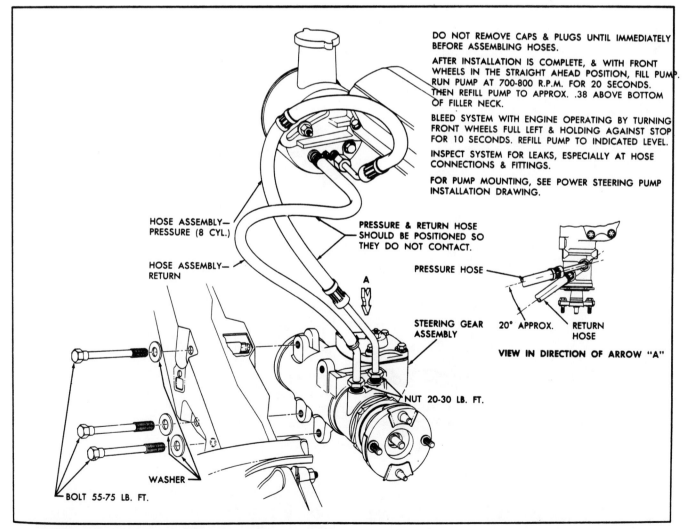

Installation and alignment of 1965 power steering pump and gearbox. Note alignment of pressure and return hoses on steering gear assembly.

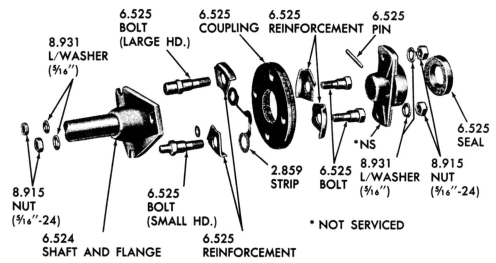

8.931 L/WASHER (5/16")

6.525 BOLT (LARGE HD.)

6.525 COUPLING

6.525 REINFORCEMENT

6.525 PIN

6.525 SEAL

8.915 NUT (5/16"-24)

6.524 SHAFT AND FLANGE

6.525 BOLT (SMALL HD.)

6.525 REINFORCEMENT

2.859 STRIP

6.525 BOLT

*NS

8.931 L/WASHER (5/16")

8.915 NUT (5/16"-24)

* NOT SERVICED

Power steering gear coupling assembly used from 1964 to 1967, viewing the flange at left.

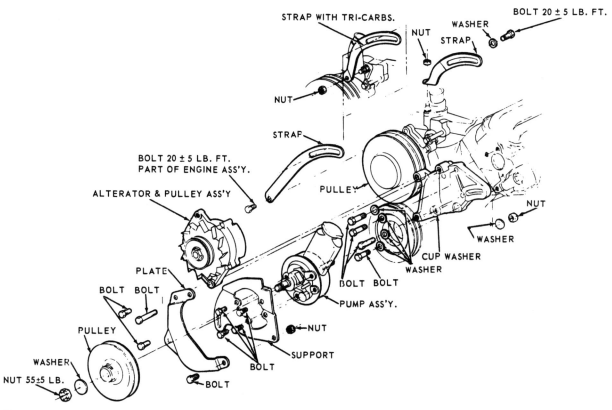

STRAP WITH TRI-CARBS.

NUT

WASHER

STRAP

BOLT 20 ± 5 LB. FT.

NUT

STRAP

BOLT 20 ± 5 LB. FT. PART OF ENGINE ASS'Y.

PULLEY

ALTERATOR & PULLEY ASS'Y.

NUT

WASHER

PLATE

CUP WASHER

WASHER

BOLT   BOLT

PULLEY

BOLT   BOLT

PUMP ASS'Y.

WASHER

NUT 55±5 LB.

NUT

SUPPORT

BOLT

BOLT

Diagram of 1966 power steering and alternator mounting procedures. The pump mounting bracket (part number 9778848, 9782660 with AIR) was natural aluminum in appearance. All other brackets, plates and supports, including alternator straps, were painted 60° gloss black.

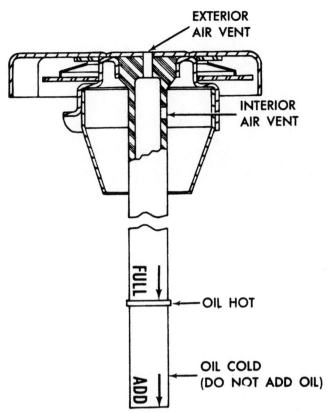

Power steering pump leaks can be caused by an overfull condition. Before overhauling the power steering to correct oil leaks, check oil level and look for a plugged vent, as shown. Check for a plugged interior vent by holding finger over exterior vent and blowing through the tube. Replace cap if the interior vent is not open. (Information and illustration taken from Dealer Service Information Bulletin number 65-104, dated 6-7-65.)

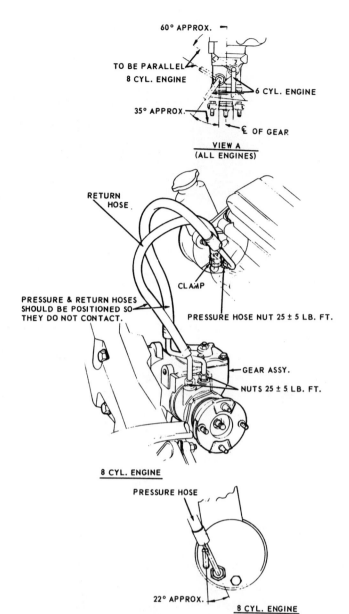

REAR VIEW OF POWER STEERING PUMP

DO NOT REMOVE CAPS & PLUGS UNTIL IMMEDIATELY BEFORE ASSEMBLING HOSES.

AFTER INSTALLATION IS COMPLETE & WITH FRONT WHEELS IN STRAIGHT AHEAD POSITION. FILL PUMP RESERVOIR TO FULL MARK.

BLEED SYSTEM WITH ENGINE OPERATING BY TURNING FRONT WHEELS FULL LEFT & RIGHT. REFIL PUMP TO INDICATED LEVEL.

INSPECT SYSTEM FOR LEAKS. ESPECIALLY AT HOSE CONNECTIONS & FITTINGS.

Installation instructions for 1966 power steering pump and related assemblies. Note alignment of pressure hose (part number 5694588) and return hose (part number 5693395).

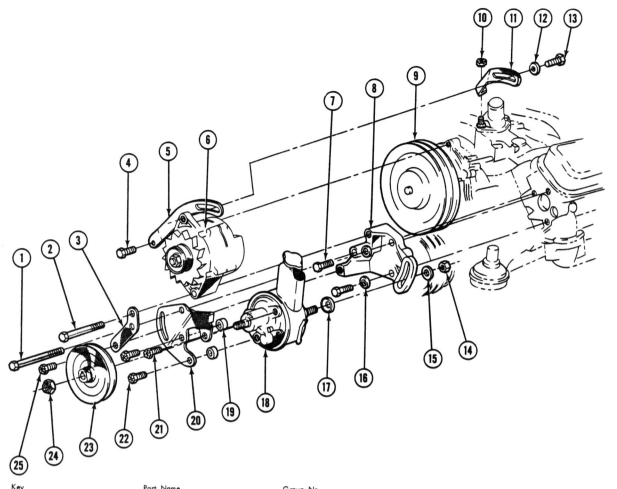

Key	Part Name	Group No.
1 — BOLT, Mounting Plate to Cyl. Head (3/8" - 16 x 5-1/2")		8.900
2 — BOLT, Bracket to Cylinder Head (3/8" - 16 x 3-1/4")		8.900
3 — BRACE, Alternator Pivot		2.277
4 — BOLT, Strap to Water Pump & Timing Chain Cover (5/16" - 18 x 1-3/8")		N.S.
5 — STRAP, Alternator Adjusting - Front		2.317
6 — DELCOTRON ASSEMBLY		2.275
7 — BOLT, Bracket to Cyl. Head (3/8" - 16 x 1-7/8")		8.900
8 — BRACKET, Steering Pump Mounting		6.606
9 — PULLEY, Water Pump & Fan		1.062
10 — NUT, Strap to Inlet Stud (3/8" - 16)		8.915
11 — STRAP, Alternator Adjusting - Rear		2.317
12 — WASHER, Adjusting Strap to Alternator (11/32" I.D. x 3/4" O.D. x 3/32")		2.317
13 — BOLT, Strap to Alternator (5/16" - 18 x 1-1/4")		8.900
14 — NUT, Pump to Bracket (3/8" - 16)		8.915
15 — WASHER, Pump to Mounting Bracket (13/32" I.D. x 7/8" O.D. x 5/32")		6.606
16 — WASHER, Pump Bracket to Cyl. Head (13/32" I.D. x 3/4" O.D. x 1/8")		6.606
17 — WASHER, Pump to Bracket-Cup (3/8" I.D. x 1-3/16" O.D. x 3/16")		6.606
18 — PUMP ASM., Power Steering		6.605
19 — SPACER, Pump to Mounting Plate		6.606
20 — PLATE, Steering Pump Mounting		6.606
21 — BOLT, Pump to Plate (3/8" - 16 x 3/4")		8.900
22 — BOLT, Pump to Plate (3/8" - 16 x 1-1/8")		8.900
23 — PULLEY, Steering Pump		6.655
24 — NUT, Steering Pump Pulley		6.655
25 — BOLT, Plate to Bracket (3/8" - 16 x 1-3/8")		8.900

Detail of 1967 power steering pump mounting and related hardware. Note redesign of pump mounting bracket (part number 9786903) with adjustment now done vertically. Its appearance was natural aluminum. All other straps, plates and braces for the alternator and pump were 60° gloss black.

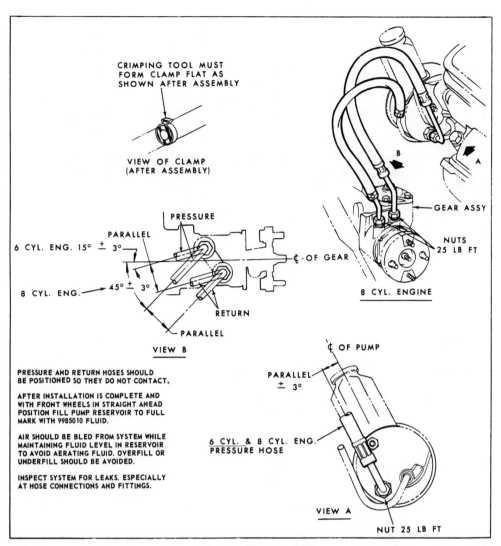

CRIMPING TOOL MUST FORM CLAMP FLAT AS SHOWN AFTER ASSEMBLY

VIEW OF CLAMP (AFTER ASSEMBLY)

PRESSURE

PARALLEL

6 CYL. ENG. 15° ± 3°

8 CYL. ENG. 45° ± 3°

RETURN

PARALLEL

℄ OF GEAR

VIEW B

GEAR ASSY

NUTS 25 LB FT

8 CYL. ENGINE

℄ OF PUMP

PARALLEL ± 3°

6 CYL. & 8 CYL. ENG. PRESSURE HOSE

VIEW A

NUT 25 LB FT

PRESSURE AND RETURN HOSES SHOULD BE POSITIONED SO THEY DO NOT CONTACT.

AFTER INSTALLATION IS COMPLETE AND WITH FRONT WHEELS IN STRAIGHT AHEAD POSITION FILL PUMP RESERVOIR TO FULL MARK WITH 9985010 FLUID.

AIR SHOULD BE BLED FROM SYSTEM WHILE MAINTAINING FLUID LEVEL IN RESERVOIR TO AVOID AERATING FLUID. OVERFILL OR UNDERFILL SHOULD BE AVOIDED.

INSPECT SYSTEM FOR LEAKS. ESPECIALLY AT HOSE CONNECTIONS AND FITTINGS.

Installation and correct alignment of 1968-69 power steering pump hoses. View B shows alignment of pressure hoses at gearbox for the six-cylinder engine. A six-cylinder power steering gearbox used a 17.5:1 ratio box; 1969 GTO used a 15:1 box, which was more desirable.

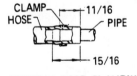

CLAMP — 11/16
HOSE — PIPE
15/16

TYPICAL HOSE CLAMPING

INSTALL PIPE AGAINST EDGE OF BRACKET

PRESSURE HOSE

CLAMP

NUT 35 LB. FT.

COVER

GEAR ASM.

RETURN HOSE

NUTS 25 LB. FT.

INSTALL PIPE AGAINST SIDE OF COVER.

PRESSURE AND RETURN HOSES SHOULD BE POSITIONED SO THEY DO NOT CONTACT.

AFTER INSTALLATION IS COMPLETE AND WITH FRONT WHEELS IN STRAIGHT AHEAD POSITION FILL PUMP RESERVOIR TO FULL MARK WITH 9985010 FLUID.

AIR SHOULD BE BLED FROM SYSTEM WHILE MAINTAINING FLUID LEVEL IN RESERVOIR TO AVOID AERATING FLUID. OVERFILL OR UNDERFILL SHOULD BE AVOIDED.

INSPECT SYSTEM FOR LEAKS. ESPECIALLY AT HOSE CONNECTIONS AND FITTINGS.

Routing of 1970 power steering hoses. While installation was almost identical to 1968-69, note pressure hose pipe to gearbox. Pipe lays against top cover of gearbox; 1968-69 version does not.

EXHAUST

1964-65

Manual transmission 1965 GTOs had built-in resonators in the tail pipes, which were 2.25 inches wide at the pipe. Exhaust systems for 1964 and 1965 had the head pipes a natural metal, the mufflers bright galvanized and the tail pipes aluminized.

The optional exhaust-splitter extension was available in both 1964 and 1965. There were accounts of an early-production "short-splitter," but no factory reference to it. However, the parts for it were listed: RPO number (422), the package part number (LH 984334, RH 984333) and the replacement part number (LH 9778487, RH 9776484). The hangers were the same for both years (LH 9776489 and RH 9776488), as were the splitters themselves, numbers included.

Exhaust

Year	Part	Part Number RH	Part Number LH	Dimensions RH	Dimensions LH	Inches In RH	Inches In LH	Inches Out RH	Inches Out LH
1964	Head pipe	9774010	9774012	2.25x0.076	2.25x0.076	—	—	—	—
	Muffler	9777030	9774546	—	—	2.25	2.25	2.0	2.0
	Tail pipe	9776706	9774315	2.00x0.055	2.00x0.055	—	—	—	—
1965	Head pipe								
	Standard	9774010	9774012	2.25x0.075	2.25x0.075	—	—	—	—
	Tri-Power								
	automatic	9774010	9774012	2.25x0.075	2.25x0.075	—	—	—	—
	manual	9774010	9774012	2.25x0.075	2.25x0.075	—	—	—	—
	Muffler								
	Standard	9777465	9777466	—	—	2.25	2.25	2.0	2.0
	Tri-Power								
	automatic	9777465	9777466	—	—	2.25	2.25	2.0	2.0
	manual	9781705	9781705	—	—	2.25	2.25	2.25	2.25
	Tail pipe								
	Standard	9776706	9774315	2.0x0.049	2.0x0.049	—	—	—	—
	Tri-Power								
	automatic	9776706	9774315	2.0x0.049	2.0x0.049	—	—	—	—
	manual	9781710	9781711	2.25x0.055	2.25x0.055	—	—	—	—

1966-67

The 1966 GTO used reverse-flow mufflers with separate resonators. The exhaust pipe was 2.00 inches in diameter and had a wall thickness of 0.060 inch. The tail pipe resonator assembly was 2.00x0.045 inches at the resonator inlet and 2.25x0.048 inches at the outlet, and was aluminized. The 1967 mufflers were also reverse-flow and galvanized (as were the 1966 mufflers). The 1967 exhaust pipe measured 2.00x0.060 inches—except for HO or Ram Air engine use, in which case 2.25x0.076 inch pipes with a three-bolt flange were used. Automatic-equipped GTOs continued to use the 1966-style resonator and tail pipe assembly. The manual transmission GTO dispensed with the resonator and ran a regular tail pipe measuring 2.25x0.048 inches.

Available for 1966 and 1967, the chrome exhaust extensions (RPO 482) were a trumpet design, with the inner edge rolled in, and extended out the rear under the bumper. The following chart indicates numbers and interchangeability.

Year	Trans.	Replacement Part Number	Accessory Package No.	Diameter (inches)
1966	All	9785205	984718	2.00
1967	Auto.	9785205	984718	2.00
1967	Man.	9789224	984860	2.25

1968-70

Reverse-flow mufflers were used during 1968-70. However, only the 1969 automatic-transmission-equipped GTO used resonators. A unique "tuner" pipe was used on the 1968 GTO equipped with automatic transmission; it took the place of a regular resonator.

All three years used exhaust pipes measuring 2.00x0.060 inches. All automatic-equipped GTOs used tail pipes measuring 2.00x0.048 inches, while manual transmission models used 2.25x0.048 inch pipes.

Exhaust extensions were an extra-cost option in 1968 (RPO 482) and 1969 (RPO 482 UPC N25). Their design was similar to the 1966-67 units. The split chromed extensions were standard in 1970.

Year	Trans.	Replacement Part Number	Accessory Package No.	Diameter (inches)
1968	Auto.	9785205	984979	2.00
1968	Man.	9789224	N/A	2.25
1969	Man.	9797245	988503	2.25
1970		478022	N/A	

Extension pipe part number 9793747 was used for the chrome exhaust extension for 2.00 inch pipes, and part number 9793746, for 2.25 inch pipes.

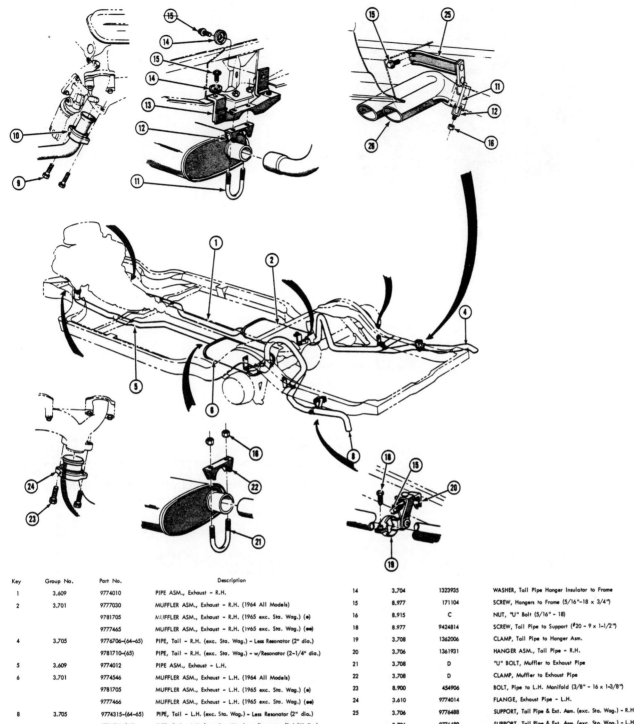

Key	Group No.	Part No.	Description
1	3.609	9774010	PIPE ASM., Exhaust – R.H.
2	3.701	9777030	MUFFLER ASM., Exhaust – R.H. (1964 All Models)
		9781705	MUFFLER ASM., Exhaust – R.H. (1965 exc. Sta. Wag.) (•)
		9777465	MUFFLER ASM., Exhaust – R.H. (1965 exc. Sta. Wag.) (••)
4	3.705	9776706–(64–65)	PIPE, Tail – R.H. (exc. Sta. Wag.) – Less Resonator (2" dia.)
		9781710–(65)	PIPE, Tail – R.H. (exc. Sta. Wag.) – w/Resonator (2-1/4" dia.)
5	3.609	9774012	PIPE ASM., Exhaust – L.H.
6	3.701	9774546	MUFFLER ASM., Exhaust – L.H. (1964 All Models)
		9781705	MUFFLER ASM., Exhaust – L.H. (1965 exc. Sta. Wag.) (•)
		9777466	MUFFLER ASM., Exhaust – L.H. (1965 exc. Sta. Wag.) (••)
8	3.705	9774315–(64–65)	PIPE, Tail – L.H. (exc. Sta. Wag.) – Less Resonator (2" dia.)
		9781711–(65)	PIPE, Tail – L.H. (exc. Sta. Wag.) – w/Resonator (2-1/4" dia.)
9	8.900	186678	BOLT, Pipe to R.H. Manifold (3/8-16 x 1")
10	3.610	9771005	FLANGE, Exhaust Pipe to Manifold – R.H.
11	3.708	C	"U" BOLT, Muffler to Tail Pipe
12	3.708	C	CLAMP, Muffler to Tail Pipe
13	3.706	9783845	HANGER ASM., Muffler Tail Pipe – R.H.
	3.706	9783634	HANGER ASM., Muffler Tail Pipe – L.H.
14	3.704	1323935	WASHER, Tail Pipe Hanger Insulator to Frame
15	8.977	171104	SCREW, Hangers to Frame (5/16"-18 x 3/4")
16	8.915	C	NUT, "U" Bolt (5/16" - 18)
18	8.977	9424814	SCREW, Tail Pipe to Support (#20 - 9 x 1-1/2")
19	3.708	1362006	CLAMP, Tail Pipe to Support
20	3.706	1361931	HANGER ASM., Tail Pipe – R.H.
21	3.708	D	"U" BOLT, Muffler to Exhaust Pipe
22	3.708	D	CLAMP, Muffler to Exhaust Pipe
23	8.900	454906	BOLT, Pipe to L.H. Manifold (3/8" - 16 x 1-3/8")
24	3.610	9774014	FLANGE, Exhaust Pipe – L.H.
25	3.706	9776488	SUPPORT, Tail Pipe & Ext. Asm. (exc. Sta. Wag.) – R.H.
	3.706	9776489	SUPPORT, Tail Pipe & Ext. Asm. (exc. Sta. Wag.) – L.H.
26	3.705	9776486	EXTENSION, Tail Pipe (exc. Sta. Wag.) – R.H.
	3.705	9776487	EXTENSION, Tail Pipe (exc. Sta. Wag.) – L.H.

(•) 2¼" INLET & OUTLET
(••) 2¼" INLET & 2" OUTLET
"C" INCLUDED IN 9777024 CLAMP PKG.—3.708
"D" INCLUDED IN 9784416 CLAMP PKG.—3.708

Installation diagram and part numbers for 1964-65 GTO dual exhaust system.

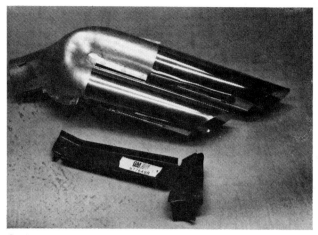

Optional exhaust splitter (RPO 422) with correct bracket. Splitter was an option in both 1964 and 1965.

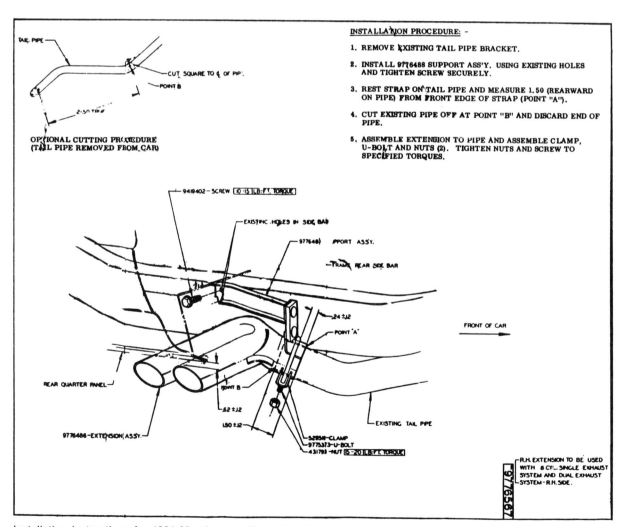

TAIL PIPE

CUT SQUARE TO ℄ OF PIPE

POINT B

2.50 THK F

OPTIONAL CUTTING PROCEDURE
(TAIL PIPE REMOVED FROM CAR)

INSTALLATION PROCEDURE: -

1. REMOVE EXISTING TAIL PIPE BRACKET.

2. INSTALL 9776488 SUPPORT ASS'Y. USING EXISTING HOLES AND TIGHTEN SCREW SECURELY.

3. REST STRAP ON TAIL PIPE AND MEASURE 1.50 (REARWARD ON PIPE) FROM FRONT EDGE OF STRAP (POINT "A").

4. CUT EXISTING PIPE OFF AT POINT "B" AND DISCARD END OF PIPE.

5. ASSEMBLE EXTENSION TO PIPE AND ASSEMBLE CLAMP, U-BOLT AND NUTS (2). TIGHTEN NUTS AND SCREW TO SPECIFIED TORQUES.

9419402 - SCREW 10-15 LB-FT TORQUE

EXISTING HOLES IN SIDE BAR

9776488 - SUPPORT ASS'Y.

FRAME REAR SIDE BAR

24 ±12

POINT "A"

FRONT OF CAR

REAR QUARTER PANEL

POINT B

EXISTING TAIL PIPE

9776486 - EXTENSION ASS'Y.

52 ±12

150 ±12

3289# - CLAMP
9775373 - U-BOLT
431793 - NUT 15-20 LB-FT TORQUE

R.H. EXTENSION TO BE USED WITH 8 CYL. SINGLE EXHAUST SYSTEM AND DUAL EXHAUST SYSTEM - R.H. SIDE.

9776587

Installation instructions for 1964-65 exhaust splitters showing correct alignment.

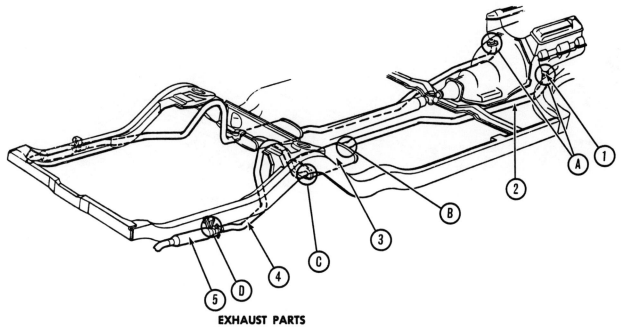

EXHAUST PARTS

1	3.610	1	9785597	FLANGE, Exhaust Pipe to Manifold – L.H.
	–	–	N.S.	FLANGE, Exhaust Pipe to Manifold – R.H.
2	3.609	1	9784895	PIPE, Exhaust – R.H.
	3.609	1	9788715	PIPE, Exhaust – L.H.
3	3.701	1	9784158	MUFFLER ASM., Exhaust – R.H.
	3.701	1	9784159	MUFFLER ASM., Exhaust – L.H.
4	3.705	1	9785676	PIPE, Tail – R.H.
	3.705	1	9785677	PIPE, Tail – L.H.
5	3.702	2	9784890	RESONATOR ASM., Exhaust

ATTACHING PARTS

A	8.900	2	179839	BOLT, Flange to Manifold – R.H. (3/8"-16 x 1")
	8.900	2	186678	BOLT, Flange to Manifold – L.H. (3/8"-16 x 1 3/8")
B	3.708	1	9784415	CLAMP PKG., Exhaust Pipe to Muffler (2" Pipe)
C	3.706	1	9783845	HANGER ASM., Muffler – R.H.
	3.706	1	9783634	HANGER ASM., Muffler – L.H.
	8.977	4	9419402	SCREW, Hanger to Frame (5/16"-18 x 3/4")
	3.704	4	1323935	WASHER, Hanger to Frame (7/16")
	3.708	2	9784416	CLAMP PKG., Tail Pipe to Muffler (2 1/4" Pipe)
D	3.706	1	1361931	HANGER ASM., Tail Pipe – Rear – R.H.
	3.706	1	9785678	HANGER ASM., Tail Pipe – Rear – L.H.
	8.977	2	9419402	SCREW, Hanger to Frame (5/16"-18 x 3/4")
	3.708	2	9784420	CLAMP PKG., Hanger to Tail Pipe (2 1/2" Pipe)

Detail drawing of 1966 dual exhaust system used on GTO.

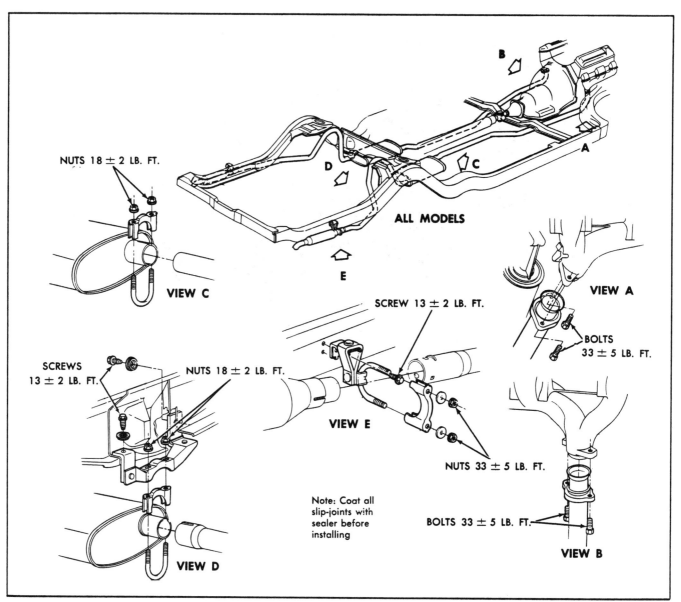

NUTS 18 ± 2 LB. FT.

VIEW C

ALL MODELS

D

C

E

SCREWS
13 ± 2 LB. FT.

NUTS 18 ± 2 LB. FT.

VIEW D

SCREW 13 ± 2 LB. FT.

VIEW E

Note: Coat all
slip-joints with
sealer before
installing

NUTS 33 ± 5 LB. FT.

BOLTS 33 ± 5 LB. FT.

VIEW B

VIEW A

BOLTS
33 ± 5 LB. FT.

1966 exhaust system, noting positioning and torque specifications for clamps. Note especially view E and position of hanger and clamp assembly. LH muffler was smaller than RH muffler to combat condensation due to heat riser.

A comparison of 1966 extension (left) and 1967 manual transmission extension. Note enlargement of extension on right to accommodate the 1967 2.25 inch tail pipe.

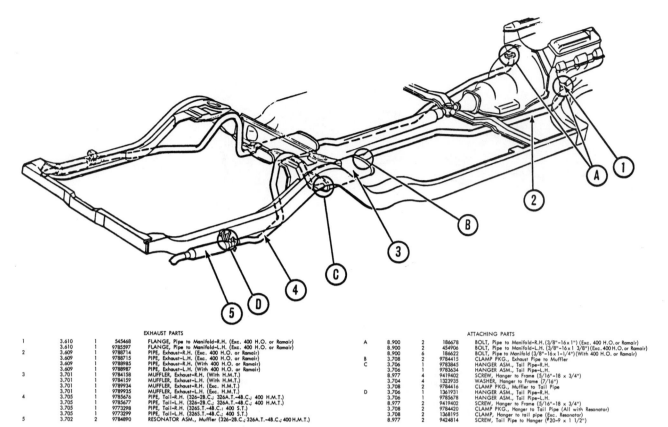

				EXHAUST PARTS
1	3.610	1	545468	FLANGE, Pipe to Manifold-R.H. (Exc. 400 H.O. or Ramair)
	3.610	1	9785597	FLANGE, Pipe to Manifold-L.H. (Exc. 400 H.O. or Ramair)
2	3.609	1	9788714	PIPE, Exhaust-R.H. (Exc. 400 H.O. or Ramair)
	3.609	1	9788715	PIPE, Exhaust-L.H. (Exc. 400 H.O. or Ramair)
	3.609	1	9788985	PIPE, Exhaust-R.H. (With 400 H.O. or Ramair)
	3.609	1	9788987	PIPE, Exhaust-L.H. (With 400 H.O. or Ramair)
3	3.701	1	9784158	MUFFLER, Exhaust-R.H. (With H.M.T.)
	3.701	1	9784159	MUFFLER, Exhaust-L.H. (With H.M.T.)
	3.701	1	9789934	MUFFLER, Exhaust-R.H. (Exc. H.M.T.)
	3.701	1	9789935	MUFFLER, Exhaust-L.H. (Exc. H.M.T.)
4	3.705	1	9785676	PIPE, Tail-R.H. (326-2B.C.; 326A.T.-4B.C.; 400 H.M.T.)
	3.705	1	9785677	PIPE, Tail-L.H. (326-2B.C.; 326A.T.-4B.C.; 400 H.M.T.)
	3.705	1	9773298	PIPE, Tail-R.H. (326S.T.-4B.C.; 400 S.T.)
	3.705	1	9773299	PIPE, Tail-L.H. (326S.T.-4B.C.; 400 S.T.)
5	3.702	2	9784890	RESONATOR ASM., Muffler (326-2B.C.; 326A.T.-4B.C.; 400 H.M.T.)

				ATTACHING PARTS
A	8.900	2	186678	BOLT, Pipe to Manifold-R.H. (3/8"-16 x 1") (Exc. 400 H.O. or Ramair)
	8.900	2	454906	BOLT, Pipe to Manifold-L.H. (3/8"-16 x 1 3/8") (Exc. 400 H.O. or Ramair)
	8.900	6	186622	BOLT, Pipe to Manifold (3/8"-16 x 1-1/4") (With 400 H.O. or Ramair)
B	3.708	2	9784415	CLAMP PKG., Exhaust Pipe to Muffler
C	3.706	1	9783845	HANGER ASM., Tail Pipe-R.H.
	3.706	1	9783634	HANGER ASM., Tail Pipe-L.H.
	8.977	4	9419402	SCREW, Hanger to Frame (5/16"-18 x 3/4")
	3.704	4	1323935	WASHER, Hanger to Frame (7/16")
	3.708	2	9784416	CLAMP PKG., Muffler to Tail Pipe
D	3.706	1	1361931	HANGER ASM., Tail Pipe-R.H.
	3.706	1	9785678	HANGER ASM., Tail Pipe-L.H.
	8.977	2	9419402	SCREW, Hanger to Frame (5/16"-18 x 3/4")
	3.708	2	9784420	CLAMP PKG., Hanger to Tail Pipe (All with Resonator)
	3.708	2	1368195	CLAMP, Hanger to tail pipe (Exc. Resonator)
	8.977	2	9424814	SCREW, Tail Pipe to Hanger (#20-9 x 1 1/2")

1967 exhaust system, showing resonator used in automatic-equipped GTO. Manual-transmission-equipped models used an open tail pipe. Note difference in part numbers for transmission application.

Comparison of 1968 two-inch and 2¼ inch exhaust extensions. Pipe was enlarged on extension at right to accept 2¼ inch tail pipe used with manual transmissions.

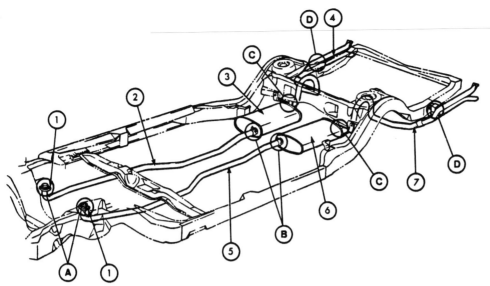

Key	Group No.	Qty.	Part No.	Description
1	3.610	2	9789096	FLANGE, Pipe to Manifold (Exc. 400 H.D. or Ramair)
2	3.609	1	9790828	PIPE, Exhaust - R.H. (Exc. 400 H.D. or Ramair)
	3.609	1	9791683	PIPE, Exhaust - R.H. (w/400 H.D. or Ramair)
3	3.701	1	9784158	MUFFLER, Exhaust - R.H. (Exc. G.T.O. w/M.T.)
	3.701	1	9793150	MUFFLER, Exhaust - R.H. (G.T.O. w/M.T.)
4	3.705	1	9790293	PIPE, Tail - R.H. (Exc. G.T.O. w/M.T.)
	3.705	1	9792198	PIPE, Tail - R.H. (G.T.O. w/M.T.)
5	3.609	1	9790829	PIPE, Exhaust - L.H. (Exc. 400 H.D. or Ramair)
	3.609	1	9782586	PIPE, Exhaust - L.H. (w/400 H.D. or Ramair)
6	3.701	1	9784159	MUFFLER, Exhaust - L.H. (Exc. G.T.O. w/M.T.)
	3.701	1	9793151	MUFFLER, Exhaust - L.H. (G.T.O. w/M.T.)
7	3.705	1	9790294	PIPE, Tail - L.H. (Exc. G.T.O. w/M.T.)
	3.705	1	9792199	PIPE, Tail - L.H. (G.T.O. w/M.T.)

Detail and part numbers for 1968 exhaust.

ATTACHING PARTS

Key	Group No.	Qty.	Part No.	Description
A	3.613	4	9777812	BOLT, Pipe to Manifold (3/8"-16 x 1 5/8") (Exc. 400 H.D. or Ramair)
	8.900	3	9420462	BOLT, Pipe to Manifold - R.H. (3/8"-16 x 1 1/4") (w/400 H.D. or Ramair)
	8.900	2	9420462	BOLT, Pipe to Manifold - L.H. (3/8"-16 x 1 1/4") (w/400 H.D. or Ramair)
B	3.708	2	3754883	CLAMP PKG., Exhaust Pipe to Muffler
C	3.704	1	9790493	HANGER ASM., Tail Pipe - L.H.
	3.704	1	9790492	HANGER ASM., Tail Pipe - R.H.
	8.977	4	9419402	SCREW, Hanger to Frame (5/16"-18 x 3/4")
	3.704	4	1323935	WASHER, Hanger to Frame (7/16")
	3.708	2	3754883	CLAMP PKG., Muffler to Tail Pipe
D	3.706	2	1382598	HANGER ASM., Tail Pipe
	3.706	2	9793544	CLAMP, Tail Pipe to Hanger (Exc. G.T.O. - w/M.T.)
	3.708	2	9793545	CLAMP, Tail Pipe to Hanger (G.T.O. - w/M.T.)
	8.977	2	9419402	SCREW, Hanger to Frame (5/16"-18 x 3/4")
	8.977	2	9429462	SCREW, Tail Pipe to Hanger (#20-9 x 1 1/2")

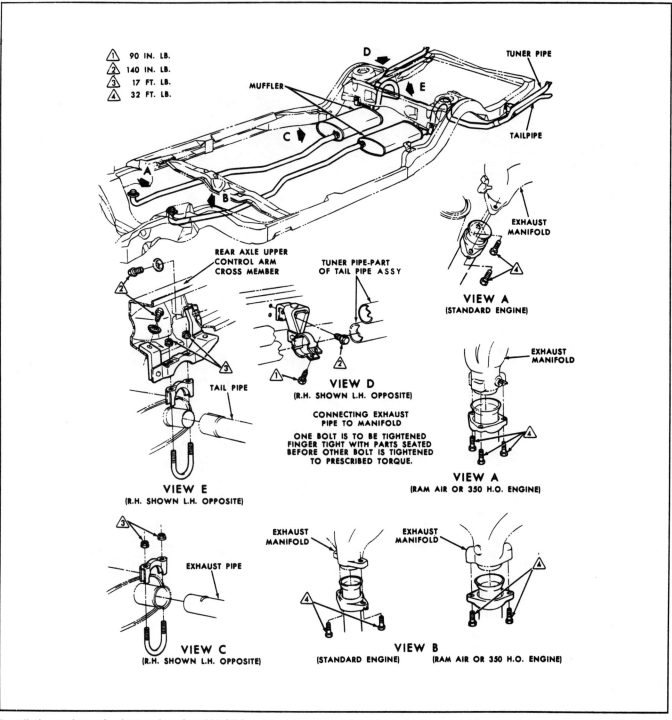

△1 90 IN. LB.
△2 140 IN. LB.
△3 17 FT. LB.
△4 32 FT. LB.

MUFFLER

D

TUNER PIPE

E

TAILPIPE

C

A

B

REAR AXLE UPPER
CONTROL ARM
CROSS MEMBER

TUNER PIPE-PART
OF TAIL PIPE ASSY

EXHAUST
MANIFOLD

VIEW A
(STANDARD ENGINE)

TAIL PIPE

VIEW D
(R.H. SHOWN L.H. OPPOSITE)

CONNECTING EXHAUST
PIPE TO MANIFOLD

ONE BOLT IS TO BE TIGHTENED
FINGER TIGHT WITH PARTS SEATED
BEFORE OTHER BOLT IS TIGHTENED
TO PRESCRIBED TORQUE.

EXHAUST
MANIFOLD

VIEW A
(RAM AIR OR 350 H.O. ENGINE)

VIEW E
(R.H. SHOWN L.H. OPPOSITE)

EXHAUST PIPE

EXHAUST
MANIFOLD

EXHAUST
MANIFOLD

VIEW C
(R.H. SHOWN L.H. OPPOSITE)

VIEW B
(STANDARD ENGINE)   (RAM AIR OR 350 H.O. ENGINE)

Installation and torquing instructions for 1968 GTO exhaust system. Note three-bolt flange used for Ram Air exhaust manifold. 350 HO was for Tempest. Also note tuner pipe used for Hydramatic-equipped models.

259

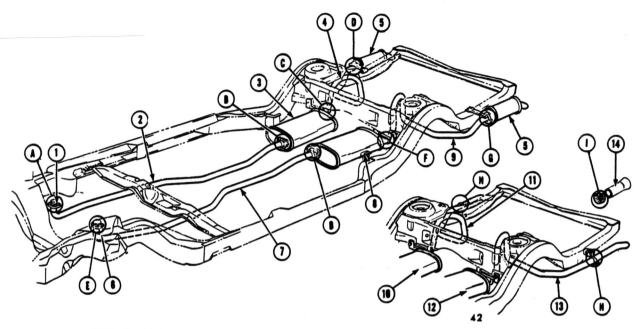

EXHAUST PARTS			
3.609	1	9789096	FLANGE, Pipe to Manifold (Exc. 400 or Ram Air)
3.609	1	9797116	PIPE, Exhaust - R.H. (S.W.B.) (Exc. 400 H.O. or Ram Air)
3.609	1	9797117	PIPE, Exhaust - R.H. (L.W.B.) (Exc. 400 H.O. or Ram Air)
3.609	1	9791683	PIPE, Exhaust - R.H. (S.W.B.) (w/400 H.O. or Ram Air)
3.701	1	9798592	MUFFLER, Exhaust - R.H. (Exc. G.T.O.-M.T.)
3.705	1	9796974	PIPE, Tail - R.H. (Exc. G.T.O.-M.T.)
3.702	2	9798957	RESONATOR & PIPE ASM., (Exc. G.T.O.-M.T.)
3.609	1	9789096	FLANGE, Pipe to Manifold (Exc. 400 H.O. or Ram Air)
3.609	1	9790829	PIPE, Exhaust - L.H. (S.W.B.) (Exc. 400 H.O. or Ram Air)
3.609	1	9788715	PIPE, Exhaust - L.H. (L.W.B.) (Exc. 400 H.O. or Ram Air)
3.609	1	9782586	PIPE, Exhaust - L.H. (S.W.B.) (w/400 H.O. or Ram Air)
3.701	1	9798593	MUFFLER, Exhaust - L.H. (Exc. G.T.O.-M.T.)
3.705	1	9796975	PIPE, Tail - L.H. (Exc. G.T.O.-M.T.)
3.701	1	9798590	MUFFLER, Exhaust - R.H. (G.T.O.-M.T.)
3.705	1	9795621	PIPE, Tail - R.H. (G.T.O.-M.T.)
3.701	1	9798591	MUFFLER, Exhaust - L.H. (G.T.O.-M.T.)
3.705	1	9795622	PIPE, Tail - L.H. (G.T.O.-M.T.)
3.705	2	9797245	EXTENSION, Tail Pipe (G.T.O.-M.T.) (2-1/4" I.D.)
N.S.	2	–	EXTENSION, Tail Pipe (2" I.D.)

Diagram and part numbers of 1969 exhaust system.

ATTACHING PARTS			
3.613	2	9777812	BOLT, Exhaust Pipe (3/8"-16 x 1-5/8")
3.708	2	3754883	CLAMP PKG., Exhaust Pipe to Muffler (2")
3.704	1	9790492	HANGER, Muffler - Rear - R.H.
3.708	1	3633128	CLAMP PKG., Muffler - Rear (2-1/2")
8.977	2	9423284	SCREW, Hanger to Frame (5/16"-12 x 7/8")
3.704	2	1323935	WASHER, Hanger to Frame
3.706	1	9797009	SUPPORT, Resonator - R.H.
3.708	1	3633128	CLAMP PKG., Resonator Support (2-1/2")
8.977	1	9423284	SCREW, Support to Frame (5/16"-12 x 7/8")
3.613	2	9777812	BOLT, Exhaust Pipe (3/8"-16 x 1-5/8")
3.704	1	9790493	HANGER, Muffler - Rear - L.H.
3.708	1	3633128	CLAMP PKG., Muffler - Rear (2-1/2")
8.977	2	9423284	SCREW, Hanger to Frame (5/16"-12 x 7/8")
3.704	2	1323935	WASHER, Hanger to Frame
3.706	1	9797010	SUPPORT, Resonator - L.H.
3.708	1	3633128	CLAMP PKG., Resonator Support (2-1/2")
8.977	1	9423284	SCREW, Support to Frame (5/16"-12 x 7/8")
3.706	2	1382598	HANGER, Tail Pipe - Rear
8.977	2	9429462	SCREW, Tail Pipe Clamp
8.977	2	9423284	SCREW, Hanger to Frame (5/16"-12 x 7/8")
3.706	2	9793545	CLAMP, Extension to Tail Pipe (G.T.O.-M.T.)
8.977	2	9429462	SCREW, Extension Clamp (#20-9 x 1-1/2")

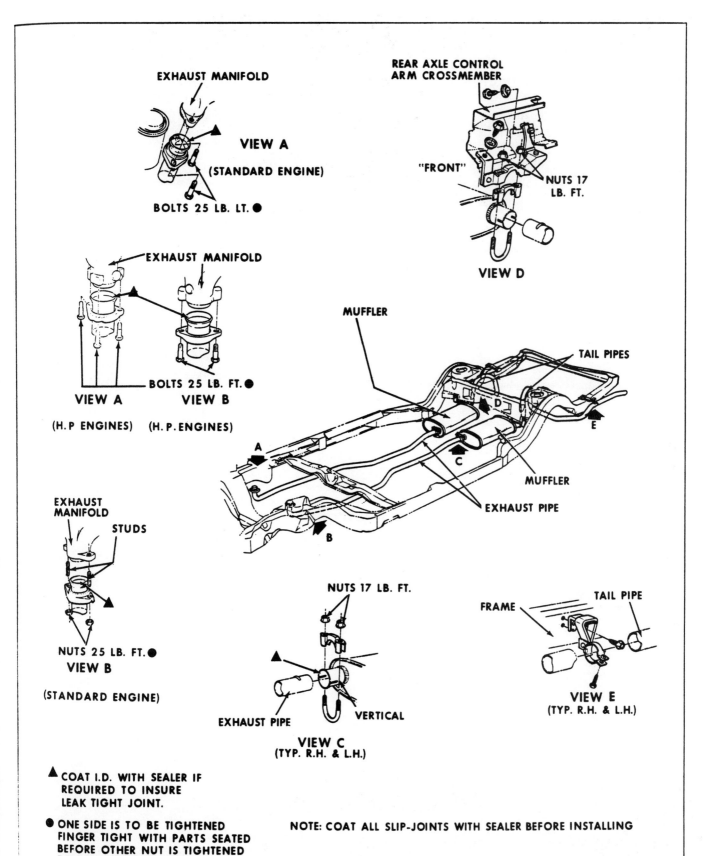

EXHAUST MANIFOLD

VIEW A

(STANDARD ENGINE)

BOLTS 25 LB. LT. ●

REAR AXLE CONTROL ARM CROSSMEMBER

"FRONT"

NUTS 17 LB. FT.

VIEW D

EXHAUST MANIFOLD

BOLTS 25 LB. FT. ●

VIEW A   VIEW B

(H.P ENGINES)   (H.P. ENGINES)

MUFFLER

TAIL PIPES

A

B

C

D

E

MUFFLER

EXHAUST PIPE

EXHAUST MANIFOLD   STUDS

NUTS 25 LB. FT. ●

VIEW B

(STANDARD ENGINE)

NUTS 17 LB. FT.

EXHAUST PIPE   VERTICAL

VIEW C
(TYP. R.H. & L.H.)

FRAME   TAIL PIPE

VIEW E
(TYP. R.H. & L.H.)

▲ COAT I.D. WITH SEALER IF
REQUIRED TO INSURE
LEAK TIGHT JOINT.

● ONE SIDE IS TO BE TIGHTENED
FINGER TIGHT WITH PARTS SEATED
BEFORE OTHER NUT IS TIGHTENED
TO PRESCRIBED TORQUE.

NOTE: COAT ALL SLIP-JOINTS WITH SEALER BEFORE INSTALLING

Detail of installation of 1969 GTO exhaust system, including torque specifications.

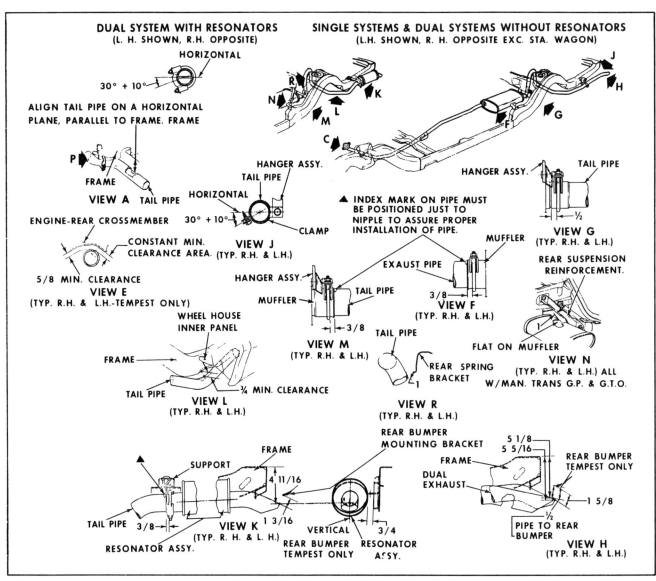

DUAL SYSTEM WITH RESONATORS
(L. H. SHOWN, R.H. OPPOSITE)

SINGLE SYSTEMS & DUAL SYSTEMS WITHOUT RESONATORS
(L.H. SHOWN, R. H. OPPOSITE EXC. STA. WAGON)

HORIZONTAL

30° + 10°

ALIGN TAIL PIPE ON A HORIZONTAL PLANE, PARALLEL TO FRAME. FRAME

P

FRAME

VIEW A TAIL PIPE

ENGINE-REAR CROSSMEMBER

CONSTANT MIN. CLEARANCE AREA.

5/8 MIN. CLEARANCE
VIEW E
(TYP. R.H. & L.H.-TEMPEST ONLY)

HANGER ASSY.

TAIL PIPE

HORIZONTAL

30° + 10°

VIEW J
(TYP. R.H. & L.H.)

CLAMP

▲ INDEX MARK ON PIPE MUST BE POSITIONED JUST TO NIPPLE TO ASSURE PROPER INSTALLATION OF PIPE.

HANGER ASSY.

TAIL PIPE

½

VIEW G
(TYP. R.H. & L.H.)

EXAUST PIPE

MUFFLER

HANGER ASSY.

MUFFLER

TAIL PIPE

3/8

VIEW F
(TYP. R.H. & L.H.)

REAR SUSPENSION REINFORCEMENT.

WHEEL HOUSE INNER PANEL

FRAME

TAIL PIPE

VIEW M
(TYP. R.H. & L.H.)

3/8

FLAT ON MUFFLER

VIEW N
(TYP. R.H. & L.H.) ALL W/MAN. TRANS G.P. & G.T.O.

TAIL PIPE

REAR SPRING BRACKET

VIEW R
(TYP. R.H. & L.H.)

¾ MIN. CLEARANCE
VIEW L
(TYP. R.H. & L.H.)

REAR BUMPER MOUNTING BRACKET

5 1/8
5 5/16

FRAME

DUAL EXHAUST

REAR BUMPER TEMPEST ONLY

▲ SUPPORT

FRAME

4 11/16

1 5/8

TAIL PIPE 3/8

VIEW K
(TYP. R. H. & L.H.)

RESONATOR ASSY.

1 3/16

VERTICAL

REAR BUMPER TEMPEST ONLY

3/4

RESONATOR ASSY.

½

PIPE TO REAR BUMPER

VIEW H
(TYP. R.H. & L.H.)

Detailed clearance requirements for installation of 1969 GTO exhaust system.

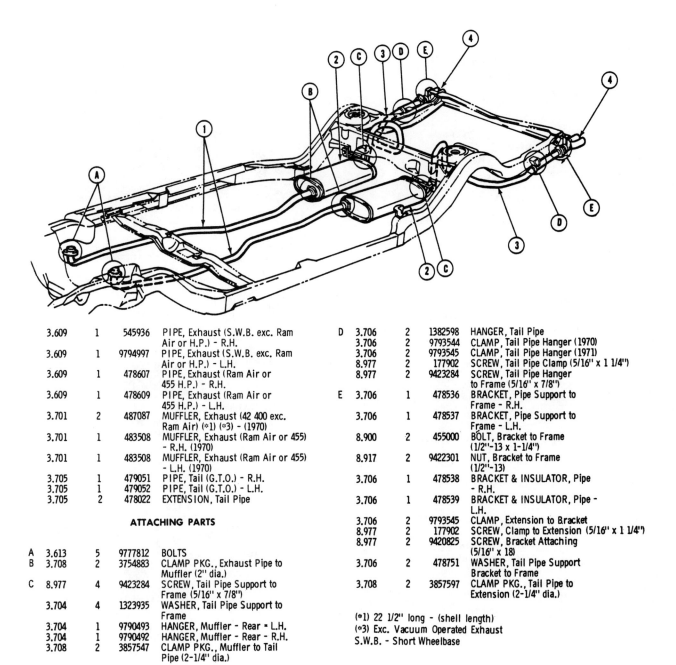

	3.609	1	545936	PIPE, Exhaust (S.W.B. exc. Ram Air or H.P.) - R.H.
	3.609	1	9794997	PIPE, Exhaust (S.W.B. exc. Ram Air or H.P.) - L.H.
	3.609	1	478607	PIPE, Exhaust (Ram Air or 455 H.P.) - R.H.
	3.609	1	478609	PIPE, Exhaust (Ram Air or 455 H.P.) - L.H.
	3.701	2	487087	MUFFLER, Exhaust (42 400 exc. Ram Air) (*1) (*3) - (1970)
	3.701	1	483508	MUFFLER, Exhaust (Ram Air or 455) - R.H. (1970)
	3.701	1	483508	MUFFLER, Exhaust (Ram Air or 455) - L.H. (1970)
	3.705	1	479051	PIPE, Tail (G.T.O.) - R.H.
	3.705	1	479052	PIPE, Tail (G.T.O.) - L.H.
	3.705	2	478022	EXTENSION, Tail Pipe

ATTACHING PARTS

A	3.613	5	9777812	BOLTS
B	3.708	2	3754883	CLAMP PKG., Exhaust Pipe to Muffler (2" dia.)
C	8.977	4	9423284	SCREW, Tail Pipe Support to Frame (5/16" x 7/8")
	3.704	4	1323935	WASHER, Tail Pipe Support to Frame
	3.704	1	9790493	HANGER, Muffler - Rear - L.H.
	3.704	1	9790492	HANGER, Muffler - Rear - R.H.
	3.708	2	3857547	CLAMP PKG., Muffler to Tail Pipe (2-1/4" dia.)

Diagram and part numbers of 1970 GTO exhaust system.

D	3.706	2	1382598	HANGER, Tail Pipe
	3.706	2	9793544	CLAMP, Tail Pipe Hanger (1970)
	3.706	2	9793545	CLAMP, Tail Pipe Hanger (1971)
	8.977	2	177902	SCREW, Tail Pipe Clamp (5/16" x 1 1/4")
	8.977	2	9423284	SCREW, Tail Pipe Hanger to Frame (5/16" x 7/8")
E	3.706	1	478536	BRACKET, Pipe Support to Frame - R.H.
	3.706	1	478537	BRACKET, Pipe Support to Frame - L.H.
	8.900	2	455000	BOLT, Bracket to Frame (1/2"-13 x 1-1/4")
	8.917	2	9422301	NUT, Bracket to Frame (1/2"-13)
	3.706	1	478538	BRACKET & INSULATOR, Pipe - R.H.
	3.706	1	478539	BRACKET & INSULATOR, Pipe - L.H.
	3.706	2	9793545	CLAMP, Extension to Bracket
	8.977	2	177902	SCREW, Clamp to Extension (5/16" x 1 1/4")
	8.977	2	9420825	SCREW, Bracket Attaching (5/16" x 18)
	3.706	2	478751	WASHER, Tail Pipe Support Bracket to Frame
	3.708	2	3857597	CLAMP PKG., Tail Pipe to Extension (2-1/4" dia.)

(*1) 22 1/2" long - (shell length)
(*3) Exc. Vacuum Operated Exhaust
S.W.B. - Short Wheelbase

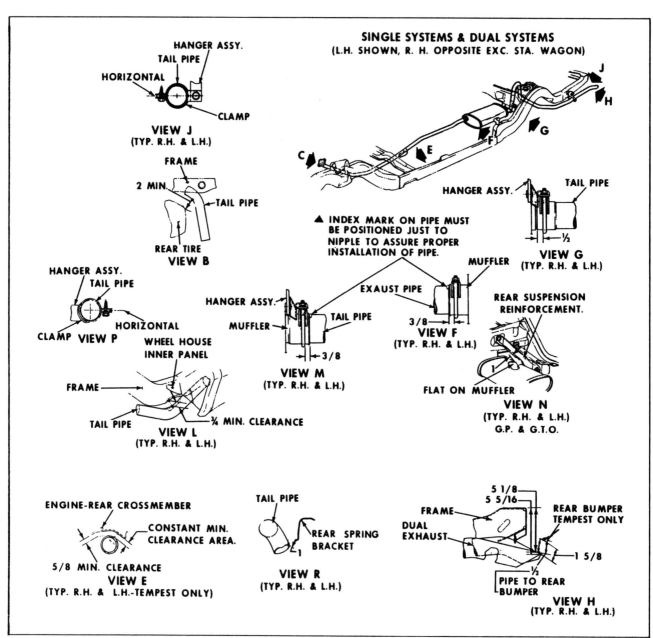

SINGLE SYSTEMS & DUAL SYSTEMS
(L.H. SHOWN, R. H. OPPOSITE EXC. STA. WAGON)

HANGER ASSY.
TAIL PIPE
HORIZONTAL
CLAMP

VIEW J
(TYP. R.H. & L.H.)

FRAME
2 MIN.
TAIL PIPE
REAR TIRE

VIEW B

▲ INDEX MARK ON PIPE MUST
BE POSITIONED JUST TO
NIPPLE TO ASSURE PROPER
INSTALLATION OF PIPE.

HANGER ASSY.
TAIL PIPE
½

VIEW G
(TYP. R.H. & L.H.)

HANGER ASSY.
TAIL PIPE
CLAMP **VIEW P**
HORIZONTAL

MUFFLER
EXAUST PIPE

HANGER ASSY.
MUFFLER
TAIL PIPE
3/8

VIEW F
(TYP. R.H. & L.H.)

REAR SUSPENSION
REINFORCEMENT.

WHEEL HOUSE
INNER PANEL
FRAME
TAIL PIPE
¾ MIN. CLEARANCE

VIEW L
(TYP. R.H. & L.H.)

3/8

VIEW M
(TYP. R.H. & L.H.)

FLAT ON MUFFLER

VIEW N
(TYP. R.H. & L.H.)
G.P. & G.T.O.

ENGINE-REAR CROSSMEMBER
CONSTANT MIN.
CLEARANCE AREA.
5/8 MIN. CLEARANCE

VIEW E
(TYP. R.H. & L.H.-TEMPEST ONLY)

TAIL PIPE
REAR SPRING
BRACKET

VIEW R
(TYP. R.H. & L.H.)

5 1/8
5 5/16
FRAME
DUAL
EXHAUST
REAR BUMPER
TEMPEST ONLY
1 5/8
½
PIPE TO REAR
BUMPER

VIEW H
(TYP. R.H. & L.H.)

1970 GTO exhaust system installation and clearance requirements.

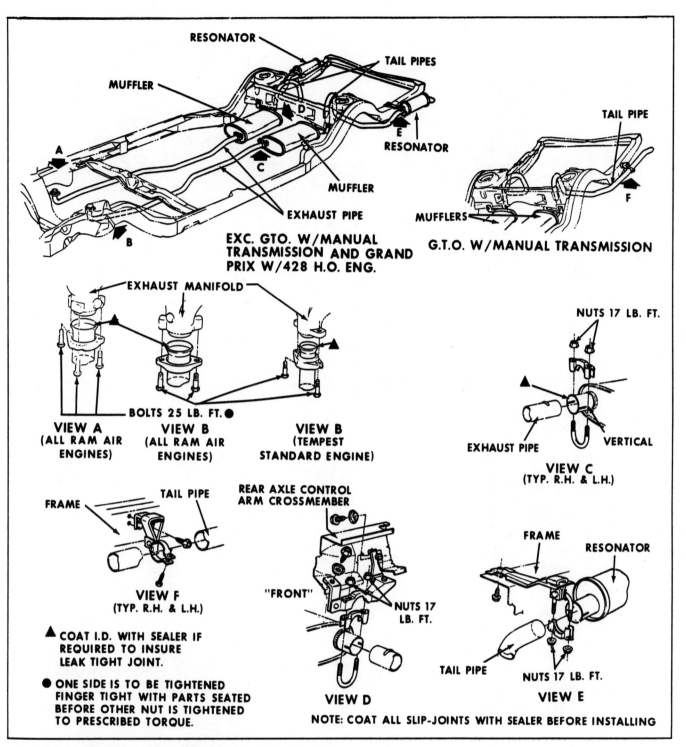

RESONATOR

TAIL PIPES

MUFFLER

TAIL PIPE

RESONATOR

MUFFLER

EXHAUST PIPE

EXC. GTO. W/MANUAL TRANSMISSION AND GRAND PRIX W/428 H.O. ENG.

G.T.O. W/MANUAL TRANSMISSION

MUFFLERS

EXHAUST MANIFOLD

BOLTS 25 LB. FT. ●

VIEW A
(ALL RAM AIR ENGINES)

VIEW B
(ALL RAM AIR ENGINES)

VIEW B
(TEMPEST STANDARD ENGINE)

NUTS 17 LB. FT.

EXHAUST PIPE

VERTICAL

VIEW C
(TYP. R.H. & L.H.)

FRAME

TAIL PIPE

VIEW F
(TYP. R.H. & L.H.)

▲ COAT I.D. WITH SEALER IF REQUIRED TO INSURE LEAK TIGHT JOINT.

● ONE SIDE IS TO BE TIGHTENED FINGER TIGHT WITH PARTS SEATED BEFORE OTHER NUT IS TIGHTENED TO PRESCRIBED TORQUE.

REAR AXLE CONTROL ARM CROSSMEMBER

"FRONT"

NUTS 17 LB. FT.

VIEW D

NOTE: COAT ALL SLIP-JOINTS WITH SEALER BEFORE INSTALLING

FRAME

RESONATOR

TAIL PIPE

NUTS 17 LB. FT.

VIEW E

Installation details of 1970 GTO exhaust system. Note Ram Air exhaust manifold with two- and three-bolt flanges.

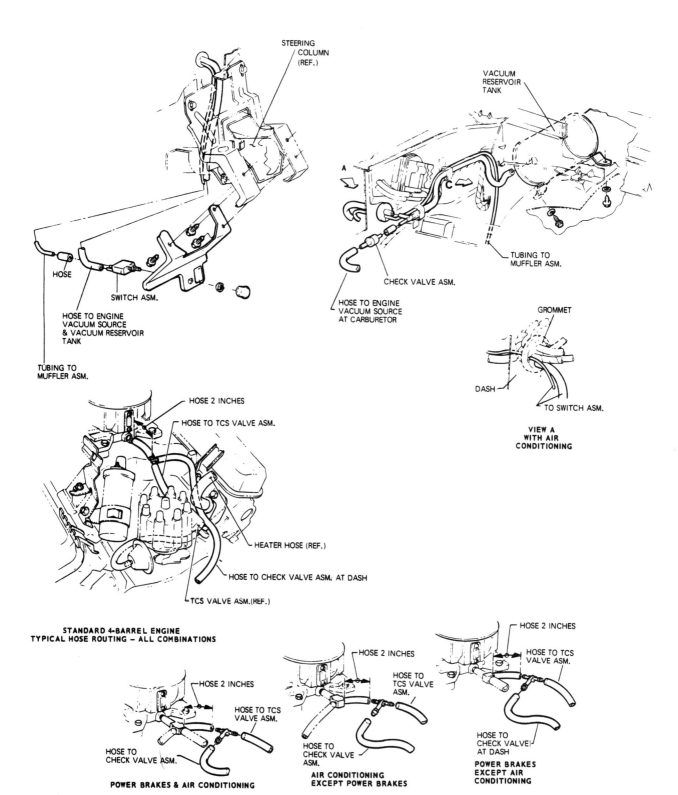

STEERING COLUMN (REF.)

HOSE

SWITCH ASM.

HOSE TO ENGINE VACUUM SOURCE & VACUUM RESERVOIR TANK

TUBING TO MUFFLER ASM.

VACUUM RESERVOIR TANK

TUBING TO MUFFLER ASM.

CHECK VALVE ASM.

HOSE TO ENGINE VACUUM SOURCE AT CARBURETOR

GROMMET

DASH

TO SWITCH ASM.

VIEW A WITH AIR CONDITIONING

HOSE 2 INCHES

HOSE TO TCS VALVE ASM.

HEATER HOSE (REF.)

HOSE TO CHECK VALVE ASM. AT DASH

TCS VALVE ASM.(REF.)

STANDARD 4-BARREL ENGINE TYPICAL HOSE ROUTING – ALL COMBINATIONS

HOSE 2 INCHES

HOSE TO TCS VALVE ASM.

HOSE TO CHECK VALVE ASM.

POWER BRAKES & AIR CONDITIONING

HOSE 2 INCHES

HOSE TO TCS VALVE ASM.

HOSE TO CHECK VALVE ASM.

AIR CONDITIONING EXCEPT POWER BRAKES

HOSE 2 INCHES

HOSE TO TCS VALVE ASM.

HOSE TO CHECK VALVE AT DASH

POWER BRAKES EXCEPT AIR CONDITIONING

Two views of the rare 1970 vacuum-operated exhaust. A faint view of the bracket and cable is found in the 1970 performance brochure. The view in the brochure shows a Pontiac crest on the decal (number 5).

266

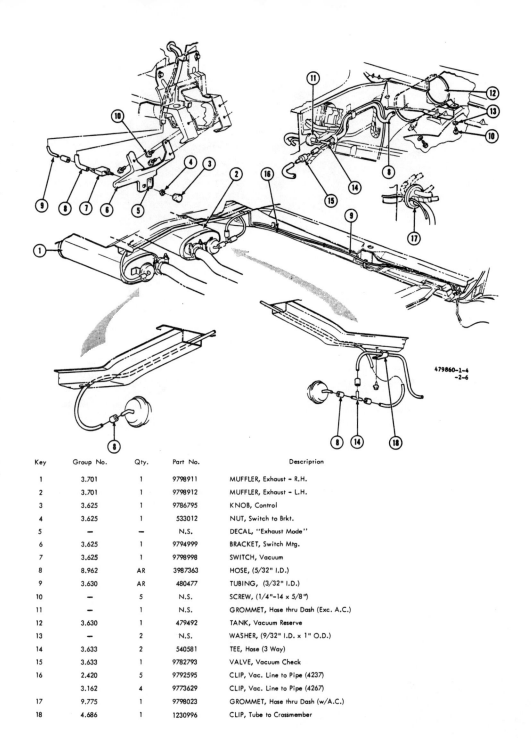

479860-1-4
-2-6

Key	Group No.	Qty.	Part No.	Description
1	3.701	1	9798911	MUFFLER, Exhaust – R.H.
2	3.701	1	9798912	MUFFLER, Exhaust – L.H.
3	3.625	1	9786795	KNOB, Control
4	3.625	1	533012	NUT, Switch to Brkt.
5	–	–	N.S.	DECAL, "Exhaust Mode"
6	3.625	1	9794999	BRACKET, Switch Mtg.
7	3.625	1	9798998	SWITCH, Vacuum
8	8.962	AR	3987363	HOSE, (5/32" I.D.)
9	3.630	AR	480477	TUBING, (3/32" I.D.)
10	–	5	N.S.	SCREW, (1/4"-14 x 5/8")
11	–	1	N.S.	GROMMET, Hose thru Dash (Exc. A.C.)
12	3.630	1	479492	TANK, Vacuum Reserve
13	–	2	N.S.	WASHER, (9/32" I.D. x 1" O.D.)
14	3.633	2	540581	TEE, Hose (3 Way)
15	3.633	1	9782793	VALVE, Vacuum Check
16	2.420	5	9792595	CLIP, Vac. Line to Pipe (4237)
	3.162	4	9773629	CLIP, Vac. Line to Pipe (4267)
17	9.775	1	9798023	GROMMET, Hose thru Dash (w/A.C.)
18	4.686	1	1230996	CLIP, Tube to Crossmember

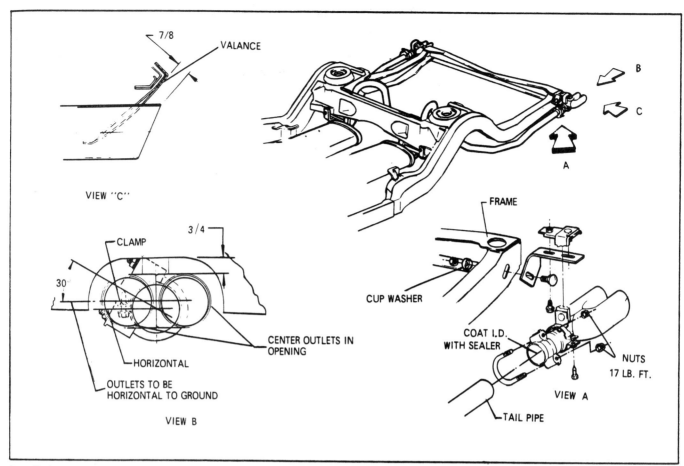

Installation instructions for 1970 exhaust extension. Note clearance requirement for valance panel.

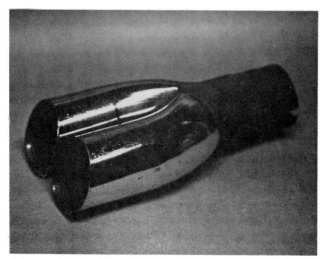

Detail of 1970 chrome exhaust split extension.

DRIVETRAIN

Chapter 5

CLUTCH AND PEDAL ASSEMBLY

1964-65

The clutch and pedal assembly was virtually the same in 1964 and 1965, along with frame brackets, countershaft and gold cadmium shift rods. The clutch return spring was extended around the fork and hooked to the exhaust flange.

The 1964 clutch disc was 10.4 inches in diameter and carried part number 544185. Its diameter remained the same for 1965, but carried a new number, 9777438.

Bellhousings were completely different for the two years, with the 1964 (part number 9774030) using a more rounded case than the 1965 (9785581). Both were aluminium. The shield was gloss black for both years, and again carried a separate number (9773870 for 1964) and was shaped differently for 1965 (9779664). Finally, the flywheels were different: The 1964 part used number 9773498, and the 1965 flywheel carried number 9779232.

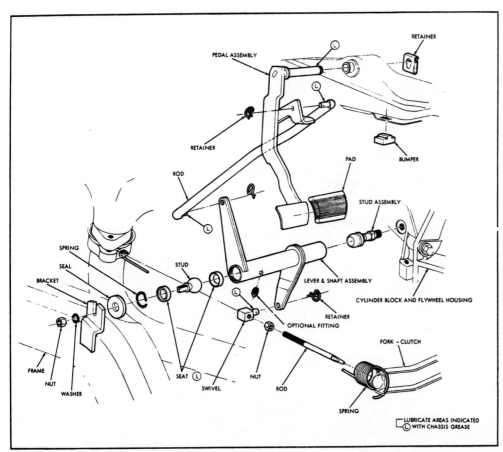

Installation of 1964 clutch control linkage. Pedal assembly was painted 60° gloss black, while countershaft was natural metal in appearance. Pedal pad in illustration is incorrect. Clutch rod was gold cadmium.

1966-67

The clutch and pedal assemblies were virtually identical in all respects to the 1965 GTO. The only difference was the 1967 pedal assembly, as the pedal arm and the clutch rod were redesigned.

The flywheel, bellhousing and disc, as well as the rest of the componentry, were identical to the 1965, and used the same part numbers.

1968-70

The clutch and pedal assembly for 1968-70 was identical in all respects to the 1965-67 components. The only exception to this was that with the 1970 455 engine, an 11 inch plate was installed, instead of the standard 10.4 inch plate.

The countershaft and related components were virtually redesigned in 1968, and used through 1970.

The clutch and pedal assembly, intermediate rod and mounting bracket were the same for 1968-70. The clutch pedal pad (part number 9776819) was also the same for all three years. A trim plate (part number 9778267) was used in GTOs equipped with power brakes.

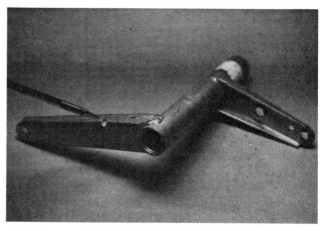

Detail of replacement clutch control countershaft (part number 9785392). Original countershafts for 1964-65 did not have hole as shown in photo. Hole was used in replacement countershafts to accommodate 1966 return spring locations.

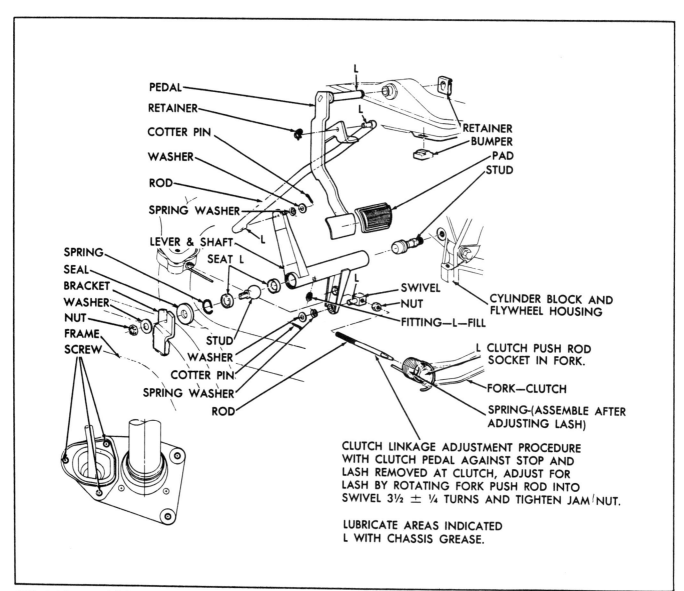

1965 clutch control linkage was almost identical to 1964 unit. Note instructions for pedal adjustment and correct pedal pad.

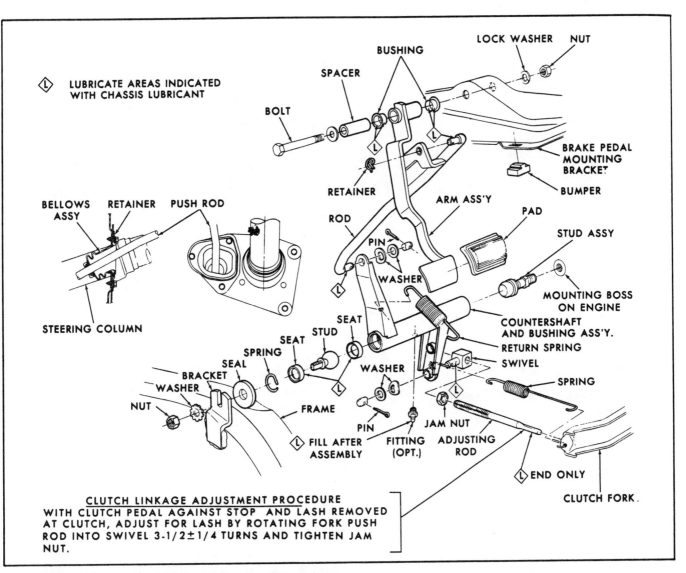

◇ LUBRICATE AREAS INDICATED WITH CHASSIS LUBRICANT

LOCK WASHER   NUT
BUSHING
SPACER
BOLT
BRAKE PEDAL MOUNTING BRACKET
BUMPER
RETAINER
ARM ASS'Y
PAD
STUD ASSY
BELLOWS ASSY   RETAINER   PUSH ROD
ROD
PIN
WASHER
MOUNTING BOSS ON ENGINE
COUNTERSHAFT AND BUSHING ASS'Y.
RETURN SPRING
STEERING COLUMN
SEAT
SWIVEL
SEAT   STUD
SPRING
SPRING
SEAL
BRACKET
WASHER
NUT
WASHER
FRAME
PIN
FILL AFTER ASSEMBLY
FITTING (OPT.)
JAM NUT
ADJUSTING ROD
END ONLY
CLUTCH FORK.

CLUTCH LINKAGE ADJUSTMENT PROCEDURE
WITH CLUTCH PEDAL AGAINST STOP AND LASH REMOVED AT CLUTCH, ADJUST FOR LASH BY ROTATING FORK PUSH ROD INTO SWIVEL 3-1/2±1/4 TURNS AND TIGHTEN JAM NUT.

Clutch linkage assembly for 1966 GTO. Note design of arm assembly compared to 1967 design, and change of return and retention springs from 1965 application.

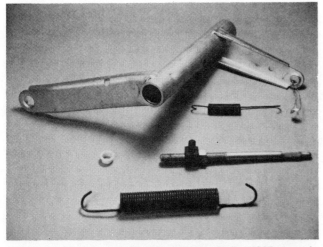

Detail of 1967 countershaft and related hardware. 1967 was only year to use bushing from pedal rod at countershaft.

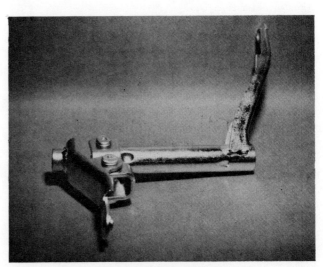

1968-70 countershaft (part number 9792271).

271

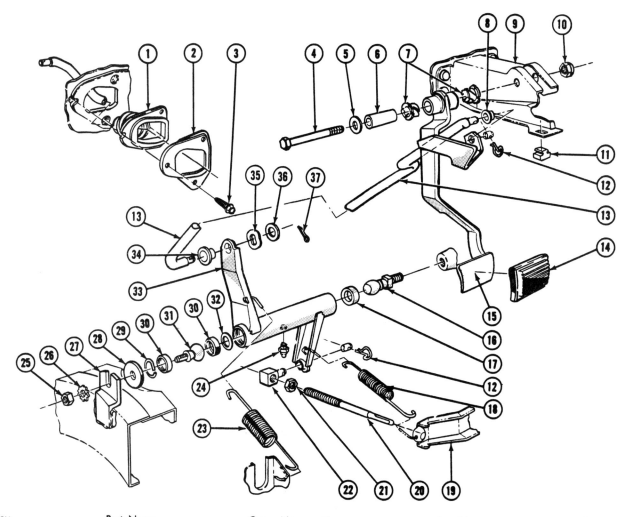

Key	Part Name	Group No.
1 — BELLOWS ASM., Clutch Pedal Rod		0.854
2 — RETAINER, Clutch Rod Bellows		0.854
3 — SCREW, Retainer to Dash (1/4"-14 x 3/4")		8.977
4 — BOLT, Clutch Pedal Pivot (7/16"-14 x 4-7/16")		8.900
5 — WASHER, Clutch Pedal Pivot (15/32" I.D. x 59/64" O.D. x 1/16")		N.S.
6 — SPACER, Clutch Pedal		0.852
7 — BUSHING, Clutch Pedal		0.831
8 — BUSHING, Clutch Pedal Push Rod (5/16" I.D.)		0.854
9 — BRACKET, Brake & Clutch Pedal		4.634
10 — NUT, Pivot Bolt (7/16"-14)		8.916
11 — BUMPER, Clutch Pedal		0.829
12 — CLIP, Clutch Fork & Pedal Rods		0.793
13 — ROD, Clutch Pedal Push		0.854
14 — PAD, Brake & Clutch Pedal		4.630
15 — ARM ASM., Clutch		0.830
16 — STUD ASM., Clutch Lever Shaft Ball to Engine		0.852
17 — WASHER, Countershaft Inner Stud (1/2" I.D. x 7/8" O.D. x 3/16")		0.852
18 — SPRING, Clutch Fork Push Rod Anti-Rattle		0.844
19 — FORK ASM., Clutch		0.795

Key	Part Name	Group No.
20 — ROD, Clutch Fork Push		0.787
21 — NUT, Push Rod Adjusting (3/8"-16)		8.916
22 — SWIVEL, Clutch Fork Push Rod		0.787
23 — SPRING, Clutch Linkage Return		0.844
24 — FITTING, Countershaft Grease		N.S.
25 — NUT, Countershaft to Frame (3/8"-16)		8.915
26 — LOCKWASHER, Countershaft to Frame		8.932
27 — BRACKET, Clutch Lever & Shaft		0.852
28 — SEAL, Clutch Control Countershaft		0.851
29 — SPRING, Shaft Ball Stud Seat Retainer		0.851
30 — SEAT, Lever Shaft Ball Stud		0.851
31 — STUD, Shaft Ball to Frame		0.851
32 — WASHER, Clutch Lever Ball Stud Seat (17/32" I.D. x 7/8" O.D. x 1/6")		0.852
33 — COUNTERSHAFT ASM., Clutch Control		0.852
34 — BUSHING, Clutch Pedal Push Rod - Lower		0.854
35 — WAVE WASHER, Pedal Rod to Countershaft		N.S.
36 — WASHER, Clutch Pedal to Countershaft (13/32" I.D. 13/16" O.D. x 1/16")		0.854
37 — COTTER PIN, Pedal Rod to Countershaft (3/32" x 5/8")		8.938

Exploded view of 1967 clutch linkage assembly. Compare design of pedal arm to 1966 design. Clutch rods for the two years were also different.

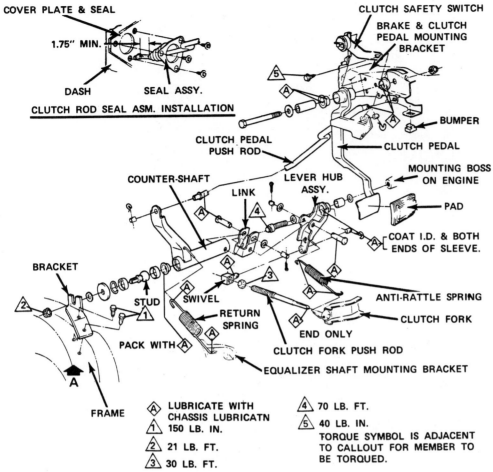

COVER PLATE & SEAL

1.75" MIN.

DASH   SEAL ASSY.

CLUTCH ROD SEAL ASM. INSTALLATION

CLUTCH SAFETY SWITCH

BRAKE & CLUTCH PEDAL MOUNTING BRACKET

⑤

△A

BUMPER

CLUTCH PEDAL PUSH ROD

CLUTCH PEDAL

COUNTER-SHAFT

LINK

④

LEVER HUB ASSY.

MOUNTING BOSS ON ENGINE

PAD

△A

COAT I.D. & BOTH ENDS OF SLEEVE.

BRACKET

△2

STUD △1

SWIVEL

③

RETURN SPRING

△A

ANTI-RATTLE SPRING

CLUTCH FORK

△A

PACK WITH △A

FRAME

END ONLY

CLUTCH FORK PUSH ROD

EQUALIZER SHAFT MOUNTING BRACKET

△A LUBRICATE WITH CHASSIS LUBRICATN
△1 150 LB. IN.
△2 21 LB. FT.
△3 30 LB. FT.
④ 70 LB. FT.
⑤ 40 LB. IN.

TORQUE SYMBOL IS ADJACENT TO CALLOUT FOR MEMBER TO BE TORQUED.

Exploded view of 1968-70 clutch and pedal. Pedal assembly was painted 60° gloss black (part number 1231313). Intermediate rod, countershaft and hub assembly were silver cadmium.

TRANSMISSION, THREE-SPEED MANUAL

1964-65

Standard on all 1964 GTOs was a three-speed floor-mounted box with all forward gears synchromeshed. The code for this transmission was X, and was found on the RH case. All 1964 GTOs used a Hurst shifter (part number 9775835). It is important to note that while all GTOs in 1964 were equipped with Hurst shifters, not all of the shifters came with the Hurst name stamped on the lever; some were installed with blank shift levers.

Transmissions built after date stamp S50564 (found on RH side of case at rear) used a 1¾ inch magnet installed at the bottom of the case. This was used to collect shavings that could damage the transmission.

For 1965, two three-speeds were offered: a Muncie (code X) was standard; a Ford-built heavy-duty Dearborn (code S) was optional. The Dearborn was available after March 1, 1965, and could be identified by the cover plate on the top of the case.

The Hurst shifter part number was again 9775835. Two different shift levers were used. Console applications used part number 9781448. Non-console-equipped cars had the curved lever (part number 9775834).

It is recommended that reinforcement brackets, part number 3869875(F) left side and 3869876(F) right side, be installed on all GTOs with manual transmissions. These reinforcement brackets were designed to provide extra rigidity and improved load distribution in the frame rear cross-member and lower control arm area. They attached between these two components, on each side, utilizing the forward upper and lower control arm attachments. Be sure to check for proper brake line clearance. (This information was taken from Pontiac Service News Flash number 65-108, dated 6-24-65.)

1966-67

Standard equipment for all 1966 GTOs was a column-shift three-speed all-synchromesh Muncie manual transmission. The code for this transmission was 5, and it was located on the RH transmission case. It was available with a 3.55:1 rear—except for cars equipped with air conditioning; then the rear was 3.23:1. Rears from 3.08:1 to 4.33:1 could be ordered with this transmission, although there were mandatory options such as speedo adapters, metallic linings and Safe-T-Track rear—and air conditioning was not available with rears over 3.23:1. The column shifter lever was part number 9779399.

Optional was the code S Ford-built Dearborn three-speed transmission with a Hurst floor-mounted shifter (RPO 785, assembly part number 9785094). Shifter lever knobs were either white with a three-speed pattern (part number 9776441) or black with a three-speed pattern (part number 9781840). The ratios available for rear gearing were the same as for the code 5 transmission. If the optional bench seat was ordered, a different shifter (part number 9785199) was available.

For 1967, the column shift was still the standard configuration, but the lever part number was changed to 9787097, due to column redesign, and was chrome with a black plastic knob. Rear end ratio information was unchanged from 1966. The code for this transmission was 5, and it was located on the RH transmission case. The manufacturer was Muncie.

The optional heavy-duty three-speed (RPO 785) was designated code S. The shifter assembly was part number 9789764, and the Hurst shift lever (part number 9789783) could be ordered separately for servicing in 1967. The shifter knob (part number 9781840) was black with the three-speed pattern inlaid in white. The accessory catalog listed a three-speed shift lever knob in walnut (part number 984848) but not much research has been done relative to this knob. It had the Pontiac crest emblem and the three-speed shift pattern on the face of the knob. It was apparently shaped the same as the four-speed walnut knob.

1968-70

Standard equipment on all 1968-70 GTOs was a three-speed manual transmission with Hurst shifter. The Ford-built Dearborn gearbox was used in both 1968 and 1969, and was identified as code DB. This two-letter code was painted on the RH case. The transmission was available as replacement part number 9793425.

Standard gearing was a 3.55:1 rear—except with air conditioning, in which case the gearing was 3.23:1. A 3.08:1 rear could be ordered with or without air condition-

ing. A 3.36:1, 3.90:1 or 4.33:1 rear was available. However, an RPO 591 speedometer adapter and an RPO 361 Safe-T-Track limited slip differential were mandatory options with rears above 3.36:1.

The shifter assembly (without shift lever) was part number 9792433 for 1968 and 9798722 for 1969. Two shift levers were used: Bench-seat models (without console) used part number 9787944; bucket-seat applications used part number 9792434 (with or without console).

The Dearborn transmission was replaced in 1970 with a Muncie-built heavy-duty three-speed box. This transmission was coded DG, and was identified in the same fashion as in previous years. The replacement part number of the Muncie unit was 477781. It was available with the same rear axle ratios as the 1968-69 unit (except for 3.36:1 ratios), and mandatory options for performance rears remained the same.

The shifter assembly for 1970 was part number 478437. One shift lever was used, part number 9784385.

A variety of shifter knobs was offered. A black knob with the shift pattern inlaid in white (part number 9781840) was used in 1968 and 1969. In 1969 and 1970, a walnut knob (part number 9794301) was available. This knob had no shift pattern on it. A black knob (part number 9794506) was used in 1970. A Hurst T-handle was standard in 1969-70 Judges and was available in the GTO.

All three years used the same shifter seal, or boot (part number 9795407). The retaining plate (part number 9780055) that held the boot to the floor was chromed (without console). When the optional console was ordered, a black plate (part number 9780054) was installed. Shifter seals (boots) and retaining plates were the same for three- or four-speed transmissions.

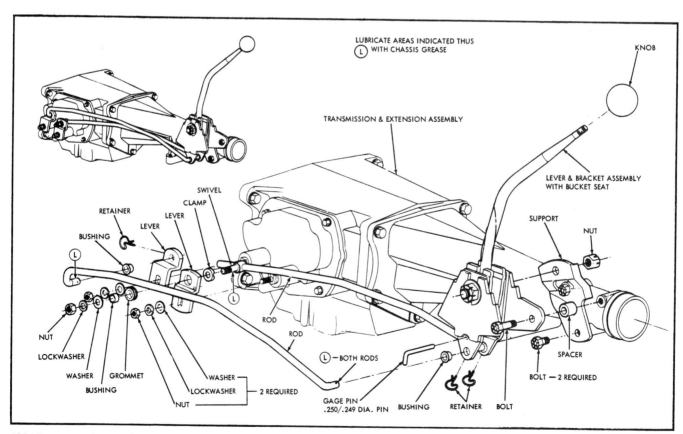

1964 three-speed manual transmission was the Muncie gearbox. Retaining clips were used to attach shift rods to shifter.

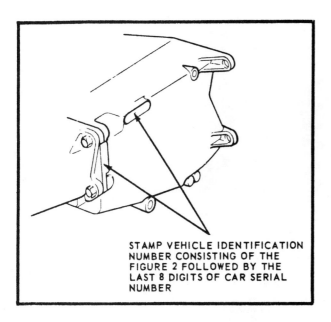

STAMP VEHICLE IDENTIFICATION NUMBER CONSISTING OF THE FIGURE 2 FOLLOWED BY THE LAST 8 DIGITS OF CAR SERIAL NUMBER

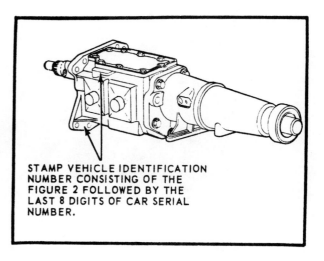

STAMP VEHICLE IDENTIFICATION NUMBER CONSISTING OF THE FIGURE 2 FOLLOWED BY THE LAST 8 DIGITS OF CAR SERIAL NUMBER.

MANUAL TRANSMISSION IDENTIFICATION

An identifying code is marked in yellow paint on all manual transmissions. This code consists of two letters, 2 inches high, on the R.H. side of the transmission case.

The vehicle identification number is also stamped on the transmission case, as shown.

Location of numbers on Muncie transmission, 1964-70 (left) and 1965-69 Ford-built Dearborn heavy-duty three-speed transmission (right).

DEARBORN 3-SPEED MANUAL TRANSMISSION IDENTIFICATION

An identifying code is marked in yellow paint on all three-speed manual transmissions. This code consists of two letters, 2 inches high, on the R.H. side of the case.

The vehicle identification number is also stamped on the transmission case, as shown.

REAR AXLE RATIO		SPEEDO. DRIVEN GEAR			TIRE SIZE		SPEEDO. ADAPTER				SLEEVE
		PART NO.	RATIO	COLOR		7.50 x 14	MODEL NO.	RATIO	PART NO.	COLOR	
1964 TEMPEST SPEEDOMETER GEAR USAGE CHART											
3-SPEED MANUAL TRANSMISSION											
43:10	4.30	3987921	21:8	RED			666-AJ	.7692	9775435	YELLOW	NOT REQ'D.
		3987920	20:8	BLUE		X	666-AJ	.7692	9775435	YELLOW	NOT REQ'D.
41:11	3.73	3987920	20:8	BLUE			666-AJ	.8653	9775436	BLUE	NOT REQ'D.
		3987919	19:8	NATURAL		X	666-AJ	.8653	9775436	BLUE	NOT REQ'D.
39:11	3.55	3987919	19:8	NATURAL			666-AJ	.8653	9775436	BLUE	NOT REQ'D.
		3987918	18:8	BROWN		X	666-AJ	.8653	9775436	BLUE	NOT REQ'D.
39:10	3.90	3987921	21:8	RED			666-AJ	.8653	9775436	BLUE	NOT REQ'D.
		3987920	20:8	BLUE		X	666-AJ	.8653	9775436	BLUE	NOT REQ'D.
42:13	3.23	3987920	20:8	BLUE							
		3987919	19:8	NATURAL		X					
40:13	3.08	3987919	19:8	NATURAL				NOT REQUIRED			
		3987918	18:8	BROWN		X					
37:11	3.36	3987921	21:8	RED							
		3987920	20:8	BLUE		X					

1964 Tempest speedometer gear usage chart.

View of 1965-69 Dearborn three-speed manual transmission. The Dearborn unit was easily recognized by the top cover.

View of 1965-69 Dearborn transmission. Code was stenciled in yellow. This transmission was coded DA, identifying it for use in Pontiac models. Code DB was used for the GTO.

1965 TEMPEST SPEEDOMETER GEAR USAGE CHART										
REAR AXLE RATIO	DRIVEN GEAR OR GEAR & SHAFT			TIRE SIZE			SPEEDOMETER ADAPTER			
	PART NO.	TEETH	COLOR		7.75 x 14		MODEL	RATIO	PART NO.	COLOR
3-SPEED MANUAL TRANSMISSION										
37:11	3.36	3987920	20	Blue		X				
37:11	3.36	3987920	20	Blue			●6660-AJ	.9705	9777006	Red
37:11	3.36	3987920	20	Blue			●777-S▲	.9705	9775437	Black & Yellow
37:11	3.36	3987921	21	Red						
39:9	4.33	3987920	20	Blue		X	666-AJ	.7692	9775435	Yellow
39:9	4.33	3987920	20	Blue		X	777-S▲	.7692	535615	Yellow
39:10	3.90	3987918	18	Brown			666-AJ	.7692	9775435	Yellow
39:10	3.90	3987918	18	Brown			777-S▲	.7692	535615	Yellow
39:10	3.90	3987919	19	Natural			666-AJ	.7692	9775435	Yellow
39:10	3.90	3987919	19	Natural			777-S▲	.7692	535615	Yellow
39:11	3.55	3987919	19	Natural			666-AJ	.8653	9775436	Blue
39:11	3.55	3987919	19	Natural			777-F▲	.8653	535617	Blue
39:11	3.55	3987920	20	Blue			666-AT	.8653	9775436	Blue
39:11	3.55	3987920	20	Blue			777-F▲	.8653	535617	Blue
39:11	3.55	3987921	21	Red		X				
40:13	3.08	3987918	18	Brown						
40:13	3.08	3987919	19	Natural		X				
40:13	3.08	3860343	20	Blue						
42:13	3.23	3987920	19	Natural		X				
42:13	3.23	3860343	20	Blue						
42:13	3.23	3987920	21	Red						

(●) Use with Police   (▲) Use with Heavy Duty Trans.

1965 Tempest speedometer gear usage chart.

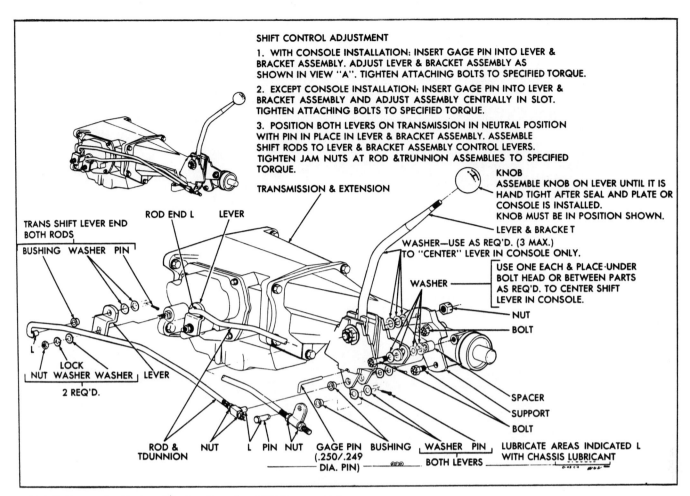

SHIFT CONTROL ADJUSTMENT

1. WITH CONSOLE INSTALLATION: INSERT GAGE PIN INTO LEVER & BRACKET ASSEMBLY. ADJUST LEVER & BRACKET ASSEMBLY AS SHOWN IN VIEW "A". TIGHTEN ATTACHING BOLTS TO SPECIFIED TORQUE.

2. EXCEPT CONSOLE INSTALLATION: INSERT GAGE PIN INTO LEVER & BRACKET ASSEMBLY AND ADJUST ASSEMBLY CENTRALLY IN SLOT. TIGHTEN ATTACHING BOLTS TO SPECIFIED TORQUE.

3. POSITION BOTH LEVERS ON TRANSMISSION IN NEUTRAL POSITION WITH PIN IN PLACE IN LEVER & BRACKET ASSEMBLY. ASSEMBLE SHIFT RODS TO LEVER & BRACKET ASSEMBLY CONTROL LEVERS. TIGHTEN JAM NUTS AT ROD & TRUNNION ASSEMBLIES TO SPECIFIED TORQUE.

TRANSMISSION & EXTENSION

KNOB
ASSEMBLE KNOB ON LEVER UNTIL IT IS HAND TIGHT AFTER SEAL AND PLATE OR CONSOLE IS INSTALLED. KNOB MUST BE IN POSITION SHOWN.

LEVER & BRACKET

WASHER—USE AS REQ'D. (3 MAX.) TO "CENTER" LEVER IN CONSOLE ONLY.

WASHER

USE ONE EACH & PLACE UNDER BOLT HEAD OR BETWEEN PARTS AS REQ'D. TO CENTER SHIFT LEVER IN CONSOLE.

NUT
BOLT

TRANS SHIFT LEVER END BOTH RODS
BUSHING WASHER PIN
ROD END L   LEVER

L
LOCK
NUT WASHER WASHER LEVER
2 REQ'D.

ROD & TDUNNION   NUT   L PIN NUT   GAGE PIN (.250/.249 DIA. PIN)   BUSHING   WASHER PIN BOTH LEVERS

SPACER
SUPPORT
BOLT

LUBRICATE AREAS INDICATED L WITH CHASSIS LUBRICANT

Installation and adjustment instructions for 1965 three-speed transmission shifter. Note that transmission used for illustration is standard Muncie unit.

1966 TEMPEST SPEEDOMETER GEAR USAGE CHART											
REAR AXLE RATIO		DRIVEN GEAR OR GEAR & SHAFT			TIRE SIZE		SPEEDOMETER ADAPTER				TRANS. TYPE	
		PART NO.	TEETH	COLOR		7.75 x 14	MODEL	RATIO	PART NO.	COLOR	STD.	H.D.
3-SPD. MANUAL TRANSMISSION												
37:11	3.36	3987919	19	Natural							X	
37:11	3.36	3987918	18	Brown		X					X	
37:11	3.36	3987921	21	Red		X						X
39:9	4.33	3987920	20	Blue		X	777-S	.7692	535615	Yellow		X
39:10	3.90	3987921	21	Red		X					X	
39:10	3.90	3987919	19	Natural			777-S	.7692	535615	Yellow		X
39:10	3.90	3987918	18	Brown		X	777-S	.7692	535615	Yellow		X
39:11	3.55	3987920	20	Blue							X	
39:11	3.55	3987919	19	Natural		X					X	
39:11	3.55	3987919	19	Natural		X	777-F	.8653	535617	Blue		X
39:11	3.55	3987921	21	Red		X						X
40:13	3.08	3987917	17	Purple		X					X	
40:13	3.08	3987919	19	Natural		X						X
42:13	3.23	3987918	18	Brown							X	
42:13	3.23	3987917	17	Purple		X					X	
42:13	3.23	3987920	20	Blue		X						X

1966 Tempest speedometer gear usage chart.

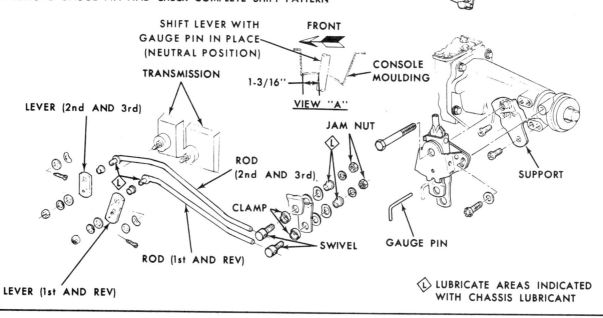

SHIFT CONTROL ADJUSTMENT

1. POSITION SELECTOR LEVER IN NEUTRAL POSITION.

2. LOOSEN SWIVEL JAM NUTS ON TRANSMISSION GEAR SHIFT CONTROL RODS.

3. PLACE TRANSMISSION LEVER AND BRACKET ASSEMBLY IN NEUTRAL POSITION AND INSTALL GAUGE PIN AS ILLUSTRATED.

NOTE: WITH CONSOLE: SHIFT LEVER IN CAR WILL BE AS ILLUSTRATED IN VIEW "A".

WITHOUT CONSOLE: SHIFT LEVER IN CAR WILL BE CENTRALLY LOCATED IN FLOOR BOOT.

4. POSITION LEVERS ON TRANSMISSION IN NEUTRAL.

5. RETORQUE JAM NUTS 22+3 LB. FT.

6. REMOVE GAUGE PIN AND CHECK COMPLETE SHIFT PATTERN

LEVER AND BRACKET ASS'Y (BENCH SEAT)

"FRONT"

LEVER AND BRACKET ASS'Y (BUCKET SEAT)

SHIFT LEVER WITH GAUGE PIN IN PLACE (NEUTRAL POSITION)

FRONT

TRANSMISSION

CONSOLE MOULDING

1-3/16"

VIEW "A"

LEVER (2nd AND 3rd)

JAM NUT

ROD (2nd AND 3rd)

SUPPORT

CLAMP

SWIVEL

GAUGE PIN

ROD (1st AND REV)

LEVER (1st AND REV)

Ⓛ LUBRICATE AREAS INDICATED WITH CHASSIS LUBRICANT

Drawing of 1966 three-speed transmission and gearshift mounting. Note different shifter designs for bench and bucket seat applications, and use of Dearborn gearbox.

1967 TEMPEST SPEEDOMETER GEAR USAGE CHART											
										78-2-1	
REAR AXLE RATIO		DRIVEN GEAR OR GEAR & SHAFT ASM.			TIRE SIZE	SPEEDOMETER ADAPTER				TRANS. TYPE	
		PART NO.	TEETH	COLOR	F70 x 14	MODEL	RATIO	PART NO.	COLOR	STD.	H.D.
3-SPEED MANUAL TRANSMISSION											
37:11	3.36	3987918	18	Brown	X					X	
37:11	3.36	3987921	21	Red	X						X
39:9	4.33	3987920	20	Blue		777-S	.7692	535615	Yellow		X
39:9	4.33	3987921	21	Red	X	777-S	.7692	535615	Yellow		X
39:10	3.90	3987921	21	Red	X					X	
39:10	3.90	3987921	21	Red	X	777-F	.8653	535617	Blue		X
39:10	3.90	3987918	18	Brown		777-S	.7692	535615	Yellow		X
39:11	3.55	3987919	19	Natural	X					X	
39:11	3.55	3987919	19	Natural	X	777-F	.8653	535617	Blue		X
39:11	3.55	3987921	21	Red							X
40:13	3.08	3987917	17	Purple	X					X	
40:13	3.08	3987919	19	Natural	X						X
42:13	3.23	3987917	17	Purple						X	
42:13	3.23	3987918	18	Brown	X					X	
42:13	3.23	3987920	20	Blue	X						X

1967 Tempest speedometer gear usage chart.

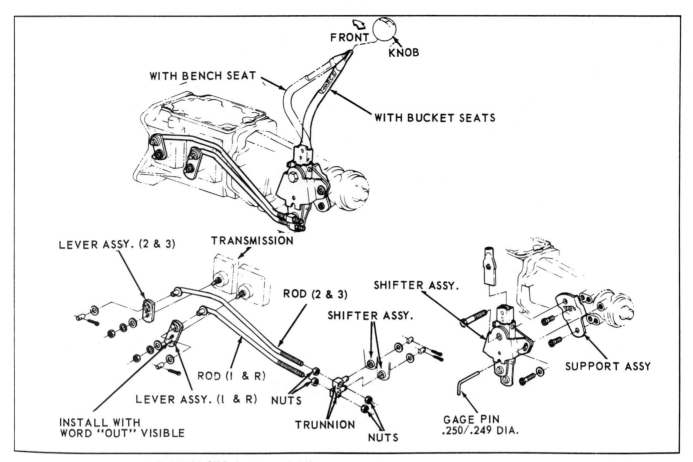

Installation and adjustment of 1967-68 GTO three-speed shifter and rods.

REAR AXLE RATIO	*	DRIVEN GEAR			*	TIRE SIZE			SPEEDOMETER ADAPTER				DRIVE GEAR
		PART #	TEETH	COLOR		G70 X 14	205R X 14	G77 X 14	*MODEL	RATIO	PART #	COLOR	*TEETH
40:13 3.08		3987918	18	BROWN				X					8
40:13 3.08		3987919	19	NATURAL		X	X						8
42:13 3.23		3987920	20	BLUE		X	X						8
42:13 3.23		3987919	19	NATURAL			X						8
37:11 3.36		3987921	21	RED		X	X						8
37:11 3.36		3987919	19	NATURAL				X					8
39:11 3.55		3987921	21	RED		X	X	X					8
39:10 3.90		3987918	18	BROWN		X	X	X	777-S	.7692	535615	YELLOW	8
39:9 4.33		3987920	20	BLUE		X	X	X	777-S	.7692	535615	YELLOW	8

1968 GTO speedometer gear usage chart, three-speed manual transmission.

HURST PERFORMANCE, INC.

SERVICE SPECIFICATIONS

MAINTENANCE
AND
LUBRICATION

THREE SPEED AND FOUR SPEED
PONTIAC SHIFTER ASSEMBLIES

GENERAL:

These units are manufactured and assembled under a rigid quality environment. All parts (except housing) are heat-treated for maximum strength and durability. All parts exceed the established corrosion tests for coating of these types. This assembly is supplied under a REMOVE AND REPLACE WARRANTY. Warranty is VOID if unit is dis-assembled.

SERVICE DIAGNOSIS CHART		
CONDITION	POSSIBLE CAUSE	CORRECTION
HARD SHIFTING	Lack of Lubrication Mounting bolts too tight	Lubricate — Para. 3 Check bolt torque - Para. 1
ROUGH NEUTRAL CROSS-OVER	Out of alignment Bent Rod	Check alignment - Para. 2 Replace rod
NOISE	Loose Assembly	Check bolt torque - Para. 1. Also check carriage pivot bolt locknut and tighten if loose (Fig. 4).
LOCKS IN TWO GEARS AT SAME TIME	Out of Alignment Bent Rod	Check alignment - Para. 2 Replace rod.

3. LUBRICATION

All shifters are greased at time of manufacture.* Due to exposure under vehicle, it is necessary to periodically replenish this lubrication. Lubrication of the shifter should be included when the vehicle is in for regular oil changes and/or suspension lubrication.

Use a needle fitting grease gun adapter on grease gun nozzle to direct grease into vital areas. Use grease liberally.

PROCEDURE:

Pry dust cover off with screwdriver blade. Perform the following operation on each lever, one at a time. Move lever all the way forward (Fig. 2). Inject grease behind lever. Move lever all the way to the rear. Inject grease ahead of lever.

After all lever areas have been greased, replace dust cover. CAUTION: DO NOT OVER-BEND DUST COVER.

Recommended lubricant - water resistant E P Chassis Lubricant.

4. GEARSHIFT CONTROL LEVER REMOVAL

The control lever can be released by inserting a thin rule or a piece of .015" to .020" thick shim stock into the socket alongside the base of the lever on the driver's side. Insert to a depth of at least one inch (Fig. 3). Lift the lever and the rule up out of the shifter socket.

Replace lever. Bayonet retainer will lock lever automatically.

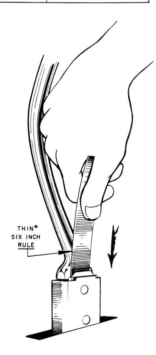

THIN*
SIX INCH
RULE

FIG. 3
CONTROL LEVER REMOVAL

* MAXIMUM THICKNESS—.020"

1. MOUNTING BOLTS - TORQUING LIMITS.

Do not exceed maximum torque limits specified for grade of bolt used (Figs. 1 & 4).

7/16" Dia. Bolt   40 - 45 Ft. Lb.

3/8" Dia. Bolt   25 - 30 Ft. Lb.

Tightening of the mounting bolts beyond the limits specified above could cause distortion of housing which would bind mechanism.

Flatwashers should be installed between split-type lockwashers and housing.

2. ASSEMBLY ALIGNMENT

Move all levers to Neutral positions. "Neutral" position is the mid-position of travel of shifter levers. Insert alignment tool (or suitable 1/4" dia. rod) into shifter alignment holes (Fig. 1).

IMPORTANT

Be sure that tool reaches notch in far side of housing.

Withdraw alignment tool completely, then re-insert. If tool enters all holes through housing and levers freely, shifter is correctly aligned.

A lever that does not accept insertion of tool is out of alignment. Observe levers while inserting tool — a lever that moves when tool is inserted is slightly mis-aligned and should be adjusted correctly.

NOTE: Some four speed units do not have an alignment hole in their reverse lever. Such units are aligned when the front edges of levers are perfectly parallel with the front edge of the shifter frame.

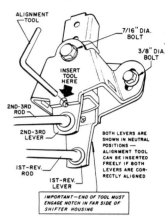

IMPORTANT—END OF TOOL MUST ENGAGE NOTCH IN FAR SIDE OF SHIFTER HOUSING

FIG. 1 SHIFTER ALIGNMENT

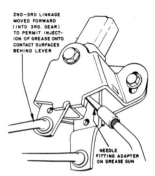

FIG. 2 LUBRICATING SHIFTER

SOUND DAMPENING TYPE DESIGN

FIG. 4   FOUR SPEED SHIFTER ASSEMBLY

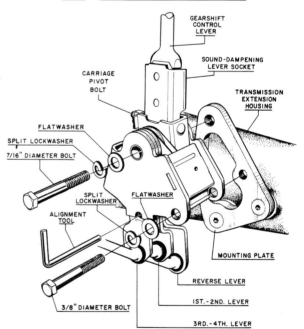

Pontiac provided dealers with this data in cooperation with Hurst Performance, Inc. It covered the maintenance and lubrication of both three- and four-speed shifter assemblies, plus detailed instructions on removal of 1967 and later shift handles from the control assembly.

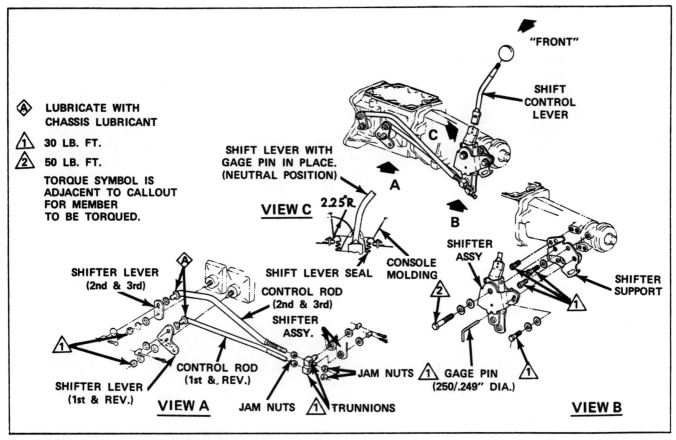

Dearborn unit was used in GTOs through the 1969 model year.
Note rod alignment and torque requirements.

THREE SPEED MANUAL TRANSMISSION

| REAR AXLE RATIO | * | DRIVEN GEAR | | | * TIRE SIZE | | | SPEEDOMETER ADAPTER | | | DRIVE GEAR |
		PART #	TEETH	COLOR	G78 X 14	G70 X 14	*MODEL	RATIO	PART #	COLOR	*TEETH
40:13 3.08		3987919	19	NATURAL	X	X					8
42:13 3.23		3987920	20	BLUE	X	X					8
42:13 3.23		3987919	19	NATURAL	X						8
37:11 3.36		3987920	20	BLUE	X	X					8
37:11 3.36		3987921	21	RED		X					8
39:11 3.55		3987921	21	RED	X						8
39:11 3.55		3987919	19	NATURAL		X			535617	BLUE	8
39:10 3.90		3987918	18	BROWN	X				535615	YELLOW	8
39:10 3.90		3987921	21	RED		X			535617	BLUE	8
39:9 4.33		3987920	20	BLUE	X	X			535615	YELLOW	8
39:9 4.33		3987921	21	RED		X			535615	YELLOW	8

1969 GTO speedometer gear usage chart, three-speed manual
transmission.

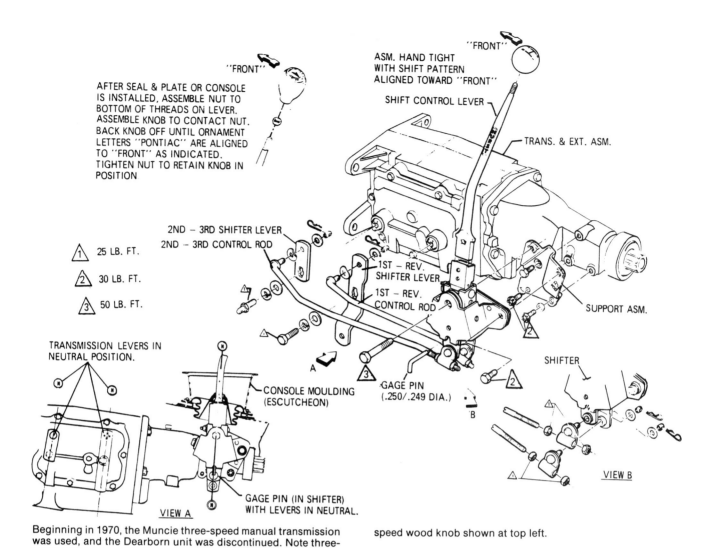

AFTER SEAL & PLATE OR CONSOLE
IS INSTALLED, ASSEMBLE NUT TO
BOTTOM OF THREADS ON LEVER.
ASSEMBLE KNOB TO CONTACT NUT.
BACK KNOB OFF UNTIL ORNAMENT
LETTERS "PONTIAC" ARE ALIGNED
TO "FRONT" AS INDICATED.
TIGHTEN NUT TO RETAIN KNOB IN
POSITION.

"FRONT"

ASM. HAND TIGHT
WITH SHIFT PATTERN
ALIGNED TOWARD "FRONT"
"FRONT"

SHIFT CONTROL LEVER

TRANS. & EXT. ASM.

2ND – 3RD SHIFTER LEVER
2ND – 3RD CONTROL ROD

1ST – REV.
SHIFTER LEVER

1ST – REV.
CONTROL ROD

SUPPORT ASM.

△1 25 LB. FT.
△2 30 LB. FT.
△3 50 LB. FT.

TRANSMISSION LEVERS IN
NEUTRAL POSITION.

A

CONSOLE MOULDING
(ESCUTCHEON)

GAGE PIN
(.250/.249 DIA.)
B

SHIFTER

VIEW B

GAGE PIN (IN SHIFTER)
WITH LEVERS IN NEUTRAL.

VIEW A

Beginning in 1970, the Muncie three-speed manual transmission was used, and the Dearborn unit was discontinued. Note three-speed wood knob shown at top left.

THREE SPEED MANUAL TRANSMISSION

REAR AXLE RATIO	* DRIVEN GEAR			* TIRE SIZE			SPEEDOMETER ADAPTER		DRIVE GEAR
	PART #	TEETH	COLOR	G70 X 14	G78 X 14	*MODEL	RATIO	PART #	COLOR	*TEETH
40:13 3.08	3987917	17	PURPLE	X	X					7
40:13 3.23	3987917	17	PURPLE	X	X					7
43:13 3.31	3987918	18	BROWN	X	X					7
39:11 3.55	3987919	19	NATURAL	X	X					7
39:10 3.55	3987921	21	RED	X	X					7
39:10 3.90	3987921	21	RED	X	X					7
39:9 4.33	3987917	17	PURPLE	X				535615	YELLOW	7
39:9 4.33	3987917	21	PURPLE		X			535614	RED	7

1970 GTO speedometer gear usage chart, three-speed manual transmission.

TRANSMISSION, FOUR-SPEED MANUAL

1964-65

The optional Muncie M-20 wide-ratio four-speed all-synchromesh transmission code for the 1964 was W, for use with the following rear ratios: 3.08:1, 3.23:1, 3.36:1, 3.55:1. The M-21 close-ratio, code 9, was used with 3.90:1 or 4.33:1 rear axle ratios in 1964.

A change was made in manual-shift GTOs produced after October 7, 1963, relative to shift control cover screw locations. (See Service Bulletin number 64-20.)

Hurst shifters were standard equipment on all four-speed-equipped GTOs in both years. An unknown number of shift levers came through in early 1964 production without the Hurst name on the lever. The 1964 shifter was part number 9781846. In 1965, two different lever assemblies were used: Part number 9781846 was used with console, and part number 9774366, without.

The code for the 1965 Muncie M-20 was W for the wide-ratio unit, and was used with the following rear axle ratios: 3.08:1, 3.23:1, 3.36:1, and 3.55:1. This code was applicable regardless of carburetion.

The 1965 M-21 close-ratio used different codes depending on carburetion: code 9 for four-barrel engines only; code 8 or 9 with Tri-Power engines. The M-21 was used only with 3.90:1 or 4.33:1 rear axle ratios.

The Safe-T-Track limited slip differential was mandatory with the close-ratio, as were a heavy-duty fan and metallic brake linings (RPO 692), in both years. The 4.33:1 ratio was available only as a dealer-installed option in 1964, but became a factory item in 1965.

1966-67

GTOs of 1966 and 1967 continued to use the Muncie M-20 four-speed wide-ratio gearbox (RPO 784). The code for the 1966 was W for use with the following rear end ratios: F 3.08:1, G 3.23:1, H 3.36:1, K 3.55:1, P 3.90:1. (Only the F and G rears were available if air conditioning was ordered.)

The M-21 close-ratio gearbox (RPO 778), code 8, was used with P 3.90:1 and S 4.33:1 rears only. When the P and S code rears were used with the M-21, the RPO 514 heavy-duty fan, RPO 484 metallic brake linings and RPO 731 Safe-T-Track limited slip rear were mandatory options, and no air conditioning could be ordered.

Hurst shifters were standard equipment on all four-speed GTOs for both years. The shifter assembly part number for 1966 was 9784845 when bucket seats were ordered, and 9774366 when the optional bench seat was ordered. The bench seat shifter for 1967 used the same assembly as the 1967 bucket seat shifter, but the shift lever was serviced separately by part number 9787944. The shifter for bucket seat use was part number 9787222; the shift lever part number was 9789783.

The code for the 1967 M-20 wide-ratio four-speed transmission was W, and it was used with the following rear axle ratios: F 3.08:1, G 3.23:1, H 3.36:1, K 3.55:1, P 3.90:1, S 4.33:1. Air conditioning was available with gearing up to 3.23:1. The same mandatory options were required as in 1966 for higher-performance rear axles.

The M-21 close-ratio four-speed was available as code 8, and came with 3.90:1 or 4.33:1 rear axles. The mandatory options required with these performance rears were the same as in 1966.

A 4.11:1 rear axle was available as a dealer-installed option for both years. The RPO numbers for the transmissions were the same for both years.

There were two different shift lever knobs used 1964-67: a white ball with the four-speed pattern inlaid in black (part number 9776121) and a black ball with the four-speed pattern inlaid in white (part number 9781795). A walnut lever knob (RPO 524, dealer accessory part number 984700) was available from 1966 to 1968.

1968-70

Both the 1968 and the 1969 GTOs with Muncie M-20 wide-ratio four-speed gearboxes used the same code, FO, stenciled in yellow paint on the RH side of the transmission case. The M-20 was offered with the following rear axle ratios for both years: F 3.08:1, G 3.23:1 H 3.36:1, K 3.55:1, P 3.90:1.

Only the 3.08:1 and the 3.23:1 rears were available with air conditioning. The 1968 Ram Air and the 1969 Ram Air IV were not available with the M-20. The P 3.90:1 rear was not available with the 1969 M-20. When the 1968 P rear was ordered, RPO 361 heavy-duty Safe-T-Track limited slip differential was a mandatory option.

The codes were changed in 1970, and rear axle availability was decreased. The code DJ M-20 was offered with the standard engine; the Ram Air III was offered with the 3.55:1 rear (standard) or the 3.23:1 (with air conditioning). The only other available rear was a 3.08:1, and it came only with the base engine.

The M-21 close-ratio box used in 1968 and 1969 was designated code FT. It was offered with the standard and HO engines with rears of 3.90:1 and 4.33:1 only in 1968. The RPO 361 heavy-duty Safe-T-Track was mandatory.

For 1969, slight changes were made in rear axle combinations with the M-21, and it was available with standard and Ram Air engines. Both the standard engine and the Ram Air III, when mated to the M-21, could use either a 3.90:1 or a 4.33:1 rear. The RPO 701 heavy-duty radiator and RPO 361 Safe-T-Track were mandatory options. The Ram Air IV came standard with the M-21 and a 3.90:1 rear, along with the mandatory RPO 361. A 4.33:1 was the only other rear available, and required a speedometer adapter and RPO 361 option.

For 1970, two different close-ratios were offered depending on engine choice. The code DL M-21 gearbox was available in the base engine and the Ram Air III, and was standard with the Ram Air IV. Another close-ratio box, code DP, was used in conjunction with the 455 engine only.

The code DL M-21 used only two rears, the 3.90:1 and the 4.33:1. Air conditioning was not available, and the usual pair of mandatory options was required. The DP M-21 used a 3.31:1 rear and the only available optional rear was a 3.55:1. Air conditioning was offered with the 3.31:1 rear only. All 1970 GTOs equipped with the 455 engine used the C-type twelve-bolt rear.

The Hurst shifter was again standard equipment in 1968-70.

Year	Shifter Assembly	Shift Lever
1968	9790772	9787944 (bench seat)*
		9792434 (bucket seat)*
1969	9798725	
1970	478436	9784385

*used in 1968 and 1969.

A variety of shift lever knobs was used for these three years. The walnut knob (accessory part number 984700) was carried over from 1967 for use in 1968. It was redesigned in 1969 (part number 9794300) and used the four-speed shift pattern. This shift pattern design was carried over into 1970 (accessory part number 988605).

A black knob with the shift pattern inlaid in white (part number 9781795) was used in 1968 and 1969. It was changed slightly in 1970, and used part number 9794505. The Hurst T-handle (part number 9794532) was offered in 1969 and 1970. This T-handle was standard on the Judge.

The shifter seal (part number 9795407) was the same for all three years. A chrome retaining plate (part number 9780055) was used in nonconsole applications. A black-painted plate (part number 9780054) was used with consoles.

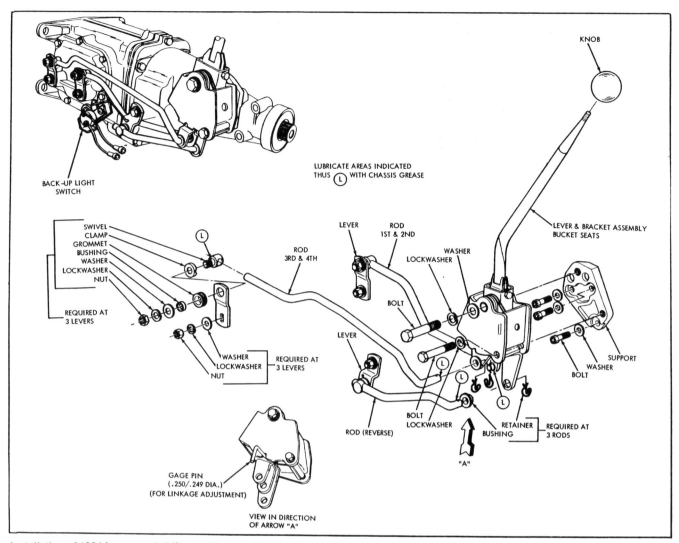

Installation of 1964 four-speed shifter and linkage. Note installation of backup light switch and harness. 1965 GTO four-speed shifter and linkage were virtually the same as 1964, although extra hardware was used to retain the rods to the transmission.

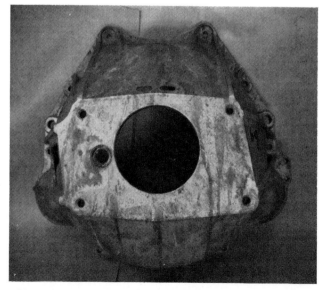

1964 bellhousing used with standard transmission and optional four-speed manual transmission. 1964 bell housing did not have extra mounting holes for Dearborn transmission. It was completely round with no hole at bottom for inspection.

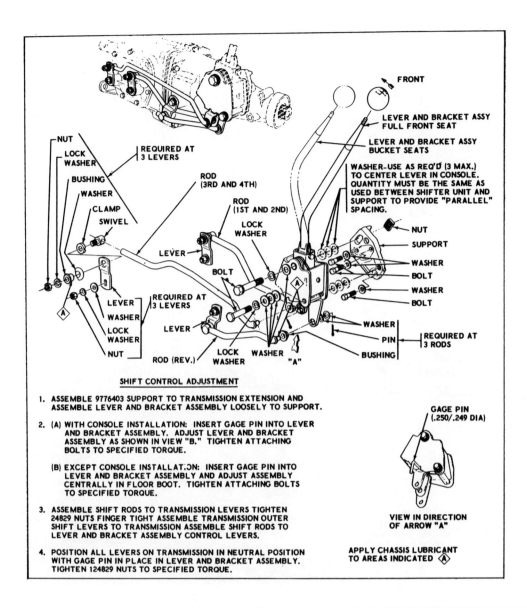

SHIFT CONTROL ADJUSTMENT

1. ASSEMBLE 9776403 SUPPORT TO TRANSMISSION EXTENSION AND ASSEMBLE LEVER AND BRACKET ASSEMBLY LOOSELY TO SUPPORT.

2. (A) WITH CONSOLE INSTALLATION: INSERT GAGE PIN INTO LEVER AND BRACKET ASSEMBLY. ADJUST LEVER AND BRACKET ASSEMBLY AS SHOWN IN VIEW "B." TIGHTEN ATTACHING BOLTS TO SPECIFIED TORQUE.

   (B) EXCEPT CONSOLE INSTALLATION: INSERT GAGE PIN INTO LEVER AND BRACKET ASSEMBLY AND ADJUST ASSEMBLY CENTRALLY IN FLOOR BOOT. TIGHTEN ATTACHING BOLTS TO SPECIFIED TORQUE.

3. ASSEMBLE SHIFT RODS TO TRANSMISSION LEVERS TIGHTEN 24829 NUTS FINGER TIGHT ASSEMBLE TRANSMISSION OUTER SHIFT LEVERS TO TRANSMISSION ASSEMBLE SHIFT RODS TO LEVER AND BRACKET ASSEMBLY CONTROL LEVERS.

4. POSITION ALL LEVERS ON TRANSMISSION IN NEUTRAL POSITION WITH GAGE PIN IN PLACE IN LEVER AND BRACKET ASSEMBLY. TIGHTEN 124829 NUTS TO SPECIFIED TORQUE.

GAGE PIN (.250/.249 DIA)

VIEW IN DIRECTION OF ARROW "A"

APPLY CHASSIS LUBRICANT TO AREAS INDICATED Ⓐ

Longer bracket attaching bolts have been released to provide greater adjustment on the 1964 Tempest (with console) 4-speed shift lever (see illustration).

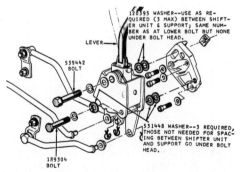

These bolts provide space for a maximum of three additional washers between the shifter bracket and transmission extension.

If three washers are not needed for adjustment at the lower bolt, place the excess under the bolt head to take up bolt length. Use the same number of washers on the top bolt to provide parallel spacing. It is not necessary to place the excess under the top bolt head. Continue using the original lock washers.

	Bolts	Washers
Upper	539442 (M)	120395 (M)
Lower	189304 (MF)	531448 (F)

This information from a Pontiac Service News Flash (number 64-63 dated 1-29-64) dealt with the longer bolts for the four-speed shift lever released in 1964.

REAR AXLE RATIO		SPEEDO. DRIVEN GEAR			TIRE SIZE	SPEEDO. ADAPTER				SLEEVE
		PART NO.	RATIO	COLOR	7.50 x 14	MODEL NO.	RATIO	PART NO.	COLOR	
4-SPEED MANUAL TRANSMISSION										
43:10	4.30	543800	19:6	ORANGE	X					
41:11	3.73	9771729	18:6	GREEN						
		9771902	17:6	BLACK	X					
39:11	3.55	3987921	21:8	RED	X	NOT REQUIRED				
39:10	3.90	9771729	18:6	GREEN						
		9771902	17:6	BLACK	X					
42:13	3.23	3987920	20:8	BLUE						
		3987919	19:8	NATURAL	X					
40:13	3.08	3987919	19:8	NATURAL						
		3987918	18:8	BROWN	X					
37:11	3.36	3987921	21:8	RED						
		3987920	20:8	BLUE	X					

1964 Tempest speedometer gear usage chart.

Close-up of 1965-70 bellhousing (part number 9785581). Housing was all aluminum.

Close-up of part number tag from cover of Muncie M-20 case. Transmission was 1965 vintage.

4 SPEED MANUAL TRANSMISSION

REAR AXLE RATIO		DRIVEN GEAR			TIRE SIZE
		PART #	TEETH	COLOR	7.75 X 14
37:11	3.36	3987920	20	BLUE	X
39:9	4.33	9781826	19	ORANGE	X
39:10	3.90	9780523	17	BLACK	X
39:11	3.55	3987921	21	RED	X
40:13	3.08	3987919	19	NATURAL	X
42:13	3.23	3987919	19	NATURAL	X

1965 GTO speedometer gear usage chart, four-speed manual transmission.

Detail of numbers stamped on transmission case of Muncie M-20, matching the VIN.

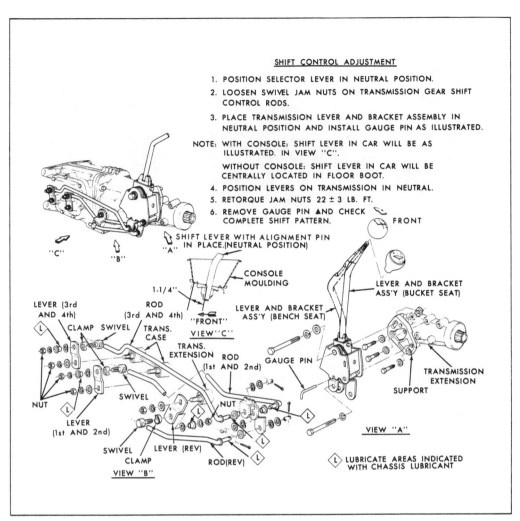

SHIFT CONTROL ADJUSTMENT

1. POSITION SELECTOR LEVER IN NEUTRAL POSITION.
2. LOOSEN SWIVEL JAM NUTS ON TRANSMISSION GEAR SHIFT CONTROL RODS.
3. PLACE TRANSMISSION LEVER AND BRACKET ASSEMBLY IN NEUTRAL POSITION AND INSTALL GAUGE PIN AS ILLUSTRATED.

NOTE: WITH CONSOLE: SHIFT LEVER IN CAR WILL BE AS ILLUSTRATED. IN VIEW "C".

WITHOUT CONSOLE: SHIFT LEVER IN CAR WILL BE CENTRALLY LOCATED IN FLOOR BOOT.

4. POSITION LEVERS ON TRANSMISSION IN NEUTRAL.
5. RETORQUE JAM NUTS 22 ± 3 LB. FT.
6. REMOVE GAUGE PIN AND CHECK COMPLETE SHIFT PATTERN.

Instructions for shift control adjustment and view of linkage and mounting shifter assembly on transmission for 1966 GTO.

1966 Hurst four-speed shifter assembly (part number 9784845) used with bucket seat applications.

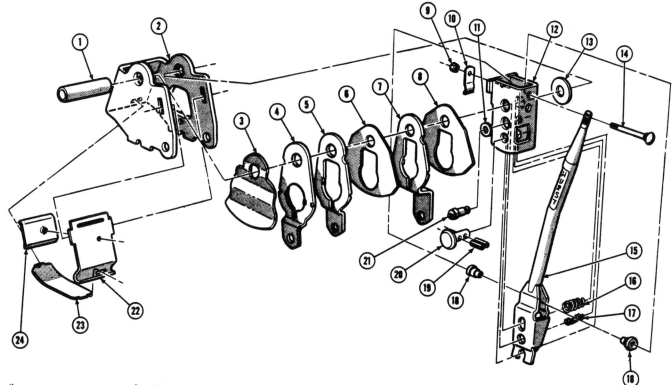

Key	Part Name	Group No.
1 — SLEEVE, Control Lever Carrier		4.008
2 — HOUSING, Control Asm.		N.S.
3 — PLATE, Control Asm. Pressure		4.010
4 — LEVER, Gearshift Shaft Control - 3rd. & 4th.		4.030
5 — LEVER, Gearshift Shaft Control - 1st. & 2nd.		4.030
6 — PLATE, Control Lever Interlock		4.010
7 — LEVER, Gearshift Shaft Control - Reverse		4.030
8 — PLATE, Control Lever Reverse Interlock		4.010
9 — NUT, Control Lever to Carrier (1/4"-28)		8.915
10 — SPRING, Control Carrier Asm.		N.S.
11 — WASHER, Control Lever Reverse Interlock Plunger		4.008
12 — CARRIER, Trans. Control Lever		N.S.
13 — WASHER, Carrier to Trans. Control Housing		N.S.
14 — BOLT, Lever & Bracket to Carrier (1/4"-28 x 2-1/4")		N.S.
15 — LEVER ASM., Trans. Control		N.S.
16 — SPRING, Control Lever Pressure		4.008
17 — SPRING, Reverse Interlock Plunger		4.008
18 — BUSHING, Control Carrier Sleeve		4.032
19 — PIN, Control Lever Selector Pin Roll (5/32" x 1-1/4" x .032)		N.S.
20 — PIN, Control Lever Selector (31/64" x 1-27/32")		4.008
21 — PLUNGER, Control Lever Reverse Interlock		4.008
22 — PLATE, Control Housing Spacer		N.S.
23 — COVER, Lever & Bracket Asm.		N.S.
24 — SPRING, Interlock Plate Anti-Rattle		N.S.

Exploded view of 1966 Hurst shifter assembly. Lever could be serviced separately beginning in 1967.

REAR AXLE RATIO		DRIVEN GEAR OR GEAR & SHAFT			TIRE SIZE	7.75 x 14
		PART NO.	TEETH	COLOR		
4-SPD. MANUAL TRANSMISSION						
37:11	3.36	3987919	19	Natural		
37:11	3.36	3987918	18	Brown		X
39:9	4.33	3860329	20	Yellow		X
39:10	3.90	3987921	21	Red		X
39:10	3.90	9780522	18	Green		X
39:11	3.55	3987920	20	Blue		
39:11	3.55	3987919	19	Natural		X
40:13	3.08	3987917	17	Purple		X
42:13	3.23	3987918	18	Brown		
42:13	3.23	3987917	17	Purple		X

1966 Tempest speedometer gear usage chart.

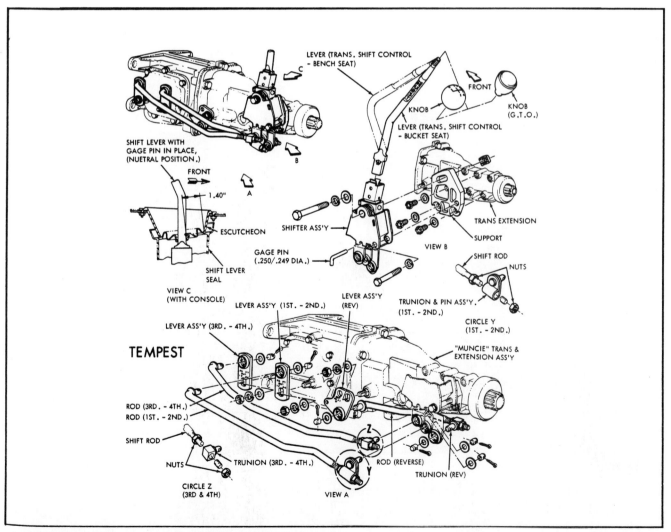

Installation and adjustment of 1967 GTO Hurst shifter and linkage. Shift lever was now serviced separately from the shifter assembly.

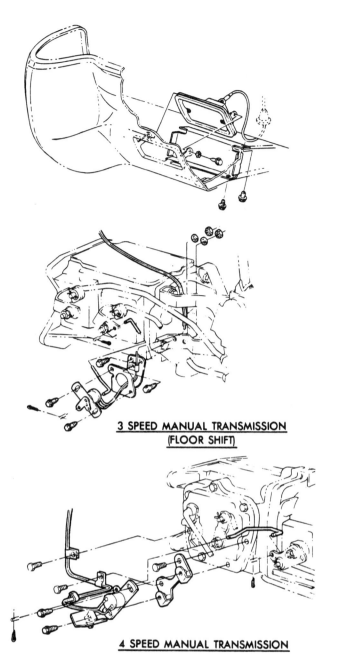

**3 SPEED MANUAL TRANSMISSION
(FLOOR SHIFT)**

4 SPEED MANUAL TRANSMISSION

Backup lamp switch assembly for 1967 GTO floor-mounted shift-er. Assemblies shown were typical for 1966 as well, with the exception of the backup lamps in the bumper.

REAR AXLE RATIO		DRIVEN GEAR OR GEAR & SHAFT			TIRE SIZE	SPEEDOMETER ADAPTER			
		PART NO.	TEETH	COLOR	F70 x 14	MODEL	RATIO	PART NO.	COLOR
4-SPEED MANUAL TRANSMISSION									
37:11	3.36	3987918	18	Brown	X				
39:9	4.33	3860329	20	Yellow	X				
39:10	3.90	3987921	21	Red	X				
39:10	3.90	9780522	18	Green	X				
39:11	3.55	3987919	19	Natural	X				
40:13	3.08	3987917	17	Purple	X				
42:13	3.23	3987917	17	Purple					
42:13	3.23	3987918	18	Brown	X				

1967 Tempest speedometer gear usage chart.

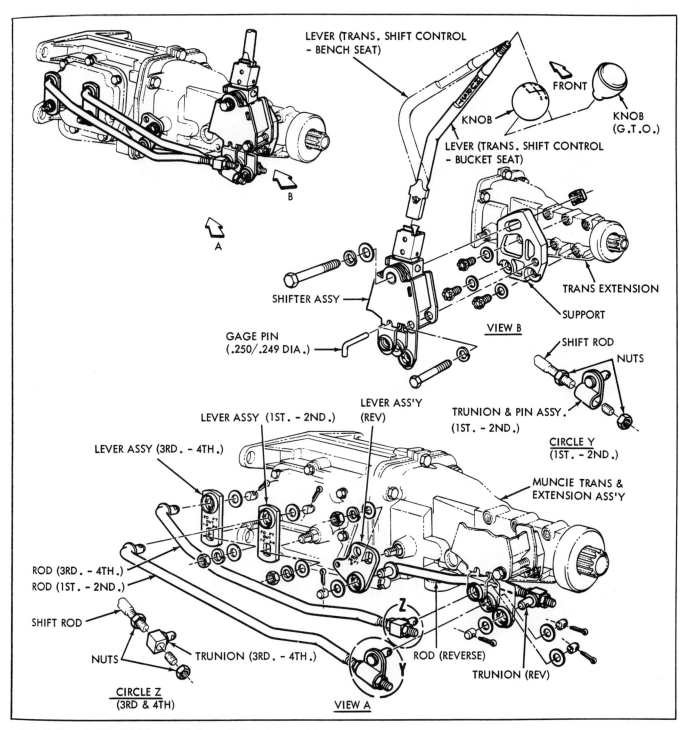

LEVER (TRANS. SHIFT CONTROL - BENCH SEAT)

FRONT

KNOB

KNOB (G.T.O.)

LEVER (TRANS. SHIFT CONTROL - BUCKET SEAT)

TRANS EXTENSION

SHIFTER ASSY

SUPPORT

VIEW B

GAGE PIN (.250/.249 DIA.)

SHIFT ROD

NUTS

TRUNION & PIN ASS'Y. (1ST. - 2ND.)

CIRCLE Y (1ST. - 2ND.)

LEVER ASS'Y (REV)

LEVER ASSY (1ST. - 2ND.)

LEVER ASSY (3RD. - 4TH.)

MUNCIE TRANS & EXTENSION ASS'Y

ROD (3RD. - 4TH.)

ROD (1ST. - 2ND.)

SHIFT ROD

Z

Y

NUTS

TRUNION (3RD. - 4TH.)

ROD (REVERSE)

TRUNION (REV)

CIRCLE Z (3RD & 4TH)

VIEW A

Installation of 1968 shift lever and linkage. Shift rods were either gold or black cadmium plated. Note bench seat shift lever.

291

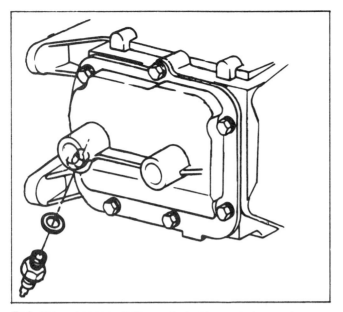

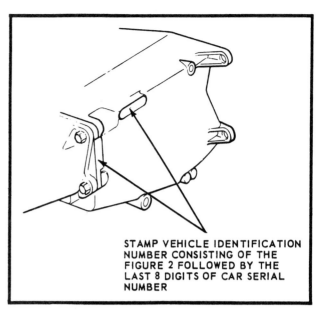

STAMP VEHICLE IDENTIFICATION
NUMBER CONSISTING OF THE
FIGURE 2 FOLLOWED BY THE
LAST 8 DIGITS OF CAR SERIAL
NUMBER

To further enhance emission controls, a transmission spark control switch (TCS) was added to the transmission which didn't allow the vacuum advance to operate until the car was in high gear.

An identifying code was marked in yellow paint on all four-speed manual transmissions. This code consisted of two letters, one inch high, on the top of the case.

4 SPEED MANUAL TRANSMISSION

REAR AXLE RATIO	* DRIVEN GEAR PART #	TEETH	COLOR	* TIRE SIZE G70 X 14	205R X 14	G77 X 14	SPEEDOMETER ADAPTER *MODEL	RATIO	PART #	COLOR	DRIVE GEAR *TEETH
40:13 3.08	3987917	17	PURPLE	X	X						7
40:13 3.08	3987918	18	BROWN			X	777-S	1.1250	540474	NONE	7
42:13 3.23	3987917	17	PURPLE	X	X	X					7
37:11 3.36	3987918	18	BROWN	X	X	X					7
39:11 3.55	3987919	19	NATURAL	X	X	X					7
39:10 3.90	9780522*	18	GREEN	X	X						6
39:10 3.90	9780523*	17	BLACK		.	X					6
39:9 4.33	3860329*	20	YELLOW	X	X						6
39:9 4.33	9781826*	19	ORANGE			X					6

* USED WITH CODE FT M21 MUNCIE CLOSE RATIO 4 SPEED TRANSMISSION ONLY.

1968 GTO speedometer gear usage chart, four-speed manual transmission.

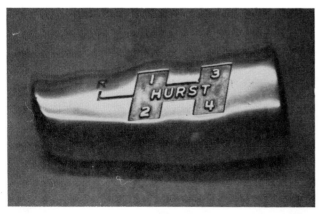

Hurst T-handle (part number 9794532) was standard equipment on the Judge in 1969 and 1970, and was available in the GTO as well.

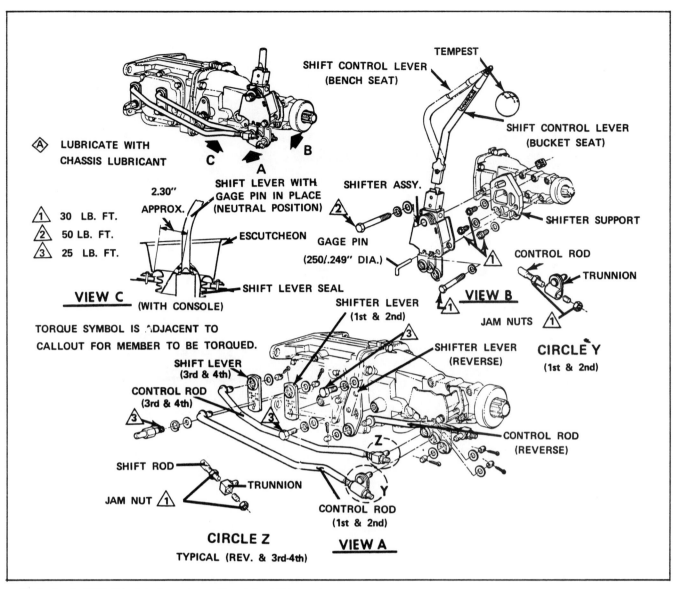

LUBRICATE WITH CHASSIS LUBRICANT ⚑Ⓐ

△1 30 LB. FT.
△2 50 LB. FT.
△3 25 LB. FT.

2.30" APPROX.

SHIFT CONTROL LEVER (BENCH SEAT)

TEMPEST

SHIFT CONTROL LEVER (BUCKET SEAT)

SHIFT LEVER WITH GAGE PIN IN PLACE (NEUTRAL POSITION)

SHIFTER ASSY.

SHIFTER SUPPORT

ESCUTCHEON

GAGE PIN (250/.249" DIA.)

CONTROL ROD

TRUNNION

SHIFT LEVER SEAL

VIEW C (WITH CONSOLE)

VIEW B

JAM NUTS △1

CIRCLE Y (1st & 2nd)

TORQUE SYMBOL IS ADJACENT TO CALLOUT FOR MEMBER TO BE TORQUED.

SHIFTER LEVER (1st & 2nd)

SHIFTER LEVER (REVERSE)

SHIFT LEVER (3rd & 4th)

CONTROL ROD (3rd & 4th)

CONTROL ROD (REVERSE)

SHIFT ROD

JAM NUT △1

TRUNNION

CONTROL ROD (1st & 2nd)

CIRCLE Z TYPICAL (REV. & 3rd-4th)

VIEW A

Beginning in 1969, ⅜ inch bolts were used to retain shift levers to shifter forks.

4 SPEED MANUAL TRANSMISSION

REAR AXLE RATIO	DRIVEN GEAR			TIRE SIZE		SPEEDOMETER ADAPTER				DRIVE GEAR
	PART #	TEETH	COLOR	G78 X 14	G70 X 14	*MODEL	RATIO	PART #	COLOR	*TEETH
40:13 3.08	3987919	19	NATURAL	X		–	–	540474	–	7
40:13 3.08	3987917	17	PURPLE		X					7
42:13 3.23	3987917	17	PURPLE	X	X					7
37:11 3.36	3987918	18	BROWN	X	X					7
39:11 3.55	3987919	19	NATURAL	X	X					7
39:10 3.90	9780522*	18	GREEN	X	X					6
39:9 4.33	3860329*	20	YELLOW	X	X					6

* USED WITH CODE FT M21 MUNCIE CLOSE RATIO 4 SPEED TRANSMISSION ONLY.

1969 GTO speedometer gear usage chart, four-speed manual transmission.

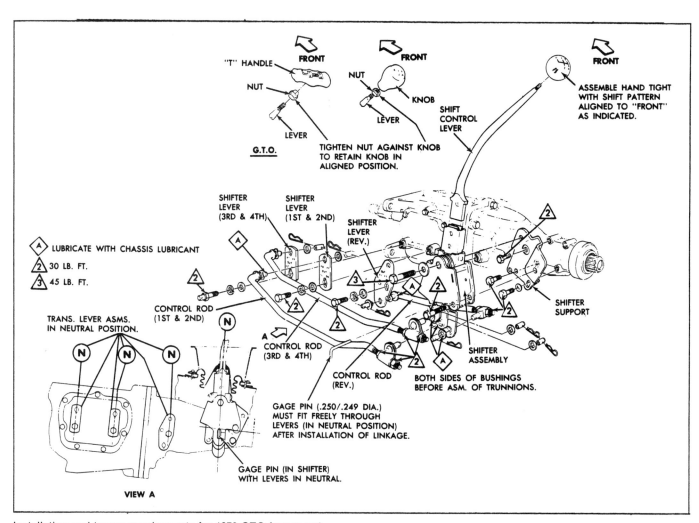

Installation and torque requirements for 1970 GTO four-speed
transmission. M-20 and M-21 shared the same shift components.

4 SPEED MANUAL TRANSMISSION

REAR AXLE RATIO	* DRIVEN GEAR			* TIRE SIZE		SPEEDOMETER ADAPTER			DRIVE GEAR		
	PART #	TEETH	COLOR	G78 X 14	G70 X 14	*MODEL RATIO	PART #	COLOR	*TEETH		
40:13 3.08	3987917	17	PURPLE	X	X				7		
40:13 3.08	3987917	17	PURPLE	X		–	–	9775739	B/WHITE	7	
42:13 3.23	3987917	17	PURPLE	X	X				7		
39:11 3.55	3987919	19	NATURAL	X	X				7		
39:10 3.90	9780522*	18	GREEN	X	X				6		
39:9 4.33	3860329*	20	YELLOW	X	X				6		

* USED WITH CODE DL M21 MUNCIE CLOSE RATIO 4 SPEED TRANSMISSION ONLY.

1970 GTO speedometer gear usage chart, four-speed manual
transmission.

TRANSMISSION, AUTOMATIC

1964-65

The automatic transmission (1373422), offered as an option in 1964 and 1965, was a two-speed unit with a 2.20:1 torque converter. GTOs in 1964 used the code J; pertinent information on transmission model, assembly date and model year was located on the lower servo cover. The 1965 GTO had the identification information located in the same spot, but code designation was slightly changed. While the J designation was retained, the T code was used for those equipped with air conditioning.

Standard transmission shifter location was on the steering column. The placement of the shifter on the floor was available only with the optional console, and at extra cost.

All of the components interchanged between the two years, although there was a slight difference in the part numbers for the console-mounted shift lever. In 1964, parts were ordered on an individual basis, but in 1965 the entire lever assembly was serviced as one number. The shift lever knob (part number 581962) and shift lever knob button (part number 9777515) were the same and were interchangeable for the two years.

Transmission cooler lines were routed along the RH side of the engine. They ran under a retainer bracket bolted to the front RH frame rail, and were then routed to the lower radiator tank. The vacuum pipe was routed from a fitting at the carburetor, along the right top side of the transmission, to the vacuum modulator. Two different carburetor fittings were used depending on carburetion, and another two were used depending on use of power brakes. Cars with four-barrel carbs used part number 535247 (with power brakes) or 9770910 (with standard brakes). These were the same for both years. The Tri-Power in 1964 used part number 544775 for all applications, and the 1965 Tri-Power number was 538958.

1966-67

The 1966 two-speed automatic (designated model NA) used part number 1373422. The code for the 1966 transmission was J; transmission model, assembly date and model year information was found on the lower servo cover.

The standard rear with the non-air-conditioned GTO was 3.55:1. Air-conditioned models used a 3.23:1 rear. The rear axle availability was the same as for the four-speed. However, along with the mandatory options for the higher-performance axles, the heavy-duty radiator (RPO 681) was required.

Standard shift location was on the column, with or without tilt column.

	Shift Lever	Dial	Retainer
With Tilt	9776102	9775618	9775620
Without Tilt	9780215	9781369	9776668

The shift lever was chromed, as was the indicator retainer. The dial was clear plastic, and the shift indicator letters were white against a dark background.

Note that the absence of a forced downshift on 1966 Tempest automatics may be caused by an improperly set downshift switch. To reset the switch, push the plunger all the way forward toward the firewall. When the accelerator is fully depressed, the switch will now automatically adjust itself to the linkage travel.

There was a major change in automatic transmissions with the introduction of the Turbo Hydra-matic for 1967. The transmission support cross-member was moved back six inches to accommodate the Turbo 400. Three different Turbo 400 models were used in 1967. An identification plate was located on the RH side of the transmission case. The codes for 1967 GTO applications were PS (part number 9777928), PT (part number 9777927) and PQ (part number 9789928).

A revision was made to the PQ model, beginning with serial number PQ-67-1143. The clutch-driven wave plate (part number 8623851) was eliminated, and the new direct clutch assembly contained five flat-steel clutch-driven plates (part number 8625197).

Also, late in the production year, the PS model was replaced by the PX, which was redesigned to complement the higher torque output in GTO engines. Service replacement parts for the PX transmission were the same as for the PS, with the exception of the following. (This information taken from Service Bulletin number 67-I-76.)

Group Number	Part Name	PS	PX
4.003	Transmission Assembly	9777928 (F-3)	9791682 (F-3)
4.265	Control Valve Assembly	8625616 (1MF-3)	8625784 (FOL-LX)
4.233	Front Accumulator Piston Spring	8623654 (F-BX)	8624358 (FOL-LX)

All 1967 GTO models equipped with the Turbo Hydra-matic came with the new Hurst Dual Gate shifter. (The shifter components and console hardware are described in the Interior chapter.)

When the floor-mounted shifter and console were not ordered, the transmission shifter and indicator were mounted on the steering column.

	Shift Lever	Dial	Retainer
With Tilt	9787108	3009590	9787711
Without Tilt	9787108	9788744 (one assembly)	

The shift lever was chrome with a black plastic knob. The retainer was chrome, and the dial was clear plastic, with the shift indicator letters in white.

Only the GTO came equipped with the Turbo Hydra-matic; The LeMans and Tempest used the two-speed automatic. Nothing was interchangeable between the GTO and the other models in 1967.

Bound-up console-equipped automatic-transmission shift cables have been traced to loose, poorly connected or missing body-to-engine ground straps, which forced the shift cable to act as the ground and allowed high electrical currents to melt the plastic liners.

When replacing the cable assembly due to this type of failure, check to be sure that all ground straps are not only in place but also that they are not insulated by paint, sealer, masking tape and so on. Check connections at the rear of *each* cylinder head-to-dash panel, or rear of left cylinder-head-to-dash panel and the ignition-coil-bracket-to-dash panel (when equipped with radio).

A limited number of 1967 Hydra-matic transmission assemblies was produced incorporating a second-design oil strainer, intake pipe and transmission bottom pan. Whether a unit contains a first- or second-design strainer can be determined by the contour of the pan, and the number of "dimples" in the pan. The parts or assemblies involved in this change were the following.

Group Number	Part Name	Second Design	First Design
4.197	Strainer Assembly*	6437741 (Z-BX)	5579822
4.222	Pipe Assembly, intake	8625428 (1MF-BX)	None
4.197	Bolt, strainer retaining	8625769 (M-BX)	None
4.195	Pan, transmission oil	8625766 (Z-BX)	8623778
4.197	Grommet, strainer to pipe	6437746 (1MF-CX)	None
4.197	O Ring, pipe to case	1363951 (Z-BX)	1363951

*The 6437741 strainer assembly included 6437746 grommet.

The serial numbers of the second-design units were: PQ67-1164 and up, PS67-23118 and up, PT67-3884 and up, PX67-20279 and up.

1968-70

The M-40 Turbo Hydra-matic transmission was used for all GTO automatic applications from 1968 to 1970. An identification plate was attached to the RH side of the transmission case. Three different M-40 transmissions were used in 1968: Code PT was used with the 265 hp two-barrel 400 cid engine. Code PX was used with the standard 350 hp engine and the 360 hp HO. The Ram Air engine mated to the code PQ transmission.

The PT transmission came standard with a 2.93:1 rear. If air conditioning was included, the standard rear was 2.78:1. A 3.23:1 or 2.56:1 rear was also available; however, air conditioning was not offered with the 2.56:1 rear.

The PX transmission, when coupled to the standard engine, came with a 3.36:1 ratio, or 2.93:1 with air conditioning. Ratios of 3.23:1, 3.55:1, 3.90:1 and 4.33:1 were available. The RPO 591 (speedometer adapter) and RPO 361 (heavy-duty Safe-T-Track rear) were required with either the 3.90:1 or the 4.33:1 axle.

When mated to the HO engine, the PX transmission used a standard rear of 3.55:1, or 3.23:1 with air conditioning. The optional rears were the same as those used with the standard engine.

The Ram Air transmission (code PQ) was available with only one rear, 4.33:1. Air conditioning was not offered, and RPO 361 was a mandatory option.

For 1969, the code PT transmission was used with the two-barrel engine. The rear axle ratios were identical to those used in 1968. The standard engine was mated to code PX and all rear ratios were the same—with one exception: The standard rear used without air conditioning was changed to 3.55:1 for better performance.

The PX transmission was also used with the Ram Air III, and used the same rear ratios—except the 3.08:1, which was not offered. The Ram Air IV used the code PQ M-40, and came standard with a 3.90:1 rear. The RPO 361 heavy-duty Safe-T-Track was required. A 4.33:1 was the only optional rear ratio. The usual mandatory options were required.

In 1970, there were three M-40s used: code PY for the standard engine; code PD for both Ram Air engines; and code PR for the 455 powerplant.

The standard rear with both the standard engine and the Ram Air III was 3.55:1, with 3.23:1 offered on cars equipped with air conditioning. Rears of 3.23:1, 3.90:1 and 4.33:1 were available on the standard engine. The Ram Air III was not offered with the 3.23:1. The usual mandatory options were required when the 3.90:1 or the 4.33:1 ratios were ordered.

For the Ram Air IV, the 3.90:1 was standard, with the 4.33:1 available. The 455 cid engine came standard with a 3.07:1 rear, and the 3.31:1 was available—although air conditioning could not be ordered with this rear.

Standard shift location was on the column for all three years. Shift levers were as follows.

	With Tilt Column	Without Tilt Column
1968	9798737	9792626
1969	9798737	9798732
1970	546354	546355

The shift lever was chromed, had a black knob (part number 9792623) and was used for 1968-70. The shift indicator lens was clear with white characters.

Bound-up and/or breaking shift cables on console-equipped automatic transmissions can be traced directly to loose, poorly connected or missing engine-to-body ground straps. When the ground strap is missing or has poor contact to the body, body electrical currents are forced to flow through the shift cable to ground, heating the cable and melting its plastic liner.

In *all* 1969 models, only *one* engine-to-body ground strap was used. In all V-8 engines, the ground strap was connected between the right cylinder head and the firewall. In 1968 and previous V-8 models, one ground strap was used between the left cylinder head and the firewall on cars not equipped with radio. On radio-equipped V-8 cars, two ground straps were used; that is, one ground strap from each cylinder head to the firewall.

Engine-to-body ground straps should be checked for damage, and any problems should be corrected, on all cars where this condition has been reported.

To assist in servicing of the Tempest automatic transmission, for the GTO option, listed below are the significant differences peculiar to this transmission:

1. High Output Governor - Increases upshift speed and rpm.

2. Increased Clutch Capacity - One more clutch plate in both the high and reverse clutch.

3. Oil Pump - GTO option oil pump incorporates a coast downshift timing valve (see illustration).

4. High Speed Downshift Valve - Has a heavier spring.

For part numbers on the above, consult the Master Parts Catalog.

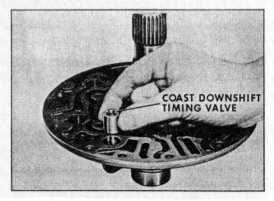

COAST DOWNSHIFT TIMING VALVE

1964 Pontiac Service News Flash number 64-28 (dated 11-13-63) outlined these GTO transmission differences.

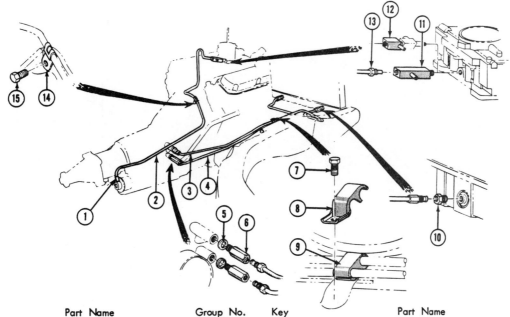

Key	Part Name	Group No.
1 — TUBE, Trans. Vacuum Pipe to Trans.		N.S.
2 — PIPE, Carb. to Trans. Vacuum		4.205
3 — PIPE ASM., Trans. Oil Cooler - Inlet		4.128
4 — PIPE ASM., Trans. Oil Cooler - Outlet		4.128
5 — WASHER, Oil Cooler Lines to Connector - Copper .		4.128
6 — CONNECTOR, Trans. Oil Cooler Pipes to Trans. . .		4.128
7 — SCREW, Pipe Clip to Frt. Cross Member (5/16"-18 x 3/4")		8.900
8 — CLIP, Trans. Oil Cooler Pipes to Frt. Cross Member .		4.128

Key	Part Name	Group No.
9 — INSULATOR, Oil Cooler Pipe (Part of #3-4)		N.S.
10 — CONNECTOR, Oil Cooler Pipes to Trans. Case . .		4.128
11 — FITTING, Vacuum Hose Pipe to Carb. at Mfld. (3-Way)		3.278
12 — FITTING, Vacuum Hose & Pipe to Carb. - w/Power Brakes		3.278
13 — SLEEVE, Vacuum Pipe to Carb. (1/4")		3.278
14 — CLIP, Trans. Vacuum Pipe to Flywheel Hsg.		4.205
15 — BOLT, Clip to Flywheel Hsg. (1/2"-13 x 1-1/2") . .		8.900

Routing of cooler and vacuum lines for 1964-66 automatic transmission.

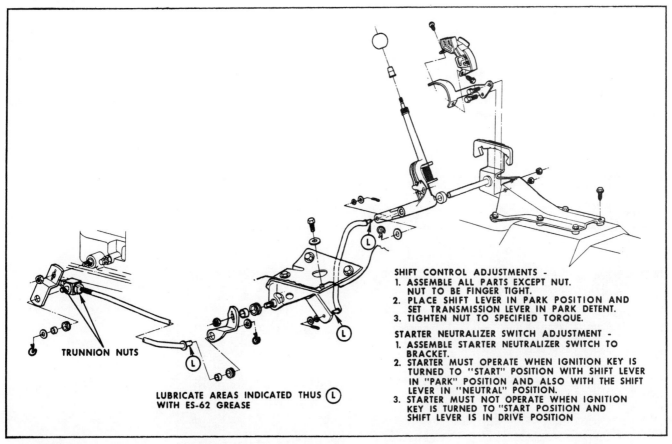

SHIFT CONTROL ADJUSTMENTS -
1. ASSEMBLE ALL PARTS EXCEPT NUT. NUT TO BE FINGER TIGHT.
2. PLACE SHIFT LEVER IN PARK POSITION AND SET TRANSMISSION LEVER IN PARK DETENT.
3. TIGHTEN NUT TO SPECIFIED TORQUE.

STARTER NEUTRALIZER SWITCH ADJUSTMENT -
1. ASSEMBLE STARTER NEUTRALIZER SWITCH TO BRACKET.
2. STARTER MUST OPERATE WHEN IGNITION KEY IS TURNED TO "START" POSITION WITH SHIFT LEVER IN "PARK" POSITION AND ALSO WITH THE SHIFT LEVER IN "NEUTRAL" POSITION.
3. STARTER MUST NOT OPERATE WHEN IGNITION KEY IS TURNED TO "START POSITION AND SHIFT LEVER IS IN DRIVE POSITION

TRUNNION NUTS

LUBRICATE AREAS INDICATED THUS (L) WITH ES-62 GREASE

Installation and adjustment of 1964 automatic transmission shifter and linkage.

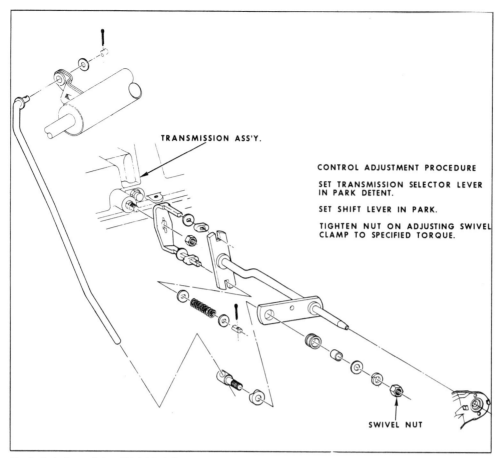

TRANSMISSION ASS'Y.

CONTROL ADJUSTMENT PROCEDURE

SET TRANSMISSION SELECTOR LEVER IN PARK DETENT.

SET SHIFT LEVER IN PARK.

TIGHTEN NUT ON ADJUSTING SWIVEL CLAMP TO SPECIFIED TORQUE.

SWIVEL NUT

Exploded view of the 1964-66 shift control linkage for column-mounted automatics.

REAR AXLE RATIO		SPEEDO. DRIVEN GEAR			TIRE SIZE	SPEEDO. ADAPTER				SLEEVE
		PART NO.	RATIO	COLOR	7.50 x 14	MODEL NO.	RATIO	PART NO.	COLOR	
AUTOMATIC TRANSMISSION										
41:11	3.73	9775187	45:18	LT. BLUE		777-S	.8653	535617	BLUE	1362285
		1362196	43:18	PURPLE	X	777-S	.8653	535617	BLUE	1362285
39:11	3.55	1362196	43:18	PURPLE		777-S	.8653	535617	BLUE	1362285
		1362195	41:18	YELLOW	X	777-S	.8653	535617	BLUE	1362285
37:11	3.36	1362195	41:18	YELLOW		777-S	.8653	535617	BLUE	1362285
		1359273	39:18	BROWN	X	777-S	.8653	535617	BLUE	1362284
42:13	3.23	9775187	45:18	LT. BLUE						1362285
		1362196	43:18	PURPLE	X					1362285
40:13	3.08	1362196	43:18	PURPLE						1362285
		1362195	41:18	YELLOW	X		NOT				1362285
41:14	2.93	1362195	41:18	YELLOW		REQUIRED				1362285
		1359273	39:18	BROWN	X						1362284
39:14	2.78	1359273	39:18	BROWN						1362284
		1359271	37:18	RED	X						1362284
41:16	2.56	1359270	36:18	WHITE						1362284
		9774413	34:18	LT. GREEN	X						1362284
39:10	3.90	1359273	39:18	BROWN		777-S	.7333	535614	RED	1362284
		1359273	38:18	BROWN	X	777-S	.7333	535614	RED	1362284

1964 Tempest speedometer gear usage chart.

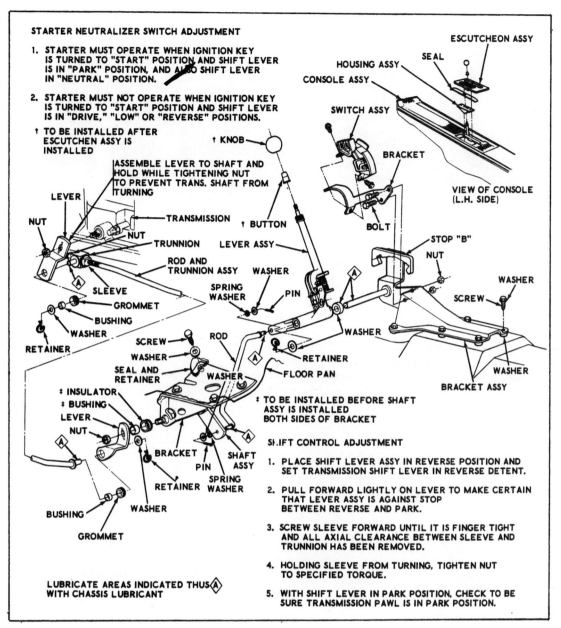

STARTER NEUTRALIZER SWITCH ADJUSTMENT

1. STARTER MUST OPERATE WHEN IGNITION KEY IS TURNED TO "START" POSITION AND SHIFT LEVER IS IN "PARK" POSITION, AND ALSO SHIFT LEVER IN "NEUTRAL" POSITION.

2. STARTER MUST NOT OPERATE WHEN IGNITION KEY IS TURNED TO "START" POSITION AND SHIFT LEVER IS IN "DRIVE," "LOW" OR "REVERSE" POSITIONS.

† TO BE INSTALLED AFTER ESCUTCHEN ASSY IS INSTALLED

ASSEMBLE LEVER TO SHAFT AND HOLD WHILE TIGHTENING NUT TO PREVENT TRANS. SHAFT FROM TURNING

ESCUTCHEON ASSY
SEAL
HOUSING ASSY
CONSOLE ASSY
SWITCH ASSY
† KNOB
BRACKET
BOLT
VIEW OF CONSOLE (L.H. SIDE)

LEVER
NUT
NUT
TRANSMISSION
† BUTTON
TRUNNION
LEVER ASSY
ROD AND TRUNNION ASSY
WASHER
STOP "B"
NUT
SLEEVE
SPRING WASHER
PIN
WASHER
WASHER
SCREW
GROMMET
BUSHING
WASHER
WASHER
RETAINER
SCREW
ROD
RETAINER
WASHER
WASHER
FLOOR PAN
BRACKET ASSY
SEAL AND RETAINER
‡ INSULATOR
‡ BUSHING
LEVER
NUT
‡ TO BE INSTALLED BEFORE SHAFT ASSY IS INSTALLED BOTH SIDES OF BRACKET
BRACKET
PIN
SHAFT ASSY
RETAINER
SPRING WASHER
BUSHING
WASHER
GROMMET

SHIFT CONTROL ADJUSTMENT

1. PLACE SHIFT LEVER ASSY IN REVERSE POSITION AND SET TRANSMISSION SHIFT LEVER IN REVERSE DETENT.

2. PULL FORWARD LIGHTLY ON LEVER TO MAKE CERTAIN THAT LEVER ASSY IS AGAINST STOP BETWEEN REVERSE AND PARK.

3. SCREW SLEEVE FORWARD UNTIL IT IS FINGER TIGHT AND ALL AXIAL CLEARANCE BETWEEN SLEEVE AND TRUNNION HAS BEEN REMOVED.

4. HOLDING SLEEVE FROM TURNING, TIGHTEN NUT TO SPECIFIED TORQUE.

5. WITH SHIFT LEVER IN PARK POSITION, CHECK TO BE SURE TRANSMISSION PAWL IS IN PARK POSITION.

LUBRICATE AREAS INDICATED THUS △ WITH CHASSIS LUBRICANT

LH view of 1965 automatic transmission shifter and linkage assembly, with adjustment instructions.

AUTOMATIC TRANSMISSION

REAR AXLE RATIO	*	DRIVEN GEAR			*	TIRE SIZE 7.75 X 14	*MODEL	SPEEDOMETER ADAPTER				SLEEVE & SEAL ASM
		PART #	TEETH	COLOR				RATIO	PART #	COLOR	*	
39:10 3.90		1362195	41	YELLOW		X	777-S	.8653	535617	BLUE		1362285
39:11 3.55		1362196	43	PURPLE		X						1362285
40:13 3.08		1362049	42	GREEN		X						1362285
42:13 3.23		1359273	39	BROWN		X						1362284

1965 GTO speedometer gear usage chart, automatic transmission.

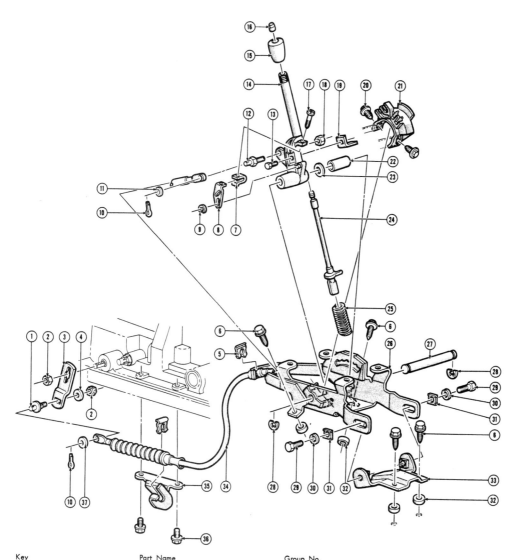

Key	Part Name	Group No.
1 — PIN, Control Cable to Range Selector Lever		4.047
2 — NUT, Cable and Lever to Trans. (3/8"-16)		8.915
3 — LEVER, Range Selector - Outer		4.045
4 — WASHER, Control Cable to Range Selector Lever (13/32" I.D. x 47/64" O.D. x 1/16")		N.S.
5 — RETAINER, Control Cable to Mounting Bracket (Yoke)		4.037
6 — SCREW, Mounting Bracket to Body (1/4"-14 x 7/8")		8.977
7 — NUT, Adjusting Screw to Lever Asm. (3/16")		N.S.
8 — LEVER, Neutral Safety Switch		N.S.
9 — RETAINER, Neutral Safety Switch Lever		4.054
10 — COTTER PIN, Cable to Levers (3/32" x 5/8")		8.938
11 — WASHER, Cable Asm. to Lever (9/32" I.D. x 1/2" O.D. x 1/32")		N.S.
12 — PIN, Control Cable to Shift Lever		4.047
13 — BOLT, Pawl Guide to Lever (1/4"-28 x 1/2")		8.900
14 — LEVER ASM., Gear Shift Control (Inc. #7-8-9-12-13-17-18-19-24-25)		4.006
15 — KNOB, Shift Lever		4.006
16 — BUTTON, Shift Lever Knob		4.006
17 — SCREW, Switch Lever Adjusting (#10-32 x 3/4")		N.S.
18 — NUT, Shift Lever Pin to Lever (1/4"-20)		8.915
19 — GUIDE, Shift Lever Pawl Rod		4.006
20 — SCREW, Switch to Switch Bracket (#10-24 x 1/2")		8.977
21 — SWITCH ASM., Trans. Neutralizer and Back-Up Lamp		4.054
22 — SPACER, Shift Lever to Bracket		4.008
23 — WASHER, Shift Lever to Bracket		4.032
24 — ROD, Shift Lever Pawl		4.006
25 — SPRING, Shift Lever Pawl Retaining		4.006
26 — BRACKET ASM., Shift Lever Mounting		4.010
27 — PIN, Shift Lever to Bracket Retaining		4.008
28 — RING, Shift Lever Retaining Pin (7/16")		4.008
29 — BOLT, Mounting Bracket to Bracket (5/16"-18 x 3/4")		8.900
30 — LOCKWASHER, Mounting Bracket to Bracket (5/16")		8.931
31 — LOCATOR, Shift Lever Mounting Bracket to Console Bracket		4.010
32 — WASHER, Console Mounting Bracket to Body		4.037
33 — BRACKET ASM., Console Mounting		10.240
34 — CABLE ASM., Trans. Control		4.047
35 — BRACKET, Control Cable Mounting - Lower		4.010
36 — SCREW, Cable Mounting Bracket to Trans.		N.S.
37 — WASHER, Cable to Lever Pin		N.S.

1966 automatic shift lever used for console application. Note that 1966 used a cable shift linkage.

Close-up of 1965 column-shifted automatic transmission gear-shift indicator assembly.

Components used in the 1966 floor-mounted console with automatic transmission. Note design of shift lever knob; it was unique to 1966.

AUTOMATIC TRANSMISSION

REAR AXLE RATIO	*	DRIVEN GEAR			*	TIRE SIZE 7.75 × 14	SPEEDOMETER ADAPTER				*	SLEEVE & SEAL ASM
		PART #	TEETH	COLOR			*MODEL	RATIO	PART #	COLOR		
37:11 3.36		1362195	41	YELLOW	×		777-S	.8653	535617	BLUE		1362285
39:9 4.33		1362195	41	YELLOW	×		777-S	.7692	535615	YELLOW		1362285
39:10 3.90		1362195	41	YELLOW	×		777-S	.8653	535617	BLUE		1362285
39:11 3.55		1362196	43	PURPLE	×							1362285
40:13 3.08		1359271	37	RED	×							1362284
42:13 3.23		1359273	39	BROWN	×							1362284

1966 GTO speedometer gear usage chart, automatic transmission.

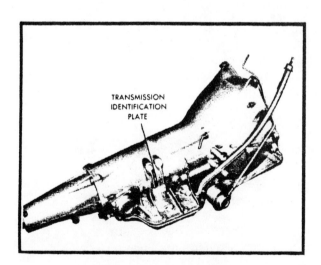

TRANSMISSION IDENTIFICATION PLATE

TURBO HYDRA-MATIC TRANSMISSION IDENTIFICATION

The Turbo Hydra-Matic transmission identification plate is located on the right side of the transmission case. The serial number begins with the letter P meaning Pontiac, followed by a letter code designating engine usage. The numerical code, following the two-letter codes represents the model year.

Location of identification information for the Turbo Hydra-matic (left) used from 1967 to 1970, and two-speed automatic from 1964 to 1966 (right).

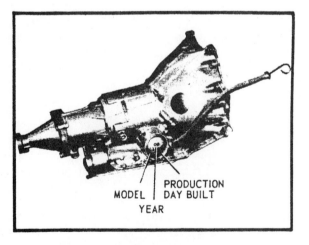

MODEL YEAR | PRODUCTION DAY BUILT

AUTOMATIC TRANSMISSION IDENTIFICATION

The identification data is located on the right side of the transmission. The transmission model, model year and the assembly date code appear on the low servo cover. Whenever the servo cover is replaced, it will be necessary to stamp all of the above information on the new cover.

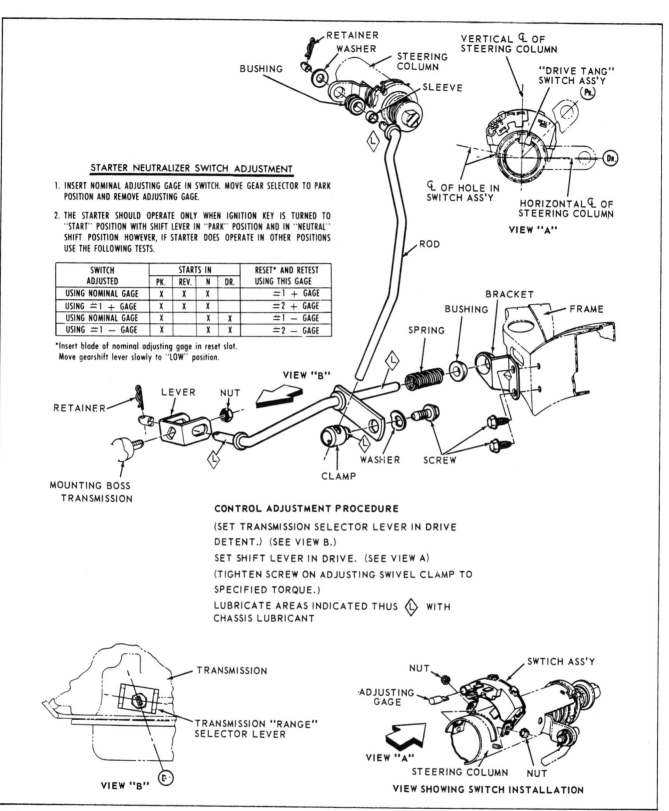

STARTER NEUTRALIZER SWITCH ADJUSTMENT

1. INSERT NOMINAL ADJUSTING GAGE IN SWITCH. MOVE GEAR SELECTOR TO PARK POSITION AND REMOVE ADJUSTING GAGE.

2. THE STARTER SHOULD OPERATE ONLY WHEN IGNITION KEY IS TURNED TO "START" POSITION WITH SHIFT LEVER IN "PARK" POSITION AND IN "NEUTRAL" SHIFT POSITION. HOWEVER, IF STARTER DOES OPERATE IN OTHER POSITIONS USE THE FOLLOWING TESTS.

SWITCH ADJUSTED	STARTS IN				RESET* AND RETEST USING THIS GAGE
	PK.	REV.	N	DR.	
USING NOMINAL GAGE	X	X	X		±1 + GAGE
USING ±1 + GAGE	X	X	X		±2 + GAGE
USING NOMINAL GAGE	X		X	X	±1 − GAGE
USING ±1 − GAGE	X		X	X	±2 − GAGE

*Insert blade of nominal adjusting gage in reset slot. Move gearshift lever slowly to "LOW" position.

CONTROL ADJUSTMENT PROCEDURE

(SET TRANSMISSION SELECTOR LEVER IN DRIVE DETENT.) (SEE VIEW B.)

SET SHIFT LEVER IN DRIVE. (SEE VIEW A)

(TIGHTEN SCREW ON ADJUSTING SWIVEL CLAMP TO SPECIFIED TORQUE.)

LUBRICATE AREAS INDICATED THUS ⬩ WITH CHASSIS LUBRICANT

Exploded view of 1967 column shift linkage for Turbo Hydra-matic.

302

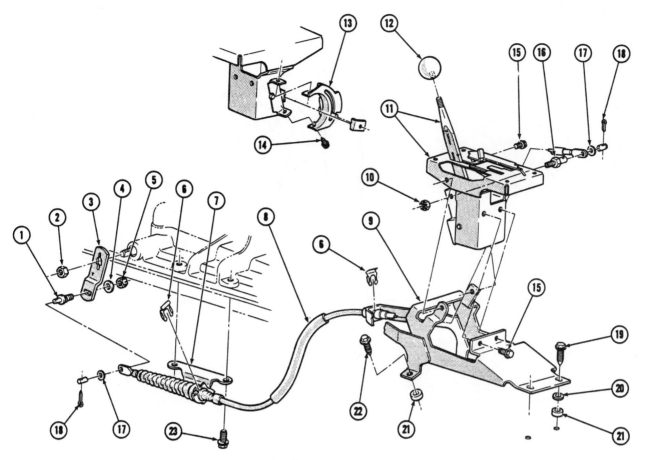

Key	Part Name	Group No.
1 — PIN, Trans. Control Cable to Shift Lever		4.047
2 — NUT, Range Selector Lever to Shaft (3/8"-16)		8.917
3 — LEVER, Range Selector - Outer		4.045
4 — WASHER, Control Cable to Lever (13/32" I.D. x 3/4" O.D.)		8.929
5 — NUT, Control Cable to Lever (3/8"-16)		8.917
6 — YOKE, Control Cable to Mtg. Bracket		4.047
7 — BRACKET, Trans. Control Cable Mounting		4.047
8 — CABLE ASM., Trans. Control		4.047
9 — BRACKET ASM., Shift Lever Mounting		4.010
10 — NUT, Control Cable Pin to Lever (1/4"-20)		8.915
11 — LEVER ASM., Shift		4.006
12 — KNOB, Shift Lever		4.006

Key	Part Name	Group No.
13 — SWITCH ASM., Trans. Neutralizer & Back-Up Lamp		4.054
14 — SCREW, Trans. Neutralizer Switch (#10-24 x 1/2")		8.977
15 — SCREW, Shift Lever Arm to Mtg. Bracket (1/4"-20 x 3/8")		8.977
16 — PIN, Control Cable to Shift Lever		4.047
17 — WASHER, Control Cable to Lever (9/32" I.D. x 1/2" O.D.)		N.S.
18 — COTTER PIN, Control Cable to Lever (3/32" x 1/2")		8.938
19 — SCREW, Shift Lever Mtg. Brkt. to Body (1/4"-14 x 1-1/4")		N.S.
20 — WASHER, Shift Lever Mtg. Brkt. to Body (17/64" I.D. x 1" O.D.)		N.S.
21 — WASHER, Mounting Bracket to Body		10.240
22 — SCREW, Mounting Bracket to Body (1/4"-14 x 7/8")		8.977
23 — SCREW & WASHER ASM., Cable Mtg. Bracket to Trans.		N.S.

Drawing of components used in the 1967 Hurst Dual Gate Turbo Hydra-matic floor-mounted shifter.

1967 Hurst Campbell Dual Gate Turbo Hydra-matic floor-mounted shifter. Phillips-head screws were used to retain shifter escutcheon to assembly.

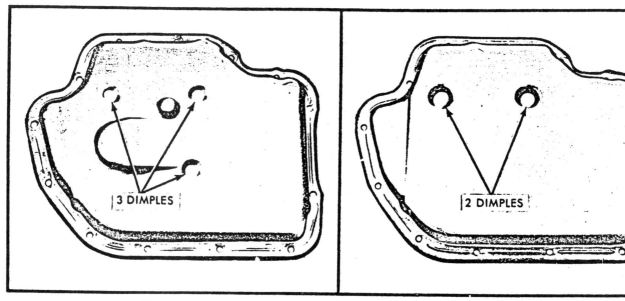

1ST TYPE PAN

2ND TYPE PAN

Note the differences in the dimples that help differentiate between the two designs of 1967 M-40 Turbo transmissions. The dimples were located on the transmission oil pan. (This information and illustration taken from Dealer Service Information Bulletin number 67-16, dated 7-31-67.)

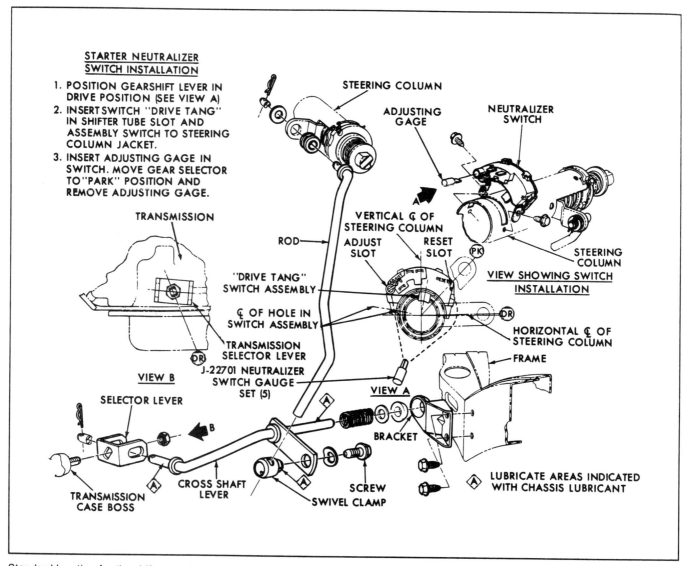

Standard location for the shift control was on the column; console location was optional. Shown here are the alignment and components used in the 1968 GTO column shift. 1969-70 GTO was similar.

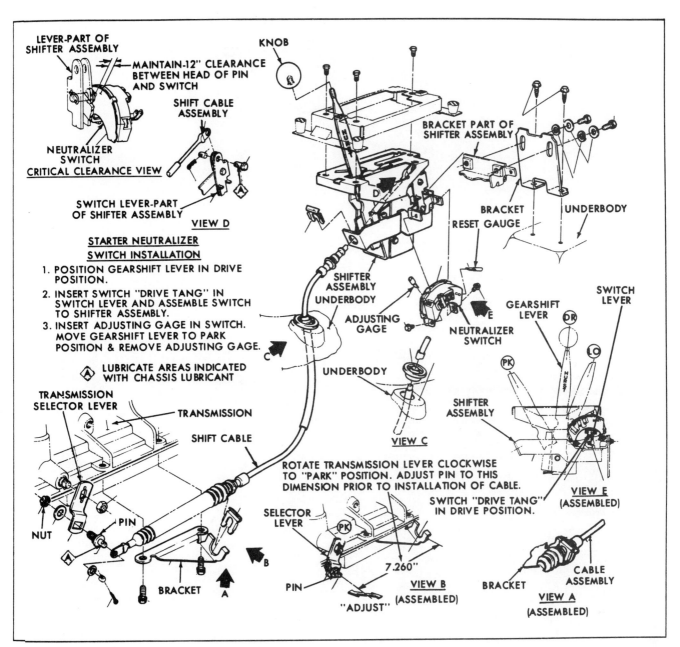

LEVER-PART OF
SHIFTER ASSEMBLY

MAINTAIN-12" CLEARANCE
BETWEEN HEAD OF PIN
AND SWITCH

KNOB

SHIFT CABLE
ASSEMBLY

NEUTRALIZER
SWITCH
CRITICAL CLEARANCE VIEW

BRACKET PART OF
SHIFTER ASSEMBLY

SWITCH LEVER-PART
OF SHIFTER ASSEMBLY
VIEW D

BRACKET
RESET GAUGE

UNDERBODY

SHIFTER
ASSEMBLY
UNDERBODY

SWITCH
LEVER

GEARSHIFT
LEVER

**STARTER NEUTRALIZER
SWITCH INSTALLATION**

1. POSITION GEARSHIFT LEVER IN DRIVE
   POSITION.
2. INSERT SWITCH "DRIVE TANG" IN
   SWITCH LEVER AND ASSEMBLE SWITCH
   TO SHIFTER ASSEMBLY.
3. INSERT ADJUSTING GAGE IN SWITCH.
   MOVE GEARSHIFT LEVER TO PARK
   POSITION & REMOVE ADJUSTING GAGE.

ADJUSTING
GAGE

NEUTRALIZER
SWITCH

SHIFTER
ASSEMBLY

LUBRICATE AREAS INDICATED
WITH CHASSIS LUBRICANT

UNDERBODY

TRANSMISSION
SELECTOR LEVER

TRANSMISSION

SHIFT CABLE

VIEW C

VIEW E
(ASSEMBLED)

ROTATE TRANSMISSION LEVER CLOCKWISE
TO "PARK" POSITION. ADJUST PIN TO THIS
DIMENSION PRIOR TO INSTALLATION OF CABLE.
SWITCH "DRIVE TANG"
IN DRIVE POSITION.

NUT

PIN

SELECTOR
LEVER

BRACKET

A

B

7.260"

VIEW B
(ASSEMBLED)

PIN

"ADJUST"

BRACKET

CABLE
ASSEMBLY

VIEW A
(ASSEMBLED)

Installation of 1968 GTO Hurst Dual Gate shifter and linkage.

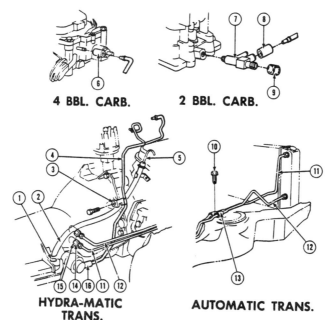

4 BBL. CARB.   **2 BBL. CARB.**

HYDRA-MATIC TRANS.   **AUTOMATIC TRANS.**

Key	Part Name	Group No.
1—SEAL, Oil Filler Pipe to Case	. . . .	4.133
2—PIPE ASM., Oil Filler	. . . .	4.133
3—CLIP, Vacuum Pipe to Flywheel Housing	. . . .	4.205
4—PIPE, Carb. to Trans. Vacuum	. . . .	4.205
5—INDICATOR ROD, Trans. Oil Level	. . . .	4.133
6—HOSE, Pipe to Carb. (7/32" I.D. x 1 5/16") (1968)		8.962
7—FITTING, Carb. Vacuum Connector	. . . .	3.278
8—HOSE, Pipe to Fitting (7/32" I.D. 1 5/16")	. . . . .	8.962
9—CAP, Carb. Vacuum Tube	. . . .	3.764

Key	Part Name	Group No.
10—SCREW, Pipe Clip to Frame (5/16"-18 x 3/4")	. . . .	8.977
11—PIPE ASM., Oil Cooler - Outlet	. . . .	4.128
12—PIPE ASM., Oil Cooler - Inlet	. . . .	4.128
13—CLIP, Oil Cooler Pipe	. . . .	4.128
14—CONNECTOR, Oil Cooler Pipe to Trans.	. . . .	4.128
15—WASHER, Cooler Line to Connector - Copper	. . . .	4.128
16—HOSE, Vacuum Line to Modulator (7/32" I.D. x 1 5/16")	. . . .	8.962

Routing and parts nomenclature for 1968-69 M-40 cooler and vacuum lines.

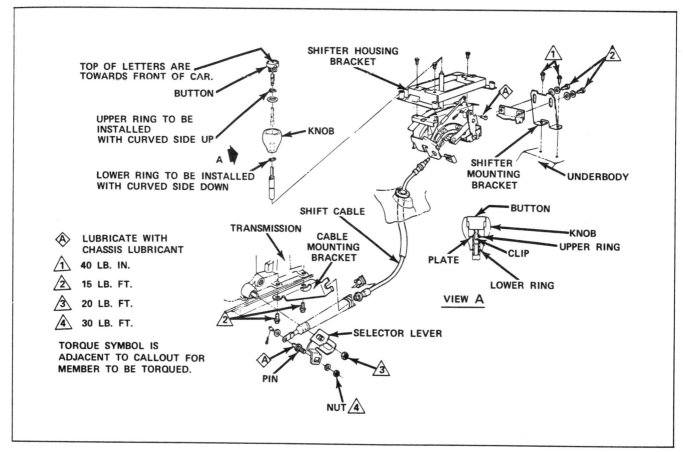

Installation of 1969 and 1970 Rally Sport shifter. Dual Gate was discontinued after the end of 1968 production.

REAR AXLE

1964-65

All GTOs in 1964 and 1965 used a ten-bolt, semifloating hypoid rear axle. A limited slip differential (Safe-T-Track) was optional. The differential ratio could be determined by a stamping on the rear of the RH axle tube. In 1964, the ratio itself was stamped on the tube. In 1965, a letter code was used. However, some early-production 1965 models used 1964 rears, carrying the numerical stamp.

Rears equipped with the optional Safe-T-Track limited slip (RPO 731) can be determined by two methods. One is the location of a warning tag for use of special lubricant in the limited slip. (The tag was attached to the lower RH carrier cover plate bolt.) The second (and more accurate) is determination of the rear axle code. In 1965, metallic brakes were not available with the 3.08:1 rear.

All 1965 models had their propeller shaft indexed to the companion flange for optimum balance to minimize driveline vibrations. Any time the two are disconnected, be sure to reassemble them in the same position. Scribing a mark that will align is the best method to ensure this. (Pontiac Service News Flash number 65-6, dated 9-18-64, reported this information.)

1966-67

Rear axle design was unchanged for 1966-67 although the 1967 rear tread was widened one inch.

The differential information was again stamped on the rear of the RH axle tube. However, due to a stamping machine breakdown, the code stamp was moved to the top of the LH axle tube (refer to Service Bulletin 66-73). This malfunction occurred toward the end of the 1966 production year, so the change should appear on GTOs dated O7C and later. It is not known if this malfunction affected any early-production 1967 GTOs.

A white sticker with red letters was also applied to the LH rear brake drum with the appropriate rear axle code in 1966 and 1967.

1968-70

The axle ratio identification stamp was moved in 1968 to the rear of the LH axle tube near the carrier. A sticker was also located on the LH brake drum face as in previous years.

Some 1969 Tempests built after June 25, 1969, had a new ring gear, ring gear bolt and differential case. These parts were changed to increase durability.

To determine if a car has the new parts, examine the ring gear retaining bolts. The old bolt was ⅜ inch with 11/16 inch head, RH thread. The new bolt was 7/16 inch with ¾ inch head, LH thread; the letter L stamped in the center of the bolt head.

The old bolt, case and ring gear are *not interchangeable* with the new parts (take care not to use the ⅜ inch bolt and corresponding ring gear with a case that uses the 7/16 inch bolt). Also, the new Tempest bolts were not interchangeable with the later Pontiac bolts, which were 0.19 inch longer.

These new ring gear bolts should be torqued to 90 lb. ft.

The major change came in 1970, with the introduction of a twelve-bolt rear for use with the 455 engine when ordered. Consequently, two carrier and tube assemblies were used in 1970. Part number 479724 took care of the ten-bolt rear, and the C-type rear used part number 3981669. The differential cover with part number 9777035 was used for all 1968-70 ten-bolt carriers, and part number 3852998 distinguished the C-type twelve-bolt unit.

Two different types of axle shaft bearings were used in original 1970 ten-bolt production. One type was the straight roller design; the other was the tapered roller type. The two bearings were interchangeable and one of each type may be found on the same vehicle. The straight roller type was the only one available for service use.

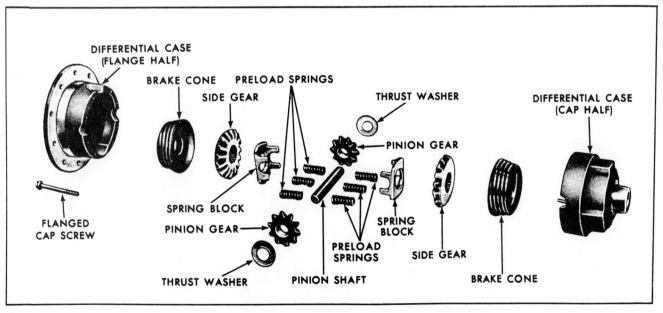

Exploded view of 1964-70 two-pinion Safe-T-Track limited slip rear.

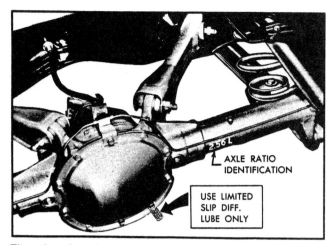

The axle ratio code was stamped on the rear of the RH axle tube for 1964. The location of the warning tag used on rears equipped with limited slip differential is also shown.

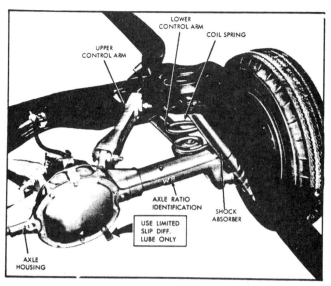

1965-67 rear axle code was stamped in same location as 1964 but used a two-letter code. The limited slip warning tag was again placed in same location on differential cover. Overall length of 1964-65 rear from backing plate to backing plate was 53¼ inches.

REAR AXLE GEAR		TRANS			AIR COND		STANDARD DIFFERENTIAL		SAFE-T-TRACK DIFFERENTIAL	
COMBINATION	RATIO	3 SPEED M.T.	4 SPEED M.T.	AUTOMATIC	WITHOUT	WITH	COLOR	CODE	COLOR	CODE
40:13	3.08			X		X	YELLOW	2D	GREEN & YELLOW	3D
42:13	3.23			X	X	X	BROWN	2K	GREEN & BROWN	3K
40:13	3.08	X	X	X	X	X	YELLOW	2D	GREEN & YELLOW	3D
37:11	3.36	X	X	X	X		WHITE	2E	GREEN & WHITE	3E
39:11	3.55	X	X	X	X		BLUE	2F	GREEN & BLUE	3F

1964 Tempest rear axle usage and identification chart with standard brakes.

REAR AXLE GEAR		TRANS			AIR COND		STANDARD DIFFERENTIAL		SAFE-T-TRACK DIFFERENTIAL	
COMBINATION	RATIO	3 SPEED M.T.	4 SPEED M.T.	AUTOMATIC	WITHOUT	WITH	COLOR	CODE	COLOR	CODE
42:13	3.23	X	X	X	X	X	BROWN	2L	GREEN & BROWN	3L
37:11	3.36	X	X	X	X		WHITE	2M	GREEN & WHITE	3M
39:11	3.55	X	X	X	X		BLUE	2N	GREEN & BLUE	3N
39:10	3.90	X	X	X	X		NOT AVAILABLE		GREEN & GREEN	3D

1964 Tempest rear axle usage and identification chart with metallic brakes.

REAR AXLE GEAR		TRANS			AIR COND		STANDARD DIFFERENTIAL	SAFE-T-TRACK DIFFERENTIAL
COMBINATION	RATIO	3 SPEED M.T.	4 SPEED M.T.	AUTOMATIC	WITHOUT	WITH	CODE	CODE
40:13	3.08			X		X	WE	YE
42:13	3.23	X	X	X	X	X	WF	YF
39:11	3.55	X	X	X	X		WH	YH
37:11	3.36	X	X	X	X	X	WG	WG

1965 GTO rear axle usage and identification chart with standard brakes.

REAR AXLE GEAR		TRANS			AIR COND		STANDARD DIFFERENTIAL	SAFE-T-TRACK DIFFERENTIAL
COMBINATION	RATIO	3 SPEED M.T.	4 SPEED M.T.	AUTOMATIC	WITHOUT	WITH	CODE	CODE
42:13	3.23			X	X	X	XF	ZF
39:11	3.55	X	X	X	X		XH	ZH
40:13	3.08	X	X	X	X	X	XE	ZE
37:11	3.36	X	X	X	X		XG	ZG
39:10	3.90	X	X	X	X		N/A	ZK
39:9	4.33	X	X	X			N/A	ZL

1965 GTO rear axle usage and identification chart with metallic brakes.

Close-up of warning tag used on Safe-T-Track limited slip rear axle.

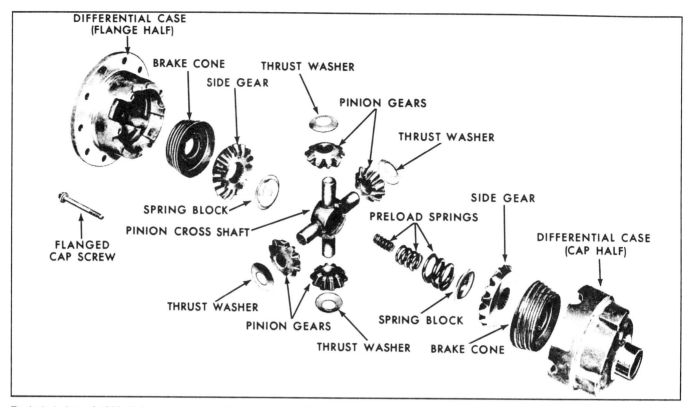

Exploded view of 1966-70 four-pinion Safe-T-Track limited slip
differential.

REAR AXLE GEAR		*	TRANS			*	AIR COND		*	STANDARD DIFFERENTIAL	*	SAFE -T - TRACK DIFFERENTIAL
C O M B I N A T I O N	R A T I O	* *	3 S P E E D M . T .	4 S P E E D M . T .	A U T O M A T I C	*	W I T H O U T	W I T H	*	C O D E	*	C O D E
40:13	3.08				×			×		WE		YE
42:13	3.23		×	×	×		×	×		WF		YF
39:11	3.55		×	×	×		×	×		WH		YH
37:11	3.36		×	×	×		×	×		WG		YG

1966 GTO rear axle usage and identification chart with standard
brakes.

| REAR AXLE GEAR | | TRANS | | | AIR COND | | STANDARD DIFFERENTIAL | SAFE-T-TRACK DIFFERENTIAL |
COMBINATION	RATIO	3 SPEED M.T.	4 SPEED M.T.	AUTOMATIC	WITHOUT	WITH	CODE	CODE
40:13	3.08	X	X	X	X	X	XE	ZE
42:13	3.23	X	X	X	X	X	XF	ZF
39:11	3.55	X	X	X	X	X	XH	ZH
39:9	4.33	X	X	X	X		N/A	ZL
37:11	3.36	X	X	X	X		XG	ZG
39:10	3.90	X	X	X	X		N/A	ZK

1966 GTO rear axle usage and identification chart with metallic brakes.

| REAR AXLE GEAR | | TRANS | | | AIR COND | | STANDARD DIFFERENTIAL | SAFE-T-TRACK DIFFERENTIAL |
COMBINATION	RATIO	3 SPEED M.T.	4 SPEED M.T.	AUTOMATIC	WITHOUT	WITH	CODE	CODE
41:16	2.56			X	X		WB	YB
39:14	2.78			X		X	WC	YC
41:14	2.93			X	X	X	WD	YD
42:13	3.23	X	X	X	X	X	WF	YF
37:11	3.36			X	X		WG	YG
39:11	3.55	X	X	X	X		WH	YH
39:9	4.33	X		X	X		N/A	YL
40:13	3.08	X	X		X	X	WE	YE
39:10	3.90	X	X	X	X		WK	YK

1967 GTO rear axle usage and identification chart.

COMBINATION	RATIO	3 SPEED M.T.	4 SPEED M.T.	AUTOMATIC	WITHOUT	WITH	4 BBL.	4 BBL. H.O.	2 BBL.	STD DIFF CODE	LOCK DIFF CODE
41:16	2.56			X	X				X	WB	YB
39:14	2.78			X		X			X	WC	YC
41:14	2.93			X	X				X	WD	YD
42:13	3.23			X	X	X			X	WF	N/A
42:13	3.23	X	X			X	X	X	X	WF	N/A
42:13	3.23	X	X	X	X	X	X	X		WF	N/A
37:11	3.36	X	X	X	X		X	X		WG	ZG
39:11	3.55	X	X	X	X	X	X			WH	ZH
39:11	3.55	X	X	X	X			X		WH	ZH
39:9	4.33		X		X			X		N/A	ZL
40:13	3.08	X	X		X	X	X	X		WE	YE
39:10	3.90	X	X	X	X		X	X		WK	ZK

1968 GTO rear axle usage and identification chart.

COMBINATION	RATIO	3 SPEED M.T.	4 SPEED M.T.	AUTOMATIC	WITHOUT	WITH	4 BBL.	4 BBL. RAM AIR	2 BBL.	STD DIFF CODE	LOCK DIFF CODE
41:16	2.56			X	X	X			X	WB	XB
39:14	2.78			X		X			X	WC	XC
41:14	2.93			X	X				X	WD	XD
42:13	3.23	X	X	X	X	X	X	X	X	WF	XF
39:11	3.55	X	X	X	X	X	X	X		WH	XH
39:10	3.90	X	X*	X	X			X		WK	XK
40:13	3.08	X	X	X	X	X	X	X		WE	XE
37:11	3.36	X	X	X	X		X	X		WG	XG
39:10	3.90	X	X*	X	X		X	X		N/A	XK
39:9	4.33	X	X*	X	X		X	X		N/A	XM

*M21 CLOSE RATIO ONLY AVAILABLE 4 SPEED GEARBOX WITH THIS REAR AXLE RATIO

1969 GTO rear axle usage and identification chart.

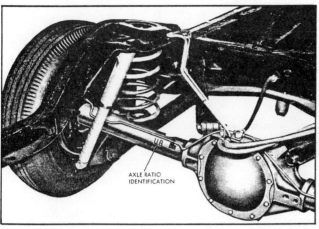

Location of axle identification code for 1968-70.

1970 AXLE IDENTIFICATION

TYPE "C"	STD. AXLE
12 BOLTS	10 BOLTS

Comparison of 12-bolt and 10-bolt carrier covers used in 1970.
The type C was used with all 455 engines installed in GTOs.

REAR AXLE GEAR		* TRANS *			* AIR COND *		* ENGINE *400*			STD DIFF	LOCK DIFF
COMBINATION	RATIO	3 SPEED M.T.	4 SPEED M.T.	AUTOMATIC	WITHOUT	WITH	4 BBL.	4 BBL. RAM AIR	455 4 BBL.	CODE	CODE
43:14	3.07			X	X	X			X	WT	XT
42:13	3.23	X	X	X	X	X	X	X		WF	XF
43:13	3.31	X	X*	X	X	X			X	WU	XU
39:11	3.55	X	X	X	X	X	X	X		WH	XH
39:10	3.90		X*	X	X			X		WK	YK
40:13	3.08	X	X		X	X	X			WE	XE
39:11	3.55	X	X		X	X			X	WV	XV
39:10	3.90	X	X	X	X		X	X		N/A	XK
39:9	4.33	X	X*		X		X	X		N/A	XM
39:9	4.33		X*		X			X		N/A	XM
39:9	4.33		X*		X			X		N/A	7N

*M21 CLOSE RATIO ONLY AVAILABLE 4 SPEED GEARBOX WITH THIS REAR AXLE RATIO

1970 GTO rear axle usage and identification chart.

Chapter 6

ENGINES

BATTERY

1964-67

There were two batteries available in 1964. The standard GTO battery was the Delco DC-12. A heavy-duty option (RPO 582), rated at 61 amps, was available in the last two-thirds of the model year. It appeared on Special Equipment charts dated December 1963, but did not appear on price sheets until March 9, 1964. It is not known if early-production 1964 GTOs had this option available.

Both the standard and the optional batteries used the same tray in 1964 (part number 9774139). However, since the optional battery stood just over ½ inch taller, a different retainer and bolt were necessary.

	Standard	Optional
Retainer	9775086	9776982
Bolt	9775068	9775067

The heavy-duty battery, with different retainer and bolt, was used in all air-conditioned GTO models as part of the RPO 581 Tri-Comfort option.

For 1965, battery tray part number 9779380 was used. For 1966 and 1967 first-design models, battery tray part number 9784231 was used. With the introduction of the R-59 Delco Energizer in 1965, the 1964 heavy-duty battery retainer and bolt were used from 1965 through mid-1967.

During the 1967 production year, the battery tray was redesigned in conjunction with changes in the core support. The tray (part number 9788900) utilized a lower clamping device (part number 9788712), which was mounted at the base of the battery tray. A ½ inch hex-head bolt held the clamp to the tray and secured the battery from the bottom, thus eliminating the corrosive effects of the upper retainer method. All 1964-67 battery trays were painted 60° gloss black, as were the bolt and the 1967 clamp.

A thirty-inch battery ground cable (part number 2978482) was used from 1964 to 1967. The positive cable in 1964 (part number 2987242) was eleven inches long and ran from the battery terminal to a junction block mounted on the top of the LH fender skirt. The junction block and its wire assembly to the starter were part number 2987929.

In 1965, the junction block was eliminated, and the positive cable (part number 6286151) ran directly to the starter solenoid. This cable was used through 1967 for all applications except when equipped with power windows or seats, or when in convertibles. These applications used a forty-two-inch cable (part number 6286152). In 1967, all GTOs with HO and Ram Air used a forty-four-inch cable (part number 6289157 without ground strap, and 6289158 with ground strap).

Pontiac Service News Flash number 65-38, dated 11-11-64, reported that some early-production 1965 mod-

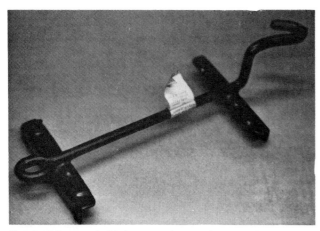

Detail of battery hold-down retainer or bracket. Retainer was dipped in black rubber, used from 1964 to mid-1967.

View of R-59 Delco Energizer battery used from 1965 to 1970. Caps shown here are incorrect, being the charcoal vent variety used in the early seventies. Correct caps had Delco emblem on top.

els had an incorrect engine wire harness. Be sure your harness is routed inboard of the spark plug wire bracket and is retained in this position by clip number 535938(F) on the throttle control cross-shaft bracket. The starter solenoid wires must drop behind the head and not come in contact with the sharp edge of the rocker cover. The correct length of the ground strap is six inches (it should not be any longer). And it should extend from the coil bracket to a hole 3½ inches to the left of and 2 11/64 inches down from the dash insulator retainer, as viewed from the front of the car.

1968-70

The R-59 Delco Energizer battery was standard for 1968-70. A heavy-duty, 61 amp battery (R59S) was available as an option. It was standard when air conditioning was ordered.

The 60° gloss-black battery tray (part number 9790366) was the same for 1968 and 1969. The tray was redesigned slightly for 1970 (part number 9790161). A hold-down clamp (part number 9790345) was used to secure the battery to the tray. The battery ground cable was thirty-six inches long in 1968 (part number 2978483) and 1969 (part number 2978482). If the 455 cid engine was used in 1970, cable part number 6299883 was used.

Two positive cables were offered in 1968. For standard engines, part number 2982498 was employed. Ram Air or HO engines used a heavier-duty cable (part number 2982499). This cable was used in 1969 and 1970 for standard engine applications. Ram Air engines used part number 6297957 in 1969. For 1970, the Ram Air engine used cable part number 8901070, and the 455 cid engine used positive cable part number 6299885.

A black plastic clip (part number 3816659) was used in 1968 and 1969 to route the battery cable along the fender skirt. Another clip (part number 9772827) was used for the positive battery cable in 1968 HO or Ram Air GTOs. Two clips were used on the 1970 Ram Air IV. Clip part number 478654 retained the cable at the front of the LH side of the block. Part number 478655 also retained the cable just ahead of the starter. The front clip was also used on the 1970 Ram Air III.

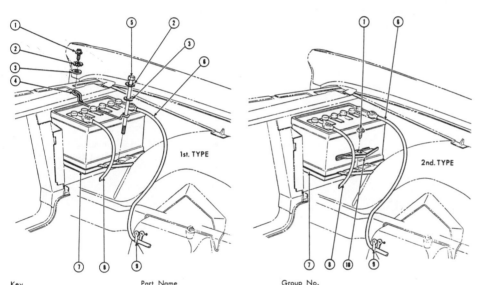

1st. TYPE

2nd. TYPE

Key	Part Name	Group No.
1 - SCREW, Retainer or Clamp Hold-Down (5/16"-18 x 7/8")		8.977
2 - LOCKWASHER, Battery Hold-Down		2.334
3 - WASHER, Battery Hold-Down-Lead Plated		2.334
4 - RETAINER, Battery (1st Type)		2.335
5 - BOLT, Battery Hold Down (5/16"-18 x 8 3/8")		2.334
6 - CABLE ASM., Battery Ground		2.341
7 - TRAY, Battery		2.333
8 - CABLE ASM., Battery Positive		2.342
9 - CLIP, Harness to Fender Cross Brace & Baffle (2 1/4" Plastic)		2.482
10 - CLAMP, Battery Hold-Down (2nd Type)		2.335

Detail of 1966 and 1967 GTO battery mounting (left) and second-design for 1967 (right). Illustration is for Tempest six-cylinder applications; consequently, battery assembly is on RH side and battery ground cable (number 6) is routed along cross-member. GTO mounted battery on LH side and did not use clip (number 9).

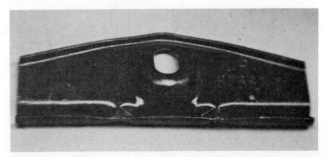

Close-up of second-design battery hold-down retainer (part number 9788712). Part number was stamped on RH side of retainer.

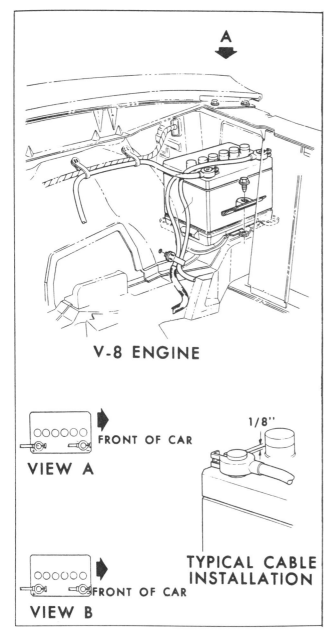

V-8 ENGINE

VIEW A

FRONT OF CAR

VIEW B

FRONT OF CAR

TYPICAL CABLE INSTALLATION

1/8"

Factory drawing of correct battery cable routing for 1968 GTO. Note alignment of cable and placement of clamp height. Alignment was also correct for 1969.

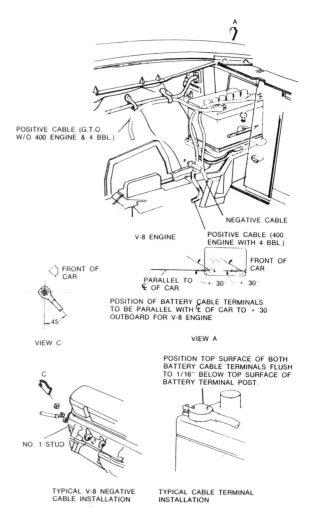

POSITIVE CABLE (G.T.O. W/O 400 ENGINE & 4 BBL.)

NEGATIVE CABLE

V-8 ENGINE

POSITIVE CABLE (400 ENGINE WITH 4 BBL.)

FRONT OF CAR

FRONT OF CAR

PARALLEL TO ℄ OF CAR

+ 30°   + 30°

POSITION OF BATTERY CABLE TERMINALS TO BE PARALLEL WITH ℄ OF CAR TO + 30° OUTBOARD FOR V-8 ENGINE

45°

VIEW C

VIEW A

POSITION TOP SURFACE OF BOTH BATTERY CABLE TERMINALS FLUSH TO 1/16" BELOW TOP SURFACE OF BATTERY TERMINAL POST.

C

NO. 1 STUD

TYPICAL V-8 NEGATIVE CABLE INSTALLATION

TYPICAL CABLE TERMINAL INSTALLATION

Installation of 1970 battery and routing and alignment of positive and negative battery cables. Note positioning of negative cable at block at a 45° angle.

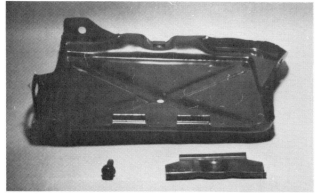

Close-up of 1968 battery tray (part number 9790366). Tray was used for 1969 as well. Clamp for battery hold-down (part number 9790345) was used from 1968 to 1970.

UNDERHOOD LAMP

1964-70

The underhood lamp for 1964-65 (RPO 404) was available as a separate option or as part of the optional Lamp Group (084 in 1964, 074 in 1965). It was also available as an accessory package (984143 in 1964 and 984483 in 1965). The 1965 replacement part number for the lamp assembly was 9780477. The wire-to-lamp switch, which ran from the fuse block to the underhood lamp switch, was part number 9774463 in 1964 and 9780449 in 1965. It was mounted to the firewall by hex-head black cadmium screws. The top of the lamp housing and the switch bracket were 0° gloss black. The switch itself and the inside reflector side of the lamp housing were bright-metal.

The 1966-67 underhood lamp option (RPO 421) was similar in design to the 1965 unit. The lamp switch mounting bracket (part number 9780754) was used for both years, and was painted black. The lamp assembly for 1966 was part number 9780477; for 1967, 9788584.

The underhood lamp option for 1968 through 1970 shared the same RPO number (671). It was also available as a dealer-installed option. The 1968 accessory package part number was 984906. The wiring design was revised slightly for 1969-70, warranting a new package number (988681). The lamp assembly was finished in the same appearance as previous years, and was mounted to the firewall by two ¼ inch black cadmium hex-head screws.

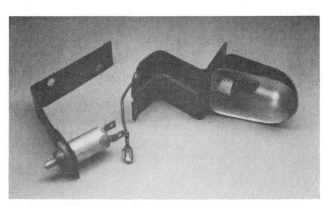

Detail of underhood lamp (RPO 421) used for 1964-67 GTO.

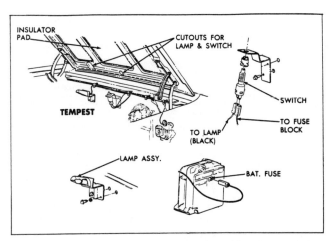

Installation of underhood lamp option for 1968-70 (accessory package part number 988681). The top of the lamp and the bracket were painted 60° gloss black. The switch was natural metal.

STANDARD AIR CLEANER

1964-65

The standard GTO engine for 1964 used an air cleaner quite similar to standard cleaners, except that it was chrome plated (part number 6420754). The 1965 air cleaner (part number 6421289) was redesigned, and was almost identical to the Corvette's. This was an extremely low-profile design, measuring 1½ inches in height and 14¾ inches in diameter. Around the circumference were twelve sets of louvers, with three louvers per set. The original element for the 1964 air cleaner was A119C. The 1965 used a foam element (A98C) with a wire mesh screen retainer. Replacement paper elements carried the AC number A350C.

A GTO built after January 1, 1964, for sale in California, used a closed positive crankcase ventilation (CPCV) system to comply with California emissions standards. In these cars, an element assembly (part number 6424145) was incorporated into the air cleaner and vented to the left rocker arm cover. The oil filler cap was moved to the right valve cover. The closed system called for a revised air cleaner design—still chromed (part number 6420765 in 1964 and 6420984 in 1965). The 1965 CPCV system air cleaner was unlike the forty-nine-state unit. Only the top was chromed, and it was quite similar to later-model Ram Air air cleaners.

Pontiac Service News Flash number 64-57, dated 1-14-64, reported on the "California Type" closed positive crankcase ventilation system. This system incorporated a sealed oil filler cap and a special filter assembly in the air cleaner, except on the Tri-Power. The Tri-Power engine had a flame arrester in the air cleaner on the center carburetor. Servicing and cleaning of this system should be performed yearly or every 12,000 miles.

1966-67

The standard forty-nine-state air cleaner assembly for 1966 was identical in all respects to the 1965 GTO four-barrel air cleaner.

The CPCV system used in 1966 was quite similar to that used in 1965. The air cleaner (part number 6420984) was painted gloss black except for the lid, which was chromed. A vent hose (part number 9784800) went from the LH side of the air cleaner assembly to a chromed oil filler cap (part number 6421919) on the LH chrome valve cover. The air cleaner element was A154C.

For GTOs built for sale in California, an air injector reactance (AIR) system was introduced in 1966 to comply with that state's stringent emission-control requirements. The air cleaner used in the AIR system was identical to the CPCV, except for a tube running from the RH side of the air cleaner to the air injector pump. The CPCV vent hose and oil filler assembly were used in this system as well. The AIR system was complex, and few were produced. (See the correct factory service material for details of theory of operation and maintenance.)

With the introduction of the 1967 GTO, a host of major changes appeared in the air cleaners. The standard forty-nine-state 400 cubic inch engine used the familiar pancake-style air cleaner, as did 1965-66. However, as the Rochester Quadra-Jet carburetor was now used, its base was redesigned, with different indentations to allow clearance for the Quadra-Jet. The part number for this air cleaner was 6422168. The optional two-barrel forty-nine-state air cleaner (part number 6424571) was the same unit used on B-body Pontiac two-barrel applications, and was painted 60° gloss black. A heavy-duty air cleaner assembly (part number 6424574) was available at extra cost.

The CPCV system was again used for 1967. The two-barrel air cleaner used part number 6424572 for standard use and 6424575 with the heavy-duty option. Two assemblies were also used for the standard four-barrel engine (part number 6423210, and 6423280 for heavy-duty use). The chrome oil filler cap (part number 6410204) was still located on the LH chrome valve cover.

For California use, the AIR system was retained for 1967. However, only the oil filler cap and its attaching vent tube were carried over from the CPCV. The air cleaner assemblies were entirely different, as both a CPCV vent tube and an AIR hose eminated from the air cleaner.

Size	Application	Part Number
Two-barrel	Standard	6424573
Two-barrel	Heavy-duty	6424576
Four-barrel	Standard	6423211
Four-barrel	Heavy-duty	6423209

Air cleaner elements were not as varied. The standard forty-nine-state two-barrel used a polyurethane filter

(A154C) and a retainer screen (part number 5648477). The heavy-duty filter (A277C) was paper and polyurethane. The standard forty-nine-state four-barrel used either A274C or the polyurethane A98C. Heavy-duty versions used A279C. The same numbers were applicable for AIR or CPCV.

1968-70

The AIR system was eliminated in 1968 as the redesigned cylinder head combustion chamber was more efficient in burning the air and fuel mixture. The closed positive crankcase ventilation system (CPCV) was continued, along with the new controlled combustion system (CCS). The CPCV utilized a vent pipe (part number 9790092) which ran from the air cleaner to the RH valve cover. The air cleaner used a "snorkel" design, and was painted 60° gloss black; the lid was chromed.

The two-barrel engine, available in 1968 and 1969, used the same air cleaner (part number 6424820). The four-barrel air cleaner used a different part number for 1968 to 1970 (1968, 6424827; the 1969, 6484994; and 1970, 6485778).

A preheater assembly was used for all three years. A shroud was bolted above the LH intake manifold (part number 9791546), and used a tube or duct (part number 9791541 in 1968-69 and 478373 in 1970), which ran to the air cleaner snorkel. A vent tube breather element (part number 6484966, AC part number FB 59) was inside the air cleaner.

There were basically two air cleaner elements used from 1968 through 1970. For the two-barrel air cleaner, the standard element was AC 331C or part number 6483536, while heavy-duty use saw part number 6424138 or AC 277C. The four-barrel air cleaners used part number 6421746 or AC 212CW, and heavy-duty use called for part number 6424140 or AC 279C.

Detail of 1965-67 GTO four-barrel chromed air cleaner. Assembly had black base that was changed in 1967 to accommodate the Rochester Quadra-Jet carburetor.

Close-up of base of four-barrel air cleaner assembly for 1965-66. Note instructions for use of A98C element.

1964 GTO standard four-barrel air cleaner used a single-snorkel design. Both the base and the top of the air cleaner were chromed.

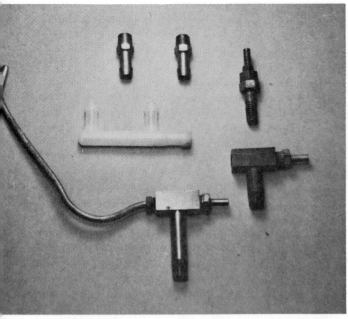

Detail of A98C used in 1965-67 standard four-barrel air cleaner. Note retainer used with polyurethane element.

1964-66 vacuum fittings top to bottom: 1965-66 vent-hose-to-manifold fitting (1966 fittings were pressed into manifold); right-rear-center carburetor mounting stud with vacuum for air-conditioning applications. Center: crankcase vent hose connector (left), 1966 center carburetor vacuum tee (right). Bottom: 1964-65 center carburetor vacuum tee with modulator line.

Close-up of AIR distributor vacuum advance showing two vacuum fittings—one for advancing and one for retarding the timing.

View of 1970 engine compartment showing standard engine dual-snorkel air cleaner assembly.

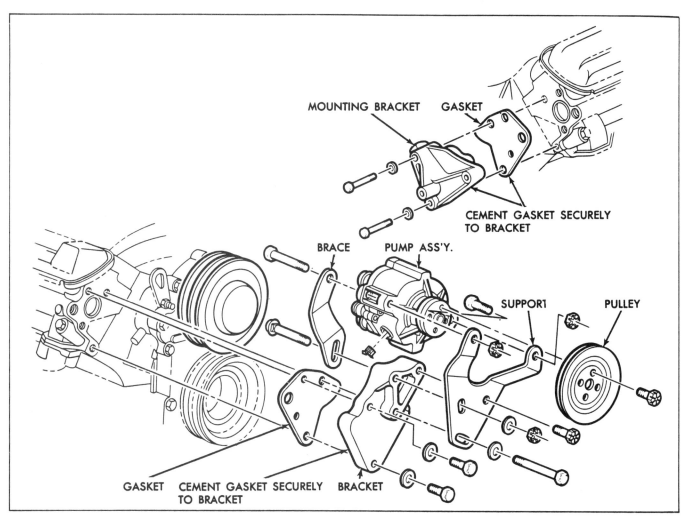

MOUNTING BRACKET   GASKET

CEMENT GASKET SECURELY
TO BRACKET

BRACE   PUMP ASS'Y.

SUPPORT   PULLEY

GASKET   CEMENT GASKET SECURELY
TO BRACKET   BRACKET

Detail of AIR pump mounting hardware. Pump was aluminum in
appearance, as were bracket and bolts. The pulley, brace and
support were 60° gloss black.

Underhood of 1967 GTO with AIR system. Note breather tube
from air cleaner to RH valve cover, and use of snorkel-type air
cleaner with chrome lid.

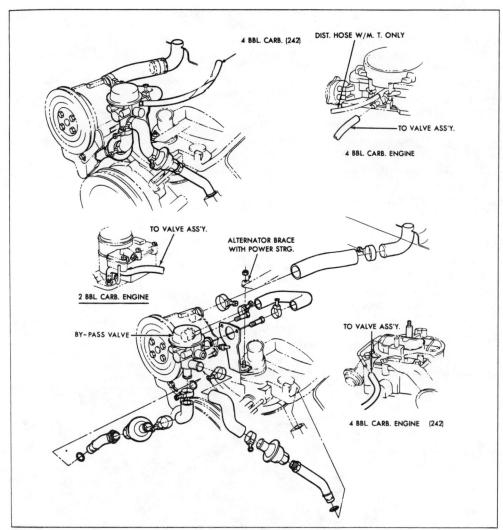

Detail of 1967 AIR mounting and hardware. Again for 1967, tower-type clamps were used on all hoses in AIR system.

STANDARD CARBURETION

1964-65

Standard carburetion for 1964 was a 500 cfm Carter AFB four-barrel. The identification tag was located on the rear of the air horn's right-center screw. The manual-transmission-equipped GTOs used part number AFB3647S; automatics used AFB3649S.

The 1965 GTO used the same cfm-rated Carter AFB. The tag was in the same location. The number for the manual transmission was AFB3895S; for automatics, AFB3898S. The Carter AFB was aluminum bodied, and so should be brought back to a natural-aluminum finish.

The fuel line for both years was routed the same: from the front-mounted fuel pump, along the driver's side of the water pump, and up to the left top of the carb. A fuel filter was housed within the carb inlet. The fuel line was finished in natural aluminum.

The throttle cable brackets for 1965 were mounted with two bolts. In 1964, both legs of the bracket were mounted to the intake bolts. For 1965, one leg was mounted from the intake to the head bolt, and the other to a boss in the intake. The bracket was painted the engine color. The 1964 bracket was number 9775928; the 1965,

9779968. Throttle linkage cables were different (1964, 9777042; 1965, 9779930).

1966-67

The 1966 GTO used a Carter AFB four-barrel carburetor for the standard 335 hp engine. Four different AFBs were used.

Transmission	49-State	AIR
Manual	AFB4033S	AFB4041S
Automatic	AFB4034S	AFB4030S

The fuel line was routed in the same manner as on the 1965 GTO. Note that the body of the AFB was finished in a dull aluminum, and the fuel filter element was part number 7013404.

The throttle linkage bracket (part number 9783285) was mounted in the same fashion as on the 1965. The throttle linkage cable (part number 9783230) was used for the standard engine. The bracket was painted engine-blue the cable was natural metal in all exposed areas and the insulator was black.

The two-barrel engine in 1967 used a Rochester 2GC design carburetor (part number 7027061 in forty-nine-state versions, replacement part number 7037162 in

AIR versions). This engine was only available with automatic transmission.

The standard 335 hp engine used the Rochester Quadra-Jet carburetor. Four different versions of the Quadra-Jet were available. Replacement numbers were stamped on the LH side of the float bowl.

Transmission	49-State	AIR
Manual	7027263	7037263
Automatic	7027262	7037262

The carburetor air horns and bodies were finished in a dull gold cadmium.

The throttle bracket (part number 9787163) was mounted in the same fashion as in earlier years, and the throttle linkage cable was part number 9788674. The fuel line ran from the fuel pump up the LH front of the block to the fuel filter (part number 5651119, AC-GF-414), which sat above the front of the intake manifold and ran to the front fuel inlet of the Quadra-Jet.

1968-70

The Rochester Quadra-Jet carburetor was used for 1968 through 1970 in standard engines. The Rochester 2GC two-barrel was used for the low-compression engine option. In 1968, the carburetor used for the two-barrel engine was part number 7028060. The last year for the two-barrel option was 1969, and two different part numbers were used (7029060 and 7029070). These engines were available only with Turbo Hydra-matic. The throttle linkage was the same for 1968-69 (part number 9791208). The throttle linkage bracket (part number 9792068) was also the same for 1968-69.

The standard carburetor for all three years was different for the transmission applications.

Year	Transmission	Part Number
1968	Manual	7028263
	Hydra-matic	7028268
1969	Manual	7029263
	Hydra-matic	7029268
1970	Manual	7040263
	Hydra-matic	7040264
1970 EES	Manual	7040563
	Hydra-matic	7040564

The identifying numbers for the Rochester carbs were located on the LH side of the float bowl. The carburetor air horns and bodies were finished in a dull zinc chromate.

The four-barrel throttle linkage bracket was the same for 1968 and 1969 (part number 9792069) and part number 479789 for 1970. The cable was the same for all three years (part number 9791207). The bracket was painted engine-blue.

Standard G.T.O. Engine, 325 H.P. w/4 bbl. carb.

Optional G.T.O. Engine, 348 H.P. w/Tri-Power

Detail of 1964 four-barrel engine. Note spark plug wire routing and clutch fan.

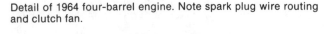

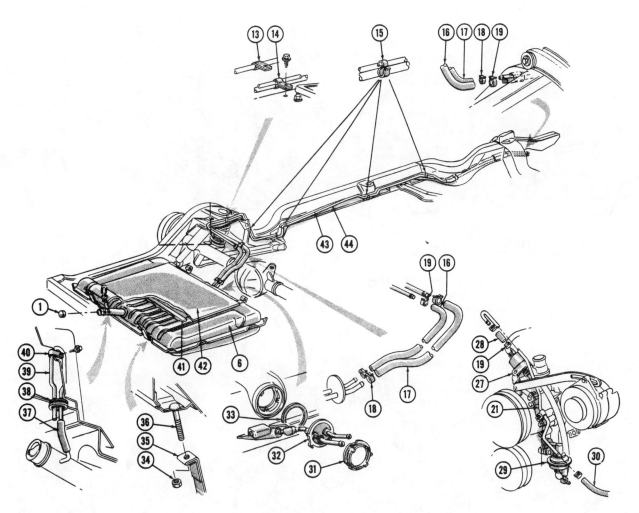

Key	Part Name	Group No.	Key	Part Name	Group No.
1 — CAP, Fuel Tank Filler		3.028	30 — HOSE, Vapor Return Pipe Connector		
6 — TANK, Fuel		3.001	(7 3/4" x 1/4" I.D.)		3.163
13 — CLIP, Fuel Pipe to Frame		N.S.	31 — CAM, Gauge to Tank		3.107
14 — CLIP, Return Pipe to Rear Spring Seat		3.162	32 — GAUGE, Fuel (Tank Unit)		3.107
15 — CLIP, Vapor Return Pipe to Fuel Pipe		3.162	33 — GASKET, Fuel Tank Fuel Gauge		3.112
16 — HOSE, Fuel Pipe to Fuel Pump (5/16" I.D.)		3.163	34 — NUT, Fuel Tank Supt. Strap to Body		3.023
17 — HOSE, Fuel Pipe to Return Pipe (1/4" I.D.)		3.163	35 — STRAP, Fuel Tank Support		3.022
18 — CLAMP, Vapor Return Hose		3.163	36 — BOLT, Fuel Tank Strap		3.023
19 — CLAMP, Fuel Hose		N.S.	37 — HOSE, Fuel Tank Filler Pipe Vent		
20 — HOSE, Vapor Pipe to Return Pipe			(3 3/4" x 1/4" I.D.)		3.163
(13 1/2" x 1/4" I.D.)		3.003	38 — GROMMET, Fuel Tank Vent Pipe		3.008
21 — PIPE, Vapor Div. to Return Pipe (1/4" I.D.)		8.964	39 — PIPE, Fuel Tank Vent		3.003
26 — FILTER & VAPOR SEPARATOR ASM., Fuel		3.890	40 — CLIP, Fuel Tank Vent Pipe to Body		3.004
27 — BRACKET, Vapor Div. Support		3.890	41 — BEAD, Fuel Tank to Underbody		N.S.
28 — HOSE, Vapor Div. to Return Pipe			42 — INSULATOR, Fuel Tank to Body		3.022
(1 1/2" x 1/4" I.D.)		3.163	43 — PIPE, Fuel Return (1/4" I.D.)		8.964
29 — FUEL PUMP, Package		3.900	44 — PIPE, Fuel Main (5/16" I.D.)		8.964

Overall detail of 1964-66 fuel system used with air-conditioned models. Note positioning of fuel filter and bracket (number 27), part number 9785328, used in four-barrel air-conditioned applications.

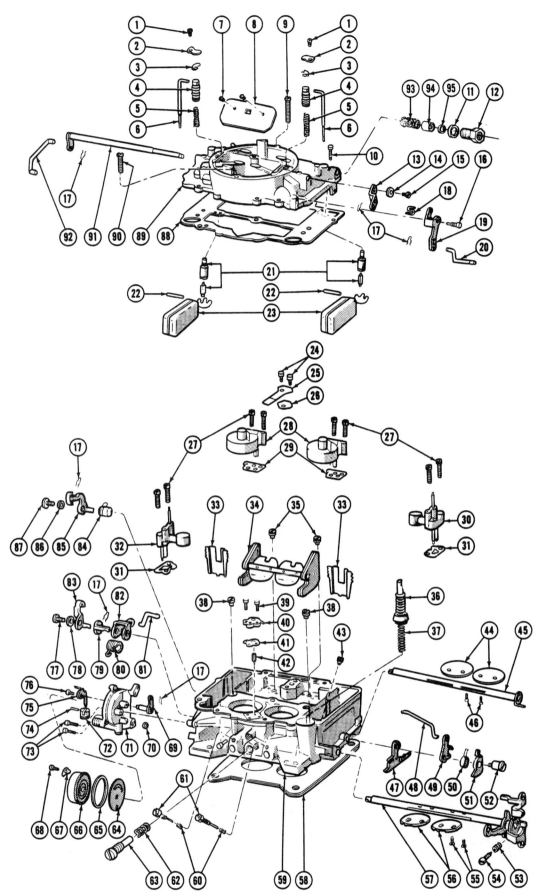

Exploded view and parts nomenclature of 1964-66 Carter AFB
four-barrel carburetor, used on all standard GTO engines.

Key	Part Name	Group No.
1 — SCREW & WASHER, Step-Up Piston Cover Plate		3.858
2 — PLATE, Step-Up Piston Cover		3.858
3 — SPRING, Step-Up Rod Retainer		3.810
4 — PISTON, Carb. Step-Up		3.858
5 — SPRING, Carb. Vacuum Piston	(▲)	3.859
6 — ROD, Carb. Step-Up	(▲)	3.806
7 — SCREW, Choke Valve (#3-48 x 7/32")		3.751
8 — VALVE, Carb. Choke		3.751
9 — SCREW ASM., Air Horn (#10-30 x 15/16")		3.730
10 — SCREW ASM., Air Horn		3.730
11 — GASKET, Strainer Nut	(★)(■)	3.740
12 — NUT, Fuel Inlet		3.740
13 — LEVER, Choke Shaft		3.752
14 — WASHER, Choke Shaft		3.752
15 — SCREW, Choke Shaft Lever Attaching (#6-32 x 5/16")		3.752
16 — SCREW, Pump Arm Attaching		3.845
17 — RETAINER SPRING, Pump Conn. Link		3.843
18 — LINK, Carb. Pump Connector		3.843
19 — ARM & COLLAR, Carb. Pump		3.845
20 — ROD, Throttle Connector		3.762
21 — NEEDLE & SEAT, Carb. Intake	(■)(▲)	3.814
22 — PIN, Carb. Float Lever		3.747
23 — FLOAT, Carburetor		3.745
24 — SCREW & WASHER, Thermostatic Valve Attaching		3.820
25 — VALVE, Thermostatic		3.820
26 — GASKET, Thermostatic Valve	(★)(■)	3.820
27 — SCREW, Venturi Attaching (#10-32 x 1")		3.786
28 — VENTURI ASM., Secondary - Pump Side & Choke Side		3.786
29 — GASKET, Venturi Cluster - Secondary	(★)(■)(▲)	3.790
30 — VENTURI ASM., Primary - Pump Side		3.786
31 — GASKET, Venturi Cluster - Primary	(★)(■)(▲)	3.790
32 — VENTURI ASM., Primary - Choke Side		3.786
33 — BAFFLE: Fuel Bowl		N.S.
34 — SHAFT, VALVE & WEIGHT ASM., Auxiliary Throttle		3.759
35 — JET, Secondary		3.792
36 — PLUNGER & ROD, Carb. Pump	(■)(▲)	3.838
37 — SPRING, Pump Return		3.841
38 — JET, Primary	(▲)	3.792
39 — SCREW & WASHER, Dust Cover		3.858
40 — JET & HOUSING, Carb. Pump		3.844
41 — GASKET, Pump Jet Housing	(★)(■)(▲)	3.844
42 — NEEDLE, Pump Discharge Check (1965)		3.832
BALL, Pump Discharge Check (1966)		3.826
43 — CHECK ASM., Pump Intake Ball		3.826
44 — VALVE, Carb. Throttle - Secondary		3.758
45 — SHAFT & LEVER, Carb. Throttle - Secondary		3.759
46 — SCREW, Throttle Valve & Lever - Secondary		3.761
47 — DOG, Secondary Throttle Shaft Lockout		3.762

Key	Part Name	Group No.
48 — ROD, Connector		3.768
49 — LEVER, Cam Trip		3.752
50 — SPRING, Fast Idle Arm		3.767
51 — CAM, Fast Idle		3.766
52 — SCREW, Cam Attaching		3.767
53 — SPRING, Idle Adjusting Screw		3.823
54 — SCREW, Fast Idle Adjusting		3.766
55 — SCREW, Throttle Valve & Lever - Primary		3.761
56 — VALVE, Carb. Throttle - Primary		3.758
57 — SHAFT & LEVER, Carb. Throttle Primary		3.759
58 — GASKET, Carb. to Manifold	(★)(■)(▲)	3.726
59 — BODY ASM., Carb. Throttle		N.S.
60 — SPRING, Idle Adjusting Screw		3.823
61 — SCREW, Idle Adjusting		3.822
62 — SPRING, Idle Air Screw		3.823
63 — SCREW, Idle Air Adjusting		3.822
64 — PLATE, Coil Housing Baffle		3.750
65 — GASKET, Coil Housing	(★)(■)(▲)	3.750
66 — HOUSING & COIL ASM., Carb. Thermostatic		3.750
67 — RETAINER, Housing Stat Cover		3.750
68 — SCREW, Coil Housing (#8-32 x 1/4")		3.750
69 — SHAFT & LEVER, Choke Piston Housing		3.752
70 — GASKET, Piston Housing	(★)(■)	3.750
71 — HOUSING ASM., Choke		3.750
72 — PISTON, Carb. Choke		3.752
73 — SCREW, Choke Housing		3.750
74 — PIN, Choke Piston		3.752
75 — LEVER & LINK ASM., Choke		3.752
76 — SCREW, Choke Piston Lever (#6-32 x 5/16")		3.752
77 — SCREW, Throttle Shaft Arm		3.762
78 — WASHER, Throttle Shaft Arm Primary		3.762
79 — DOG, Primary Throttle Shaft		3.762
80 — SPRING, Throttle Flex		3.763
81 — ROD, Throttle Operating		3.762
82 — ARM, Primary Throttle Shaft - Inner		3.762
83 — ARM, Primary Throttle Shaft - Outer		3.762
84 — SPRING, Secondary Return		3.763
85 — LEVER, Secondary Shaft Operating		3.762
86 — WASHER, Throttle Shaft Arm Secondary		3.762
87 — SCREW, Throttle Shaft Arm		3.762
88 — GASKET, Air Horn	(★)(■)(▲)	3.738
89 — AIR HORN, Carburetor		3.730
90 — SCREW ASM., Air Horn		3.730
91 — SHAFT & LEVER, Carb. Choke		3.752
92 — ROD, Choke		3.752
93 — SPRING, Fuel Inlet Filter		3.740
94 — STRAINER, Fuel Inlet		3.740
95 — GASKET, Fuel Inlet Strainer		3.740

(▲) NOTE: INCLUDED IN REPAIR KIT-3.725
(■) NOTE: INCLUDED IN KLEANOUT KIT-3.725
(★) NOTE: INCLUDED IN GASKET PACKAGE-3.724

Location of identification tag on Carter AFB carburetors.

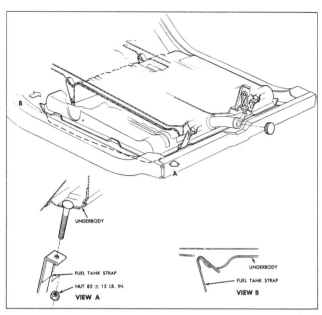

Correct positioning and retainment of fuel tank for 1964-67. GTO in 1967 did not use a bolt to hold front of strap to the underbody. The fuel tank straps (part number 396711) were cadmium plated.

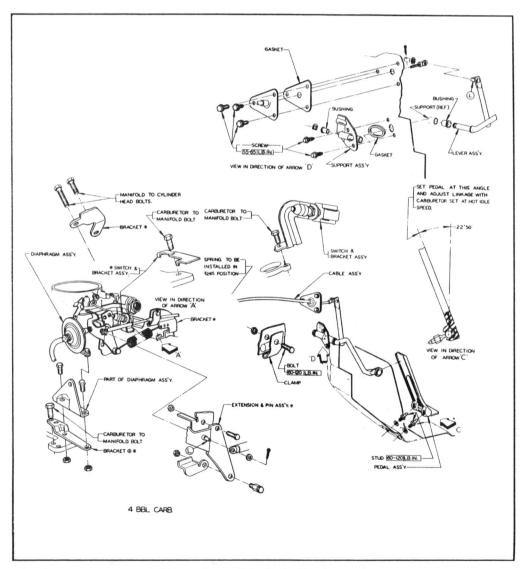

Installation and alignment of 1964 accelerator linkage, showing pedal, cable and throttle components.

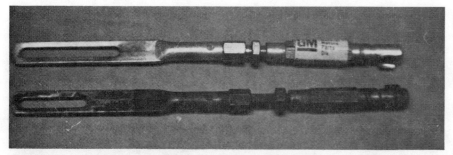

Detail of throttle control rods showing correct original short slot design used on 1966 Tri-Power (bottom) and standard 1965 long-slot rod (top). Long-slot (part number 9777328) was used for 1966 replacement, which required replacement of carb lever extension (part number 9777290).

Close-up of 1966 Carter AFB carburetor, AFB4034S, used on Baltimore 242176B105833. Fuel line pipe into carburetor was shorter than pictured in factory drawing.

Close-up detail of 1966 four-way fuel fitting and line routing. Cap (part number 9781338) was used on front carb bleed-off tube for 1965-66 manual transmission applications only.

Four-barrel intake and carb for 1966. Casting date indicated manifold was cast March 14, 1966. This unit has "ridges" along top of second runner. Not all 1966 intakes used such ridges.

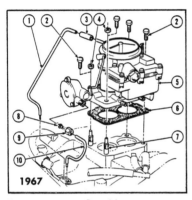

1967

Key	Part Name	Group No.
1 —	TUBE, Carb. to Manifold Choke Heat . . .	3.603
2 —	BOLT, Carb. to Manifold (5/16"-18 x 1")	8.900
3 —	HOSE, Carb. to Choke Heat Tube (7/32" x 1 1/4")	3.765
4 —	NUT, Carb. to Manifold Stud (5/16"-24)	8.916
5 —	CARBURETOR ASM., Rochester-2-Bbl. . . .	3.725
6 —	GASKET, Carb. to Manifold	3.726
7 —	STUD, Carb. to Manifold (5/16"-18 x 5/16"-24 x 1 13/16") . . .	3.288
8 —	SLEEVE, Heat Tube to Choke (1/4") . . .	8.963
9 —	NUT, Heat Tube to Choke (1/4")	8.963
10 —	TUBE, Manifold to Carb. Choke Heat . . .	3.603

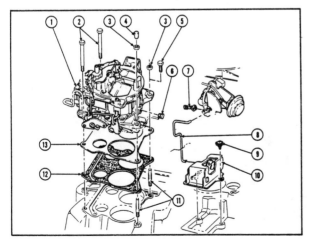

Routing and nomenclature for 1967 two-barrel and four-barrel carburetor and choke parts.

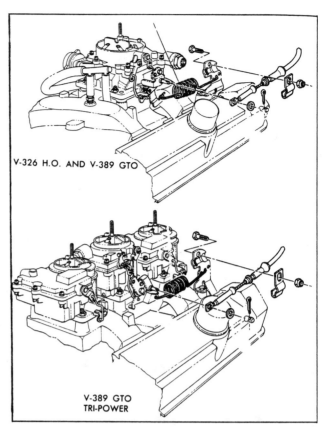

V-326 H.O. AND V-389 GTO

V-389 GTO
TRI-POWER

Instructions for attaching throttle linkage cable for 1966 GTO. Throttle return spring (part number 9789460) was painted yellow by factory.

Key	Part Name	Group No.
1 —	CARBURETOR ASM., Rochester - 4-Bbl. .	3.725
2 —	BOLT, Carb. to Manifold (5/16"-18 x 3 5/8").	N.S.
3 —	NUT, Carb. to Manifold (5/16"-24) . . .	8.916
4 —	CAP, Vacuum Stud	3.764
5 —	BOLT, Carb. to Manifold (5/16"-18 x 1")	8.900
6 —	PLUG, Carb. Vacuum Hole (1/8")	3.278
7 —	CLIP, Choke Rod to Carb.	3.752
8 —	ROD, Choke Thermo Lever to Carb. Choke Lever	3.752
9 —	SCREW ASM., Choke to Manifold (1/4"-20 x 5/16")	N.S.
10 —	THERMOSTAT ASM., Automatic Choke . .	3.750
11 —	STUD, Carb. to Manifold (5/16"-18 x 2 1/8"-Hollow).	3.288
12 —	GASKET, Carb. to Manifold	3.726
13 —	BAFFLE, Carb. to Manifold Gasket (1967)	3.726

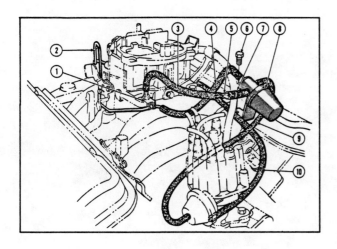

MANUAL TRANS. WITH AIR INJECTION

Key	Part Name	Group No.
1	CLIP, Dist. Vacuum Pipe to Carb.	N.S.
2	PIPE, Carb. to Dist. Vacuum (3/16" I. D. – Steel)	8.964
3	HOSE, Stud to Tee (5/32" x 8")	2.420
4	HOSE, Pipe to Valve (5/32" x 9")	2.420
5	TEE, Carb. to Dist. Vac. Pipe – 3 Way (1/4" x 3/16" x 3/16") (Pontiac)	3.278
	REDUCER, Stud Vac. Hose (1/4" to 3/16") (Tempest)	3.765
6	BOLT, Valve to Mfld. (5/16" – 18 x 5/8")	8.900
7	HOSE, Valve to Tee (7/32" x 1-1/4") . . .	2.420
8	VALVE ASM., Dist. Vacuum Advance . . .	2.410
9	HOSE, Dist. to Valve (5/32" x 18")	2.420
10	HOSE, Carb. to Dist. (5/32" x 18")	2.420

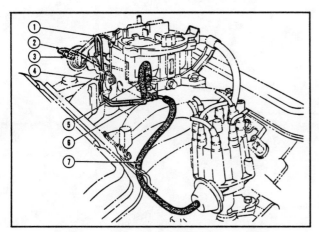

MANUAL TRANS. EXC. AIR INJECTION

Key	Part Name	Group No.
1	PIPE, Carb. to Dist. Vacuum (3/16" I.D. – Steel)	8.964
2	PIPE, Diaphragm Asm. Vacuum (3/16" – I.D. – Steel)	8.964
3	HOSE, Diaphragm Pipe to Diaphragm (5/32" x 1-3/8")	3.765
4	CLIP, Diaphragm Pipe to Dist. Vac. Pipe .	2.420
5	HOSE, Vac. Pipe to Carb. Stud (5/32" x 6-13/32")	3.765
6	CLIP, Dist. Vacuum Pipe to Carb.	N.S.
7	HOSE, Carb. to Dist. (5/32" x 14-3/4") . .	2.420

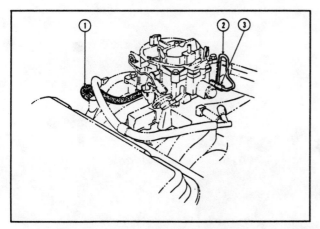

Factory drawings of 1967 GTO four-barrel carburetor and distributor vacuum hose routing. Dual vacuum lines on AIR system were used for distributor vacuum advance.

REAR VIEW

Key	Part Name	Group No.
1	HOSE, Carb. to Dist. (5/32" x 18")	2.420
2	PIPE, Carb. to Dist. Vacuum (3/16" I/D. – Steel)	8.964
3	HOSE, Diaphragm to Vac. Pipe (5/32" x 1-3/8")	3.765

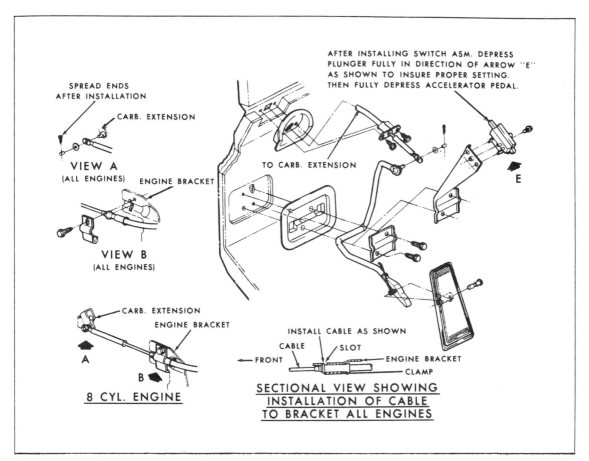

SPREAD ENDS
AFTER INSTALLATION

CARB. EXTENSION

VIEW A
(ALL ENGINES)

ENGINE BRACKET

VIEW B
(ALL ENGINES)

CARB. EXTENSION
ENGINE BRACKET

A

B

8 CYL. ENGINE

AFTER INSTALLING SWITCH ASM. DEPRESS
PLUNGER FULLY IN DIRECTION OF ARROW "E"
AS SHOWN TO INSURE PROPER SETTING.
THEN FULLY DEPRESS ACCELERATOR PEDAL.

TO CARB. EXTENSION

E

INSTALL CABLE AS SHOWN
CABLE
SLOT
FRONT
ENGINE BRACKET
CLAMP

**SECTIONAL VIEW SHOWING
INSTALLATION OF CABLE
TO BRACKET ALL ENGINES**

Exploded assembly instructions for 1968-70 accelerator pedal
and linkage. Note alignment of cable to bracket.

Detail of 1968-69 throttle linkage cable bracket (part number
9792069). Bracket was painted engine-blue.

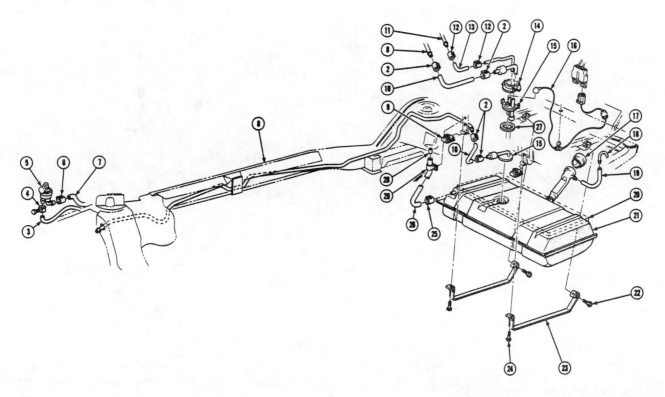

Key	Part Name	Group No.
3 — HOSE, Pump to Return Pipe (1/4" I.D. x 13") . . .		3.163
4 — CLAMP, Vacuum Hose		1.166
5 — FUEL PUMP, Package - 8 Cyl.		3.900
6 — CLAMP, Fuel Hose (5/8" - Green)		3.163
7 — HOSE, Pump to Fuel Pipe (11/32" I.D. x 10") . . .		3.163
8 — PIPE ASM., Fuel Main (5/16" I.D.)		8.964
9 — NUT, Support Strap to Saddle (3/8"-16)		3.023
10 — HOSE, Tank to Fuel Pipe (5/16" I.D. x 4 1/2")		3.163
11 — PIPE, Fuel Return (1/4" I.D.)		8.964
12 — CLAMP, Vapor Return Hose (1/2" - Red)		3.163
13 — HOSE, Tank to Return Pipe (1/4" x 4 1/2")		3.163
14 — CAM, Fuel Gauge to Tank		3.107
15 — GAUGE ASM., Fuel (Tank Unit)		3.107

Key	Part Name	Group No.
16 — WIRE ASM., Fuel Gauge		2.480
17 — CAP, Filler Pipe Filler		3.028
18 — PIPE, Filler Pipe Vent		3.003
19 — HOSE, Fuel Tank Vent (1/4" I.D. x 7 3/4")		3.003
20 — INSULATOR, Fuel Tank to Body		3.022
21 — TANK ASM., Fuel		3.001
22 — SCREW, Strap to Rear Cross Bar (1/4"-14 x 1") . . .		3.023
23 — STRAP, Fuel Tank Support		3.022
24 — BOLT, Support to Saddle (3/8"-16 x 3 3/4") . . .		3.023
25 — CLAMP, Fuel Tank Vent Hose (3/8")		3.003
26 — HOSE, Fuel Tank Vent (1/2" I.D. x 9 1/2")		N.S.
27 — GASKET, Fuel Tank Fuel Gauge		3.112
28 — RESTRICTOR, Fuel Tank Vent Hose		3.003

Exploded view of 1968 GTO fuel system, with parts nomenclature.

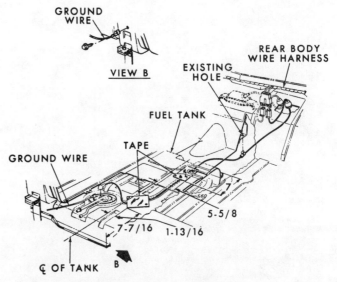

Diagram for routing fuel gauge wiring along floor pan to fuel tank in 1969 GTO.

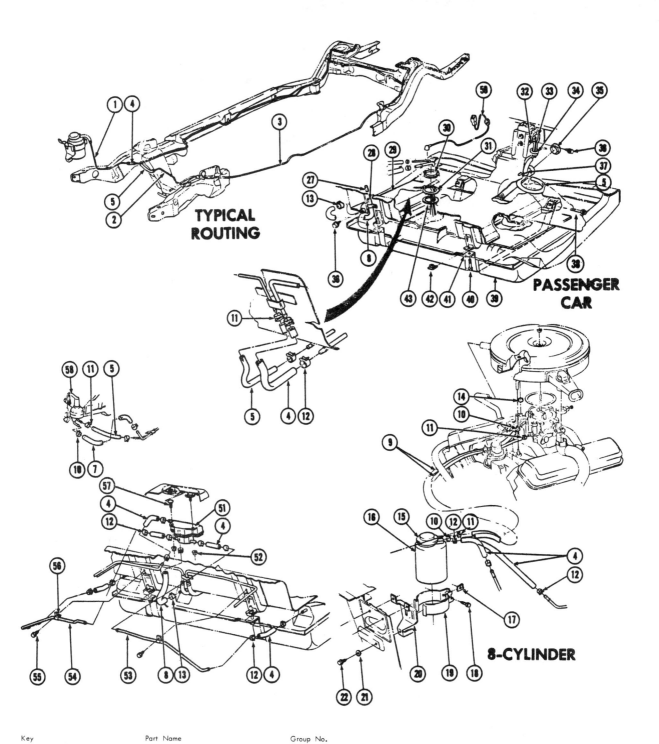

Key	Part Name	Group No.
1 — PIPE, Canister (5/16" O.D.)		8.964
2 — PIPE, Vapor (1/4" O.D.)		8.964
3 — PIPE, Fuel (5/16" O.D.)		8.964
4 — HOSE, Fuel or Vapor (5/16")		3.130
5 — HOSE, Fuel or Vapor (1/4")		3.130
7 — HOSE, Fuel or Vapor (3/8")		3.130
8 — HOSE, Fuel or Vapor (1/2")		8.962
9 — HOSE ASM., Carb. to Canister		3.130
10 — CLAMP, Hose (5/16")		1.166
11 — CLAMP, Hose (1/2")		1.166
12 — CLAMP, Fuel Hose (5/16" O.D.)		1.166
14 — GASKET, Air Cleaner to Carb. Vent Switch Valve		3.403
15 — CANISTER, Vapor		3.130
16 — ELEMENT, Vapor Canister Filter		3.130
17 — NUT, Mounting Strap (1/4"-14 "U")		8.921
18 — SCREW, Mounting Strap (1/4"-14 x 1 1/4")		N.S.
19 — STRAP, Canister Mounting		3.130
20 — BRACKET, Canister Mounting		3.130
21 — WASHER, Bracket to Baffle (9/32" I.D x 3/4" O.D.)		8.929
22 — SCREW, Bracket to Baffle (1/4"-14 x 3/4")		1.269
27 — RESTRICTOR, Fuel Tank Vent		3.003
28 — CLIP, Vent Hose		3.003
29 — INSULATOR, Fuel Tank to Body		3.022
30 — CAM, Fuel Tank Gauge to Tank		3.107
31 — GAUGE, Fuel Tank		3.107
32 — CLIP, Fuel Tank Vent Pipe to Body		3.003
33 — PIPE, Fuel Tank Vent		3.003
34 — GROMMET, Fuel Tank Vent Pipe (1 3/4" O.D.)		3.008
35 — CAP, Fuel Tank Filler		3.028
36 — SCREW, Clip to Underbody (#10-16 x 1/2")		8.977
37 — CLIP, Hose to Panel (2 1/4" Plastic)		2.559
38 — SCREW, Fuel Tank Strap to Rr. Cross Bars (1/4"-14 x 1")		3.023
39 — TANK, Fuel		3.001
40 — BOLT, Fuel Tank Strap to Frt. Saddle (3/8"-16 x 3 3/4")		3.023
41 — STRAP, Fuel Tank		3.022
42 — NUT, Fuel Tank Supt. Strap to Saddle (3/8"-16)		3.023
43 — GASKET, Fuel Tank Outlet Fittings to Tank		3.112
51 — SEPARATOR, Liquid		3.120
52 — NUT, Plate to Separator		N.S.
53 — PIPE, Liquid Separator to Fuel Tank - L.H.		3.120
54 — PIPE, Liquid Separator to Fuel Tank - R.H.		3.120
55 — SCREW, Clip to Panel (5/16"-12 x 5/8")		8.977
56 — CLIP, Liquid Separator		N.S.
57 — BOLT, Seperator to Underbody		3.130
58 — PUMP, Fuel		3.900

Routing of fuel and evaporative emissions system (EES) for 1970, with parts nomenclature.

OPTIONAL CARBURETION, TRI-POWER

1964-65

The three two-barrel Rochester carburetors used in 1964 had chromed air cleaner lids, with foam elements using wire mesh screens and wire screen retainers, and black bases. The foam elements were AC number A193C, and were used in both 1964 and 1965. Replacement paper filters were introduced in 1968, superseding the foams and designated A220C.

Pontiac Service News Flash number 65-25, dated 10-12-64, reported a change in the service specifications for the 1965 Rochester carbs as follows: Float level for the front and rear Tri-Power should be 21/32 inch, plus or minus 1/16 inch, the center float level should be 11/16 inch, plus or minus 1/16 inch. Where equipped with an automatic transmission, the center vacuum switch should be 1 3/32 inches, plus or minus 1/64 inch.

Effective with GTOs built after January 1, 1964, for sale in California, Tri-Powers also came equipped with a closed PCV system. The outer air cleaner bases used a pipe that went through the wall of the throat and then vented to the center carb base, which had an element and a black assembly routed by way of a vent tube to the left valve cover. The closed system used the same foam air cleaner as the open system (A193C).

Pontiac Service News Flash number 64-14, dated 10-17-63, announced a new accelerating pump outer lever having two pump rod holes for the 1964 Tri-Power models. The rod should be located in the inside hole for normal operation. For hot weather or high altitude the pump rod may be relocated to the outside hole without readjusting the pump setting. This change was identified on the carburetors by the tag letter A. A pump modification kit (7028758, code F) was made available for previous installations.

Rochester two-barrel carburetors were used in both 1964 and 1965. The identification tag was located on the left-front air horn screw. The correct carbs for the respective years are listed below.

Year	Application	Part Number
1964	Manual/automatic (front)	7024178
	Manual (center)	7024175
	Automatic (center)	7024173
	Manual/automatic (rear)	7024179
1965	Manual/automatic (front)	7024178
	Manual (center)	7025175
	Automatic (center)	7025177
	Manual/automatic (rear)	7024179

Different throttle cable brackets were used in 1964 for automatic (9776283) and manual (9777062) transmission GTOs. Brackets were painted engine-blue in 1964 and 1965. The bracket for 1965 (part number 9779969) was the same regardless of transmission. The throttle cable was part number 9777043 in 1964. Manual transmission GTOs in 1965 utilized part number 9781587; automatics used 9779930.

The fuel line was run from the fuel pump along the water pump, crossing to the right side of the block and up to the fuel block on the front carburetor. The choke tubes were steel and were not the same for both years. The choke housing was natural, the choke face plate was 60° gloss black.

1966-67

The Tri-Power for 1966 (RPO 802) was revised significantly from 1965. The center carburetor, a Rochester 2GC (as were all other Tri-Power carbs), was enlarged.

Transmission	Part Number		
	Front	Center	Rear
Manual	7025178	7026075	7025179
Automatic	7024178	7026074	7024179
Manual with AIR		7036175	

1964-66 Tri-Power air cleaner components. Air cleaner base at lower LH corner had vent tube used for California CCS.

In the forty-nine-state version of the Tri-Power, the air cleaner assemblies (three required) all carried the same part number (6424292). Both the CPCV and AIR systems used part number 6424294 for the center air cleaner assembly and 6424293 for the front and rear assemblies. (Refer to 1965 CPCV system for detail.) The bases were gloss black, the top lids and wing nuts were chrome.

The A193C foam element (superseded by the A220C replacement introduced in 1968) was used in all applications, and a screen and flame arrester (part number 6420618 and AIR, 6424267) was installed in the air cleaner assembly for the forty-nine-state version.

The CPCV vent hose (part number 9784820) ran from the center carburetor base to the oil filler cap (part number 6421919), which was chromed and located on the chrome LH valve cover.

The 1966 California AIR-equipped Tri-Powers used a system unique to that year alone. While the CPCV was again retained in conjunction with the AIR, a separate air cleaner for the injector pump was utilized (part number 6422732). The filter element was A224C, and an AIR decal (part number 9785012) identified the system.

The throttle linkage bracket (part number 9783286) was mounted on the rear LH intake-to-head bolt and a boss on the intake. The bracket was painted engine-blue. Two throttle linkage cables were used. The automatic-transmission-equipped GTO used part number 9783230, while manual transmissions used 9783231.

Detail of reproduction A193C foam air cleaner element used for 1964-66 Tri-Power.

Comparison of original screen used with A193C foam element (right) with current reproduction being sold.

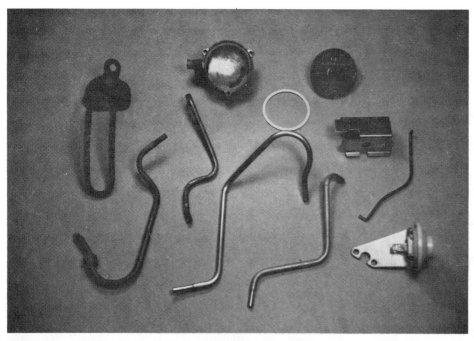

Choke components used for 1964-66 Tri-Power: three components at left were for 1964 application; tubes at center, for 1965 usage; housing and cover at top used for 1964-65; and coil, rod and choke pull-off at right used for 1966.

Close-up detail of correct Weatherhead four-way fuel fitting used with 1964-66 Tri-Power. Note squared-off shoulders, length of

thread and Weatherhead logos stamped on back of block running from top to bottom.

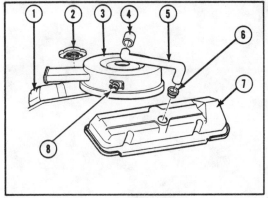

Key	Part Name	Group No.
1 — COVER, Valve Rocker Arm – R.H.		0.386
2 — CAP, Oil Filler		1.758
3 — CLEANER & SILENCER, Carburetor Air		3.402
4 — HOSE, Vent to Air Cleaner		1.762
5 — PIPE, Crankcase Ventilator		1.762
6 — GROMMET, Vent Pipe to Rocker Arm Cover		1.745
7 — COVER, Valve Rocker Arm – L.H.		0.386
8 — ELEMENT ASM., Air Filter (In Air Cleaner)		1.745

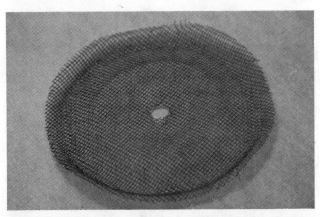

Wire-mesh screen was used as a flame arrester (part number 6424267) in 1965-66 Tri-Power, and was located in center of the A193C foam element screen.

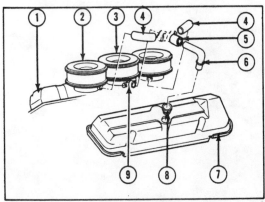

Key	Part Name	Group No.
1 — COVER, Valve Rocker Arm – R.H.		0.386
2 — CLEANER & SILENCER, Carburetor Air – Front & Rear		3.402
3 — CLEANER & SILENCER, Carburetor Air – Center		3.402
4 — HOSE, Center to End Air Cleaner		1.762
5 — HOSE, Vent to Center Air Cleaner		1.762
6 — PIPE, Crankcase Ventilator		1.762
7 — COVER, Valve Rocker Arm – L.H.		0.386
8 — GROMMET, Vent Pipe to Rocker Arm Cover		1.745
9 — ELEMENT ASM., Air Filter (In Air Cleaner)		1.745

California AIR-equipped GTOs used a positive closed crankcase system. The 1964 systems for both four-barrel and Tri-Power applications are shown.

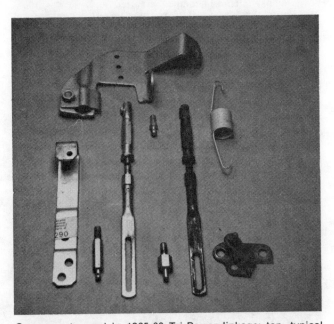

Components used in 1965-66 Tri-Power linkage: top, typical throttle mounting bracket; from left to right, 1965 extension lever, 1965 throttle cable stud, 1965 long slot (1966 replacement) throttle control rod; center top, control rod rear mounting stud; center bottom, 1965-66 control rod front stud; bottom left, 1966 original short slot throttle control rod; top right, accelerator return spring (painted yellow); and bottom right, non-serviced 1966 accelerator cable mounting bracket.

Comparison of Rochester two-barrel carburetors. Left: 1964-65 Pontiac Tri-Power. Note fuel inlet design. Center: 1966 Pontiac Tri-Power center carb. Note enlarged inlet design. Right: average 1956-67 Chevrolet two-barrel carburetor. Novice restorers can be fooled by not paying attention to differences in air-horn design between Pontiac and Chevrolet; Tri-Power center carbs had fuel inlet facing forward, and outer carbs had inlet facing toward RH side, without provision for enlarged fuel filter nut.

Vacuum linkage control components used for Tri-Power, 1964-66: carburetor actuator switch (top) used for all three years; front carburetor vacuum source fitting (center left); manifold block-off plate (center right); front cover (bottom left) used for thermostatic vacuum switch (bottom center) with gasket (bottom right).

View of complete 1965 Tri-Power intake with carburetors and mechanical linkage used with stick-shift models. Note installation of linkage, especially throttle control rod.

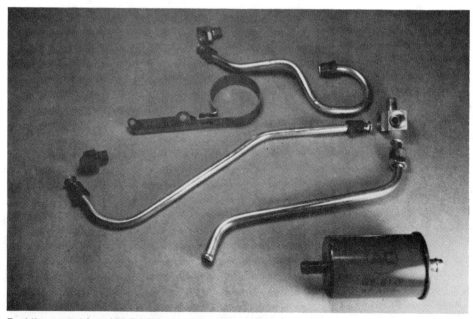

Fuel lines used for 1965 Tri-Power, with carburetor fitting, fuel block and filter. Fuel filter bracket at top was used for 1966 only. Fuel lines were made from aluminum tubing.

RH view of 1965 Tri-Power GTO engine. Note length of dipstick
tube used for 1964-65. Also note shape of front and rear actuating
lever on end carbs—1964 levers had a straighter back area.

1966 Tri-Power intake manifold, illustrating intake date casting
number. Number reads C246: Intake was cast March 24, 1966.
Number was found in front of rear throttle bore; carburetor must
be removed from intake for it to be seen.

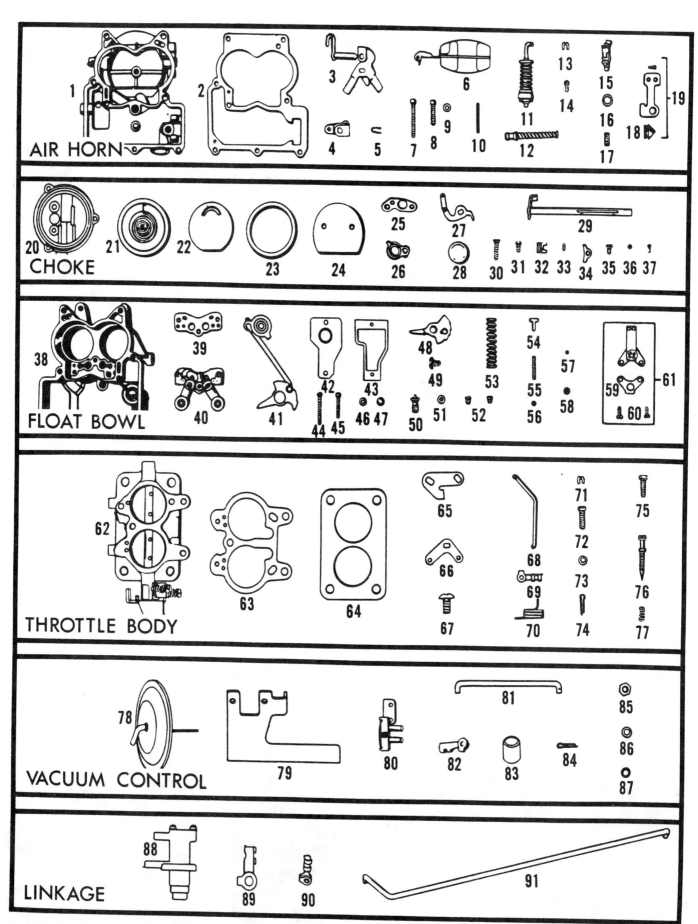

AIR HORN

1 2 3 4 5 6 7 8 9 10 11 12 13 14 15 16 17 18 19

CHOKE

20 21 22 23 24 25 26 27 28 29 30 31 32 33 34 35 36 37

FLOAT BOWL

38 39 40 41 42 43 44 45 46 47 48 49 50 51 52 53 54 55 56 57 58 59 60 61

THROTTLE BODY

62 63 64 65 66 67 68 69 70 71 72 73 74 75 76 77

VACUUM CONTROL

78 79 80 81 82 83 84 85 86 87

LINKAGE

88 89 90 91

Individual components used for 1964-66 Tri-Power. There were a few variations from stock, as illustrated. Bowl vent (number 19) is used here on center carb; hot idle compensator (numbers 42-47 and 56-60) were used on most center carbs. Return spring (number 70) was used on front and rear carbs only. Number 81 is incorrectly illustrated, as is number 91 front. Rear carb link is configured wrong for GTO application.

Key	Part Name	Group No.
1 — AIR HORN, Carburetor		3.730
2 — GASKET, Air Horn to Bowl .(●)(★)(▲)		3.738
3 — SHAFT & LEVER ASM., Pump Operating		3.842
4 — LEVER, Pump Inside		3.842
5 — RETAINER, Pump Lever (3/16") .(▲)		3.842
6 — FLOAT, Carburetor		3.745
7 — SCREW, Air Horn-Long		3.730
8 — SCREW, Air Horn-Short		3.730
9 — LOCKWASHER, Air Horn Screw (#10)		3.730
10 — PIN, Float Lever		3.747
11 — PLUNGER & ROD, Pump .(★)(▲)		3.838
12 — PISTON, Power		3.858
13 — RETAINER, Pump Plunger .(★)(▲)		N.S.
14 — SCREW, Pump Lever		N.S.
15 — NEEDLE & SEAT, Intake .(★)(▲)		3.814
16 — GASKET, Needle Seat .(●)(▲)		3.832
17 — STRAINER, Needle Seat .(▲)		3.740
18 — VALVE, Idle Vent		3.852
19 — VALVE KIT, Idle Vent		3.852
20 — HOUSING ASM., Choke		3.750
21 — COVER & COIL, Thermostatic		3.750
22 — PLATE, Coil Housing Baffle		3.750
23 — GASKET, Choke Cover .(★)(▲)		3.750
24 — VALVE, Choke		3.751
25 — GASKET, Choke Housing .(★)(▲)		3.750
26 — LEVER, LINK & CAM ASM., Choke		3.752
27 — LEVER & LINK ASM., Choke Piston-Replace w/Item #41		3.752
28 — PLUG, Choke Hsg. Expansion (5/8" dia.)		3.750
29 — SHAFT & LEVER, Choke		3.752
30 — SCREW, Choke Housing (#8-32 x 13/16")		3.750
31 — SCREW, Choke Lever (#6-32 x 5/16")		3.752
32 — PISTON, Choke		3.752
33 — PIN, Choke Piston		3.752
34 — RETAINER, Choke Cover		3.750
35 — SCREW, Choke Cover		3.750
36 — PLUG, Choke		N.S.
37 — SCREW, Choke Valve Attaching (#6-32 x 9/32")		3.751
38 — BOWL ASM., Carb Float		3.734
39 — GASKET, Venturi Cluster .(●)(★)(▲)		3.790
40 — VENTURI, ASM., Carburetor		3.786
41 — LEVER, LINK & CAM ASM., Choke		3.752
42 — COVER ASM., Idle Compensator		3.820
43 — GASKET, Compensator Cover to Bowl .(★)(▲)		3.820
44 — SCREW, Venturi Cluster (#8-32 x 1-3/16")		3.786
45 — SCREW, Venturi Cluster (#8-32 x 15/16")		3.786
46 — GASKET, Venturi Cluster Center Screw .(●)(★)		3.786
47 — LOCKWASHER, Venturi Cluster Screw (#8)		3.786
48 — CAM, Fast Idle-Replace w/Item #41		N.S.
49 — SCREW, Cam Attaching		3.767
50 — VALVE, Power .(▲)		3.858
51 — GASKET, Power Valve .(★)(▲)		3.858
52 — JET, Metering		3.792
53 — SPRING, Pump Return .(▲)		3.841
54 — GUIDE, Pump Discharge Spring .(▲)		3.825
55 — SPRING, Pump Discharge .(▲)		3.825
56 — BALL, Pump Discharge .(▲)		3.825
57 — BALL, Pump Check .(▲)		3.826
58 — SCREEN, Pump Inlet .(▲)		3.841
59 — GASKET, Idle Compensator .(★)(▲)		3.820
60 — SCREW, Idle Compensator		3.820
61 — KIT, Idle Compensator		3.820
62 — BODY ASM., Throttle		3.729
63 — GASKET, Throttle Body to Float Bowl .(●)(★)(▲)		3.735
64 — GASKET, Carburetor to Manifold .(●)(★)(▲)		3.726
65 — LEVER, Rear Carb. Actuating		3.762
66 — LEVER, Front Carb. Actuating		3.762
67 — SCREW, Actuating Lever Ret. (#8-32 x 5/16")		3.762
68 — ROD, Pump Lever Actuating		3.843
69 — CLIP, Pump Rod .(▲)		3.838
70 — SPRING, Throttle Return		3.763
71 — CLIP, Pump Rod .(★)(▲)		3.838
72 — SCREW, Throttle Body to Float Bowl (#12-28 x 13/16")		3.741
73 — LOCKWASHER, Throttle Body Screw (#12)		3.741
74 — COTTER PIN, Pump Rod (3/64" x 5/16") .(▲)		8.938
75 — SCREW, Idle Adjusting (#10-32 x 1")		3.766
76 — SCREW, Idle Air Adjusting .(▲)		3.822
77 — SPRING, Idle Adjusting Needle		3.823
78 — CONTROL ASM., Front Carb. Vacuum		3.764
79 — BRACKET, Carb. Vacuum Control		3.765
80 — SWITCH, Carb. Vacuum		3.764
81 — LINK, Vacuum Control Actuating		3.765
82 — CLIP, Link Retaining .(▲)		N.S.
83 — SPACER, Vacuum Control Bracket		3.765
84 — COTTER PIN, Link Retaining (3/64" x 5/16")		8.938
85 — NUT, Control Bracket Attaching (#10-32)		8.915
86 — LOCKWASHER, Control Bracket Attaching (#10)		8.931
87 — WASHER, Vacuum Actuating Link		3.762
88 — CONTROL ASM., Thermostatic Vacuum		3.764
89 — CLIP, Carb. Rod to Front Carb.		3.425
90 — CLIP, Carb. Rod to Rear Carb.		3.425
91 — LINK, Front Carb. to Rear Carb.		3.762

(▲) NOTE: INCLUDED IN MAJOR REPAIR KIT-3.725
(★) NOTE: INCLUDED IN MINOR REPAIR KIT-3.725
(●) NOTE: INCLUDED IN GASKET PACKAGE-3.724

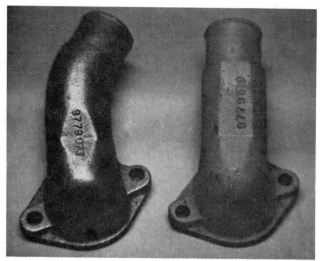

Comparison of 1966 (left) and 1965 Tri-Power intake manifold outlets. Note part number cast into outlets, which were painted engine-blue.

Passenger-side view of 1966 mechanical linkage Tri-Power assembly, showing correct fuel lines and choke assembly.

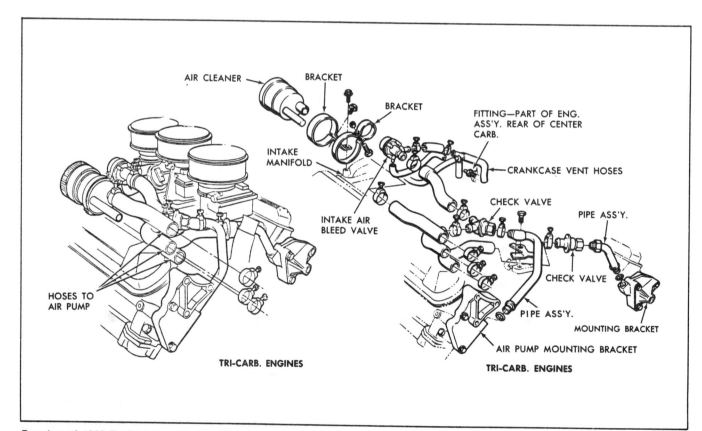

Drawing of 1966 Tri-Power used with Air Injector Reactance (AIR) system. Note separate air cleaner assembly for air pump. Tower-type hose clamps were used for AIR hoses.

Profile of 1966 Tri-Power setup. Note location of fuel filter bracket and inlet line.

QUADRA POWER (HO)

1967-68

The HO engine (RPO 802) was a new option for the GTO in 1967. The forty-nine-state-version air cleaner was part number 6424590. This number also applied to the 1967 Ram Air.

For the CPCV and AIR systems, the HO came equipped with the standard carburetor's heavy-duty air cleaner (part number 6423280 CCS and 6423209 AIR). The same vent hose and oil filler cap were used as in the standard CCS or the AIR system.

The forty-nine-state air cleaner for the HO was part number A212CWX. For CPCV or AIR, the A279C element was utilized.

Dealer Service Information Bulletin number 67-I-28, dated 2-6-67, advised of the new Quadra-Jet carb (7037271, identified by a yellow tag coded XG) on the Ram Air option for automatic transmission models. It replaced part number 7027262, code XP. Service specifications remained the same, except the fast idle which was increased to 2800 rpm. The Quadra-Jet vacuum break adjustment on 400 and 428 engines (automatic transmission) with and without AIR was also revised, to 0.160 inch.

The HO engine was carried over from 1967. The Rochester carburetor for the HO engine was part number 7028267 for manual transmission applications and 7028268 for use with Turbo Hydra-matic.

The standard air cleaner (part number 6484827) was used for the HO, and the appropriate element for this air cleaner was employed. The standard throttle linkage bracket and cable were used, and there was no difference in the CPCV components.

The optional Ram Air systems were more than just carburetor options, as they were an integral part of the Ram Air engine and air induction system. (See Ram Air section.)

Only two Rochester Quadra-Jet carburetors were used in all HO applications, either forty-nine-state or AIR.

Transmission	Carburetor Part Number
Manual	7037263
Automatic	7037262

The standard four-barrel carburetor throttle bracket and linkage cable were used for the HO.

1967 HO and Ram Air air cleaner assembly, with optional heavy-duty foam element.

Solenoid heat shield (part number 9789465) used for 1967 HO and Ram Air applications.

1967 HO air cleaner assembly with standard A212 CWX paper element. This setup was also used on 1967 Ram Air engines when shroud and seal assembly was not in place, usually when the car was used during inclement weather.

Air cleaner used on 1968 GTO with standard engine and HO option. Note chrome lid; remainder of air cleaner was painted 60° gloss black. CCS vent tube is in left foreground.

INTAKE MANIFOLD

1964-65

All GTO intake manifolds for 1964 and 1965 were *not* interchangeable because they had different intake bolt patterns. Casting numbers were as follows.

	1964	1965
Four-barrel	9770274	9782895
Tri-Power	9775088	9778815

Tri-Power casting dates were located in front of the rear throttle bore, and consisted of a letter code for the month of casting, followed by numbers for the day of the month and the year. For example, an intake cast on February 13, 1965, would read B135.

The waternecks had the part number cast in the front running vertically down the neck. The 1964 and 1965 both used number 544745 for four-barrel applications. The Tri-Powers carried number 9776276 in 1964 and 9779580 in 1965. Waternecks and attaching bolts were painted engine-blue.

1966-67

All 1966 and 1967 intake manifolds were painted engine-blue. The 1965 and 1966 four-barrel intakes were interchangeable. However, care must be taken to ensure that the correct casting date appears for the respective year, and that the correct engine-blue is used. The casting number on the four-barrel intake was located between the waterneck and the temperature gauge sending unit on the front LH runner.

The 1966 Tri-Power was unique (part number 9782898, replacement part number 9784440). The casting date appeared in the same location and used the same coding information as the 1965 Tri-Power intake.

For the 1967 two-barrel engine, intake part number 9784437 was used. All four-barrel applications used part number 9786285. The intakes on all 1967 GTOs were painted engine-blue.

The manifold inlet assemblies (waternecks) for 1966 used part number 9779072 for four-barrel manifolds and part number 9779073 for the Tri-Power. One part number (9779072) sufficed for all 1967 applications.

1968-70

All intake manifolds were painted engine-blue with the exception of the 1969 and 1970 Ram Air IV manifolds, which were aluminum in appearance. Care must be taken when selecting the correct intake manifold, as casting dates should match up between the block, heads and intake for correctness. (A difference of ten days to two weeks between the codings on the engine components is acceptable, as the factory often assembled engines in this fashion.) The casting code on the intake manifold was located on the front water passage between the waterneck and the water temperature sensor.

The same intake was used for two-barrel models in 1968 and 1969 (part number 9799067). The standard four-barrel intake for 1968 and 1969 was part number 9794234. The 1970 GTO used part number 9799068.

Water inlet assemblies, or waternecks, were the same for all three years (part number 9779072). They were painted engine-blue.

Correct four-barrel intake manifold outlet (part number 544745 for 1964-65) was made of aluminum and painted engine-blue.

Standard 335 hp four-barrel manifold used in 1965-66 GTO. Choke tubes are below manifold for illustration purposes. Note angle of waterneck. Some 1966 manifolds had a ridge along the front upper runner. Casting date code is just visible between waterneck and sending unit boss.

Tri-Power intake manifold used on 1966 GTO. Note location of casting and part numbers.

1966 Tri-Power intake manifold. Note casting date of J255, indicating intake was cast September 25, 1965. Part number was directly below cast date.

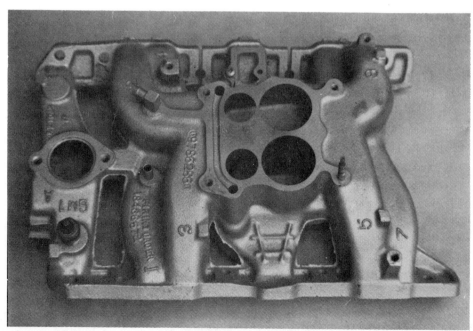

1967 GTO four-barrel intake manifold. Carburetor heat holes were located behind front carburetor mounting bolt holes. 1967 was only year that utilized this heat passage under the carburetor.

Location of casting date code on intake manifolds from 1968-70.

CYLINDER HEAD

1964-65

Cylinder heads for 1964 and 1965 were different. The cast number for 1964 was 9770716, and was located on the center exhaust port. There were two heads used in 1965. Originals carried the cast number 77 on the front exhaust port. The part number for this head was 9778777. According to Service Bulletin number 66-12, 093 heads were the correct replacements for 1965 GTO 389 engines. These 093 heads (part number 9784212) were used in 1966 production. A 1965 engine showing a 093 cast number on the cylinder heads would not be incorrect in restoration.

The 1965 cylinder heads could be identified by the code number cast on the right exhaust port. The complete production part number was also cast just below the rocker cover sealing edge. The 389 and 421 engines carried identification code number 77 and production part number 9778777. Note that service part numbers differed for various heads; they shouldn't be ordered by production part number. (This data was reported in Service News Flash number 65-62, dated 1-12-65.

Intake valves for both years were the same (number 9770713). Exhausts for 1964 carried number 9770712; for 1965, 9778747. A production change in valve spring applications for 1964 produced two sets of numbers. Prior to engine number 190810 (December 19, 1963), inners were 519112, outers were 519113. Heavier-duty springs (524598 inner and 524593 outer) were used thereafter, and were identified by a dab of yellow paint. The 1965 springs were different, depending on transmission application. Automatic-equipped cars used 9779008 inner and 9779009 outer. Manual-transmission and heavy-duty use carried 9781476 inner and 9779009 outer. All GTOs used 1.5 inch rockers.

Service News Flash number 65-117, dated 7-22-65, advised that valve spring cups on 1965 models with four-barrel carbs and manual transmission should be replaced with cups numbered 540833(Z). These cups were identified by their pink color and had been heat-treated to withstand more severe usage.

1966-67

Only one cylinder head was used in 1966 (part number 9784212). The cast number, 093, appeared above the center exhaust ports. The 9784212 part number was the replacement part number issued by Pontiac for servicing 1966 GTO heads. The production part number and the first-generation replacement part number differed, but—because of Service Bulletin 66-17—the first-generation part numbers were superseded, and the 9784212 number was used.

Pontiac Service News Flash number 66-17, dated 11-12-65, reported the correct identification codes for the 1966 engines as follows: The 389 and the 421 HO had

Comparison of oil filler cap design. On left is original dimpled design, on right is AC Delco replacement. 1964 push-on style was part number 6419454; 1965-67 twist-lock style was part number 6420359.

identification number 093. Also reported in Pontiac Service News Flash number 66-12, dated 11-8-65, was that two types of cylinder head castings were used for the 1966 389 engine. One type had an internal air galley required for the California cars. The 1966 cylinder head, 9784212(M), was used to service 1965 421 HO engines. When this head was used on 1965 engines a special head bolt, 9782913(MF), was required in the lower center bolt hole—it had an extended head which allowed for proper torquing.

In 1967, all GTOs used head part number 9788067, cast number 670—except two-barrel engines, which used head part number 9788064. However, very late in the production year, starting with engine serial number 646616, all Ram Air engines switched to head part number 9783657, cast number 97.

All GTOs in 1966 and 1967 used standard valve stems. The second-design Ram Air head valve applications used different numbers, as their specifications were revised.

Valve Springs

Year	Engine Type	Inner	Outer
1966	Manual	9781476	9779009
1966	Automatic	9779008	9779009
1966	XS*	9785720	and damper
1967	Manual	9781476	9779009
1967	Automatic	9779008	9779009
1967	Ram Air Automatic	9785720	and damper
1967	Ram Air**	9785999	9785998

*Optional Ram Air engine.
**Second-design used with cast number 97 heads.

Valves

Year	Engine Type	Intake	Dia.	Exhaust	Dia.
1966	All	9770713	1.96"	9778747	1.66"
1967	Two-barrel	9778752	2.11"	9787590	1.77"
1967	Four-barrel	9787587	2.11"	9787584	1.77"
1967	HO + RA	9789725	2.11"	9787584	1.77"
1967	RA*	9792316	2.11"	9792313	1.77"

*Second-design used with cast number 97 heads.

All 1966 and 1967 GTO cylinder heads used 1.5 inch rockers. The 1967 head was redesigned, with a different valve angle, longer pushrod and longer rocker arms. A stamped steel pushrod guide plate was used in 1967.

1968-70

In 1968, for two-barrel engines, head part number 9792266 was used. This head was carried over into 1969 for two-barrel applications. The standard four-barrel engine used part number 9790118, cast number 16. The head and cast numbers were carried over into 1969 for Hydra-matic-equipped applications. The manual transmission 1969 models used head part number 9795043, cast number 48. The 1970 GTO sported two different head part numbers for use with different transmissions. With manual transmissions, head part number 9799496, cast number 12 was used; GTOs equipped with Turbo Hydra-matic used head part number 9799497, cast number 13. The 455 cid engine used head part number 9799362, cast number 64.

Dealer Service Information Bulletin 68-I-19, dated 11-1-67, reported that the 1968 cylinder heads could not be identified in the same way as the 1967 heads. The casting number was located on the center exhaust port. But, for 1968, the cast stamp consisted of only two digits (it was three in 1967).

The following chart lists the valve springs used for all 1968-70 GTO engines. (See also the Ram Air section.)

Year	Transmission	Engine Type	Part Number Inner	Outer
1968	Hydra-matic	2bbl	9779008	9779009
	Manual	4bbl/HO	9781476	9779009
	Hydra-matic	4bbl/HO	9779008	9779009
		RA I	9785999	9785998
		RA II	9794044	9794045
1969	Hydra-matic	2bbl	9779008	9779009
	Manual	4bbl	9781476	9779009
	Hydra-matic	4bbl	9779008	9779009
		RA III*	9794934	9794939
		RA III**	9781476	9779009
		RA IV	9796789	9796790
1970	Manual	4bbl	9781476	9779009
	Hydra-matic	4bbl	9779008	9779009
		RA III	9781476	9779009
		RA IV	9796789	9796790
		455	9779008	9779009

*Used up until engine serial number 709185. Camshaft part number 9785744 was used with this spring.
**Beginning with engine serial number 709186. The change was made, according to Milt Schornack, because a particular Pontiac engineer didn't care for the poor starts and rough running of the Ram Air III in cold Michigan winters!

Valves

Year	Transmission	Engine Type	Part Number Intake	Exhaust
1968	Hydra-matic	2bbl	546384	9792332
	All	4bbl	9792344	9792340
		HO/RA	9792426	9792424
		RA II	9794021	9794019
1969	Hydra-matic	2bbl	546384	9792332
	All	4bbl	9792344	9792340
	All	RA III	9792344	9792340
	All	RA IV	9794021	9794019
1970	Hydra-matic	4bbl	478354	478348
	Manual	4bbl	478354	9792332
	All	RA III	9792344	9792340
	All	RA IV	9794021	9794019
	All	455	9799370	9799367

All valves were the same diameter, 2.11 inches for the intake and 1.77 inches for the exhaust. All engines used 1.5 inch rockers, with the exception of the Ram Air IV engines, which took 1.65 inch rockers.

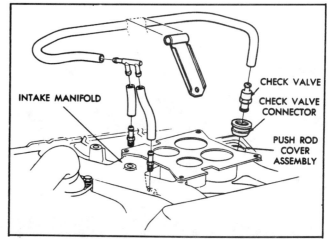

Components and installation of 1964-66 PCV system. Bracket was painted engine-blue.

The 093 heads from 24217B105833. Casting number was on center exhaust port as well as on inside top of head. Casting date code indicated head was cast September 12, 1965. This correlated with data plate on firewall, indicating car was built third week of October 1965.

Detail of 1966 GTO valve covers. Note hole for oil filler cap on LH cover (part number 9776742). RH cover (part number 9782999) was blank. "Hump" on valve covers was eliminated beginning in 1967.

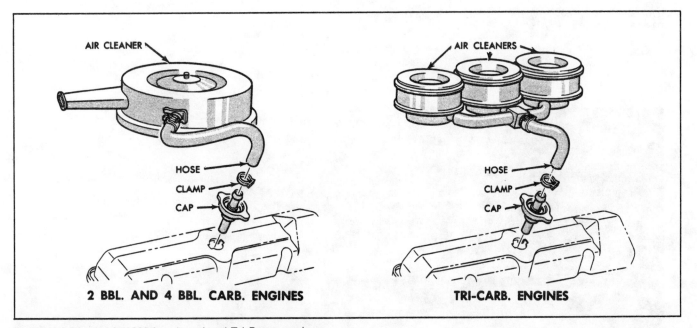

Detail of CCS used in 1966 four-barrel and Tri-Power engines, and in 1967 two-barrel and four-barrel engines. Drawing shows 1966 valve covers. Oil filler cap was located on LH valve cover.

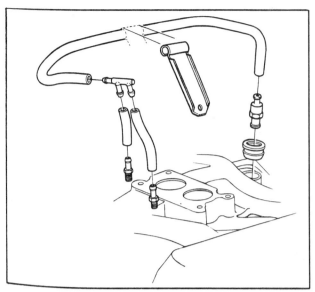

Positive crankcase ventilation for use in 1967 GTO two-barrel applications.

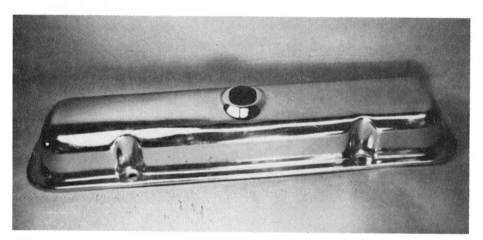

1967-and-up valve covers were of a new raised design to clear the new valvetrain geometry.

1967 GTO heads with casting number 670. Note guide plates and casting date in center between plates.

BLOCK

1964-65

All factory-installed Pontiac GTO blocks had both the engine production number and the engine code located on the RH bank of the block, on a machined pad. All GTOs in 1964 and 1965 came from the factory with engines of 389 cid. No 421 cid engines were released to the public for sale in a GTO. A number of dealers installed the 421 cid engine at the point of purchase, but unless substantiated by the restorer as so equipped, this conversion is incorrect.

To assist in determining correctness of a GTO block, the casting date and block part number were located on the top rear of the block, near the distributor shaft hole. The casting date was read exactly as the intake manifold casting date, beginning with a letter for the month, followed by numbers for the day and year.

Pontiac engines used in production for 1964 and 1965 were painted blue. The correct DuPont number was 93-76981; Ditzler, 11561; and Rinshed-Mason, 62-015.

Pontiac Service News Flash number 64-16 (10-18-63) and 65-53 (12-22-64) verified that the oil capacity on all V-8 engines should be five quarts—six quarts with a filter change. Some 1964 models were manufactured with a four-quart dipstick; the five-quart dipstick, part number 9776085 (code MF), should be installed. It is easily identified by the five-quart tag on the handle.

Pushrod guide wear in 1965 engines was reported in Pontiac Service News Flash 65-65, dated 1-20-65. The solution presented in this bulletin was to enlarge the holes in the guide to 0.005 inch larger than the diameter of the rocker arm studs. This was later amended by News Flash 65-125, dated 8-17-65, which reported that a pushrod guide plate, 9777594(MF-3), had been released to solve the problem without modifying the regular guides.

1966-67

As in 1964 and 1965, all GTO engine blocks for 1966-67 had both the engine production number and the engine manifest code located on the RH bank at the front of the block on a machined pad. The 1966 GTO was equipped with the 389 cid block. The 1967 GTO used the 400 cid block. No 421 cid or 428 cid blocks were released by the factory for sale in a GTO. A number of dealers installed a 421 cid or 428 cid engine at the time of purchase, but unless substantiated by the restorer as so equipped, this conversion is incorrect.

P&A Extra number 67-24, dated 10-30-67, reported that the new Ram Air engine block was available, part number 9794075(F-3). The new block featured four-bolt bearing cap construction—blocks with the two-bolt bearing cap design should not be used for these cars.

Pontiac Service News Flash number 66-5, dated 10-15-65, reported that the 1966 owner's guide and shop manuals were incorrect regarding GTO oil capacity. The correct capacity was six quarts; seven with a filter change.

Research indicates the use of a sticker affixed to the RH front of the block indicating the engine manifest code in 1967 GTOs assembled at the Pontiac, Michigan, assembly plant. The sticker was white with red letters, and appeared quite similar to the rear axle code sticker on the LH rear brake drum.

Dealer Technical Bulletin number 67-T-6, dated 11-30-66, pointed out the importance that all four-barrel, 428 HO and manual transmission engines use the 60 psi oil pressure regulator spring, regardless of the distributor gear used. This was part number 534652 (NP3), Group number 1.609. Also, if a failure of the distributor drive gear occurs it should be replaced with gear part number 1968683 (M3), Group number 2.374.

Pontiac engines used in production for 1966 and 1967 were painted engine-blue. The correct DuPont number was 181-97219; Ditzler, 13255; and Rinshed-Mason, 266T21. (To determine the engine casting code date, refer to the 1964-65 engine block information.)

1968-70

The engine manifest code and serial number locations were unchanged from previous years. Beginning in 1968, the last eight digits of the vehicle's serial number appeared on a machined pad next to the timing chain cover.

No engines other than the 400 cid were released from the assembly line for sale to the public in 1968 or 1969. There were a number of dealers (such as Royal Pontiac) who could perform an engine conversion, switching the 400 for a 428. Unless documented, this would be an incorrect restoration. The 455 was first released in the 1970 GTO.

The same white-with-red-letters stickers found on earlier models were found on 1970 GTOs produced in the Pontiac assembly plant. These stickers were located on the RH front of the block. Engine casting date codes were coded the same as before.

All engines built between the beginning of the 1968 production year and the end of the 1970 production year were the same color of engine-blue. The correct DuPont number was 181-97219; Ditzler, 13255; and Rinshed-Mason, 266T21.

HORSEPOWER	ENGINE CODE	250	350	400	MANUAL	AUTOMATIC	1 BBL (MV)	2 BBL (2GV)	4 BBL (4MV)	8.6:1	9.0:1	9.2:1	10.5:1	10.75:1	9790826	9792539	9796327	9777254	9785744	9779067	9779068	9794041	1110474	1110475	1111940	1111946 (b)	1111942	1111952 (b)	1111941 (b)	1111960	SINGLE	STD.-DUAL	H.D.-DUAL	H.D. SPEC.-DUAL	RAM AIR IV-DUAL	SMALL VALVE	LARGE VALVE
350	YS			X		X			X				X					X							X							X					X
350	WT			X	X				X				X							X								X				X					X
366	YZ			X	X	X			X				X							X					X								X				X
366	WS			X	X	X			X			X									X					X							X				X
265	(a) XM XX			X	X	X	X			X							X						X								X					X	
370	XP			X		X			X				X								X					X								X		X	X
370	WW			X	X				X				X								X					X								X		X	X

(a) Early Production (small valve) Engines with 30° intake valve seat angle. Later Production (small valve) Engines use 45° intake valve seat.
NOTE: All large valve engines use 30° intake valve seat.
(b) Uses hardened drive gear for use with 60 p.s.i. oil pump and high tension distributor points.

GTO engine chart.

Identification Letter Code stamped immediately below production engine number on front of right hand side of block. Do not order engines or parts from this chart.
Z-S.M.T. (3-Spd.-215 Eng.) 5-S.M.T. (3-Spd.-326 Eng.) X-SM (3-Spd.-389 Eng.)
Y-Auto. (215 Eng.) O-Auto. (326 Eng.) J-Auto. (389 Eng.)
R.P.O.-Regular Production Option

79J	78X	77J	76X	LETTER CODE
A.T.	S.M.	A.T.	S.M.	TRANS. TYPE
				215 Cubic Inch
				326 Cubic Inch
X	X	X	X	389 Cubic Inch
Std. G.T.O.	Std. G.T.O.	R.P.O. G.T.O.	R.P.O. G.T.O.	USAGE
X	X	X	X	10:75:1 Comp. Ratio
				10:5 Comp. Ratio
				8:6 Comp. Ratio
				6:9 Comp. Ratio
				1 Bbl. Carb.
				2 Bbl. Carb.
X	X			4 Bbl. Carb.
		X	X	3/2 Bbl. Carb.
				Single Valve Spring
				Two Valve Springs
X	X	X	X	H.D. Valve Spring
				Camshaft (3788506)
				Camshaft (537441)
X	X	X	X	Camshaft (524009)
				Distributor (1110316)
				Distributor (1111052)
X	X	X	X	Distributor (1111054)
	X		X	H.D. Clutch
X	X	X	X	Special Valve Lifter
325	325	348	348	Horsepower

1964 Tempest engine identification chart.

Typical 1964-67 two-piece harmonic balancer and pulley assembly. Note 1966-67 timing chain cover.

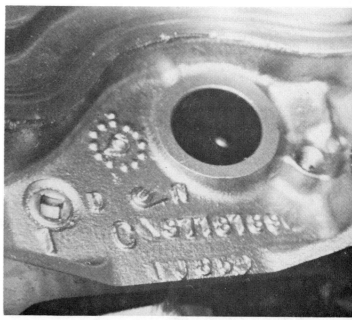

Close-up of rear of block on 242176B105833. Casting date again confirmed correctness of block; casting was dated September 8, 1965, and firewall plate had time-built code of 10C.

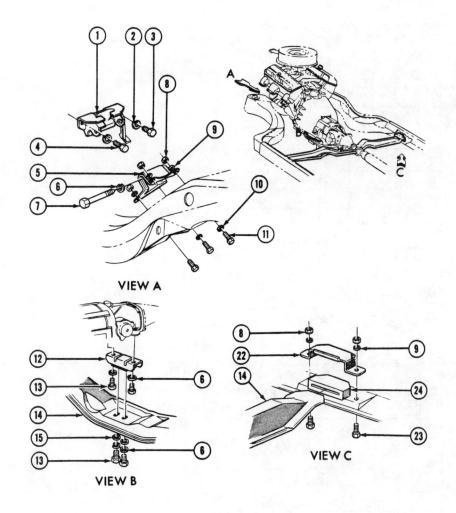

VIEW A

VIEW B

VIEW C

Key	Part Name	Group No.
1 — INSULATOR ASM., Engine Front Mounting		0.027
2 — LOCKWASHER, Insulator to Cylinder Block (7/16")		8.931
3 — BOLT, Insulator to Cylinder Block (7/16"-14 x 1-1/8")		0.002
4 — BOLT, Insulator to Cyl. Block (7/16"-14 x 7/8")		0.002
5 — BRACKET, Engine Front Support		0.029
6 — LOCKWASHER, Insulator to Supt. Brkt. (7/16")		8.931
7 — BOLT, Front Insulator to Support Bracket		0.002
8 — NUT, Bracket to Frame (3/8"-16)		8.915
9 — LOCKWASHER, Bracket to Frame (3/8")		8.931
10 — WASHER, Engine Mounting Frame Bracket (13/32" I.D. x 47/64" O.D. x 1/16")		N.S.

Key	Part Name	Group No.
11 — BOLT, Engine Mounting Frame Bracket (3/8"-16 x 7/8")		8.900
12 — MOUNTING ASM., Trans. Support		4.081
13 — BOLT, Trans. Mtg. to Supt. Brkt. (7/16"-14 x 1")		8.900
14 — MEMBER, Engine Rear Support Frame Cross		7.011
15 — WASHER, Trans. Support Mtg. to Bracket		0.002
22 — RETAINER, Rear Cross Member Frame Insulator		0.029
23 — BOLT, Insulator Retainer to Frame (3/8"-16 x 3/4")		8.900
24 — INSULATOR, Rear Cross Member Frame		0.027

Factory drawing of installation of engine and transmission insulators for 1964-70.

Identification Letter Code stamped immediately below production engine number on front of right hand side of block. Do not order engines or parts from this chart.

W - S.M.T. Y - A.T. S - Standard O - Option or Spec. Equipment

| WT | YS | WS | YR | LETTER CODE |
S.M.T.	A.T.	S.M.T.	A.T.	TRANS. TYPE
				215 Cubic Inch
				326 Cubic Inch
X	X	X	X	389 Cubic Inch
78	79	76	77	Engine No. (Last Two Digits)
				3300 Series
				3500 Series
				3700 Series
S	O	O	O	G.T.O. Option
				Taxi
				Police
X	X	X	X	10:75 Comp. Ratio
				10:5 Comp. Ratio
				8:6 Comp. Ratio
				6.9 Comp. Ratio
				1 Bbl. Carb.
				2 Bbl. Carb.
X	X			4 Bbl. Carb.
		X	X	Triple Carbs.
				Camshaft (3788492)
				Camshaft (537441)
X	X			Camshaft (9779067)
		X	X	Camshaft (9779068)
				Single Valve Spring
				Std. Two Valve Springs
X	X	X	X	H.D. Two Valve Springs
				Distributor (1110328)
X	X	X	X	Distributor (1111054)
				Distributor (1111079)
X		X		H.D. Clutch
335	335	360	360	Horsepower

1965 Tempest engine identification chart.

Y - A.T.   S - Standard   O - Option or Spec. Equipment

YS	WT	YR	WS	XE	WW	WV	XS	LETTER CODE
AT	MAN	AT	MAN	AT	MAN	MAN	MAN	TRANS. TYPE
X	X	X	X	X	X	X	X	389 Cubic Inch
79	78	77	76	75	74	73	70	ENGINE NO. (Last Two Digits)
O	O	S	O	O	O	O	O	4207-17-67
X	X	X	X	X	X	X	X	10:75 Comp. Ratio
X	X			X	X			4 Bbl. Carb.
		X	X			X	X	Triple Carbs.
X	X			X	X			Camshaft (9779067)
		X	X			X	X	Camshaft (9779068)
							X	Camshaft (9785744)
							X	Single Valve Spring (w/Damper)
							X	Std. Two Valve Springs
X	X	X	X	X	X	X		H.D. Two Valve Springs
								Distributor (1110341)
		X	X				X	Distributor (1111054)
X	X		X					Distributor (1111078)
						X	X	Distributor (1111103)
335	335	360	360	335	335	360	360	Horsepower

1966 Tempest engine identification chart.

Close-up of rear of block showing location of casting code. Bolt and washer assembly covering distributor hole was for dust protection, only while block was stored. Letters D and N with arrow indicated that block was cast at night.

S – Standard Equipment   O – Option or Special Equipment

XP	XM	XL	YS	WT	XS	WS	WW	WV	YR	YZ	LETTER CODE
HMT	HMT	HMT	HMT	MAN	MAN	MAN	MAN	MAN	MAN	HMT	TRANS. TYPE
X	X	X	X	X	X	X	X	X	X	X	400 Cubic Inch
81	83	82	79	78	77	76	74	73	72	71	Engine No. (Last Two Digits)
O	O	O	O	S	O	O	O	O	O	O	4200 Styles
	X	X									8.6 Comp. Ratio
X			X	X	X	X	X	X	X	X	10.75 Comp. Ratio
	X	X									2-Bbl. Carb.
X			X	X	X	X	X	X	X	X	4-Bbl. Carb.
			X				X	X	X		Calif. Air Injection Eng.
			X	X							Camshaft (9779066)
	X	X									Camshaft (537441)
			X				X				Camshaft (9779067)
					X		X			X	Camshaft (9779068)
X				X				X			Camshaft (9785744)
X				X				X			Valve Spring (w/Damper)
											Distributor (1111164)
						X	X	X			Distributor (1111252)
X			X	X	X	X				X	Distributor (1111250)
▶			▶	▶	▶	▶				▶	Distributor (1111243)
					▶		▶	▶			Distributor (1111244)
		X									Distributor (1111261)
▶			▶	▶	▶	▶				▶	Distributor (1111183)
							▶	▶	▶		Distributor (1111237)
											Distributor (1110398)
▶			▶	▶	▶	▶				▶	Distributor (1111245)
360	255	255	335	335	360	360	335	360	360	360	Horsepower

▶NOTE: Production Alternate

1967 Tempest engine identification chart.

FIG 1.

POSSIBLE OIL LEAK AREAS

FIG 2.

NEOPRENE TABS
9793833

MAKE SURE
TABS LAY
FLAT.

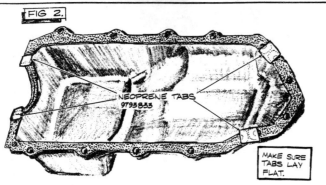

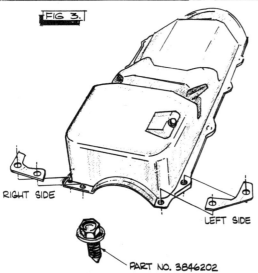

FIG 3.

RIGHT SIDE

LEFT SIDE

PART NO. 3846202

Dealer Technical Bulletin 70-T-15, dated 5-28-70, reported a fix for the problem of oil leaking from the rear area of the oil pan on all 1965-70 engines. Oil pan reinforcement package (484083) should be installed by first removing the oil pan and all the old gaskets. Then check the pan rail (both sides) for flatness; make sure the bolt holes haven't been deformed. Next install the new gaskets, using the supplied neoprene tabs in all four corners (figure 2). Now position the pan on the engine and start all bolts except the rear two on each side. Place the reinforcement straps in position on the pan (figure 3) and install the new bolts (figure 4) included in the package. Snug all bolts then torque evenly to 12 lb. ft., including the rear ones. Last, tighten the new rear bolts to 20 lb. ft. Be sure not to overtorque the bolts.

1968 TEMPEST SERVICE PART NUMBER AND CODE IDENTIFICATION CHART—GROUP 1.219				
	BL 3019205	PB Use BT		
	BN 3019205	PC Use BT		
BI 3019205	PA Use BT	PE Use BT	VE 3014757	BT-3025764

1968 Tempest service part number and code identification chart (Group 1.219).

1968 FIREBIRD & TEMPEST 8-CYL. ENGINE   IDENTIFICATION CHART

IDENTIFICATION LETTER CODE STAMPED IMMEDIATELY BELOW PRODUCTION ENGINE NUMBER ON FRONT OF RIGHT HAND SIDE OF BLOCK. DO NOT ORDER ENGINES OR PARTS FROM THIS CHART.

S - STANDARD EQUIPMENT   O - OPTIONAL OR SPECIAL EQUIPMENT   02-1-5 & 04-1-5

Letter Code	Trans. Type	400 Cubic Inch	Engine No. (Last Two Digits)	2 Bbl. Carb.	4 Bbl. Carb. (Quadrajet)	8.6 Comp. Ratio	10.75 Comp. Ratio		4237-67	Camshaft (9777254)	Camshaft (9779067)	Camshaft (9779068)	Camshaft (9785744)	Camshaft (9794041)	Distributor (1111270)	Distributor (1111272) ■	Distributor (1111449)	Distributor (1111940) ●	Distributor (1111165)	Distributor (1111941)	Valve Springs (Std.)	Valve Springs (H.D.)	Valve Springs (Ram Air)	Horsepower
YZ	HMT	X	71		X		X		O		X					▲						X			350
WY	MAN	X	73		X		X		X				X										X	X	360
XW	HMT	X	74		X		X		O			X											X	X	360
WS	MAN	X	76		X		X		O				X										X		360
XS	MAN	X	77		X		X		O					X					▲				X		360
WT	MAN	X	78		X		X		S	X									▲			X			360
YS	HMT	X	79		X		X		O		X					▲						X			350
XP	HMT	X	81		X		X		O				X			▲							X		360
XM	HMT	X	83	X		X			O	X								X	X			X			265

▲NOTE: With 60 P.S.I. Oil Pump Spring   ■ Early Production   ● Late Production

1968 Firebird and Tempest eight-cylinder engine identification chart.

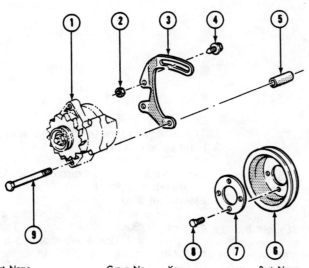

Key	Part Name	Group No.	Key	Part Name	Group No.
1	— DELCOTRON & PULLEY ASM.,	2.275	6	— PULLEY, C/Shaft-(7-1/4" dia.) Single	0.659
2	— NUT, Delcotron Mounting Plate to Cyl. Head (3/8"-24)	8.917	7	— PLATE, C/Shaft Pulley Reinforcement	0.660
3	— PLATE, Delcotron Mounting	2.277	8	— BOLT, C/Shaft Pulley Reinforcement Plate to Pulley (5/16"-24 x 3/4")	2.275
4	— SCREW, Delcotron to Plate-(5/16"-18 x 1-1/4").	8.977	9	— BOLT, Delcotron to Plate & Cyl. Head (3/8"-16 x 6")	2.275
5	— SPACER, Delcotron to Plate & Cyl. Head (3-7/16" long)	2.277			

View of 1968-70 manual steering alternator mounting and single-groove balancer pulley (part number 9790947). Alternator bracket was painted 60° gloss black, balancer was painted engine-blue and pulley was 60° gloss black.

LUBRICATION SYSTEM

Type .... Pressure

Oil Pressure-

Pontiac exc. large valve 455	35 psi above 2600 rpm
Pontiac with large valve 455	60 psi above 2600 rpm
6-Cyl.	50 to 65 psi at 2000 rpm
350	35 psi above 2600 rpm
G.T.O. and Ram-Air III & IV	60 psi above 2600 rpm

Engine Lubricant Capacity

When Refilling-8 Cyl	5 qts. (6 qts. if filter element is changed)
When Refilling-6-Cyl	4 qts. (5 qts. if filter element is changed)

Oil Pump Type .... Spur Gear

1970 lubrication system.

355

1970 ALL ENGINE IDENTIFICATION CHART

8-Cylinder identification letter code is located beneath the production engine number on a machined pad on the right hand bank of the engine block.

6-Cylinder engine code is stamped on the distributor mounting pad at the right side of the block.

DO NOT ORDER ENGINES FROM THIS CHART.

Letter Code	Engine Number (Last Two Digits)	Manual	M-40 HMT	400 (8-Cyl.)	455 (8-Cyl.)	Ram Air III	Ram Air IV	4 BBL.	10.5	10.25	Horsepower
					TEMPEST						9799601-7 9799603-4
YZ	71		X	X		X		X	X		366
XP	75		X	X		X	X	X	X		370
WS	76	X		X		X		X	X		366
WW	77	X		X		X	X	X	X		370
WT	78	X		X				X		X	350
YS	79		X	X				X		X	350
WA	10	X			(1)			X	X		370
YA	13		X		(1)		X	X		X	370

☐ Production Code Change to CG
☐☐ Production Code Change to RF

(1) Large Valve   (2) Small Valve

1970 engine identification chart for all Tempests.

CAMSHAFT

1964-65

The 1964 GTO used one camshaft for both 325 and 348 hp versions. The correct factory part number for the cam was 524009, and it carried a letter code, C, stamped ⅛ inch high on the front end.

Two different camshafts were used in 1965, either standard or Tri-Power. Standard four-barrel cams were numbered 9779067, letter stamp P. Tri-Power cams were number 9779068, letter stamp S.

1966-67

Three camshafts were used in 1966. The correct factory part number for the standard four-barrel 335 hp application was 9779067. It carried a letter stamp, P, ⅛ inch high on the front end of the camshaft.

Two different camshafts were used in Tri-Power engines. The RPO 802 engine used camshaft part number 9779068, while the special-order XS engine used 9785744.

Detail of pushrod guide referred to in Service Bulletin 65-65. Guide plate part number was 522937, replaced by 9777594.

The letter code for the 068 cam was S, and the 744 cam letter code was H.

The camshaft for the 1967 low-compression two-barrel engine was part number 537441, and it carried one of two letter codes, F or U. The U-stamped camshaft was used more often.

The standard 335 hp engine used camshaft part number 9779066, letter stamp N. The HO camshaft was part number 9779068, letter stamp S. The Ram Air used camshaft part number 9785744, letter stamp H.

1968-70

A multitude of camshafts was used for 1968-70. All cams carried the same letter identifying stamp as used in previous years.

Year	Transmission	Engine Type	Part Number	Letter Stamp
1968	Hydra-matic	2bbl	537441	E or U
	Hydra-matic	4bbl	9779067	P
	Manual	4bbl	9779067	P
	All	HO	9779068	S
	Manual	RA I	9785744	H
	Hydra-matic	RA I	9779068	S
	Manual	RA II	9794041	T
1969	Hydra-matic	2bbl	537441	E or U
	Hydra-matic	4bbl	9779067	P
	Manual	4bbl	9779068	S
	Manual	RA III	9785744*	H
	Manual	RA III	9779068**	S
	Hydra-matic	RA III	9779068	S
	All	RA IV	9794041	T
1970	All	4bbl	9779067	P
	All	RA III	9779068	S
	All	RA IV	9794041	T
	Hydra-matic	455	9779067	P
	Manual	455	9779068	S

*Used until engine serial number 709185.
**Used in engine serial number 709186 and up.

ENGINE COOLING

1964-65

In 1964, two radiators were used for the GTO.

Size	Application	Production Part Number	Replacement Part Number
2x17½ inches	Standard four-barrel, no air conditioning	3002157 3003450	3001257
2⅝x17½ inches	Air conditioning and Tri-Power only	3002158 3003459	3001258

Radiator Mounting Brackets

Size	Upper	Lower
2 inches	9775034	Not serviced, part of core support
2⅝ inches	9773439	Not serviced, part of core support

Radiator Mounting Bracket Insulators

Size	Upper	Lower
2 inches	9775033	9775033
2⅝ inches	9773436	9773436

Two clips held the overflow tube in place along the LH side of the support. A fifteen-pound pressure cap was used for both years (original part number 3886283, RC-15; replacement part number 861050).

The core support (part number 9775061) was unique to the GTO alone, and was not interchangeable with that of the 1964 LeMans or Tempests, unless these cars were equipped with air conditioning. The 1965 GTO core support used two part numbers: 9779849 with air conditioning, 9779848 for standard models. All core supports, braces and hardware were painted 60° gloss black.

Radiator hoses were molded, and both years used the same bottom hose (part number 3897878). Because of the change in the thermostat cover and waterneck design, different hoses were used for the two years for inlet application.

Year	Application	Part Number
1964	Tri-Power	9776277
	4-bbl	9775909
1965	Tri-Power	9779581
	4-bbl	9779582

The original "tower" type of radiator clamp was used on the assembly line only. These were not used when hoses were replaced, and consequently were not serviced by a Pontiac Motor Division part number.

Air-conditioned GTOs used a seal and retaining assembly made of black rubber along the core support.

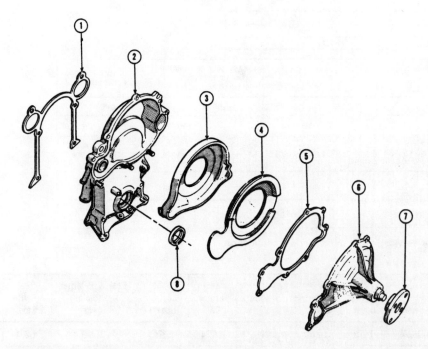

Key	Part Name	Group No.
1 — GASKET, Timing Chain Cover (Part of 9775217 Gasket Pkg.-0.207)		N.S.
2 — COVER ASM., Timing Chain - Inc. #8		0.206
3 — HOUSING, Water Pump		1.069
4 — DIVIDER, Water Pump		1.069
5 — GASKET, Water Pump to Timing Chain Cover		1.079
6 — PUMP ASM., Water - Inc. #5		1.069
7 — HUB, Water Pump and Fan		1.062
8 — SEAL, Timing Chain Cover Oil		0.213

Exploded view of 1964-68 water pump and timing chain cover (1964-65 shown). Outer components were painted engine-blue.

1966-67

A 60° gloss-black fan shield (part number 9781494) was used for all non-air-conditioned applications. A fan caution sticker may or may not have been affixed to the shield.

For all air-conditioned applications in 1966 and 1967, a plastic shroud cast in black, part number 9783757, was used with the nineteen-inch fan. Although factory literature indicated use of the 9783757 shroud with 1967 Ram Air engines, research shows that not *all* Ram Air engines came with the shroud.

The RC-15 pressure cap was again used (part number 861050). Two overflow clips routed the hose down the LH side of the core support next to the radiator.

The core supports for the 1966 and 1967 were the same for standard use (part number 9784743). The air-conditioning core support (part number 9788904) was also interchangeable. The 1967 Ram Air-equipped GTO used the air-conditioning core support, although air conditioning was not offered with the Ram Air option. A second-design core support for non-air-conditioned applications (part number 9788903) was used during the course of 1967 production. However, it is not known exactly when the change was made. All core supports for both years were painted 60° gloss black.

Radiator hoses were molded, and both years used the same lower hose (part number 3897878). Different inlet (upper) hoses were used.

Year	Application	Part Number
1966	Standard steering 4bbl	9782744
	Power steering 4bbl	9782745
	Standard steering 3x2	9782941
	Power steering 3x2	9782940
1967	Standard steering 4bbl	9782744
	Power steering 4bbl	9788796

The original tower type of radiator clamp was used on assembly line production only. These were discarded when hoses were replaced, and were not serviced by a PMD part number. Correct restorations should use this type of clamp.

Air-conditioned GTOs used a seal assembly made of black rubber along the core support.

1968-70

For non-air-conditioned models in 1968, a 60° gloss-black fan shield (part number 9790150) was used. A fan caution sticker may have been applied to the shield. Air-conditioned models used a fan shroud (part number 9790785). In 1969 and 1970, two fan shrouds were used, as the fan shield was eliminated. With heavy-duty radiator use (part number 9795194), the shroud was used. With the heavy-duty 2 11/16 inch radiator, part number 9795359 was employed.

The RC-15 pressure cap was used for all three years (part number 3886273). Since Pontiac went to a cross-flow radiator design beginning in 1968, the same core support was utilized for air-conditioned and non-air-conditioned cars. The core support was painted 60° gloss black, and used part number 9790330 in 1968, 975474 in 1969, and 477774 in 1970.

Radiator hoses were molded, and all had a 1½ inch inside diameter. The lower hose was the same for all three years (part number 9790277). The letters NL were stamped on the hose. The upper hose was the same for 1968 and 1969 (part number 9796090), and was stamped NH. The hose used in 1970 was part number 546498, and measured 1½ inch inside diameter. The tower-type hose clamps were used through 1970.

TR	3005254	TX	3005258
TT	3005254	TN	3005156
TV	3005258		

TRANS-MISSION	SERIES AND SPEC. OPTIONS	STANDARD			HEAVY DUTY COOLING TRAILER PROVISION SPECIAL AXLE RATIO		AIR CONDITIONING	
		ENGINE			ENGINE		ENGINE	
			389 (GTO)			389 (GTO)		389 (GTO)
			4 Bbl.	Tri-Carb		4 Bbl. and Tri-Carb		4 Bbl. and Tri-Carb
3 & 4 Speed Manual	Except Station Wagon		TN	TT		TT		TV
Automatic	Except Station Wagon		TR	TT		TT		TX

1965 Tempest radiator service part number, code identification and usage chart.

Radiator	Bracket		Insulators		Shroud	Seal (Frame Bar)	Seal (Radiator Upper)	Seal & Retainer (Radiator Lower)	Seal (Baffle Side)	Seal & Retainer (Radiator Lower Outer)
	Upper	Lower	Upper	Lower						
1.219	1.274	1.274	1.270	1.270	1.277	1.274	1.274	1.270	1.274	7.865
3005156	9779536	9773437	9775033	539476	9774621(●)					
3005254	9779536	9773439	9773436	9773436	9774621(▲)					
3005258	9779536	-	9773436	9773436	9775959	9775943	9781123	9781487R.H.	9781077	9774419R.H. 9774420L.H.

●NOTE: Use w/Police Car.
▲NOTE: Use w/All Police (Heavy Duty), Taxi, & Trailer Provision.

1965 Tempest radiator mounting parts.

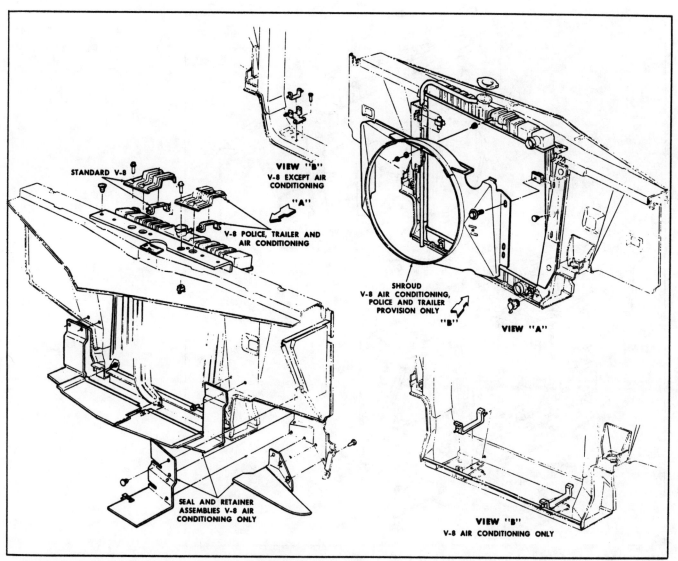

STANDARD V-8

V-8 POLICE, TRAILER AND
AIR CONDITIONING

VIEW "B"
V-8 EXCEPT AIR
CONDITIONING

"A"

SHROUD
V-8 AIR CONDITIONING,
POLICE AND TRAILER
PROVISION ONLY

"B"

VIEW "A"

SEAL AND RETAINER
ASSEMBLIES V-8 AIR
CONDITIONING ONLY

VIEW "B"
V-8 AIR CONDITIONING ONLY

Exploded view of 1965 core support, radiator brackets, upper and lower air-conditioning baffling and fan shroud. 1964-65 air-conditioning fan shroud was metal; all components were painted 60° gloss black.

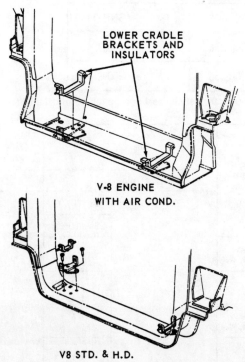

LOWER CRADLE
BRACKETS AND
INSULATORS

V-8 ENGINE
WITH AIR COND.

V8 STD. & H.D.

Lower radiator brackets and insulators used in 1966 and 1967 GTOs.

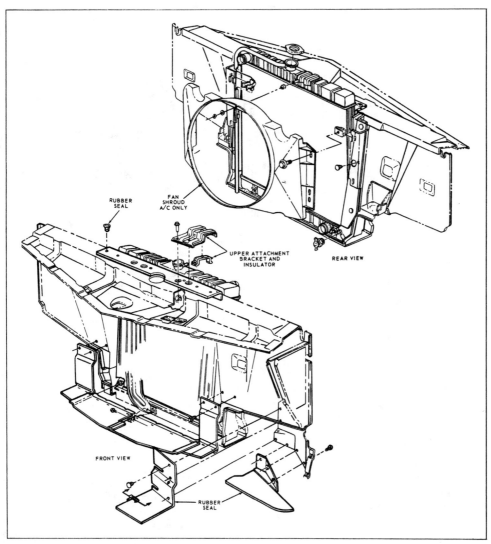

Core support and related hardware for 1966-67 GTO. Note placement of fan shroud and rubber seals for air-conditioned applications.

TY	3009875	TS	3008354
TP	3008356	TT	3008354
TR	3008356	TV	3009875

1966 Tempest radiator service part number and code identification chart.

Trans-mission	Series and Special Options	Standard			Heavy Duty Cooling Trailer Provisions Special Axle Ratio		Air Conditioning	
		Engine			Engine		Engine	
			389 (G.T.O.)			389 (G.T.O.)		389 (G.T.O.)
			4-Bbl.	Tri-Carb.				
3 & 4 Speed Manual	33 Series Exc. Sta. Wag.		–	–		–		–
	3335 35, 37, 42		TP	TS		TS		TV
Auto-Matic	33 Series Exc. Sta. Wag.		–	–		–		–
	3335 35, 37, 42		TR	TT		TT		TY

1966 Tempest radiator chart.

1966 Tempest radiator mounting parts.

Radiator	Bracket		Insulator		Shroud	Seal (Frame Bar)	Seal (Radiator Upper)	Seal & Retainer Asm. (Radiator Lower)	Seal (Baffle Side)	Seal & Retainer Asm. (Radiator Lower Outer)
	Upper	Lower	Upper	Lower						
Group 1.219	Group 1.274	Group 1.274	Group 1.270	Group 1.270	Group 1.277	Group 1.274	Group 1.274	Group 1.274	Group 1.274	Group 7.865
3008354	9779536	9773439	9773436	9773436	9774621 (▲)					
3009875	9779536	—	9773436	9773436	9783757	9775943	9781123	9783075R 9783076L	9781077	9774419R 9774420L

(▲) NOTE: Use w/Trailer Provision.
* Effective in Production Approx. Nov. 1, 1965.

TR	3010456	TV	3010455
TS	3010454	TY	3010455
TT	3010454		

1967 Tempest radiator service part number and code identification chart (GRP. 1.219).

Transmission	Series & Regular Production Options	STANDARD			Heavy Duty Rad., Special Axle Ratios, Trailer Provisions	AIR CONDITIONING	
		Engine			Engine	Engine	
				400	400		400
		2-Bbl.	Ram Air	4-Bbl. HO	All		All
Manual Trans.	42	-	-	-	-		-
		-	TV	TS	TS		TV
Automatic Trans.	42	-	-	-	-		-
		TR	-	TT	TT		TY
Hydramatic Trans.	42 Series	TR	TY	TT	TT		TY

▲NOTE: California cars w/A.I.R. use TY Radiators.

1967 Tempest radiator usage chart.

Radiator	Bracket		Insulators		Shroud	Seal (Frame Bar)	Seal (Rad. Upper)	Seal & Ret. (Rad. Lwr.)	Seal (Baffle Side)	Seal & Ret. (Rad. Lwr. Outer)
	Upper	Lower	Upper	Lower						
Group 1.219	Group 1.274		Group 1.270		Grp. 1.277	Grp. 1.274	Grp. 1.274	Grp. 1.274	Grp. 1.274	Grp. 7.865
3010456 (TE & TL Prod. Rad.)	9780177	9775049	539476	9775033			■9781123		■9781077	
3010456 (TJ-TN-TP-TR Prod. Rad.)	9779536	9773437	9775033	539476	▲9774621					
3010454	9779536	9773439	9773436	9773436	▲9774621					
3010455	9779536	-	9773436	9773436	9783757	9775943	9781123	9783075RH 9783076LH	9781077	9774419RH 9787788LH

▲NOTE: Used with Heavy Duty Radiator and Shroud
■NOTE: Used with TL Production Radiator

1967 Tempest radiator mounting parts.

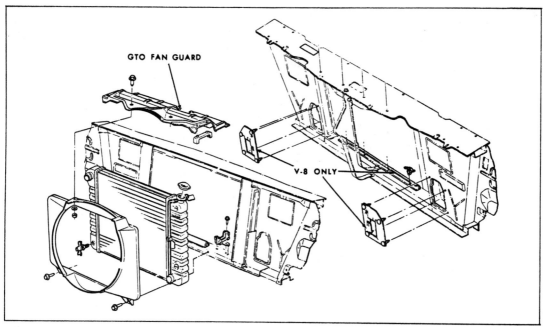

1968 radiator mounting, fan shield and fan shroud. Shield was used on non-air-conditioned GTOs, and was painted 60° gloss black.

		1968 TEMPEST RADIATOR USAGE CHART												
		Standard					Heavy Duty				Air Conditioning			
		Engine					Engine				Engine			
Trans-mission	Series		400					400				400		
			2 Bbl.	4 Bbl.	Ram Air	H.O.		4 Bbl.	2 Bbl.	H.O.		2 Bbl.	4 Bbl.	H.O.
3 & 4 Spd. Manual Trans.	42 (G.T.O.)	–	–	PC	PA	PC	–	PA	–	PA	–	–	PA	PA
Automatic														
Hydra-matic	42 (G.T.O.)	–	BI	BN	PB	PE	–	PE	BL	PB	–	PB	PB	FB

1968 Tempest radiator usage chart.

		1968 TEMPEST RADIATOR MOUNTING PARTS							
Radiator	Bracket	Insulators		Shroud	Radiator Seals			Filler (Cross Brace to Bpr.)	
	Lower Only	Upper	Lower		Rad. Supt.	R.H. Baffle	L.H. Baffle		42 (G.T.O.)
Grp. 1.219	Grp. 1.274	Group 1.270		Grp. 1.277	Group 1.274			Group 8.155	
3014622	9790403	9790387	9780011					9796411●	
3014757	9790402	9790388	9780011					9796411▲	
3019205	9790742RH	9790390RH	9780010RH	9790785	9783550	9791834●	9791834●	9796411▲	9793487▲
	9790743LH	9790391LH	9780011LH						
3025764	9790744	9790389	9780010	9790785	9783550	9791834●	9791834●	9796411●	9793487▲●

▲ Note: Used with Heavy Duty Radiator

● Note: Used with Air Conditioning

1968 Tempest radiator mounting parts.

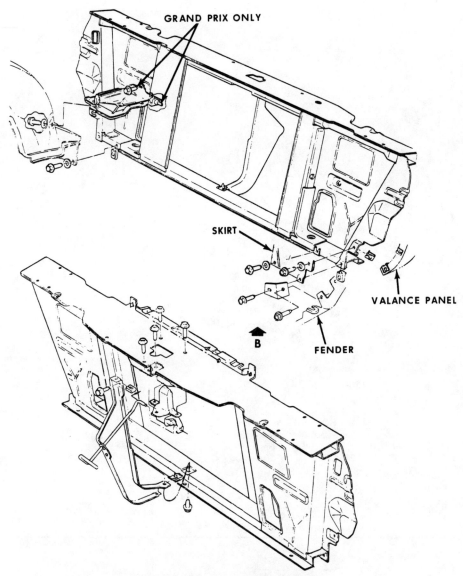

GRAND PRIX ONLY

SKIRT

VALANCE PANEL

B

FENDER

Core support components and installation for 1969 GTO. Grand Prix battery tray installation did not apply to GTO. Entire assembly was painted 60° gloss black. Bolts were black cadmium.

Series	Engine		Standard		Heavy ▲ Duty Radiator		Air Cond. Radiator		Super Cooling Radiator	
	Cubic Inch	Description	M.T.	A.T.	M.T.	A.T.	M.T.	A.T.	M.T.	A.T.
39	350	4 Bbl.	BE	BN	BO	BK	PA	PB	N/A	N/A
42	8-Cyl. 400	4 Bbl. Std.	BO	BS	PA	PB	PA	PM	N/A	N/A
		2 Bbl.	N/A	BN	N/A	BH	N/A	PM	N/A	N/A
		HO	BO	BS	PA	PB	PA	PB	N/A	N/A
		Ram Air	PA	PB	N/A	N/A	N/A	N/A	N/A	N/A

▲Tempest, Firebird & Grand Prix require H.D. Radiator with Axle Ratios above 3.55

1969 radiator usage chart (1.219) for all models.

BL-BN-BI-BH BO-BS-BU-BG	Use 3019205
PA-PB-PP	Use 3025764
PD	Use 3017248
PM	Use 3021744

Service radiators.

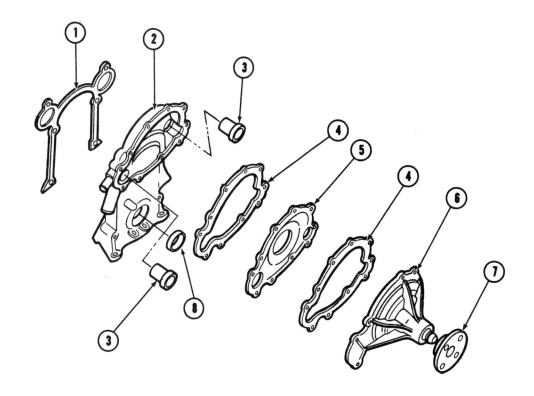

Key	Part Name	Group No.	Key	Part Name	Group No.
1 — GASKET PKG., Timing Chain Cover		0.207	5 — HOUSING, Pump Internal		1.069
2 — COVER ASM., Timing Chain		0.206	6 — PUMP ASM., Water (Incl. #4)		1.069
3 — SLEEVE & SEAL ASM., Pump Outlet		1.069	7 — HUB, Water Pump and Fan		1.062
4 — GASKET, Pump to Timing Chain Cover		1.079	8 — SEAL, Timing Chain Cover Oil		0.213

Exploded view of 1969-70 water pump and divider plate. Assembly was changed from 1968 design.

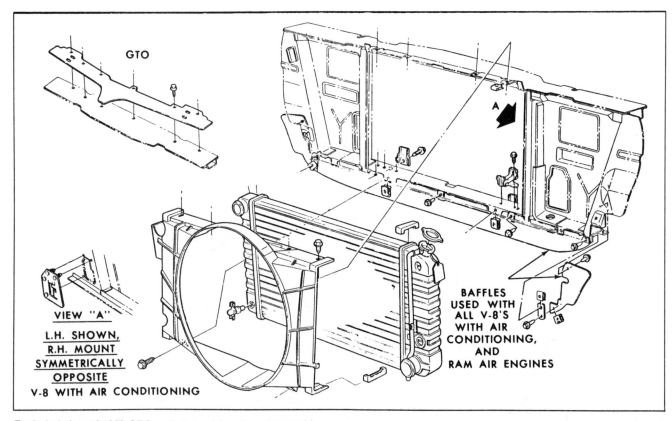

Exploded view of 1969 GTO radiator and fan shroud assembly.
Baffles were used with air-conditioned models.

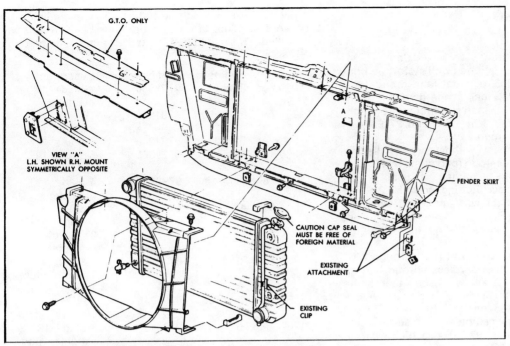

Exploded drawings of 1969-70 radiator and shroud. The same core support was used for all applications, as Pontiac began using cross-flow radiators in 1968.

Service Radiator Number	Radiator Panel & Brackets		Insulators		Fan Shroud
	Top Panel Asm.	Lower Bracket	Top	Bottom	
3019205	–	–	9795948-9	9795948-9	9795359 ▲
3025764	–	–	9795948	9795948	9795359 ▲
3017248	–	–	9795948	9795948	9795359 ▲

▲ For Grand Prix 9795182 Shroud Replaces 9795359 Shroud

Radiator mounting parts.

1970 RADIATOR USAGE CHART—1.219										477749-36
SERIES	ENGINE		STANDARD		HEAVY ▲ DUTY RADIATOR		AIR COND. RADIATOR		SUPER COOLING RADIATOR	
	Cubic Inch	Description	M.T.	A.T.	M.T.	A.T.	M.T.	A.T.	M.T.	A.T.
TEMPEST										
42	8-Cyl. 400	Ram Air - III	BO	BL	PA	PM	PA	PM	N/A	N/A
	8-Cyl. 400	Ram Air - IV	PA	PD	N/A	N/A	N/A	N/A	N/A	N/A
	8-Cyl. 455	4 Bbl.	BO	BL	PA	PD	PA∞	PD∞	N/A	N/A

▲ Tempest, Firebird & Grand Prix require H.D. Radiators with Axle Ratios above 3.55.
∞ Use PS Radiator for Spec. Ord. Locking & Non-Locking Axles.

1970 radiator usage chart (1.219).

SERVICE RADIATORS
BI-BL-BH-BO Use 3019205 (BR)
PD Use 3017248 (PD)
PA Use 3025764 (BT)
PM Use 3021744 (PM)

Service radiators.

RADIATOR MOUNTING PARTS					
Service Radiator Number	RADIATOR PANEL & BRACKETS		INSULATORS		Fan Shroud
	Top Panel Asm.	Lower Bracket	Top	Bottom	
3025764 (BT)	–	–	9795948	9795948	9795359∞
3021744 (PM)	–	–	9795948	9795948	9795359
3019205 (BR)	–	–	9795948-9	9795948-9	9795359∞
3017248 (PD)	–	–	9795948	9795948	9795359∞

Radiator mounting parts.

FAN AND FAN SHROUD

1964-67

Three different fan shrouds were used during 1964-67 GTO production. When equipped with factory air conditioning in 1964 and 1965, a metal fan shroud (part number 9775959) with a 21½ inch inside-diameter opening for the fan was used. A 19½ inch seven-blade declutching fan (part number 9777013 in 1964, and 9779004 in 1965) was used with this shroud.

For 1966 and 1967 models with factory-installed air conditioning, a black plastic shroud (part number 9783757) with an inside diameter of 21½ inches was used. A 19½ inch diameter seven-blade declutching fan with a 2¼ inch pitch (part number 9784546) was employed with this shroud. In 1967, when the Ram Air engine was installed, this fan shroud was also used, but with a four-blade fan (part number 519834).

A third shroud was utilized from 1964 through 1967 (part number 9774621). This fiberglass shroud had an inside diameter of 19½ inches, and was used either for the optional trailer package or for field-installed air conditioning. It could also be used on any 1964-67 non-air-conditioned GTO utilizing an eighteen-inch seven-blade declutching fan (part number 9777014), which was the standard fan on 1964-67 GTOs.

A 60° gloss-black metal fan shield was used for non-air-conditioned 1965-67 GTOs (part number 9781494).

When the Tri-Power engine or the heavy-duty radiator was ordered in 1965, fan shield part number 9781680 was installed. This shield had the radiator cap opening on its RH side.

Year	Engine	Part Number	Description
1968	2bbl	9798940	4-blade, 19" diameter
1968-69	2bbl HD	9791346	19", 2⅜" variable pitch
1968-70	Standard	9791346	5-blade
1968	4bbl HD	9779005	5-blade, 19½", 2¼" pitch
1967-68	Ram Air	9798940	4-blade, 19", diameter
1968-69	AC	9784546	7-blade, square tip, 19" 2¼" pitch, therostatic
1968	RPO 514	9777012	7-blade, Thermo Pitch, 19½", 1⅞" pitch
1969	Ram Air	9791346	19", 2⅜" variable pitch
1969	HD	9796135	7-blade, 19", 2¼" variable pitch
1970	AC	9796134	7-blade, round tip, 19½"

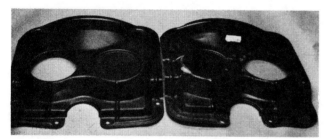

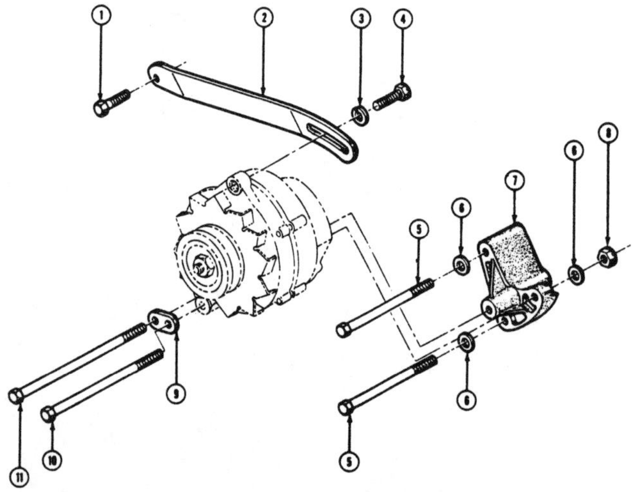

1965 GTOs used a fan shield (part number 9781494) for four-barrel applications (right) and Tri-Power applications (9781680), left. Shield was painted 60° gloss black. Some production cars had the fan caution sticker applied to the shield, others to the top of the core support. Either was correct.

Key	Part Name	Group No.
1 — BOLT, Cover to Manifold (5/16"-18 x 3-3/4")		0.206
2 — STRAP, Delcotron Adjusting		2.317
3 — LOCKWASHER, Strap to Delcotron (3/4 O.D.)		8.931
4 — BOLT, Strap to Delcotron (5/16"-18 x 7/8")		8.900
5 — BOLT, Delcotron Bracket to Cyl. Head (3/8"-16 x 3-1/4")		8.900
6 — WASHER, Delcotron Mtg. Brkt. to Cyl. Head (3/8")		3.275
7 — BRACKET, Delcotron Mounting		2.277
8 — NUT, Bolt to Brkt. Mtg. Lock (3/8"-16)		8.917
9 — PLATE, Delcotron Extension Plate		2.277
10 — BOLT, Plate to Brkt. (3/8"-16 x 4-1/2")		N.S.
11 — BOLT, Plate to Brkt. and Cyl. Head (3/8"-16 x 5-1/2")		8.900

View of 1964-67 alternator and mounting hardware. The adjusting strap used without power steering or air conditioning in 1964 was part number 9774774. The 1965-67 strap was the same, part number 9779013. The natural-aluminum mounting bracket used without power steering or air conditioning, 1964-67, was part number 9774773. When the AIR system was used for the California GTO in 1966 and 1967, a different bracket, (part number 9782667 in 1966 and 9786904 in 1967) was used.

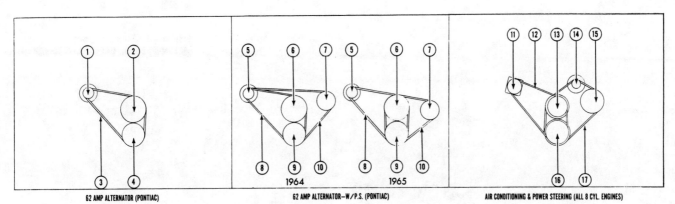

62 AMP ALTERNATOR (PONTIAC)   **62 AMP ALTERNATOR—W/P.S. (PONTIAC)** — 1964 / 1965   **AIR CONDITIONING & POWER STEERING (ALL 8 CYL. ENGINES)**

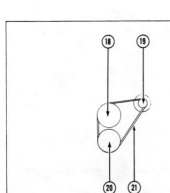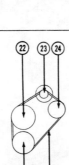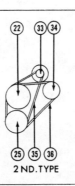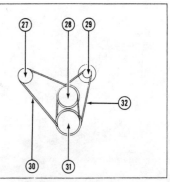

STANDARD CAR (ALL 8 CYL. ENGINES)   **POWER STEERING (ALL 8 CYL. ENGINES)** — 1ST. TYPE / 2ND. TYPE   **AIR CONDITIONING (ALL 8 CYL. ENGINES)**

Key	Group No.	Part No. 1964	Part No. 1965	Description	Size
1	–	N.S.		Pulley (2-Groove)	3 7/16" dia.
			9779456	Pulley (2-Groove)	3 7/16" dia.
2	1.062	538547		Fan Pulley (2-Groove)	8 1/32" dia.
			9778808	Fan Pulley (2-Groove)	8" dia.
3	1.066	9772317	9772317	Belt (2 Required)	1/2" x 62"
4	0.659	9775627		Balancer (2-Groove)	7 9/32" dia.
			9778802	Balancer (2-Groove)	7 1/4" dia.
5	–	N.S.		Pulley (2-Groove)	3 7/16" dia.
			9779456	Pulley (2-Groove)	3 7/16" dia.
6	1.062	538547		Fan Pulley (2-Groove)	8 1/32" dia.
			9778808	Fan Pulley (2-Groove)	8" dia.
7	6.655	9774775		Pulley (2-Groove – 1st Type)	5 7/8" dia.
		9778378		Pulley (1-Groove – 2nd Type)	5 7/8" dia.
			9777401	Pulley (1-Groove)	5 7/8" dia.
8	1.066	9772317	9772317	Belt (2-Required)	1/2" x 62"
9	0.659	9775627		Balancer (2-Groove)	7 9/32" dia.
			9778802	Balancer (2-Groove)	7 1/4" dia.
10	1.066	9775643		Belt	3/8" x 77"
			9779019	Belt	3/8" x 51 1/2"
11	9.180	5914730	5914730	Pulley and Bearing Asm.	4 7/8" dia.
12	1.066	9772317	9772317	Belt	1/2" x 62"
13	1.062	544594		Fan Pulley (2-Groove)	7 13/32" dia.
			9781739	Fan Pulley (2-Groove)	7 3/8" dia.
14	2.274	1949357		Pulley (1-Groove)	2 3/4" dia.
		1949358		Pulley (1-Groove)	3" dia.
			1949355	Pulley (1-Groove) W/P.S.	2 1/2" dia.
			1949357	Pulley (1-Groove) Exc. P.S.	2 3/4" dia.
15	6.655	544840		Pulley (Tempest)	6 21/32" dia.
		9774454		Pulley (Pontiac)	7 5/8" dia.
			9779020	Pulley (Pontiac & Tempest)	7 3/8" dia.
16	0.659	9775626		Balancer (2-Groove)	8 9/32" dia.
			9781740	Balancer (2-Groove)	8 5/16" dia.
17	1.066	3861956		Belt (Tempest)	3/8" x 59"
			9775522	Belt (Pontiac)	1/2" x 60 1/2"
		9789342		Belt (Pontiac & Tempest)	1/2" x 56 1/2"
18	1.062	544595	544595	Fan Pulley (1-Groove)	8" dia.
19	2.274	1949357	1949357	Pulley (1-Groove)	2 3/4" dia.
20	0.659	9775627		Balancer (2-Groove)	7 9/32" dia.
			9778802	Balancer (2-Groove)	7 1/4" dia.
21	1.066	9790635		Belt	3/8" x 53 1/2"
			542881	Belt	3/8" x 54"
22	1.062	538547		Fan Pulley (2-Groove)	8" dia.
			9778808	Fan Pulley (2-Groove)	8" dia.
23	2.274	1962998		Pulley (2-Groove – 1st Type)	2 5/8" dia.
24	6.655	9774775		Pulley (2-Groove – 1st Type)	5 7/8" dia.
25	0.659	9775627		Balancer (2-Groove)	7 9/32" dia.
			9778802	Balancer (2-Groove)	7 1/4" dia.
26	1.066	9775476		Belt Pkg. (Set of 2 Belts – 1st Type)	3/8" x 57 1/2"
27	9.180	5914730	5914730	Pulley & Bearing Asm.	4 7/8" dia.
28	1.062	544594		Fan Pulley (2-Groove)	7 13/32" dia.
			9781739	Fan Pulley (2-Groove)	7 3/8" dia.
29	2.274	1949357		Pulley (1-Groove)	2 3/4" dia.
		1949358		Pulley (1-Groove)	3" dia.
			1949357	Pulley (1-Groove)	2 3/4" dia.
30	1.066	9772317	9772317	Belt	1/2" x 62"
31	0.659	9775626		Balancer (2-Groove)	8 9/32" dia.
			9781740	Balancer (2-Groove)	8 5/16" dia.
32	1.066	548659		Belt	13/32" x 53 3/8"
			542881	Belt	3/8" x 54"
33	2.274	1949357		Pulley (1-Groove) (2nd Type 1964)	2 3/4" dia.
34	6.655	9778378		Pulley (1-Groove) (2nd Type)	5 7/8" dia.
			9777401	Pulley (1-Groove)	5 7/8" dia.
35	1.066	9779017		Belt	3/8" x 50 1/2"
			9779017	Belt	3/8" x 50 1/2"
36	1.066	9776573		Belt (2nd Type)	3/8" x 55 1/2"
			9779019	Belt	3/8" x 51 1/2"

Here are the belt arrangements and specifications for the 1964 and 1965 GTO.

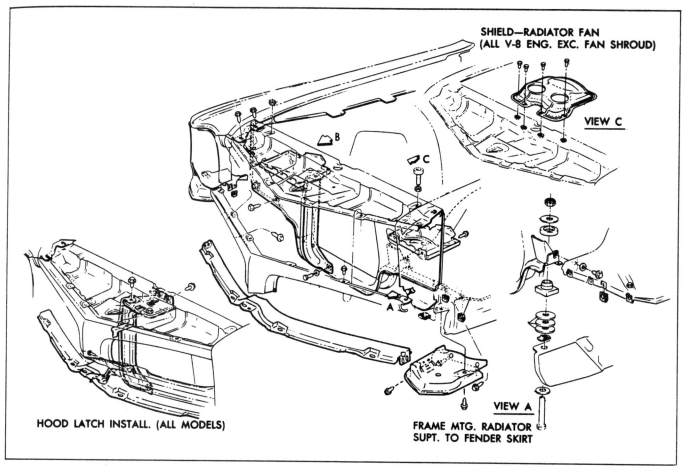

SHIELD—RADIATOR FAN (ALL V-8 ENG. EXC. FAN SHROUD)

VIEW C

B

C

A

VIEW A

HOOD LATCH INSTALL. (ALL MODELS)

FRAME MTG. RADIATOR SUPT. TO FENDER SKIRT

Drawing of installation of fan shield, core-support mounting hardware, and mounting of core support to front end sheet metal.

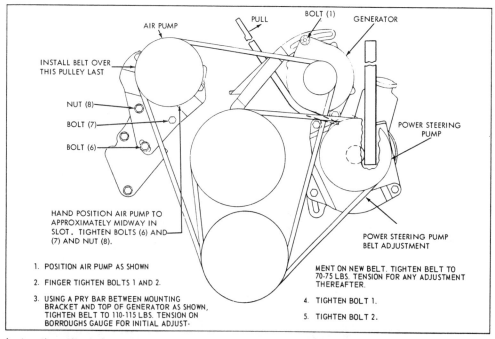

AIR PUMP

PULL

BOLT (1)

GENERATOR

INSTALL BELT OVER THIS PULLEY LAST

NUT (8)

BOLT (7)

BOLT (6)

POWER STEERING PUMP

HAND POSITION AIR PUMP TO APPROXIMATELY MIDWAY IN SLOT. TIGHTEN BOLTS (6) AND (7) AND NUT (8).

POWER STEERING PUMP BELT ADJUSTMENT

1. POSITION AIR PUMP AS SHOWN

2. FINGER TIGHTEN BOLTS 1 AND 2.

3. USING A PRY BAR BETWEEN MOUNTING BRACKET AND TOP OF GENERATOR AS SHOWN, TIGHTEN BELT TO 110-115 LBS. TENSION ON BORROUGHS GAUGE FOR INITIAL ADJUST-

MENT ON NEW BELT. TIGHTEN BELT TO 70-75 LBS. TENSION FOR ANY ADJUSTMENT THEREAFTER.

4. TIGHTEN BOLT 1.

5. TIGHTEN BOLT 2.

Instructions for belt tension adjustments for 1966 GTO with power steering and AIR.

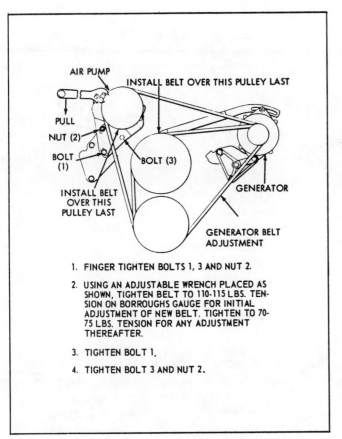

1. FINGER TIGHTEN BOLTS 1, 3 AND NUT 2.

2. USING AN ADJUSTABLE WRENCH PLACED AS SHOWN, TIGHTEN BELT TO 110-115 LBS. TENSION ON BORROUGHS GAUGE FOR INITIAL ADJUSTMENT OF NEW BELT. TIGHTEN TO 70-75 LBS. TENSION FOR ANY ADJUSTMENT THEREAFTER.

3. TIGHTEN BOLT 1.

4. TIGHTEN BOLT 3 AND NUT 2.

Instructions for adjusting belt tension on AIR 1966 GTOs when not equipped with power steering.

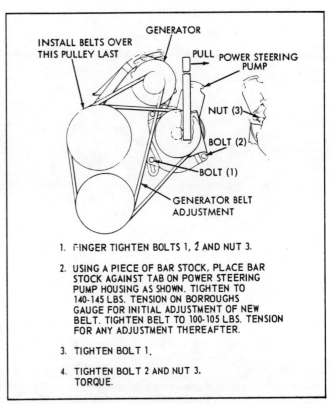

1. FINGER TIGHTEN BOLTS 1, 2 AND NUT 3.

2. USING A PIECE OF BAR STOCK, PLACE BAR STOCK AGAINST TAB ON POWER STEERING PUMP HOUSING AS SHOWN. TIGHTEN TO 140-145 LBS. TENSION ON BORROUGHS GAUGE FOR INITIAL ADJUSTMENT OF NEW BELT. TIGHTEN BELT TO 100-105 LBS. TENSION FOR ANY ADJUSTMENT THEREAFTER.

3. TIGHTEN BOLT 1.

4. TIGHTEN BOLT 2 AND NUT 3.
TORQUE.

Illustration of belt-tightening procedure for the 1966 GTO equipped with power steering.

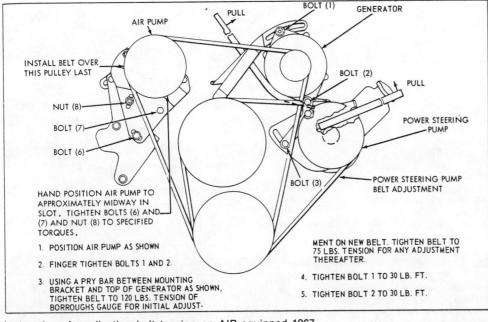

HAND POSITION AIR PUMP TO APPROXIMATELY MIDWAY IN SLOT. TIGHTEN BOLTS (6) AND (7) AND NUT (8) TO SPECIFIED TORQUES.

1. POSITION AIR PUMP AS SHOWN

2. FINGER TIGHTEN BOLTS 1 AND 2.

3. USING A PRY BAR BETWEEN MOUNTING BRACKET AND TOP OF GENERATOR AS SHOWN, TIGHTEN BELT TO 120 LBS. TENSION OF BORROUGHS GAUGE FOR INITIAL ADJUST-

MENT ON NEW BELT. TIGHTEN BELT TO 75 LBS. TENSION FOR ANY ADJUSTMENT THEREAFTER.

4. TIGHTEN BOLT 1 TO 30 LB. FT.

5. TIGHTEN BOLT 2 TO 30 LB. FT.

Instructions for adjusting belt tension on AIR-equipped 1967 GTO.

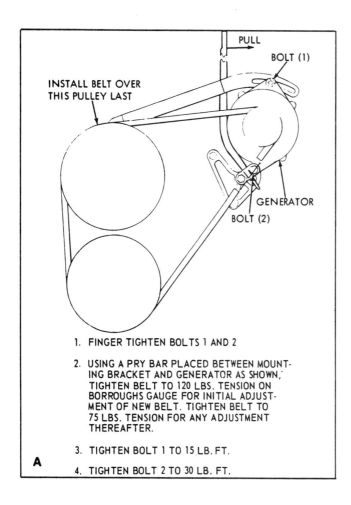

A

1. FINGER TIGHTEN BOLTS 1 AND 2

2. USING A PRY BAR PLACED BETWEEN MOUNT-
   ING BRACKET AND GENERATOR AS SHOWN,
   TIGHTEN BELT TO 120 LBS. TENSION ON
   BORROUGHS GAUGE FOR INITIAL ADJUST-
   MENT OF NEW BELT. TIGHTEN BELT TO
   75 LBS. TENSION FOR ANY ADJUSTMENT
   THEREAFTER.

3. TIGHTEN BOLT 1 TO 15 LB. FT.

4. TIGHTEN BOLT 2 TO 30 LB. FT.

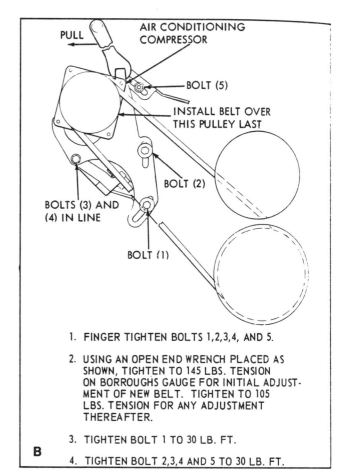

B

1. FINGER TIGHTEN BOLTS 1,2,3,4, AND 5.

2. USING AN OPEN END WRENCH PLACED AS
   SHOWN, TIGHTEN TO 145 LBS. TENSION
   ON BORROUGHS GAUGE FOR INITIAL ADJUST-
   MENT OF NEW BELT. TIGHTEN TO 105
   LBS. TENSION FOR ANY ADJUSTMENT
   THEREAFTER.

3. TIGHTEN BOLT 1 TO 30 LB. FT.

4. TIGHTEN BOLT 2,3,4 AND 5 TO 30 LB. FT.

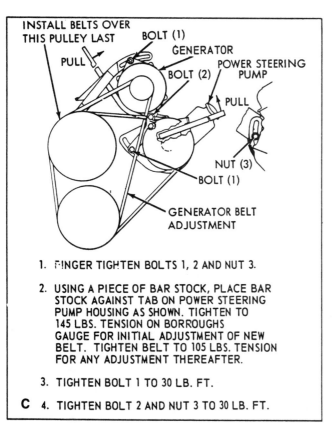

C

1. FINGER TIGHTEN BOLTS 1, 2 AND NUT 3.

2. USING A PIECE OF BAR STOCK, PLACE BAR
   STOCK AGAINST TAB ON POWER STEERING
   PUMP HOUSING AS SHOWN. TIGHTEN TO
   145 LBS. TENSION ON BORROUGHS
   GAUGE FOR INITIAL ADJUSTMENT OF NEW
   BELT. TIGHTEN BELT TO 105 LBS. TENSION
   FOR ANY ADJUSTMENT THEREAFTER.

3. TIGHTEN BOLT 1 TO 30 LB. FT.

4. TIGHTEN BOLT 2 AND NUT 3 TO 30 LB. FT.

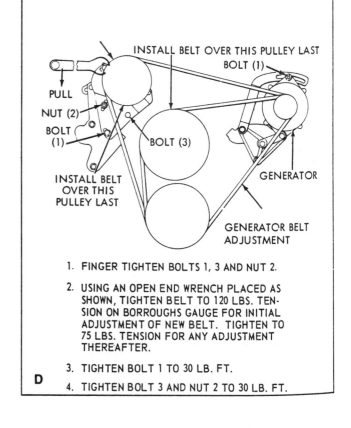

D

1. FINGER TIGHTEN BOLTS 1, 3 AND NUT 2.

2. USING AN OPEN END WRENCH PLACED AS
   SHOWN, TIGHTEN BELT TO 120 LBS. TEN-
   SION ON BORROUGHS GAUGE FOR INITIAL
   ADJUSTMENT OF NEW BELT. TIGHTEN TO
   75 LBS. TENSION FOR ANY ADJUSTMENT
   THEREAFTER.

3. TIGHTEN BOLT 1 TO 30 LB. FT.

4. TIGHTEN BOLT 3 AND NUT 2 TO 30 LB. FT.

1966-67 manual-steering alternator belt tightening specifications
(A). 1966-67 air-conditioning compressor belt tension specifications (B). 1967 power steering and alternator belt tightening specifications (C). 1966-67 manual-steering and AIR belt tightening
specifications (D).

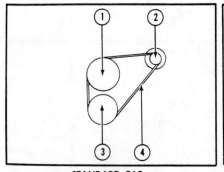

STANDARD CAR

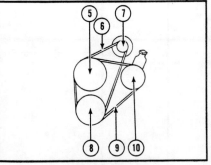

POWER STEERING

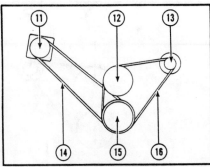

AIR CONDITIONING

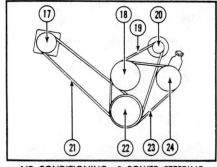

AIR CONDITIONING & POWER STEERING

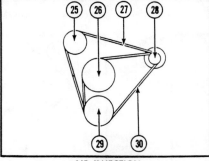

AIR INJECTION

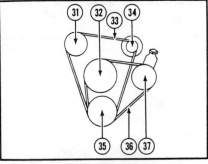

AIR INJECTION & POWER STEERING

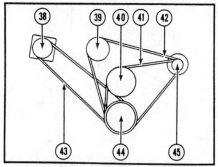

AIR CONDITIONING & AIR INJECTION

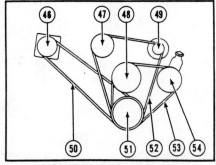

AIR CONDITIONING, AIR INJECTION POWER STEERING

Key	Group No.	1966	1967	Description	1966	1967
1	1.062	544595	544595	FAN PULLEY (1-Groove)	8" dia.	8" dia.
2	2.274	1949357	1949357	PULLEY (1-Groove)	2 3/4" dia.	2 3/4" dia.
3	0.659	9783144	9786714	BALANCER (2-Groove)	7 1/4" dia.	7 5/16" dia.
4	1.066	542881	542881	BELT	3/8" x 54"	3/8" x 54"
5	1.062	9778808	9786819	PULLEY (2-Groove)	8" dia.	8" dia.
6	1.066	9779017	9786983	BELT	3/8" x 50 1/2"	3/8" x 50"
7	2.274	1949357	1949357	PULLEY (1-Groove)	2 3/4" dia.	2 3/4" dia.
8	0.659	9783144	9786714	BALANCER (2-Groove)	7 1/4" dia.	7 5/16" dia.
9	1.066	9783071	9778558	BELT	1/2" x 52 1/2"	1/2" x 52"
10	6.655	9777401	9786900	PULLEY	5 7/8" dia.	5 7/8" dia.
11	9.180	5914730	5914730	PULLEY & BEARING ASM.	4 7/8" dia.	4 7/8" dia.
12	1.062	9782679	9786909	PULLEY	7" dia.	7 1/8" dia.
13	2.274	1949357	1949357	PULLEY (1-Groove)	2 3/4" dia.	2 3/4" dia.
14	1.066	9782705	9782705	BELT	1/2" x 59"	1/2" x 59"
15	0.659	9782703	9786908	BALANCER (3-Groove)	8" dia.	8" dia.
16	1.066	542881	542881	BELT	3/8" x 54"	3/8" x 54"
17	9.180	5914730	5914730	PULLEY & BEARING ASM.	4 7/8" dia.	4 7/8" dia.
18	1.062	9782679	9786909	PULLEY	7" dia.	7 1/8" dia.
19	1.066	9779017	9786983	BELT	3/8" x 50 1/2"	3/8" x 50"
20	2.274	1949357	1949357	PULLEY (1-Groove)	2 3/4" dia.	2 3/4" dia.
21	1.066	9782705	9782705	BELT	1/2" x 59	1/2" x 59
22	0.659	9782703	9786908	BALANCER (3-Groove)	8" dia.	8" dia.
23	1.066	9782706	9786985	BELT	1/2" x 53 1/2"	1/2" x 53 1/2"
24	6.655	9782671	9786901	PULLEY	7 3/8" dia.	7 1/8" dia.
25	3.650	9785478	9785478	PULLEY	6 1/8" dia.	6 1/8" dia.
26	1.062	9778808	9786819	PULLEY (2-Groove)	8" dia.	8" dia.
27	1.066	9782708	9786812	BELT	3/8" x 68"	3/8" x 69"
28	2.274	1966002	1967651	PULLEY	2 27/32" dia.	2 3/4" dia.
29	0.659	9783144	9786714	BALANCER (2-Groove)	7 1/4" dia.	7 5/16" dia.
30	1.066	9772704	9786714	BELT	3/8" x 56"	1/2" x 57"
31	3.650	9785478	9785478	PULLEY (1-Groove)	6 1/8" dia.	6 1/8" dia.
32	1.062	9778808	9786819	PULLEY (2-Groove)	8" dia.	8" dia.
33	1.066	9782709	9786982	BELT	3/8" x 62"	3/8" x 61 3/16"
34	2.274	1949357	1949357	PULLEY (1-Groove)	2 3/4" dia.	2 3/4" dia.
35	0.659	9783144	9786714	BALANCER (2-Groove)	7 1/4" dia.	7 5/16" dia.
36	1.066	9785071	9778558	BELT	1/2" x 52 1/2"	1/2" x 52"
37	6.655	9777401	9786900	PULLEY	5 7/8" dia.	5 7/8" dia.
38	9.180	5914730	5914730	PULLEY & BEARING	4 7/8" dia.	4 7/8" dia.
39	3.650	9782664	9782664	PULLEY (1-Groove)	5 5/8" dia.	5 5/8" dia.
40	1.062	9782679	9788886	PULLEY (2-Groove)	7" dia.	5 11/16" dia.
41	1.066	9772704	9789342	BELT	3/8" x 56"	1/2" x 56 5/8"
42	1.066	9782708	9786812	BELT	3/8" x 68"	3/8" x 69"
44	0.659	9782703	9786908	BALANCER (3-Groove)	8" dia.	8" dia.
45	2.274	1966003	1967651	PULLEY (2-Groove)	2 27/32" dia.	2 3/4" dia.
46	9.180	5914730	5914730	PULLEY & BEARING ASM.	4 7/8" dia.	4 7/8" dia.
47	3.650	9782664	9782664	PULLEY (1-Groove)	5 5/8" dia.	5 5/8" dia.
48	1.062	9782679	9788886	PULLEY (2-Groove)	7" dia.	5 11/16" dia.
49	2.274	1949357	1949357	PULLEY (1-Groove)	2 3/4" dia.	2 3/4" dia.
50	1.066	9782705	9782705	BELT	1/2" x 59"	1/2" x 59"
51	0.659	9782703	9786908	BALANCER (3-Groove)	8" dia.	8" dia.
52	1.066	9782709	9786982	BELT	3/8" x 62"	3/8" x 61 3/16"
53	1.066	9782706	9786985	BELT	1/2" x 54"	1/2" x 53 1/2"
54	6.655	9782671	9786901	PULLEY (1-Groove)	7 3/8" dia.	7 1/8" dia.

Complete nomenclature and part number descriptions for 1966-67 pulley and belt applications.

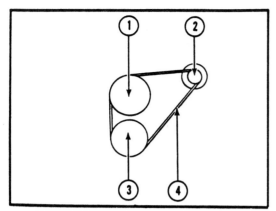

STANDARD CAR

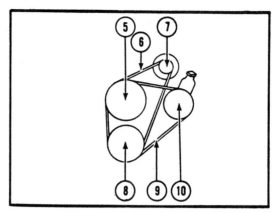

POWER STEERING

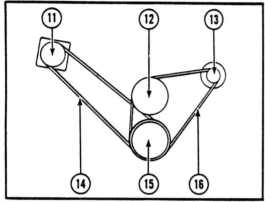

AIR CONDITIONING

1968

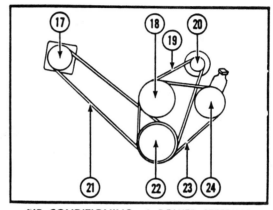

AIR CONDITIONING & POWER STEERING

1969

Key	Group No.	Part No.	Description	Size
1	1.062	9790946	Pulley (1-Groove)	8" dia.
2	2.274	1949357	Pulley (1-Groove)	2-3/4" dia.
3	0.659	477682	Balancer (less pulley)	6-13/16" dia.
	0.659	9790947	Pulley (1-Groove)	7-1/4" dia.
4	1.066	539130	Belt	3/8" x 47-1/2"
5	1.062	9786819	Pulley (2-Groove)	8" dia.
6	1.066	391201	Belt (Tempest & Firebird Exc. A. T.)	3/8" x 50"
	1.066	3909819	Belt (Tempest & Firebird w/A. T.)	3/8" x 49-1/2"
7	2.274	1949357	Pulley (1-Groove)	2-3/4" dia.
8	0.659	477682	Balancer (less pulley)	6-13/16" dia.
	0.659	9790846	Pulley (2-Groove)	7-5/16" dia.
9	1.066	9789230	Belt	1/2" x 52"
10	6.655	9786900	Pulley.	5-7/8" dia.
11	9.180	5914730	Pulley & Bearing Asm.	4-7/8" dia.
12	1.062	9788886	Pulley	5-11/16" dia.
13	2.274	1949357	Pulley (1-Groove)	2-3/4" dia.
14	1.066	9782705	Belt	1/2" x 59"
15	0.659	477682	Balancer (less pulley)	6-13/16" dia.
	0.659	9790843	Pulley (1-Groove)	7-5/16" dia.
	0.659	9790842	Pulley (2-Groove)	8" dia.
16	1.066	539130	Belt	3/8" x 47-1/2"
17	9.180	5914730	Pulley & Bearing Asm.	4-7/8" dia.
18	1.062	9788886	Pulley	5-11/16" dia.
19	1.066	3909819	Belt	3/8" x 49-1/2"
20	2.274	1949357	Pulley (1-Groove)	2-3/4" dia.
21	1.066	9782705	Belt	1/2" x 59"
22	0.659	477682	Balancer (less pulley)	6-13/16" dia.
	0.659	9790843	Pulley (1-Groove)	7-5/16" dia.
	0.659	9790842	Pulley (2-Groove)	8" dia.
23	1.066	1375404	Belt (Firebird w/A. T.)	1/2" x 53"
	1.066	9786985	Belt (Tempest & Firebird Exc. A. T.)	1/2" x 53-1/2"
24	6.655	9786900	Pulley.	5-7/8" dia.

Key	Group No.	Part No.	Description	Size
1	1.062	9796059	Pulley (1-Groove)	8" dia.
2	2.274	1949357	Pulley (1-Groove)	2-3/4" dia.
3	0.659	477682	Balancer (less pulley) exc. Ram Air	6-13/16" dia.
	0.659	9794058	Balancer (less pulley) Ram Air	6-13/16" dia.
	0.659	9790947	Pulley (1-Groove)	7-1/4" dia.
4	1.066	539130	Belt	3/8 x 47-1/2
5	1.062	9796060	Pulley (2-Groove)	8" dia.
6	1.066	391201	Belt	3/8" x 50"
7	2.274	1949357	Pulley (1-Groove)	2-3/4" dia.
8	0.659	477682	Balancer (less pulley) exc. Ram Air	6-13/16" dia.
	0.659	9794058	Balancer (less pulley) Ram Air	6-13/16" dia.
	0.659	9790846	Pulley (2-Groove)	7-5/16" dia.
9	1.066	9789230	Belt	1/2" x 52"
10	6.655	9786900	Pulley	5-7/8" dia.
11	9.180	5914730	Pulley & Brg. Asm.	4-7/8" dia.
12	1.062	9796062	Pulley – (2-Groove) exc. F/8 H.T. (M40) less V.P. fan	7-3/16" dia.
	1.062	9796061	Pulley – (2-Groove) F/8 H.T. (M40) less V.P. fan	6-1/2" dia.
13	2.274	1949357	Pulley (1-Groove)	2-3/4" dia.
14	1.066	9782705	Belt	1/2" x 59-1/2"
15	0.659	477682	Balancer (less pulley)	6-13/16" dia.
	0.659	9790843	Pulley (1-Groove)	7-5/16" dia.
	0.659	9790842	Pulley (2-Groove)	8" dia.
16	1.066	539130	Belt	3/8" x 47-1/2"
17	9.180	5914730	Pulley & Brg. Asm.	4-7/8" dia.
18	1.062	9796062	Pulley – (2-Groove) exc. F/8 H.T. (M40) less V.P. fan	7-3/16" dia.
	1.062	9796061	Pulley – (2-Groove) F/8 H.T. (M40) less V.P. fan	6-1/2" dia.
19	1.066	3909819	Belt	3/8 x 49-1/2"
20	2.274	1949357	Pulley – (1-Groove)	2-3/4" dia.
21	1.066	9782705	Belt	1/2" x 59"
22	0.659	477682	Balancer (less pulley)	6-13/16" dia.
	0.659	9790843	Pulley (1-Groove)	7-5/16" dia.
	0.659	9790842	Pulley (2-Groove)	8" dia.
23	1.066	1375404	Belt	1/2" x 53"
24	6.655	9786901	Pulley	7-3/32" dia.

1968 and 1969 Tempest eight-cylinder engine pulley and belt application.

DRIVE BELTS			
Belt Width		**Belt Tension New**	**Belt Tension Used**
8 CYLINDER			
3/8"	Water Pump and Generator Belt	110–125	70–75
1/2"	Power Steering Belt	135–150	100–105
1/2"	Air Conditioning Belt	135–150	100–105

1970 drive belts.

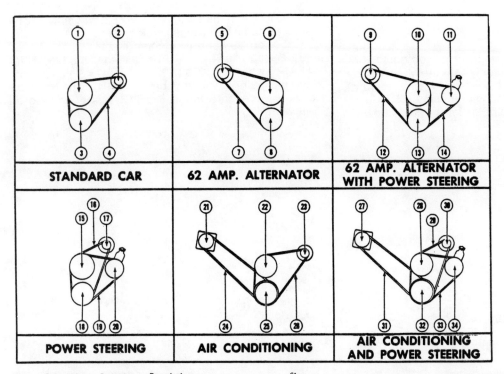

STANDARD CAR		62 AMP. ALTERNATOR		62 AMP. ALTERNATOR WITH POWER STEERING		
POWER STEERING		AIR CONDITIONING		AIR CONDITIONING AND POWER STEERING		

Key	Group No.	Part No.	Description	Size
1	1.062	9799129	Pulley (1-Groove) . . . . 8" dia.	
2	2.274	1949357	Pulley (1-Groove) . . . . 2 3/4" dia.	
	0.659	477682	Balancer (less pulley) . . . . . . 6 13/16" dia.	
	0.659	9790747	Pulley (1-Groove) . . . . 7 1/4" dia.	
4	1.066	539130	Belt . . . . 3/8" x 47 1/2"	
5	2.274	9787141	Pulley (2-Groove) (P/8) . . . . 3 37/64" dia.	
6	1.062	9799127	Pulley (2-Groove) (P/8) . . . . 8" dia.	
7	1.066	9772317	Belt (P/8 exc. Police) . . . . . . 1/2" x 62"	
	1.066	9792634	Belt Set (P/8 Police) . . . . 1/2" x 62"	
	0.659	477682	Balancer (less pulley) . . . . . . 6 13/16" dia.	
	0.659	9790846	Pulley (2-Groove) (P/8) . . . . . 7 1/4" dia.	
9	2.274	9787141	Pulley (2-Groove) (P/8) . . . . 3 37/64" dia.	
10	1.062	9799127	Pulley (2-Groove) (P/8) . . . . 8" dia.	
11	6.655	9786900	Pulley (1-Groove) (P/8) . . . . 5 7/8" dia.	
12	1.066	9772317	Belt . . . . 1/2" x 62"	
	0.659	477682	Balancer (less pulley) . . . . . . 6 13/16" dia.	
	0.659	9790846	Pulley (2-Groove) . . . . 7 1/4" dia.	
14	1.066	9789230	Belt . . . . 1/2" x 52"	
15	1.062	9799127	Pulley (2-Groove) . . . . 8" dia.	
16	1.066	391201	Belt . . . . 3/8" x 50"	
17	2.274	1949357	Pulley (1-Groove) . . . . 2 3/4" dia.	
	0.659	477682	Balancer (less pulley) . . . . . . 6 13/16" dia.	
	0.659	9790846	Pulley (2-Groove) . . . . 7 1/4" dia.	
19	1.066	9789230	Belt . . . . 1/2" x 52"	
20	6.655	9786900	Pulley (1-Groove) . . . . 5 7/8" dia.	
21	9.180	5914730	Pulley & Bearing . . . . 4 7/8" dia.	
22	1.062	9799128	Pulley (2-Groove) . . . . 6 7/8" dia.	
23	2.274	1949357	Pulley (1-Groove) . . . . 2 3/4" dia.	
24	1.066	478012	Belt . . . . 15/32" x 59 1/4"	
25	0.659	477682	Balancer (less pulley) . . . . . . 6 13/16" dia.	
	0.659	9790843	Pulley (1-Groove) . . . . 7 5/16" dia.	
	0.659	9790842	Pulley (2-Groove) . . . . 8" dia.	
26	1.066	539130	Belt . . . . 3/8" x 47 1/2"	
27	9.180	5914730	Pulley & Bearing . . . . 4 7/8" dia.	
28	1.062	9799128	Pulley (2-Groove) . . . . 6 7/8" dia.	
29	1.066	539130	Belt . . . . 3/8" x 50"	
30	2.274	1949357	Pulley (1-Groove) . . . . 2 3/4" dia.	
31	1.066	478012	Belt . . . . 15/32" x 59 1/4"	
32	0.659	477682	Balancer (less pulley) . . . . . . 6 13/16" dia.	
	0.659	9790843	Pulley (1-Groove) . . . . 7 5/16" dia.	
	0.659	9790842	Pulley (2-Groove) . . . . 8" dia.	
33	1.066	9786985	Belt . . . . 1/2" x 53 1/2"	
34	6.655	9786900	Pulley (1-Groove) . . . . 5 7/8" dia.	

1970 eight-cylinder engine pulley and belt application.

FAN TYPES AND USAGE		
FAN		USAGE
No. Blades	Diameter X Pitch	
4		
	19" x 2"	350, 400 M.T. w/o A/C
5	19" x 2 3/8"	GTO, G.P. w/o A/C Catalina, Executive, Bonneville w/455 C.I. w/o A/C
7		
	19" x 2 1/2"	GTO & G.P. w/455 M.T. w/A/C 455 HO All
	19 1/2" x 2 1/4"	TEMP w/350 or 400 & A/C GTO & G.P. w/400 or 455 A.T. w/A/C Catalina, Executive Bonneville w/A/C All w/K02

1970 fan types and usage.

CRUISE CONTROL

1967-70

Cruise control was offered as an option from 1967 through 1970. It was available only with the M-40 Turbo Hydra-matic transmission. The lever and switch assembly was the same for all four years (part number 6465256). A button was located at the end of the lever to activate the control. A switch (part number 9794682) was activated by the brake pedal to disengage the system.

The cruise-control regulator was the same for 1967 and 1968 (part number 9787978, RPO 441); the 1969 (RPO 441, UPC K30) and 1970 (RPO 481, UPC K30) units were interchangeable (part number 9797504). The vacuum-release switch (part number 6465213) was the same for all four years.

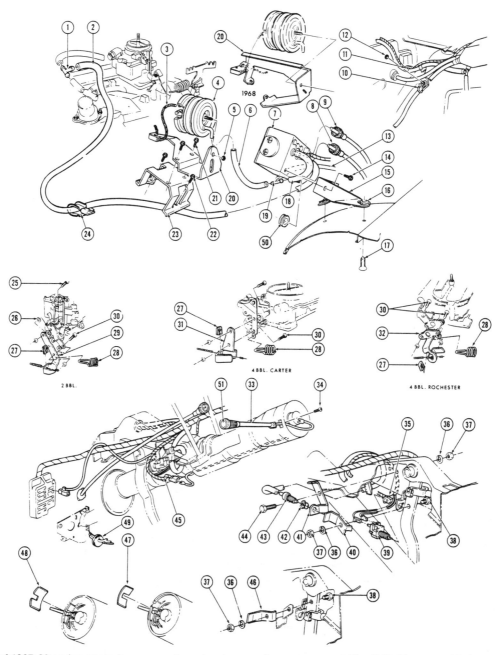

Exploded view of 1967-68 cruise-control components and parts nomenclature. Note the mounting of the 1967 servo (part number 9787977) to a servo support bracket (part number 9787979) which was mounted to a bracket attached to the valve cover retaining bolts (part number 9780749). The brackets for all years were painted 60° gloss black. Two speedometer cables, upper and lower, were used. The 1967-68 upper cable (part number 6454759) measured 32⅛ inches long. The lower cable for 1967 was part number 6476588. The 1968-70 lower cable (part number 6476811) measured 49½ inches long. The 1969-70 upper cable was the same (part number 6477421).

Key	Part Name	Group No.
1 — TEE, Cruise Control Hose Vacuum Source-3 Way		3.885
2 — HOSE, Tee to Regulator (7/32" x 39")		3.885
3 — CHAIN ASM., Cruise Control-Bead		3.885
4 — SERVO ASM., Cruise Control Vacuum		3.887
5 — NUT, Servo to Mounting Bracket (1/4"-20)		8.915
6 — HOSE, Tee to Servo (9/32" x 9 1/4")		3.885
7 — REGULATOR ASM., Cruise Control		3.885
8 — CABLE & CASING ASM., Speedometer-Upper		4.342
9 — CABLE & CASING ASM., Speedometer-Lower		4.342
10 — CLIP, Speedometer Cable		N.S.
11 — STRAP, Cruise Control Switch Hose to Wire Harness		3.885
12 — NUT, Cable Clip to Fender Skirt (5/16"-18)		8.915
13 — HOSE, Tee to Release Switch (7/32" x 53")		3.885
14 — SCREW, Regulator to Brkt. (1/4"-20 x 1/2")		8.977
15 — BRACKET, Cruise Control Regulator		3.885
16 — NUT, Regulator Bracket to Skirt (5/16"-12 "U" Shape)		8.921
17 — SCREW, Regulator Bracket to Skirt (5/16"-12 x 5/8")		8.977
18 — HOSE, Regulator to Tee (9/32" x 7 3/4")		3.885
19 — TEE, Cruise Control Vacuum Hose Release Switch		3.885
20 — BRACKET ASM., Cruise Control Servo Support		3.885
21 — SCREW, Servo Bracket to Power Unit Brkt. (1/4"-20 x 1/2")		8.977
22 — BOLT, Rocker Arm Cover		0.413
23 — BRACKET, Cruise Control Power Servo		3.885
24 — CLIP, Regulator Hose to Servo Supt. Brkt.		N.S.
25 — BOLT, Carb. Lever Extension (1/4"-20 x 3/4")		8.900
26 — WASHER, Carb. Lever Extension (11/32" I.D. x 3/4" O.D. x 3/32")		2.277
27 — CLIP, Bead Chain to Carb. Extension		3.885
28 — SPRING, Throttle Control Return		3.459
29 — EXTENSION, Carb. Lever (4 Holes) (326-2 B.C.)		3.454
30 — BOLT, Carb. Lever Extension (1/4"-20 x 5/8")		8.900
31 — EXTENSION, Carb. Lever (3 Holes) (326-4 B.C.)		3.454
32 — EXTENSION, Carb. Lever (400-4 B.C.)		3.454
33 — LEVER & SWITCH ASM., Direction Signal		3.887
34 — SCREW, Lever to Switch (#8-32 x 5/8")		8.977
35 — CLIP, Stop Light Switch to Bracket		2.447
36 — LOCKWASHER, Striker to Pedal (5/16")		8.931
37 — NUT, Striker to Pedal (5/16"-18)		8.915
38 — BOLT, Striker to Pedal (5/16"-18 x 7/8")		8.900
39 — SWITCH ASM., Stop Light & Cruise Control Release		2.447
40 — STRIKER, Cruise Control Vacuum Release Valve (S.B.)		3.880
41 — BRACKET, Cruise Control Vacuum Release Valve		3.880
42 — CLIP, Release Switch to Bracket		3.885
43 — SWITCH ASM., Cruise Control Vacuum Release		3.883
44 — BOLT, Valve Bracket to Pedal Bracket (5/16"-18 x 3/4")		8.900
45 — WIRE ASM., Cruise Control		3.887
46 — STRIKER, Cruise Control Vacuum Release Valve (P.B.)		3.880
47 — SHIELD, Cruise Cont. Engage Switch Wire (Tilt Wheel)		3.885
48 — SHIELD, Cruise Cont. Engage Switch Wire (Exc. Tilt Wheel)		3.885
49 — GROMMET, Speedo Cable Through Dash - 2" Wide		9.775
50 — GROMMET, Cruise Control Regulator Bracket		3.885
51 — BUTTON, Cruise Control Switch		3.883

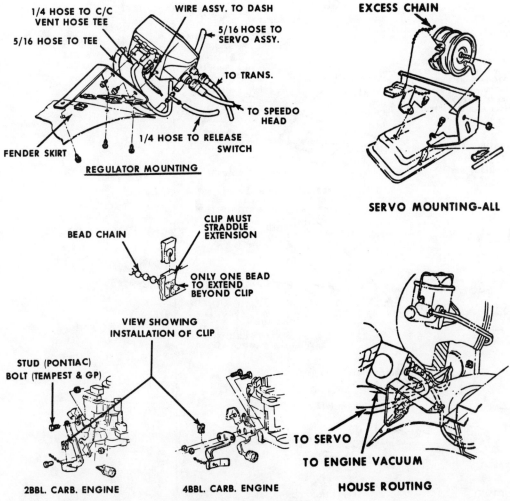

Diagram of 1969 cruise control, with servo part number 9787977 mounting and regulator mounting. Vacuum hoses are routed correctly here.

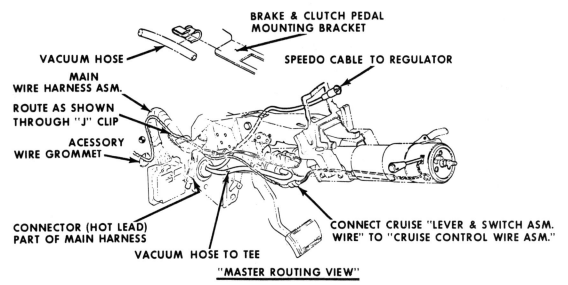

BRAKE & CLUTCH PEDAL MOUNTING BRACKET

VACUUM HOSE

SPEEDO CABLE TO REGULATOR

MAIN WIRE HARNESS ASM.

ROUTE AS SHOWN THROUGH "J" CLIP

ACESSORY WIRE GROMMET

CONNECTOR (HOT LEAD) PART OF MAIN HARNESS

VACUUM HOSE TO TEE

CONNECT CRUISE "LEVER & SWITCH ASM. WIRE" TO "CRUISE CONTROL WIRE ASM."

"MASTER ROUTING VIEW"

View of vacuum hose, speedometer cable and harness routing for 1969 cruise control.

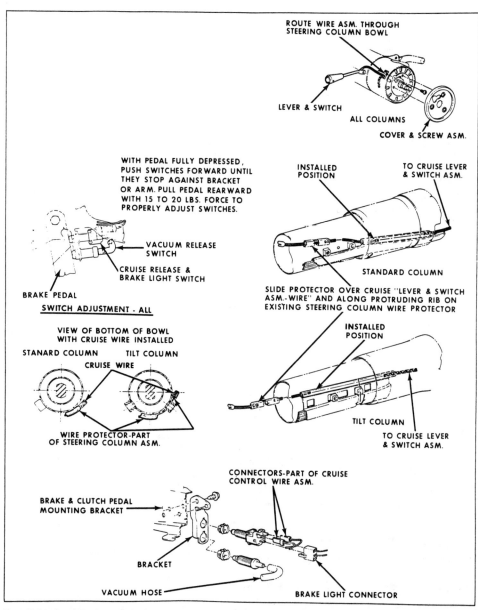

ROUTE WIRE ASM. THROUGH STEERING COLUMN BOWL

LEVER & SWITCH

ALL COLUMNS

COVER & SCREW ASM.

WITH PEDAL FULLY DEPRESSED, PUSH SWITCHES FORWARD UNTIL THEY STOP AGAINST BRACKET OR ARM. PULL PEDAL REARWARD WITH 15 TO 20 LBS. FORCE TO PROPERLY ADJUST SWITCHES.

INSTALLED POSITION

TO CRUISE LEVER & SWITCH ASM.

VACUUM RELEASE SWITCH

CRUISE RELEASE & BRAKE LIGHT SWITCH

BRAKE PEDAL

SWITCH ADJUSTMENT - ALL

STANDARD COLUMN

SLIDE PROTECTOR OVER CRUISE "LEVER & SWITCH ASM.-WIRE" AND ALONG PROTRUDING RIB ON EXISTING STEERING COLUMN WIRE PROTECTOR

VIEW OF BOTTOM OF BOWL WITH CRUISE WIRE INSTALLED

STANARD COLUMN   **TILT COLUMN**

CRUISE WIRE

WIRE PROTECTOR-PART OF STEERING COLUMN ASM.

INSTALLED POSITION

TILT COLUMN

TO CRUISE LEVER & SWITCH ASM.

CONNECTORS-PART OF CRUISE CONTROL WIRE ASM.

BRAKE & CLUTCH PEDAL MOUNTING BRACKET

BRACKET

VACUUM HOSE

BRAKE LIGHT CONNECTOR

Detail for installation of 1969 cruise-control switch and lever assembly and column wiring.

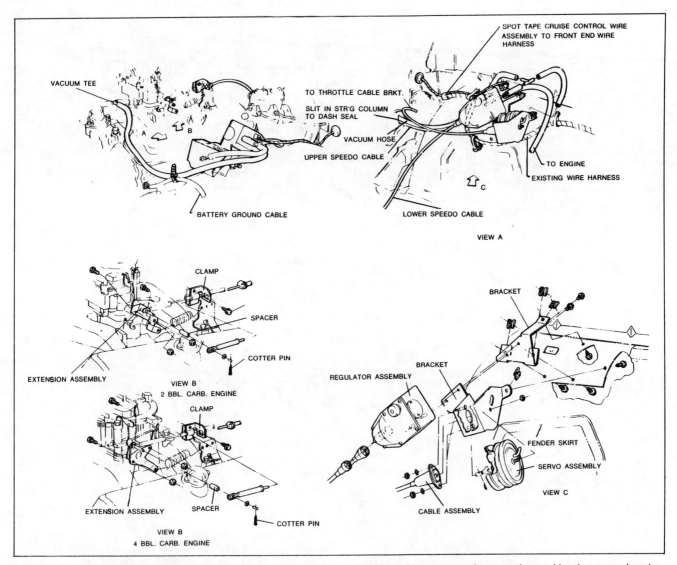

VACUUM TEE

SPOT TAPE CRUISE CONTROL WIRE ASSEMBLY TO FRONT END WIRE HARNESS

TO THROTTLE CABLE BRKT.

SLIT IN STR'G COLUMN TO DASH SEAL

VACUUM HOSE

UPPER SPEEDO CABLE

A   B

C

TO ENGINE

EXISTING WIRE HARNESS

BATTERY GROUND CABLE

LOWER SPEEDO CABLE

VIEW A

CLAMP

SPACER

COTTER PIN

EXTENSION ASSEMBLY

VIEW B
2 BBL. CARB. ENGINE

CLAMP

EXTENSION ASSEMBLY   SPACER

COTTER PIN

VIEW B
4 BBL. CARB. ENGINE

BRACKET

BRACKET

REGULATOR ASSEMBLY

FENDER SKIRT

SERVO ASSEMBLY

VIEW C

CABLE ASSEMBLY

Installation instructions for 1970 cruise control. Note mounting of 1970 servo (part number 9799871) and bracket (part number 9799941). Note vacuum hose routing and hookup to carburetor. Brackets were painted 60° gloss black.

377

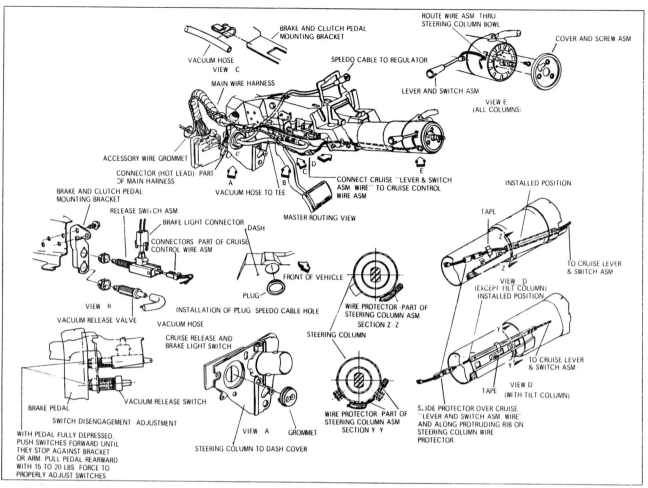

Installation of underdash hardware and harness for 1970 cruise control.

RAM AIR

1965

One of the most-sought-after 1965 GTO accessories was the Ram Air package, which was released on August 17, 1965. It made use of the hood scoop and included a hood ornament that was to be cut out and painted by the customer; a "tub" or shroud with sealing gasket; and instructions. As the release date dictated, it was only an accessory package, and no Ram Air 1965 GTOs were built by the factory.

A new 1965 combination air scoop and cleaner was announced in Pontiac P&A Extra number 65-19, dated 8-17-65. It was designed only for the 3-2 barrel engine option. The package (part number 984716) included air scoop, gasket, replacement ornament and instructions.

P&A Extra number 66-8, dated 1-31-66, listed a similar device for the 1966 model; still only for the 3-2 barrel engine. This was part number 98471, and it only fit the 1966 GTO.

1966-67

The 1966 Ram Air system was available half way through the production year. It came in one of two versions, either as a dealer-installed package or as an RPO option.

The dealer accessory package was released on January 31, 1966. The 1966 Ram Air pan differed greatly from the 1965 version with the addition of three triangular inserts around the carburetor opening to secure the

cleaner elements and minimize element movement. The panel was totally flat—unlike the 1965 panel which curved downward—and had a rolled lip up around it to retain the foam seal. The seal itself (part number 9777619) was the same for 1965 and 1966. The instructions for modifying the placement of the fuel filter to accommodate the pan differed. The ornament supplied with the package had to be modified (opened) by the installer, as did the under-hood bracing.

The Ram Air option, released in February 1966, consisted of this Ram Air panel and the XS-coded block. The engine was different from the RPO 802 Tri-Power engine in several respects.

Pontiac P&A Extra listed the parts and part numbers for the XS Ram Air Tri-Power engine that differed from the WS Tri-Power unit. They were: camshaft (9785744), valve spring and damper assembly—replaced inner & outer valve springs—(9785720), four-way fuel fitting (9785755) and fuel line fitting (538570). This notice was numbered 66-11, dated 2-28-66.

While there are no accurate accountings from Pontiac as to exactly how many packages and XS-equipped GTOs were sold in 1966, a few estimates have been made. Approximately 25-35 XS models were produced, and about 300 Ram Air dealer packages were sold. (These are only estimates; the exact numbers are not known.)

The XS package came delivered from the factory with the panel, extra ornament and instructions in the trunk. It was then assembled either by the dealer or by the customer.

The 1967 Ram Air was available as an RPO. However, no RPO number was issued by the factory for it. This was often the case when the factory was unsure of an option and allowed itself a contingency to withdraw the option within a certain time span. Mandatory options when the Ram Air was ordered were a heavy-duty 4.33:1 rear with RPO 731 Safe-T-Track limited slip rear and code 591 speedometer adapter. The block code on the 1967 Ram Air engine was XS for four-speed-transmission use, YR for California AIR use or XP for Turbo Hydra-matic use.

The camshaft and valve springs were carried over from the 1966 XS engine. (See Engine chapter.)

Once again a Ram Air package was available over the counter in 1967 (part number 984837). This package consisted of an ornament, an air filter element, a panel and seal, a black air cleaner lid, a closed-system breather tube and instructions.

The panel and seal assembly was serviced by replacement part number 9788921, and the seal itself could be ordered as part number 9788922. The Ram Air engine shared the 400 HO exhaust manifolds, and used the air-conditioning core support and radiator.

Toward the end of the 1967 production year, starting with engine serial number 646616, a second type of Ram Air cylinder head was used (part number 9783657, cast number 97). The cylinder head casting number was not in the usual center exhaust port placement. Instead (if viewing the head from the LH side), the cast number was next to the lower head bolt and behind the center exhaust port.

This cylinder head incorporated a taller valve spring stack height (1.712 inches). A different valve spring was used for the 97 head only (part number 9785999 inner, and 9785998 outer). Different valves were used for the 97 head application (part number 9792316 intake, and 9792313 exhaust).

The 1967 HO and Ram Air models used a removable lower flange on the standard steering column to clear the exhaust manifold, facilitating removal of the column. This flange was the same in appearance as the tilt column flange.

1968-70

The Ram Air system began to mature in 1968 into a sophisticated air-induction system. The 1968 was unique, while the 1969 and 1970 systems were virtually identical.

There were two separate Ram Air engines used in 1968. The first, known today as the Ram Air I, was designed with the standard D-port head design (part number 9792700, cast number 37).

The first-design head was an open-chambered version of the second-design 1967 Ram Air head, using taller valve spring stack heights. The intake manifold was part number 9794234. The exhaust manifolds were different from standard 1968 manifolds, and quite similar to the 1967 Ram Air exhaust manifolds. In fact, the RH manifold (part number 9777641) was the same as in 1967, and used a three-bolt flange. The LH manifold (part number 9791637) used a two-bolt flange and had a slightly different runner design.

The 1968 Ram Air I system used the Rochester Quadra-Jet (part number 7036342, Rochester part number 7028274) when the Turbo Hydra-matic was used. The manual transmission models used part number 7036343 (Rochester part number 7028275).

On March 15, 1968, Pontiac introduced the 1968½ Ram Air, or Ram Air II as it is known today. This engine replaced the RA I, and all cars ordered with Ram Air engines were equipped with the RA II after April 1, 1968. The round port head carried part number 9794040, cast number 96, and had the same intake manifold (9794234) as the Ram Air I. The changes made were in the camshaft, pistons, valve springs, head design and exhaust manifolds.

Internally, the Ram Air II used a revised camshaft (part number 9794041) and forged pistons. The standard D-port head configuration with "siamesed" center ports was discarded, and round ports were used. The valve and valve springs were changed (see Engine chapter).

Underhood view of 1965 Ram Air package. Leading edge of pan was curved downward.

With the introduction of the round-port head design, the pushrod diameter was changed, incorporating larger slotted pushrod guide plates (part number 9794042). The pushrods were part number 9794043. The 1.5 inch rockers were serviced as a package (part number 9794325). The exhaust manifolds (9794033 RH, 9794035 LH) were redesigned to fit the round port heads.

Carburetion was again the Rochester Quadra-Jet. Research indicates two part numbers that apparently fit the 1968½ Ram Air II: 7036485 (Rochester part number 7028273) and 7016949 (Rochester part number 7028270). The first number may have been for manual transmission applications only.

The 1968½ Ram Air II was also available with Hydramatic.

The air-induction system used in the 1968 Ram Air was unchanged through the entire production year. The open scoops (part number 9794281 RH and 9794282 LH) were unique to 1968, and were not interchangeable with 1969 or 1970. A three-stud arrangement was used, so the scoops could be changed without removing the baffle. The 1968 open scoops were a "fair weather" system; the factory advised that the driver use the standard closed scoops during cold or inclement weather.

The rest of the 1968 Ram Air system was quite simple and effective. A pentagon-shaped baffle (part number 9792984) was bolted to the underside of the hood and used a seal (part number 9792986) between the hood and the baffle. A shroud (part number 9793163) fit on the air cleaner (part number 6424398). The air cleaner and lid were painted 60° gloss black. A replacement package, consisting of a replacement seal and shroud, was listed under part number 9792987. Finally, the 1968 Ram Air package was the last to be offered as a dealer accessory package (number 988505).

Since the 1968½ Ram Air II was introduced on March 15, 1968, the restorer must be careful that the time-built code of the car be close to the casting codes of the Ram Air II heads. An early-production 1968 GTO would not have the Ram Air II engine, so to install this engine in an early-production car would be incorrect. However, to install the accessory induction package would be considered acceptable.

Two Ram Air engines were introduced in 1969, and were carried over to 1970. The air-induction system was also completely revised from 1968.

The Ram Air III had a D-port head configuration, and the head part number for 1969 was 9795043, cast number 48. This head was also used on the manual transmission 350 hp engine. The 1970 Ram Air III head carried part number 9799496, cast number 12. The 1969-70 Ram Air III intake was cast iron (part number 9794234). This intake was also used on all 1968 and 1969 standard engines.

Since the Ram Air III heads were the same as the standard manual transmission heads, there was nothing exotic about their makeup. The only major change to the 1969 heads was a valve spring and camshaft alteration made during the 1969 production year. (See Engine chapter.)

The Ram Air III used Rochester Quadra-Jet carburetion. The manual-transmission-equipped Ram Air III used part number 7016853 (Rochester part number 7029273). When the Turbo Hydra-matic was used, part number 7016949 (Rochester part number 7029270) was installed. For 1970, the manual transmission carb was part number 7036914 (Rochester part number 7040273) and for the Turbo, part number 7036912 (Rochester part number 7040270). (The camshaft part numbers are listed in the Engine chapter.)

Also introduced in 1969 and used in 1970 was the Ram Air IV, which was probably the finest, best-balanced all-around street-performance engine ever built. The Ram Air IV engine was also known as the round-port engine because it used the same design as the 1968½ Ram Air II engine.

The head part number for the 1969 Ram Air IV was 9796721, cast number 722. The 1970 head was part number 9799498, cast number 614. Both years used large guide plates. A longer pushrod (part number 9782370) was used, and a special, deep-socket, anti-pump-up lifter

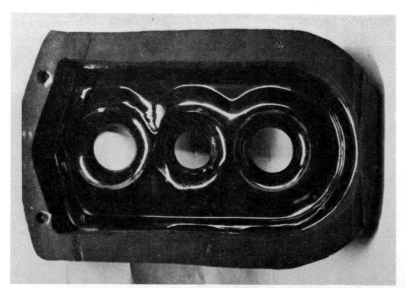

Detail of 1965 Ram Air pan (replacement part number 9777618). The pan was available as accessory package 984716. It was identifiable from the 1966 pan, as the 1965 unit did not have triangular-shaped air filter retainers stamped into the pan, and the center hole was smaller.

(part number 5232675) was employed. The Ram Air IV used the 1.65 inch rocker (package part number 9798429).

The rocker arm studs (part number 9796512) used a special double-locking nut (part number 546212 and 9422300). A rocker arm oil deflector (part number 9782500) was held to the stud with a nut (part number 9420169). All of this was stuffed under a standard GTO valve cover.

To allow for clearance, a taller valve cover gasket (part number 9797580) was used, in conjunction with a longer valve-cover-to-cylinder-head bolt (part number 9784378). All of the parts for the two years of Ram Air IV production were interchangeable.

Carburetion was the Rochester Quadra-Jet, and it used the same part numbers as the Ram Air engine, with a few exceptions. With the advent of the EES (evaporative emissions system) in 1970, the GTO equipped with Ram Air used carb part number 7036915 with the manual transmission (Rochester part number 7040573) and 7036913 with the Turbo Hydra-matic (Rochester part number 7040570).

Also in 1970, when the 455 engine was ordered with Ram Air induction, different carbs were used. For use without the EES, when equipped with manual transmission, carburetor part number 7036914 (Rochester part number 7040279) was installed. When the Turbo 400 was used, part number 7036912 (Rochester part number 7040278) was installed. Finally, the EES required part number 7036915 (Rochester part number 7040579) with manual transmission, and part number 7036913 (Rochester part number 7040578) with the Turbo Hydra-matic.

The Ram Air IV intake manifold was aluminum (part number 9796614 in 1969 and 9799084 in 1970). A separate cast-iron heat crossover with a one-piece elbow and a flex hose were used to the air inlet shroud. A LH exhaust manifold preheater assembly was used to operate the sensors in the shroud, as the aluminum intake was so efficient

in heat dissipation. The Ram Air III and the 455 Ram Air used the cast-iron manifold and only one duct to the shroud, coming from the LH preheater.

The exhaust manifolds for the Ram Air III were shuffled around as replacement parts began to disappear. The original part numbers for the 1969 Ram Air III manifolds were 9797072 (RH) and 9791637 (LH). The 1970 manifolds were part number 9799720 (RH) and 478140 (LH).

The Ram Air IV exhaust manifolds were part number 9797075 (RH) and 9794035 (LH) for 1969. The 1970 manifold part numbers were 9799721 (RH) and 478141 (LH).

The Ram Air induction system will not be explained in great length here, as the accompanying illustrations and part numbers suffice. There are, however, a few important aspects that should be mentioned.

The 455 engine was available with the air induction (RPO 601) in 1970. However, the 455 engine was *not* offered in the Judge. The hood scoops were painted to match the body trim on GTOs—with the exception of the 1970 Judge scoops, which were matte black. The 1969 and 1970 Ram Air systems used a cable control, actuated by the driver, to open or close the hood scoops. When the scoops were open, fresh air flowed to the carburetor; when closed, warm underhood air went to the carb.

Finally, the Ram Air IV Super Duty: Research indicates that approximately seventy of these engines may have been released for public consumption in 1970. The Ram Air IV Super Duty consisted of a Ram Air V bottom end and Ram Air IV heads, intake manifold and carburetion. No Ram Air V engines were released from the factory for public consumption, although it was possible to order all the necessary Ram Air V components over the counter. Occasionally a Ram Air V will turn up, but it was not built on the assembly line for sale in a 1970 GTO. Evidence also indicates the installation of a few RA IV SD engines in 1970 Trans Ams.

When Ram Air pan was installed, the air cleaner bases were not used, as the pan provided for air cleaner element retention.

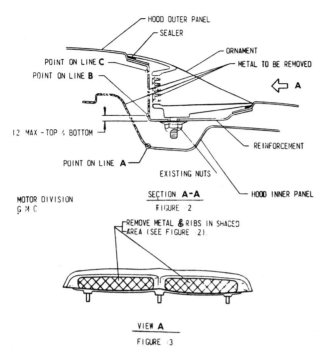

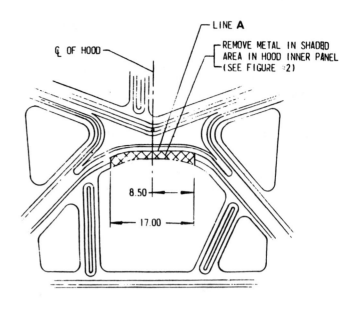

VIEW **A**
FIGURE 3

VIEW **B**
FIGURE 4

Instructions for opening the hood ornament for the 1965-67 Ram Air package.

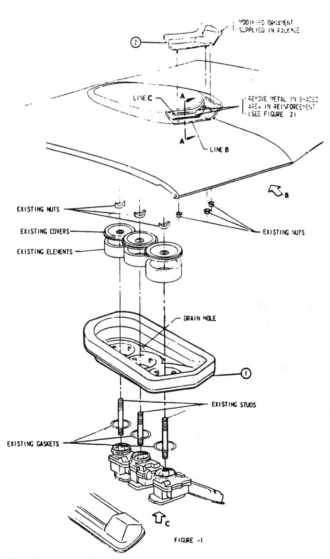

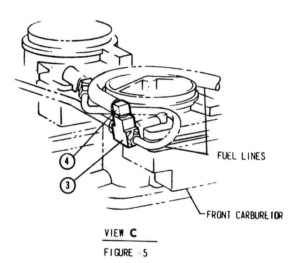

VIEW **C**
FIGURE 5

Instruction from the 1966 Ram Air package advising the installer to modify the underhood bracing and the fuel filter.

Directions from the 1966 instruction sheet for installing the Ram Air pan and carburetor assembly and the hood ornament after it has been modified. Note inserts in pan around carburetor openings, indicating pan was for 1966.

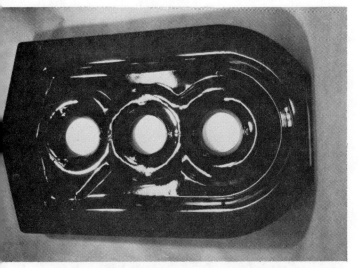

View of 1967 Ram Air pan with correct black filter lid. Note AIR vent tube in pan.

1966 Ram Air pan. Dimples around carb openings were used to keep air cleaners from shifting around in pan.

Comparison of 1967-68 Ram Air I, 1968 Ram Air II and 1969-70 Ram Air IV intake and exhaust valves. Intake valve on left had deep tulip design and was swirl polished to promote airflow. Exhaust valve on right had less-pronounced tulip and was also swirl polished.

Underhood view of 1967 Ram Air package. Breather tube from air pan to valve cover was not used in all applications.

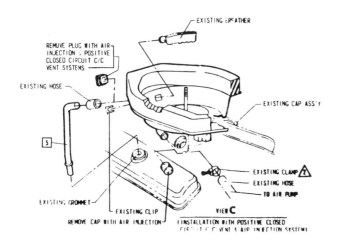

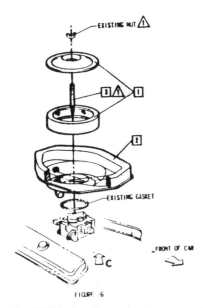

Directions from the 1967 instructions, showing removal of plug from air cleaner for installation of breather tube for models with the Controlled Combustion System (CCS) or AIR.

Comparison of 1967 and 1968 LH Ram Air D-port exhaust manifolds. There was a significant change in front and rear runner designs, and the 1967 manifold had a three-bolt flange.

Low compression pressures obtained on GTO, 421-H.O., or 428-H.O. engines are not a valid indication of engine condition. Due to the long valve overlap period with camshafts used in these engines, compression pressure readings (at cranking speeds) as low as 120 PSI are considered normal.

An engine should not be condemned as faulty on the basis of these low compression pressures alone. The readings obtained from all eight cylinders should be taken and recorded. If the lowest cylinder is not less than 80% of the highest, the engine compression is probably okay.

If there is still some doubt, the engine may be tested using a cylinder leak tester. If leakage at TDC on the compression stroke is not over 20%, the cylinder is okay.

Compression pressures should be checked as follows:

1. Run engine until completely normalized - 15 minutes minimum.

2. Shut off engine and hook up primary tachometer.

3. Remove all spark plugs.

4. Disconnect coil tower lead at coil and ground to engine.

5. Block choke valve and throttle open fully.

6. Install compression tester in No. 1 spark plug hole and crank engine at least five compression strokes. Observe cranking speed and record highest pressure obtained.

7. Repeat for other cylinders. Be certain cranking speed is the same for each check (within 10 RPM) and is at least 150 RPM.

8. Take 80% of highest reading. If no other reading is below this figure, engine is probably okay.

Dealer Service Information Bulletin number 67-I-27, dated 2-3-67, outlined this procedure for checking compression on high-performance engines.

View of 1968 Ram Air air cleaner and shroud. Entire air cleaner assembly was painted 60° gloss black.

1968 Ram Air hood baffle (part number 9792984). Baffle fit to underside of hood and was sealed by foam. Tangs near bottom of baffle were used to facilitate installation.

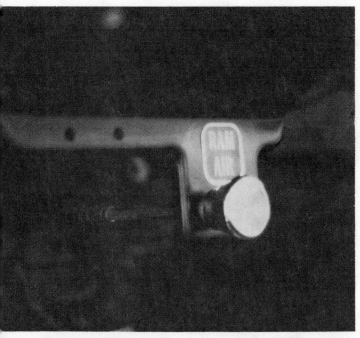

Underhood view of 1968 Ram Air baffle and seal assembly. Holes in front of baffle allowed removal of hood scoops without removal of baffle.

Close-up of Ram Air cable, handle and bracket assembly (part number 546526). The Ram Air decal was available separately (part number 9798222).

View of 1968 Ram Air engine, showing circular pan and 60° gloss-black air cleaner lid.

View of 1969 Ram Air III cylinder head. Cast number 48 was located at center ports. Casting date code is visible above center right spark plug hole.

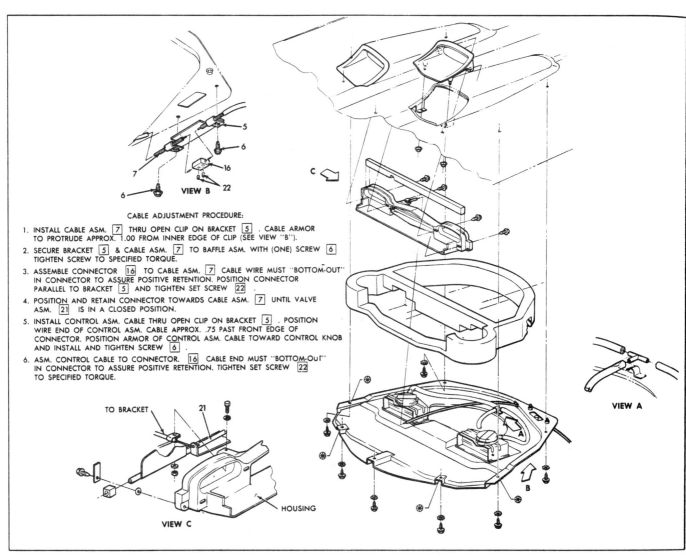

CABLE ADJUSTMENT PROCEDURE:

1. INSTALL CABLE ASM. [7] THRU OPEN CLIP ON BRACKET [5]. CABLE ARMOR TO PROTRUDE APPROX. 1.00 FROM INNER EDGE OF CLIP (SEE VIEW "B").

2. SECURE BRACKET [5] & CABLE ASM. [7] TO BAFFLE ASM. WITH (ONE) SCREW [6] TIGHTEN SCREW TO SPECIFIED TORQUE.

3. ASSEMBLE CONNECTOR [16] TO CABLE ASM. [7] CABLE WIRE MUST "BOTTOM-OUT" IN CONNECTOR TO ASSURE POSITIVE RETENTION. POSITION CONNECTOR PARALLEL TO BRACKET [5] AND TIGHTEN SET SCREW [22].

4. POSITION AND RETAIN CONNECTOR TOWARDS CABLE ASM. [7] UNTIL VALVE ASM. [21] IS IN A CLOSED POSITION.

5. INSTALL CONTROL ASM. CABLE THRU OPEN CLIP ON BRACKET [5]. POSITION WIRE END OF CONTROL ASM. CABLE APPROX. .75 PAST FRONT EDGE OF CONNECTOR. POSITION ARMOR OF CONTROL ASM. CABLE TOWARD CONTROL KNOB AND INSTALL AND TIGHTEN SCREW [6].

6. ASM. CONTROL CABLE TO CONNECTOR. [16] CABLE END MUST "BOTTOM-OUT" IN CONNECTOR TO ASSURE POSITIVE RETENTION. TIGHTEN SET SCREW [22] TO SPECIFIED TORQUE.

Exploded view of 1969-70 Ram Air baffle and hood scoop installation. Note cable adjustment instructions.

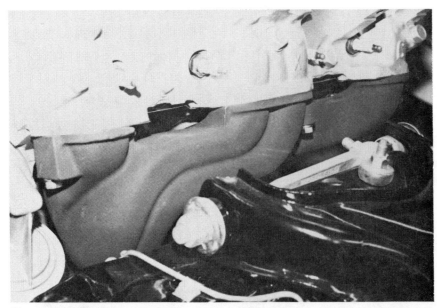

Close-up of 1969-70 Ram Air IV RH exhaust manifold.

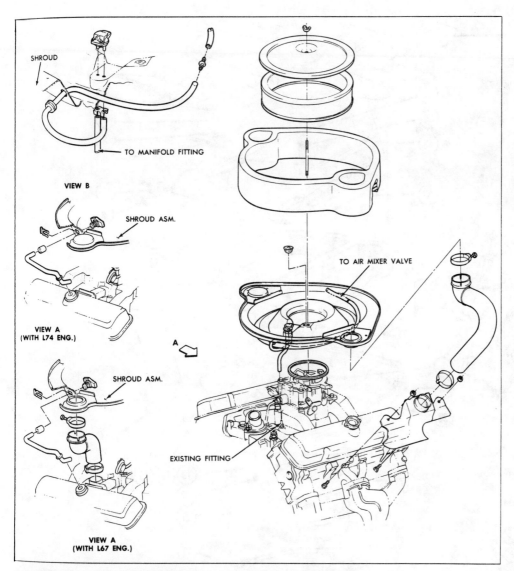

SHROUD

TO MANIFOLD FITTING

VIEW B

SHROUD ASM.

VIEW A
(WITH L74 ENG.)

SHROUD ASM.

VIEW A
(WITH L67 ENG.)

TO AIR MIXER VALVE

A

EXISTING FITTING

Installation instructions for 1969-70 Ram Air III and Ram Air IV air cleaner and shroud assemblies. Ram Air IV shroud had two pre-heaters. Ram Air III, which used the standard cast-iron intake manifold, required only LH preheater. Consequently, the Ram Air III shroud had only one preheater hole on LH side.

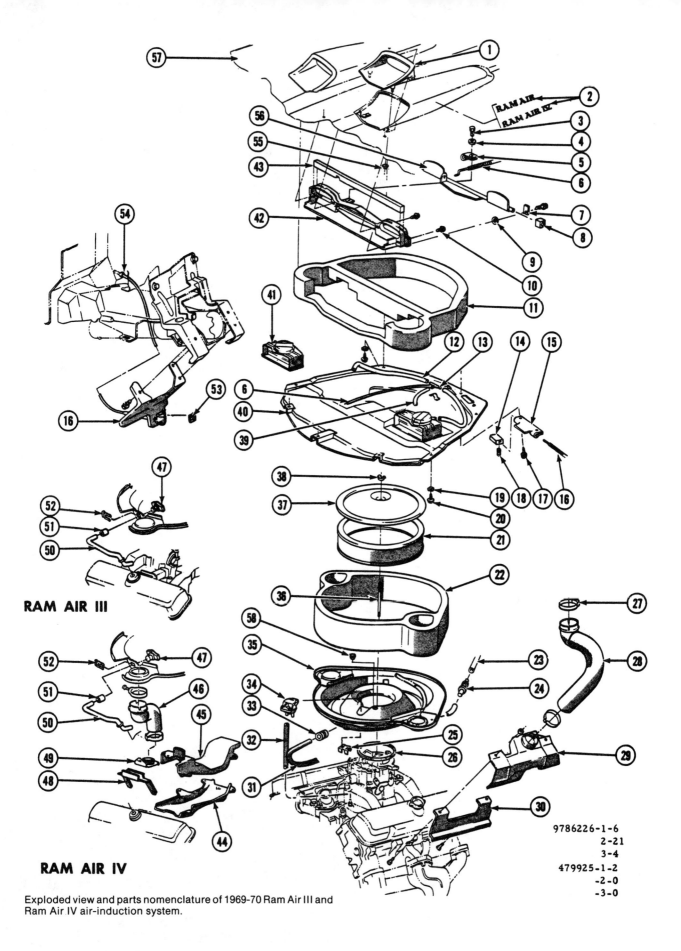

RAM AIR III

RAM AIR IV

9786226-1-6
2-21
3-4
479925-1-2
-2-0
-3-0

Exploded view and parts nomenclature of 1969-70 Ram Air III and Ram Air IV air-induction system.

Key	Part Name	Part No. 1969	Part No. 1970	Group No.
1	ORNAMENT, Hood Vent	546327RH-546328LH	546327RH-546328LH	8.030
2	DECAL, Hood Name "Ram Air" – Red	9794722	9794722	8.030
	"Ram Air" – White	9794723	9794723	8.030
	"Ram Air" – Black	9794721	9794721	8.030
	"Ram Air IV" – Red	9789042	9789042	8.030
	"Ram Air IV" – White	9789043	9789043	8.030
	"Ram Air IV" – Black	9789041	9789041	8.030
3	BOLT, Cable to Housing (1/4" – 20 x 1/2")	180016	180016	8.900
4	WASHER, Cable to Housing (9/32" I.D. x 47/64" O.D.)	—	—	N.S.
5	CLIP, Cable to Housing	—	—	N.S.
6	CABLE, Valve to Splice Brkt.	546524	546524	3.415
7	RETAINER, Valve Shaft Bushing	9797419	9797419	3.415
8	BUSHING, Inlet Valve Shaft	9797418	9797418	3.415
9	WASHER, Retainer to Valve Hsg. (13/64" I.D. x 13/32" O.D.)	—	—	N.S.
10	SCREW, Retainer to Valve Hsg. (#10-16 x 3/4")	—	—	N.S.
11	SEAL, Baffle to Hood	9797423	9797423	3.410
12	HOSE, Tee to Air Mix Valve (5/32" I.D. x 15")	3987363	3987363	8.962
13	TEE, Sensor Hose (3/16" x 3/16" x 3/16")	540581	540581	3.440
14	CONNECTOR, Cable Splice (2nd Type)	546516	546516	3.415
15	BRACKET, Cable Mounting (2nd Type)	546517	546517	3.415
16	CONTROL, Air Inlet (See Catalog Note)	546526	546526	3.415
17	SCREW, Bracket to Baffle (1/4"-20 x 5/8")	—	—	N.S.
18	SET SCREW, Cable to Connector (#8-32 x 3/16")	192208	192208	8.975
19	LOCKWASHER, Baffle to Inner Panel (5/16" Ext.)	138485	138485	8.932
20	SCREW, Baffle to Inner Panel (5/16"-12 x 5/8")	9422232	9422232	8.977
21	ELEMENT, Air Cleaner	6485166	6485166	3.410
22	SEAL, Baffle to Shroud	9797429	9797429	3.410
23	HOSE, Sensor to Tee (5/32" I.D. x 14")	3987363	3987363	8.962
24	CONNECTOR, Inlet Vac. Hose	3923213	3923213	1.745
25	NUT, Inlet Thermal Sensor	6484435	6484435	3.415
26	GASKET, Cleaner to Carb.	3919812	3919812	3.403
27	CLAMP, Shroud Adapter	9793132	9793132	3.417
28	DUCT, Preheater to Inlet Shroud	9797496	9797496	3.417
29	SHROUD, Preheater – Ram Air IV (Outer)	9794047	9794047	3.417
	SHROUD, Preheater – Ram Air III or HO	9791627	478461	3.417
30	SHROUD, Preheater – Inner	9794046	478460	3.417
31	HOSE, Sensor to Tee (5/32" I.D. x 22")	3987363	3987363	8.962
32	HOSE, Sensor to Vac. Fitting (5/32" I.D. x 6 1/2")	3987363	3987363	8.962
33	GROMMET, Inlet Sensor Hose	9797816	9797816	3.415
34	SENSOR ASM., Air Inlet Thermal	6484242	6484242	3.415
35	SHROUD, Air Inlet – Ram Air IV	9794639	478135	3.410
	SHROUD, Air Inlet – Ram Air III or HO	9794638	478136	3.410
36	STUD, Air Cleaner	546515	546515	3.403
37	COVER, Air Cleaner Element	6485198	6485198	3.410
38	NUT, Cleaner to Carb. (1/4"-20)	219281	219281	8.920
39	HOSE, Sensor to Tee (5/32" I.D. x 14")	3987363	3987363	8.962
40	BAFFLE, Hood Inlet	9797436	9797436	3.410
41	DIAPHRAGM, Air Cleaner	6485087RH-6485088LH	6485087RH-6485088LH	3.415
42	HOUSING, Inlet to Hood Valve	9797435	9797435	3.415
43	SEAL, Valve Housing to Hood	9797622	9797622	3.415
44	SHROUD, Preheater – Lower	9798520	9798520	3.417
45	SHROUD, Preheater – Upper	9798519	9798519	3.417
46	DUCT, Preheater to Inlet Shroud	9798523	9798523	3.417
47	ELEMENT, Air Filter	6484966	6484966	3.410
48	BRACKET, Switch Harness Supt.	9798517	9798517	3.765
49	COVER, Preheater Shroud	9798518	9798518	3.417
50	PIPE, Crankcase Vent	9796460	9796460	1.762
51	HOSE, Pipe to Carb. (3/4" I.D. x 1 1/2")	9776770	9776770	1.762
52	RETAINER, Filter Element	6420265	6420265	3.410
53	DECAL, Inlet Control	9798222	9798222	3.415
54	GROMMET, Cable thru Dash (2nd Type)	546525	546525	3.415
55	NUT, Ornament to Hood (#10-24)	441239	441239	8.921
56	VALVE, Air Inlet	9797428	9797428	3.415
57	PANEL, Hood	9797791	9797791	8.000
58	PLUG, Shroud Hole	—	478131	3.410

In 1969 and 1970, GTOs and Judges equipped with Ram Air III engines used this decal on the outboard sides of the hood scoops.

RH view of 1969 Ram Air III engine compartment. Note cast-iron intake used with Ram Air III and CCS vent pipe running from rear of air cleaner to valve cover. Cable ran from air cleaner to underhood controls to air inlet valves.

LH view of 1969 Ram Air III, showing preheater shroud and tube assembly to air pan.

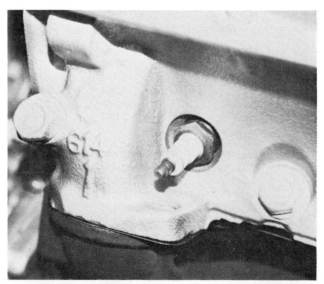

Close-up of 614 casting on 1970 Ram Air IV cylinder head.

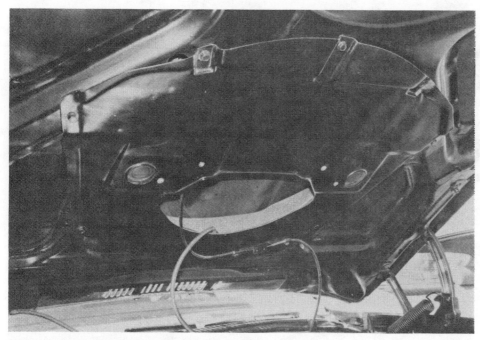

Underhood view of 1969-70 Ram Air baffle and seal assembly with cable running to air inlet valves. Baffle was painted 60° gloss black.

Should it become necessary to disassemble, repair, or readjust valve train components on Ram Air IV engine, it will be necessary to perform one of the following valve adjustment procedures. It is not possible on this engine to tighten the rocker arm adjusting nut until it seats on the shoulder of the rocker arm stud to obtain the correct valve setting.

The procedure to be followed will depend upon whether the engine has remained in the car or has been removed for necessary repair. In cases where the engine has been removed, the second procedure should be used and the valve adjustment made before attempting to start the engine.

ENGINE IN CAR

1. After necessary repair has been made, tighten affected rocker arm adjusting nut (s) sufficiently snug so that rocker arm (s) will not jump off valve stem or pushrod when engine is started.

2. Start engine and retighten rocker arm nut on any valve that is noisy or clattering. Tighten only enough so that noise disappears. If noise is noted in a valve assembly which has not been disassembled, it will be necessary to remove the lock nut and tighten the rocker arm adjusting nut as described above.

   NOTE: You may find it desirable to purchase a set of oil deflector clips to eliminate excessive oil splash from the rocker arm oil feed holes while engine is running. These clips are available commercially from most independent auto parts suppliers.

3. After allowing engine sufficient time to reach normal operating temperature (approximately 5 minutes), and with engine running, individually loosen each rocker arm adjusting nut until the valve assembly begins to clatter or becomes noisy.

4. Retighten rocker arm adjusting nut until noise disappears. This will bring the pushrod just slightly into the top of the lifter travel.

5. Being sure the rocker arm adjusting nut does not change position, install lock nut and tighten to 30-40 lb. ft. torque.

6. Having performed adjustment on all valve assemblies upon which it was necessary, install rocker arm splash shields and retaining nuts and torque to 60-90 lb. in.

ENGINE OUT-OF-CAR

After all necessary work has been performed and train components have been reassembled:

1. Turn crankshaft until No. 1 piston is at TDC on compression stroke (Distributor rotor at No. 1 firing position) and timing mark on balancer is aligned with 0° mark on timing cover.

2. Tighten rocker arm adjusting nuts on two valves on this cylinder until .008" clearance is obtained between rocker arm and top of valve stem.

3. Tighten adjusting nut an additional 1/8 turn + 5°.

4. Install lock nuts and tighten to 30-40 lb. ft. torque.

For each succeeding cylinder in the firing order (1, 8, 4, 3, 6, 5, 7, 2), rotate crankshaft 90° to bring piston up to TDC on its' firing stroke, and repeat steps 2 through 4.

Dealer Service Information Bulletin number 69-I-62, dated 4-17-69, reported that owners should use this procedure for valvetrain adjustment on the 1969 models equipped with the Ram Air IV.

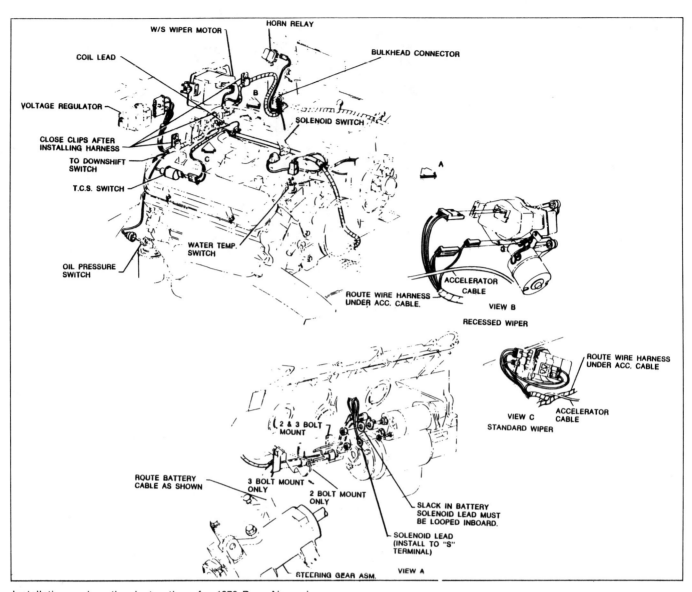

COIL LEAD
VOLTAGE REGULATOR
W/S WIPER MOTOR
HORN RELAY
BULKHEAD CONNECTOR
SOLENOID SWITCH
CLOSE CLIPS AFTER INSTALLING HARNESS
TO DOWNSHIFT SWITCH
T.C.S. SWITCH
WATER TEMP. SWITCH
OIL PRESSURE SWITCH
ROUTE WIRE HARNESS UNDER ACC. CABLE.
ACCELERATOR CABLE
VIEW B
RECESSED WIPER
ROUTE WIRE HARNESS UNDER ACC. CABLE
VIEW C
STANDARD WIPER
ACCELERATOR CABLE
ROUTE BATTERY CABLE AS SHOWN
2 & 3 BOLT MOUNT
3 BOLT MOUNT ONLY
2 BOLT MOUNT ONLY
SLACK IN BATTERY SOLENOID LEAD MUST BE LOOPED INBOARD.
SOLENOID LEAD (INSTALL TO "S" TERMINAL)
STEERING GEAR ASM.
VIEW A

Installation and routing instructions for 1970 Ram Air engine wiring harness. Clips were used to retain harness going to starter—Ram Air III used one clip; Ram Air IV used two.

Chapter 7

ELECTRICS

IGNITION, STANDARD

1964-65

The standard ignition used a single black wire, running from the engine harness to the positive side of the coil. The coil (original part number 1115134, current part number 1115238) was mounted to the rear of the RH cylinder head by a white metal bracket (part number 1963479 in 1964 and 1964715 in 1965). If the optional tachometer was used, a brown tachometer jumper wire with a white fuse holder (part number 2989272) went to the negative side of the coil along with the distributor lead wire. A copper ground strap bolted to the coil bracket and ran to the firewall. It was retained by a hex-head silver cadmium bolt.

The spark plug wires ran from the distributor to the cylinder heads, routed by spark plug wire brackets. The 1964 brackets were mounted on a boss on the RH rear of the intake manifold and the rear intake manifold to cylinder head bolt on the LH side. The LH bracket was part number 548969 and the RH bracket was part number 9773969. The 1965 wires were routed differently: The spark plug wire brackets were mounted to the rear of the cylinder heads on both sides. The LH bracket was part

number 9781140 and the RH bracket was part number 9779162. As the plug wires made their way to the respective plugs toward the front of the heads, they were separated by wire retainers holding three and then two wires.

Both 1964 and 1965 used the same distributor (part number 1111054), regardless of which engine was used. A red part number band was used around the distributor housing.

1966-67

The standard ignition in 1966-67 used a single black wire and a white, braided resistance wire from the engine harness to the positive terminal of the coil. The coil (original part number 1115134, current part number 1115238) was mounted on the rear of the RH cylinder head by a natural-metal-appearing bracket (part number 1966527 in 1966 and 1968034 in 1967). A braided copper ground strap ran from the coil bracket to the firewall, and was secured by a silver cadmium hex-head bolt.

If the optional tachometer was ordered in either year, a brown wire assembly with a white inline fuse and a white plastic female connector was used. The wire assembly fed from the accessory grommet along the firewall, routed by the firewall harness retaining clips to the coil. In

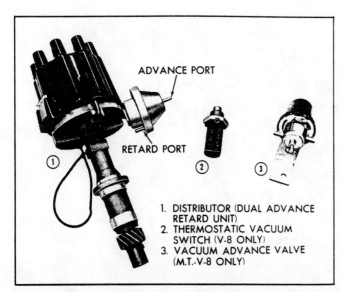

Components of the Controlled Combustion System (CCS). Note use of advance and retard port on vacuum-advance assembly, and advance valve used on manual transmission models.

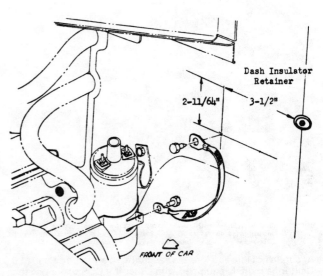

The length and location of early 1965 ground straps may be incorrect. Correct length was six inches—installed as shown here.

1966, a short jumper wire, also brown, ran from the negative coil terminal and used a white plastic male connector for a positive connection to the tachometer wire. The 1967 wire assembly dispensed with the short brown jumper as used in 1966. Instead, the brown lead from the tachometer ran directly to the negative coil terminal, using the same routing as in 1966.

Also, in 1967, when the dealer-installed hood tachometer was ordered, a special harness (part number 6468461) was used. (See 1968-70 ignitions for more detail.)

Dealer Service Information Bulletin number 67-I-9 dated 11-9-66, reported a revision in the hot idle specifications for 1967 engines. The 376 and 360 hp engines with automatic transmission should be set at 650 rpm in "Drive." The throttle return check was unnecessary on these vehicles. The Ram Air engines with manual transmission should be set at 1200 rpm. (It is necessary to reduce idle speed to 700 rpm when checking or adjusting ignition timing.)

The spark plug wire set (part number 6289618) was routed from the distributor to the cylinder heads by way of plug wire brackets, which were white metal in appearance with black rubber-coated tops. The 1966 brackets were bolted to the rear of the cylinder heads, and used part number 9783878 (RH) and 9784140 (LH). The 1967 brackets were changed slightly: The RH bracket (part number 9786278) was mounted on the rear of the cylinder head; the LH bracket (part number 9785669) was retained by the inside rear valve cover screw. On 1967 two-barrel engines, an additional bracket (part number 9789550) was mounted by the outside front valve cover retaining screw, and held plug wires number 1 and number 3. As the plug wires made their way to the front of the heads, they were secured by retainers—part number 3702799 for four wires and 2977417 for two wires.

Distributor applications became somewhat confusing in 1966 and 1967. (Refer to distributor application segment of engine chart in Engine chapter.) A red part number band was used around the distributor housing.

1968-70

All GTOs from 1968 through 1970 used the same coil (part number 1115238), mounted in a natural-metal bracket (part number 1971782). When the optional tachometer was ordered, a brown wire with a white inline fuse holder was routed through the accessory grommet to the firewall along a harness bracket to the negative coil terminal.

When the hood-mounted tachometer was ordered, a special harness (part number 6295973) was used for 1968. One end plugged to the connector on the tach harness. The other end had three leads: The gray lead was routed through the accessory grommet in the firewall to the lamp rheostat. The black lead was grounded to the top screw holding the horn relay to the firewall. The black and pink wire had a white plastic inline fuse holder and went through the harness bracket to the negative coil terminal.

The routing and color codes were similar for 1969. The hood tach harness (part number 6299178) was routed the same, with the exception of the ground lead, which was longer and used the top RH voltage-regulator-to-firewall hex-head screw for a ground.

The 1970 harness (part number 546694) mounted the same way. However, the grounding location was moved back to the horn relay.

The plug wires were retained by plug wire brackets (part number 9793050 RH and 9792380 LH), used in 1968 and 1969. They were mounted to the cylinder head, and had rubber-coated tops, natural-metal bottoms. In 1970, the brackets (part number 9789666) were mounted to the rocker arm covers.

The 1968 voltage regulator (part number 1119511) was painted 60° gloss black, and the bracket was natural metal or silver cadmium. The 1969-70 regulator (part number 1119515) was the same in appearance. If the Delcotron CSI alternator (RPO 681, UPC K81) was used in 1970, regulator part number 1116384 was employed.

Six different distributors were used in 1970.

Engine	Transmission	Part Number
Standard	Manual	1111176
Standard	Hydra-matic	1111148
RA III	Manual	1112010
RA III	Hydra-matic	1112009
RA IV	All	1112011
455	All	1112010

Hot Idle Specs.

	V-8	V-8 (H.O.)	G.T.O. (Ram-Air)
AT	600	650	650
AT/A.C.	600	650	650
MT	700	700	1200
MT/A.C.	700	700	1200

CAUTION: On G.T.O. Ram-Air (MT only) cars, distributor centrifugal advance mechanism is operating at 1200 rpm making it necessary to reduce the idle speed to 700 rpm when checking or adjusting ignition timing.

Accurate hot idle and ignition settings are very important in 1967 California models equipped with either the CCS or AIR system. When setting ignition timing on engines with dual-acting distributor, disconnect and plug both hoses to the advance unit. These specifications are from Dealer Service Information Bulletin number 67-I-20, dated 1-12-67.

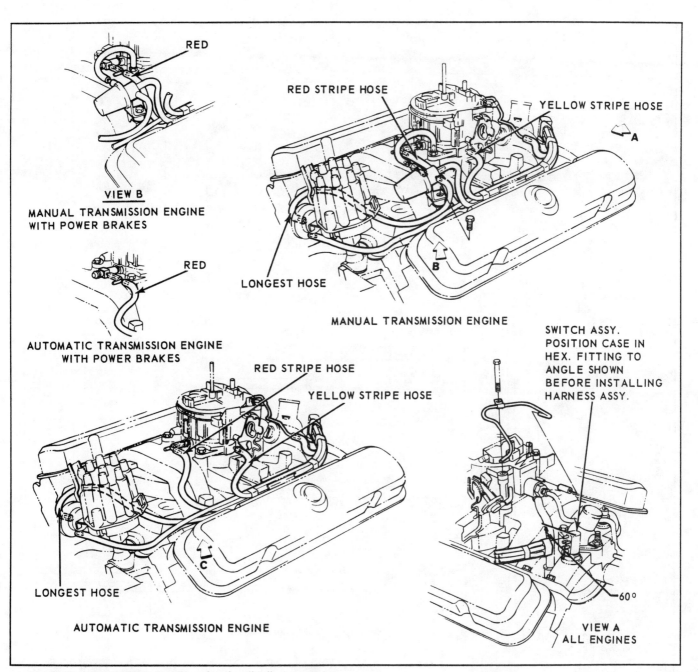

RED

VIEW B
MANUAL TRANSMISSION ENGINE
WITH POWER BRAKES

RED

AUTOMATIC TRANSMISSION ENGINE
WITH POWER BRAKES

RED STRIPE HOSE

YELLOW STRIPE HOSE

A

LONGEST HOSE

B

MANUAL TRANSMISSION ENGINE

RED STRIPE HOSE

YELLOW STRIPE HOSE

C

LONGEST HOSE

AUTOMATIC TRANSMISSION ENGINE

SWITCH ASSY.
POSITION CASE IN
HEX. FITTING TO
ANGLE SHOWN
BEFORE INSTALLING
HARNESS ASSY.

60°

VIEW A
ALL ENGINES

Installation and routing directions for the distributor vacuum
hoses, typical of 1968 through 1970 models. Note use of electrical
friction tape to bundle the hoses together.

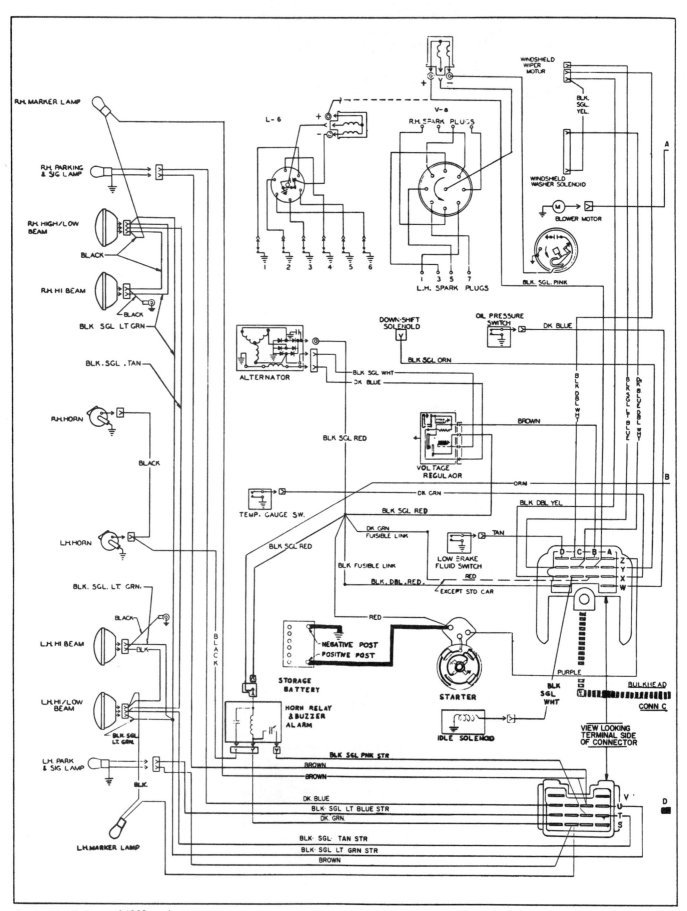

Schematic diagram of 1969 engine compartment wiring.

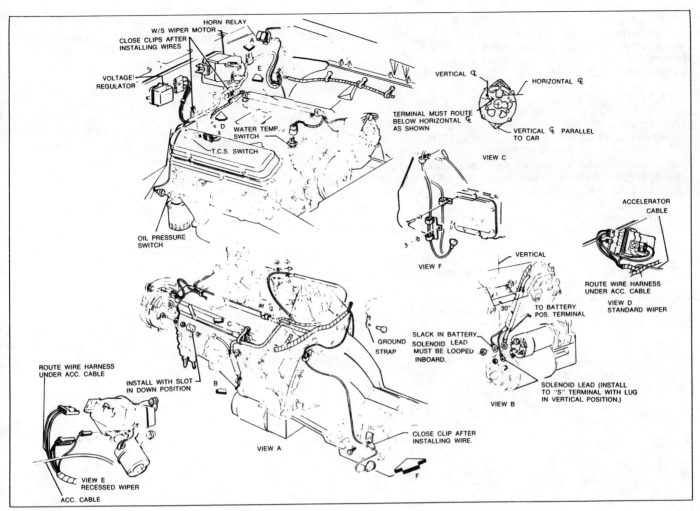

Installation and routing of standard engine harness for 1970 GTO.

IGNITION, TRANSISTORIZED

1964-65

In design and application, the 1964 transistorized ignition (RPO 671) stood alone. Some components were not used in 1965; others were not interchangeable with 1965 versions.

The 1964 system used a static voltage regulator assembly (part number 1116366) mounted on the LH skirt shield (part number 9774745). The control amplifier (part number 1115005) was mounted on the RH skirt shield (part number 9774744). A cover plate (part number 9775015) was used over the regulator and the amplifier. The harness for the amplifier was routed along the underside of the top of the core support, through clips (part number 545249), along the top of the LH fender skirt to a plug, and then into the firewall accessory grommet. The regulator harness and the amplifier harness ran along the fender skirt top, then along the firewall to a relay (part number 1115827) mounted near the normal voltage regulator location.

The original control amplifier was replaced by part number 1115008 if service was required. When the amplifier was replaced, it was necessary to discard the existing control amplifier harness and use the harness that came with the replacement amplifier. It was possible to replace the control amplifier harness separately, using part number 2986209.

The remainder of the 1964 components were the distributor (part number 1111047), which used a pole piece (original part number 1958674, replacement part number 1960779) and the coil (part number 1115207). There was no firewall-mounted voltage regulator, transistorized or otherwise, used in the 1964 transistorized ignition.

The transistorized ignition for 1965 was redesigned and was much simpler. The control amplifier (original part number 1115007, replacement 1115008) was mounted on the LH splash shield (part number 9779294) and protected by the plate cover (part number 9775015). One harness was used from the amplifier to the regulator, distributor harness and firewall connector. This harness was routed between the fender and the fender skirt. A junction block (part number 9781110) was mounted on the firewall behind the coil. Two distributors were used: for the standard engine, distributor part number 1111080; for the optional Tri-Power engine, distributor part number 1111047. The original coil part number was 1115215 (with bracket), and the replacement part number was 1115207 (without bracket).

A transistorized voltage regulator (RPO 662) was available with or without transistorized ignition in 1965. It was mounted in the same location as the standard regulator, and carried part number 1116378. It was available only as a factory-installed option.

1966-67

The 1966 transistorized ignition (RPO 671) was similar in theory and layout to the 1965 system, but there were some subtle differences. The 1966 coil was part number 1115207 (Delco part number D514 was the 1965 replacement number). The coil mounting bracket (part number 1966527) had to be ordered separately. The coil was gloss black and the bracket was natural metal. The assembly was again mounted to the rear of the RH cylinder head. The LH splash shield for the 1966 was part number 9782626, and had provision for mounting the control amplifier.

The 1967 GTO transistorized ignition was completely redesigned. The system used a capacitive discharge (CD) control unit (part number 1115010). It was mounted on the LH splash shield (part number 9787753) and was protected by a cover (part number 9787094). The control unit wire harness ran through a grommet (part number 9786871), along the LH upper fender skirt—retained by the headlamp harness clips—and to the distributor and coil. The harness rested along the firewall harness clips.

The ignition coil (part number 1115248, Delco part number D516) was bright red. The natural-metal-appearing coil bracket (part number 1968034) was mounted to the rear of the RH cylinder head. The distributor cap (part number 1968018) was also bright red. The 1967 CD system was not available with GTOs equipped with AM/FM radios.

The transistorized voltage regulator (RPO 664) was available on both the 1966 and 1967 GTO not equipped with air conditioning. It was available only as a factory-installed option. The replacement part number was 1116378, Delco part number D-639. The transistorized voltage regulator could be ordered with or without transistorized ignition, and no modifications had to be made to the existing harness.

There were no transistorized ignitions or transistorized voltage regulators offered in 1968 or 1969. A Delcotron CSI alternator was optional in 1970 only.

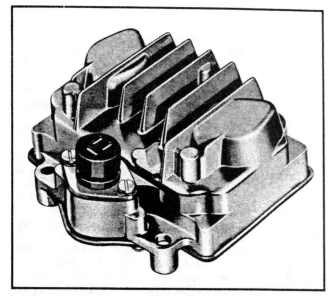

Ignition pulse amplifier for 1964 and distributor for 1964-66 transistorized ignition. The 1965-66 distributor was basically the same.

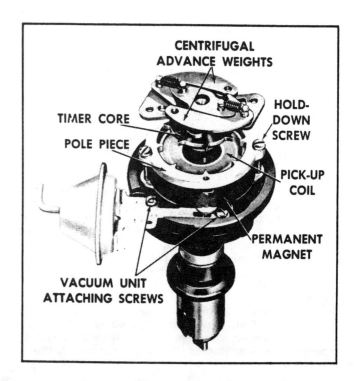

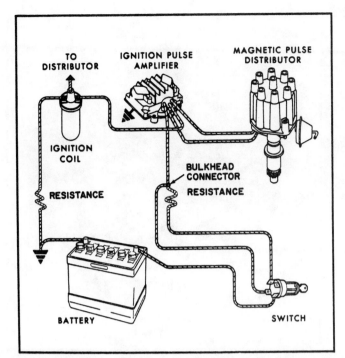

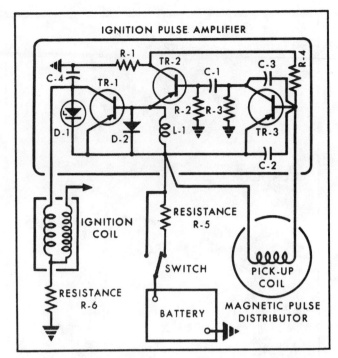

Theory of operation and schematic for 1964 transistorized ignition. Many replacement transistorized and solid-state components can be found at electronics shops.

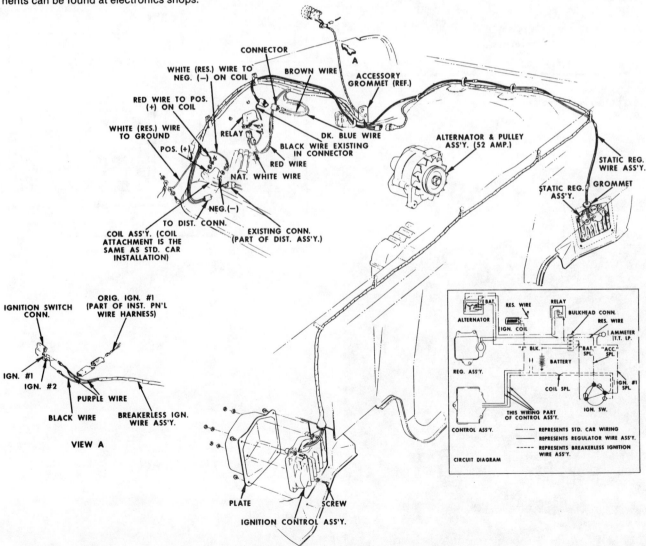

Installation of 1964 transistorized ignition harness and component location. Relay was on firewall in place of standard ignition voltage regulator.

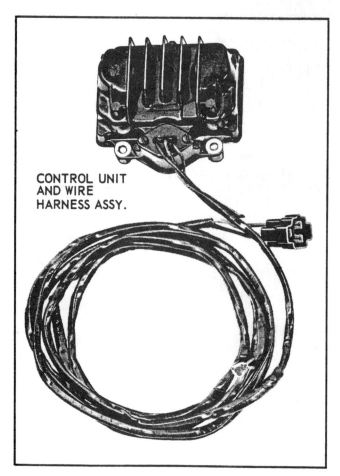

CONTROL UNIT AND WIRE HARNESS ASSY.

1965-66 distributor used for transistorized ignition was basically similar to 1964 units. Control amplifier for 1965-66 was serviced with the harness.

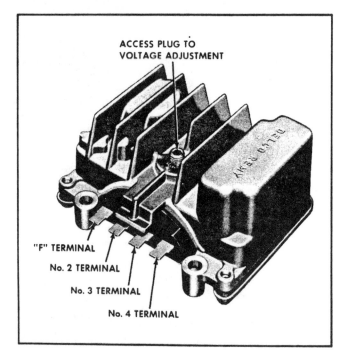

ACCESS PLUG TO VOLTAGE ADJUSTMENT

"F" TERMINAL

No. 2 TERMINAL

No. 3 TERMINAL

No. 4 TERMINAL

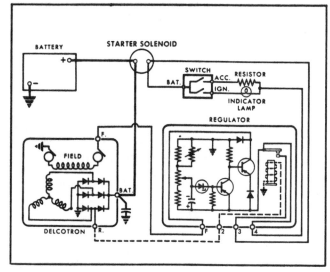

Views of transistorized voltage regulator used from 1965-66 and schematic of the regulator in the charging circuit. The transistorized voltage regulator was not available in 1964.

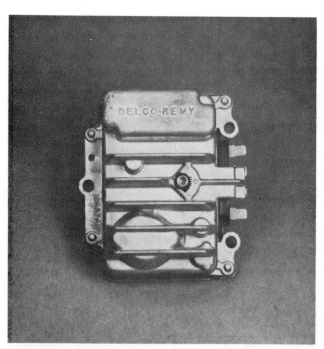

Detail of transistorized voltage regulator used 1965-67.

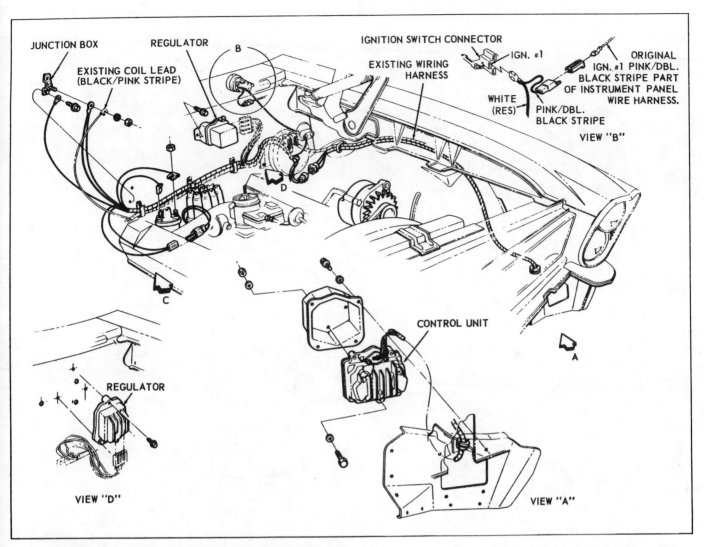

JUNCTION BOX

REGULATOR

B

EXISTING COIL LEAD
(BLACK/PINK STRIPE)

IGNITION SWITCH CONNECTOR

IGN. #1

EXISTING WIRING
HARNESS

ORIGINAL
IGN. #1 PINK/DBL.
BLACK STRIPE PART
OF INSTRUMENT PANEL
WIRE HARNESS.

WHITE
(RES)

PINK/DBL.
BLACK STRIPE

VIEW "B"

D

C

A

CONTROL UNIT

REGULATOR

VIEW "D"

VIEW "A"

Installation and routing of 1965 transistorized ignition harness
and location of components. Note that regulator was mounted
approximately ¾ inch higher than standard regulator.

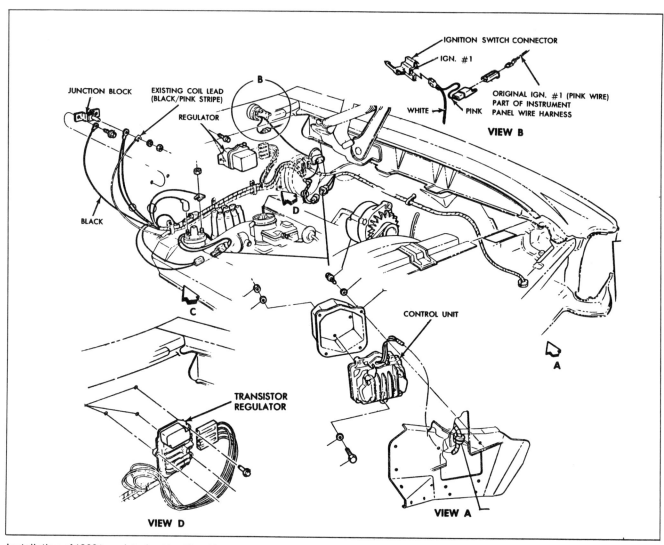

Installation of 1966 transistorized ignition. Note junction block on firewall and grommet in radiator core support (part number 9775265).

Close-up of 1966 replacement transistorized ignition coil. Original coils did not have part numbers in bold white letters.

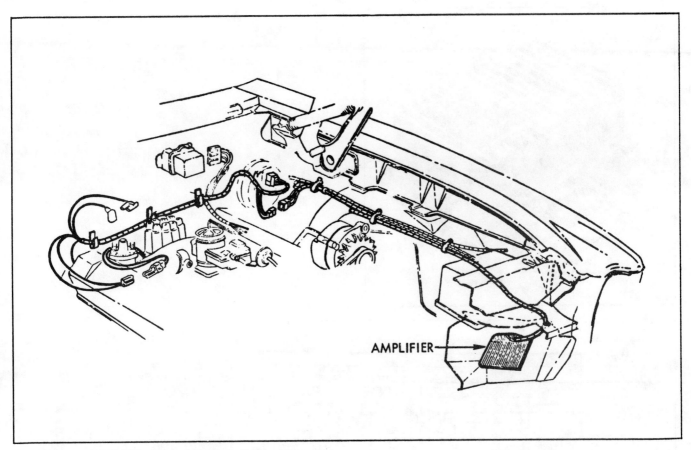

Installation of 1967 CD ignition system, including harness routing.

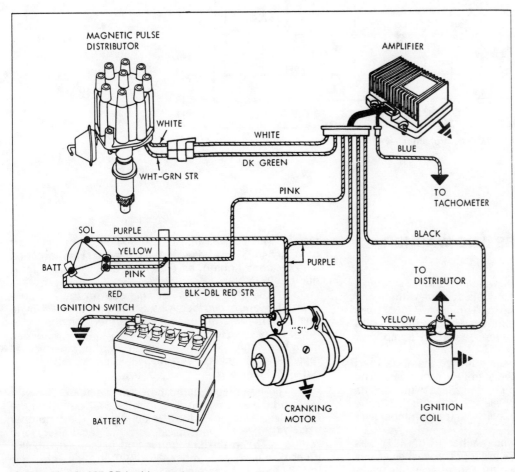

Schematic of 1967 CD ignition system.

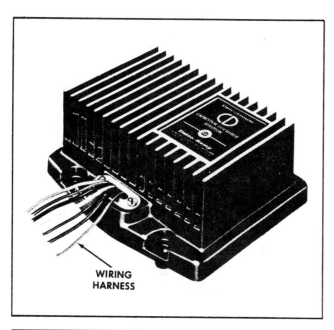

WIRING
HARNESS

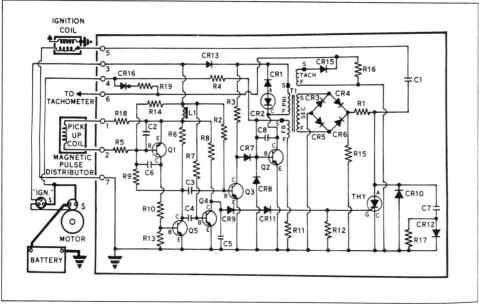

Exterior view and schematic of 1967 CD control amplifier.

WINDSHIELD WIPERS AND WASHER

1964-65

The standard one-speed windshield wiper was used on both 1964 and 1965 GTO models. It came without any washer provision. A dash knob (part number 9773857) was used for both years. The motor case on the firewall was 60° gloss black with a cap over the washer pump gear shaft.

The wiper arm itself was polished stainless (part number 383284), and was the same for both years. The base of the wiper arm was chrome diecast metal. The housing and link assembly was the same for both the one- and two-speed wiper systems (part number RH 4913654, LH 4913655).

A dual-speed wiper and washer (RPO 421) was offered as an option for 1964 and 1965. The washer jar was mounted on the RH core support and was opaque white

plastic. The lid was black. The standard bracket (part number 548935) was used in 1964. If the car was equipped with air conditioning, an extension arm was used (part number 9775728).

In 1965 the washer jar was still on the RH core support, in one of two locations. Some used the 1964-style flush mount (part number 548935) farther from the radiator. Others used a second type with uneven extended mounting legs, positioned closer to the radiator. All replacement brackets used the 548935 part number, without any extensions.

The hose was routed between the upper radiator tank and the core support—and in 1965 GTOs, under the fan shield—and joined by a connector (part number 9780771). It was then looped around the battery and routed between the LH fender and fender skirt to the pump by clips (part number 535938). Two clips were used in 1964, one was used in 1965.

The pump cover was plastic and painted 60° gloss black. The inlet/outlet valve package (part number 3840766) was white plastic. The hoses to the nozzles were routed through a clip (part number 545249) and then along the lower cowl screen edge and the rear hood seal. They were held in place by metal spring clips (part number 3829994) screwed to the cowl screen. The clips and screws were black cadmium in color. The washer jets were silver cadmium. The pump was activated by a button (part number 533396) in the center of the wiper knob (part number 9773848). The motor cover for the wiper was painted 60° gloss black, the same as the standard wiper motor cover.

1966-67

A two-speed electric windshield wiper with washer was standard on the 1966 and 1967 GTOs. The washer jar (replacement part number 3840083) was white opaque plastic with a black cap (part number 3798372). Original jars were supplied to GM in either white or black. The jar was mounted on the RH core support in 1966 by means of a 60° gloss-black bracket (part number 548935). Air-conditioned GTOs used the same jar and bracket mounted farther away from the radiator on the RH core support to clear the air conditioning receiver-indicator assembly.

The 1967 washer jar was mounted in either of two locations: GTOs equipped with air-injection reactors (the AIR system) mounted the redesigned white plastic washer jar (part number 9788109) on the RH core support with a 60° gloss-black bracket (part number 9788021). When equipped with air conditioning, the jar and bracket were moved farther to the right to clear the air conditioning receiver-indicator assembly. Non-AIR-equipped GTOs mounted the washer jar at the front of the LH fender inner skirt next to the power steering pump with two 16x⅝ inch hex-head screws.

For all 1966 and 1967 AIR GTOs, the 7/32 inch inside-diameter washer hose ran from, and was routed along, the top of the core support, under the upper radiator fan shield. It was retained by black plastic clips (part

number 3829994). The washer hose joined a connector (part number 9780771) near the battery, and then was routed between the LH fender and fender skirt. It was retained to the fender lip by two ½x1 inch clips (part number 535938) and continued on to the pump.

The pump package (part number 4912365) was identical to the 1964-65 optional two-speed wiper washer. The pump cover was 60° gloss-black plastic. The inlet/outlet valve package (part number 4914357) was white plastic. The 3/32 inch inside-diameter hoses to the washer spray nozzles were routed along the lower cowl screen edge and held in place by three cadmium-plated metal spring clips (part number 545249) screwed to the cowl screen with cadmium-plated hex-head screws. The washer spray nozzles (part number 3840766) were silver cadmium.

The 1966 pump was activated by a button (part number 9783683) in the windshield wiper knob (part number 9783679). The 1967 switch (part number 1993372) was redesigned without a button to activate the washer. Instead, the knob (part number 9786797) was depressed to activate the washer pump. A chromed bezel (part number 9782425 in 1966 and 9786941 in 1967) was used under the wiper knob.

The wiper motor assembly (part number 4911476) was identical to the 1964-65 unit in all respects. The motor case on the firewall was painted 60° gloss black. The wiper arm (part number 393832) was brushed stainless. The base of the arm was diecast metal and was satin finished. The housing and link assembly was identical to the 1964-65 unit and used the same part numbers.

1968-70

All 1968-70 GTOs came equipped with two-speed recessed park windshield wipers and washer.

The washer jar, part number 9791348, used a black cap (part number 3798372) and mounted on the front of the RH inner fender skirt by two number 10 16x½ inch hex-head screws. The 7/32 inch inside-diameter washer hose ran from the cap between the skirt and fender, came out under the RH hood hinge and looped across the blower motor case. It was retained by a plastic clip on the upper blower case screw and was then routed to the pump.

The pump package (part number 4918180) had a plastic cover painted 60° gloss black. The inlet/outlet valve package (part number 4914356) was white plastic. The assembly mounted to the firewall on a 60° gloss-black adapter plate (part number 3913663). This plate was not used on 1970 models.

Detail of 1964-67 two-speed windshield washer pump and wiper motor assembly, with clip, nozzle and retaining screw in foreground.

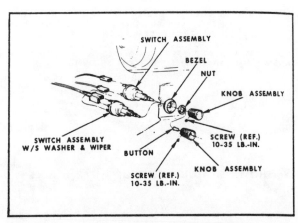

Installation of 1964-65 washer/wiper knob for two-speed wiper system.

The 5/32 inch inside-diameter hoses were routed through the firewall to the top vent screen and to the nozzle located on the underside of the hood. The 1968-69 nozzles were the same (part number 9791310 RH and 9791311 LH). They were held to the hood underside by two number 10 16x⅜ inch hex-head screws. The 1970 nozzles (part number 479525 RH and 479526 LH) were mounted in the same location, but used one number 10 16x⅜ inch hex-head screw per side.

The pump was activated by a switch located in the instrument panel. The knob for the 1968 control was part number 9790960. The word washer appeared across the face of the knob. One of two bezels with the word wiper was used: The letters appeared in white on bezel part number 9791114, and in black on bezel part number 9786941.

In 1969, the knob was changed to a rocker switch (part number 1993449). The switch was black with white letters reading off, wash, and wipe. This was changed to a slide switch in 1970 (part number 9794087). The switch was depressed to activate the washer.

The wiper motor assembly (part number 4918438, superseded by 4939586) was the same for all three years. The wiper motor assembly was natural metal.

The wiper arm (part number 3913612 RH and 3913613 LH) was dull stainless steel. The housing and link assembly (part number 4918758 RH and 4918624 LH) was the same in 1968-70.

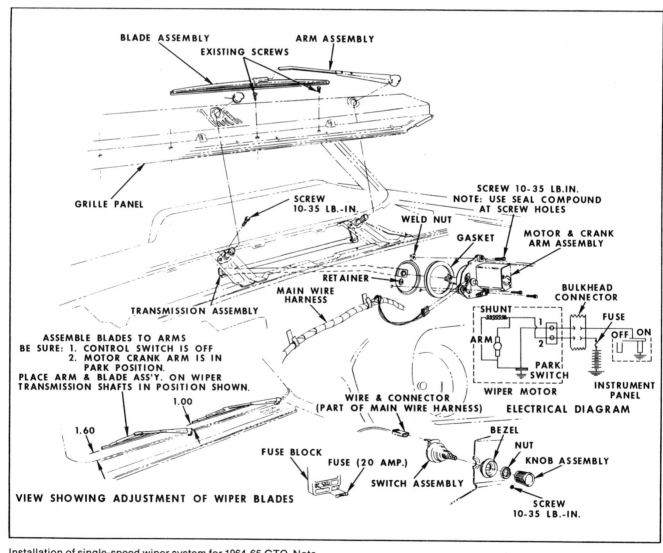

VIEW SHOWING ADJUSTMENT OF WIPER BLADES

Installation of single-speed wiper system for 1964-65 GTO. Note alignment of wiper blades.

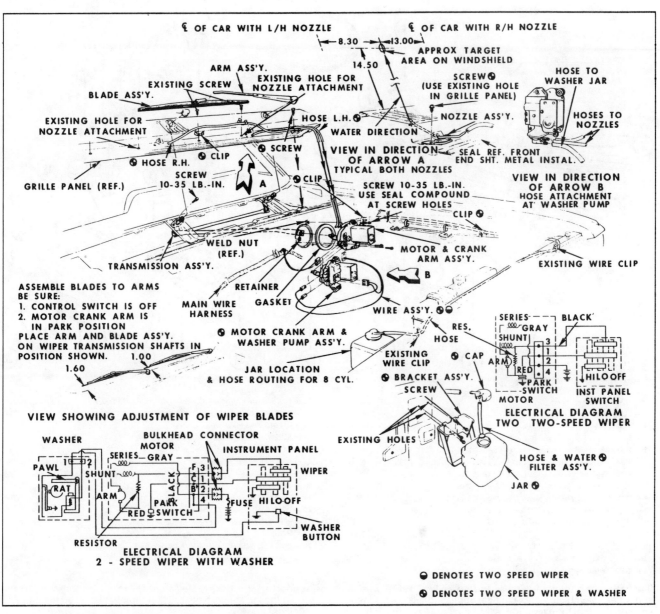

View showing adjustment of wiper blades. Electrical diagram 2-speed wiper with washer. Electrical diagram two two-speed wiper.

Installation and alignment instructions for 1964-65 optional two-speed wiper and washer system. Note routing of washer hoses from jar to pump and from pump to nozzles.

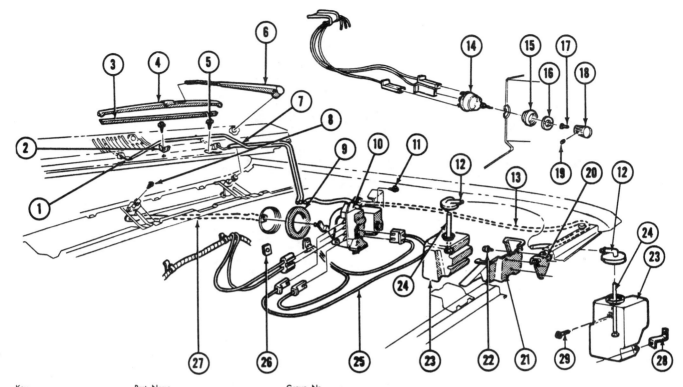

Key	Part Name	Group No.
1 — NOZZLE, Washer Spray		10.156
2 — CLIP, Hose		10.155
3 — INSERT ASM., Wiper Blade		10.146
4 — BLADE, Windshield Wiper		10.146
5 — SCREW & WASHER, Louver Panel to Cowl		N.S.
6 — ARM, Windshield Wiper		10.147
7 — HOSE, Pump to Nozzle (3/32" I.D. x 42" Long)		10.155
8 — SCREW, WASHER & SEALER, Wiper Trans. to Shroud		10.160
9 — GASKET, Wiper Motor to Shroud		10.152
10 — MOTOR ASM., Windshield Wiper		10.150
11 — SCREW, Wiper Motor to Shroud		N.S.
12 — CAP, Washer Jar		10.154
13 — HOSE, Pump to Jar (7/32" I.D. x 91" Long)		10.155
14 — SWITCH ASM., Two-Speed-Wiper & Washer		10.163
15 — BEZEL, Wiper Switch		10.166
16 — NUT, Windshield Wiper Control (1/2"-28 x 5/8" O.D.)		10.166
17 — BUTTON, Control Knob		10.164
18 — KNOB, Windshield Wiper Control		10.164
19 — SCREW, Wiper Control Knob (#8-32 x 5/32")		N.S.
20 — EXTENSION, Washer Jar Mounting Bracket		10.153
21 — BRACKET ASM., Washer Jar		10.154
22 — SCREW, Bracket to Baffle (#10-16 x 1/2")		8.977
23 — JAR, Washer		10.154
24 — FILTER ASM., Washer Jar (Less Hose)		10.154
25 — WIRE ASM., Wiper & Washer		10.150
26 — RETAINER, Wiper Drive Link to Motor		10.160
27 — HOUSING & LINK ASM., Wiper Trans.		10.159
28 — BRACKET, Washer Jar (T/8 w/A.I.R.)		10.154
29 — SCREW, Washer Jar to Skirt (#10-16 x 5/8")		8.977

Illustration of routing of harness and hoses for 1964-67 washer and wiper assemblies for six-cylinder application. GTO assembly was similar, with the exception of the jar mounted on the RH core support and the hose routed along the top of the core support and under the fan shield. Note bracket (number 28) used for 1967 AIR applications.

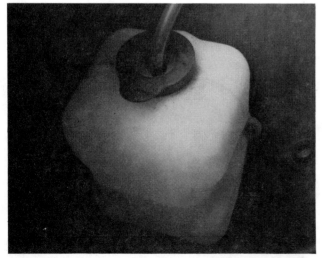

Close-up of 1968-70 washer jar (part number 9791348) located on front of RH fender skirt. Washer jar cap pictured is original. Replacements used the 1964-67 cap because the 1968-70 cap was not serviced.

Detail of 1966 washer jar and bracket assembly. Original jars were either black or white, but were of the same design.

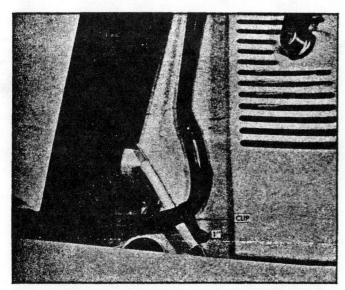

The windshield washer hoses on some 1964 Tempests have been pinched between the hood reinforcement and the flange at the left end of the cowl vent grille. This causes the washer to be inoperative or damages the hoses. To correct, drill a 0.250-inch-diameter hole through the vent grille next to the rolled flange, approximately 1 9/16 inches from left end of the grille and one inch from the vertical wall behind the hood. Replace hoses if necessary. Clip hoses at this location with one number 545249 (code F-3) clip (same as used to clip wire harness to front fender cross-brace).

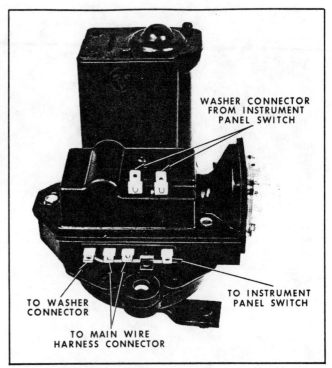

1964-67 washer pump assemblies, showing identification of harness terminals.

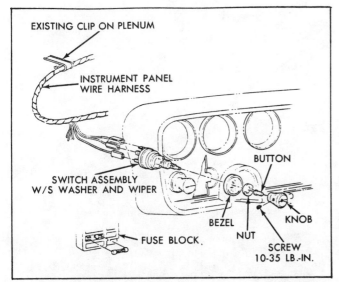

Installation instructions for 1967 windshield wiper and washer control knob in instrument panel. A button was no longer used to activate washer; knob was depressed to start the washer pump.

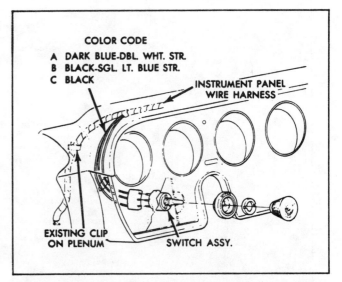

Installation instructions for 1966 windshield washer and wiper knob and button on instrument panel.

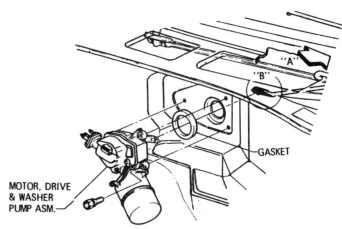

1970 GTO did not use adapter plate for mounting motor to firewall.

MOTOR, DRIVE & WASHER PUMP ASM.

GASKET

"A"
"B"

Detail of 1968-70 washer pump and wiper motor assembly. Motor and bracket were natural metal in appearance, and the pump cover was 60° gloss black.

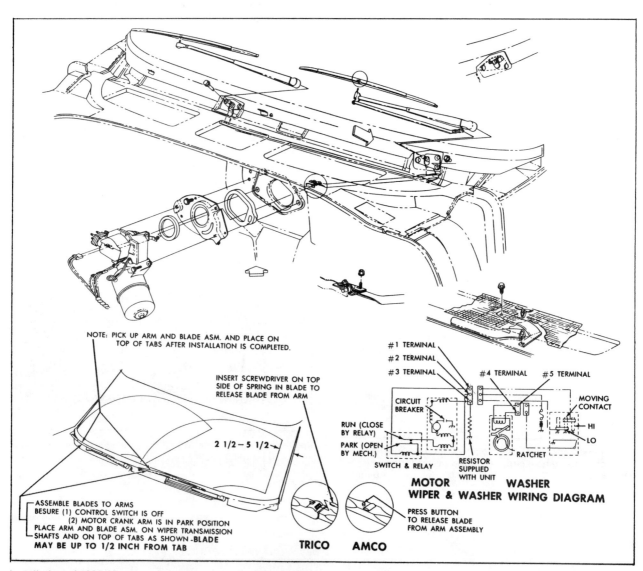

NOTE: PICK UP ARM AND BLADE ASM. AND PLACE ON TOP OF TABS AFTER INSTALLATION IS COMPLETED.

INSERT SCREWDRIVER ON TOP SIDE OF SPRING IN BLADE TO RELEASE BLADE FROM ARM

2 1/2 - 5 1/2

ASSEMBLE BLADES TO ARMS
BE SURE (1) CONTROL SWITCH IS OFF
(2) MOTOR CRANK ARM IS IN PARK POSITION
PLACE ARM AND BLADE ASM. ON WIPER TRANSMISSION
SHAFTS AND ON TOP OF TABS AS SHOWN - BLADE
MAY BE UP TO 1/2 INCH FROM TAB

TRICO   AMCO

PRESS BUTTON
TO RELEASE BLADE
FROM ARM ASSEMBLY

#1 TERMINAL
#2 TERMINAL
#3 TERMINAL
#4 TERMINAL   #5 TERMINAL

CIRCUIT BREAKER

MOVING CONTACT

RUN (CLOSE BY RELAY)
PARK (OPEN BY MECH.)

HI
LO

SWITCH & RELAY

RESISTOR SUPPLIED WITH UNIT

RATCHET

MOTOR   WASHER
WIPER & WASHER WIRING DIAGRAM

Installation of 1968-69 motor and pump assembly. Note instructions for alignment of wiper blades, and use of either Amco or Trico blades as original equipment.

HEATER

1964-65

The Circ-L-Aire heater was standard for 1964 and 1965. The blower motor cover, mounted on the firewall, was painted 30° gloss black. The blower motor wire was routed through the engine harness, through clips mounted at the cover retainer screws at the top of the cover, to the motor connector.

Heater hoses were routed differently for the two years. In 1964, the heater inlet hose was run to the front of the intake manifold to a connecting elbow (part number 9776906). The hose was held in place by a bracket (part number 9774644) painted black and bolted to the head, just above the center port on the RH bank.

In 1965, with the new design, the heater inlet hose (part number 9780120) was molded and ran to a pipe on the top rear of the RH cylinder head. The outlet hose was retained by a redesigned bracket (part number 9780957) bolted to the RH front cylinder head, and was painted black. Air-conditioned GTOs routed the heater hose along the top of the RH fender skirt. Corbin-type ring clamps were used in 1964 and 1965 to secure heater hoses.

The underdash heater core cover assembly was painted dark metallic gray at a 60° gloss. The heater core part number used for 1964 and 1965 was 3022069; 3004817 for air-conditioned cars.

A heater deletion option (RPO 584) was available in both 1964 and 1965. A heater opening cover plate (part number 9774373 in 1964 and 9777185 in 1965) was installed on the instrument panel in place of the heater control assembly. On the firewall, two plates were used. One covered the upper hole (part number 3823111 for both years), and another covered the lower hole (part number 3860114 for both years). The firewall heater cover plates were painted 30° gloss black, and were retained by sheet metal screws to the firewall.

1966-67

The Circ-L-Aire heater was standard equipment for 1966-67. The blower motor cover was mounted on the firewall and was painted 30° gloss black. The blower motor wire ran from a grommet in the firewall directly above the heater core pipes. It was routed under the blower cover by clips attached to the cover, to the firewall mounting nuts, and then to the blower motor connector.

The heater inlet hose measured ⅝ inch inside diameter by thirteen inches, and used part number 9780120. The hose was a preformed curve and ran to the inlet pipe on the RH rear of the engine block. The outlet hose was supported by a 60° gloss-black bracket (part number 9780957) which was bolted to the front of the RH cylinder head. GTOs equipped with air conditioning routed the outlet hose along the RH upper fender skirt and retained it with a clip (part number 9774218).

Research indicates that 1966 and 1967 GTOs used tower-type heater-hose clamps (instead of the Corbin type of ring clamp now being used by restorers) at both ends of the heater hoses.

The underdash heater core cover assembly was painted 30° gloss black. The heater core part number for non-air-conditioned GTOs was 3006266; 3014949 for those equipped with air conditioning.

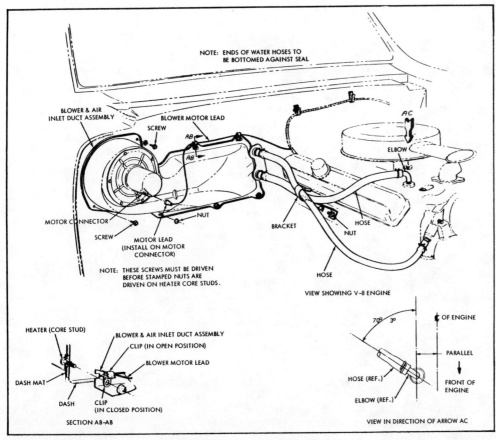

Installation and routing of heater hose and wire assemblies for 1964 GTO without air conditioning. Bracket was painted 60° gloss black.

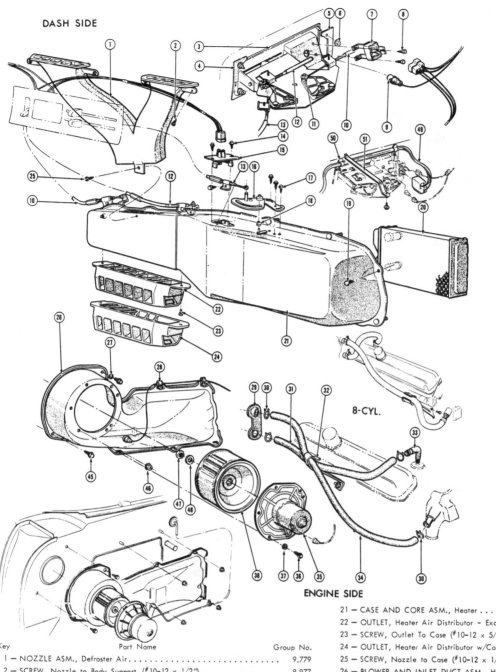

DASH SIDE

8-CYL.

ENGINE SIDE

Key	Part Name	Group No.
1 — NOZZLE ASM., Defroster Air		9.779
2 — SCREW, Nozzle to Body Support (#10-12 x 1/2")		8.977
3 — CONTROL ASM., Heater (Inc. #7)		8.849
4 — BRACKET, Heater Control Mounting-R.H.		8.866
5 — BRACKET, Heater Control Mounting-L.H.		8.866
6 — NUT, Control to Inst. Panel (3/16")		8.921
7 — SWITCH, Heater Blower Motor		8.852
8 — SCREW, Switch to Control Asm.		N.S.
9 — BULB, Heater Control Panel Lamp (#1895)		8.991
10 — CABLE ASM., Heater Defroster Air-Yellow Staple (25-1/2" long)		9.779
11 — NUT, Cable to Control (1/4"-20)		N.S.
12 — CABLE ASM., Heater Air Inlet-Black Staple (25" long)		8.866
13 — CABLE ASM., Heater Temperature Control-Red Staple (16" long)		8.866
14 — SCREW, Resistor to Case (#10-12 x 5/8")		8.977
15 — RESISTOR ASM., Heater Blower		8.852
16 — CAM AND SUPPORT ASM., Heater Temperature		8.866
17 — SCREW, Cam and Support to Case		N.S.
18 — BEARING, Heater Control Shaft		8.866
19 — SCREW, Case and Core to Dash (1/4"-14 x 7/8")		8.977
20 — CORE ASM., Heater - w/Fittings		8.854

Exploded view and parts nomenclature for 1964-65 heater and defroster assemblies. For 1964, heater hose was retained by bracket mounted to side of cylinder head; for 1965, hose was retained by bracket mounted on front of head. Blower motor wire was routed along top of cover in 1964; 1965 wire was routed under cover and was retained by metal clip fastened to cover bolt. (Pontiac motor cover is shown here).

Key	Part Name	Group No.
21 — CASE AND CORE ASM., Heater		8.845
22 — OUTLET, Heater Air Distributor - Exc. Console		8.845
23 — SCREW, Outlet To Case (#10-12 x 5/8")		8.977
24 — OUTLET, Heater Air Distributor w/Console		8.845
25 — SCREW, Nozzle to Case (#10-12 x 1/2")		8.977
26 — BLOWER AND INLET DUCT ASM., Heater		8.857
27 — LOCKWASHER, Duct to Dash (1/4" Ext.)		8.932
28 — CLIP, Blower Motor Wire		N.S.
29 — SEAL, Heater Core Tubes to Dash		8.846
30 — CLAMP, Heater Hose		8.846
31 — HOSE, Heater Water Inlet (3/4" I.D. x 37" long)		8.846
32 — BRACKET, Heater Water Hose		8.846
33 — ELBOW, Hose to Intake Manifold		8.866
34 — HOSE, Heater Water Outlet (5/8" I.D. x 32-1/4" long)		8.846
35 — MOTOR ASM., Heater Blower		8.855
36 — SCREW, Motor to Duct (#8-18 x 3/8")		8.977
37 — LOCKWASHER, Motor to Duct (#8)		8.932
38 — IMPELLER, Blower		8.857
39 — NIPPLE, Heater Hose to Thermostat Hsg.(5/8")		8.866
40 — HOSE, Heater Water Inlet (5/8" I.D. x 37" long)		8.846
41 — BRACKET, Heater Water Hose		8.846
42 — LOCKWASHER, Bracket to Cylinder Head (3/8")		8.931
43 — BOLT, Bracket to Cylinder Head (3/8"-16 x 5/8")		8.900
44 — HOSE, Heater Water Outlet (5/8" I.D. x 32-1/4" Long)		8.846
45 — SCREW, Duct to Dash (1/4"-14 x 3/4")		8.977
46 — NUT, Case Studs to Duct (1/4"-20)		8.915
47 — NUT, Impeller to Motor (#10-32)		8.915
48 — LOCKWASHER, Impeller to Motor (#10)		8.932
49 — WIRE ASM., Heater Control to Blower & Relay (1966)		8.866
50 — CLIP, Inst. Panel Wiring (1966-67)		2.482
51 — BRACKET, Heater Control to Inst. Panel (1967)		8.866

Two interior duct-outlet designs were used in 1966. GTOs not equipped with the center console used outlet part number 9773829; console-equipped cars used part number 9774479. The differences in the outlets were slight, although research shows some of the nonconsole outlets had the Chevrolet bow-tie emblem stamped on the case.

In 1967, three outlets were used. The 1966 numbers were duplicated; however, if the stereo tape player was ordered, a Y-shaped outlet (part number 9788192) was installed. (Refer to radio section, component 8 in stereo tape player illustration, for outlet detail.) All outlet ducts were black plastic.

As in 1964 and 1965, the heater deletion option (RPO 584) was available for 1966-67. The heater opening cover plate for the instrument panel was part number 9785373 in 1966 and 9777674 in 1967. The upper and lower hole covers for the firewall were the same as in 1964-65.

1968-70

The blower motor cover mounted on the firewall was painted 30° gloss black. The blower motor wire was routed through a grommet in the firewall and then under the blower motor cover. It was retained by two clips attached to the cover retaining nuts, and then routed to the motor terminal.

A preformed inlet hose (part number 9792569) was used on GTOs without air conditioning. Air-conditioned cars used hose part number 527928. A 60° gloss-black bracket (part number 9780957) retained the outlet hose, which was routed to the water pump and bolted to the front of the RH cylinder head. When equipped with air conditioning, a clip (part number 3825416) was mounted on the RH fender skirt and retained the hose as it was routed to the water pump.

As in 1966 and 1967, tower-type hose clamps were used on all heater hoses.

The underdash heater core cover was painted 30° gloss black. Two different heater cores were used in 1969 non-air-conditioned models. A 2½-inch-wide core (part number 3017152) was used in 1968. It was replaced during the 1969 production year by a two-inch core (part number 3014782), which was used until the end of the 1970 production year. On air-conditioned models, core part number 3017156 was used in 1968. This was replaced in 1969 by part number 3014083, which was used until the end of the 1970 production year. This core measured two inches in width.

On non-air-conditioned GTOs, a sponge-rubber seal (part number 9776917) was used to seal the heater core tubes to the firewall. Although two different width cores were used, the case assemblies were unaffected.

The heater duct outlet was black plastic, and was the same for all three years. The standard straight design (part number 9790487) was used on most applications. If the stereo tape player option was ordered, but not with air conditioning, a U-shaped duct (part number 9791750) was used. If air conditioning and the stereo tape player were ordered together, duct part number 9793675 was utilized.

While there was no heater deletion credit available as in previous years, the components were available to cover the holes if the 1968-70 heater hardware was removed. Components and detail for the firewall were the same as for 1964-65. The heater control assembly plate cover was part number 9791132 for 1968, 9796811 for 1969, and 9799793 for 1970.

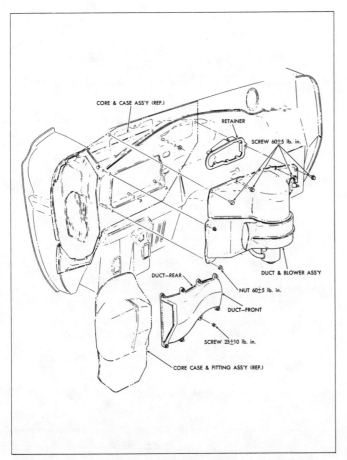

(1) Disconnect battery cable and heater blower wire at the motor.

(2) Using a 1/4 inch socket and extension, through the front opening and between the right front fender and fender inner panel, remove 5 blower motor to blower housing retaining bolts.

(3) Remove the motor and impeller assembly from the blower housing and position with impeller facing toward the engine below the right hood hinge.

(4) Remove the blower to impeller retaining nut and washer and separate.

NOTE: IT MAY BE NECESSARY TO TAP LIGHTLY ON THE MOTOR SHAFT WITH A WOOD OR PLASTIC TOOL HANDLE.

(5) Move the motor and then the impeller separately along the top of the right front fender inner panel to the front opening and remove.

NOTE: IT WILL BE NECESSARY TO POSITION THE MOTOR WITH THE SHAFT DOWN, AND THE LARGE FLAT ON THE SIDE OF THE MOTOR FLANGE TOWARD THE OUTSIDE OF THE FENDER.

(6) Reinstall by reversing the above procedure.

(7) Test operation.

Pontiac Service News Flash number 65-127, dated 9-8-65, reported the above revised procedure for removal and replacement of the heater blower motor on 1964 and 1965 models. Note that this method does not require removal of the front fender.

Components of 1964-67 cover assemblies, and torque specifications. All covers were painted 60° gloss black.

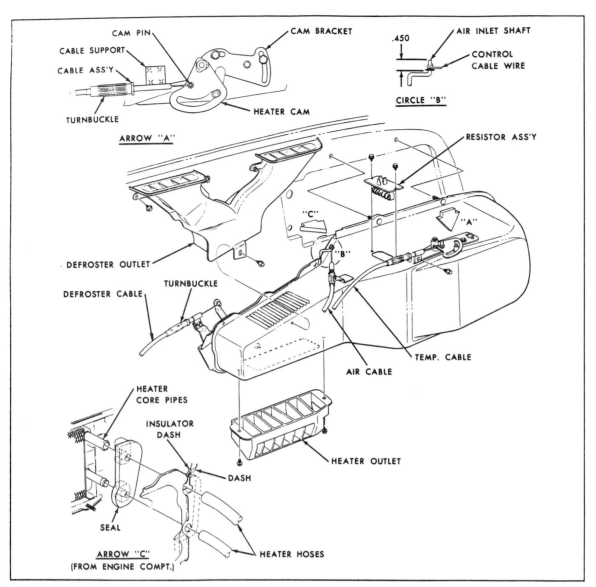

CAM PIN
CABLE SUPPORT
CABLE ASS'Y
TURNBUCKLE
CAM BRACKET
HEATER CAM

.450
AIR INLET SHAFT
CONTROL CABLE WIRE
CIRCLE "B"

ARROW "A"
RESISTOR ASS'Y
"C"
"A"
"B"
DEFROSTER OUTLET
TURNBUCKLE
DEFROSTER CABLE
TEMP. CABLE
AIR CABLE

HEATER CORE PIPES
INSULATOR DASH
DASH
SEAL
ARROW "C"
(FROM ENGINE COMPT.)
HEATER HOSES
HEATER OUTLET

Detail of interior heater components, 1964-67.

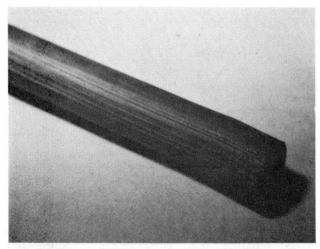

Detail of heater hose still available from GM (part number 495692). Note three-groove design used from 1964–70.

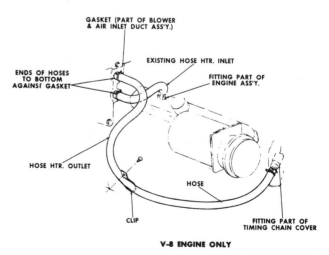

GASKET (PART OF BLOWER & AIR INLET DUCT ASS'Y.)
EXISTING HOSE HTR. INLET
ENDS OF HOSES TO BOTTOM AGAINST GASKET
FITTING PART OF ENGINE ASS'Y.
HOSE HTR. OUTLET
HOSE
CLIP
FITTING PART OF TIMING CHAIN COVER
V-8 ENGINE ONLY

Routing of heater hoses for 1965 GTO with air conditioning. Clip retained outlet hose to RH inner fender skirt.

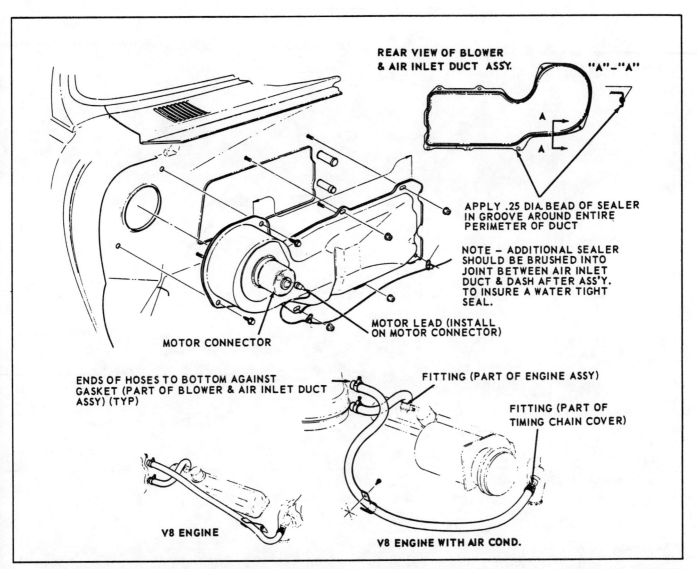

REAR VIEW OF BLOWER
& AIR INLET DUCT ASSY.

"A"—"A"

APPLY .25 DIA. BEAD OF SEALER
IN GROOVE AROUND ENTIRE
PERIMETER OF DUCT

NOTE — ADDITIONAL SEALER
SHOULD BE BRUSHED INTO
JOINT BETWEEN AIR INLET
DUCT & DASH AFTER ASS'Y.
TO INSURE A WATER TIGHT
SEAL.

MOTOR LEAD (INSTALL
ON MOTOR CONNECTOR)

MOTOR CONNECTOR

ENDS OF HOSES TO BOTTOM AGAINST
GASKET (PART OF BLOWER & AIR INLET DUCT
ASSY) (TYP)

FITTING (PART OF ENGINE ASSY)

FITTING (PART OF
TIMING CHAIN COVER)

V8 ENGINE

V8 ENGINE WITH AIR COND.

Detail of heater blower cover assembly and hose routing for 1966-67. Note wire routing to blower motor connector, and heater outlet hose bracket used on standard cars, with retainer (part number 3825416) to skirt mount for air-conditioning-equipped GTOs.

415

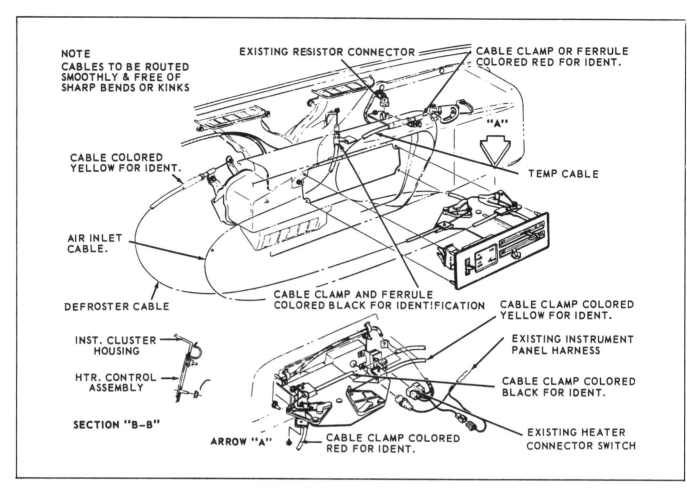

NOTE
CABLES TO BE ROUTED
SMOOTHLY & FREE OF
SHARP BENDS OR KINKS

EXISTING RESISTOR CONNECTOR

CABLE CLAMP OR FERRULE
COLORED RED FOR IDENT.

"A"

TEMP CABLE

CABLE COLORED
YELLOW FOR IDENT.

AIR INLET
CABLE.

DEFROSTER CABLE

CABLE CLAMP AND FERRULE
COLORED BLACK FOR IDENTIFICATION

CABLE CLAMP COLORED
YELLOW FOR IDENT.

EXISTING INSTRUMENT
PANEL HARNESS

CABLE CLAMP COLORED
BLACK FOR IDENT.

EXISTING HEATER
CONNECTOR SWITCH

INST. CLUSTER
HOUSING

HTR. CONTROL
ASSEMBLY

SECTION "B-B"

ARROW "A"

CABLE CLAMP COLORED
RED FOR IDENT.

Detail of 1966-67 heater control assembly and related cables.
Note harness attachment.

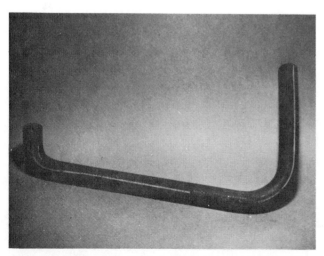

Preformed heater hose used on all non-air-conditioned GTOs
from 1968 to 1970 (part number 9792569).

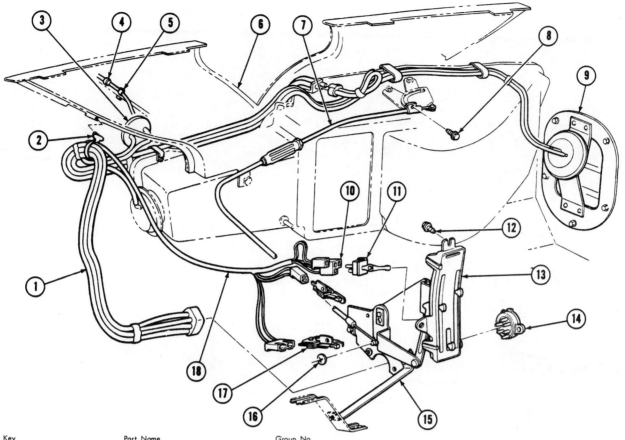

Key	Part Name	Group No.
1 — HARNESS ASM., Vacuum Hose		9.281
2 — CLIP, Harness to Brace (1/4" Plastic)		2.559
3 — GROMMET, Vacuum Hose & Wires Thru Dash		9.775
4 — VALVE ASM., Vacuum Check		9.281
5 — CLIP, Hose to Vapor Return & Fuel Pipe		3.162
6 — NOZZLE ASM., Defroster Air		9.779
7 — CABLE ASM., Air Conditioning & Heater Temperature Control		9.281
8 — SCREW, Cable to Cam & Support (#10-16 x 5/8")		9.281
9 — INLET & VALVE ASM., Air		9.215

Key	Part Name	Group No.
10 — SWITCH ASM., Control Master		9.275
11 — SWITCH ASM., Blower Motor		9.275
12 — SCREW, Control to Inst. Panel (#8-32 x 1/2")		8.977
13 — CONTROL ASM., Air Conditioner & Heater		9.273
14 — VALVE ASM., Heater Control Vacuum		8.850
15 — BRACKET, Heater & Air Conditioner Control Stabilizer		9.787
16 — NUT, Control Cable to Inlet Shaft		9.281
17 — SWITCH ASM., Clutch Control		9.275
18 — WIRE ASM., Air Conditioner Control		9.276

1968 vacuum and electrical controls and harness. The heater control assembly was mounted vertically for 1968 only.

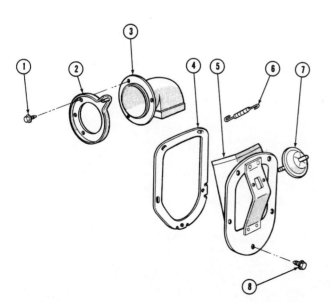

Key	Part Name	Group No.	Part No.	1968	1969	1970-72
1 — SCREW (#10-16 x 3/4")		—	N.S.	X	X	⌐
2 — PIN & FLANGE, Mounting		9.215	3014871	X	X	X
3 — DUCT, Inlet		9.215	3014866	X	X	X
4 — GASKET, Duct		9.215	3014867	X		
			3018642		X	X
5 — INLET & VALVE, Air		9.215	3014079	X		
	("A")		3018596		X	X
	("G")		3017842		X	X
6 — SPRING, Valve		9.215	3014868	X	X	X
7 — DIAPHRAGM, Air Inlet		9.281	1998939	X		
	("A")		1998942		X	X
	("G")		1998943		X	X
8 — SCREW (#10-16 x 1")		—	N.S.	X	X	X

Drawing of 1968-70 blower inlet valve mounted inside RH cowl panel.

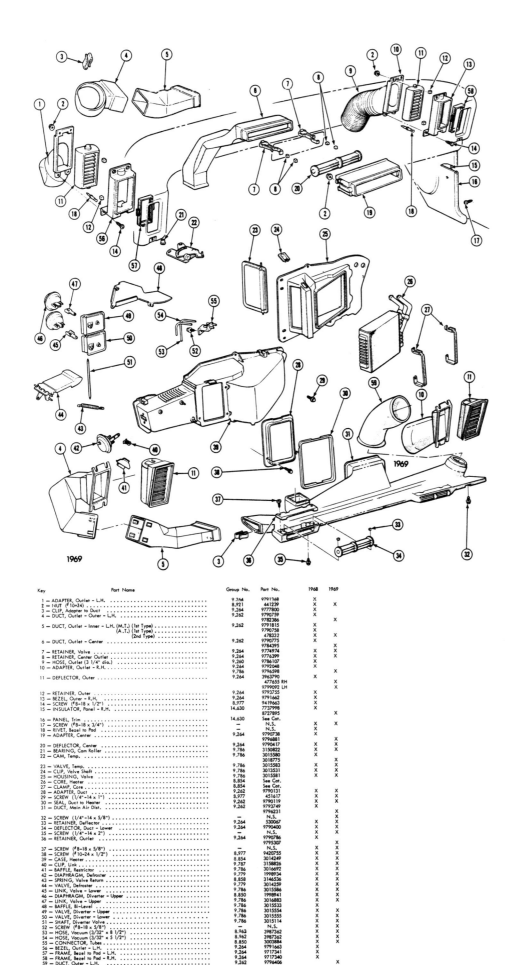

Key	Part Name	Group No.	Part No.	1968	1969
1 — ADAPTER, Outlet - L.H.		9.264	9791368	X	
2 — NUT (#10-24)		8.921	441239	X	X
3 — CLIP, Adapter to Duct		9.264	9777800	X	
4 — DUCT, Adapter to Duct - L.H.		9.262	9790759		X
			9782386	X	
5 — DUCT, Outlet - Inner - L.H. (M.T.) (1st Type)		9.262	9791815	X	
	(A.T.) (1st Type)		9790758	X	
	(2nd Type)		478332	X	X
6 — DUCT, Outlet - Center		9.262	9790775	X	
			9784395		X
7 — RETAINER, Valve		9.264	9774974	X	X
8 — RETAINER, Center Outlet		9.264	9776399	X	X
9 — HOSE, Outlet (3 1/4" dia.)		9.260	9786107	X	X
10 — ADAPTER, Outlet - R.H.		9.264	9792048	X	
			9.786	9796598		X
11 — DEFLECTOR, Outer		9.264	3963790	X	
				477655 RH		X
			9799092 LH		X
12 — RETAINER, Outer		9.264	9793755	X	
13 — BEZEL, Outer - R.H.		9.264	9791662	X	
14 — SCREW (#8-18 x 1/2")		8.977	9419663	X	
15 — INSULATOR, Panel - R.H.		14.630	7737998		X
				8727895		X
16 — PANEL, Trim		14.630	See Cat.	X	X
17 — SCREW (#8-18 x 3/4")		—	N.S.	X	
18 — RIVET, Bezel to Pad		—	N.S.	X	
19 — ADAPTER, Center		9.264	9790738	X	
			9796881		X
20 — DEFLECTOR, Center		9.264	9790417	X	X
21 — BEARING, Cam Roller		9.786	3150822	X	X
22 — CAM, Temp.		9.786	3015580	X	X
			3018775		X
23 — VALVE, Temp.		9.786	3015583	X	X
24 — CLIP, Valve Shaft		9.786	3013531	X	X
25 — HOUSING, Valve		9.786	3015581	X	X
26 — CORE, Heater		8.854	See Cat.		
27 — CLAMP, Core		8.854	See Cat.		
28 — ADAPTER, Duct		9.262	9790131	X	X
29 — SCREW (1/4"-14 x 1")		8.977	451617	X	X
30 — SEAL, Duct to Heater		9.262	9790119	X	X
31 — DUCT, Main Air Dist.		9.262	9793749	X	
			9796231		X
32 — SCREW (1/4"-14 x 5/8")		—	N.S.	X	X
33 — RETAINER, Deflector		9.264	530067	X	X
34 — DEFLECTOR, Duct - Lower		9.264	9790400	X	X
35 — SCREW (1/4"-14 x 2")		—	N.S.	X	X
36 — RETAINER, Outlet		9.264	9790786	X	X
			9795303		X
37 — SCREW (#8-18 x 5/8")		—	N.S.	X	X
38 — SCREW (#10-24 x 1/2")		8.977	9420755	X	X
39 — CASE, Heater		8.854	3012249	X	X
40 — CLIP, Link		9.787	3158826	X	X
41 — BAFFLE, Restrictor		9.786	3016692	X	X
42 — DIAPHRAGM, Defroster		9.779	1998934	X	X
43 — SPRING, Valve Return		8.858	3146536	X	X
44 — VALVE, Defroster		9.779	3014259	X	X
45 — LINK, Valve - Lower		9.786	3015586	X	X
46 — DIAPHRAGM, Diverter - Upper		8.850	1998941	X	X
47 — LINK, Valve - Upper		9.786	3016883	X	X
48 — BAFFLE, Bi-Level		9.786	3015533	X	
49 — VALVE, Diverter - Upper		9.786	3015554	X	X
50 — VALVE, Diverter - Lower		9.786	3015555	X	X
51 — SHAFT, Diverter Valve		9.786	3015114	X	X
52 — SCREW (#8-18 x 5/8")		—	N.S.	X	X
53 — HOSE, Vacuum (3/32" x 8 1/2")		8.962	3987362	X	X
54 — HOSE, Vacuum (3/32" x 5 1/2")		8.962	3987362	X	X
55 — CONNECTOR, Tubes		8.850	3003884	X	
56 — BEZEL, Outlet - L.H.		9.264	9791663	X	
57 — FRAME, Bezel to Pad - L.H.		9.264	9717341	X	
58 — FRAME, Bezel to Pad - R.H.		9.264	9717340	X	
59 — DUCT, Outer - L.H.		9.262	9796406		X

Drawing of 1968-69 interior ductwork with part names and part numbers. Lower air duct (number 31) was painted interior color at 0° gloss. Heater case (number 39) was cast black fiberglass.

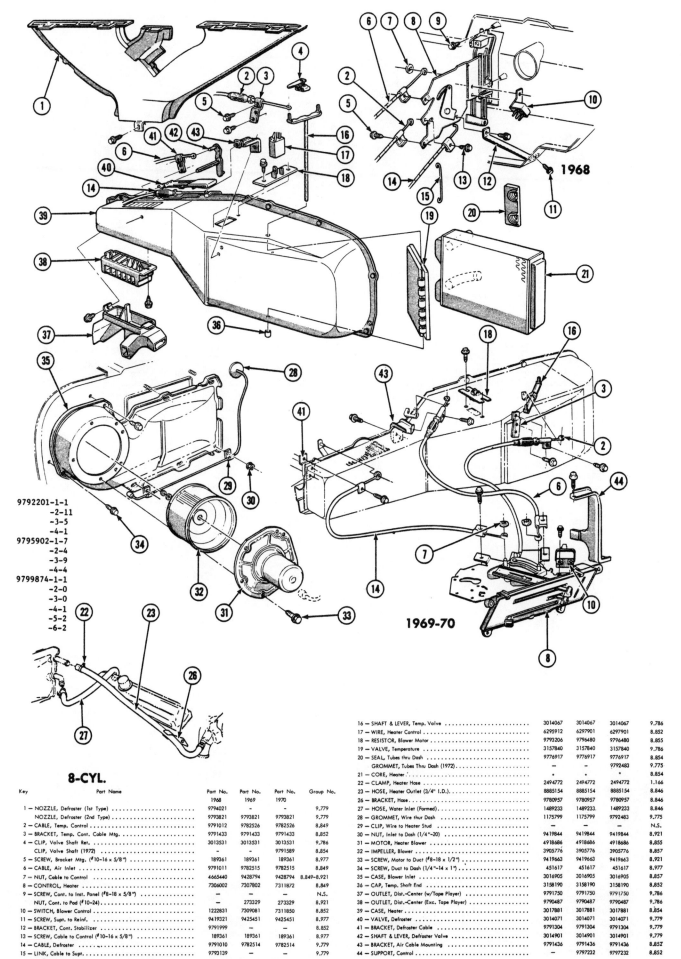

9792201-1-1
     -2-11
     -3-5
     -4-1
9795902-1-7
     -2-4
     -3-9
     -4-4
9799874-1-1
     -2-0
     -3-0
     -4-1
     -5-2
     -6-2

1968

1969-70

8-CYL.

Key	Part Name	Part No. 1968	Part No. 1969	Part No. 1970	Group No.
1 —	NOZZLE, Defroster (1st Type)	9794021	—	—	9.779
	NOZZLE, Defroster (2nd Type)	9793821	9793821	9793821	9.779
2 —	CABLE, Temp. Control	9791012	9782526	9782526	8.849
3 —	BRACKET, Temp. Cont. Cable Mtg.	9791433	9791433	9791433	8.852
4 —	CLIP, Valve Shaft Ret.	3013531	3013531	3013531	9.786
	CLIP, Valve Shaft (1972)	—	—	9791589	8.854
5 —	SCREW, Bracket Mtg. (#10-16 x 5/8")	189361	189361	189361	8.977
6 —	CABLE, Air Inlet	9791011	9782515	9782515	8.849
7 —	NUT, Cable to Control	4665440	9428794	9428794	8.849-8.921
8 —	CONTROL, Heater	7306002	7307802	7311872	8.849
9 —	SCREW, Cont. to Inst. Panel (#8-18 x 5/8")	—	—	—	N.S.
	NUT, Cont. to Pad (#10-24)	—	273329	273329	8.921
10 —	SWITCH, Blower Control	1222831	7309081	7311850	8.852
11 —	SCREW, Supt. to Reinf.	9419321	9425451	9425451	8.977
12 —	BRACKET, Cont. Stabilizer	9791999			8.852
13 —	SCREW, Cable to Control (#10-16 x 5/8")	189361	189361	189361	8.977
14 —	CABLE, Defroster	9791010	9782514	9782514	9.779
15 —	LINK, Cable to Supt.	9793139	—	—	9.779

Key	Part Name	Part No. 1968	Part No. 1969	Part No. 1970	Group No.
16 —	SHAFT & LEVER, Temp. Valve	3014067	3014067	3014067	9.786
17 —	WIRE, Heater Control	6295912	6297901	6297901	8.852
18 —	RESISTOR, Blower Motor	9793206	9796480	9796480	8.855
19 —	VALVE, Temperature	3157840	3157840	3157840	9.786
20 —	SEAL, Tubes thru Dash	9776917	9776917	9776917	8.854
	GROMMET, Tubes Thru Dash (1972)	—	—	9792483	9.775
21 —	CORE, Heater			*	8.854
22 —	CLAMP, Heater Hose	2494772	2494772	2494772	1.166
23 —	HOSE, Heater Outlet (3/4" I.D.)	8885154	8885154	8885154	8.846
26 —	BRACKET, Hose	9780957	9780957	9780957	8.846
27 —	HOSE, Water Inlet (Formed)	1489233	1489233.	1489233	8.846
28 —	GROMMET, Wire thru Dash	1175799	1175799	9792483	9.775
29 —	CLIP, Wire to Heater Stud	—	—	—	N.S.
30 —	NUT, Inlet to Dash (1/4"-20)	9419844	9419844	9419844	8.921
31 —	MOTOR, Heater Blower	4918686	4918686	4918686	8.855
32 —	IMPELLER, Blower	3905776	3905776	3905776	8.857
33 —	SCREW, Motor to Duct (#8-18 x 1/2")	9419663	9419663	9419663	8.921
34 —	SCREW, Duct to Dash (1/4"-14 x 1")	451617	451617	451617	8.977
35 —	CASE, Blower Inlet	3016905	3016905	3016905	8.857
36 —	CAP, Temp. Shaft End	3158190	3158190	3158190	8.852
37 —	OUTLET, Dist.-Center (w/Tape Player)	9791750	9791750	9791750	9.786
38 —	OUTLET, Dist.-Center (Exc. Tape Player)	9790487	9790487	9790487	9.786
39 —	CASE, Heater	3017881	3017881	3017881	8.854
40 —	VALVE, Defroster	3014071	3014071	3014071	9.779
41 —	BRACKET, Defroster Cable	9791304	9791304	9791304	9.779
42 —	SHAFT & LEVER, Defroster Valve	3014901	3014901	3014901	9.779
43 —	BRACKET, Air Cable Mounting	9791436	9791436	9791436	8.852
44 —	SUPPORT, Control	—	9797232	9797232	8.852

Exploded view of 1968-70 heater components and part numbers.

*See Group 8.854

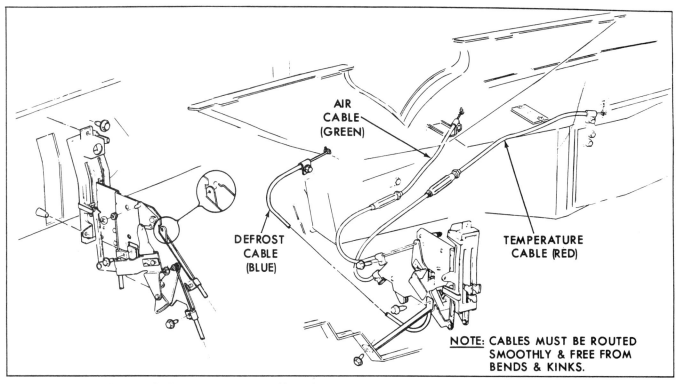

AIR
CABLE
(GREEN)

DEFROST
CABLE
(BLUE)

TEMPERATURE
CABLE (RED)

NOTE: CABLES MUST BE ROUTED
SMOOTHLY & FREE FROM
BENDS & KINKS.

Routing instructions for 1968 GTO heater control assembly and cables.

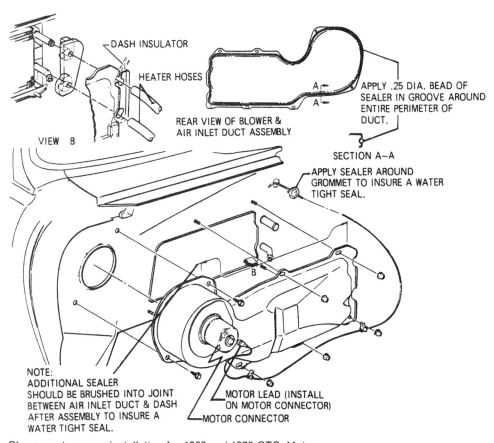

DASH INSULATOR

HEATER HOSES

VIEW B

REAR VIEW OF BLOWER &
AIR INLET DUCT ASSEMBLY

A
A

APPLY .25 DIA. BEAD OF
SEALER IN GROOVE AROUND
ENTIRE PERIMETER OF
DUCT.

SECTION A—A

APPLY SEALER AROUND
GROMMET TO INSURE A WATER
TIGHT SEAL.

NOTE:
ADDITIONAL SEALER
SHOULD BE BRUSHED INTO JOINT
BETWEEN AIR INLET DUCT & DASH
AFTER ASSEMBLY TO INSURE A
WATER TIGHT SEAL.

MOTOR LEAD (INSTALL
ON MOTOR CONNECTOR)
MOTOR CONNECTOR

Blower motor cover installation for 1969 and 1970 GTO. Motor
lead ran from grommet near heater core tubes and around to
bottom of case.

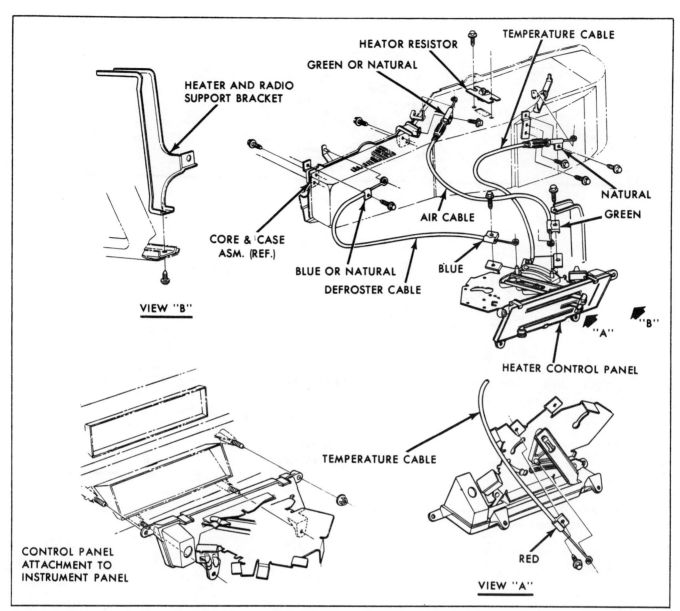

HEATER RESISTOR
TEMPERATURE CABLE
GREEN OR NATURAL
HEATER AND RADIO SUPPORT BRACKET
CORE & CASE ASM. (REF.)
BLUE OR NATURAL DEFROSTER CABLE
AIR CABLE
BLUE
NATURAL
GREEN
VIEW "B"
"A"
"B"
HEATER CONTROL PANEL
TEMPERATURE CABLE
CONTROL PANEL ATTACHMENT TO INSTRUMENT PANEL
RED
VIEW "A"

Detail of routing for 1969–70 GTO heater cable. Note use of radio and heater support bracket.

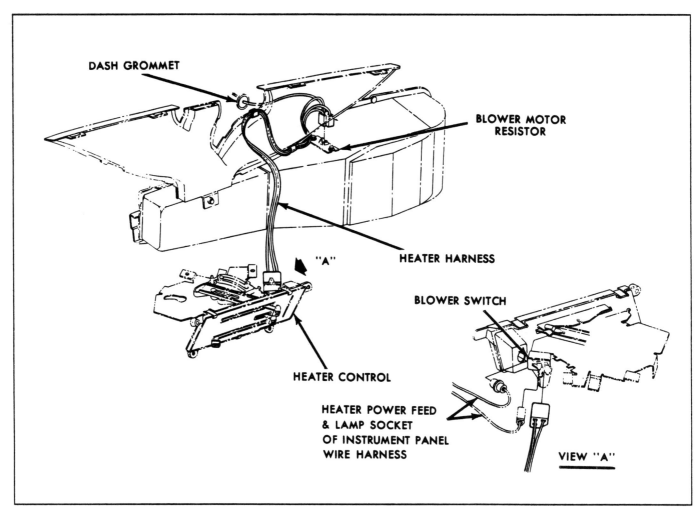

DASH GROMMET

BLOWER MOTOR RESISTOR

HEATER HARNESS

"A"

BLOWER SWITCH

HEATER CONTROL

HEATER POWER FEED & LAMP SOCKET OF INSTRUMENT PANEL WIRE HARNESS

VIEW "A"

Routing of 1969-70 heater harness.

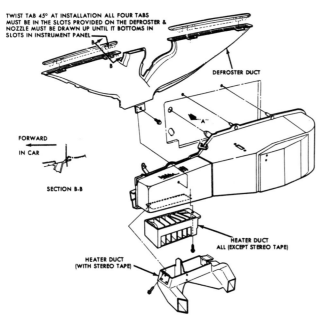

TWIST TAB 45° AT INSTALLATION ALL FOUR TABS MUST BE IN THE SLOTS PROVIDED ON THE DEFROSTER & NOZZLE MUST BE DRAWN UP UNTIL IT BOTTOMS IN SLOTS IN INSTRUMENT PANEL

DEFROSTER DUCT

FORWARD IN CAR

SECTION B-B

HEATER DUCT ALL (EXCEPT STEREO TAPE)

HEATER DUCT (WITH STEREO TAPE)

Installation of 1969-70 core cover and ducts. Note use of U-shaped duct with stereo tape player.

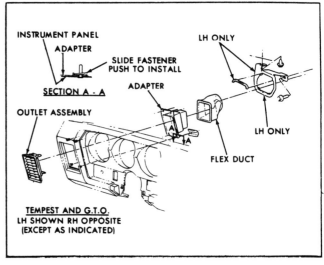

INSTRUMENT PANEL ADAPTER

SLIDE FASTENER PUSH TO INSTALL

LH ONLY

SECTION A - A

ADAPTER

OUTLET ASSEMBLY

LH ONLY

FLEX DUCT

TEMPEST AND G.T.O. LH SHOWN RH OPPOSITE (EXCEPT AS INDICATED)

Exploded view of upper air ventilation system in 1969 and 1970 GTOs.

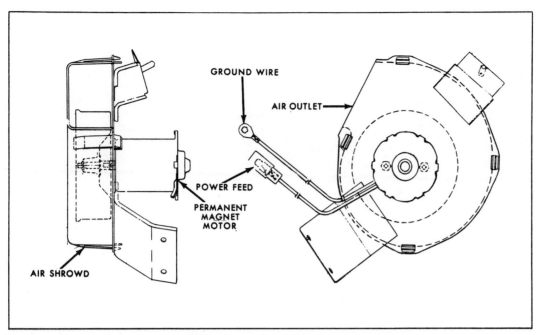

The Power Flow ventilation option was available in 1969 and 1970. Two small motors and impellers forced air through the upper instrument panel outlets. The motors were located in the kick panels.

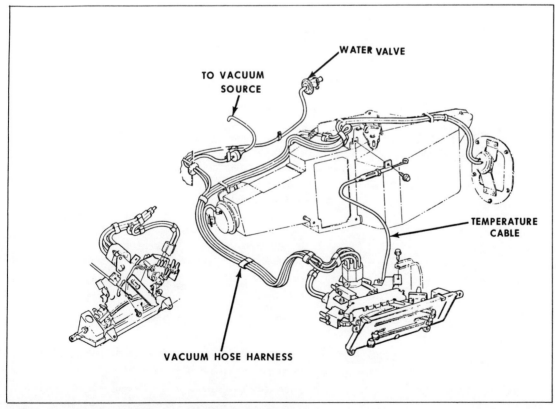

1969 cable (part number 9784763 in 1969-70) with vacuum harness and valves. Note check valve in vacuum source line (part number 9787802).

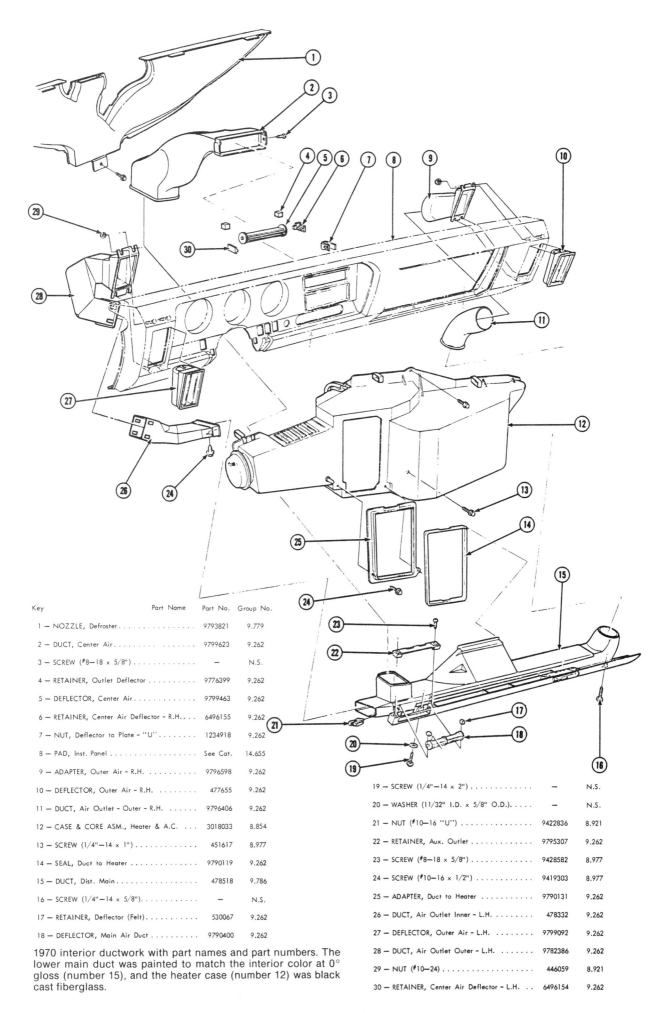

Key	Part Name	Part No.	Group No.
1 — NOZZLE, Defroster		9793821	9.779
2 — DUCT, Center Air		9799623	9.262
3 — SCREW (#8—18 x 5/8")		—	N.S.
4 — RETAINER, Outlet Deflector		9776399	9.262
5 — DEFLECTOR, Center Air		9799463	9.262
6 — RETAINER, Center Air Deflector - R.H.		6496155	9.262
7 — NUT, Deflector to Plate - "U"		1234918	9.262
8 — PAD, Inst. Panel		See Cat.	14.655
9 — ADAPTER, Outer Air - R.H.		9796598	9.262
10 — DEFLECTOR, Outer Air - R.H.		477655	9.262
11 — DUCT, Air Outlet - Outer - R.H.		9796406	9.262
12 — CASE & CORE ASM., Heater & A.C.		3018033	8.854
13 — SCREW (1/4"—14 x 1")		451617	8.977
14 — SEAL, Duct to Heater		9790119	9.262
15 — DUCT, Dist. Main		478518	9.786
16 — SCREW (1/4"—14 x 5/8")		—	N.S.
17 — RETAINER, Deflector (Felt)		530067	9.262
18 — DEFLECTOR, Main Air Duct		9790400	9.262
19 — SCREW (1/4"—14 x 2")		—	N.S.
20 — WASHER (11/32" I.D. x 5/8" O.D.)		—	N.S.
21 — NUT (#10—16 "U")		9422836	8.921
22 — RETAINER, Aux. Outlet		9795307	9.262
23 — SCREW (#8—18 x 5/8")		9428582	8.977
24 — SCREW (#10—16 x 1/2")		9419303	8.977
25 — ADAPTER, Duct to Heater		9790131	9.262
26 — DUCT, Air Outlet Inner - L.H.		478332	9.262
27 — DEFLECTOR, Outer Air - L.H.		9799092	9.262
28 — DUCT, Air Outlet Outer - L.H.		9782386	9.262
29 — NUT (#10—24)		446059	8.921
30 — RETAINER, Center Air Deflector - L.H.		6496154	9.262

1970 interior ductwork with part names and part numbers. The lower main duct was painted to match the interior color at 0° gloss (number 15), and the heater case (number 12) was black cast fiberglass.

REAR WINDOW DEFOGGER

1964-65

A two-speed rear window defogger (RPO 541) was available as an option for both years. The accessory package part number for 1964 was 984138, and 984474 for 1965. The defogger was mounted on the LH rear package shelf, and the grille was painted to match the interior color trim at 60° gloss. The wire was run under the carpet on the passenger side, and routed under the instrument panel. The switch (part number 9775544 in 1964 and 9780999 in 1965) was mounted in the same location for both years—just to the left of the steering column opening on the lower dash panel.

1966-67

A two-speed rear window defogger (RPO 374) was available for both years as a factory- or dealer-installed option. The accessory package part number was 984625 for 1966 and 1967.

The wire assembly (part number 2988544, field) was routed in the same manner as in 1964-65. The switch and wire assembly (part number 9783122) was the same for both years, as were the chrome switch bezel (part number 9784643) and the chrome switch knob (part number 9784535). The switch and bezel assembly was mounted under the instrument panel pad, between the far-left and center-left instrument pods.

1968-70

A two-speed rear window defogger (RPO 404 in 1968-69, RPO 541 in 1970, UPC C50 in 1969-70) was available for 1968-70 as either a dealer- or factory-installed option. The replacement package part number for 1968 was 3014891; 3017807 for 1969-70. The accessory package part number for 1969 was 988643; 988720 for 1970.

The wire assembly (part number 7720084, field) measured 174 inches and was routed under the carpet along the passenger side. The defogger grille was mounted on the LH side of the package tray, and was painted to match the interior trim at 60° gloss.

The switch and wire assembly (part number 9793177) was mounted under the dash pad ledge between the LH and center instrument pods in 1968. The switch and wire assembly in 1969 (part number 9797083) and 1970 (part number 9799923) was mounted in the panel below the RH instrument pod.

An electric rear-window defroster (RPO 534, UPC C49) was available in 1970 only. The rear window was impregnated with electric coils, and was actuated by a switch and wire assembly (part number 479050).

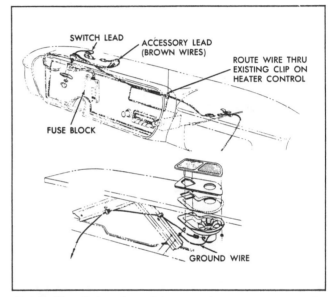

Detail of installation of rear defogger, switch and wire routing for 1966-67 GTO. Clips used to secure wire to seat support were not serviced by Pontiac.

Detail of 1964-65 rear defogger switch and wire assembly (part number 9780999).

Close-up comparison of the two different bezel designs used for 1966-67 rear window defogger switch assemblies. Both units carried the same part number (9784643), which was also used for Pontiac models and A-bodies.

425

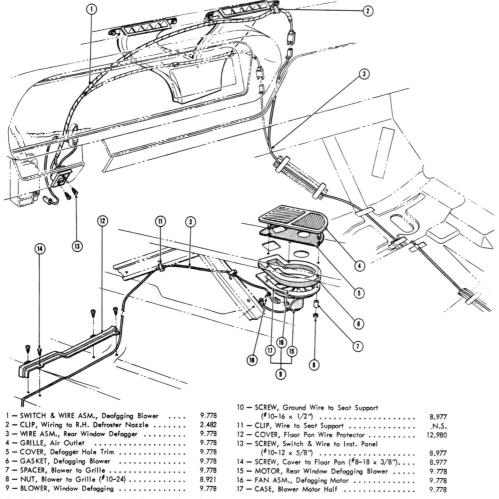

1 — SWITCH & WIRE ASM., Deofgging Blower 9.778	10 — SCREW, Ground Wire to Seat Support
2 — CLIP, Wiring to R.H. Defroster Nozzle 2.482	(#10-16 x 1/2") 8.977
3 — WIRE ASM., Rear Window Defogger 9.778	11 — CLIP, Wire to Seat Support .... N.S.
4 — GRILLE, Air Outlet 9.778	12 — COVER, Floor Pan Wire Protector 12.980
5 — COVER, Defogger Hole Trim 9.778	13 — SCREW, Switch & Wire to Inst. Panel
6 — GASKET, Defogging Blower 9.778	(#10-12 x 5/8") 8.977
7 — SPACER, Blower to Grille 9.778	14 — SCREW, Cover to Floor Pan (#8-18 x 3/8").... 8.977
8 — NUT, Blower to Grille (#10-24) 8.921	15 — MOTOR, Rear Window Defogging Blower 9.778
9 — BLOWER, Window Defogging 9.778	16 — FAN ASM., Defogging Motor 9.778
	17 — CASE, Blower Motor Half 9.778

Installation and routing of rear window defogger wire assembly.
Floor pan wire protector cover was used, and tape was used to
retain wire to floor pan.

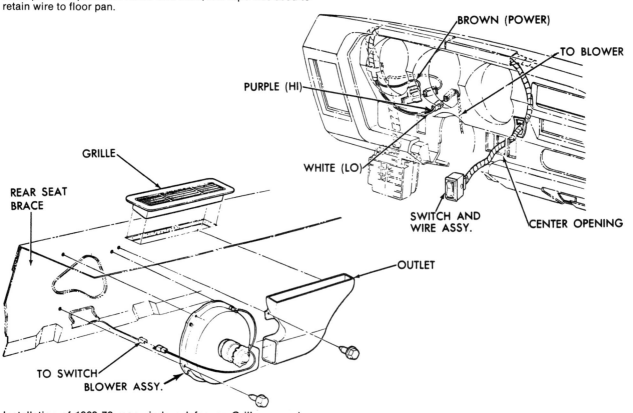

Installation of 1969-70 rear window defogger. Grille was redesigned (part number 1386075). Switch location was the same for
both years.

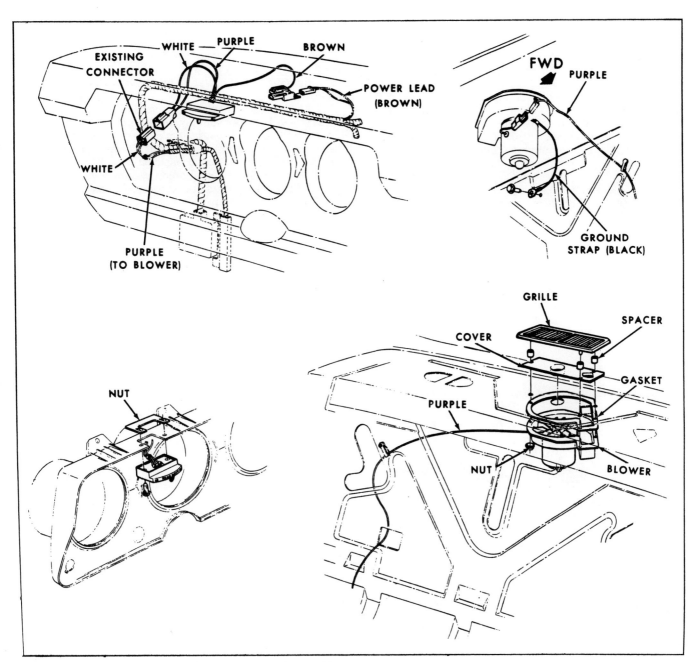

Installation instructions for 1968 rear window defogger. Note location of switch assembly at instrument panel.

AIR CONDITIONING

1964-70

Because of the complexities of Pontiac air conditioning (RPO 581 in 1964, RPO 582 in 1965), only parts of the system will be covered here. It is recommended that further reference be made to the factory manuals, and work be done by qualified personnel.

All GTOs equipped with Tri-Comfort air conditioning used a 55 amp alternator—except transistorized ignition applications, which used a 61 amp model. The 1965 system used a 30 amp inline fuse at the alternator. The 1964 system did not have the fuse located at the alternator; it didn't use one. The 1964 control assembly had three levers on the instrument panel, the 1965 had two. Both years shared the same blower switch.

The heater hoses in air-conditioning-equipped GTOs were routed through metal clips (part number 9774218) screwed to the top of the RH fender skirt. All 1964 and first-design 1965 air conditioning systems used a vacuum-controlled refrigerant valve (part number 5910533). It can be identified by the stamp 0533. The second-design 1965 used a pilot-operated absolute-suction throttling valve (part number 5910508). It can be identified by the stamp 0508.

The plenum blower case assembly was painted gloss black. The door vacuum diaphragm was white plastic on originals and black plastic on replacements. The heater core assembly cover located under the dash was of fiberglass construction, and was cast in dark gray.

The 1966-67 air conditioning system (RPO 582) was identical in all respects to the 1965 second-design system. The interior core and case assembly was painted 30° gloss black.

The theory of operation and basic design of components for the air conditioning system for 1968-70 was the same as in the 1965 second-design. Code for 1968-70 was RPO 582; 1969-70, UPC C60.

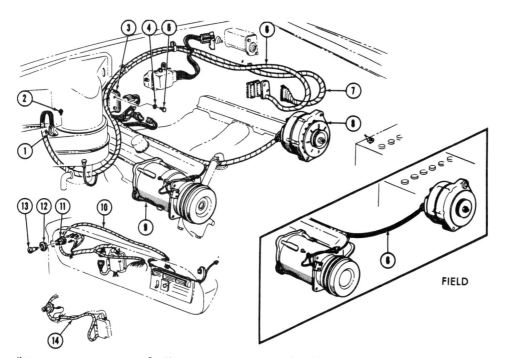

FIELD

Key	Part Name	Group No.
1 — RESISTOR, Blower Motor		9.275
2 — SCREW, Resistor to Case (#10-12 x 5/8")		8.977
3 — RELAY ASM., Master		9.275
4 — LOCKWASHER, Relay to Duct (1/4")		8.932
5 — SCREW, Relay to Duct (#12-11 x 1/2")		8.977
6 — WIRE HARNESS, Air Cond. Jumper Wire (64" Long)		9.276
7 — WIRE HARNESS, Engine		2.480
8 — DELCOTRON ASSEMBLY		2.275
9 — COMPRESSOR, Air Conditioner		9.170
10 — HARNESS, Instrument Panel		2.480
11 — SWITCH, Starter & Ignition		2.188
12 — FERRULE, Ignition Switch		2.192
13 — CYLINDER, Ignition Lock		2.188
14 — WIRE HARNESS, Air Cond. Main (Field)		9.276

1964 air-conditioning electrical factory and field wiring. Note difference in air-conditioning jumper wire harness for field installation. Harness was routed along RH side of engine and then over to alternator.

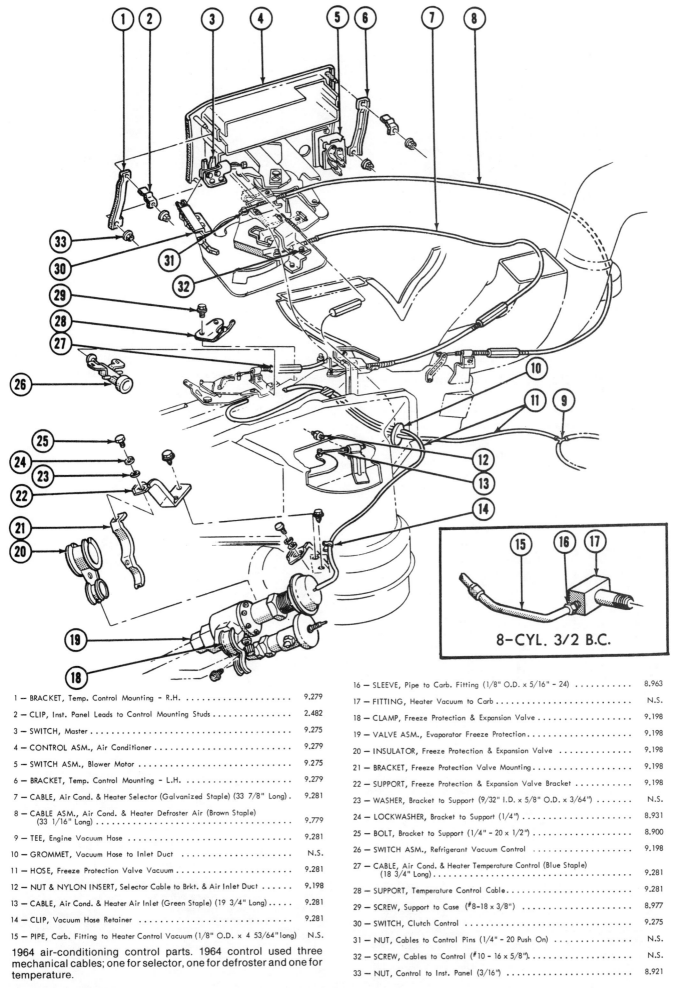

1 — BRACKET, Temp. Control Mounting – R.H. 9.279

2 — CLIP, Inst. Panel Leads to Control Mounting Studs 2.482

3 — SWITCH, Master 9.275

4 — CONTROL ASM., Air Conditioner 9.279

5 — SWITCH ASM., Blower Motor 9.275

6 — BRACKET, Temp. Control Mounting – L.H. 9.279

7 — CABLE, Air Cond. & Heater Selector (Galvanized Staple) (33 7/8" Long) . 9.281

8 — CABLE ASM., Air Cond. & Heater Defroster Air (Brown Staple)
(33 1/16" Long) 9.779

9 — TEE, Engine Vacuum Hose 9.281

10 — GROMMET, Vacuum Hose to Inlet Duct . . . . N.S.

11 — HOSE, Freeze Protection Valve Vacuum 9.281

12 — NUT & NYLON INSERT, Selector Cable to Brkt. & Air Inlet Duct 9.198

13 — CABLE, Air Cond. & Heater Air Inlet (Green Staple) (19 3/4" Long) 9.281

14 — CLIP, Vacuum Hose Retainer 9.281

15 — PIPE, Carb. Fitting to Heater Control Vacuum (1/8" O.D. x 4 53/64" long) N.S.

1964 air-conditioning control parts. 1964 control used three
mechanical cables; one for selector, one for defroster and one for
temperature.

16 — SLEEVE, Pipe to Carb. Fitting (1/8" O.D. x 5/16" - 24) 8.963

17 — FITTING, Heater Vacuum to Carb . . . . N.S.

18 — CLAMP, Freeze Protection & Expansion Valve 9.198

19 — VALVE ASM., Evaporator Freeze Protection 9.198

20 — INSULATOR, Freeze Protection & Expansion Valve 9.198

21 — BRACKET, Freeze Protection Valve Mounting 9.198

22 — SUPPORT, Freeze Protection & Expansion Valve Bracket 9.198

23 — WASHER, Bracket to Support (9/32" I.D. x 5/8" O.D. x 3/64") . . . . . N.S.

24 — LOCKWASHER, Bracket to Support (1/4") 8.931

25 — BOLT, Bracket to Support (1/4" - 20 x 1/2") 8.900

26 — SWITCH ASM., Refrigerant Vacuum Control 9.198

27 — CABLE, Air Cond. & Heater Temperature Control (Blue Staple)
(18 3/4" Long) 9.281

28 — SUPPORT, Temperature Control Cable 9.281

29 — SCREW, Support to Case (#8-18 x 3/8") 8.977

30 — SWITCH, Clutch Control 9.275

31 — NUT, Cables to Control Pins (1/4" - 20 Push On) . . . . N.S.

32 — SCREW, Cables to Control (#10 - 16 x 5/8") . . . . N.S.

33 — NUT, Control to Inst. Panel (3/16") 8.921

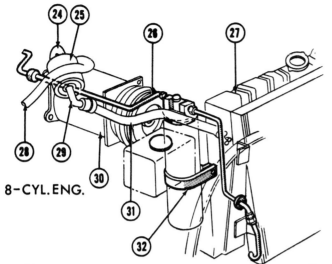

8-CYL. ENG.

1 — CORE & CASE ASM., Evaporator (See Exploded View) 9.210
2 — GASKET, Evaporator Outlet to Temp. Reg. Valve (3/4" O.D.) 9.211
3 — GASKET, Suction Tube to Temp. Reg. Valve (5/8" O.D.) 9.211
4 — VALVE ASM., Evaporator Freeze Protection 9.198
5 — GASKET, Evaporator Freeze Protection Valve (3/16" I.D. x 39/32") 9.210
6 — GASKET, Receiver to Evaporator Tubes (3/8" O.D.) 9.211
11 — SCREW, Condenser to Baffle (5/16"-18 x 3/4") 8.977
12 — CONDENSER ASM., Refrigerant 9.190
22 — TUBE ASM., Freeze Protection Valve to Comp. Suction Hose 9.229
23 — SCREW, Core & Case to Shroud & Dash (1/4"-14 x 1") 8.977

24 — HOSE, Compressor Discharge Freon – Rear (7" Long) 9.225
25 — BUMPER, Discharge Hose Muffler 9.225
26 — TUBE ASM., Receiver to Evaporator 9.231
27 — RADIATOR ASM., W/Over Flow Tube & Clips 1.219
28 — HOSE, Compressor Freon Suction 9.229
29 — MUFFLER ASM., Discharge Hose 9.226
30 — COMPRESSOR, Air Conditioner 9.170
31 — HOSE, Compressor Discharge Freon – Front (10-1/2" Long) 9.225
32 — CLAMP, Receiver Support 9.206

1964 air-conditioning refrigeration system and parts nomenclature. Plenum cover was cast in black fiberglass.

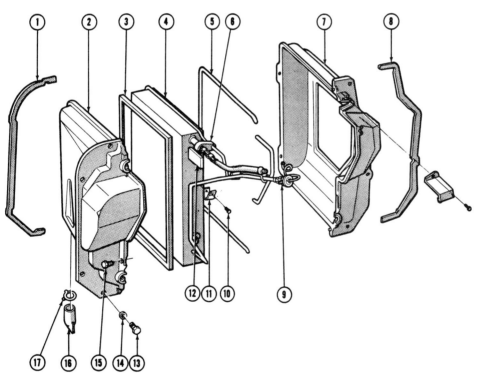

1 — GASKET, Evaporator Case to Dash – Outer 9.211
2 — CASE, Evaporator – Outer 9.211
3 — SEAL, Evaporator Core to Case 9.211
4 — CORE & CASE ASM., Evaporator – w/Fittings 9.210
5 — SEAL, Evaporator Case 9.211
6 — GROMMET, Evaporator Outlet Pipe 9.775
7 — CASE, Evaporator – Inner 9.211
8 — GASKET, Evaporator Case to Dash – Inner 9.211
9 — VALVE ASM., Expansion 9.213

10 — SCREW, Pipe Clamp to Case (#10 – 124 1/2") 8.977
11 — CLAMP, Discharge Hose Tube to Condenser 9.242
12 — INSULATION, Expansion Valve Bulb 9.213
13 — SCREW, Evaporator to Shroud & Dash (1/4" – 14 x 1") 8.977
14 — WASHER, Evaporator to Shroud & Dash (5/16" I.D. x 3/4" O.D.) 8.929
15 — SCREW, Inner Case to Outer Case . . . . N.S.
16 — TUBE, Evaporator Drain 9.211
17 — CLAMP, Evaporator Case Drain Tube 9.211

1964-67 evaporator case and core assembly with parts nomenclature. Corbin-type clamp was used for evaporator drain tube.

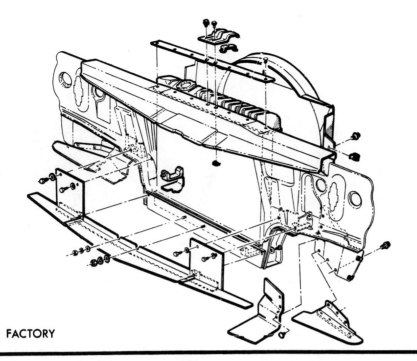

FACTORY

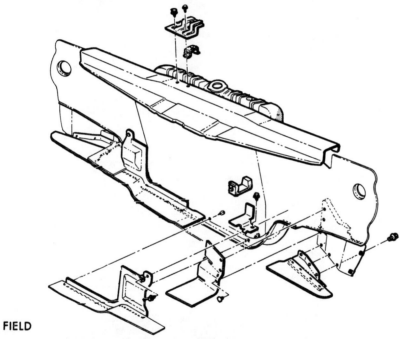

FIELD

Installation of metal and rubber baffles used in engine compartment for air-conditioning system used in 1964-65 (1964 shown).
Note difference in factory and field installations.

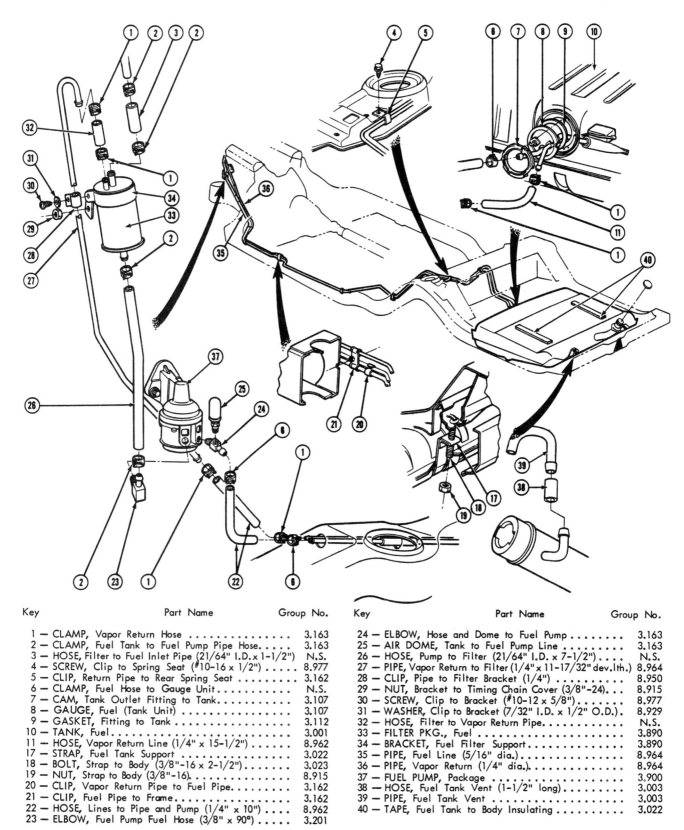

Key	Part Name	Group No.
1 — CLAMP, Vapor Return Hose		3.163
2 — CLAMP, Fuel Tank to Fuel Pump Pipe Hose		3.163
3 — HOSE, Filter to Fuel Inlet Pipe (21/64" I.D. x 1-1/2")		N.S.
4 — SCREW, Clip to Spring Seat (#10-16 x 1/2")		8.977
5 — CLIP, Return Pipe to Rear Spring Seat		3.162
6 — CLAMP, Fuel Hose to Gauge Unit		N.S.
7 — CAM, Tank Outlet Fitting to Tank		3.107
8 — GAUGE, Fuel (Tank Unit)		3.107
9 — GASKET, Fitting to Tank		3.112
10 — TANK, Fuel		3.001
11 — HOSE, Vapor Return Line (1/4" x 15-1/2")		8.962
17 — STRAP, Fuel Tank Support		3.022
18 — BOLT, Strap to Body (3/8"-16 x 2-1/2")		3.023
19 — NUT, Strap to Body (3/8"-16)		8.915
20 — CLIP, Vapor Return Pipe to Fuel Pipe		3.162
21 — CLIP, Fuel Pipe to Frame		3.162
22 — HOSE, Lines to Pipe and Pump (1/4" x 10")		8.962
23 — ELBOW, Fuel Pump Fuel Hose (3/8" x 90°)		3.201

Key	Part Name	Group No.
24 — ELBOW, Hose and Dome to Fuel Pump		3.163
25 — AIR DOME, Tank to Fuel Pump Line		3.163
26 — HOSE, Pump to Filter (21/64" I.D. x 7-1/2")		N.S.
27 — PIPE, Vapor Return to Filter (1/4" x 11-17/32" dev.lth.)		8.964
28 — CLIP, Pipe to Filter Bracket (1/4")		8.950
29 — NUT, Bracket to Timing Chain Cover (3/8"-24)		8.915
30 — SCREW, Clip to Bracket (#10-12 x 5/8")		8.977
31 — WASHER, Clip to Bracket (7/32" I.D. x 1/2" O.D.)		8.929
32 — HOSE, Filter to Vapor Return Pipe		N.S.
33 — FILTER PKG., Fuel		3.890
34 — BRACKET, Fuel Filter Support		3.890
35 — PIPE, Fuel Line (5/16" dia.)		8.964
36 — PIPE, Vapor Return (1/4" dia.)		8.964
37 — FUEL PUMP, Package		3.900
38 — HOSE, Fuel Tank Vent (1-1/2" long)		3.003
39 — PIPE, Fuel Tank Vent		3.003
40 — TAPE, Fuel Tank to Body Insulating		3.022

Fuel system for 1964-65 with air conditioning. Note ¼ inch return line and fuel filter assembly that mounted to timing chain cover.

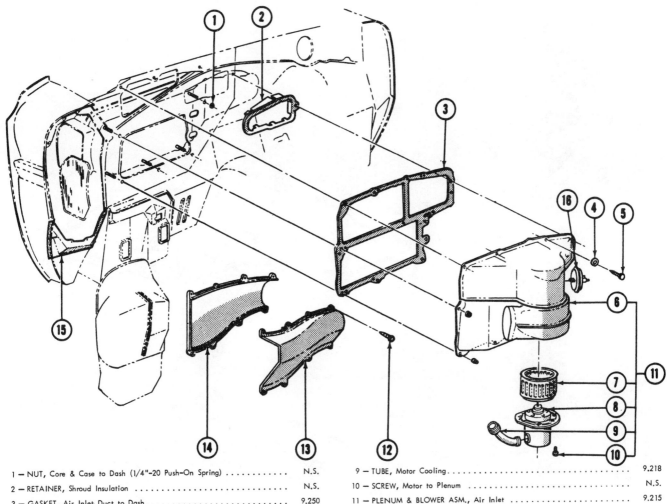

1 – NUT, Core & Case to Dash (1/4"-20 Push-On Spring) . . . . N.S.	9 – TUBE, Motor Cooling 9.218
2 – RETAINER, Shroud Insulation . . . . N.S.	10 – SCREW, Motor to Plenum . . . . N.S.
3 – GASKET, Air Inlet Duct to Dash 9.250	11 – PLENUM & BLOWER ASM., Air Inlet 9.215
4 – LOCKWASHER, Duct to Shroud (1/4") 8.932	12 – SCREW, Front Duct to Rear Duct (#10-24 x 3/4") 8.977
5 – SCREW, Duct to Shroud (1/4"-14 x 7/8") 8.977	13 – DUCT ASM., Blower to Evaporator - Front 9.215
6 – PLENUM, Air Inlet . . . . N.S.	14 – DUCT ASM., Blower to Evaporator - Rear 9.215
7 – IMPELLER ASM., Blower Motor 9.216	15 – PANEL, Lower Filler - Evaporator Lower 9.215
8 – MOTOR ASM., Blower 9.215	16 – DIAPHRAGM ASM., Air Inlet Duct Vacuum 9.281

Exploded view of firewall hardware and parts nomenclature for 1964-67 air-conditioning system.

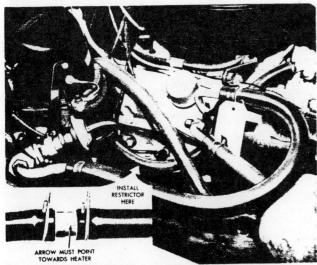

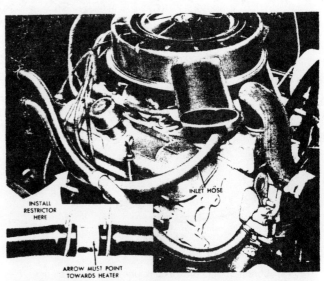

To reduce the possibility of repeat heater core leaks of air-conditioning-equipped cars, restrictor 3005030 (MAC) should be installed in the inlet hose between the engine block and the lower heater core inlet tube, at the time of heater core repair. Install the restrictor in the inlet hose, not the outlet hose, on air-conditioned cars as shown in Figure 1, and GTOs and HOs as shown in Figure 2. The arrow on the restrictor must point in the direction of flow

(toward the heater). The restrictor is a one-way-type valve and will not regulate pressures unless properly installed. Note: If restrictor is installed with coolant in radiator, pinch hose at both sides of where cut is to be made, or keep this spot above level of coolant in radiator to minimize loss of coolant. (This information taken from Pontiac Service News Flash number 64-107, dated 9-21-64.)

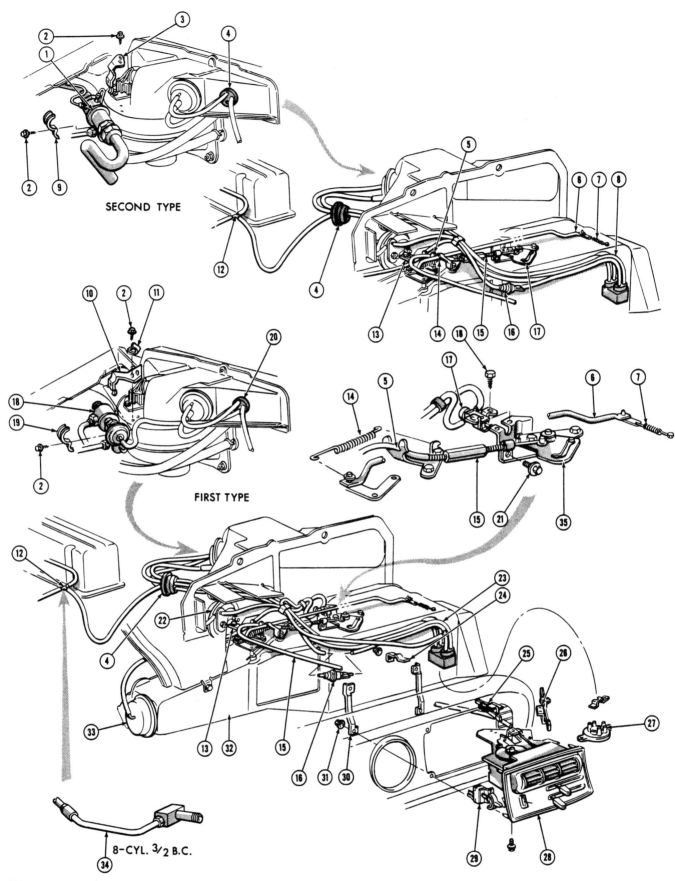

SECOND TYPE

FIRST TYPE

8-CYL. ³/₂ B.C.

1965 air-conditioning control components and parts nomenclature. Note that 1965 system used one control cable for temperature control; all other components were vacuum operated.

Second-design used a nonvacuum throttle suction valve; first-design was carried over from 1964.

434

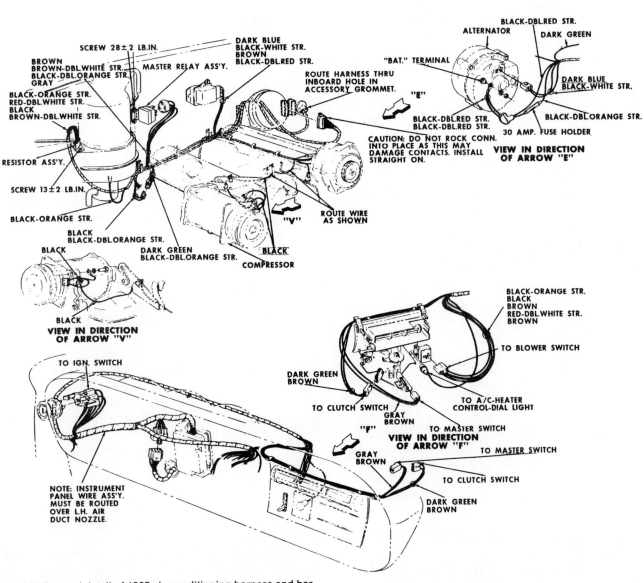

Installation and detail of 1965 air-conditioning harness and harness routing, including torque specifications for component mounting.

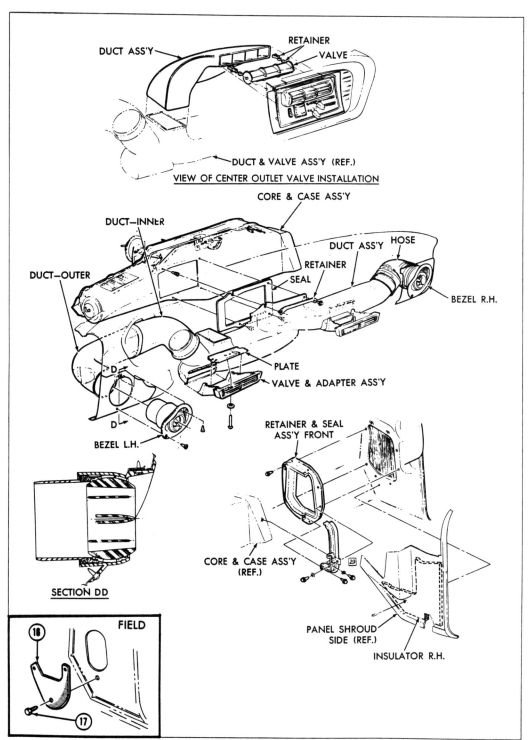

RETAINER

DUCT ASS'Y

VALVE

DUCT & VALVE ASS'Y (REF.)

VIEW OF CENTER OUTLET VALVE INSTALLATION

CORE & CASE ASS'Y

DUCT—INNER

DUCT ASS'Y HOSE

RETAINER

DUCT—OUTER

SEAL

BEZEL R.H.

PLATE

VALVE & ADAPTER ASS'Y

RETAINER & SEAL
ASS'Y FRONT

BEZEL L.H.

CORE & CASE ASS'Y
(REF.)

SECTION DD

PANEL SHROUD
SIDE (REF.)

INSULATOR R.H.

FIELD

Installation of 1964 and 1965 air-conditioning ductwork and kick
panel assembly. Note field-installed kick panel vent cover.

436

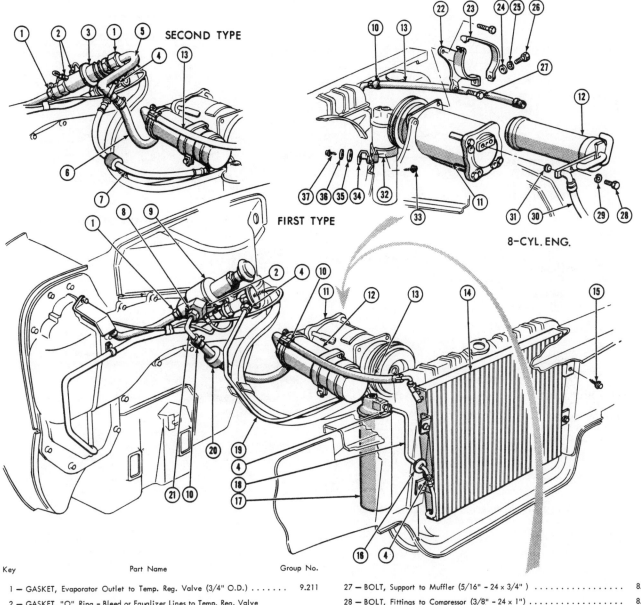

SECOND TYPE

FIRST TYPE

8-CYL. ENG.

Key	Part Name	Group No.
1	GASKET, Evaporator Outlet to Temp. Reg. Valve (3/4" O.D.)	9.211
2	GASKET, "O" Ring - Bleed or Equalizer Lines to Temp. Reg. Valve (3/16" I.D. x 5/16" O.D.)	9.210
3	VALVE ASM., Suction Throttle - Stamped 0508	9.198
4	SEAL, Evaporator Connector - "O" Ring (3/8" I.D.)	9.210
5	TUBE ASM., STV to Suction Hose - w/0508 Valve	9.229
6	HOSE, Compressor Freon Suction	9.229
11	COMPRESSOR, Air Conditioner	9.170
12	FITTINGS ASM., Compressor - w/Muffler	9.226
22	SUPPORT, Muffler to Compressor	9.242
23	CLAMP, Muffler to Compressor Support	9.242
24	WASHER, Clamp to Support (11/32" I.D. x 5/8" O.D. x 1/16")	N.S.
25	LOCKWASHER, Clamp to Support (5/16")	8.931
26	BOLT, Clamp to Support (5/16" - 24 x 1")	8.900
27	BOLT, Support to Muffler (5/16" - 24 x 3/4")	8.900
28	BOLT, Fittings to Compressor (3/8" - 24 x 1")	8.900
29	LOCKWASHER, Fittings to Compressor (3/8")	8.931
30	HOSE, Compressor Freon Suction	9.229
31	SEAL, Compressor Valve Body to Compressor "O" Ring	9.240
32	CLAMP, Receiver Support	9.206
33	SCREW, Receiver Support (5/16" - 18 x 3/4")	8.977
34	BRACKET, Receiver Clamp to Fan Shroud - Field	9.206
35	WASHER, Receiver to Support (11/32" I.D. x 5/8" O.D. x 1/16")	N.S.
36	LOCKWASHER, Receiver to Support (5/16")	8.931
37	SCREW, Receiver to Support (5/16" - 18 x 7/8")	8.977
38	SCREW, Support to Fan Shroud (5/16" - 18 x 3/4")	8.977
39	SPACER, Support to Compressor	N.S.
40	NUT, Support to Shroud (5/16" - 18")	8.921

1965 air-conditioning refrigeration system. The muffler was natural metal in appearance; the compressor was painted 60° gloss black, as was the receiver assembly. Note difference in first- and second-design suction throttle valves used in 1965.

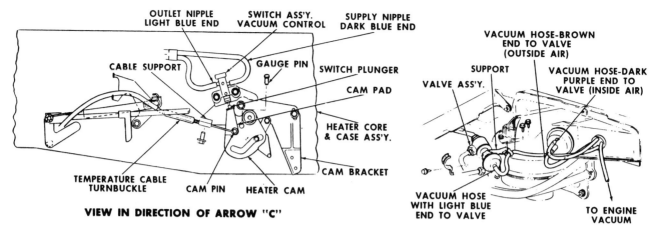

OUTLET NIPPLE
LIGHT BLUE END

SWITCH ASS'Y.
VACUUM CONTROL

SUPPLY NIPPLE
DARK BLUE END

CABLE SUPPORT

GAUGE PIN

SWITCH PLUNGER

CAM PAD

HEATER CORE
& CASE ASS'Y.

CAM BRACKET

TEMPERATURE CABLE
TURNBUCKLE

CAM PIN

HEATER CAM

VIEW IN DIRECTION OF ARROW "C"

VACUUM HOSE-BROWN
END TO VALVE
(OUTSIDE AIR)

SUPPORT

VACUUM HOSE-DARK
PURPLE END TO
VALVE (INSIDE AIR)

VALVE ASS'Y.

VACUUM HOSE
WITH LIGHT BLUE
END TO VALVE

TO ENGINE
VACUUM

VIEW IN DIRECTION OF ARROW "B"

TO CENTER CARB.

VACUUM HOSE-DARK
BLUE END TO PIPE

VIEW IN CIRCLE "A"
(V8 ENGINE WITH TRI CARBS.)

TO DISTRIBUTOR OR
VACUUM DIAPHRAGM

TO ENGINE VACUUM

VACUUM HOSE-DARK
BLUE END TO TEE

VIEW IN CIRCLE "A"
(WITH V8 ENGINE
EXC. TRI CARBS.)

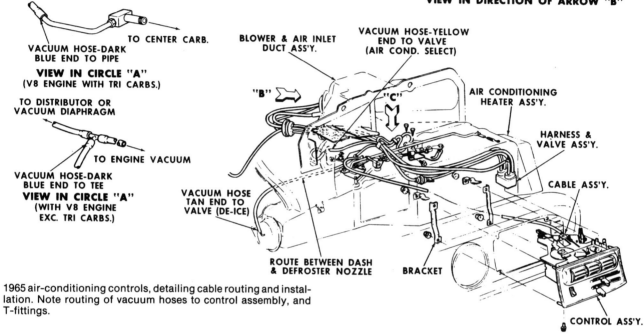

BLOWER & AIR INLET
DUCT ASS'Y.

VACUUM HOSE-YELLOW
END TO VALVE
(AIR COND. SELECT)

"B"

"C"

AIR CONDITIONING
HEATER ASS'Y.

HARNESS &
VALVE ASS'Y.

CABLE ASS'Y.

VACUUM HOSE
TAN END TO
VALVE (DE-ICE)

ROUTE BETWEEN DASH
& DEFROSTER NOZZLE

BRACKET

CONTROL ASS'Y.

1965 air-conditioning controls, detailing cable routing and installation. Note routing of vacuum hoses to control assembly, and T-fittings.

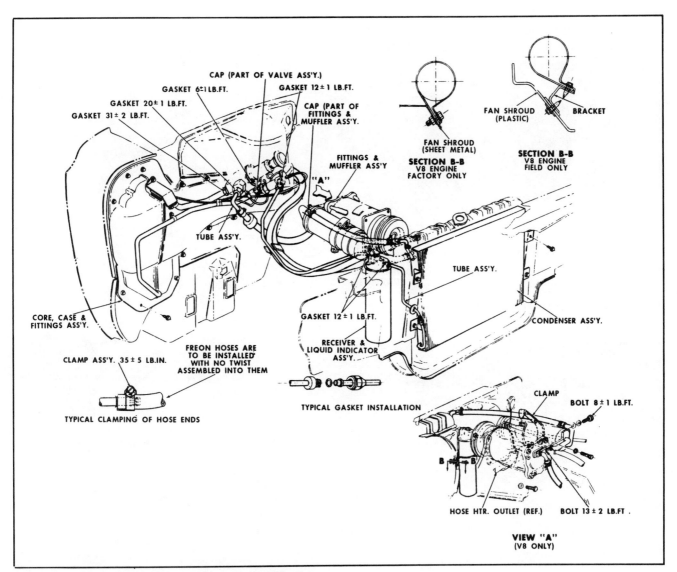

GASKET 31 ± 2 LB.FT.
GASKET 20 ± 1 LB.FT.
GASKET 6 ± 1 LB.FT.
CAP (PART OF VALVE ASS'Y.)
GASKET 12 ± 1 LB.FT.
CAP (PART OF FITTINGS & MUFFLER ASS'Y.
FITTINGS & MUFFLER ASS'Y
"A"

FAN SHROUD (SHEET METAL)
SECTION B-B
V8 ENGINE
FACTORY ONLY

FAN SHROUD (PLASTIC)   BRACKET
SECTION B-B
V8 ENGINE
FIELD ONLY

TUBE ASS'Y.

TUBE ASS'Y.

CONDENSER ASS'Y.

CORE, CASE & FITTINGS ASS'Y.

GASKET 12 ± 1 LB.FT.

RECEIVER & LIQUID INDICATOR ASS'Y.

CLAMP ASS'Y. 35 ± 5 LB.IN.

FREON HOSES ARE TO BE INSTALLED WITH NO TWIST ASSEMBLED INTO THEM

TYPICAL CLAMPING OF HOSE ENDS

TYPICAL GASKET INSTALLATION

CLAMP
BOLT 8 ± 1 LB.FT.

HOSE HTR. OUTLET (REF.)   BOLT 13 ± 2 LB.FT.

VIEW "A"
(V8 ONLY)

Drawing of 1965 refrigeration system with torque specifications.
Note installation of receiver/evaporator assembly bracket, with
factory metal fan shroud and field-installed plastic shroud.

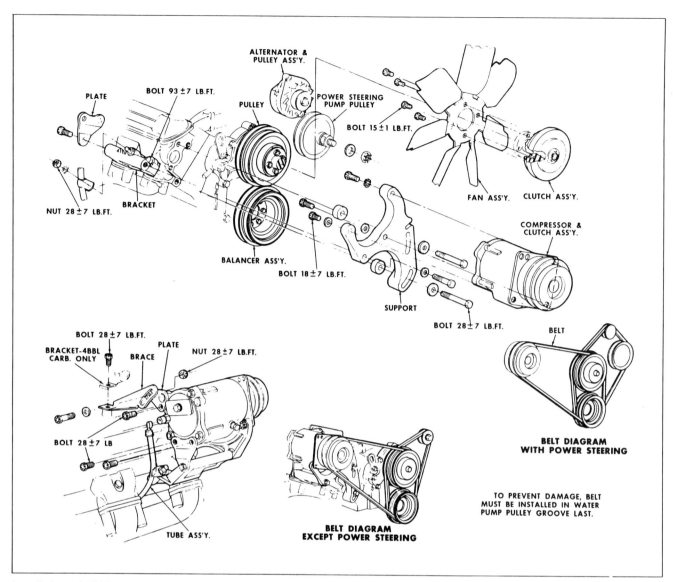

PLATE

BOLT 93±7 LB.FT.

ALTERNATOR &
PULLEY ASS'Y.

PULLEY

POWER STEERING
PUMP PULLEY

BOLT 15±1 LB.FT.

NUT 28±7 LB.FT.

BRACKET

FAN ASS'Y.

CLUTCH ASS'Y.

BALANCER ASS'Y.

BOLT 18±7 LB.FT.

COMPRESSOR &
CLUTCH ASS'Y.

SUPPORT

BOLT 28±7 LB.FT.

BELT

BOLT 28±7 LB.FT.

BRACKET-4BBL
CARB. ONLY

BRACE

PLATE

NUT 28±7 LB.FT.

BOLT 28±7 LB

BELT DIAGRAM
WITH POWER STEERING

TO PREVENT DAMAGE, BELT
MUST BE INSTALLED IN WATER
PUMP PULLEY GROOVE LAST.

TUBE ASS'Y.

BELT DIAGRAM
EXCEPT POWER STEERING

Installation of 1965 compressor, with mounting brackets and torque specifications. All front mounting hardware was natural aluminum in appearance. Fan blade was natural aluminum, all pulleys and brackets were 60° gloss black, dipstick tube was engine-blue, bolts were black cadmium in appearance.

440

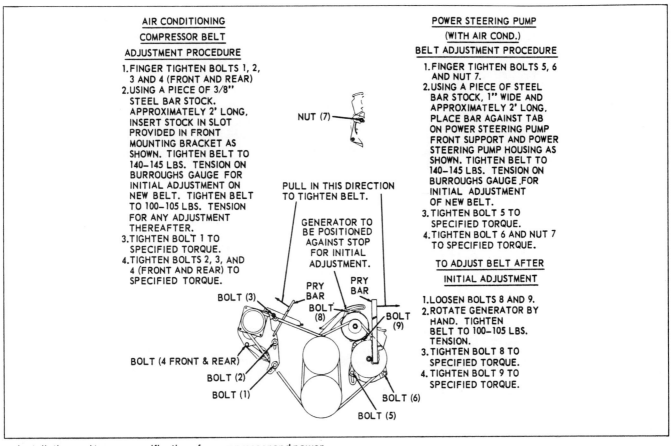

AIR CONDITIONING
COMPRESSOR BELT
ADJUSTMENT PROCEDURE

1. FINGER TIGHTEN BOLTS 1, 2, 3 AND 4 (FRONT AND REAR)
2. USING A PIECE OF 3/8" STEEL BAR STOCK. APPROXIMATELY 2' LONG, INSERT STOCK IN SLOT PROVIDED IN FRONT MOUNTING BRACKET AS SHOWN. TIGHTEN BELT TO 140–145 LBS. TENSION ON BURROUGHS GAUGE FOR INITIAL ADJUSTMENT ON NEW BELT. TIGHTEN BELT TO 100–105 LBS. TENSION FOR ANY ADJUSTMENT THEREAFTER.
3. TIGHTEN BOLT 1 TO SPECIFIED TORQUE.
4. TIGHTEN BOLTS 2, 3, AND 4 (FRONT AND REAR) TO SPECIFIED TORQUE.

NUT (7)

PULL IN THIS DIRECTION TO TIGHTEN BELT.

GENERATOR TO BE POSITIONED AGAINST STOP FOR INITIAL ADJUSTMENT.

PRY BAR   PRY BAR

BOLT (3)
BOLT (8)
BOLT (9)

BOLT (4 FRONT & REAR)
BOLT (2)
BOLT (1)
BOLT (6)
BOLT (5)

POWER STEERING PUMP
(WITH AIR COND.)
BELT ADJUSTMENT PROCEDURE

1. FINGER TIGHTEN BOLTS 5, 6 AND NUT 7.
2. USING A PIECE OF STEEL BAR STOCK, 1" WIDE AND APPROXIMATELY 2' LONG, PLACE BAR AGAINST TAB ON POWER STEERING PUMP FRONT SUPPORT AND POWER STEERING PUMP HOUSING AS SHOWN. TIGHTEN BELT TO 140–145 LBS. TENSION ON BURROUGHS GAUGE FOR INITIAL ADJUSTMENT OF NEW BELT.
3. TIGHTEN BOLT 5 TO SPECIFIED TORQUE.
4. TIGHTEN BOLT 6 AND NUT 7 TO SPECIFIED TORQUE.

TO ADJUST BELT AFTER
INITIAL ADJUSTMENT

1. LOOSEN BOLTS 8 AND 9.
2. ROTATE GENERATOR BY HAND. TIGHTEN BELT TO 100–105 LBS. TENSION.
3. TIGHTEN BOLT 8 TO SPECIFIED TORQUE.
4. TIGHTEN BOLT 9 TO SPECIFIED TORQUE.

Installation and torque specifications for compressor and power-steering belts for 1965.

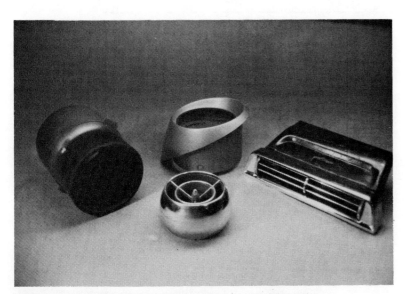

Components of 1966-67 air-conditioning system. Left is retainer adapter (part number 9782270), center rear is bezel assembly (part number 9782330 RH and 9782331 LH). The face of the bezel was painted to match instrument panel trim. Center front is the plastic chrome deflector (part number 9782269). At far right is the air distributor deflector assembly.

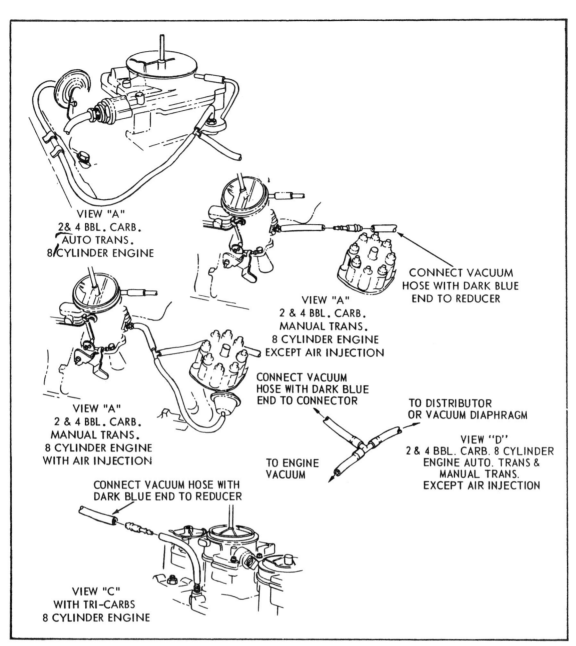

VIEW "A"
2 & 4 BBL. CARB.
AUTO TRANS.
8 CYLINDER ENGINE

VIEW "A"
2 & 4 BBL. CARB.
MANUAL TRANS.
8 CYLINDER ENGINE
EXCEPT AIR INJECTION

CONNECT VACUUM
HOSE WITH DARK BLUE
END TO REDUCER

CONNECT VACUUM
HOSE WITH DARK BLUE
END TO CONNECTOR

TO DISTRIBUTOR
OR VACUUM DIAPHRAGM

VIEW "D"
2 & 4 BBL. CARB. 8 CYLINDER
ENGINE AUTO. TRANS &
MANUAL TRANS.
EXCEPT AIR INJECTION

TO ENGINE
VACUUM

VIEW "A"
2 & 4 BBL. CARB.
MANUAL TRANS.
8 CYLINDER ENGINE
WITH AIR INJECTION

CONNECT VACUUM HOSE WITH
DARK BLUE END TO REDUCER

VIEW "C"
WITH TRI-CARBS
8 CYLINDER ENGINE

Detail of vacuum sources for air-conditioning system used in
1966 four-barrel and Tri-Power engines.

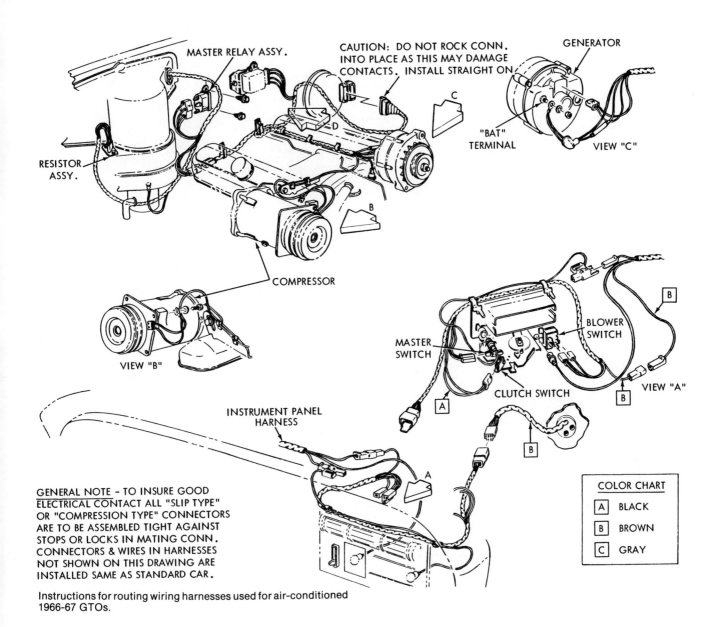

MASTER RELAY ASSY.

CAUTION: DO NOT ROCK CONN. INTO PLACE AS THIS MAY DAMAGE CONTACTS. INSTALL STRAIGHT ON

GENERATOR

C

RESISTOR ASSY.

D

B

"BAT" TERMINAL

VIEW "C"

COMPRESSOR

VIEW "B"

MASTER SWITCH

BLOWER SWITCH

B

CLUTCH SWITCH

B

VIEW "A"

A

INSTRUMENT PANEL HARNESS

A

B

GENERAL NOTE – TO INSURE GOOD ELECTRICAL CONTACT ALL "SLIP TYPE" OR "COMPRESSION TYPE" CONNECTORS ARE TO BE ASSEMBLED TIGHT AGAINST STOPS OR LOCKS IN MATING CONN. CONNECTORS & WIRES IN HARNESSES NOT SHOWN ON THIS DRAWING ARE INSTALLED SAME AS STANDARD CAR.

COLOR CHART	
A	BLACK
B	BROWN
C	GRAY

Instructions for routing wiring harnesses used for air-conditioned 1966-67 GTOs.

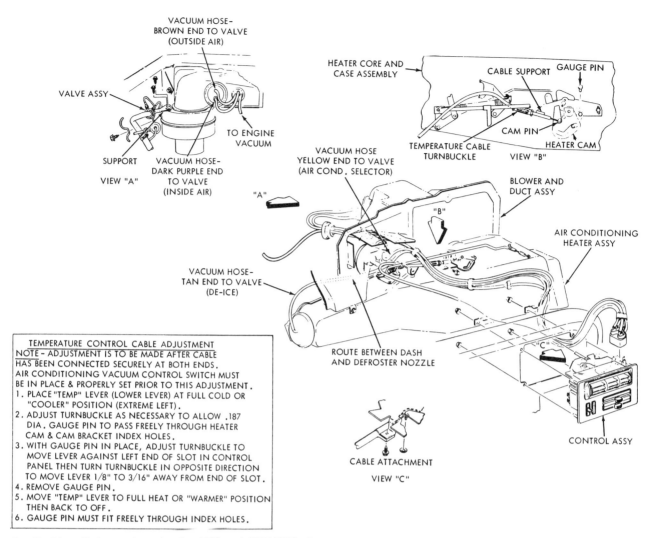

VACUUM HOSE-
BROWN END TO VALVE
(OUTSIDE AIR)

VALVE ASSY

TO ENGINE
VACUUM

SUPPORT

VACUUM HOSE-
DARK PURPLE END
TO VALVE
(INSIDE AIR)

VIEW "A"

HEATER CORE AND
CASE ASSEMBLY

CABLE SUPPORT   GAUGE PIN

CAM PIN

TEMPERATURE CABLE
TURNBUCKLE

HEATER CAM

VIEW "B"

VACUUM HOSE
YELLOW END TO VALVE
(AIR COND. SELECTOR)

BLOWER AND
DUCT ASSY

"A"

"B"

AIR CONDITIONING
HEATER ASSY

VACUUM HOSE-
TAN END TO VALVE
(DE-ICE)

ROUTE BETWEEN DASH
AND DEFROSTER NOZZLE

"C"

CONTROL ASSY

TEMPERATURE CONTROL CABLE ADJUSTMENT
NOTE – ADJUSTMENT IS TO BE MADE AFTER CABLE
HAS BEEN CONNECTED SECURELY AT BOTH ENDS.
AIR CONDITIONING VACUUM CONTROL SWITCH MUST
BE IN PLACE & PROPERLY SET PRIOR TO THIS ADJUSTMENT.
1. PLACE "TEMP" LEVER (LOWER LEVER) AT FULL COLD OR
   "COOLER" POSITION (EXTREME LEFT).
2. ADJUST TURNBUCKLE AS NECESSARY TO ALLOW .187
   DIA. GAUGE PIN TO PASS FREELY THROUGH HEATER
   CAM & CAM BRACKET INDEX HOLES.
3. WITH GAUGE PIN IN PLACE, ADJUST TURNBUCKLE TO
   MOVE LEVER AGAINST LEFT END OF SLOT IN CONTROL
   PANEL THEN TURN TURNBUCKLE IN OPPOSITE DIRECTION
   TO MOVE LEVER 1/8" TO 3/16" AWAY FROM END OF SLOT.
4. REMOVE GAUGE PIN.
5. MOVE "TEMP" LEVER TO FULL HEAT OR "WARMER" POSITION
   THEN BACK TO OFF.
6. GAUGE PIN MUST FIT FREELY THROUGH INDEX HOLES.

CABLE ATTACHMENT

VIEW "C"

Detail of installation and service for 1966 and 1967 GTO air-
conditioning controls.

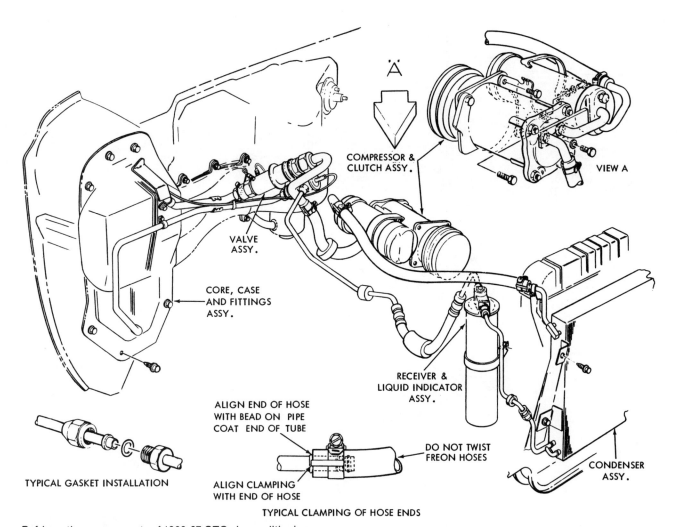

VIEW A

COMPRESSOR & CLUTCH ASSY.

VALVE ASSY.

CORE, CASE AND FITTINGS ASSY.

RECEIVER & LIQUID INDICATOR ASSY.

CONDENSER ASSY.

ALIGN END OF HOSE WITH BEAD ON PIPE COAT END OF TUBE

DO NOT TWIST FREON HOSES

TYPICAL GASKET INSTALLATION

ALIGN CLAMPING WITH END OF HOSE

TYPICAL CLAMPING OF HOSE ENDS

Refrigeration components of 1966-67 GTO air-conditioning system. Windshield washer jar and bracket were moved farther to right to clear receiver and liquid indicator assembly.

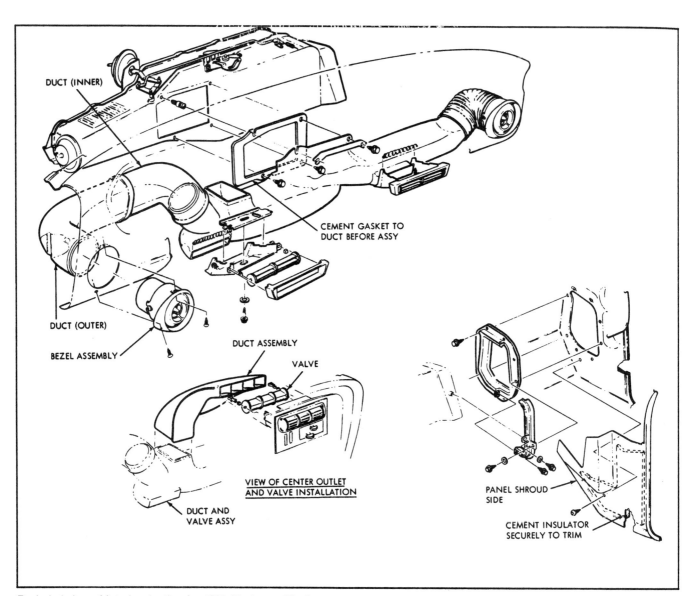

DUCT (INNER)

CEMENT GASKET TO
DUCT BEFORE ASSY

DUCT (OUTER)

BEZEL ASSEMBLY

DUCT ASSEMBLY

VALVE

VIEW OF CENTER OUTLET
AND VALVE INSTALLATION

DUCT AND
VALVE ASSY

PANEL SHROUD
SIDE

CEMENT INSULATOR
SECURELY TO TRIM

Exploded view of interior ducting for 1966-67 air conditioning.
Note configuration of RH kick panel on air-conditioned models.

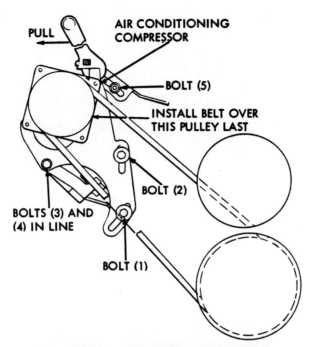

PULL

AIR CONDITIONING COMPRESSOR

BOLT (5)

INSTALL BELT OVER THIS PULLEY LAST

BOLT (2)

BOLTS (3) AND (4) IN LINE

BOLT (1)

1. FINGER TIGHTEN BOLTS 1,2,3,4, AND 5.

2. USING AN ADJUSTABLE WRENCH PLACED AS SHOWN, TIGHTEN TO 140-145 LBS. TENSION ON BORROUGHS GAUGE FOR INITIAL ADJUSTMENT OF NEW BELT. TIGHTEN TO 100-105 LBS. TENSION FOR ANY ADJUSTMENT THEREAFTER.

3. TIGHTEN BOLT 1 TO 30   LB. FT. TORQUE.

4. TIGHTEN BOLT 2,3, 4 AND 5 TO 30   LB. FT. TORQUE.

Instructions for belt tension adjustment for compressor drive belt on 1966-67 models with air conditioning.

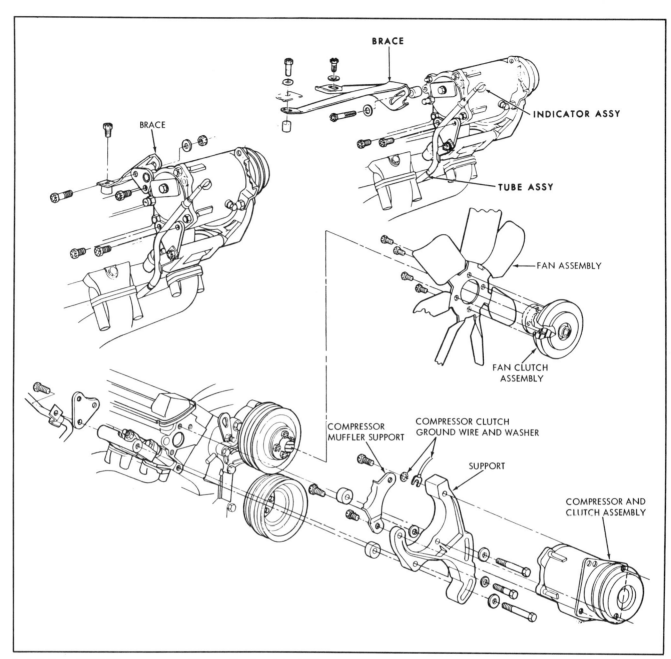

BRACE

INDICATOR ASSY

TUBE ASSY

BRACE

FAN ASSEMBLY

FAN CLUTCH ASSEMBLY

COMPRESSOR MUFFLER SUPPORT

COMPRESSOR CLUTCH GROUND WIRE AND WASHER

SUPPORT

COMPRESSOR AND CLUTCH ASSEMBLY

Installation of 1966-67 compressor with mounting brackets. 1966 brace at rear of compressor was a different design than the 1967 brace. Detailing of components was identical to that of the 1965 unit.

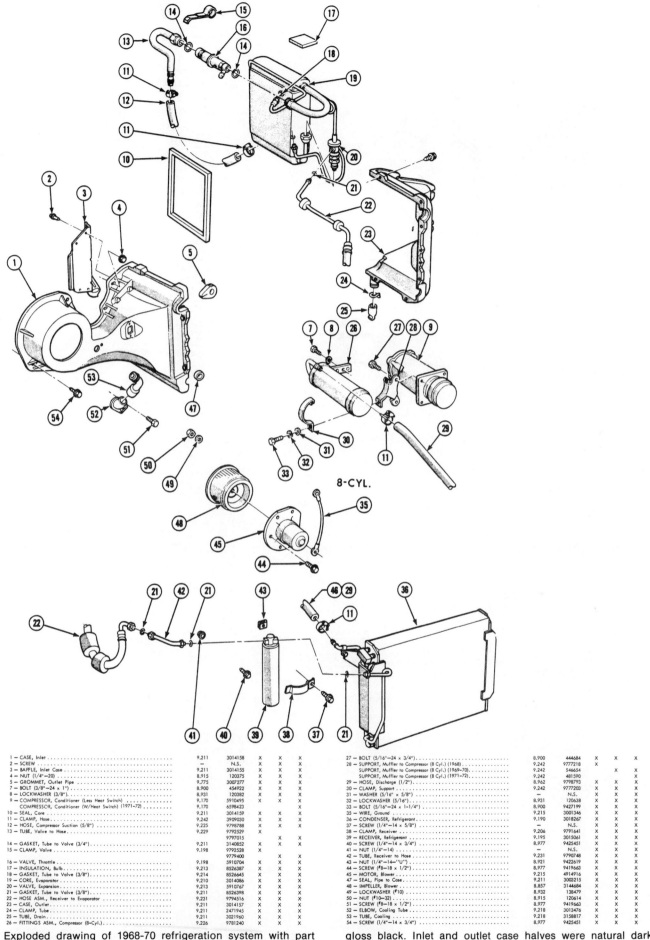

8-CYL.

1 — CASE, Inlet	9.211	3014158	X	X	X
2 — SCREW	—	N.S.	X	X	X
3 — BAFFLE, Inlet Case	9.211	3014155	X	X	X
4 — NUT (1/4"—20)	8.915	120375	X	X	X
5 — GROMMET, Outlet Pipe	9.775	3007277	X	X	X
7 — BOLT (3/8"—24 x 1")	8.900	454922	X	X	X
8 — LOCKWASHER (3/8")	8.931	120382	X	X	X
9 — COMPRESSOR, Conditioner (Less Heat Switch)	9.170	5910495	X	X	X
COMPRESSOR, Conditioner (W/Heat Switch) (1971-72)	9.170	6598423			X
10 — SEAL, Core	9.211	3014159	X	X	X
11 — CLAMP, Hose	9.242	3909030	X	X	X
12 — HOSE, Compressor Suction (5/8")	9.225	9798788	X	X	X
13 — TUBE, Valve to Hose	9.229	9792529	X		
		9797015		X	X
14 — GASKET, Tube to Valve (3/4")	9.211	3140852	X		
15 — CLAMP, Valve	9.198	9792528	X		
		9779400		X	X
16 — VALVE, Throttle	9.198	5910704	X	X	X
17 — INSULATION, Bulb	9.213	8526387	X	X	X
18 — GASKET, Tube to Valve (3/8")	9.214	8526645	X	X	X
19 — CORE, Evaporator	9.210	3014086	X	X	X
20 — VALVE, Expansion	9.213	3014767	X	X	X
21 — GASKET, Tube to Valve (3/8")	9.211	8526398	X	X	X
22 — HOSE ASM., Receiver to Evaporator	9.231	9794516	X	X	X
23 — CASE, Outlet	9.211	3014157	X	X	X
24 — CLAMP, Tube	9.211	2471945	X	X	X
25 — TUBE, Drain	9.211	3021960	X	X	X
26 — FITTINGS ASM., Compressor (8-Cyl.)	9.226	9781240	X	X	X
27 — BOLT (5/16"—24 x 3/4")	8.900	444684	X	X	X
28 — SUPPORT, Muffler to Compressor (8 Cyl.) (1968)	9.242	9777218	X		
SUPPORT, Muffler to Compressor (1969-70)	9.242	546654		X	X
SUPPORT, Muffler to Compressor (1971-72)	9.242	481590			X
29 — HOSE, Discharge (1/2")	8.962	9798793	X	X	X
30 — CLAMP, Support	9.242	9777203	X	X	X
31 — WASHER (5/16" x 5/8")	—	N.S.	X	X	X
32 — LOCKWASHER (5/16")	8.931	120638	X	X	X
33 — BOLT (5/16"—24 x 1-1/4")	8.900	9427199	X	X	X
35 — WIRE, Ground	9.215	3001346	X	X	X
36 — CONDENSER, Refrigerant	9.190	3018267	X	X	X
37 — SCREW (1/4"—14 x 5/8")	—	N.S.	X	X	X
38 — CLAMP, Receiver	9.206	9791641	X	X	X
39 — RECEIVER, Refrigerant	9.195	3015061	X	X	X
40 — SCREW (1/4"—14 x 3/4")	8.977	9425451	X	X	X
41 — NUT (1/4"—14)	—	N.S.	X	X	X
42 — TUBE, Receiver to Hose	9.231	9790748	X	X	X
43 — NUT (1/4"—14—"U")	8.921	9422619	X	X	X
44 — SCREW (#8—18 x 1/2")	8.977	9419663	X	X	X
45 — MOTOR, Blower	9.215	4914916	X	X	X
47 — SEAL, Pipe to Case	9.211	3003215	X	X	X
48 — IMPELLER, Blower	8.857	3144684	X	X	X
49 — LOCKWASHER (#10)	8.932	138479	X	X	X
50 — NUT (#10—32)	8.915	120614	X	X	X
51 — SCREW (#8—18 x 1/2")	8.977	9419663	X	X	X
52 — ELBOW, Cooling Tube	9.218	3013476	X	X	X
53 — TUBE, Cooling	9.218	3158817	X	X	X
54 — SCREW (1/4"—14 x 3/4")	8.977	9425451	X	X	X

Exploded drawing of 1968-70 refrigeration system with part names and part numbers. All metal tubes and fittings were natural in appearance. Muffler was natural metal, receiver dryer was 60° gloss black. Inlet and outlet case halves were natural dark fiberglass.

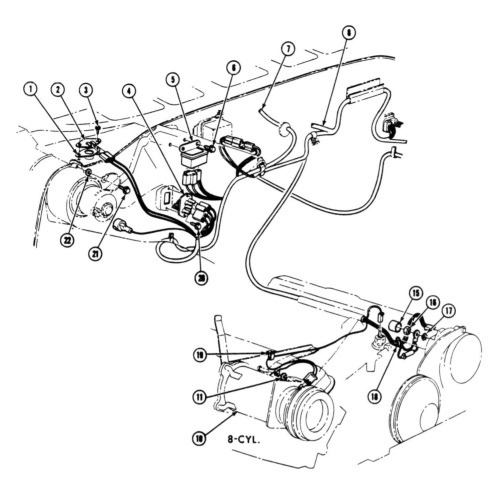

Key	Part Name	Group No.	Part No.	1968	1969	1970-72
1 —	GASKET, Ambient Switch	9.275	3917361	X	X	X
2 —	SWITCH, Ambient	9.275	9792638	X	X	X
3 —	SCREW, (#8—18 x 1/2")	8.977	9419663	X	X	X
4 —	RESISTOR, Motor.	9.277	9791201	X		
	RESISTOR, Motor	9.277	9798125		X	X
5 —	RELAY, Motor.	9.277	9788001	X	X	X
6 —	SCREW (#10—16 x 1/2")	8.977	9419303	X	X	X
7 —	WIRE, Control.	9.276	6293303	X		
			6299115+		X	X
			8903755++			X
	(8-Cyl.)		6292074	X		
	(8-Cyl.) (Jumper)	9.276	6297482		X	
		2.480	See Cat.			X
9 —	FITTING ASM., Comp. (6-Cyl.)	9.226	479339	X	X	X
	(8-Cyl.)		9781240	X	X	X
10 —	COMPRESSOR, Conditioner (Less Heat Switch)	9.170	5910495	X	X	X
	COMPRESSOR, Conditioner (w/Heat Switch) (1971-72)	9.170	6598423			X
11 —	LOCKWASHER (5/16")	8.932	138485	X	X	X
15 —	COVER, Terminal	2.313	1483218	X	X	X
16 —	NUT (#12—24)	8.915	121743	X	X	X
17 —	LOCKWASHER (#12)	—	N.S.	X	X	X
18 —	CLIP, Wire	2.482	1484957	X		
19 —	CLIP, Wire	—	N.S.	X	X	X
20 —	SCREW (#10—16 x 5/8")	8.977	9419321	X	X	X
21 —	SCREW (1/4"—14 x 1")	8.977	451617	X	X	X
22 —	WASHER (1/4" x 3/4")	8.977	N.S.	X	X	X

+Exc. Rear Window Defogger
++w/Rear Window Defogger

1968-70 air-conditioning electrical components with part names and part numbers.

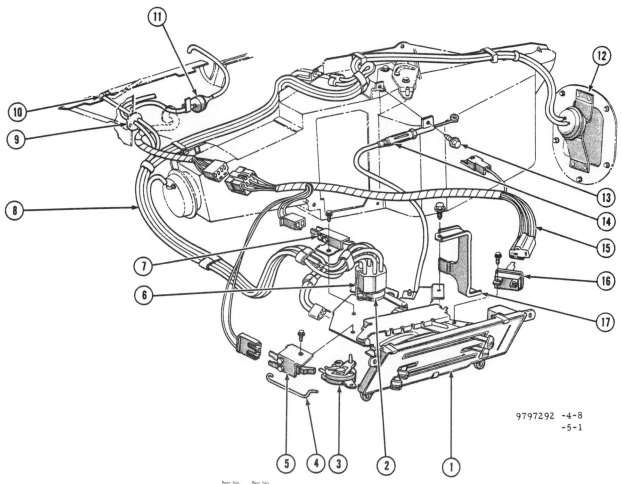

Key	Part Name	Part No. 1969	Part No. 1970	Group No.
1 — CONTROL, Air Conditioner (With Water Valve)		7307822	7311882	9.273
2 — VALVE, Heater Control Vacuum (Upper)		7309067	7309067	8.850
3 — VALVE, Heater Control Vacuum (Lower) (Use With Water Valve)		7309068	7309068	8.850
4 — CLIP, Vacuum Hose Retaining (Long)		545883	—	9.281
5 — SWITCH, Heater Control—Vent		7308859	7308859	9.275
6 — CLIP, Vacuum Hose Retaining (Short)		545884	—	9.281
7 — SWITCH, Master		7308858	7308858	9.275
8 — HARNESS, Vacuum Hose (With Water Valve) (1971)		9796776	9796776	9.281
9 — GROMMET, Hose thru Dash		9798023	9798023	9.775
10 — CLIP, Hose to Vacuum Line		540029	—	3.162
11 — VALVE, Vacuum Check		9787802	9787802	9.281
12 — INLET & VALVE, Air		3018596	3018596	9.789
13 — SCREW, Cable to Bracket (#10—16 x 1/2")		9419303	9419303	8.977
14 — CABLE, A.C. & Heater Temp. Cont.		3862203	3862203	9.787
15 — WIRE, A.C. & Temperature Control		6299116	6299116+	9.276
		—	8903756++	9.276
16 — SWITCH, Blower Motor		7308842	7311845	9.275
17 — SUPPORT, Control		9797232	9797232	8.852

+Exc. Rear Window Defogger   ++w/Rear Window Defogger

Exploded view of 1968-70 vacuum and electrical controls and
harness with part names and part numbers.

Hot water valve (1968-70) and bracket assembly used in air-
conditioned models.

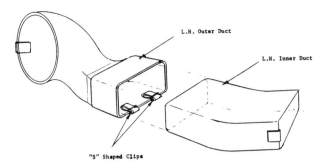

L.H. Outer Duct

L.H. Inner Duct

"S" Shaped Clips

On some air-conditioned 1968 cars, the left duct extension may be loose and become disengaged. This condition can be corrected by installing two S-shaped clips (part number 9777800, F-3, Gp. No. 9.264) as shown here. (This information taken from Dealer Technical Bulletin number 68-T-16 dated 6-12-68.)

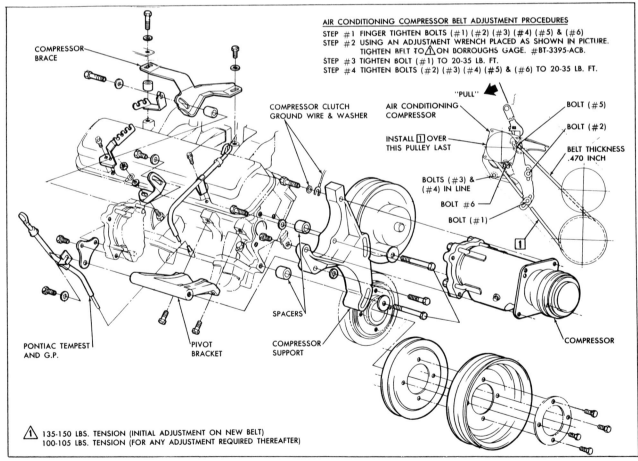

COMPRESSOR BRACE

COMPRESSOR CLUTCH GROUND WIRE & WASHER

AIR CONDITIONING COMPRESSOR BELT ADJUSTMENT PROCEDURES
STEP #1 FINGER TIGHTEN BOLTS (#1) (#2) (#3) (#4) (#5) & (#6)
STEP #2 USING AN ADJUSTMENT WRENCH PLACED AS SHOWN IN PICTURE. TIGHTEN BELT TO △ ON BORROUGHS GAGE. #BT-3395-ACB.
STEP #3 TIGHTEN BOLT (#1) TO 20-35 LB. FT.
STEP #4 TIGHTEN BOLTS (#2) (#3) (#4) (#5) & (#6) TO 20-35 LB. FT.

"PULL"

AIR CONDITIONING COMPRESSOR

INSTALL 1 OVER THIS PULLEY LAST

BOLTS (#3) & (#4) IN LINE

BOLT #6

BOLT (#1)

BOLT (#5)

BOLT (#2)

BELT THICKNESS .470 INCH

1

SPACERS

COMPRESSOR SUPPORT

COMPRESSOR

PONTIAC TEMPEST AND G.P.

PIVOT BRACKET

△ 135-150 LBS. TENSION (INITIAL ADJUSTMENT ON NEW BELT)
100-105 LBS. TENSION (FOR ANY ADJUSTMENT REQUIRED THEREAFTER)

1969 compressor mounting. The 1968 was mounted the same, except the pivot bracket mounted to the cylinder head bolts (like the 1964-67 units). The compressor support was natural aluminum in appearance; all other brackets and braces were painted 60° gloss black. The spacers were natural metal, while the dipstick and dipstick tube were engine-blue. The 1968 pivot bracket was part number 9788304, the 1969-70 part number was 9785787. The compressor support was the same for all three years (part number 9782661), as was the rear brace (part number 9786452).

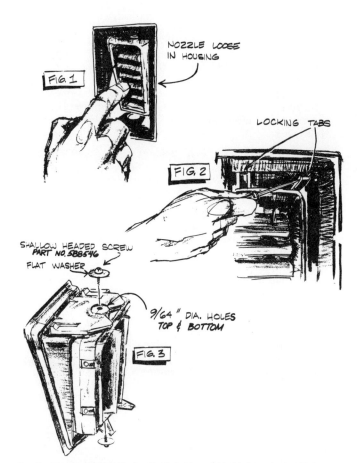

NOZZLE LOOSE IN HOUSING

FIG. 1

LOCKING TABS

FIG. 2

SHALLOW HEADED SCREW PART NO. 588546

FLAT WASHER

9/64" DIA. HOLES TOP & BOTTOM

FIG. 3

Dealer Technical Bulletin 69-T-6, dated 10-30-68, reported that the two upper-left or right air nozzles may come loose inside their housings on 1969 vehicles with air conditioning or upper-level ventilation. To correct, first remove the instrument panel by inserting a screwdriver between the two upper locking tabs and housing (Figure 2). While prying down the locking tabs, pull the assembly out of the instrument panel. Separate the air nozzle from the housing and drill a 0.140 inch (9/64 inch) diameter hole in each end of the nozzle (there is a small dimple on each nozzle where hole is to be drilled). Now, position nozzle into housing and install a shallow-headed screw (588546) and a regular number 10 flat steel or fiber washer approximately 3/16 inch inside diameter by 9/16 inch outside diameter and 3/32 inch thick in each end of the nozzle (Figure 3). Then install the unit back into opening in the instrument panel. In some cases, after two washers and screws are installed, there may be insufficient clearance for the unit to fit into the instrument panel opening. Therefore, it will be necessary to file a small notch in the center of the upper end of the instrument panel opening to allow the screw head to pass through the opening. It is important that the notch be filed only in the center of the opening.

RADIO

1964-65

In 1964 there was a choice of four different radio and antenna combinations. Part of the 061 Basic group was the standard AM push-button radio with manual fender-mount antenna. This could be ordered separately as RPO 392. An AM manual-tune radio with manual antenna (RPO 398), an AM push-button with electric rear quarter mount (RPO 393), and an AM with manual control and electric rear quarter mount (RPO 399) were also available. The switch for the electric antenna was mounted under the dash pad ledge between the RH instrument pod and the heater control assembly.

Although there was no reference made to availability, it has been reported that AM/FM radios were made a dealer-installed option in the last weeks of the model year. It has also been reported that some of the last 1964 GTOs off the assembly line could have had AM/FM radios installed. This information has never been substantiated. There is no RPO or dealer information available at this time relative to the 1964 AM/FM radio. Installation of an AM/FM radio by restorers in any 1964 GTO is therefore incorrect.

A rear speaker option known as Separa-Phonic (RPO 401) was available, with a switch to select speaker usage mounted under the top edge of the instrument cluster housing assembly between the center-right and far-right pods. If the RPO 474 Verba-Phonic reverberation option was ordered, the reverb switch was mounted in the same location as the Separa-Phonic switch. The reverberation box was mounted under the package shelf in the trunk on the rear seatback diagonal brace. Neither Separa-Phonic nor Verba-Phonic was available with the convertible GTO.

The front speaker used for 1964-65 was a 10 ohm 4x10 inch oval. The front-fender-mount antenna was round. The wiring for the reverb, Separa-Phonic and rear electric antenna ran under the carpet along the passenger side of the floor pan.

The 1965 GTO used the same radio and antenna combination RPO numbers, except for the addition of the AM/FM. With manual antenna it was RPO 394, and with rear-quarter-mount electric antenna, RPO 395 was used. The 1965 went with an oval front speaker, and the new-design oval antenna (part number 9776979) was introduced. Again, as in 1964, neither rear speaker option was available with convertible models.

The rear-mount, electric antenna used a 188 inch cable to the radio. The replacement mast part number was 541963. The replacement part number for the entire antenna motor assembly was 9770160. The dealer-installed accessory package was 984518. The 1964 and 1965 electric antennas and components were completely interchangeable.

Any GTO ordered with no radio came with a block-off plate from the factory. It matched the adjoining molding trim in style and color. The 1964 plate (part number 9775395) had the familiar bluish-gray tint; the 1965 plate (part number 9781068) was painted black between the ribs.

Detail of speaker enclosure used for all rear seat radio applications in 1964-67 GTO. Enclosure was clipped to rear seat speaker magnet.

1966-67

There were six different radio and antenna combinations in 1966. Four were AM radio and antenna packages: a push-button AM with manual RH front-fender-mount antenna (RPO 342, accessory package 984594), which was also available as part of the 061 Basic group; a push-button AM radio with electric RH rear-quarter-mount antenna (RPO 342); a manual-control AM with manual RH front-fender-mount antenna (RPO 348, accessory package 984595); a manual-control AM with electric RH rear-quarter-mount antenna (RPO 349). Two were AM/FM radio and antenna combinations: RPO 344 identified the AM/FM manual antenna mounted on the RH front fender; RPO 345 was used for the AM/FM radio with electric RH rear-quarter-mount antenna.

The electric antenna switch and wire assembly (part number 9784131) was mounted under the dash pad ledge. The wire was routed by clips behind the instrument panel, under the RH side of the floor, through the rear seat divider board, along the RH rear wheelhouse to the antenna assembly. The 188 inch antenna cable (part number 9771297) was routed from the radio to the antenna in the same manner as the wire. The antenna assembly (part number 9782945) was also available as a dealer-installed option (accessory package number 984591). Replacement mast assemblies were available as part number 541963.

The rear seat speaker option, known as Separa-Phonic (RPO 351), was available either factory or dealer installed. The switch bezel (part number 9784642) was mounted in the same manner as the power antenna. The switch and wire assembly (part number 7297142) was routed by clips behind the instrument panel, and ran along the RH floor pan, through the cardboard rear seat divider clipped to the diagonal rear seat brace, and to the speaker.

A GTO ordered with the Separa-Phonic option installed at the factory used a weave-design package shelf with holes drilled in the cardboard backing for the speaker. This shelf was finished in a 0° gloss to match the interior trim (except when the interior trim was parchment, in which case the shelf was painted black). Dealer-installed rear seat speaker (accessory package number 984574) used a speaker grille (part number 7295996), which was painted to match the package shelf trim color. The package shelf in a GTO ordered without RPO 351 used a plain cardboard shelf painted low gloss to match the interior trim, (with the exception of a parchment interior, in which case the shelf was painted black).

Available as either a factory- or dealer-installed option (accessory package number 984679), the Verba-Phonic amplifier (RPO 352) and rear seat speaker were available on all 1966 GTOs, with the exception of convertibles.

The switch bezel (part number 9784638) was mounted on the dash. The switch and wire assembly (part number 7297152) was routed behind the instrument panel and along the RH floor pan, through the cardboard rear seat divider, along clips, up the rear seat diagonal brace and to the reverberation amplifier. A 162 inch replacement wire assembly (part number 4414620) was available. The amplifier box was mounted on the rear seatback diagonal brace by a bracket (part number 7284943) measuring 4⅝ inches long.

The front speaker assembly (part number 7286462) measured 4x10 inches, and was rated at 10 ohms. The rear speaker measured 6x9 inches and was also rated at 10 ohms. The rear speaker used one terminal, as the chassis mount provided the ground. An enclosure (part number 9784559) made of cardboard and lined with insulation clipped to the rear speaker magnet, and was used in all rear seat applications, except convertibles.

Whenever wires for rear speaker, defogger or power antenna applications were run on the RH floor pan, a wire protector (part number 4414997) was used. This applied to all 1965 through 1967 GTOs. (See defogger illustration in heater section for detail.)

For 1967, the radio options, RPO numbers, switch and wire assemblies, bezels and electric antenna information were all identical to 1966, with the exception of the following:

1967 Verba-Phonic accessory package—984849
AM/FM radio—984729
Separa-Phonic rear seat speaker—984818

The Separa-Phonic and Verba-Phonic options were available in 1967 on convertible models. The rear speaker was mounted behind the rear seat and used a special speaker enclosure (part number 3904844). The reverberation amplifier was mounted on the front of the rear compartment pan assembly.

Also new for 1967 was the stereo tape player (RPO 354, dealer accessory package number 984824). The eight-track player had a separate amplifier, and used the front and rear speakers as described above. It was available in all body styles, with all radio options, but could not be ordered with the RPO heater deletion option. A special Y-shaped heater outlet was used when the stereo tape player was ordered. (See heater section for more detail.)

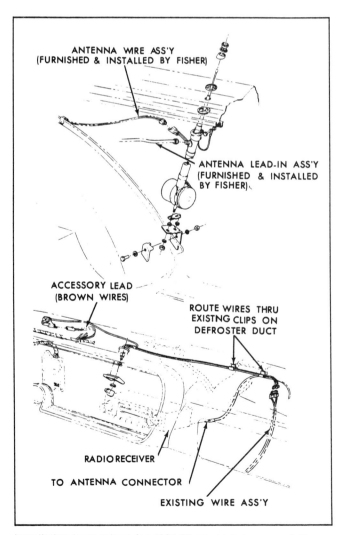

Installation instructions for 1964-67 power antenna and directions for routing switch wire behind instrument panel for 1966-67.

The player mounted to the underside of the instrument panel using a rubber filler (part number 9788206). It could be ordered with or without a transmission floor console. An insert (part number 9788395) was used to match the instrument cluster wood grain on the face of the player. The Separa-Phonic and Verba-Phonic options were not available when the stereo tape player was ordered.

To combat radio noise, several supression devices were used by the factory to filter and dampen ignition interference. A capacitor and bracket (part number 1964110) were mounted to the firewall and connected to the standard voltage regulator. This was not used with transistorized voltage regulators or transistorized ignition. A capacitor and bracket (part number 9781723) were mounted on the heater blower motor cover, connected to the blower terminal, for AM/FM radio applications only. A nine-inch static collector strap (part number 537715) was connected to the cylinder head and the firewall.

A GTO ordered without a radio used a radio opening cover plate (part number 9782742 in 1966 and 9777675 in 1967).

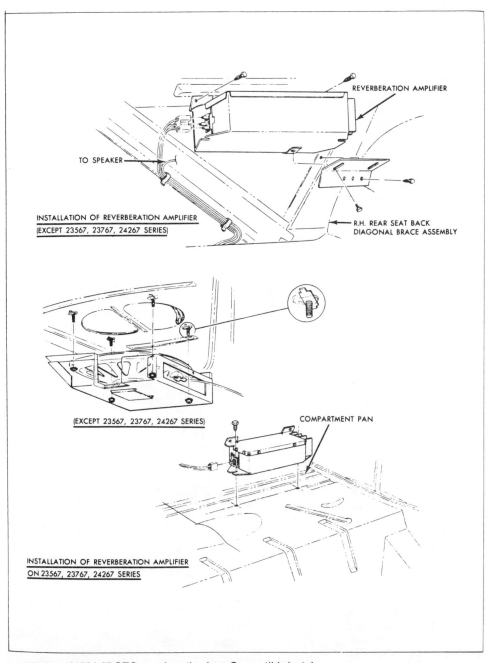

INSTALLATION OF REVERBERATION AMPLIFIER
(EXCEPT 23567, 23767, 24267 SERIES)

REVERBERATION AMPLIFIER

TO SPEAKER

R.H. REAR SEAT BACK
DIAGONAL BRACE ASSEMBLY

(EXCEPT 23567, 23767, 24267 SERIES)

COMPARTMENT PAN

INSTALLATION OF REVERBERATION AMPLIFIER
ON 23567, 23767, 24267 SERIES

Installation of 1964-67 GTO reverberation box. Convertible installation was new for 1967. Box had to be mounted to right to clear top motor and hydraulic pump. Note use of clips to retain three conductor wires to brace.

1968-70

There were six different radio and antenna combinations offered in 1968-69 and three in 1970.

Year	Description	RPO Code	UPC Code	Access. Package Number
1968	AM—PB, MA	382	—	984978
	AM—PB, EA	383	—	984978
	AM/FM—PB, MA	384	—	984976
	AM/FM—PB, EA	385	—	984976
	AM/FM stereo—MA	388	—	984987
	AM/FM stereo—EA	389	—	984987
1969	AM—PB, MA	382	U63	988588
	AM—PB, EA	383	U75-U63	988588
	AM/FM—MA	384	U69	988586
	AM/FM—EA	385	U69-U75	988586
	AM/FM stereo—MA	388	U58	988587
	AM/FM stereo—EA	389	U58-U75	988587
1970	AM—PB, WS	401	U63	988742
	AM/FM—WS	402	U69	988740
	AM/FM stereo—WS	404	U58	988741

PB-push button, MA-manual antenna, EA-electric antenna, WS-windshield antenna.

The electric antenna switch and wire assembly (part number 9793183) was mounted under the dash pad ledge in 1968. A rocker-style switch (part number 9797084) was used in 1969. The wire was routed in the same fashion as in 1966-67. The electric antenna assembly (part number 9779935) was also available as a dealer-installed option, in 1968 only. The replacement mast assembly was part number 541963. No electric antenna was available in 1970.

A rear speaker option was available for all three years. The 1968 Separa-Phonic option (RPO 391) used a switch and wire assembly (part number 9793182) mounted at the underside of the dash pad ledge to the instrument panel. The wire was routed in the same manner as the 1966-67 unit. A speaker enclosure (part number 9784559) was used for all three years, and clipped to the speaker magnet.

The 1969 and 1970 rear seat speaker option (RPO 391, UPC U80 in 1969; RPO 411, UPC U80 in 1970) used a fader control and control bezel. The 1969-70 fader control (part number 7309432 in 1969 and 7309422 in 1970) was mounted at the radio tuning control. The bezel (part number 9784359) was the same for both years. The rear seat speaker option was not available when AM/FM stereo radio or the stereo tape player was ordered.

The Verba-Phonic rear seat speaker option was available in 1968 and 1969. The 1968 unit (RPO 392) used a switch and wire assembly (part number 9793178) mounted under the dash pad ledge at the instrument panel. The amplifier was mounted behind the glovebox, using an adapter (part number 988560).

In 1969, the Verba-Phonic (RPO 392, UPC U84) used a rocker-type switch (part number 9795669). The amplifier was mounted above the glovebox, using an adapter package (part number 988648). The wire was routed to the rear speaker in almost the same fashion as the 1967 unit; however, it went directly to the speaker, as the amplifier was no longer located in the rear. The Verba-Phonic was available as a dealer-installed option for both years. The accessory package part numbers were 984888 for 1968 and 988633 for 1969.

The rear seat speaker and Verba-Phonic rear seat speaker were available for convertible installation. A speaker adapter package (part number 984985) was used for all three years for any convertible rear seat speaker application. The Verba-Phonic was not available when the AM/FM stereo radio or stereo tape player was ordered. If the Power Flow ventilation system was ordered, Verba-Phonic was not available.

For all three years, only one 6x9" rear seat speaker was employed, even with stereo radio or tape player. The factory did not install dual rear seat speakers at any time, with any radio or stereo tape player.

The stereo tape player option was available for all three years. The 1968 unit (RPO 394) was similar to the 1967 unit, except it carried additional padding around the front edges, and the woodgrain insert was different. The 1968 stereo tape player was available with any radio, but was not available with floor-mounted manual transmission.

For 1969, the tape player (RPO 394, UPC U57) was redesigned and was more compact. It was available with any radio. However, it could not be ordered with the bench seat and manual transmission combination. The 1970 unit (RPO 412, UPC U57) was identical to the 1969 unit and was available as an accessory package (988754 without console and 988752 with console). A heater outlet duct (part number 9793675) was used with nonconsole installations to allow air to flow unimpeded by the player.

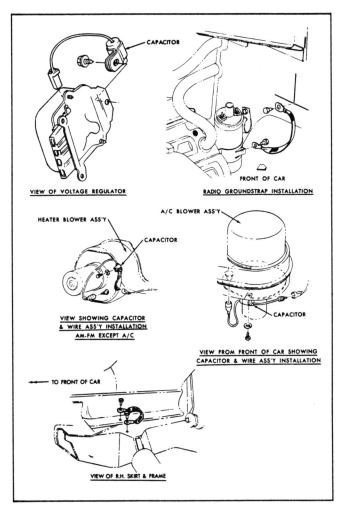

VIEW OF VOLTAGE REGULATOR

RADIO GROUNDSTRAP INSTALLATION

CAPACITOR

FRONT OF CAR

HEATER BLOWER ASS'Y

A/C BLOWER ASS'Y

CAPACITOR

CAPACITOR

VIEW SHOWING CAPACITOR & WIRE ASS'Y INSTALLATION AM-FM EXCEPT A/C

VIEW FROM FRONT OF CAR SHOWING CAPACITOR & WIRE ASS'Y INSTALLATION

TO FRONT OF CAR

VIEW OF R.H. SKIRT & FRAME

Capacitors and ground straps were used in 1964-67 to combat radio interference caused by ignition. The AM/FM suppression equipment did not apply to 1964.

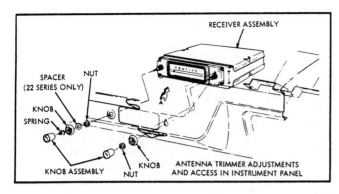

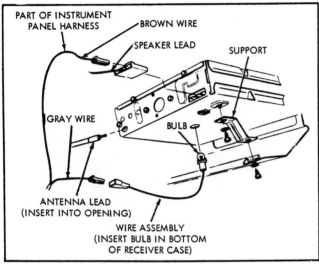

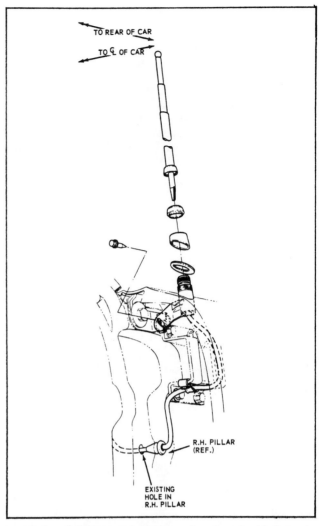

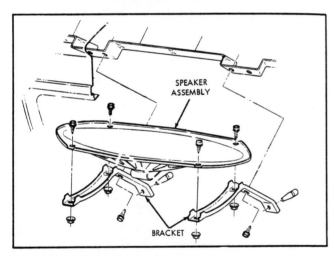

Installation of 1964 radio, harness and front speaker (part number 7286462).

Installation of 1964 manual antenna and routing of cable through pillar. Mast assemblies were either round (part number 520124) or oval (part number 9776979) in 1964. Different antenna support bodies were used for the round mast (9774445) and oval mast (9776919).

1964-67 Verba-Phonic and bracket were mounted on cross-brace behind rear seat under package shelf. Not available on convertibles until 1967.

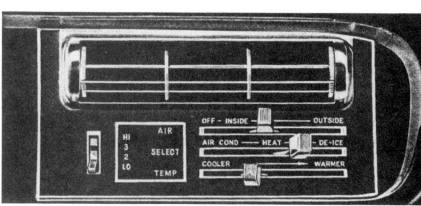

Factory artwork of 1964 manual-tune AM radio, model number 984065.

RPO 392 AM push-button radio for 1964 GTO, model number 984076.

Detail of capacitor (part number 9781723) used in 1965-67 to combat ignition noise in AM/FM radios. Unit was mounted on heater blower case cover and connected inline with blower motor lead from firewall.

1965 AM/FM radio was offered as RPO 394 with manual antenna and RPO 395 with rear quarter mount electric antenna. Model number is 7292112.

1965 AM push-button radio (RPO 392 with manual antenna and RPO 393 with rear quarter mount electric antenna), model number 7291582.

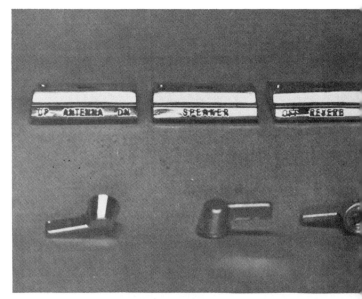

Comparison of 1964-65 power antenna, Separa-Phonic and Verba-Phonic switch bezels, and knobs.

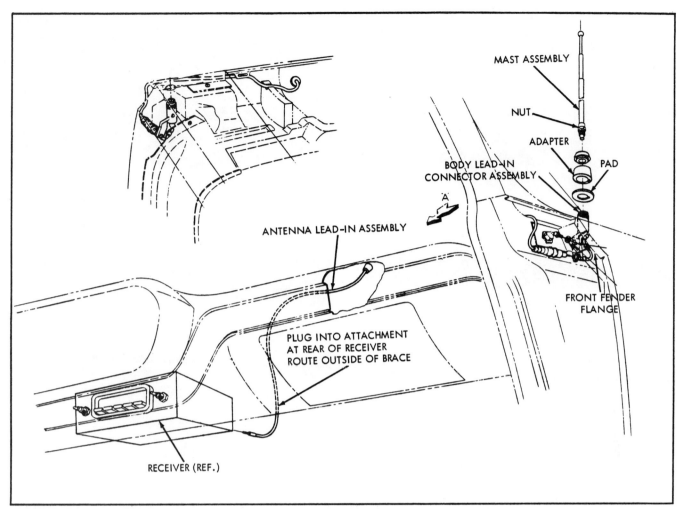

Installation of 1965 manual antenna and correct routing of antenna cable through cowl to radio.

Close-up detail of 1966-67 power antenna switch bezel (part number 9784640) and chrome knob (part number 9784535).

Radio block-off plate (rear) for 1965; standard molding for use with radio in front. 1964 plates were identical except for color between chrome ribs. Rear plate looks smaller here due to placement of display.

Close-up of 1966 AM radio with push buttons. Button had rounded fronts. Radio model number was 7293502.

Close-up of 1966 AM/FM radio (model number 7293472). Compare design of push buttons to 1967 AM/FM buttons. Slide bar with Pontiac name moved left to right, uncovering FM letters painted yellow on right, or AM letters painted white on left.

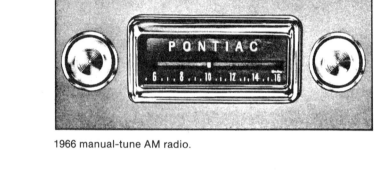

1966 manual-tune AM radio.

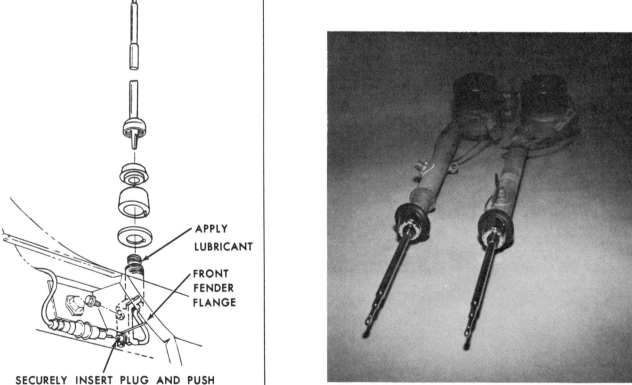

APPLY LUBRICANT

FRONT FENDER FLANGE

SECURELY INSERT PLUG AND PUSH INTO SOCKET ON BODY LEAD IN CONNECTOR ASS'Y

Exploded view of 1966 manual antenna. The 1967 manual antenna used a solid 5/16-inch-diameter base with a different part number for the antenna body.

Comparison of 1967 and 1968 (right) power antenna assemblies. Note difference in location of antenna lead-in plug and ground wire. Two designs were used in the 1968 upper adapter. The first type (part number 9782912) measured ⅞ inch in thickness. The second design for convertibles measured ¾ inch thick (part number 9793318), and was carried into 1969. For hardtops, part number 9793434 measured 11/16 inch thick, and was also used through 1969.

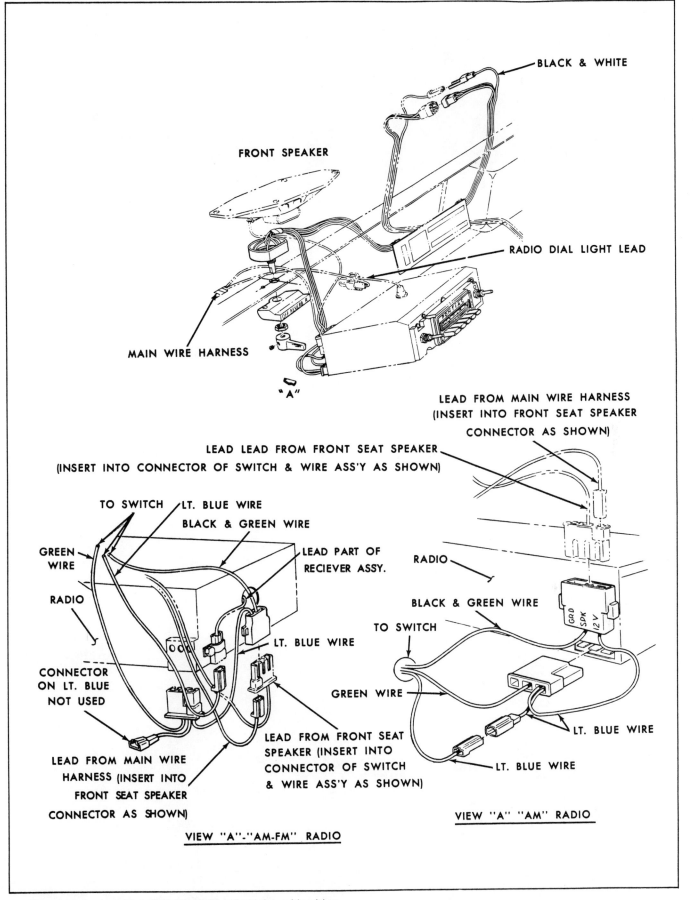

BLACK & WHITE

FRONT SPEAKER

RADIO DIAL LIGHT LEAD

MAIN WIRE HARNESS

"A"

LEAD FROM MAIN WIRE HARNESS
(INSERT INTO FRONT SEAT SPEAKER
CONNECTOR AS SHOWN)

LEAD LEAD FROM FRONT SEAT SPEAKER
(INSERT INTO CONNECTOR OF SWITCH & WIRE ASS'Y AS SHOWN)

TO SWITCH LT. BLUE WIRE

BLACK & GREEN WIRE

GREEN WIRE

LEAD PART OF
RECIEVER ASSY.

RADIO

RADIO

BLACK & GREEN WIRE

LT. BLUE WIRE

TO SWITCH

CONNECTOR
ON LT. BLUE
NOT USED

GREEN WIRE

GRD SPK 12V

LT. BLUE WIRE

LEAD FROM FRONT SEAT
SPEAKER (INSERT INTO
CONNECTOR OF SWITCH
& WIRE ASS'Y AS SHOWN)

LT. BLUE WIRE

LEAD FROM MAIN WIRE
HARNESS (INSERT INTO
FRONT SEAT SPEAKER
CONNECTOR AS SHOWN)

VIEW "A"-"AM-FM" RADIO

VIEW "A" "AM" RADIO

Directions for installing 1966 Verba-Phonic option with wiring
color codes.

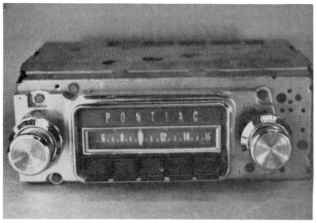

Close-up of 1967 AM push-button radio (model number 7298802).
Note design of push buttons and tone and select knobs.

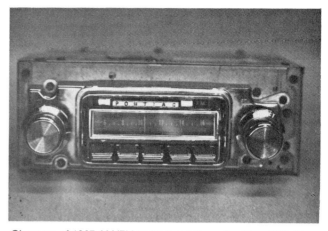

Close-up of 1967 AM/FM radio (model number 7298812). Compare knob design with 1966 knobs on AM radio.

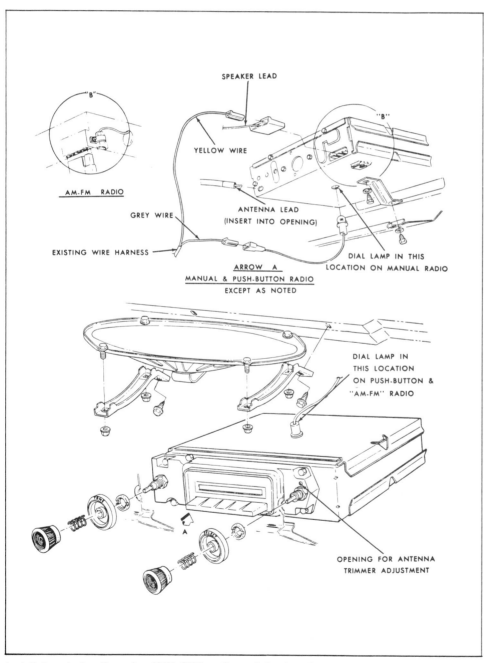

Installation instructions for 1967 GTO radio and front seat speaker. The same instructions applied for the 1966 GTO.

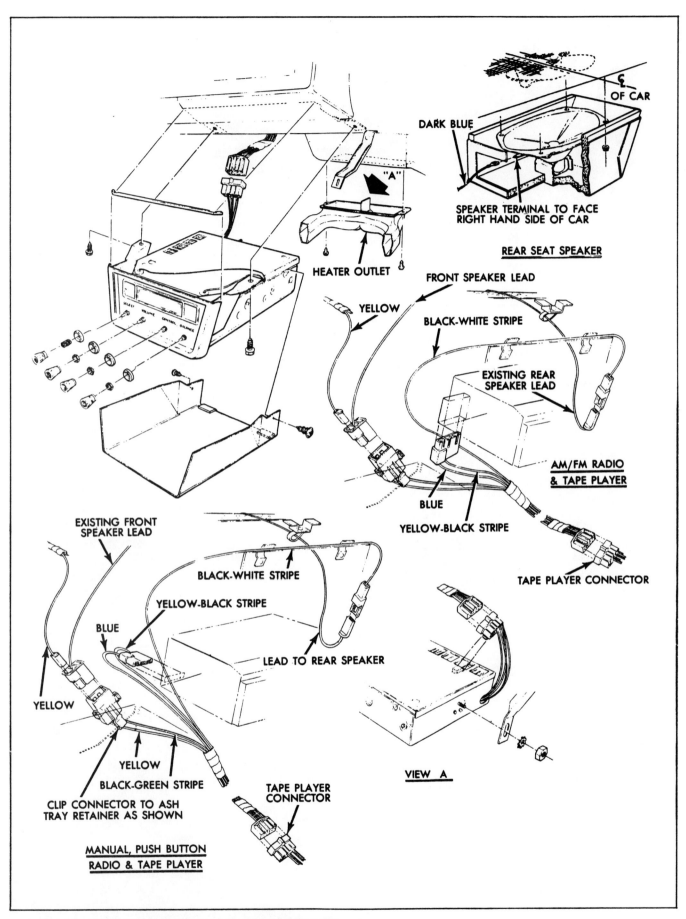

DARK BLUE

SPEAKER TERMINAL TO FACE RIGHT HAND SIDE OF CAR

OF CAR

REAR SEAT SPEAKER

HEATER OUTLET

"A"

FRONT SPEAKER LEAD

YELLOW

BLACK-WHITE STRIPE

EXISTING REAR SPEAKER LEAD

AM/FM RADIO & TAPE PLAYER

BLUE

YELLOW-BLACK STRIPE

TAPE PLAYER CONNECTOR

EXISTING FRONT SPEAKER LEAD

BLACK-WHITE STRIPE

YELLOW-BLACK STRIPE

BLUE

LEAD TO REAR SPEAKER

YELLOW

YELLOW

BLACK-GREEN STRIPE

CLIP CONNECTOR TO ASH TRAY RETAINER AS SHOWN

TAPE PLAYER CONNECTOR

VIEW A

MANUAL, PUSH BUTTON RADIO & TAPE PLAYER

Installation of 1967 stereo tape player. A Y-shaped heater outlet was used. If optional courtesy lamp was used, it had to be moved to the right to clear tape player.

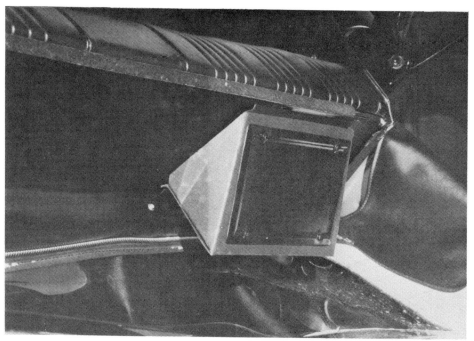

1967 convertible rear speaker enclosure, showing correct location for installation.

1970 AM/FM stereo radio with multiplex adapter. Note support bracket on multiplexer.

Close-up of face and padding of 1968 stereo tape player. The knob part number was 9786795 for all controls. This knob part number was also used for 1969 and 1970 players.

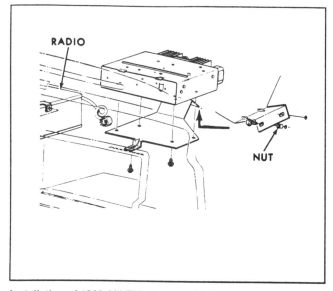

Installation of 1968 AM/FM stereo multiplex unit, using adapter bracket.

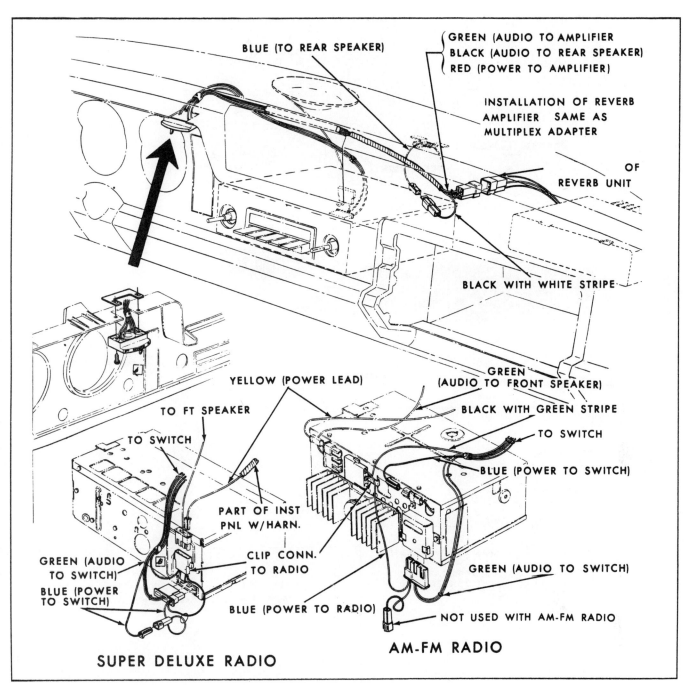

BLUE (TO REAR SPEAKER)

GREEN (AUDIO TO AMPLIFIER
BLACK (AUDIO TO REAR SPEAKER)
RED (POWER TO AMPLIFIER)

INSTALLATION OF REVERB
AMPLIFIER SAME AS
MULTIPLEX ADAPTER

OF
REVERB UNIT

BLACK WITH WHITE STRIPE

GREEN
(AUDIO TO FRONT SPEAKER)

BLACK WITH GREEN STRIPE

TO SWITCH

BLUE (POWER TO SWITCH)

YELLOW (POWER LEAD)

TO FT SPEAKER

TO SWITCH

PART OF INST
PNL W/HARN.

CLIP CONN.
TO RADIO

GREEN (AUDIO
TO SWITCH)

BLUE (POWER
TO SWITCH)

GREEN (AUDIO TO SWITCH)

BLUE (POWER TO RADIO)

NOT USED WITH AM-FM RADIO

SUPER DELUXE RADIO

AM-FM RADIO

Installation of Verba-Phonic system in 1968 GTO. Note installation of switch and wire assembly.

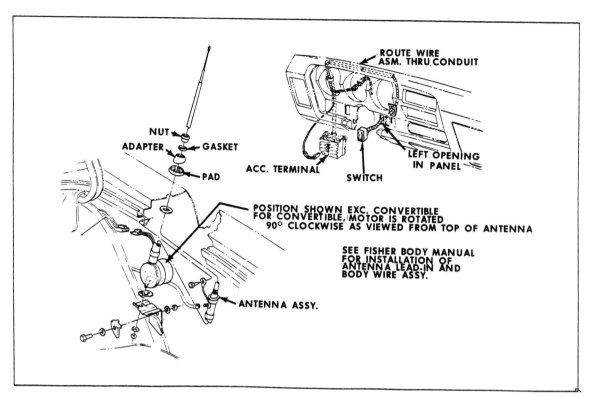

ROUTE WIRE ASM. THRU CONDUIT

NUT
ADAPTER — GASKET
PAD

ACC. TERMINAL

SWITCH

LEFT OPENING IN PANEL

POSITION SHOWN EXC. CONVERTIBLE
FOR CONVERTIBLE, MOTOR IS ROTATED
90° CLOCKWISE AS VIEWED FROM TOP OF ANTENNA

SEE FISHER BODY MANUAL
FOR INSTALLATION OF
ANTENNA LEAD-IN AND
BODY WIRE ASSY.

ANTENNA ASSY.

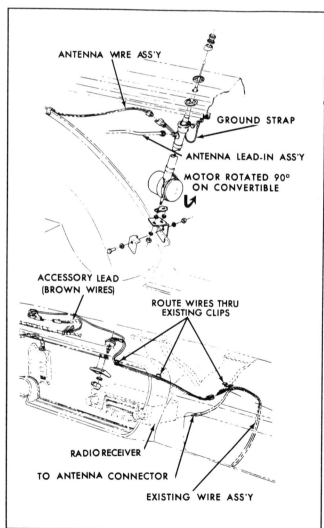

ANTENNA WIRE ASS'Y

GROUND STRAP

ANTENNA LEAD-IN ASS'Y

MOTOR ROTATED 90°
ON CONVERTIBLE

ACCESSORY LEAD
(BROWN WIRES)

ROUTE WIRES THRU
EXISTING CLIPS

RADIO RECEIVER

TO ANTENNA CONNECTOR

EXISTING WIRE ASS'Y

Installation of 1968 and 1969 power antennas was virtually identical. However, note differences in harness routing and hookup. Same part number serviced replacement assembly for both years (9779935).

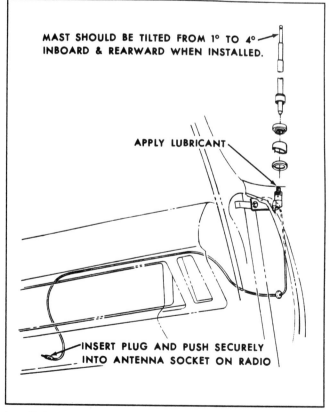

MAST SHOULD BE TILTED FROM 1° TO 4°
INBOARD & REARWARD WHEN INSTALLED.

APPLY LUBRICANT

INSERT PLUG AND PUSH SECURELY
INTO ANTENNA SOCKET ON RADIO

Installation of 1968 front fender antenna. Note alignment of front mast (part number 9794673).

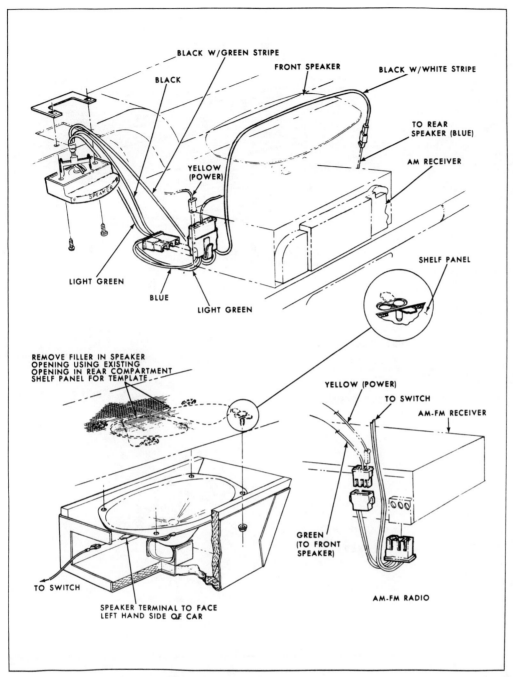

BLACK W/GREEN STRIPE
FRONT SPEAKER
BLACK W/WHITE STRIPE
BLACK
TO REAR SPEAKER (BLUE)
AM RECEIVER
YELLOW (POWER)
LIGHT GREEN
BLUE
LIGHT GREEN
SHELF PANEL

REMOVE FILLER IN SPEAKER OPENING USING EXISTING OPENING IN REAR COMPARTMENT SHELF PANEL FOR TEMPLATE

YELLOW (POWER)
TO SWITCH
AM-FM RECEIVER

GREEN (TO FRONT SPEAKER)

TO SWITCH

SPEAKER TERMINAL TO FACE LEFT HAND SIDE OF CAR

AM-FM RADIO

Installation of 1968 Separa-Phonic rear seat speaker.

467

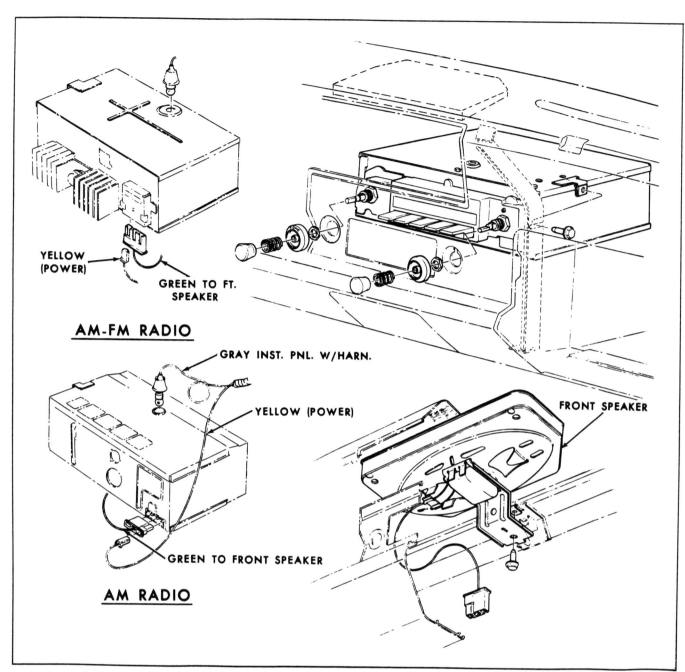

YELLOW (POWER)

GREEN TO FT. SPEAKER

AM-FM RADIO

GRAY INST. PNL. W/HARN.

YELLOW (POWER)

FRONT SPEAKER

GREEN TO FRONT SPEAKER

AM RADIO

Installation of 1968 radio and harness. 1968 was the only year to offer black letters on tone control (part number 9786943). White lettering was used on rest of 1968 through 1970 controls (part number 9791115).

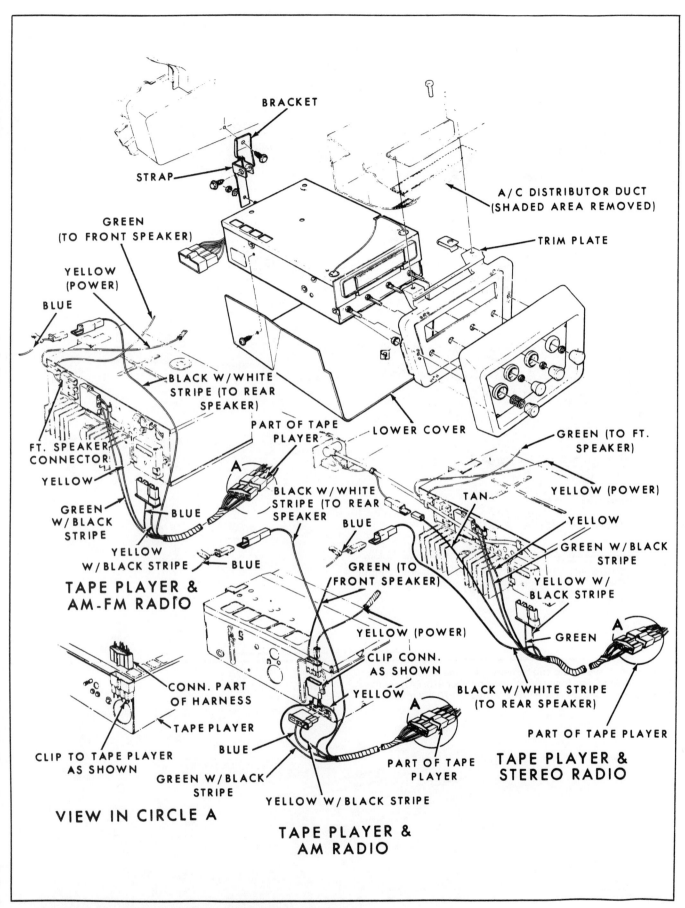

BRACKET

STRAP

A/C DISTRIBUTOR DUCT
(SHADED AREA REMOVED)

GREEN
(TO FRONT SPEAKER)

YELLOW
(POWER)

BLUE

TRIM PLATE

BLACK W/WHITE
STRIPE (TO REAR
SPEAKER)

FT. SPEAKER
CONNECTOR

YELLOW

PART OF TAPE
PLAYER

LOWER COVER

GREEN (TO FT.
SPEAKER)

YELLOW (POWER)

GREEN
W/BLACK
STRIPE

A

BLUE

BLACK W/WHITE
STRIPE (TO REAR
SPEAKER)

TAN

YELLOW

GREEN W/BLACK
STRIPE

YELLOW
W/BLACK STRIPE

BLUE

BLUE

GREEN (TO
(FRONT SPEAKER)

YELLOW W/
BLACK STRIPE

**TAPE PLAYER &
AM-FM RADIO**

YELLOW (POWER)

CLIP CONN.
AS SHOWN

GREEN

A

CONN. PART
OF HARNESS

YELLOW

BLACK W/WHITE STRIPE
(TO REAR SPEAKER)

PART OF TAPE PLAYER

TAPE PLAYER

A

**TAPE PLAYER &
STEREO RADIO**

CLIP TO TAPE PLAYER
AS SHOWN

BLUE

PART OF TAPE
PLAYER

GREEN W/BLACK
STRIPE

YELLOW W/BLACK STRIPE

VIEW IN CIRCLE A

**TAPE PLAYER &
AM RADIO**

Installation and harness connections for 1968 stereo tape player.
Heater duct was changed for installation. Note padding around
face of unit; 1967 player did not use padding.

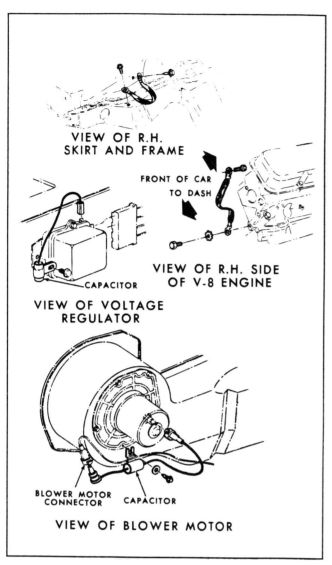

VIEW OF R.H.
SKIRT AND FRAME

FRONT OF CAR
TO DASH

VIEW OF R.H. SIDE
OF V-8 ENGINE

CAPACITOR

VIEW OF VOLTAGE
REGULATOR

BLOWER MOTOR
CONNECTOR   CAPACITOR

VIEW OF BLOWER MOTOR

Typical GTO radio suppression equipment used from 1968 through 1970. Capacitor at blower motor was used for AM/FM radios only.

SERVICE MODEL NO. 82BFM1		8	2	B	FM	1
SERIAL NO. 05-00001						
Patent numbers						
PRODUCT NO. 7303362						
LABEL		Year	Car Division	Body Size	Type Radio	Rev. No.

Dealer Service Information Bulletin number 68-I-34, dated 1-18-68, announced the application of this type of label on all Delco radios, reverb amplifiers, tape players and multiplex adapters for 1968 models.

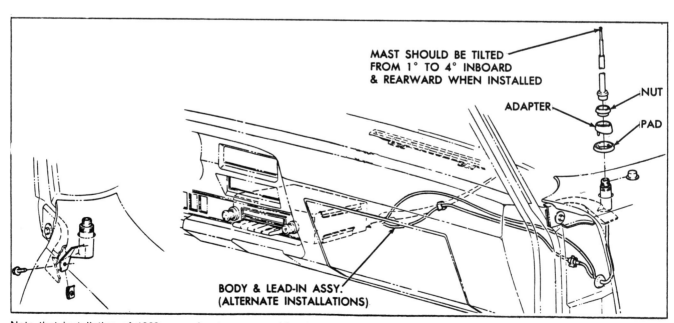

MAST SHOULD BE TILTED
FROM 1° TO 4° INBOARD
& REARWARD WHEN INSTALLED

NUT
ADAPTER
PAD

BODY & LEAD-IN ASSY.
(ALTERNATE INSTALLATIONS)

Note that installation of 1969 manual antenna assembly was somewhat different than 1968; brackets were not interchangeable.

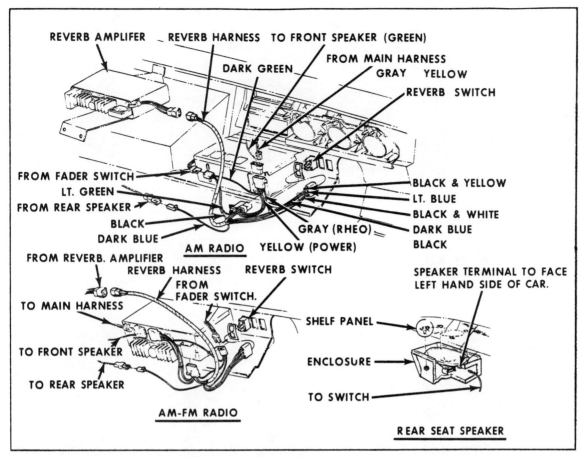

REVERB AMPLIFER   REVERB HARNESS   TO FRONT SPEAKER (GREEN)

DARK GREEN   FROM MAIN HARNESS
GRAY   YELLOW

REVERB SWITCH

FROM FADER SWITCH
LT. GREEN
FROM REAR SPEAKER
BLACK
DARK BLUE

AM RADIO

GRAY (RHEO)
YELLOW (POWER)

BLACK & YELLOW
LT. BLUE
BLACK & WHITE
DARK BLUE
BLACK

FROM REVERB. AMPLIFIER
REVERB HARNESS
FROM
FADER SWITCH.

REVERB SWITCH

TO MAIN HARNESS

TO FRONT SPEAKER

TO REAR SPEAKER

AM-FM RADIO

SPEAKER TERMINAL TO FACE
LEFT HAND SIDE OF CAR.

SHELF PANEL

ENCLOSURE

TO SWITCH

REAR SEAT SPEAKER

On 1969 Verba-Phonic system, location of amplifier was moved
slightly. Note installation of rear seat speaker, using enclosure.

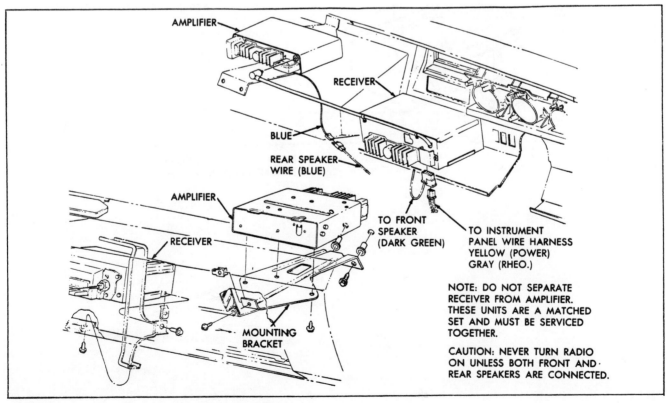

AMPLIFIER

RECEIVER

BLUE

REAR SPEAKER
WIRE (BLUE)

AMPLIFIER

RECEIVER

MOUNTING
BRACKET

TO FRONT
SPEAKER
(DARK GREEN)

TO INSTRUMENT
PANEL WIRE HARNESS
YELLOW (POWER)
GRAY (RHEO.)

NOTE: DO NOT SEPARATE
RECEIVER FROM AMPLIFIER.
THESE UNITS ARE A MATCHED
SET AND MUST BE SERVICED
TOGETHER.

CAUTION: NEVER TURN RADIO
ON UNLESS BOTH FRONT AND·
REAR SPEAKERS ARE CONNECTED.

Location of multiplex unit was moved slightly for 1969; bracket
was redesigned. Note harness connections. Installation was the
same for 1970.

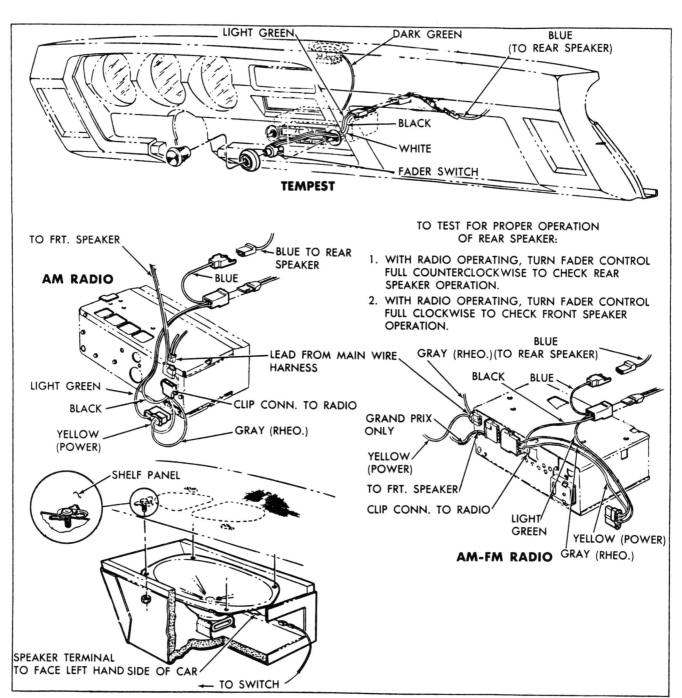

LIGHT GREEN — DARK GREEN — BLUE (TO REAR SPEAKER)

BLACK

WHITE

FADER SWITCH

TEMPEST

AM RADIO

TO FRT. SPEAKER

BLUE TO REAR SPEAKER

BLUE

LEAD FROM MAIN WIRE HARNESS

LIGHT GREEN

BLACK

YELLOW (POWER)

CLIP CONN. TO RADIO

GRAY (RHEO.)

TO TEST FOR PROPER OPERATION OF REAR SPEAKER:

1. WITH RADIO OPERATING, TURN FADER CONTROL FULL COUNTERCLOCKWISE TO CHECK REAR SPEAKER OPERATION.

2. WITH RADIO OPERATING, TURN FADER CONTROL FULL CLOCKWISE TO CHECK FRONT SPEAKER OPERATION.

BLUE

GRAY (RHEO.)(TO REAR SPEAKER)

BLACK — BLUE

GRAND PRIX ONLY

YELLOW (POWER)

TO FRT. SPEAKER

CLIP CONN. TO RADIO

LIGHT GREEN

YELLOW (POWER)

AM-FM RADIO GRAY (RHEO.)

SHELF PANEL

SPEAKER TERMINAL TO FACE LEFT HAND SIDE OF CAR

← TO SWITCH

For 1969, Separa-Phonic fader control was integrated onto tuner control of radio. Rear seat speaker installation was the same for 1968-70.

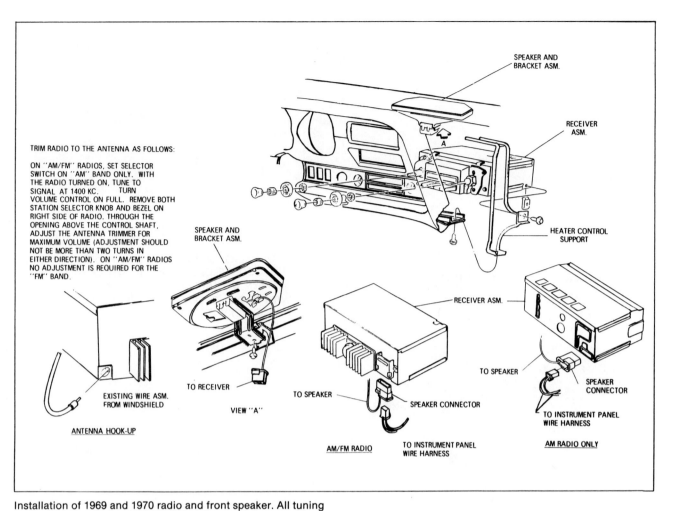

TRIM RADIO TO THE ANTENNA AS FOLLOWS:

ON "AM/FM" RADIOS, SET SELECTOR
SWITCH ON "AM" BAND ONLY. WITH
THE RADIO TURNED ON, TUNE TO
SIGNAL AT 1400 KC.   TURN
VOLUME CONTROL ON FULL. REMOVE BOTH
STATION SELECTOR KNOB AND BEZEL ON
RIGHT SIDE OF RADIO. THROUGH THE
OPENING ABOVE THE CONTROL SHAFT,
ADJUST THE ANTENNA TRIMMER FOR
MAXIMUM VOLUME (ADJUSTMENT SHOULD
NOT BE MORE THAN TWO TURNS IN
EITHER DIRECTION). ON "AM/FM" RADIOS
NO ADJUSTMENT IS REQUIRED FOR THE
"FM" BAND.

SPEAKER AND BRACKET ASM.

RECEIVER ASM.

HEATER CONTROL SUPPORT

SPEAKER AND BRACKET ASM.

RECEIVER ASM.

TO RECEIVER

EXISTING WIRE ASM. FROM WINDSHIELD

VIEW "A"

ANTENNA HOOK-UP

TO SPEAKER

SPEAKER CONNECTOR

TO INSTRUMENT PANEL WIRE HARNESS

AM/FM RADIO

TO SPEAKER

SPEAKER CONNECTOR

TO INSTRUMENT PANEL WIRE HARNESS

AM RADIO ONLY

Installation of 1969 and 1970 radio and front speaker. All tuning
and volume knobs for 1968-70 AM radios were the same (part
number 9786795). Speaker was a 10 ohm, 4x10 inch oval.

473

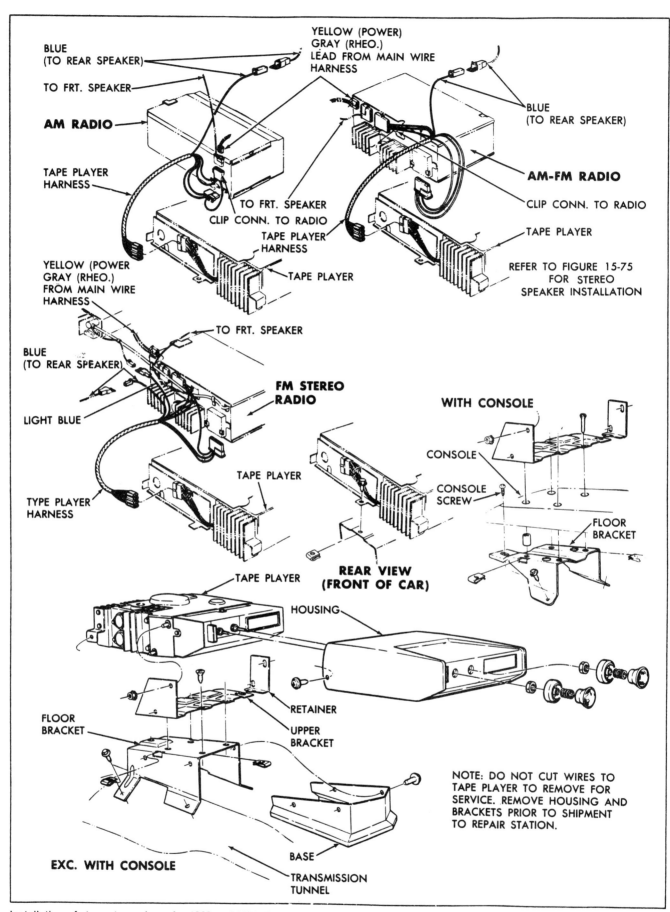

BLUE
(TO REAR SPEAKER)

TO FRT. SPEAKER

AM RADIO

TAPE PLAYER
HARNESS

YELLOW (POWER
GRAY (RHEO.)
FROM MAIN WIRE
HARNESS

YELLOW (POWER)
GRAY (RHEO.)
LEAD FROM MAIN WIRE
HARNESS

BLUE
(TO REAR SPEAKER)

AM-FM RADIO

CLIP CONN. TO RADIO

TAPE PLAYER

REFER TO FIGURE 15-75
FOR STEREO
SPEAKER INSTALLATION

TO FRT. SPEAKER
CLIP CONN. TO RADIO
TAPE PLAYER
HARNESS

TAPE PLAYER

BLUE
(TO REAR SPEAKER)

LIGHT BLUE

TO FRT. SPEAKER

**FM STEREO
RADIO**

TYPE PLAYER
HARNESS

TAPE PLAYER

WITH CONSOLE

CONSOLE

CONSOLE
SCREW

FLOOR
BRACKET

TAPE PLAYER

**REAR VIEW
(FRONT OF CAR)**

TAPE PLAYER

HOUSING

FLOOR
BRACKET

RETAINER

UPPER
BRACKET

NOTE: DO NOT CUT WIRES TO
TAPE PLAYER TO REMOVE FOR
SERVICE. REMOVE HOUSING AND
BRACKETS PRIOR TO SHIPMENT
TO REPAIR STATION.

EXC. WITH CONSOLE

BASE

TRANSMISSION
TUNNEL

Installation of stereo tape player for 1969 and 1970. Player was
mounted on console, and assembly used for mounting player
without console is shown.

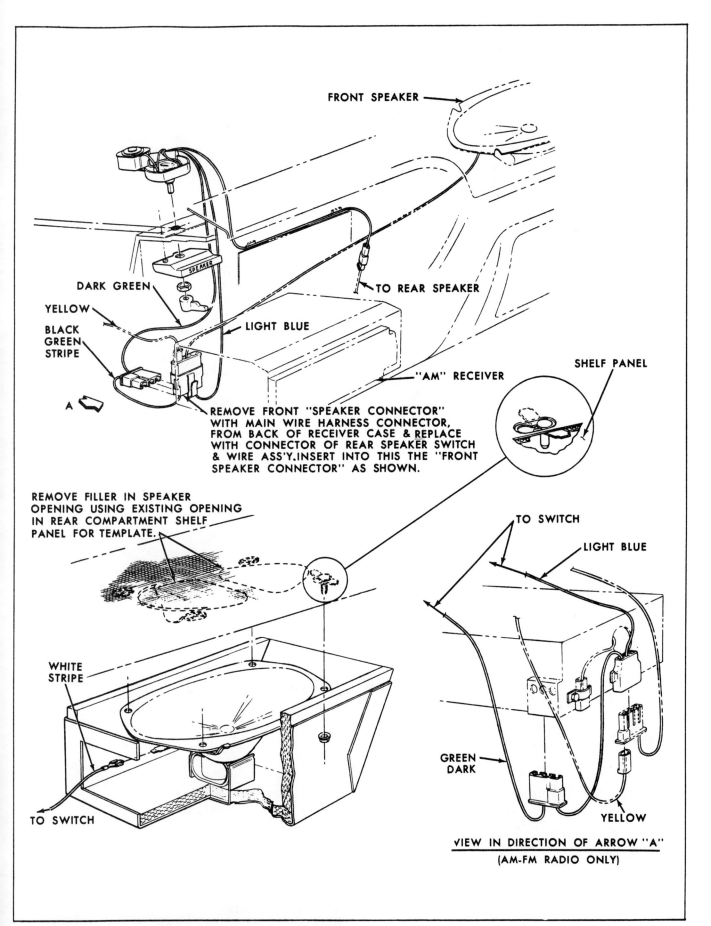

FRONT SPEAKER

TO REAR SPEAKER

DARK GREEN

YELLOW

BLACK GREEN STRIPE

LIGHT BLUE

"AM" RECEIVER

A

REMOVE FRONT "SPEAKER CONNECTOR" WITH MAIN WIRE HARNESS CONNECTOR, FROM BACK OF RECEIVER CASE & REPLACE WITH CONNECTOR OF REAR SPEAKER SWITCH & WIRE ASS'Y.INSERT INTO THIS THE "FRONT SPEAKER CONNECTOR" AS SHOWN.

SHELF PANEL

REMOVE FILLER IN SPEAKER OPENING USING EXISTING OPENING IN REAR COMPARTMENT SHELF PANEL FOR TEMPLATE.

WHITE STRIPE

TO SWITCH

TO SWITCH

LIGHT BLUE

GREEN DARK

YELLOW

VIEW IN DIRECTION OF ARROW "A"
(AM-FM RADIO ONLY)

Directions for installing Separa-Phonic rear seat speaker option. Illustration shows weave pattern for package shelf. GTOs not factory equipped with rear seat speaker used cardboard package shelf; dealer-installed grille was painted to match the shelf color when installing rear speaker.

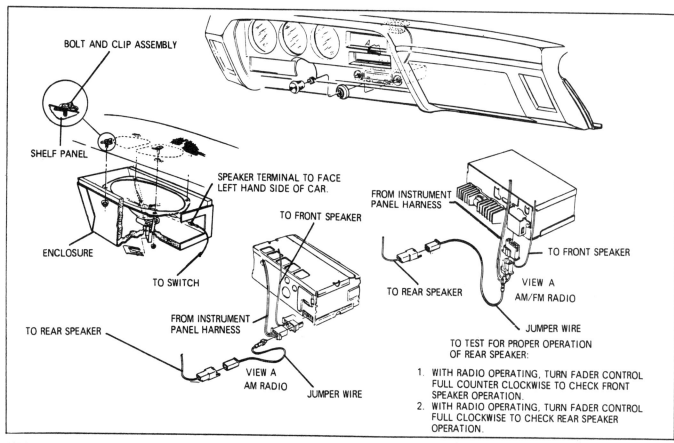

BOLT AND CLIP ASSEMBLY

SHELF PANEL

ENCLOSURE

TO SWITCH

SPEAKER TERMINAL TO FACE LEFT HAND SIDE OF CAR.

TO FRONT SPEAKER

FROM INSTRUMENT PANEL HARNESS

TO REAR SPEAKER

VIEW A
AM RADIO

JUMPER WIRE

FROM INSTRUMENT PANEL HARNESS

TO FRONT SPEAKER

TO REAR SPEAKER

VIEW A
AM/FM RADIO

JUMPER WIRE

TO TEST FOR PROPER OPERATION OF REAR SPEAKER:

1. WITH RADIO OPERATING, TURN FADER CONTROL FULL COUNTER CLOCKWISE TO CHECK FRONT SPEAKER OPERATION.
2. WITH RADIO OPERATING, TURN FADER CONTROL FULL CLOCKWISE TO CHECK REAR SPEAKER OPERATION.

1970 rear seat speaker had redesigned speaker harness interconnects for both AM and AM/FM radios.

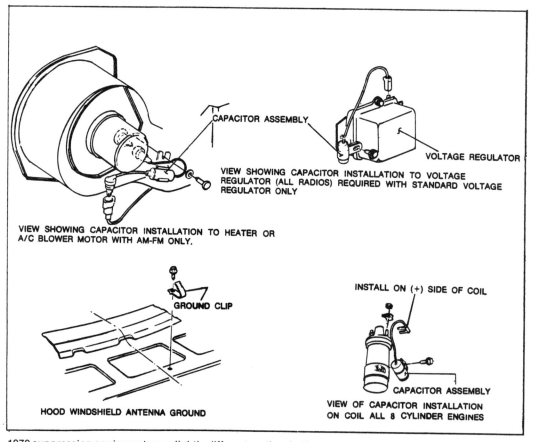

CAPACITOR ASSEMBLY

VOLTAGE REGULATOR

VIEW SHOWING CAPACITOR INSTALLATION TO VOLTAGE REGULATOR (ALL RADIOS) REQUIRED WITH STANDARD VOLTAGE REGULATOR ONLY

VIEW SHOWING CAPACITOR INSTALLATION TO HEATER OR A/C BLOWER MOTOR WITH AM-FM ONLY.

GROUND CLIP

INSTALL ON (+) SIDE OF COIL

CAPACITOR ASSEMBLY

HOOD WINDSHIELD ANTENNA GROUND

VIEW OF CAPACITOR INSTALLATION ON COIL ALL 8 CYLINDER ENGINES

1970 suppression equipment was slightly different, as the plastic cowl screen necessitated the use of a ground clip (part number 9798054) for the windshield antenna, as well as a capacitor to the coil.

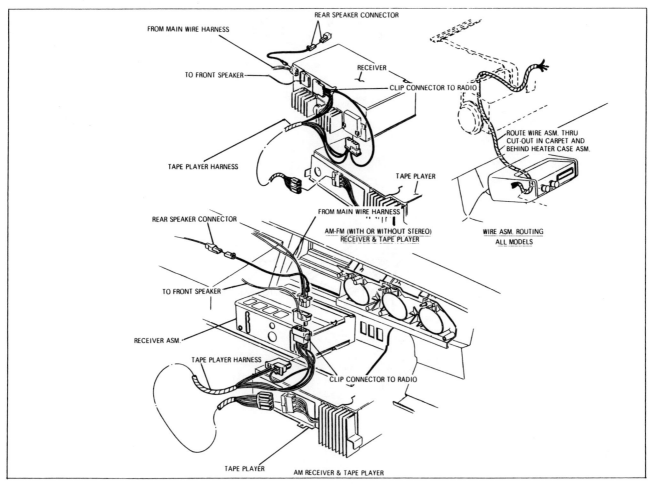

REAR SPEAKER CONNECTOR

FROM MAIN WIRE HARNESS

TO FRONT SPEAKER

RECEIVER

CLIP CONNECTOR TO RADIO

TAPE PLAYER HARNESS

TAPE PLAYER

ROUTE WIRE ASM. THRU CUT-OUT IN CARPET AND BEHIND HEATER CASE ASM.

FROM MAIN WIRE HARNESS

AM-FM (WITH OR WITHOUT STEREO) RECEIVER & TAPE PLAYER

WIRE ASM. ROUTING ALL MODELS

REAR SPEAKER CONNECTOR

TO FRONT SPEAKER

RECEIVER ASM.

TAPE PLAYER HARNESS

CLIP CONNECTOR TO RADIO

TAPE PLAYER

AM RECEIVER & TAPE PLAYER

This illustration shows routing of the wire harness through carpet and behind heater case for installation of 1970 stereo tape player.

RESTORATION NOTES

RESTORATION NOTES

MORE GREAT READING

American Car Spotter's Guide 1940-1965. Covers 66 makes—almost 3,000 illustrations. 358 pages, softbound.

American Car Spotter's Guide 1966-1980. Giant pictorial source with over 3,600 illustrations. 432 pages, softbound.

The Production Figure Book For U.S. Cars. Reflects the relative rarity of various makes, models, body styles, etc. Softbound, 180 pages.

Pontiac: The Postwar Years. One of America's most exciting makes of automobile is described in this factual 33-year history. 256 photos, 205 pages.

The Big "Little GTO" Book. All of these Great Ones by Pontiac are covered—1965-1974. Over 150 great photos, 235 pages. Large format, softbound.

Chevy Super Sports 1961-1976. Exciting story of these hot cars with complete specs and data. 176 pages, 234 illustrations, softbound. Large format.

Son of Muscle Car Mania. 176 pages of more great ads from the 1962-1974 muscle car era. All U.S. makes represented. Softbound, 250 illustrations.

Muscle Car Mania. A collection of advertisements for muscle cars 1964 through 1974. 176 pages, 250 illustrations, softbound.

Fearsome Fords 1959-1973. Over 250 photos of these great cars accompany 182 pages of interesting information. Softbound, large format.

Mighty Mopars 1960–1974. The story of these great muscle cars is told through text and over 175 great illustrations. 176 pages, softbound.

Auto Restoration From Junker to Jewel. Illustrated guide to restoring old cars. 292 pages, 289 illustrations, softbound.

Shelby's Wildlife: The Cobras and Mustangs. Complete, exciting story of the 260, 289, 427 and Daytona Cobras plus Shelby Mustangs. 224 pages, nearly 200 photos.

Classic Motorbooks Chrysler 300 1955-1961 Photofacts. Over 125 photos accompany lots of info on these cars. Softbound, 80 pages.

Classic Motorbooks Pontiac Trans Am 1969-1973 Photofacts. Over 125 great photos help tell the story. 80 pages, softbound.

Bob Bondurant on High Performance Driving. World-famous instructor teaches secrets to fast, safe driving. Over 100 illustrations, 144 pages, softbound.

Restoring Convertibles. Great tips on restoring post-WWII convertibles. 242 pages, 222 illustrations.

Classic Motorbooks Mercury Cougar 1967-1973 Photofacts. Covers all these models with over 150 illustrations. Softbound, 80 pages.

Porsches For The Road. Beautiful photo essays on 12 models. In the Survivors Series. 128 pages, 250 illustrations, 125 in color.

Automotive Fuel Injection Systems: A Technical Guide. Thorough analysis and description of current gas-engine technology. 173 illustrations, 182 pages, softbound.

The Art and Science of Grand Prix Driving. Complete analysis and discussion by World Champion Niki Lauda. Over 150 photos, 23 in color, 245 pages.

Autocourse. Large-format racing annual. Coverage of each Grand Prix and other major racing events and series. Over 200 pages with lots of color.

Illustrated Corvette Buyer's Guide. Includes 194 photos and lots of info on all these cars 1953-1982. 156 pages, softbound.

Illustrated High Performance Mustang Buyer's Guide. Covers the 1965 GT, the Shelby, through the 1973 Mach 1. Softbound, 250 illustrations, 176 pages.

How To Restore Your Collector Car. Covers all the major restoration processes in an easy to understand, easy to use format. More than 300 illustrations. Softbound, 320 pages.

Harley-Davidson Motor Company: An Official Eighty-Year History. More than 250 photos plus 8 pages of color tell the complete story of the company 1903–1983. 288 pages.

Illustrated Rolls-Royce, Bentley Buyer's Guide. Covers prewar 1907 Silver Ghost through present models including the Silver Spirit and Mulsanne. 176 pages, over 150 illustrations, softbound.

Illustrated BMW Buyer's Guide. From the early 500 through the 7-Series and the M1. 176 pages, softbound, over 175 illustrations.

Illustrated Jaguar Buyer's Guide. Includes over 160 illustrations of the SS 100 through the elegant sedans of the eighties. 156 pages, softbound.

Illustrated Maserati Buyer's Guide. Covers all models up through the Biturbo. 136 pages over 120 illustrations, softbound.

Illustrated Triumph Buyer's Guide. Features models from TR1 through TR8 including Spitfire, GT6, Stag and more. Nearly 200 illustrations, 176 pages, softbound.

Illustrated Camaro Buyer's Guide. Covers models from 1967 to 1985 with lots of information and nearly 200 illustrations. 156 pages, softbound.

Supertuning Your Z-28 Camaro. Hands-on guide to tuning, supertuning and race prepping a Z-28. 148 illustrations, 160 pages, softbound.

Engineer To Win. Latest info on racing materials technology, prevention of fatigue failure and other fascinating subjects. 280 pages, over 250 illustrations, softbound.

The New Formula One: A Turbo Age. Twice World Driving Champion Niki Lauda on aerodynamics turbos, ground effects, suspensions, racing developments and much more. 252 pages, 135 illustrations including 12 pages in color.

Corvettes For The Road. Lavish pictorial coverage, in the Survivors Series. 128 pages, over 250 photos, 100 in color.

The Ford Y-Block: Origin, Maintenance, Rebuild. Step-by-step guide to tearing down and rebuilding. Softbound, nearly 200 illustrations, 120 pages.

Restorer's Model A Shop Manual: Complete and Illustrated. Step-by-step instructions of best methods to restore these cars. 224 pages, 143 illustrations, softbound.

Mustang Performance and Handling Guide 1964–1985. Easy-to-use tips on getting more power and better cornering from your Mustang. Softbound, over 200 illustrations, 165 pages.

Motorbooks International
Publishers & Wholesalers Inc.
Osceola, Wisconsin 54020, USA